AN EYEWITNESS HISTORY OF AUSTRALIA

Harry Gordon has been an eyewitness to history as a reporter, writer and editor. He was a war correspondent in Korea during the bitterest fighting in 1950–51, covered the Algerian revolution in 1960 and wrote about five Wimbledon championships, three Olympic Games and one Commonwealth Games. He has won a number of distinctions, including a special commendation in the 1956 Walkley Awards for journalism. The first edition of *An Eyewitness History of Australia* was awarded, among other honours, the National Book Council first prize for Australian literature. For his campaigning in the field of road safety, the Royal Australasian College of Surgeons awarded him its Graeme Grove Medal in 1977. He was made a Champion of the Order of St Michael and St George (CMG) in 1981 for distinguished service to journalism. He has held senior positions on several major newspapers, including that of editor-in-chief of The Herald and Weekly Times group. He is now executive contributing editor to *Time Australia*. Mr Gordon has written seven books and contributed to many anthologies.

AN EYEWITNESS HISTORY OF AUSTRALIA

HARRY GORDON

FOREWORD BY MANNING CLARK

PENGUIN BOOKS

To the newsgatherers, past, present and future. And particularly to the memory of three good friends who died before this book was completed: Graham Perkin, Roy Macartney and Hugh Buggy.

Penguin
Penguin Books Australia Ltd
487 Maroondah Highway, PO Box 257
Ringwood, Victoria 3134, Australia
Penguin Books Ltd
Harmondsworth, Middlesex, England
Viking Penguin Inc.
40 West 23rd Street, New York, N.Y., U.S.A.
Penguin Books Canada Limited
2801 John Street, Markham, Ontario, Canada L3R 1B4
Penguin Books (N.Z.) Ltd
182-190 Wairau Road, Auckland 10, New Zealand

First published in 1976 by
John Currey, O'Neil Publishers Pty Ltd
Reprinted 1976, 1978
Second edition published 1981
Reprinted 1982
Third edition published 1986
New and revised edition published 1988

10 9 8 7 6 5 4 3 2 1

Produced by Viking O'Neil
56 Claremont Street, South Yarra, Victoria 3141, Australia
A division of Penguin Books Australia Ltd

Typeset in Baskerville
Printed in Australia by Globe Press

National Library of Australia
Cataloguing-in-Publication data

Gordon, Harry, 1925
   An eyewitness history of Australia

   4th ed.
   Bibliography
   Includes index.
   ISBN 0 140 11884 5.

   1. Australia – History – Sources. I. Title.

Foreword

One of the reasons why Australian history once held the unenviable reputation of being the dullest subject in the class-room, and providing the dullest books in a library was that its historians only used dull official material. So no wonder the subject became as lifeless, and indeed as far removed from the great pulse of life as a Government House tea party.

The great virtue of this most valuable collection of eye-witness accounts of leading events in our history is that they were written by men with an eye and an ear, even a nose for what really interests human beings, as distinct from what intellectual bullies think men and women ought to be interested in. Reading through the table of contents and sampling some of the entries reminded me of that scene in Government House, Hobart, in the late 1830s. Poor Jane, Lady Franklin, wanted to get the ladies of the colony interested in higher things, in science, in religion, in philosophy and in literature: they wanted to dance, and have fun.

The secret of the success of the good reporter of news is this awareness of what his contemporaries are really interested in. That is why Harry Gordon has made such a marvellous collection. His life as a working journalist gives him that concern with things as they are, and not as they might be or should be. All journalists live in a state of tension between the dictates of their moral passions and their obligation to come to terms with the forces in power in their society.

From the writings of Edward Smith Hall on the slaughter of Aborigines to Samuel Irwin's account of the Eureka Stockade, to the comments of Brian Fitzpatrick on the Melbourne scene or Osmar White in Rabaul, or Allan Barnes and Ben Hills on the Labor Party's return to government after twenty-three years, passion and power are nicely balanced.

Good journalists know they are hirelings, but they know, too, they have an innate dignity, a grace, and a command of language with which to conceal the realities of their position. Indeed it is just this cheek and daring, this skating close to the edge of the pond, which gives the life to their performance and enables their work to live on long after the immediate interest in the event they are describing or discussing has disappeared.

That is the other feature of this collection of material. It is a bringing together of writing that deserved to be rescued from the huge anonymous piles of old newspapers that slumber in our libraries. It is also a reminder of the simple fact that our best prose writers, with one or two exceptions, have belonged to the honourable profession of journalism.

The collection should therefore inspire the young man starting out on his career to greater things: it should be and will be a mine of information for anyone interested in Australian History: it will also remind all the workers in the field of letters that our newspapers from the *Sydney Gazette* to the present day are what a man should dip into not once, but again and again and again if he wants to understand what Australians are like, and what faith, if any, they live by.

MANNING CLARK

Contents

A Nation at War (1939—1945)

Changing Face of Australia (1946–1968)

Loss of Innocence (1969-1988)

Introduction

The primary purpose of this book is to explore the role of the reporter as a witness to history. Australia has a rich, exciting history and reporting at its highest, most enduring levels is largely the business of catching history in the act. History is to a great degree an assembly of the significant moments in our past — those which represent great events and terrible events and, once in a while, ridiculous events. These have to be trapped freshly, accurately; reporters of distinction trap great moments well.

The historian is the person who mines and preserves those moments, fossicks and disseminates, and finally relates them to our human progress. Sometimes he is concerned to examine trends rather than just events, but often these trends were first revealed in happenings that made news. The truth is that the good reporter, even though he does not always realise it, is sometimes writing for some still unborn historian.

A secondary purpose has been to discuss along the way the history of Australian journalism itself, and some of the characters who have decorated it. They are a diverse lot, the news-gatherers: not the least fascinating aspect of them is that, from Marcus Clarke to George Johnston, they have included some of our finest authors.

The desire to learn the news is as old as man. Even in the Stone Age, before men traded in products they had grown or made, they exchanged news. As early as 449 BC, official records of the transactions of the Roman Senate were kept and deposited in the Temple of Ceres; notes were taken of these — usually by intelligent slaves — and sent to provincial governors as newsletters. It was Caesar who caused the precursor of the modern daily newspaper to be published each day in the Forum.

It was called *Acta Diurna*, or the *Daily Acts*, published on a white wooden board.

The *Daily Acts* recorded births and deaths, receipts of taxes from the provinces, election news and proceedings in civil and criminal courts. The next development was the production of a larger written newspaper; professional editors would take the news of the *Daily Acts*, gather some others of their own, then dictate the news to a dozen slaves who produced a written newspaper with a circulation of twelve. In those days, long before the discovery of the printing press, the size of an edition was limited only by the number of slaves employed.

For some fourteen centuries, until the days of Gutenberg and Caxton, little advance was made on the form of the newspaper. The invention of printing made the multiplication of copies a reasonably simple and profitable business, and the reporting of events, in news-sheet form, spread rapidly on the European continent. Columbus's momentous letter of 1493, announcing the results of his first expedition, was distributed as a news broadside; so was the disaster to the Spanish Armada.

In the sixteenth century the great German banking firm of Fugger was the pre-eminent news-gathering service, sending its dispatches from the first printing presses around the shrunken world that was Europe. The first English-language news-sheets were published, on an irregular basis, in the sixteenth century, and the historian James Bonwick noted the appearance of a publication called the *English Mercury* in 1588, the year of the Armada. The first regular pamphlet, the *Corante* or *Newes from Italy, Germany &c,* appeared in 1621; the *Weekely Newes,* published by Nicholas Bourne and Thomas Archer, followed a year later and in 1623 Bourne and Archer joined with Nathaniel Butter to produce *More Newes from Europe.* The first American newspaper, John Campbell's *Boston News-Letter*, was born in April 1704, and Australia's first paper, the *Sydney Gazette and New South Wales Advertiser*, arrived in March 1803. Down the centuries have come a great procession of chroniclers, all of them adept at the craft of recording history as it happened: through Daniel Defoe (of the *Review*), Samuel Buckley (of the *Daily Courant*), Ned Ward (of the *London Spy*) and Samuel Johnson (of the *Gentleman's Magazine*); through Cobbett, Wilkes, Coleridge, Lamb, Desmoulins, Mayhew, Hazlitt, Dumas, Dickens and Hugo; through the moderns, from Kipling, Churchill, Twain, William Howard Russell, Stephen Crane, 'Chinese' Morrison, Richard Harding Davis, Henry Morton Stanley, Sir Philip Gibbs, Ellis Ashmead-Bartlett, Jack London, Arnold Toynbee and Ernest Hemingway to Rebecca West, John Hersey, Alan Moorehead, A. J. Liebling, John Hetherington, John Gunther, Alistair Cooke, James Cameron, Norman Mailer, David Halberstam and Peter Arnett.

Journalism, it has been said, is literature in a hurry. The corollary is that reporting, which is the very gut of journalism, is literature in a roaring hurry. At its highest levels, it calls for instinctive who-saw-the-bullet-hit?, where's-the the-nearest-phone?, when's-the-next-edition? reactions, plus stamina, plus perception, plus insight, plus a constantly interrogative state of mind, plus a purity of motive which asserts itself in an almost passionate search for truth. Plus — and this is maybe the most important ingredient of all — a considerable amount of luck. Some potentially wonderful reporters have lived out their entire careers without colliding once with history . . . history in the big sense. Others have discovered that a kind of dice-shuffle of time and place and people has put them close to a moment that could live for centuries; and, in doing so, the shuffle has changed their careers.

Consider, for instance, the case of the *New York Times* man Tom Wicker, who reported the assassination of President John Kennedy on 22 November 1963. Wicker was known as a promising newspaperman, attached to the Washington bureau of the *Times*, when he travelled with Kennedy to Dallas. He wrote his story in the pressroom of the Dallas air terminal, having sprinted for half a mile, lugging a typewriter and briefcase, jumping a fence along the way without even breaking his stride; he remembered all he had seen and heard after Kennedy was shot, and from all the confusion in that most deranged day of his life, he sieved the facts, assembled them, and dictated them into a phone in a voice that cracked at times with emotion. He carried no notebook that day. He heard no shots, but saw Kennedy's car speed away and watched confusion and rumor travel, turning the heads of the people from the point where Kennedy was to have addressed the crowd. It reminded him, he said, of a wind sweeping over a wheat field. Gay Talese, in his book *The Kingdom and the Power*, later wrote: 'It is probably true that Wicker's reporting from Dallas that day, one afternoon's work, will live longer than any novel, or play, or essay, or piece of reportage that he has ever written or will ever write. It was not that he had produced a classic. He had not. He had previously reported as well, written better. But the test in Dallas was like no other test; Wicker was writing for history that day.'

Reporters do not always agree about the qualities necessary for their trade. Kipling wrote that a good war correspondent needed 'the power of glib speech that neither man nor woman can resist when a meal or bed is in question, the eye of a horse coper, the skill of a cook, the constitution of a bullock, the digestion of an ostrich, and an infinite adaptability to all circumstances'. And he added: 'But many die before they attain to this degree.' Joseph and Stewart Alsop have stated: 'All reporters need sturdy constitutions, good feet, and some feeling for the English language.' George Ernest ('Chinese') Morrison, possibly the most colourful of Australian reporters, wrote of his craft: 'In spite of all that has been said to the contrary it is the noblest in my opinion of all the professions, and . . . energy, courage, temperance and truthfulness are necessary to its success.' And Keith Murdoch, another great Australian reporter, declared that 'the old journalist dies, still stretching out for better English, better cover of actualities, better comment. . .'

Certainly the most vital qualities are speed and accuracy. It is the sheer pace of reporting that separates it from most other forms of chronicling. The reporter lives with the tyranny of deadlines. Often he is forced to put together his words in awkward, inappropriate circumstances. Charles Dickens used to recall the reporting days when he used to write his stories on the palm of his hand, 'by the light of a dark lantern, in a post chaise and four, galloping through a wild country, and through the dead of night, and at the then surprising rate of fifteen miles an hour'. Dickens worked for the *Mirror of Parliament*, the *Morning Chronicle* and the *Daily News*; he used his experiences as a Bow Street reporter and his travels around Europe as a representative of the *Daily News* as a basis for many of his novels. He confessed to having been upset 'in almost every description of vehicle known in this country' and bemired on roads many miles from London, stranded in the company of exhausted horses and drunken postboys, with only one idea — meeting his paper's deadline. William Howard Russell, of *The Times*, wrote his story of the Light Brigade until the candle he used for a light 'disappeared in the bottle like a stage demon through a trapdoor'. 'Chinese' Morrison, trying to get a message to *The Times* during the siege of Peking by the Boxers, wrote one message on both sides of a scrap of very thin paper measuring five inches by less than two and a half, dipped it in oil to waterproof it, and buried it in an old dish of gruel, then gave it to a young Chinese Christian who was smuggled out of the city as a beggar.

The transition from Dickensian gallops through the night and dispatch by disguised couriers to jet planes and satellite communications has in no way lessened the harshness of the deadlines; it has simply accelerated the pressure. The methods of telling stories have changed considerably: the measured, step-by-step prose of Australia's first war correspondent, Howard Willoughby, is a long way from the explosive style of Wilfred Burchett's 'Hiroshima, which was atomic-bombed on 6 August, looks as though a monster steamroller has passed over and squashed it out of existence'. The techniques vary with the years; the integrity, the purpose and the unyielding deadlines remain.

The pieces of Australian reporting quoted in this book deserve to endure, generally because they reflect important capsules in our history, but in many cases because they also represent a special quality of craftmanship. To collect them, to stitch them into historical perspective, has involved a great deal of research, some half-dozen years of it, carried out at varying degrees of intensity. I have tried to select the best examples of literature-under-pressure — material written on the spot and at the time, where possible, rather than articles written later, in comfort and with the sharp, sure vision of hindsight. I have also tried, wherever possible, to identify the reporters concerned.

Since bylines were not fashionable for more than a century of the period under scrutiny, this has not always been easy; nor has it always been successful. Most of the research has been carried out among the musty files of the La Trobe Library in Melbourne, the Mitchell Library in Sydney, and many smaller newspaper libraries. I have studied scores of published and unpublished volumes of reminiscence (an endearing quality about many old journalists is their desire to put it all down on paper, to make some collected record of their small brushes with history, even if there is nobody willing to publish what they write). Out of old notebooks and manuscripts in forgotten, not-quite-discarded trunks, out of newspaper morgues, out of the living memories of so many journalists, have emerged identities and anecdotes.

The line-up of these men who watched and scribbled as they acted as middle-men between the moment and the reader is formidable. Sometimes, during restless nights after long exposure to their work in files that grow frailer and more yellowed with the years, they form up in one's mind — in untidy order, variously talented, with little in common but a kind of inner commitment to set it all down the best way they could. Joe Melvin, one of the very finest Australian reporters, often moves at night through the corridors of my mind, watching police and railway-men pouring bullets at the iron-clad frame of Ned Kelly; dragging the fatally-wounded Steve Hart out of the Glenrowan Inn; carrying his swag in Queensland as he covered the great shearers' strike; hiring his own train to cover a meeting. He was, according to one etching published in the *Australasian Sketcher*, a youngish man in his Kelly days, with a mournful moustache and a tweed deerstalker cap. His name is virtually unknown today. The legends about him have got lost, and the craft of journalism is poorer for that.

And there are so many others. George Howe, the mutton-chopped Creole convict who was Australia's first working journalist, hustling about the ill-made muddy streets of Sydney, meeting ships, attending hangings, selling advertisements. Howard Willoughby, our first war correspondent, jogging on horse-back into combat against the Maoris and, years later, stalking along Bourke Street towards Melbourne's Parliament House, pensive, frock-coated and quite absent-minded. Edward Smith Hall and Andrew Bent, armed with courage and an utter dedication to what they considered was the duty of the press, waging David-like struggles against governors who had the power and the desire to persecute them. Samuel Irwin, moving around the diggers' encampment at Eureka as it burned to the ground, chronicling in longhand an account that would be accepted by historians as remarkably accurate. William Jevons, conducting painstaking house-to-house surveys around the foul-smelling back streets of the dirty, boozy, lusty town that was Sydney in the 1850s. 'Chinese' Morrison, so earnestly intrepid, being speared by New Guinea blacks and shot by Boxer Chinese. The parsons' sons who became war reporters, Keith Murdoch and C. E. W. Bean, the former trying hard to conquer a nervous stammer as he set about his own Gallipoli campaign against the British military Establishment. William Lambie, riding into combat against the Saracens and later the Boers, collecting a bullet in an arm in the Sudan, and another, fatally, in the Transvaal. C. P. Smith, the former Saturday-afternoon rifle-shooting correspondent, who suddenly found himself on Anzac Cove, writing about a more meaningful kind of rifle-shooting. Frail little Harry Seekamp, a folk hero among the Ballarat miners, reacting gamely, if a little unchivalrously, when the exotic dancer Lola Montes set about him with a horsewhip. The *Argus* men of the 1880s, men like Billy Salter, Peter Symmonds and David Maling, a breed described by *Bulletin* editor J. F. Archibald

as 'all tall, thin, taciturn and well-dressed in tail-coats and bell-toppers . . . some effecting patent-leather boots and lemon-colored kid gloves'. The battle specialists, from Lambie, Donald Macdonald, Willoughby, 'Banjo' Paterson, to Alan Moorehead, Ron Monson, John Hetherington, Noel Monks, Kenneth Slessor, George Johnston . . . whole waves of them, gifted and brave and equipped with a fine sense of history. And the close-range watchers of crime and disaster, Hugh Buggy and Clyde Palmer, both of them pure specimens from the lurid, 'twenties era of journalism that was characterised by the Hecht-Macarthur play *The Front Page*. So many witnesses of distinction, and most of their work buried now, lost echoes in forgotten files.

Four Australian prime ministers — Curtin, Deakin, Scullin and Watson — worked as journalists. Two of them are represented here, and it is worth explaining why. One of the advantages of embarking on a project like this is that one can frame one's own rules. A general rule is that the reports should have appeared in Australian newspapers. Mostly, they have been written by Australians, although Ashmead-Bartlett's first dispatch from Gallipoli and Jack London's commissioned report (for the *Argus*) on the Johnson-Burns world heavyweight title fight in Sydney in 1908 have been considered significant enough, and Australian enough, to include. Preference has been given to hard news stories, rather than to features or magazine stories. Although Alfred Deakin wrote many fine leading articles for David Syme's Melbourne *Age*, it was during an extraordinary period when he was serving as Prime Minister and virtually 'moonlighting' as the anonymous Australian correspondent of the London *Morning Post* that his most historically pertinent material was written. His authorship of these dispatches, which were falsely datelined as having originated in Sydney, was a tight secret; in some of them, including the material published in this volume, the journalist Deakin was actually analysing anonymously the actions of the Prime Minister Deakin. Deakin's report, and the earliest dispatches concerning Captain Cook and the First Fleet, are the only cases in which I have bent the rule concerning publication in Australian newspapers.

The John Curtin piece is a classic example of the blurring that sometimes occurs along the border that separates news reports and feature articles. He wrote it for the Melbourne *Herald* in December 1941, making it clear that 'Australia looks to America, free of any pangs as to our traditional links or kinship with the United Kingdom'. It was intended as a feature article and, strangely, the *Herald* published it on its feature page rather than its front page, but it most certainly constituted news. It represented a change in the course of this nation's history, and its author was the man who was navigating that change.

Any study of Australian journalism is bound to leave one with a profound respect for the pioneer newspapermen, whose performance caused James Bonwick to write in 1890: 'Of all the institutions of Australia, the Press has exhibited the greatest vitality, exercised the most powerful influence, and illustrated the most decided progression.'

The early editors, like Howe of the Sydney *Gazette*, had to contend with primitive conditions. Howe used worn-out type and very coarse paper — when he could get it. When he could not obtain white paper, he used various colours. When he could find no paper his journal simply did not appear. He made his own ink, wrote his own news, set it in type, cleared the contributors' boxes he had erected in Sydney and Parramatta, worked his own woeful hand-press, and finally delivered the paper himself. Later newspapermen, like W. C. Wentworth, Robert Wardell and Edward Smith Hall (in Sydney), and Andrew Bent, Henry Melville and Gilbert Robertson (in Hobart Town) came into sharp conflict with authority in the form of governors. Governor Darling first tried to gag Wentworth, Wardell and Hall by means of a licence (to be renewed each year) and a stamp-duty of fourpence (a third of the selling price); when these measures were rejected by Chief Justice Forbes, Darling brought a series of libel actions against the editors. Hall was tried seven times, and sentenced to terms of imprisonment totalling three years. In Tasmania, Governor Arthur also instigated a series of libel actions after his other methods of shackling freedom of discuss-

ion had failed; Bent, Melville and Robertson all went to jail as a result of these actions.

I have referred to the presence, around the summit levels of the craft that is reporting, of a constantly interrogative state of mind. It is a quality which was possessed abundantly by Bert Wolfe, an amiable, double-breasted kind of man who looked like a tidier, sleeker, W. C. Fields and who was probably the most respected turf writer of his time. He demonstrated it best when he exposed, through sheer, persevering research which backed up a hunch, one of the great Australian racing scandals: the ring-in of a horse which ran under the name of Redlock.

Bert Wolfe, who wrote under the name of 'Cardigan', was much more than a wonderfully skilled reporter. He had a desire to probe and challenge. He had a detective instinct. So, too, did Billy Salter, who followed up an apparently insignificant clue and caused Frederick Deeming to be exposed as a mass murderer with a penchant for sealing his victims' bodies under hearthstones. So did Richard Hughes — a former Victorian Railways clerk who became a foreign correspondent of almost legendary reputation — when he solved the 1939 Piha Bones case and announced, rather to the chagrin of police investigators, that the apparent victim was not in fact dead.

Hughes later showed that same instinct when he achieved one of the great newspaper scoops by tracking down the British diplomat-spies Burgess and Maclean in Moscow; because this book concerns itself with events which have Australian rather than international significance, the Burgess-Maclean report has not been included in the collection which follows. Other outstanding pieces of investigative journalism which have been included are reports by Maurice Brodzky, who exposed some of the great frauds of the land boom of the 1890s, and Tom Farrell, whose efforts freed from prison a man convicted of murder.

Once in a long while, a reporter's story can affect the course of history. In three separate cases — involving the journalists Joe Alexander (1931), Alan Ramsey (1971) and Peter Game (1975) — it can reasonably be argued that individual news reports began chains of political events which led to changes of government. Political reporting has become more laced with comment in recent years, but the clean, hard-edged scoop still surfaces occasionally. Two such cases came from Laurie Oakes in recent years: the breaking in April 1974 of the unlikely news that Prime Minister Gough Whitlam intended to appoint Senator Vince Gair as an ambassador, and the disclosure in August 1980 of details of the nation's Budget — two days before the Treasurer, John Howard, was due to bring it down in Parliament.

A comparatively large amount of this book is devoted to war reporting. Too much, some might say. I have two defences. One is that it has been my purpose to show reporters in their role as the instant chroniclers of history . . . and history has a tendency to occur more readily and certainly more dramatically in war than in peace. The second is that war has given Australian reporters more opportunities than peace. Alan Moorehead, Noel Monks and Ronald Monson, for instance, were three very capable reporters whose assignments in the late 1930s included bushfires, locust plagues, murders and some fairly dreary council meetings; their talents were undoubted, but it was not until they began watching wars for Fleet Street papers that their horizons really opened. James Aldridge was a copy boy on the Melbourne *Sun* when he decided to travel; perhaps he would have become a celebrated correspondent even if he had not collided with a war in Finland, but a certain amount of scepticism on this point might be excused. C. E. W. Bean would still probably have been a historian of consequence and Keith Murdoch would still undoubtedly have become a newspaper proprietor, but their separate exposures to World War One at close range did have a large influence on their careers. Probably because of the greater opportunity it offers, in terms of distant assignments and raw life-and-death copy content, the truth is that combat overseas has spawned a disproportionately greater number of journalistic reputations than tranquillity at home or abroad.

It should be stated that Australian newspapers have shown, ever since Howard Willoughby went off to cover the Maori wars, an exceptional willingness to send correspondents on faraway assignments. European and American newspapermen are often surprised at the presence of Australian reporters at major world events. During the Algerian revolution, I recall Fleet Street men saying, 'How come a paper in Melbourne wants you on the spot here? Won't they get all they want from the wire services and the syndicated stuff?' It is the kind of comment which has greeted Australian journalists from Belfast to Sharpeville to the Israeli front line. The answer is simply that Australian newspapers, as a group, are extremely enterprising, and have shown a traditional inclination to record their history, where possible, through their own men's eyes.

Since this book was first published in 1976, it has been revised three times for new editions – in 1980, 1986 and now 1988. Deletions have been made, new events included. For each such exercise, the problem usually amounts to this: sure the event was big news a year or so ago, but will it qualify as history? No easy question, this, because history is always easier to define at a distance; at short range, through the telescope of time, values sometimes become a little distorted. A crazed gunman, killing people at random, makes huge headlines. Does his madness affect the history of the nation? How do you measure it against a political or economic happening that will affect lives less grotesquely, but more of them, and for years to come? The judgments must of course be subjective – and they are sometimes dictated by that traditional journalistic foe: limited space. Whatever the reason, the sins of omission and commission that follow rest with this writer.

Australia in the year this book was first published, was a rather different place. Malcolm Fraser was riding high, as were the Australian dollar, Ian Chappell, Dick Hamer, Don Dunstan and Joh Bjelke-Petersen. For the only time since the Second World War, Australians that year won not a single gold medal at the Olympic Games. The Belle Vue Hotel in Brisbane stood, seedily elegant, there were people in Melbourne who clung to the notion that Collins Street had a 'Paris end' and the Sydney Opera House was wondrous, and new.

In the intervening years, much has happened in terms of natural disaster, politics, economics, sport and crime. Regarding that last category, it has to be said that the last few years have seen a marked change in the nature of organised criminal activity. Corruption, crime syndicates and thuggery are not new to Australia: they have been around since the days of the Rum Corps. What is new, and extremely sinister, is the intrusion of drug trading on a massive scale, plus the steady soaking of corruption into high and seemingly respectable places. For much of our knowledge of these trends we have to thank various judicial commissioners, honest police, special investigators and a number of journalists and editors. Phone conversations taped by the New South Wales police receive a special mention in this book; they came to be known as the '*Age* tapes'. They were passed to the *Age* by crime investigator Bob Bottom, but an earlier version of them was published in the *National Times*. Later investigation by Phil Dickie, of the Brisbane *Courier-Mail*, and by Chris Masters and an ABC 'Four Corners' team, led to one of the most searching examinations of organised crime and associated police corruption ever conducted in Australia: the Fitzgerald Commission in Queensland.

Since this book was first published, one aspect of Australia that has changed quite dramatically is the nature of the media – particularly the print media. For the decade after 1976, and for a long time before, there existed three major newspaper publishing groups: the Herald and Weekly Times, News Limited, and John Fairfax and Sons. After a kind of newspaper-feeding frenzy, in which powerful players inside and outside Australia took part, the Herald and Weekly Times group, including its largest shareholder Queensland Press and the Adelaide *Advertiser*, were swallowed by Rupert Murdoch's News Limited. This gave Murdoch, United States citizen, 59 per cent of all Australian capital daily newspapers, plus the great bulk of the national news agency, Australian Associated Press. Surprisingly, few politicians, apart from the Liberals' Ian Macphee and Labor's Bill Hayden, registered much concern.

At this stage, Fairfax owned 24 per cent of the capital city circulations. Then came an internal power struggle at Fairfax, which ended with the sale of a vast number of assets by the new proprietor 27-year-old Warwick Fairfax. Along the way, in all the media turmoil, three newspapers were closed: the Brisbane *Telegraph*, the Sydney *Sun* and the *Times on Sunday*. Government regulations against crossover ownership of newspapers and television meant a big sell-off of television channels; a major winner was the former Melbourne *Sun* finance reporter Christopher Skase, who finished up controlling the Fairfax Channel 7 network.

A sad task of revision is to record the deaths of some of our most outstanding journalists of recent generations – people like the incomparable Richard Hughes, Geoffrey Hutton, Alan Moorehead, Wilfred Burchett, Douglas Lockwood, Alan Dower and many others. Many of those who died in recent years were correspondents who distinguished themselves in the Second World War. In a sense, they represent a fading breed; many of the media representatives who elbow their way close to combat these days are the TV cameramen and reporters, the agents of the small coloured screen in the living room.

Since the first edition of this book was published, newspapers have undergone great change. Typewriters have been replaced by video display terminals, white copy paper by blank screens, hot molten lead by photocomposition, inky clatter by tidy quiet. Undoubtedly as the computer revolution gathers pace, the tools of communication will continue to change. Whatever the tools, though, the essential commitment of journalists remains constant: basically, it is to disclosure and to truth. The best of them, as far back as Bean and Morrison and even Bent, have always been historians with deadlines. It is because of so many fine battalions of them that we know so much about that great procession of yesterdays that is our past.

Early settlers' bush hut, New South Wales

1771   Cook returns after discovering Australia's east coast and the First Fleet sails

UNKNOWN REPORTERS
Various contemporary journals, August 1771 and May 1787

The two most important events in early Australian history — the discovery of the east coast in 1770 by Lieutenant (later Captain) James Cook, and the departure from England of the First Fleet, under Captain Arthur Phillip, in 1787 — did not make much impact on the newspapers of the day. Sadly, in the rare mentions they did make, the newspapers got the names of the two principals wrong.

Cook and his Endeavour *returned to England on 13 July 1771, having completed one of the most eventful and significant voyages in the history of mankind. He was possibly the greatest sailing ship seaman who ever lived, and he had made tremendous sweeps through uncharted oceans and extremes of climate, zig-zagging across the world for more than three years. He had skirted the coast of South America, forged high into the Pacific to make the first real penetration of Tahiti, observed the transit of the planet Venus, headed south in search of the great southern continent, charted New Zealand, studied the life and customs of the Maoris, virtually collided with the east coast of Australia, raised England's flag in Botany Bay, satisfied himself that New Guinea was separated from New Holland, written with affection about the Aborigines of Australia, sent lengthy reports to the Admiralty from Batavia, and returned home via the Cape of Good Hope, with fifty-six men left of an original crew of ninety-four.*

The reporting of Captain Cook's return from this fateful piece of exploration was a shade low-key.

The London Evening Post *of 15 July 1771 noted the arrival of 'the Endeavour, Captain Cooke, from the East Indies'. The paper recalled that the vessel, which it wrongly labelled an 'East Indiaman', had sailed in August 1768, 'with Mr. Banks, Dr. Solander, Mr. Green and other ingenious gentlemen on board, for the South Seas'. They had since made a voyage around the world and 'touched at every coast and island where it was possible to get ashore'.*

Captain 'Cooke' received no other publicity after his arrival, although in the following couple of months the London journals paid considerable attention to Mr Joseph Banks, the the playboy botanist who accompanied Cook. The Public Advertiser *announced on 21 August 1771 that 'very great expectations are formed from the discoveries of Dr. Solander and Mr. Banks, and 'tis expected that the territories of Great Britain will be widely extended in consequence...' The* General Evening Post *reported that 'Dr. Solander and Mr. Banks ... attended at Richmond and had the honour of a conference with His Majesty on the discoveries they made on their late voyage'.*

Joseph Banks recommended Botany Bay to a House of Commons committee as an ideal place for convicts. In 1786, Lord Sydney requested the Lords Commissioners of the Treasury to prepare shipping to transport supplies, provisions and men to New Holland; Botany Bay was the solution for the evil of England's over-crowded jails.

The man chosen as Captain-General of the First Fleet and Governor-in-Chief of the proposed colony was Captain Arthur Phillip, then forty-eight years old. He had had a lively naval career, had retired on half pay, and was farming when he was offered the position of Governor of New South Wales.

It was an undertaking of massive significance ... the transport and planting of the very seed of a nation. But the departure of the First

Fleet attracted little attention in the British Isles and Western Europe. The London Chronicle *published on 12 May a dispatch dated 10 May, from Portsmouth. It read:*

> Commodore Phillips, since his arrival, has gone on board all the convict ships and storeships, in order to make a survey, and given the several captains their final instructions previous to sailing, which is now certainly to take place in a day or two.
>
> The fleet are to call, as we understand, at Madeira, and the Brazils, after which they are to steer immediately to the Southern ocean, where they say that they may arrive in five months. The convicts are healthy, and in good humour at present.

The dispatch added that orders had been given for the building of two twenty-four-gun Royal Yachts, and that the government was preparing to station extra vessels on the coasts and in the rivers 'for the better prevention of smuggling'.

A further dispatch from Portsmouth dated 13 May reported:

> Early this morning sailed the following ships, viz, the Sirius of 24 guns, Commodore Phillips, Capt. Hunter; the supply, armed brig; the Charlotte, Gilbert; Friendship, Walton; Alexander, Sinclair; Lady Penryn, Sier; Prince of Wales, Mason; Scarborough, Marshal; Fishbourne, Brown; Golden Grove, Sharp; and Borrowdale, Reed, transports and convicts ships, for Botany Bay.
>
> The Hyaena frigate, Captain Courcy, sailed with the above, and is to accompany them 100 leagues.

The Daily Telegraph Register *published basically the same item on Tuesday, 15 May, adding that the wind was from the south-west, and managing also to call Phillip 'Phillips'.*

The Dutch newspaper Amsterdamsche Courant *reported: 'Den 13 deezer is het Eskader, near de Botany-Bai in Nieuw Holland bestemd, en uit elf Zeilen bestaande, van Portsmouth derwards onder zeil gegaan' — but did not mention that it was to be a settlement for the punishment and reformation of convicts.*

A final report from Plymouth was published in the London Chronicle *on 21 May 1787. It said:*

> This afternoon passed by the Ram-head, through the Sound, the men of war, store-ships, etc., under command of Commodore Philips, for Botany-Bay; and the wind was fair, and blows strong, they must soon be out of the Channel.

This time the Governor-in-Chief's name was wrong in two places.

Phillip was not impressed with the potential of Botany Bay, and he decided, instead, to establish his colony at Sydney Cove — on a harbour which he believed to be the finest in the world. The First Fleet arrived in January 1788. The Lady Juliana *brought another 221 women convicts early in June 1790, and the second fleet landed later the same month, bringing another 757 convicts. Between 26 January 1788, and 20 November 1823, 37,606 felons embarked for New South Wales.*

Governor Arthur Phillip

1780   Captain Cook is killed in an affray with natives on Hawaii

UNKNOWN REPORTER
Drewry's Derby Mercury, 14 January 1780

Although Captain Cook's discovery of the east coast of Australia received scant coverage in the English newspapers, that was certainly not the case when news of his death on Hawaii was received — more than six months after it occurred. On 14 January 1780, Drewry's Derby Mercury *published a dispatch from the* London Gazette, *datelined Admiralty-Office, 11 January:*

Captain Clerke, of his Majesty's sloop the Resolution, in a letter to Mr. Stephens dated the 8th. of June, 1779, in the Harbour of St. Peter and St. Paul, Kampschatka, which was received yesterday, gives the melancholy account of the celebrated Captain Cook, late commander of the sloop, with four of his private mariners, having been killed on the 14th. of February last at the island of O'why'he, one of a group of new-discovered islands, in the 22nd. degree of north latitude, in an affray with a numerous and tumultuous body of the natives. Captain Clerke adds, that he had received every friendly supply from the Russian Government; and that as the companies of the Resolution and her consort the Discovery were in perfect health, and the two sloops had twelve months stores and provisions on board, he was making another attempt to secure a northern passage to Europe.

The Derby Mercury *explained, tripping just a little on the late Captain's name, that:*

O'why'hee (where the unfortunate Captain Cooke was killed) is a newly discovered island in the South Seas, lies 22 N.Lat. and 200 E.Long. from Greenwhich. The captain and his crew were at first treated as deities, but upon their revisiting that island some

proved inimical, hostilities ensued, and the above melancholy scene was the consequence.

The death of Captain Cooke will be considered by every nation in Europe as a public loss. The French at the commencement of this war gave directions that this able navigator should not be molested, if he was met with by their ships of war.

The Derby Mercury *then published this report on the tragedy:*

By the unfortunate Death of Captain Cook, the World has been deprived of a Man whose Talents and Industry were no less eminent than pointed to the Good of the Community. The Publication which has been already made of his Discoveries, proved his Capacity, and the Use of his Researches; and there was a strong probability, had he lived much longer, that he would have found out the Northern Passage to Europe, so eagerly, yet so fruitlessly, sought after by his Predecessors.

The Cause of Captain Cook's Death is said to arise from a Jealousy entertained by the Natives of O'why'he, the new-discovered Island, against some of the Ship's Crew, in respect to their Women, which brought on a Skirmish between a Party of the Sailors and Natives, and in which the ingenious Commander of the former perished.

From another Correspondent we have the following Particulars concerning the Death of Capt. Cook: That having been a considerable time at the Island where he met with his Fate, and all the while very friendly with the Inhabitants, upon sailing from thence he met with an Accident in the Mast of his Ship, and returned there to repair it. The People then shewed a different Disposition, and took away one of his Boats, which they would not return;

upon which the Captain, with a Lieutenant and nine Mariners, went on shore, when Hostilities ensued, which brought on the melancholy Catastrophe. The Lieutenant and four of the Mariners escaped.

The unhappy Murder of that famous Circumnavigator, Capt. Cook, is not only a national loss, but a Misfortune in which all Europe must naturally feel themselves deeply interested; yet we may hope, from the no less enterprising Spirit of Capt. Clerke, who succeede in Command, that the Plan laid down by his spirited Predecessor will be adopted by him with equal Vigour and Industry for the Discovery of the North West Passage, and thus much is already known, that certain Islands bordering upon Kamschatka have actually traded for these three or four Years past with the Northern Coast of America, and that the Distance is very trivial. . .

Then, scarcely pausing for breath, it announced in the next paragraph that a cartel had arrived at Dartmouth from St Maloes, with 302 prisoners.

And, in the following paragraph, this intriguing item:

A few days ago a female who had lived upwards of two years in the capacity of a coachman with Lady Dean, of Brook Street, Bath, was taken in labour and delivered of a fine girl, to the great astonishment of the whole family, who never suspected her being a woman.

The death of Captain Cook on Hawaii

1803   Australia's first editor writes about the man they couldn't hang

GEORGE HOWE
Sydney Gazette, 26 September 1803

Although the First Fleet carried a printing press to Australia in 1787, no use was made of it during the governorship of Captain Phillip. The reason: nobody on the colony knew how to work it.

The civil and military officials had been chosen for various talents, but there was among them a general ignorance of what was a fairly new craft. Nor had the sailors any knowledge of it. And the printers of England must have been a generally law-abiding lot; none of them had been transported. It is true that one young man, George Hughes, used the press to publish some mainly poor-quality handbills during the governorship of John Hunter; but it was not until George Howe arrived thirteen years after the First Fleet that Australia had a man with real printing experience. This experience enabled Howe to become Australia's first newspaper publisher, editor and news reporter.

Howe had been born at St Kitts in the West Indies in 1769. His father and brother were employed in the Government Press of the West Indies and it seems certain that he learned the rudiments of the printing trade there; later, after he travelled to London, he worked on The Times *and several other large newspapers as a typesetter.*

In April 1799, under the name of George Happy alias Happy George, he was convicted of having taken part in a robbery and was sentenced to death. The following month his sentence was commuted to transportation for the term of his natural life and he arrived in Sydney in 1800 aboard the convict ship Royal Admiral. *He was thirty-one years old, and it seems that he had managed to retain a surprisingly large fragment of ambition. In 1802 he applied for, and obtained, the vacant position of Government Printer, and the following year he successfully sought permission from Governor King to start Australia's first newspaper, the* Sydney Gazette and New South Wales Advertiser. *On 4 June 1806, he received a full pardon, thus becoming a free settler.*

James Bonwick, the historian who recorded the early struggles of the Australian Press, wrote of the first issue of Howe's (and the nation's) first newspaper, dated 5 March 1803: 'It was very badly printed on four pages of foolscap paper. It bore, at the top of the first page, its name, with a very rude little wood engraving, representing a ship with a Union Jack, and an allegorical female figure seated on the shore. It gave the date of the commencement of the colony, 1788. Around the picture these words were written. . ."Thus we hope to prosper".'

The Sydney Gazette *did not set out to be a particularly lively or outspoken newspaper; Howe's policy was an uncompromising one — 'We open no channel to political discussion or personal misadversion; information is our only purpose. . .' — and he stuck to it fairly well. Most of his comment in those early issues comes under the heading of rather pious asides; if he were covering an execution, for instance (and that was a fairly common assignment in those days), he liked to be able to say of the victim who listened attentively to the parson and failed to put on any show of defiance, 'we feel the greatest satisfaction in recording that he died a penitent'. Or when some unfortunate received 200 lashes, he would be moved to write that it was 'an example, we earnestly trust, that may deter others from the commission of similar offences'.*

George Howe would personally buy the

paper, make his own ink, write the news, set it in type, work the hand-press and finally deliver the finished product. When subscribers failed to pay their accounts, he would visit them personally. The Gazette was published once a week, and it sold at sixpence a copy.

In his early issues, Howe tried to offer something for everyone. He passed on orders and proclamations from the Governor, sifted the English newspapers for 'news from abroad', attended news events ranging from court hearings to executions, kept the port informed of all shipping news, recorded births, deaths and marriages, advertised wide varieties of goods, and published useful articles on such diverse subjects as the advantages of keeping pigs, methods of preserving meat and instructions for making wine.

There was plenty of local news material in the harsh little stockade town that was Sydney in the early 1880s. Even in the first issue of the Sydney Gazette, *published on 5 March 1803, there were reports of two really big news events: the fire at Woolwich Warren, in which were stored mortars, bombs and vast quantities of small-arms ammunition, and the escape of fifteen desperate Irish prisoners from the Castle Hill agricultural settlement. Two weeks later, when the Castle Hill insurgents were tried — thirteen of them were quickly sentenced to death — the accounts of their trials caused so much pressure on space in the* Gazette *that George Howe was forced to hold out the third article in his series on the making of wine.*

But the best news report George Howe wrote, in terms of human drama, concerned a Jewish convict who has passed rather anonymously and mistily into history as 'The Man They Couldn't Hang'. His name was Joseph Samuels, and he was found guilty of the murder of Joseph Luker, a police constable, on 25 August 1803. Luker had been investigating the theft of a desk containing valuables when he was attacked and bashed to death; his body had apparently been carried in a wheel-barrow and dumped on the road to Farm Cove. Samuels was undoubtedly an accomplice in the theft which preceded the murder and he was the only one of the four

charged men to be found guilty; one of the other three, Isaac Simmonds, managed to convince the court that the blood which stained his clothing could have come from his nose (which, he claimed, bled often) or from a fish he had cleaned or a duck he had killed. So on the morning of 26 September Joseph Samuels was taken to the gallows at Castle Hill to be hanged in company with another convicted murderer, James Hardwicke. This is George Howe's account of what happened then:

At half past nine on Monday morning, the New South Wales Corps got under arms, and proceeded to the place of execution, to which Joseph Samuels and James Hardwicke were brought, in pursuance of the sentence passed upon them on the preceeding Friday.

Both prisoners conducted themselves with becoming decency; and when the Reverend Mr. Marsden had performed the duties of his function, and quitted Hardwicke, he turned to Samuels (who being a Jew, was prepared by a person of his own profession) and questioning him on the subject of the murder of Luker, he solemnly declared, that during the interval of his confinement in the cell with Isaac Simmonds, nicknamed Hikey Bull, they in the Hebrew tongue exchanged an oath, by which they bound themselves to secrecy and silence in whatever they might then disclose.

Conjured by that God before whom he was shortly to appear, not to advance any thing in his latter moments that would endanger his salvation, he now repeated with an air of firmness what he had before declared; and appearing deeply imprest with a becoming fear of his approaching end, appealed to Heaven to bear his testimony, that Simmonds had, under the influence of the oath by which they were reciprocally bound, acknowledged to him that Luker had accidentally surprised him with the desk belonging to Mary Breeze; and that he, in consequence thereof, had "knocked him down, and given him a topper for luck!" adding at the same time, that if he had not been kept in the dark with the respect to the concealment of the money that had been taken out of the desk, that catastrophe never would have happened. But as it was, Simmonds said he would hang 500 Christians to save himself.

Simmonds, who was purposely brought from George's Head to witness the awful end of the unhappy culprit, heard what he advanced, and repeatedly endeavoured to check the declaration, which was delivered with mildness and composure, and which, as it appeared wholly untinctured with accrimony, gained credit among the spectators, in whose breasts a sentiment of abhorrence was universally awakened.

Odium and suspicion were attached to Simmonds from the very day on which the dreadful crime was perpetrated, and every eye was fixed in doubt upon his countenance when he assiduously assisted to lower the mangled corpse into the grave. Although from want of that full and sufficient evidence which the Law requires, he had escaped Condemnation at the Trial, yet he had been arraigned at the arbitrary Tribunal of Public Opinion, and most of the spectators had pronounced judgement against him in their hearts. It is not to be wondered then that the testimony like the present, proceeding from the lips of a dying man, whose only probable concern it was to ease his burthened conscience in the hour of death, should at once remove all doubt, if such remained, and the feelings of the multitude burst forth into invective.

At about ten the Criminals reascended the cart; and when about to be launched into eternity, a reprieve for James Hardwicke was received and announced by the Provost Marshall.

Samuels devoted the last awful minute allowed him to the most earnest and fervent prayer; at length the signal was given, and the cart drove from under him; but by the concussion, the suspending rope was separated about the centre, and the culprit fell to the ground, on which he remained motionless, with his face downwards. The cart returned, and the criminal was supported on each side until another rope was applied in lieu of the former. He was again launched off, but the rope unrove, and continued to slip until the legs of the sufferer trailed along the ground, the body being only half suspended. All that beheld were also moved at his protracted

sufferings; nor did some hesitate to declare, that the invisible hand of Providence was at work in the behalf of him who had revealed the circumstances, related above. To every appearance lifeless, the body was now raised and supported on men's shoulders, while the executioner prepared anew the work of death. The body was gently lowered but when left alone, again fell prostrate to the earth, this rope also having snapped short close to the neck.

Compassion could no longer bear restraint; winged with humanity, the Provost Marshall sped to His Excellency's presence, in which the success of his mission overcame him. A reprieve was announced — and if Mercy be a fault, it is the dearest attribute of God, and surely in Heaven it may find extenuation!

Samuels, when the Provost Marshall arrived with the tidings, which diffused gladness throughout every hearts, was incapable of participating in the general satisfaction. By what he had endured his reasonable faculties were totally impaired. When his nerves recovered somewhat from their feebleness, he uttered many incoherences, and was alone ignorant of what had past. Surgical assistance has since restored him; and MAY THE GRATEFUL REMEMBRANCE OF THESE EVENTS DIRECT HIS FUTURE COURSE.

Front page of George Howe's *Sydney Gazette*

THE
SYDNEY GAZETTE,
And New South Wales Advertiser.

WE HOPE TO PROSPER · THUS

PUBLISHED BY AUTHORITY.

Vol. I.   SATURDAY, MARCH 5, 1803.   Number 1.

It is hereby ordered, that all Advertisements, Orders, &c. which appear under the Official Signature of the Secretary of this Colony, or of any other Officer of Government, properly authorised to publish them in the SYDNEY GAZETTE, AND NEW SOUTH WALES ADVERTISER, are meant, and must be deemed to convey official and sufficient Notifications, in the same Manner as if they were particularly specified to any ONE Individual, or Others, to whom such may have a Reference.

By Command of His Excellency the Governor and Commander in Chief, WILLIAM NEATE CHAPMAN, Secretary.

Sydney, March 5th, 1803.

General Orders.

REPEATED Complaints having been made of the great losses sustained by the Settlers at Hawkesbury, from the vexatious conduct of the Boatmen by whom they send their Grain to Sydney, the following Regulations are to be observed.

Every person sending grain from the Hawkesbury to Sydney in an open boat, or a boat that is not trust-worthy, the Magistrates are directed to take no notice thereof.

If on proof it appears that the Master of a Boat receives more grain than the vessel ought to take with safety, the Master shall make good any quantity he may throw overboard, or otherwise damage, lose the freight of that part, and, on conviction before two Magistrates, forfeit 5l. to the Orphan Fund.

If it shall appear to the Magistrates that grain coming round to Sydney has been wetted, that it might weigh heavier or measure more than the quantity put on board, the Master will, on conviction, forfeit 5l. to the Orphan Fund.

The Commanding Officer of the New South Wales Corps will direct the Corporal of the Guard on board the Castle of Good Hope to read the General Orders that are packed off in the Extracts he is furnished with, to the Corporal, and the Party that relieves him; the said Orders are also to be read to the Guard on board the Supply Hulk.

By Command of His Excellency   W. N. CHAPMAN, Sec.
Government House, Feb. 21, 1803.

THE Receiving Granaries at Parramatta and Hawkesbury, being filled with Wheat which is spoiling, no more can be taken in at those places until further Orders, except in payment for Government Debts, and the Whalers Investments lodged in the Public Stores.

Wheat will continue to be received into the Stores at Sydney, until further Orders.

Wheat will be issued to the Civil, Military, &c. until further Orders; except to the detachments and labouring people at Castle-Hill, Seven-Hills, and other Out Posts, who will receive Flour, as they have not the convenience of Mills.

By Command, &c.   W. N. CHAPMAN, Sec
Government House,
   Feb. 24, 1803.

THE GOVERNOR having permitted Mr. Robert Campbell to land 4000 Gallons of Spirits for the domestic use of the Inhabitants, from the Castle of Good Hope, it will be divided in the following proportion, viz.

For the Officers on the Civil Establishment, (including Superintendants and Store-keepers), 1000 Gallons;

For Naval and Military Commissioned Officers, 1000 Gallons;

For the Licensed People, 1000 Gallons;

To be distributed to such Persons as the GOVERNOR may think proper to grant Permits to, 1000 Gallons.

The above to include the Civil and Military Officers at Norfolk Island.

By Command, &c.   W. N. CHAPMAN, Sec.
Government House, March 4, 1803.

ADDRESS.

Innumerable as the Obstacles were which threatened to oppose our Undertaking, yet we are happy to affirm that they were not insurmountable, however difficult the task before us.

The utility of a PAPER in the COLONY, as it must open a source of solid information, will, we hope, be universally felt and acknowledged. We have courted the assistance of the INGENIOUS and INTELLIGENT :---- We open no channel to Political Discussion, or Personal Animadversion :----Information is our only Purpose; that accomplished, we shall consider that we have done our duty in an exertion to merit the Approbation of the PUBLIC, and to secure a liberal Patronage to the SYDNEY GAZETTE.

JOHN JAQUES, TAYLOR,
At the Back of the General Hospital, Sydney,

RESPECTFULLY acquaints the PUBLIC, that in consequence of the reduction that has lately taken place in the Prices of many Articles of common Consumption, he has been enabled to make an Abatement in his Charges, and that all Orders with which he may be honoured shall be carefully and punctually executed.

1824   Freedom of the Press: Andrew Bent has a victory over Governor Arthur

ANDREW BENT
Hobart Town Gazette, 8 October 1824

One of the great running battles between authority and the individual journalist was fought in Van Diemen's Land in the mid-1820s. The protagonists: Colonel George Arthur, Lieutenant-Governor of the colony, and Andrew Bent, ex-convict, publisher of the Hobart Town Gazette *and* Van Diemen's Land Advertiser.

Bent had purchased the press plant and rights of the Gazette *from the government. Within a month of his arrival (in May 1824), Arthur requested that Bent refrain from all criticism of the government in his newspaper. Bent refused and insisted that the* Gazette, *because it published government material, was government property.*

At the time, Tasmania was still not independent of Sydney control. Bent sent an emissary to appeal to Arthur's superior, Sir Thomas Brisbane; Brisbane had recently ruled that Dr Wardell and William Wentworth could publish the Australian *in Sydney without government supervision, and he could see no reason why Bent should not do the same in Hobart. As soon as he received the good news, Bent announced his victory in the* Gazette, *and went on to describe Arthur as the 'Gibeonite of Tyranny'. Not many people in Hobart knew just what he meant. They assumed that the term simply meant an especially bad form of Tyranny. But Arthur knew about the Gibeonites — they hanged their enemies on the hill before the Lord — and he was alarmed at the possible effect of Bent's words on the convict population.*

Bent's report on his victory, republished here, marked only the first of a series of collisions with Arthur. Bent continued to criticise the administration, and was finally obliged — after Arthur had offered the posit-ion of government printer to Terry Howe (son of George Howe, of the Sydney Gazette) — *to change the name of his publication to the* Colonial Times. *Howe became publisher of the* Hobart Town Gazette, *with Dr James Ross as editor. Bent was found guilty of libel for the first time in 1825, and was sent to jail for six months. Later, in October 1827, Bent's* Colonial Times *came out with the news column blank, and the explanation that Arthur would not grant him a licence to publish news. He sold the copyright of his newspaper to Mr James Austin but Arthur still refused to grant a licence to the* Colonial Times, *because Austin had retained Bent as printer.*

Worn out by imprisonment and constant harassment, Bent was in the process of selling his type and presses when the news arrived that the British Ministry had repealed the Licence Act — the act which Arthur had used to persecute him. Again Bent announced news of a victory: 'Thus may the Freedom of the Press be considered once more to be restored to the colonists of Tasmania', the Colonial Times *of 2 January 1829 said.*

Later Bent wrote of his trials:

Dreading perpetual imprisonment under a Chancery suit, and broken in spirit and in pocket by the persecutions I had suffered, I discontinued the *Colonial Advocate*, and was thereupon released. The Press Licencing Act was disallowed by Sir George Murray, Secretary for the Colonies; the announcement of which disallowance reached the colony soon after my release from prison. But the unremitting persecution, which I had suffered from Colonel Arthur, and the determination on his part to put down all free discussion, by prosecution for alleged libels, and the certainty of conviction before a military tribunal, convinced me that to follow my occupation, as a newspaper proprietor and printer, would be attended with certain ruin to myself and family.

Bent was generally conceded to be the father of the Tasmanian Press — and more than one historian has referred to him as 'the Tasmanian Franklin'.

Here is his report on his victory over Governor Arthur:

Equally pusillanimous, equally reprehensible, are the assumption of a false claim, and the abandonment of a just one! With decision, therefore, we have chosen to resist what was jurisprudentially esteemed as a most "unwarranted invasion" of our right to the sole Proprietorship of this Gazette; and, thanks most profoundly permanent to that hallowed spirit of British Justice, which animates SIR THOMAS BRISBANE, our resistance has been consecrated by a perfect triumph. We knew, yes! well we knew, by confident, serene, and cloudless anticipation, that our legally indefeasible title would be confirmed and held intangible at Head Quarters. We were sure that the dignified Representative of England's all-liberal and erudite SOVEREIGN, (may God for ever bless him!) would scorn to sully his name or his nation by *illegally* scathing the literary edifice composed and cemented by a Patriot's industry.

At present, however, we shall only add the following explanatory paragraph, which, having appeared in the *Sydney Gazette*, by express and supreme Colonial Authority, will "speak volumes" to the prejudiced, and invest our tremulous adherents with a pleasing confidence, that *even yet* the sling of an outraged "*weak* one", when brandished against the Gibeonite of tyranny, must be *Laus deo*, irresistible: —

"The Art of Typography, when well employed, is in our estimation so mighty and benignant, that all, who would oppose its judicious operations, must surely be, as we are bold to call them — foes, rank foes, of every talent which adorns, and of every virtue that enobles mankind! Our inducement to offer the above remark, has been furnished by certain occurrences, of recent date and high importance, in relation to "*The Hobart Town Gazette*," for which *little Struggler* in the cause of the Community who patronize it, we have often denoted our esteem; and, to which, in a great degree, we attribute the improvement of their prospects. It appears, as we are credibly informed, that Mr. ANDREW BENT, Government Printer at Hobart Town, instituted the Hobart Town Gazette at his own expense, and has ever since so conducted it — feeling it to be, as of course it is, both by law and in equity, his own personal property! — It further appears that some efforts were rumoured as in progress to bereave him of the same; and, in consequence, he very properly despatched his newly appointed Editor, on a respectful embassy to Head Quarters, with such documents as could clearly establish his said Proprietorship. And lastly, it appears, as with feelings of pride and satisfaction we inform the Public, that HIS EXCELLENCY was pleased to consider Mr. BENT'S claim to publish his said Paper, on his own account, completely indisputable. "It was true," as the liberal and enlightened Representative of Our Gracious Monarch said, 'Lieutenant Governor ARTHUR *might* chuse another vehicle for the dissemination of Official Orders, &c.' — But, that the Journal itself was private property had been alledged on oaths the most sacred! and we are therefore justified in stating, that *on oath alone can it, if ever it can*, fairly be brought within the pale of question."

AN UNKNOWN GENTLEWOMAN
Hobart Town Colonial Advocate, 1 May 1828

One of the earliest pictures of life in Van Diemen's Land was given by the wife of a businessman. Before she left England, she had promised to write an article describing life in the colony and send it to a friend on the staff of the London Morning Herald.

Her story was published in the Morning Herald, *and it found its way back to the* Colonial Advocate, *a monthly journal started by Andrew Bent during one of his Arthur-induced stretches in jail. The* Colonial Advocate *published the article, which was less than flattering to Hobart Town, in its issue of 1 May 1828, under the cryptic heading, 'Female Writer'. This is an extract:*

I remember you wished me to give you a sketch of the society in this place, and that I can now do, as we are acquainted with almost every body, that is any body here. In the first place, you could hardly imagine that a country like England could produce such an illiterate cub as this Colony. Who would not have expected to find by this time a Library at least. They had one at South Carolina before it was established twelve months. Saturn is not more remote from the Sun, than Hobart Town from all Science and Literature. Variety is a word unknown in its vocabulary, and the light that surrounds you must be all from within. The mercantile classes are animated by an avaricious (or I should rather say *voracious*) spirit of money-getting, which engenders jealousy and ill-will when there is the least collision of interest or chance of rivalry. They are the democracy of the Colony, and proscribed at Government House, and hostile to all the measures that emanate thence; and looking to Murray, the Editor of the *Colonial Times*, as their political leader. The Government and Law Officers, &c. &c. form, and are, completely the Aristocracy. They are dull, reserved, punctiliously jealous of compromising their rank, all etiquette and caution. One reason for all this is, that there are a great many mushrooms amongst them; and there is no pride so stiff and ungraceful as upstarts. Entertainments are occasionally given; but, as Madame de Stael says of the Germans, they are rather ceremonies than parties of pleasure; and this remark applies to the first house in this place.

A card for a dinner party gives me the horrors; its very touch has the effect ascribed to the Torpedo. Often, very often, I had much rather stay at home; but, like the poor King of Arragon, "etiquette won't let me." I summon my fortitude and set forth. The servant that opens the door to me, says, in his manner, "you may come in, but are to say nothing." I find the chairs set in a row, and the company in as good order as a fine set of teeth — "not grinning however.". . .

There is no place of public meeting but the Church — not even a Public Walk. No books, no not so much as a Magazine, in which, if they were the lineal descendants of burgomasters, they may sometimes emerge from restraint, at least anonymously, so that any thing of a frank, open intercommunion of ideas is unknown; and the human mind here, like a soil that would refuse all vegetation for fear of growing a poison, becomes a barren waste. Caution has been in my eyes anything rather than a virtue; it may serve ignorance for a screen, and cowardice for a shield; to the suspicious, it answers the purpose of feelers, and I have always viewed it as the accompaniment and characteristic of the meaner order of animals, whether human or other, unless, indeed, it is the growth of sad experience, the correction of time upon the original character. Whenever I find it the indigenous quality of a young mind, I do not hesitate to pronounce it a sure indicative of a narrow and defective character. Accustomed, as I have been to a cultivated country, abounding with sources of interest and excitement, and in my own family to a great share of wit, humour, and originality, it is hardly possible to give you an idea how much I feel the *cimmerian dulness* of the town. To prove, however, that I can appreciate its local advantages in spite of these woeful disadvantages, I must assure you, that none can think more highly than I do of the capabilities of this country. So late as 1817, it was no more than a penal settlement; it is now a tolerable town, having a great number of respectable inhabitants, some excellent houses, most of the necessaries, and some of the luxuries of life, while many of the farms scattered in different parts of the country, are flourishing places. The climate is fine. This winter, which every one tells me is a cold one, has been little more than a cold October. In the bush, the name they give to the interior, they completely realise the old patriarchal times — flocks and herds forming all their wealth. As a struggling man, and with no further ambition than to see my sons plant cabbages and dig them up again, I should be happy to retire from the precariousness and anxieties attendant on most pursuits in England, to the quiet of this place, since to vegetate in Van Diemen's Land, is better than being kept in hot water in England. To any one asking me about settling in Hobart Town, "alias Humdrumstadt," I should say, there were good salaries attached to the public officers, and little to do; and from all I can learn, the returns in business are very fair, and the commerce increasing: but if Settlers expect beyond that, unless to eat, drink, sleep, and mope, any thing requisite to render their lives endurable, let them not attempt it. I don't think a superannuated Dutchman "although furnished with *tobacco gratis*," would stay here if he could help it. Another characteristic of this delectable town (and, I am sorry to say, I have heard it generally remarked to be the case where the English congregate) is scandal.

When in a reflective mood, I sigh to see so fair a world deformed by the bad passions of human kind. I have so often met with envy, splenetic ill nature, and rancorous detraction, where I hoped and sought to cultivate very opposite feelings, that I am continually turning from the world to my own family circle, not merely as it has been my pride, my happiness, but as my refuge. Literature, an auxiliary every where, is here an essential, with that, and the idol that my heart cherishes, I have a little Goshen of my own, to which I can always retire from the plagues of the world.

I have not yet told you any thing about the convicts — the worst feature in Van Diemen's Land, which, like an ugly nose, spoils the face of the country. — The most desperate are formed into gangs, and work upon the roads in chains. They leave and return to the gaol at stated hours, when a bell rings, and are always guarded by soldiers; you cannot imagine a more wreckless, horrid looking set of creatures than most of them; there are others engaged in the public works, who are unfettered, many are servants to the Settlers (and some good ones), and there are several instances of their returning into the pale of respectable society, realising fortunes, and marrying their children into decent families, and the bar of transportation in their escutcheons is overlooked.

The Colonial Advocate *did not last long. Governor Arthur introduced a law which prohibited any convict from writing for a newspaper; the penalty was for the writer to be sent to a penal settlement. As Bent complained later in a petition to the British parliament: 'The* Colonial Advocate *was not a newspaper; yet, on this government order, the editor was removed to a distant settlement, while it was notorious that one newspaper, which supported Governor Arthur's measures, was conducted by convicts.' Bent was compelled to give up the* Advocate. *He claimed in his petition that 'the sole object of the proceedings was to destroy every semblance of a free press in the colony'.*

1828   Tasmanian Aborigines raid the settlers: 'Let the blacks be removed or exterminated'

ANDREW BENT
Hobart Town Colonial Advocate, 1 May 1828

By 1826, Governor Arthur, who had begun his administration by urging all settlers to treat the natives with charity and compassion, was coming to the conclusion that there was no way to make peace with the Aborigines. The Aborigines were stealing property, butchering white men, and crying out during their raids: 'Fire, you white bastards.'

Andrew Bent, in his Colonial Advocate, *put the case bluntly, and brutally, on 1 May 1828. The alternatives, he wrote, were to exterminate or remove the blacks 'by whom more European blood has been spilled, within the last two years, than there was by all the bush-rangers who were ever out from the formation of the colony!!!' The three exclamation marks were Bent's. He also attacked a proclamation by Arthur which ordered that force should be used to keep natives out of settled districts only when it could not be avoided, and which stated that all Aborigines taken prisoner would be treated with the utmost humanity and compassion.*

By a fatality, over which we have no control, accounts of the outrages of these surely most savage of all savages in human shape are destined to pollute our pages of record, every succeeding month. Vain seems the expectation – futile the hope – and vague even the most-distant idea that an end will ever be put to the plunder, terror, and blood-shed occasioned by this sable race; *by whom more European blood has been spilled, within the last two years, than there was by all the bush-rangers who were ever out from the formation of the Colony!!!* Notwithstanding this truly lamentable and appalling fact, it seems that a false notion of pity and humanity – a singular tenderness of conscience, seems to keep the Executive from those positive and decided measures which at once can end all this dreadful carnage, and general terror.

Unless the blacks are *exterminated* or *removed*, it is plainly proved, by fatal and sanguinary experience, that all hope of their ceasing in their aggressions, is the height of absurdity. All the conciliations – all the mercy – all the kindnesses – all the entreaties and endeavours that have been bestowed to render these unhappy tribes sensible of the benefits of civilization, have been thrown away, and the only return they have made is to murder and plunder, and express their determination to *exterminate* every white man that comes in their way.

In the name of Heaven, is it not high time to resort to strong and decisive measures, if not of retaliation – of self-preservation? The *lex talionis* is by no means what we are about to advocate, nor is it to be supposed that we think the black monsters of sufficient value to warrant its being put in force; but if we do not retaliate, let us for Heaven's sake, rally our resources, and save our fellow countrymen from the Aboriginal spears! What signifies our boasted civilization – our vaunted wisdom – if we are to be foiled by a handful of black barbarians? Is it not a reproach to the British Government, that in a Colony where the population exceeds 17,000 whites, a tribe of Aborigines, whose aggregate number cannot be more than 2000, should spread, and continue to spread, devastation and alarm over the whole country? Is this to be said of a Colony of Englishmen?

Shall the sons of the greatest empire in the world give way before a body of savages, after having successfully repulsed the disciplined armies of all France? And that too, when the savages are not one-fifth part so numerous, calculating males and females, as the body of effective volunteers, which could be raised and well armed! This is too bad — it argues weak-mindedness on the part of the Government. It is no vain and idle theory which dictates the removal of the blacks. It is a step which is, in every sense of the word, practicable. Fit out your parties of volunteers from the Prisoners' Barracks — place tickets of leave, emancipations, and free pardons as the rewards, and soon would the blacks be hunted down and taken, *without* bloodshed — lodged in safe custody, and removed to King's, or some other of the Islands in the Straits. Then some hope might be entertained of civilizing them. . .

We predict, that unless the blacks are removed by the Government, the time is not far distant, when the whole of the Settlers, with one accord, will set about the dreadful work of Aboriginal extermination. Since our last, the following attacks have been made by these worthless creatures:—

1. — Mr. Gilles's hut attacked; the inmates saving their lives by flight.

2. — A servant of Mr. Cotterel's killed at his hut.

3. — A man on horseback attacked near the Lagoon of Islands; escaped with great difficulty.

4. — Mr. Batman's shepherd chased to his master's house, on the Ben Lomond rivulet. Mr. Batman, in conjunction with four of his own servants, three of the field police, and two soldiers, followed the tribe until the next day, when they came up with them, by creeping cautiously on their hands and knees, towards where they saw a smoke, unobserved. Mr. Batman endeavoured to make them stop, but in vain; one of them, in the act of throwing a spear, was brought to the ground by a shot from Mr. Batman, in his own defence; but he got up again, and ran off. After some further pursuit, the party succeeded in overtaking and capturing a boy, about 16 years of age. Mr. B. and his party then returned to the place which the blacks had just left, where they found the following articles:— 20 blankets, 24 knives, 2 muskets *loaded* (!) 4 pounds of buckshot (!!) a canister of gunpowder (!!!)

a bayonet, 2 pair of sheep shears, numerous waddies, spears, &c. The boy, having been taken to Mr. Pitcairn's farm, escaped during the night, up the chimney of the room in which he was confined! Three other parties, headed by Messrs. Batman, Crawley, and Cotterel, went out the following day, but did not fall in with the Natives.

5. — Mr. Kearney's stock-keepers attacked within a hundred yards of his dwelling, after having just before kindly entertained two Natives there. It was with the greatest difficulty that he escaped to the hut, where he and his companion were kept prisoners the whole of that night and the following day, the blacks guarding the door. At length, their patience exhausted, they fired at one of the savages, and wounded him about the posteriors, severely. The rest then collected and retired, carrying off their wounded companion.

6. — Having attacked another stock-hut, among the Western Mountains, and failed to kill any of the men, they proceeded to spear and drive away the cattle, 30 of which are missing, and two have died from spear wounds!

7. — One of Mr. Mackersey's men wounded to death! and the hut robbed of every moveable.

8. — Another man dangerously speared, near Mr. Presnel's new house, at Sorell Springs.

9. — Mr. Eddington's stock-hut, at Quamby's Bluff, set on fire!

10. — A man of Mr. Robertson's speared, and is missing!

11. — Another man, in the same neighbourhood, dangerously speared in *five* places!

Such, then, is the dreadful catalogue of crimes committed by the Natives, within *one* little month, which have come before the Public, and it is very probable, that there are many more instances . . .

They are too ignorant — too truly barbarous to understand any thing but *force*; and, although we cannot but admit, that a greater protection is afforded by the present Proclamation, still it is not *efficient*. The Natives are never, in our opinion, to be quieted, otherwise than by one of two methods, viz. their extermination or their removal. . .

1829 'Simon Stukely', a new columnist, shocks Hobart Town by ridiculing pomposity

HENRY SAVERY
Hobart Town Colonial Times, 5 June 1829

The Colonial Times, *edited by the uncompromising Henry Melville, was one of Tasmania's most distinguished pioneer newspapers. In his* Early Struggles of the Australian Press, *James Bonwick wrote of the journal: 'To it, more than to any other paper, has Australia been indebted for its subsequent emancipation from personal rule.'*

In June 1829, the Colonial Times *introduced its readers to one Simon Stukely — the country's first really devastating columnist. Stukely announced that his objective was to impart information about the state of manners and society in the colony of Van Diemen's Land, to hold up to deserved ridicule some of the vices and follies by which they were distinguished, and to present a mirror in which good qualities would be exhibited.*

His articles — entitled 'The Hermit in Van Diemen's Land' — began on 5 June and appeared in every issue until 25 December. Stukely did not discuss politics, or the major social problems of the time. He wrote about people. The historian C. M. H. Clark said of Stukely:

He wrote of greedy, rapacious lawyers; he wrote of the idle vapouring for which pert braggarts, idle coxcombs and empty-headed drivellers were ever distinguished. He wrote salaciously of women entering the critical age when an extra sentinel was required to be placed at every avenue leading to the heart. He wrote such lively character sketches of all the public figures of the day, of Arthur, Pedder, Hone, Kemp, Gellibrand, Gregson and Alfred Stephen, without mentioning them by name, that for a season identification became one of the sports of Hobart Town. He wrote with envy and spite of those who put on airs, or affected social graces.

Simon Stukely was in fact Henry Savery, a convict who was in jail in Hobart Town when he wrote his series of columns for the Colonial Times. *Savery, born in Somerset in 1791 into a respectable banking family, had been a merchant in Bristol before he was transported for forgery; he was sentenced to death, and reprieved twenty-four hours before the scheduled execution.*

He was transported in 1825, and locked up for common debt in 1828; in jail he met Thomas Wells, a printer, who copied his works and passed them to Henry Melville.

The 'Hermit' series caused a tremendous fuss. So caustic were Savery's observations that another newspaper, the Launceston Advertiser, *called them pen-and-ink slaughters which should be expunged from the pages of the* Colonial Times. *Four years later, after he had criticised a member of the Legislative Council in an article in the* Tasmanian, *Savery was charged with violation of a law which forbade ticket-of-leave holders from writing for the public press; he survived this crisis, wrote the three-volume novel* Quintus Servinton *(of which he was the hero), became a farmer, and failed. He again committed forgery, and was sent to the penal settlement of Port Arthur, where he took his own life by cutting his throat.*

Savery had not been in Hobart Town long when he wrote this piece for the Colonial Times:

It was a remarkably fine clear day when I landed from the ship on the wharf. What was my surprise to observe the large handsome stone buildings, into which porters were busily engaged rolling casks and other packages, and at several civil looking well dressed young men, who were standing with pens behind their ears, and memorandum books in their hands, paying the most diligent attention to what was going on. A number of other persons formed little knots or circles; and the hallooing of ferrymen, the cracking of whips, and the vociferation of carters, struck me as creating altogether a scene of bustle and activity, which indeed I had little expected. For the moment it occurred to me, that our Captain, in the hurry and confusion which the quarrels on board had occasioned, had missed his reckoning, and had made a wrong port, and accordingly seeing a fat, portly, sleek-looking apparently good-humoured Gentleman approaching, I enquired of him, with an apology, in what place I was? Judging from my manner and appearance that I must be a stranger, he very civilly replied, that I was in Hobart Town, the capital of Van Diemen's Land, adding, "Perhaps, Sir, you would like to walk into our Commercial Room, to which I can introduce you." I then accompanied my new acquaintance up a flight of stone steps into a rather elegantly fitted-up room, in which there were three or four plainly dressed Gentlemen reading Newspapers.

One of them, who appeared bordering upon sixty, wore spectacles, and had a considerable degree of eagerness in his manner, rose upon my entrance, and addressed me, "Just from England, eh, Sir. What news, Sir, when you left? The Colony is much talked of at home, Sir. Suppose you heard of our Association, but things are not now as they used to be." Before I could make a reply, he offered me a Newspaper, further acquainting me that the town maintained three such publications; one of which, said he, is so dull and prosy, that nobody reads it. Another has lately been at death's door, owing to some Government regulations, but has now, Phoenix-like, risen with redoubled splendour; and the other is made up of short paragraphs and country letters written in town, but commands an extensive circulation. . .

How great was my astonishment at the magnificent straight line of street, extending apparently for more than a mile by which my sight was greeted upon leaving the Quay. I could scarcely credit my senses that I was in a town which is only as it were of yesterday. As I proceeded along, my surprise was increased by seeing other fine streets meeting at right angles the one by which I was walking towards a handsome brick church, with a steeple like the extinguisher upon a flat candlestick, my left being flanked by well laid out gardens and shrubberies, in the centre of which stood the Governor's residence, and every here and there the right being ornamented by large two-story brick or stone houses. The church door happening to be open, I took the opportunity of judging of its interior, and I could almost have fancied myself in one of the modern churches of the metropolis of the world. Such regular well-arranged pews, so beautifully a finished pulpit and reading desk, made of wood which I at first thought was Spanish mahogany, quite astonished me; upon a nearer examination, however, and upon enquiry of a man who was dusting the aisles, I learnt that it was the produce of a tree, indigenous to the Colony, known by the name of Myrtle. While I was thus employing myself, a Gentleman wearing a Clerical hat, approached, and with much affability of manner, addressed me as a stranger, and gave me some general information respecting the religious institutions of the place. He had a lisp in his speech, which was by no means disagreeable, and his well cased ribs bore evident marks that, whatever doctrines he might preach, that of fasting was not one upon which he laid much stress, at least in its practice.

He acquainted me, that independent of the congregations belonging to this large Church, a Presbyterian Chapel, a Roman Catholic Chapel, and a Wesleyan Meeting House, were each well attended every Sunday, and it gave me great pleasure afterwards to be told of this Gentleman, as he himself had expressed of his brother labourers in the vineyard that in their lives and conduct the religion they all practised received its brightest ornament — that they each made a well formed corner stone of the superstructure they supported. Oh! thought I, this must be the effect of a virtuous and industrious population. Arts, architecture, literature, religion and commerce must here thrive so well, because so many excellent

An early view of Hobart Town

people, for whom Old England was not good enough, have congregated, and because so many others have been cleansed of their sins, and are now restored to innocence. Happy people, and thrice happy Simon Stukely, to have left your retirement, to come among them! — Everything seemed indeed greatly superior to my expectations. Well dressed and elegant ladies were promenading one street, well mounted Equestrians were galloping along another, respectably attired Pedestrians helped to add to the scene, which was still more enlivened by the relief-guard of the Military, as it approached the Main-guard House from the Barracks, and by the rapid passing and re-passing of gigs, carts, and other wheel vehicles. I was completely in a reverie scarcely knowing through which street I would perambulate, or which object best claimed my attention. The entire absence of all beggars, or indigent persons, added to my wonder, but after a little reflection, I accounted for it in my own mind, by considering that as all the inhabitants were either pure or purified, it was quite of a piece with their religion and virtue to be charitable, this being the brightest of the cardinal gems. I continued my walk for a long time, each moment more astonished than before at the progress which had been made in laying out and building the town — at the excellent shops in the different streets — at the wide well macadamised thoroughfares, and their convenient causeways, and at a hundred other matters which excited my admiration, until I found myself in a quarter of the town situated on an eminence at some distance from the Church, and where the houses and inhabitants seemed rather of an inferior description to those I had before seen. In their manners and style of conversation, upon the different subjects, respecting which I interrogated them, they exhibited however all the easy confidence of virtue. The calls of my appetite now warned me that the day was fast waning, and I applied my hand to my fob to ascertain the hour when to my utter dismay I found that one of Hawley's best gold watches, with which I had provided myself previous to my departure from England, was missing. . .

1831 Four thousand celebrate Governor Darling's recall to London

DR ROBERT WARDELL
Sydney Australian, 22 October 1831

The Sydney Gazette *had the newspaper field in Sydney to itself from its inception in 1803 until 14 October 1824, when the* Australian *was born. The proprietor of the* Australian *was the native-born W. C. Wentworth, who felt deeply that the new colony needed the stimulus of political discussion. 'An independent paper . . . which may serve to point out the rising interests of the colonists, and become the organ of their grievances and rights, their wishes and wants, is highly necessary,' he wrote.*

The man Wentworth chose to edit the new paper was Dr Robert Wardell, a barrister he had met in London. In the late 1820s Wardell was an extremely busy man; he practised constantly as a lawyer, ran a farm, held several directorships, edited and managed the Australian, *and wrote a great deal of its content. He believed strongly in the freedom of the press, and his expressed editorial aim was 'to convert a prison into a colony fit for a freeman to inhabit himself and to bequeath as an inheritance to a free posterity'.*

Wardell and Wentworth, through the Australian, *fought a running battle with Governor Ralph Darling almost from the moment of his arrival in the colony in December 1825. Darling was arrogant and despotic, and his repressive regime earned him the hatred of all except the major land-owners, whom he encouraged by granting 640 acres for every £500 invested and assigning them convicts as virtual slaves. After a soldier called Sudds died after the flogging which Darling had personally ordered, Wardell led a press crusade against the Governor. Darling tried to gag Wardell and the editor of the Sydney* Monitor *(established in 1826), Edward Smith Hall, by means of a licence (to be renewed*

each year) and a stamp-duty (a third of the selling price) on each newspaper. These measures were blocked by Chief Justice Forbes, who refused to certify that they were 'not repugnant to the law of England'. Darling denounced Wardell as being 'without principle'.

Wardell referred to Darling in print as 'an ignorant and obstinate man', and was promptly charged with libel; he conducted his own defence, and defeated Darling by persuading the jury to disagree.

Wardell, Wentworth and Hall, whose criticisms of government policy Darling tried constantly to suppress, were mainly responsible for the recall in October 1831 of the Governor. Darling's departure was celebrated at the Vaucluse home of Wentworth by more than 4,000 people who lit bonfires and fireworks to demonstrate their joy. Wardell's send-off in print took the form of an account of the 'splendid fete, brilliant illuminations and joyous festivities' at Vaucluse, plus a leading article which castigated the Governor and the 'junta of rapacious and despicable men' who manipulated him.

Three years later, while riding on his farm at Petersham, Wardell met three runaway convicts; he tried to persuade them to give themselves up, but one of them picked up a gun and shot him dead. The convicts were arrested a few days later, and two of them were tried and hanged for murder. Wardell, aged forty, was planning to return soon to England when he died.

This was Dr Wardell's account of Darling's departure, published in the Australian *on 22 October 1831:*

Rejoice, Australia! Darling's reign has passed. And HOPE, once more, re-enhances our land!

Thank God. We have shaken off the *incubus* at last. General Darling's government is now to all intents and purposes defunct. Ere this article reaches the reader's eye, perhaps the same breeze which is wafting General Bourke towards our shores, is impelling General Darling from them!

New prospects are opening to our view. Fresh impulses are teeming before us. We trust that the day which has seen us rid of the Darling dynasty, will be dated in future annals as the day on which, from a state of general disunion (unparalleled) and of embarrassment agricultural and commercial — our Colony began to bound forward with new life, new vigor — commerce and agriculture to revive and prosper, and the dissensions of rival Montagues and Capulets to merge so far that all honest Colonists would find their common interest really concerned. . .

Of Governor Bourke, it would be premature to say much either in the way of praise or otherwise. His acts will best bespeak his merits. But we do not think, after the lesson taught his predecessor, that General Bourke will feel strongly tempted to tread in his footsteps. Should Mr. McLeay continue to hold his present office, however, we fear that his counsels may, or will protract the goodly work which we anticipate.

We sincerely hope, therefore, that so Venerable a bigot — so grasping, avaricious and insatiable a pensionary, will not be allowed to burthen the civil list of the colony, or to retain office of any kind under the new Governor. Should any leaven of the late odious rule be infused into General Bourke's administration, it would spoil all, and we shall caution General Bourke, should Mr. McLeay be retained, as he values his reputation, his peace of mind, the public esteem and benefit, utterly to disregard every craft insinuation or sidewind remark of the official cormorant.

Let General Bourke, when he assumes the reins of government, but reflect for a moment on the miserably humiliating situation to which evil counsels reduced his predecessor; for to such interested advisers as the official pensioner, may be fairly traced a liberal share of the unpopularity and detestation which the

Governor Ralph Darling

community have so very strongly and unequivocally manifested towards General Darling, and nearly all his measures. Gracious Heaven! What must be the feelings of that man, when he reflects, that instead of using his little brief authority to promote as far as possible the welfare and interests of the community over whom he was sent to rule, he has been made the tool of a junta of rapacious and despicable men, and instigated by them to the commission of acts and deeds, which will enrol his name among the Caligulas of antiquity.

He may thank those evil counsellors, and his own unpardonable weakness, in having listened to them, for most of the parting demonstrations of dislike and aversion which nearly all persons have displayed to him! Does it not speak volumes, when we record, that instead of the respectful language of gratitude conferred by him on the country, and regret for his departure which by an opposite line of country he might have earned, he is burned and hanged in effigy, by all free thinking people, in divers parts of the town?!!

By four in the afternoon, after passing a most convivial time of it, the company began to retire homewards; many hundreds stopping to pass a few more witching hours, and the night being exceedingly fine, and the full orbed moon in all her majesty, an indescribable air of fascination was thrown over the whole scene. . .

1835 More than two hundred perish as women convicts' ship goes down

DR JAMES ROSS

Hobart Town Courier, 3 July 1835

One of the worst convict shipwrecks was that of the Neva *which struck a reef off King Island in Bass Strait on 13 May 1835. Of the 150 female prisoners, fifty-nine children, nine other women and a crew of twenty-six, only twenty-two survived and managed to swim ashore.*

Some died of exhaustion and some drank greedily from casks of spirits — they died victims, it was said, of their own depravity. This left only fifteen survivors (six prisoners and nine crew) from the entire complement of 244, who lived to tell the story.

Here is an account of the wreck which appeared in Dr Ross's Hobart Town Courier *on 3 July 1835:*

We have this week the melancholy task to record another most distressing shipwreck almost continuous to our island, attended with loss of life still more extensive and awful than that of the late unfortunate George the Third. The female convict ship Neva, Capt. Peck, left Cork on the 8th of Jan. last, bound to Sydney, having on board 150 female prisoners with 33 of their children, 9 free women with 26 children, and a crew of 26 persons, under the charge of Surgeon Superintendent Dr. Stevenson, R.N. They had proceeded prosperously on their voyage, until on Wednesday the 13th of May last, anticipating in a few more days to arrive at their destination, and being by the reckoning kept about 90 miles from King's island. So early as two in the morning, the man on the lookout discovered land in sight, and about four, a reef of rocks suddenly appeared right ahead.

Orders were instantly given to tack about, but while yet in stays the vessel struck and unshipped the rudder. The ship then became altogether unmanageable, and obeying the impulse of the wind only, was driven upon her larboard bow with violence on the rocks, and swinging round, immediately bilged. The boats were speedily lowered, but they had no sooner reached the water than they were upset, and in a few minutes more the vessel parted and fell asunder in four pieces, when dreadful to relate, with the exception of 22 persons who clung to the fragments, the whole on board perished.

After enduring unspeakable hardships the survivors reached King's island, but 7 of the number were so exhausted that they died soon after, leaving only 15 saved out of the entire complement of 244 — namely, 6 of the prisoners and 9 of the crew, viz. — the Capt. B. H. Peck, the first officer Joseph Bennett, Thomas Sharp, John Wilson, Edward Calthorpe, Thomas Hines, Robert Ballard, John Robinson, William Kidney, and 6 women, Ellen Galvin, Mary Stating, Ann Cullen, Rosa Heland, Rose Dunn, Margaret Drury. Mr. Charles Friend in his small vessel providentially discovered them on King's island, and has brought the whole, with the exception of one of the women and two of the crew, to Launceston. The government vessel, Shamrock, was to be dispatched immediately to bring these persons off the island, and also to secure any stores or other property that may have been washed ashore from the wreck.

It is a most melancholy and afflictive event, from the horrors of which the mind as it were turns away in vain, and coming so suddenly on the sad catastrophe that overtook the prison ship George the Third, the question very naturally suggests itself, 'what can be the reason of these successive and awful shipwrecks now, which since the first settlement of these distant colonies had never before occurred?' The investigation that took place with the circumstances attending the loss of the George the Third, shewed that that ship was almost too old and frail to have been chartered for so long a voyage with so many souls on board, and if the inquiry which, we learn, the government is now instituting into the circumstances of the present distressing wreck, should come to a similar conclusion, which from the so abruptly falling to pieces of the vessel, we almost anticipate, it will appear that some more care in these points is necessary at head quarters than appears to have been used. Neither can we shut our eyes to the fact of the recent arrangements adopted almost single eyed with a view to economy and saving, by which vessels of inferior size and quality have been engaged for the important duty. Compare the fine vessels commanded by able and experienced naval officers, which in former years were employed as transports, with the ships of the present day, and to say nothing of the present catastrophes, the successful voyages of those periods will at least be in some degree accounted for.

In many ways, Dr James Ross was the antithesis of Hobart's pioneering newspaperman Andrew Bent. Where Bent was a crusader, courageous and independent enough to battle against authority, Ross was something of a rubber stamp for Van Diemen's Land's Lieutenant-Governor, Colonel George Arthur.

Ross, who had been born in Scotland in 1787, arrived in Hobart late in 1822. When Arthur challenged Bent's right to publish material critical of the authorities in the Hobart Town Gazette, *and finally forced him to open another paper (the* Colonial Times), *Arthur installed Terry Howe as publisher of the* Hobart Town Gazette. *In 1825 Dr Ross became Howe's partner, and editor of the paper. In 1827 Dr Ross founded his own paper, the* Hobart Town Courier.

C. M. H. Clark, in his A History of Australia, *had this to say about Ross:*

He saw himself as a man for whom independence of spirit was his motto, freedom was his watchword, the happiness of his fellow-men his object, and the truth of his religion his buckler and his consolation. His enemies saw him as a man who had formerly been a negro-driver, and then spent the remainder of his days in advocating the cause of torture, triangles, and the gallows. They loathed him, and called him a great jack-ass, a perfidious, smiling, fawning, cringing slave, a carcase fatted on an island's spoil.

When Bent was sent to gaol for libel, Dr Ross supported Arthur editorially. Later, recording Bent's long and arduous fight to have the newspaper licensing system abolished, the chronicler of the pioneer Australian Press, James Bonwick, made this note: 'The Hobart Town Courier, *under Dr Ross, printer of the Government Gazette, had no share in the honour of this great press triumph.'*

Dr Ross, who would have qualified for the label 'wowser', had the term been in existence then, never wearied of moralising in his newspaper; his pet subject was drunkenness, which, as he constantly pointed out to his readers, was responsible for nine-tenths of crime.

1835   Henry Melville is jailed for attacking authorities in Van Diemen's Land

HENRY MELVILLE
Hobart Town Colonial Times, 3 November 1835

Henry Melville, a journalist of ability and independence, was one of the early press martyrs of Tasmania. He arrived in Hobart Town in 1828, and in 1830 took over the Colonial Times *from Andrew Bent. He was known to be something of an eccentric, but James Bonwick, a close friend, called him 'a man of superior education, of indomitable will, and of persistent energy'.*

Melville hated the transportation system, and in the Colonial Times *he insisted, week after week, that the only way to rescue the convicts from their vices, and the whole of society from contamination by the convicts, was to abolish the convict system. Through 1835 he wrote of Van Diemen's Land as one large jail, where felon police dispensed justice. The report published here was part of a steady tirade which antagonised Governor Arthur. For one article, in which he attacked the manner in which two men had been sentenced to death for the theft of a heifer, Melville was condemned to twelve months' imprisonment and a fine of £200. While he was in jail, he wrote a powerful pamphlet, 'The Administration of the Government by Colonel George Arthur', which amounted to a severe criticism of Arthur's policies, and an elaborate review of the legal judgement which had sent him to prison. 'Editors and such like,' he wrote, 'are condemned by Colonel Arthur as fit companions of the twice and thrice convicted felons.'*

A Tasmanian paper discussed Melville's term in prison:

On Mr. Melville being first incarcerated, he was locked up with Mr. Robertson in a condemned cell, from which the man-eater Pearce, the aborigines and some score of malefactors were taken to execution. The vermin and the confined space rendered the imprisonment the description of torture the authorities no doubt intended. All that Mr. Melville requires is a room or cell to himself, and that his wife may be allowed to remain with him. Not a great deal to ask, when a man is illegally incarcerated for an offence which he was ignorant of having committed; and convicted, too, by a man who was his own judge, his own jury, and his own prosecutor, and that man, too, one of the most prejudiced and hottest tempered in the Colony.

The 'Mr. Robertson' referred to was Gilbert Robertson, of the True Colonist, *who also challenged the verdict concerning the heifer theft. He was sent to prison for two months for libel.*

Here is one of Melville's antagonistic reports on the convicts:

The abominable system of appointing felons, of the worst description, to be constables, and preservers of the lives, properties, and morals of the free population, is becoming daily more and more disgusting, from the manner in which these felons are allowed to act. Not only are these felons allowed to enrich themselves by harrassing and tyrannising over the free, but, it would appear, that whatever these men may choose to do, they are not only authorised by law, but are more especially protected by the authorities.

One day last week, we were requested to step into the Police-office, to hear a case decided according to Van Diemen's Land law and justice. On the bench we observed the Assistant Police Magistrate, Mr. Clarke, and the *worthy* Superintendent of Convicts. At the bar was a poor creature, who, by some accident or other, had been deprived of both his hands. This man, most of our readers will recollect as selling pies in the streets, and, no doubt, they have been as much surprised as we ourselves, to guess how it was possible, a man so circumstanced, could earn a livelihood. Well, as we entered the Police-office, the business commenced. The man without hands was charged with selling a half-pint of gin, without being duly authorised, as by law, required. The information was as usual, laid by a district constable, who, by this means, was the *nominal* prosecutor; so that the *ostensible* prosecutor might appear as a witness. A man of the name of Lancashire, a felon, who arrived in this Colony by the *Royal George*, 1830, a prisoner for life, gave his evidence; but, before we allude to the same, let us just offer a word or two about the man — and, so to do, we may as well re-publish a paragraph, written by a Correspondent respecting him, which appeared in this Journal on the 25th August. It is as follows:—

"We find, by some strange and unaccountable means, (whether by the interest of a certain district constable with his patrons, we know not) that a convict, who arrived here some years since, a native of *Lancashire*, convicted of having committed, or being concerned in a most extensive robbery — and whose wife followed him with all the plunder, to an enormous amount, is now acting as a sort of sub-overseer, or constable, under this same District, in the Town Surveyor's gang. We know, from the best authority, this prisoner was sent here, under special orders from Home, to be kept under strict discipline. His wife has been repeatedly refused his assignment. He has been kept hitherto on the roads, by orders from the Head of the Government, and now, by some *"nobbing"* means, reached Hobart Town; and by *"nobbing"* again, has crept into the Town Surveyor's gang, walking about with his hands in his breeches pockets, like a gentleman. How, or in what manner, he has obtained this privilege, in direct opposition to Home orders, we should like to know? We cannot account for this sort of *"nobbing"*, which now seems very prevalent. We know

that a large *"Tulip"* stalks up and down Hampden-row, that has so much ascendancy over certain of the Authorities, that any representation he makes is taken for Gospel. This is another sort of *"nobbing,"* perhaps gratis — we hope so. It is the bane of this ill-fated Colony, and so will it remain, if authorities will listen to, and believe every interested spy — to whose bosom, honor and every good feeling are strangers. While it lasts, no man will be safe in the Colony — the honorable minded man will be doubted, through the base insinuations of such tolerated calumniators — and the finished villain become possessed of authority and prosperity. Many are the innocent victims that fall a sacrifice to these wretched acts of villainy and duplicity, before the wretched means are discovered.— *Correspondent."*

This, reader, was the witness! This convict constable stated, that he was at the defendant's house between eight and nine o'clock at night, on a certain evening, with the steward of the *Mangles*, and a man of the name of Visick. The selling of the half-pint of gin was then sworn to. In his cross-examination, Lancashire said, he called at Visick's lodging (prison discipline) for the purpose of taking him round to some houses to purchase liquors, for the purpose of lodging informations — that they were out at 12 o'clock at night — that they went to several public houses drinking — that they went also to private dwellings — this man also swore he did *not expect to get any portion of the fine!* This man's evidence having been gone through, Edward Visick was called. Visick is a regular flash character, he is a convict without any indulgence whatever, and arrived in the Colony, in the year 1832. It is generally believed, that this man was allowed to sleep out of barracks, through the intercession of an interested district constable, who has just obtained his freedom. The convict Visick was about to be sworn, when Mr. Gellibrand asked him, whether he had not heard the evidence of the last witness — after much quibbling on the part of Visick, he acknowledged he had been in the passage, and the Magistrates would not admit his evidence. This was the case for the prosecution.

Mr. Gellibrand was called on for the defence, but he replied, that a defence was not necessary, that all the evidence adduced, was that of the convict Lancashire, who was not to be credited, and that it would be an insult to their common sense, to imagine that they could convict upon such evidence. Mr. Gellibrand evidently appeared to be of opinion that the case was not proved — not so the *worthy* Superintendent of convicts, who repeatedly took an opportunity of affirming, that Lancashire did no more than his duty, and he was, as a constable, bound to hunt up such cases. After some little discussion between the Magistrates, the free man without hands, was fined £10, half to the King, and half to the informer. The defendent said, the Magistrates had better at once send him to jail, as he had not ten pence in the world, and could not raise such a sum. As to the assertion of Lancashire, that he did not expect to get any part of the fine, it is scarcely necessary to offer one word — if he did expect no remuneration, how was it he went and spent his own money, (prison discipline) in order to lay traps to get up informations for the benefit of others? Really this Mr. felon constable Lancashire must be a mighty patriotic man indeed, to squander his own money for the public good. One word or two of the real facts connected with these informations — a district constable, possessor of a license which has been obtained in a fictitious name, and which man resides with a woman who superintends the house, is prime mover in most of these cases. The owner of this public house has employed Lancashire and Visick — he is in fact their patron, and as he himself cannot come forward — District Constable Peel is allowed a finger in the pie — and there is little doubt, but that the landlord, Lancashire, Peel and Visick, all share alike in the booty thus obtained.

The Superintendent of Convicts, as we already noticed, applauded the conduct of Lancashire; now let us see what the conduct of this man was on the occasion. He took with him Visick, a prisoner without indulgence, to entrap free people. Does Mr. Spode, the Superintendent of Convicts, consider him deserving of praise for doing that which any free man would have been fined severely for so doing? Had any free man had Visick in his house, he would be subject to fines and penalties under the Harbouring Act; but not so with a felon constable. The latter may take a felon on a drinking spree, and when the parties whom they visit, during the dead hour of the night, will no longer treat them these convicted rascals get-up a case against them for selling without a license. The laxity — the easy temperament of Mr. Spode, as regards his own assigned servants, may, in a manner, account for his approving of the conduct of Jonas Lancashire, Esquire, the felon. In a late number of our Journal, a correspondent asked us, whether he would be doing wrong in following Mr. Spode's example towards his assigned servants, and instanced certain particulars as regarded a man of the name of Maddox. We did not then choose to answer the question, but we do so now — and we say, that we are decidedly of opinion, that if any man, unless he be a Government officer, were to adopt the same plan towards an assigned servant as Mr. Spode did towards the man Maddox, that man, be he whom he may, would have every assigned servant taken from him. . .

Let our readers peruse our police reports, let them watch the evening amusements of these two felons, Lancashire and Visick, on the night when the said-to-be-cause for the informations occurred — only imagine a couple of these gentry visiting all the public houses, and their private friends "keeping it up," as it is called — only imagine felons spending money on the public service in a most disinterested manner, and when, in all human probability, they were so drunk they could scarcely walk; these are the men Colonel Arthur's authorities tell us are fit men to watch over the interests of the free and the freed. . .

1838   A promise to report the news 'with the humble pen' in the new colony of Port Phillip

JOHN FAWKNER
Melbourne Advertiser, 1 January 1838

The settlement at Melbourne was peopled first from Tasmania. John Batman led the way, and others, including John Pascoe Fawkner, followed. It was Fawkner who brought out the first Melbourne newspaper – the Melbourne Advertiser. *The trouble then, in 1838, was that no printing press existed in the settlement. Fawkner, who had begun the Launceston press in 1829, was undeterred. He produced what was known as a manuscript newspaper: four pages of uncut foolscap paper, neatly handwritten down two columns to each page.*

Fawkner, who had opened the first establishment in Melbourne devoted to the sale of strong drink, could not publish more than thirty-two copies of each issue because of the time and labour involved in the hand-writing of each one. Generally, members of the public who wanted to learn the latest news had to call in at Fawkner's Hotel.

After nine manuscript numbers had been produced, publication was suspended. The first licensed newspaper to appear was the Port Phillip Gazette, *on 27 October 1838; the proprietors were George Arden, a nineteen-year-old editor of some literary accomplishment, and Thomas Strode, capable printer and publisher.*

Fawkner burst back into print (armed with a parcel of refuse type from Launceston) on 30 January 1839, with the Port Phillip Patriot and Melbourne Advertiser. *The* Patriot *was first published as a daily in May 1845, and in October 1848 its title was changed to the* Melbourne Daily News. *This paper, after purchase by Mr George Bourcicault and a merger, finally developed into the powerful* Melbourne Argus. *Fawkner used to claim to be the 'father' of the Melbourne press, and*

there is no doubt that the Argus, *for so long a paper of great stature, was a direct descendant of his humble, hand-written manuscript.*

In the first issue of the Advertiser, *dated 1 January 1838, Fawkner promised to report the news with the humble pen until printing materials arrived:*

We do opine that Melbourne cannot reasonably remain longer marked on the chart of advancing civilization without its Advertiser.

Such being *our* imperial Fiat We do intend therefore by means of this *our* Advertizer to throw the resplendent light of Publicity upon all the affairs of this New Colony, Whether of Commerce, of Agriculture, or of the Arts and Mysteries of the Grazier. All these patent roads to wealth are thrown open to the adventurous Port Phillipians. All these sources of riches are about to (or already are) become accessible to each adventurous Colonist of NOUS. The future fortunes of the rising Melburnians will be much accelerated by the dissemination of intelligence consequent upon the Press being thrown open here. But until the arrival of the printing Materials *we* will by means of the Humble pen diffuse such intelligence as may be found expedient or as may arise . . .

The energies of the present population of this rapidly rising district have never been exceeded in any of the Colonies of Britain.

Its giant like strides have filled with astonishment the minds of all the neighbouring states, The Sons of Britain languish when debarred the use of that mighty Engine the Press, A very small degree of Support timely afforded will establish a newspaper here, but until some further arrangements are made it will be merely, an advertising sheet and will be given away to Householders.

The Melbourne Advertiser Port Phillip Australia.

Written for, and Published by Jn° P. Fawkner.

Monday, January the 8th. 1838. Melbourne.

N° 2   Price Sixpence.   Vol 1.

For London direct

The fine fast sailing ship Hartly's Burthen 400 Tons will be ready to receive Wool early next month the greater part of her Cargo being engaged She will meet quick dispatch this vessel possesses very superior accommodations

For Freight or passage Apply to W. F. A. Rucker, Queen Street 29th Dec.

For Launceston

The fast Sailing Cutter Jemima will leave for the above port on the 20th. Jany. 1838

Apply to W. F. A. Rucker

Geelong Trader

The well known Schooner Lapwing will sail regularly between the above Port and Melbourne leaving the latter place every tenth day

For Freight or passage Apply to the Master on Board or to W. F. A. Rucker Queen Street

---

Lost

On the 17th Decem last between Melbourne and the Ford of the Salt Water River, A Lady's handsome Gold Ear Drop whoever will bring the lost Earring to the Office of this paper shall be handsomely rewarded

---

Wanted.

A good Serviceable Cart mare Apply at this Office 29 Decemb 1837

For Sale

Fit for Breeding or for the Butcher 20 Choice Pigs. Enquire at Fawkners Hotel.

On Sale

250 Head of prime Cattle these are adapted for breeding being choice stock. A part are fit for the Supply daily required by the Butcher Apply to John P Fawkner

January the 1st 1838.

A facsimile of the second issue of John Pascoe Fawkner's Melbourne *Advertiser*

1838   Eleven men are tried for the slaughter of Aborigines at Myall Creek

EDWARD SMITH HALL
Sydney Monitor, 19 November 1838

Edward Smith Hall has been called the 'father' of Australian civil liberties. He edited the Sydney Monitor, *campaigned strenuously against the repressive rule of Governor Ralph Darling, and did more than any other individual to secure three major reforms: trial by jury, freedom of the press and representative government.*

He did not stop fighting, using the one weapon he had: his eight-page, shilling-a-copy, once-a-week newspaper. He was the champion of convicts, and of freed prisoners — 'I consider the free and the freed as one class, possessing equal rights,' he wrote. He exposed corruption of officials and magistrates, he ridiculed the actions of Darling's chief supporter, Archdeacon Scott, he condemned the Governor's censorship of the press. Not surprisingly, Hall was convicted often of criminal libel — always by military juries, hand-picked by the Governor. As a result of these convictions, he spent more than a year in Sydney jail.

Rusden's Official History of Australia *records that: 'the Governor directed the libel law to be put in force with great rigour, and the proprietors of both the* Monitor *and the* Australian *newspapers were prosecuted, civilly and criminally, and both were heavily fined and imprisoned.'*

One of Hall's great triumphs came when Darling — mainly through the efforts of Hall, William Charles Wentworth and Dr Wardell — was recalled in 1831; Hall had received advance notice of the recall, and Darling learned of it in the columns of the Monitor.

Hall demonstrated his zeal as a crusading editor after the outrage which has become known as the Myall Creek Massacre. In June of 1838, twelve stockmen employed in cattle and sheep stations along the Big River in northern New South Wales banded together *to attack a party of forty Aborigines peacefully encamped beside a homestead on the Myall Creek station. Twenty-eight of them were cruelly and deliberately murdered, without excuse and without mercy; men, women and children were tied together and then cut down or shot in cold blood.*

It was, as Hall pointed out in his Monitor, *'a deed for which we cannot find a parallel for cold-blooded ferocity, even in the history of Cortez and the Mexicans or of Pizarro and the Peruvians'. The* Sydney Herald *(which became the* Sydney Morning Herald *eleven years after its inception in 1831) did not share such concern. Its leading articles, most of them written by the Rev. John Garvie, made it clear that it considered the blacks as pests, deserving of no more consideration than the dingo or the rat.*

On 15 November 1838, the trial of eleven men charged with the Myall Creek slaughter took place in the Supreme Court at Sydney before the Chief Justice, Sir James Dowling, and a civil jury. The Attorney-General, John Hubert Plunkett, prosecuted, and argued that 'the life of a black is as precious and valuable in the eyes of the law, as that of the highest noble in the land'. The jury took just fifteen minutes to acquit the eleven accused. It was a popular verdict, one which was seen as a triumph for common sense, progress and for the united stand of the landowners. It was not popular with Edward Smith Hall. This is what he wrote about the case on 19 November 1838:

The trial of eleven men for the slaughter of a company of Aborigines of both sexes and all ages, from sucking infants to hoary hairs, took place on the 15th inst., when they were *acquitted.*

From the violent articles published by the Colonial press during the last months against the black natives, we had been impressed with the belief, that not only had these slaughtered aborigines committed some wanton murders on our stockholders residing in their neighbourhood, but that their slaughter had been perpetrated in retaliation for such murders.

But in all the evidence given on the trial, our readers will perceive, that the eight-and-twenty persons put to the sword by the eleven stock-keepers are not accused of committing any personal violence whatever, at any time, either on these eleven men, or on their neighbours. The only thing laid to their charge by the murderers , is, that they had committed a "depredation" on some sheep *once*; and had once "rushed" the cattle in charge of *one* of the prisoners. The nature and extent of the "depredation" on the sheep is not explained. With respect to "rushing" of cattle, our readers lately arrived in the Colony will please to understand, that cattle when much left to themselves, "rush", that is, make off at full gallop to a great distance, and into the glens and passes difficult of access to their keepers, on falling in with either blacks or whites. There is however an exception to this rule as regards such cattle as are inspected once a fortnight or so, by their stock-keepers. On seeing their own keeper they will not "rush", unless his visits have been very few and far between. But if cattle see the *Blacks*, they are apt to rush on all occasions, even cattle that are reckoned to be pretty tame. If therefore the "rushing" of the cattle be in future to be considered as an apology for putting the Blacks to the sword, the whole race must soon be exterminated, inasmuch as they get their living, not by staying at home, but by hunting in their native wilds.

But the company or tribe of blacks put to the sword by these eleven men, had not only been innocent of all personal violence, but they had become domesticated *among these very men*. One of them (Kilmaister) had been the chief cause of their taking up their residence near his hut, and he himself seems to have formed a friendship for them; for, in the evening on his return from his journeys after his cattle, he was in the habit of playing and dancing with their children. One of the witnesses indeed states, that this man always denied being of the party. But the man made no attempt on his trial to prove an *alibi*; and other witnesses swore to him being of the party.

The Blacks, it appears, were residing at the hut of Kilmaister, in peace and confidence as usual, when a party of men, mounted, and armed with swords and pistols, galloped up to the place. From the *manner* of the party, the Blacks, who are by no means so deficient in intellect as they are represented in *books*, perceived danger, and ran for safety into the hut. They were taken out, and tied one by one to a long rope, used to catch cattle by the horns. Perceiving their fate, they began to weep and moan. The women, though tied, contrived to carry their infants in a net slung from their shoulders. Being all secured, men and boys, women, girls, and sucklings, one of the horsemen led the way, with the end of the rope attached to himself or horse. The other ten horsemen divided into two parties of five each, five placing themselves on one side of the rope, one behind the other, and five on the other side. The funeral procession then commenced its march, amid the tears and lamentations of the victims. It must have been a heart-rending sight to see the aged Black, named "Daddy", led to the slaughter, a man of giant-like stature, and probably brave as he was magnificent in his form; the tears rolling down his aged cheeks at the sight of his wife, children and relatives. The children perhaps scarcely knew their sufferings until the sharp steel had passed through their bodies, and put a speedy end to their troubles.

Arrived at the place chosen for the catastrophe, the slaughter began. All, however, we can glean from the evidence is, that two shots were fired. The sword it should seem did the rest without noise, except the cries of the victims. Decapitation appears to have been considered the readiest way of despatching them, from the great number of skulls afterwards found.

After the slaughter, a fire composed of dead trunks of trees, and many yards in extent, was kindled, and the headless bodies and skulls were placed on the pile. But the party did not stay to see the bodies completely consumed. Perhaps they got alarmed, or were compelled to return home in a given time. It would however have been prudent in one or two of the party to remain at the fire another day. In the course of twenty-four hours every skull and every bone, even the little bones of sucking children might, by diligent searching among the ashes, have been found and consumed, and then what yesterday formed eight-and-twenty living human beings, would have been mere heap of ashes.

A report which is gaining ground, that these men were set upon this deed of darkness by others; a deed for which we cannot find a parallel for cold-blooded ferocity, even in the history of Cortez and the Mexicans, or of Pizarro and the Peruvians. The only monsters whose conduct will furnish us with a parallel, is that of the Buccaneers of the West Indies.

It is not improper that these eleven men should have had counsel hired for them. *Three* counsel however was rather a luxurious number. But while three gentlemen, (the *masters* of these men for instance,) might have hired one counsel each *privately*, it is not to the credit of New South Wales that a *general subscription* should have been raised among the magistrates and graziers of Hunter's River, to an amount much larger than even three counsels could demand.

What was there in this murder of eight-and-twenty poor helpless betrayed men, women, and children, that should induce the magistrates and gentlemen of Hunter's River to hire Counsels for the murderers? Do they hire Counsel for other men when tried for murder? How will this fact *tell* in England, in France, in Austria, in Prussia, and in America? For we doubt not but there are men in the two Houses of Parliament who will *now* make the Colony known all over the world — in kingdoms and cities where it was scarcely heard of before.

The verdict of acquittal was *highly popular!* It was with exertion that the Chief Justice could prevent the audience *from cheering* — such was their delight! The aristocracy of the Colony, for once, joined heart and hand with the prison population, in expressions of joy at the acquittal of these men.

We tremble to remain in a country where such feelings and principles prevail. We have always dreaded an oligarchy. . . The verdict of Thursday shews, that only let a man, or a family, be sufficiently *unpopular* with the aristocracy and the prison population of the Colony *conjoined* (in this case), and their murder will pass unheeded. Money, lucre, profit — *these* are thy Gods, O Australia!

In fact, a second trial for the massacre took place before Mr Justice Burton and a civil jury on 27 November. The Crown officers had been unsatisfied with the verdict, and they indicted seven of the accused on charges of murder of Aboriginal children who had not been mentioned in the first trial. The jury found them guilty 'of the murder of a child unknown'; the prisoners appealed, and their plea was overruled by three judges who found that the jury's verdict was just. The seven were hanged on 18 December 1838.

Edward Smith Hall died in 1860. Sir Henry Parkes, Premier of New South Wales, called him 'one of Australia's noblest patriots'. Persecuted almost constantly by authority, he probably fought harder and accomplished more in terms of individual liberty than any other Australian journalist. It is a sad fact that his name is largely unknown today.

1846   Ludwig Leichhardt returns from the dead and reports exclusively on his great journey

L. LEICHHARDT, WITH EDWARD SILVESTER
Sydney Morning Herald, 27 March 1846

One of the proudest feats of the young Sydney Morning Herald was its publication of Dr Ludwig Leichhardt's own story of his expedition which started from the Condamine River in October 1844, and finished up at Port Essington fourteen months later. It was one of the first great scoops in Australian journalism.

On his trek to the Gulf of Carpentaria, Leichhardt discovered the Lawson and the Mackenzie Rivers, and later, travelling up the Burdekin, he crossed the watershed between the rivers of the east and those of the gulf. Rounding the southern shore of the gulf, he reached the river which he called the Roper; in the end the survivors of his party — the naturalist Gilbert had been killed by blacks — reached Port Essington in December 1845.

The party had been given up as lost, and, when news filtered through that they were safe and on their way back to Sydney, preparations were made for the greatest welcome the town had ever seen. They arrived on 25 March 1846; a salute of guns was fired by shore batteries and ships in the Harbour, Leichhardt's portraits were lithographed and sold by Sydney booksellers, and epitaph verses — written for Leichhardt by Sydney Morning Herald *reporter Edward K. Silvester when the explorer was thought to have perished — were read to him publicly.*

Silvester worked with Leichhardt on the exclusive story, which was published over eight long, tightly-packed columns of the Sydney Morning Herald *on 27 March 1846. F. C. Brewer, another* Herald *journalist of the day, wrote later about Leichhardt's appearance as he visited the office to correct the proofs of his story. 'He was tall and rather thin,' wrote Brewer, 'but his frame was just the build for*

endurance. His face was certainly handsome and refined. He wore a short beard and moustache, and had a distingué *air.'*

Leichhardt went on another expedition in December the same year, wandering in fairly aimless fashion around the same north-west area of what is now Queensland. Then came his last sad trip, on which he and his party vanished. The Sydney Morning Herald *published his last dispatch dated 3 April 1848, which gave no indication of which way he was heading.*

Edward Silvester began his journalism career as a contributor to the Sydney Monitor *in 1840. He worked on the* Examiner, *which rose briefly in the ruins of the* Monitor, *then moved to the* Australian *and finally the* Sydney Morning Herald. *Although he led the parliamentary reporting staff, his most memorable feat was his verse on the 'Death of Leichhardt' — written under the mistaken impression that the explorer had perished. Silvester died in December 1863.*

Here are excerpts from the Leichhardt report published on 27 March 1846:

I left Sydney the 13th of August, 1844, in the Sovereign, Captain Cape, The Hunter River Steam Navigation Company having given to me and to my party, a free passage to Moreton Bay. After recruiting my horses at Moreton Bay, I went up to Darling Downs, and stayed for a month at Mr. Campbell's station, waiting for my provisions, which the kind people of Moreton Bay had volunteered to send up to the Downs with drays.

Finding that my horses were not sufficient to move all the provisions, and considering that bullocks would give at the same time means to move our provisions, and form a

good stock of provisions themselves, I bought
three bullocks from Major North, at Laidley
Plains, and five from Mr. Hughes, at Darling
Downs. My party consisted originally of six
persons — Mr. Roper, Mr. James Calvert, John
Murphy, Phillips, and the black fellow, Harry
Brown, of Newcastle. In Moreton Bay, a
negro, Caleb, and a black of Bathurst, Charley,
joined me.

At the Downs, Mr. Hodgson and Mr.
Gilbert, increased the number of my party
to ten persons. The two latter added two
bullocks to those I had, and Messrs. Stephens
and Campbell made us a present of four young
steers and a bullock, Mr. Isaacs gave a fat
bullock. I started, therefore, from Jimba, the
farthest station of Darling Downs to the westward, on the 1st October, 1844, with 16 head
of cattle, 17 horses, and four kangaroo dogs.
Mr. Hodgson and Caleb returned with two
horses, from Kent's Lagoon, about 70 miles
from Jimba.

We travelled at first through the system of
waters of the Condamine, which goes much
farther to the northward than is laid down in
the map, as I left it about 26.44 of latitude.
I passed several creeks which evidently joined
the Condamine in latitude 26.26, and 26.16,
and 26.10, in a course north-west from Jimba;
and I have soon to mention that I came on
westerly waters again, in latitude 25.19, and
25.13, which, in all probability, go to the
westward and southward to join the Condamine, or belong to the great basin of the
Darling. . .

From latitude 16.30 to 15.51 we travelled
along a fine river with a running stream, now
narrow and shallow, now swelling into fine
long sheets of water. I called it the "Mitchell",
in honour of Sir Thomas Mitchell. A belt of
open forest accompanies its banks; farther off,
the country opens more and more, and changes
into a series of plains, extending parallel to
the river; they are limited by a forest of small
acacia trees, and several others, which I have
not yet been able to determine. Lagoons became larger and larger, and more frequent, as
we travelled down the river; the country
improved, the plains grew bigger, the forest
land richer, receding further from the river. . .

The table-land is covered by forests of
stringybark, of melaleuca-gum, and Banksia.
Several grassy flats, with a white gum (similar
to the flooded gum) were observed. The droop-
ing tea-tree grows in the swamps I mentioned,
to a great size; the grass is excellent in some
of these swamps; but a sedge is prevailing,
which, it appeared to me, was not so much
liked by our cattle and horses, as the deep
green colour of the young plant after late
burnings made me first believe.

It was very difficult to find a passage down
the table-land; but I succeeded, though the
descent was very steep even for our horses and
pack bullocks. This descent was about lat.
13.22, lon. 132 50.

I dare say that my passage over the table-
land would have been much simplified by
following the main branch of the Roper to its
head, to pass over to Snowdrops Creek, and
follow it down, notwithstanding its southing;
for Snowdrops Creek, in all probability, joins
the Flying Fox River, which I consider the
main head of the South Alligator. This route
would be practicable for cattle and horses,
which might be driven over to the west side;
I could certainly not recommend my line of
march. It is very remarkable that pegmatite
cropped out at the foot of the slope where
we made our descent, whilst at the top, as
well as all over the table land, when we met
the rock, it was found to be a fritted sandstone.

The South Alligator River is joined by a
great number of creeks, which, as far as we
could see, came down over a precipice, and
must, of course form as many waterfalls during
the rainy season. . .

The valley of the Upper East Alligator,
which I rather should call Goose River (for
nowhere we observed so many geese — and
what is called alligator is no alligator, but a
crocodile), is one of the most romantic spots
I have seen in my wanderings. A broad valley,
level, with the most luxuriant verdure, abrupt
hills and ranges rising everywhere along its
east and west sides, and closing it apparently
at its southern extremity; lagoons, forming
fine sheets of water, scattered over it; a creek,
though with salt water, winding through it.

After having crossed the river, I went to the

northward, passed a plain about eight miles long, from which I saw bluff mountain heads to the north-east, which seemed to indicate the valley of a northerly river, entered the forest land, passed several creeks, running to the eastward, (one at 12.11, with water), and followed a well-trodden footpath of the natives, which led me through rocky sandstone ridges, over numerous creeks running to the westward to the broad sandy bed of a river, with fine pools of water, which I consider to be the fresh-water branch of the East Alligator, coming from the east. Not very far from the river, we came to a fine lagoon, beyond which a large plain extended; the lat. of this lagoon (Bilge's Lagoon) was 12.6.

I passed the plain, and entered the forest land. Just where the latter commenced, on a swampy ground between sandstone rocks, the first tracks of buffaloes were observed...

We travelled in a northerly course again, through forest land, and crossed a small plain, in which a mangrove creek turned to the westward, and further on a tea-tree swamp equally to the west. On a fine plain we met a tribe of black fellows (Nywall's tribe), who guided us to a good sized lagoon. This plain extended far to the northward and westward, two isolated peaks and two low ranges were seen from it to the east and south-east. We crossed and skirted these plains in a north-north-west course, and entered the forest land, which was undulating with low ironstone ridges, from which numerous creeks went down to Van Diemen's Gulf, along which we travelled. Black fellows had guided us two days, but they left us at the neck of the Coburg Peninsula, which we entered on a fine footpath, keeping a little too much to the northward on the narrow neck, we came to westerly waters and to Montmorris Bay. I turned, however, again to the westward, to come to westerly waters. Creeks are numerous on both sides, and fresh water was frequent after the late thundershowers. I made my latitude at 11.32 on a westerly water, and at 11.26 on an easterly water (Baki Baki's Creek). Keeping a little too much to the northward from the latter creek, I came to Raffles Bay, from which black fellows familiar with the settlement

Ludwig Leichhardt

guided us round Port Essington to Victoria, which I entered at about five o'clock, the 17th December, 1845...

I entered Victoria with one pack bullock, and with eight horses. We had killed fifteen, of our bullocks and had dried their meat. Along the east coast, and at the east side of the gulf, they kept in a very good condition, and yielded a fine supply of fat meat; but at the west side long stages, bad grass, and several waterless camps, rendered them very weak, and compelled me to kill them; the heaviest bullock of the lot scarcely yielding a fortnight's supply of meat. My horses did exceedingly well, they got several times footsore in passing a very rocky country, but they soon recovered on soft flats. At the Burdekin, one broke its thigh bone, we killed it, and dried its meat; at the Lynd another died suddenly, probably by the gripes; at the Roper, four, the finest of the whole lot, were drowned, the banks being very steep and boggy, and the river very deep. The loss of these was very heavy. I had to throw away the greatest part of my botanical and geological collection, and my plans of returning over land, cutting off the angles of my route, and keeping more to the westward, were frustrated.

When our flour, our tea, our salt, our sugar was gone, we lived on dried beef and water, a and we lived well on it as long as the beef was good. But at the latter part of the journey the beef got bad, as it was very poor, and of knocked up beasts, and as the moist sea breeze made it very liable to taint. Fortunately the game became abundant round the gulf, and we caught for instance, in August, fifteen, and in September sixteen emus, every one of which provided meat for a day.

At the head of the South Alligator, black fellows came up to us, and we exchanged presents with them; they gave me the red ochre, which they seemed to consider as the best of their run. At the commencement of the plain, a large tribe of black fellows came to our camp, and one of them pointed to the northwest, when we asked where he got his tomahawk and a piece of shawl from. They knew Pitche Nelumbo (Van Diemen's Gulf). At the big Pandanus Swamp, another tribe of black fellows guided us over the swamp, and behaved very kind. They used the word peri good (very good) no good, Mankiterra (Malay). At the mouth of the East Alligator Eooanberry's and Minorelli's tribe, were equally hospitable and kind. We met another tribe in travelling up the river, and at its head. The latter were however noisy, boisterous, and inclined to theft. At the north bank of the river we met Bilge's tribe, Bilge being the most important personage amongst them. At Nywall's Lagoon, Nywall treated us with imberbi (the root of a species of convolvulus), and two black fellows guided us two days farther. At Montmorris Bay we met Baki Baki; and at Raffles Bay Bill White's tribe, and Bill White himself guided us into the settlement.

At Eooanberry's tribe we first heard the question, "what's your name," and the name for white man "Balanda." At Nywall's tribe they asked for flour, bread, rice, tobacco, and one of them even had a pipe. It is difficult to express our joy when English words were heard again, and when every sign which the black-fellows made proved that we were near the end of our journey, particularly as December advanced, and the setting in of the rainy season was to be expected every moment.

I think that the most important results of my expedition are the discovery of the Mackenzie, the Isaacks, the Downs of Peak Range, and the Suttor, that of a communication between the east coast of Australia, and of the east coast of the Gulf of Carpentaria along the river, with running water through a fine country; that of the Nonda Country, and of the Big Plains at the east side, and at the head of the Gulf; that of a communication between Limnenbight and the South Alligator River, along running streams and creeks. The future will show how far the country along the Big Rivers between the head of the Gulf and Limnenbight is available.

1850   A reporter breaks the news that Victoria has become an independent colony

EDMUND FINN
Port Phillip Herald, 11 November 1850

The news that the province of Victoria had been emancipated from the colony of New South Wales — and was, thus, a separate colony — was announced to the people of Victoria by Edmund Finn, one of the most colorful of the early reporters.

Finn, an Irishman from Tipperary, had arrived in what was then the Port Phillip district of New South Wales on 13 July 1841. The editor of the Port Phillip Herald, *George Cavenagh, offered him a job on that paper in 1845 and he remained a general reporter with the* Herald *for thirteen years. Finn recorded everything that went on — what he later described as 'whether the burning of a house or the founding of a church, a mayor-making or a prize-fight, a charity sermon or a coroboree'. At times he wrote the entire paper, excluding the shipping, commercial and advertising sections.*

Finn was described by a contemporary journalist as an expert and indefatigable reporter, who knew nearly every inhabitant of importance, and nearly everything that was going on. He was small of stature, short-sighted and quick-witted. He used to speak his native Gaelic and Latin, and he was one of the founders of the St Patrick Society. He wrote under the pseudonym of 'Garryowen'.

In November 1850, he took delivery of some newspapers which had arrived from South Australia in the Lysander. *Going through them, he found a summary of English news to 4 August, brought to Adelaide by the* Delta *from London. Squeezed among these items was the report that the Separation Bill had passed both Houses of Parliament, and required only the Royal Assent to become law.*

Finn later wrote about what happened next:

Having a good deal of my own way in the establishment, I said nothing to anybody, and as the editor (Mr. George Cavenagh) was not immediately accessible, I assumed responsibility for issuing an 'Extraordinary', prepared the matter, and placed it in the hands of the printers. . .

This was Finn's hastily written announcement:

Glorious News! Separation at Last!! We lose not a single moment in communicating to the public the soul-stirring intelligence that Separation has come at last!!! The Australian Colonies' Bill, with the amendments made in the Lords on the 5th July, was agreed to in the Commons on the 1st August, and only awaits the Queen's signature to become the law of the land.

The long-oppressed, long-buffetted Port Phillip is at length an Independent Colony, gifted with the Royal name of Victoria, and endowed with a flourishing revenue and almost inexhaustible resources; let all classes of colonists then not lose a moment in their hour of triumph in celebrating the important epoch in a suitable manner, and observing one General Jubilee.

The 'Public Rejoicings Committee' lately nominated by the citizens of Melbourne will assemble without delay; let one and all co-operate with them heart and hand in giving due effect to the enthusiastic ovations of our New-born Colony! It is an era in the existence of our adopted land which can never again occur; and the glorious opportunity once past will be irrevocable. Colonists, 'Now is the day and now is the hour!' For this act of justice to Port Phillip, and every other good gift, may God bless the Queen.

Washing at Tonkin's Well, South Australia

1851   News of the first gold discovery is kept a secret by the Government

UNKNOWN REPORTER
Sydney Morning Herald, May 1851

The twelfth of February 1851 was one of the most significant days in the history of Australia. Edward Hammond Hargraves was camped on the the Summer Hill Creek — a tributary of the Murrumbidgee — with a young bushman named Lister, and he had a strong conviction that there was gold all around them. Hargraves had succumbed to the gold fever which spread around the world from California in 1849, and had crossed the Pacific to get to the Californian diggings; while he was there he noticed the curious similarity between the natural gold-producing country in America and that of areas he had known near Bathurst. He had returned to Australia, and headed for the Blue Mountains. He wrote later of that day in February:

> After making a hasty repast I told Lister that the gold was under his feet, and that I would now find it. He stared with incredulous amazement. My own excitement was probably far more intense than his. I took the pick and scratched the gravel of a schistose dyke, which ran across the creek, at right angles with its side. I dug a panful of earth which I washed in the waterhole. The first trial produced a small piece of gold. 'Here it is,' I exclaimed, and then I washed five pansful in succession, obtaining gold from all but one.

Hargraves' pick, in fact, dug deep into the nation's history; it divided two eras: the pre-gold years and the post-gold years. William Charles Wentworth summed it up later: 'The gold discoveries precipitated the colonies into a nation.'

Although Hargraves advised the Government authorities promptly of his find, it was not disclosed to the public for several months.

The Government was concerned, following the excesses of the Californian gold rush, that the whole colony of New South Wales might explode if the gold fever ignited it. The first published reference to the discovery came in the Sydney Morning Herald *in the first week of May. It was an unobtrusive paragraph, halfway down a column devoted to 'Domestic Intelligence':*

It is no longer any secret that gold has been found in the earth in several places in the western country. The fact was first established on the 12th February, 1851, by Mr. E. H. Hargraves, a resident of Brisbane Water, who returned from California a few months since. While in California, Mr. Hargraves felt persuaded that, from the similarity of the geological formation, there must be gold in several districts of this Colony, and when he returned here his expectations were realised. What the value of the discovery may be it is impossible to say. Three men, who worked for three days with very imperfect machinery, realised £2/4/8 each per diem; whether they will continue to do so remains to be seen. The subject was brought under the consideration of the Government, who admitted Mr. Hargraves' claim for some consideration for the discovery, but, of course, could make no definite promise until the value of the goldfield was ascertained . . . At present all that is known is that there is gold over a considerable district; whether it is in sufficient quantities to pay for the trouble of obtaining it remains to be ascertained. Should it be found in large quantities, a strict system of licensing diggers will be immediately necessary.

1851   Gold mania sweeps the colony of New South Wales

VARIOUS CORRESPONDENTS
Sydney Morning Herald, May 1851

The gold mania swept through the colony swiftly and devastatingly, like a bushfire. Bathurst, the nearest centre to the diggings, became the centre of frantic activity. On 20 May 1851, the Sydney Morning Herald *published this despatch from its correspondent in the town:*

The discovery of the fact by Mr. Hargraves that the country from the mountain ranges to an indefinite extent into the interior is one immense goldfield, has produced a tremendous excitement in the town of Bathurst and the surrounding districts. For several days after our last publication the business of the town was utterly paralysed. A complete mental madness appears to have seized every member of the community, and as a natural consequence there has been an universal rush to the diggings. Any attempt to describe the numberless scenes — grave, gay and ludicrous — which have arisen out of this state of things would require the graphic pen of a Dickens, and would exceed any limit which could be assigned to it in a newspaper. Groups of people were to be seen early on Monday morning at every corner of the streets, assembled in solemn conclave, debating both possibilities and impossibilities, and eager to pounce upon any human being who was likely to give any information about the diggings. People of all trades, callings and pursuits were quickly transformed into miners, and many a hand which had been trained to kid gloves or accustomed to wield nothing heavier than the grey goose-quill became nervous to clutch the pick and crowbar, or "rock the cradle" at our infant mines. The blacksmiths of the town could not turn off the picks fast enough, and the manufactures of cradles was the second biggest business of the place. A few left town on Monday equipped for the diggings; but on Tuesday, Wednesday and Thursday, the roads to Summer Hill Creek became literally alive with new-made miners from every quarter, some armed with picks, others shouldering crowbars or shovels, and a few strung round with wash-hand basins, tin pots and collanders, garden and agricultural implements of every variety, either hung from the saddle-bow or dangled about the persons of the pilgrims to Ophir. Now and then a respectable tradesman, who had just left his bench or counter, would heave into sight, with a huge something in front of his horse, which he called a cradle and with which he was about to rock himself into fortune. Scores have rushed from their homes, provided with a "blanket" or a "damper" and a pick or grubbing hoe, full of hope that a day or two's labour would fill their pockets with the precious metal; and we have heard of a great number who have started without any provision but a blanket and some rude instrument to dig with. Such is the intensity of the excitement, that people appear almost regardless of their present comfort and think of nothing but gold. Of course, all this must end in disappointment. . .

Here is a letter from the Maitland correspondent, dated 19 May:

If the present mania for gold continues to exist for any time, this town will be literally drained of its population. Every hour some person may be seen sounding the note of preparation for the Bathurst gold diggings. Our merchants show a most laudable desire to hasten the departure of intending gold seekers. The price of all kinds of provisions has advanced within a few days at least 30 per cent.

Labour of any kind is hardly procurable. Permanent engagements are out of the question.

And another from Orange in the same issue:

A few weeks since and the plough was busy at work, and on every available piece of ground, from Frederick's Valley to Orange, the sight was gladdened and the ear cheered by the inspiriting view and voice of industrious husbandry. But now how changed! Stillness reigns without a sound or echo to break the sad and gloomy monotony.

From Goulburn came this message, published in the Herald *of 7 June:*

Pilgrimage to Ophir. — Exciting Scene. — Yesterday (June 3) Goulburn presented a most exciting appearance by the departure of about seventy of our townsmen, principally mechanics, who left this for the gold regions; there were six teams well laden, with plenty of horse-power attached to each; they all go well provided for a stay at the diggings, not only with provisions, but each company has a cradle and implements, picks, crowbars, shovels and everything requisite for the enterprise; they all seemed full of spirit and the sanguine expectation of realising a speedy fortune was seen in every face. The wives and children of some of those who left, as well as acquaintances, conveyed those who were departing some distance out of the town. The excitement was greatly enhanced by our townsman McKenzie, with his pibroch, who blew as if he would send his heart's blood into the bag. Altogether such a scene and such an occasion never presented itself in this district before. This is the third batch that has left, and a fourth goes on Friday. The town will in a few days be completely deserted. In consequence of the recent discovery of gold in the vicinity of Bathurst, wheat rose here from 8/6 to 12/6, and a little above that was given for small quantities, and there was a great demand for flour; at the mill flour rose to £35 per ton for fine, and parties apprehending a further rise were ready with their cash at that figure, to pay before delivery.

The Herald *sent its own man to the goldfields. This is an extract from his story, published on 28 May:*

The stupidity of many of these people is almost beyond belief . . . numbers I passed on the road without provision of any kind, either food or bedding; one, an Irishman, evidently, had nothing whatever but a pick without a handle, which he carried over his shoulder by the point, with the air of a second Cortez, marching upon Mexico. Many are totally unfitted for such a life, but the generality of those passed are strong, healthy men, in parties of five and six, with a fair outfit, many of them with a packhorse or cart among them. Even they, however seemed to suffer severely from laying on the damp ground in such cold frosty nights as we have . . .   What will it be when winter fairly sets in. . .

On 14 June, the Herald *drew attention to the number of men who were abandoning their wives and children as they succumbed to the lure of the goldfields:*

Few of our readers will be prepared for the announcement which we make on what we believe to be competent authority, that the number of families who have been so abandoned during the last four or five weeks, and who are at this time suffering extreme destitution, within and about this city, cannot be less than five hundred! To such an extent has the lust of gold proved stronger than the instincts of conjugal and parental love! Men who were in full and constant employment, and whose wages were maintaining their households in comfort, have recklessly thrown up their situations and hurried to the diggings, leaving their wives and children utterly unprovided with the means of subsistence. The cases of distress, in very many instances amounting almost to actual starvation, which are thus brought under the notice of the clergy, are enough to melt the hardest heart. It was bad enough during the mania for emigrating to California; it is infinitely worse under the present mania for rushing to our own goldfields.

1854   Forty men die as miners clash with police at the Eureka Stockade

SAMUEL IRWIN
Geelong Advertiser, 6 December 1854

The New South Wales gold rush caused a good deal of alarm to the founders of the newly established colony of Victoria. Settlers in the Port Phillip district were not slow to move north of the Murray River to try their fortunes in the older colony. In June the Sydney Morning Herald *reported that the first draft of southern migrants — some 240 of them — had already arrived in Sydney from Melbourne on their way to the diggings. Worried at the prospect of being entirely depopulated, a number of leading Victorian citizens formed the Gold Discovery Committee. They offered £200 to the first person who could lead them to a payable gold field within 200 miles of Port Phillip.*

The first useful discovery in Victoria was made by James Esmonds, who had been in California at the same time as Hargraves, and who had in fact returned to Australia in the same ship as Hargraves. He found gold at Clunes, Victoria, in July 1851 — some five months after Hargraves. Further discoveries followed at Bendigo, at Mount Alexander (near the present site of Castlemaine) and at Ballarat. A report in the Sydney Morning Herald *by a writer who visited the Mount Alexander field gave a picture of life at the diggings:*

Wretched tents of canvas or calico, adapted neither to keep out the sun nor the rain, with here and there a bark shed, in which no well-bred dog would have deigned to reside, were the homes of numbers of families . . . There certainly was more money among them than I have ever seen among men of their class, and they spent it with a degree of recklessness. . . They thought nothing of giving a shilling for a glass of rum or a pint of cider, at any of the numerous grog shops, which, tempted by the enormous profits of the trade, were, in spite of the risk of seizure, to be found in all directions.

By the middle of 1852, the colony of Victoria was at the peak of the gold boom. Ships were arriving from London, pumping thousands of men into the colony and off to the diggings. During that year, nearly 100,000 persons arrived in the country, and whole ship-loads of them were Chinese. Towns like Ballarat were filled with optimistic armies of gold-seekers in bright-colored shirts and moleskin vests, and honky-tonk music bounced out into the dusty street air from swing-door saloons.

By late 1854, serious disturbances were beginning to break out between the miners and authority — usually in the form of the Chief Commissioner and his men. The Government claimed that it owned all the land on which mining was taking place, and it threatened prosecution against all those who were digging without licences; the licences cost thirty shillings a month. The money thus raised was expected to cover the expenses of extra law enforcement on the goldfields. One difficulty was the seesawing fortunes of the miners. Some were able to spend £50 a night in the saloons; others could not afford a shirt. This sort of situation called for some tact — and that was not a common commodity in the police force, some members of which were brutal, corrupt bullies. Tax evasion became something of an art among a number of the diggers, and tax collecting became something of a sport among a number of the Chief Commissioner's men. The diggers referred to the foot-police as 'bloodhounds'; the police called their job of tax collecting 'man-hunting', and many of them seemed to like it.

The resentment finally erupted in a night of terrible violence — the Eureka Stockade clash. Five hundred miners had taken an oath to fight for their rights and liberties. Peter Lalor, about twenty-five, was elected leader, and under a blue flag adorned with the Southern Cross they formed up behind a hastily erected barricade. The next morning, 3 December 1854 — a Sunday — some infantry and cavalrymen and a hundred police advanced on the stockade from the government camp. Immediately, a couple of the insurgents opened fire and the police and troopers fought back hard. In twenty minutes the ugly affray was over. The untrained, badly armed miners were no match for the government forces. Six men on the government side died, and thirty-four miners were killed. The government forces were alleged to have wounded mere spectators and unresisting miners wantonly, and some wounded men were said to have been burned alive when troopers fired the miners' tents.

One of the wounded, unarmed spectators was Frank Hasleham, a reporter who had worked on the Port Phillip Herald and was then acting as a correspondent for the Geelong Advertiser. Hasleham (whose name has been spelt as Haslam in one of the accompanying reports) later described himself, when he asked for compensation, as 'native of the good town of Bedford, and son of a military officer, to wit, William Gale Hasleham, who bore His Majesty's commission in the 48th Foot at Talavera'. He was compensated by the Government later, and returned to England. Hasleham had been woken by the shooting, and was shot and then handcuffed after he ran from his tent. His friends had to send for a blacksmith to batter the handcuffs from his wrists as he lay bleeding outside the tent for two hours.

The accompanying reports include the first dispatch from the Melbourne Argus man at Ballarat, brought by horseback and published at 3.00 a.m. on the Monday; a fuller account by Samuel Irwin, of the Geelong Advertiser and Intelligencer; and a second account in the same paper by another writer. Irwin was re-garded as one of the most responsible eyewitnesses. Withers, in his History of Ballarat, credited Irwin with very full and accurate reports of the incident, and Sir Charles Hotham later used some of Irwin's accounts as portions of his dispatches to the English Secretary for the Colonies.

At the above hour [3 a.m.] a gentleman arrived at the office who had ridden through express, leaving Ballaarat at half-past one yesterday. He brings us the following disastrous report:

At four a.m. this morning (Sunday) the troopers advanced on the right of the Warraneep Gulley, and another division on the left of the Eureka line, encompassing the camp of the diggers. A shout was raised, and after a sharp firing of about twenty minutes the troopers called to the soldiers, who were advancing, that it was all over.

The camp of the diggers was constructed of piles of slabs collected from the neighbouring holes.

I enclose the official return, as known at 9 a.m. Tomorrow you shall have the real truth. I do not believe but that the loss of the military, to say nothing of the wounded, is considerably more than acknowledged.

Ballaarat, December 3rd, 1854. Sir, — I have the honor to inform you, that the casualties on the part of the military, are, 1 private of 12th regiment killed, two privates of 40th killed, Captain Wise, 40th, is dangerously wounded; Lieutenant Paul, 12th, seriously wounded. Several privates of 40th and 12th more or less wounded. No official return has yet been made, but the correspondent of the Argus can have it tomorrow, by applying at the Camp.

One hundred and twenty-five prisoners made, but the casualties on the part of the insurgents are not known.

I have the honor to be, Sir,
Your most obedient servant,
Robt. Rede,
Resident Commissioner.

In the case of Captain Wise, amputation is considered necessary, he having received two wounds in the leg. This is but the beginning of the end. The reporter of the Ballaarat Times has been taken, and his life was with difficulty saved from the hands of the infuriated soldiers. A colored man, recognised by a soldier, would have been shot at the Camp had it not been for the officers. Nearly all the ringleaders are taken.

Fifteen are lying dead in the Eureka camp. Sixteen are dangerously wounded.

A German has received five different wounds.

The Eureka Camp, as well as the stores and tents in the neighborhood, have been burnt to the ground, and considerable loss of property has ensued thereby.

A former reporter for the Herald, a Mr. Haslam, was shot in the shoulder by the troopers.

The London Hotel is the chief repository for the dead and wounded. The troopers swept the diggings, and are making several captures now at the moment of writing.

The most harrowing and heart-rending scenes among the women and children I have witnessed through this dreadful morning. Many innocent persons have suffered, and many are prisoners who were there at the time of the skirmish, but took no active part.

10 a.m. Several waggons containing wounded and confiscated property have passed on their way to the camp. At present everyone is as if stunned, and but few are to be seen about.

The flag of the diggers, "The Southern Cross," as well as the "Union Jack", which they had to hoist underneath, were captured by the foot police.

Had the diggers fired longer the loss to the military would have been immense, and they, as it were, acted with a precision and regularity admired even by the officers of the military.

Report says that only a small division of the diggers were attacked this morning, merely a guard of relief enough to protect the "Eureka camp". Of the rest, some were off duty, but the majority were in the bush, and guarding the roads to Melbourne and Geelong.

This is Samuel Irwin's account, published in the Geelong Advertiser and Intelligencer *on the Wednesday, 6 December 1854:*

The hurried note which I sent you by yesterday's express gave you, as far as I could make out from the different stories I heard, an outline somewhat near the truth.

Having heard about 50 other versions since then, I can approximate still more near the truth.

The insurgent party had been out most of Saturday on various duties, one of which was watching, after the rumoured approach of some additional force, which it was their intention of wait for, and, if possible, drive back.

Not having fallen in with this party, they returned to the encampment at Eureka, where a kind of barricade or stockade of slabs had been erected. Here, after orders when to reassemble, the whole force was ordered to go home; this most of them did, but a few, some 130 men would not go home.

Outposts were usually placed a long way out, in this instance there were none, and through some instant communication on this subject to the authorities, they were made aware of this fact and determined to surprise them.

The first intimation which was given of Her Majesty's troops was either a demand from the officer in command that the insurgents should lay down their arms, or else a trumpet at some one hundred yards distant from the stockade.

When the demand was made, either a negative answer or silence was the result; the troops were then ordered to fire, as had been agreed, on two rounds of blank cartridges. The diggers returned the fire. Five soldiers fell at the first fire. The troopers and few foot police were present, but at some distance. The main fighting part devolved on the soldiers. The diggers, as I said before, numbered some one hundred and fifty, they were in several divisions, rifle men, etc., in all five. After a contest of about from 15 to 20 minutes the whole affair was over. The insurgent party were thrown into immediate confusion, from the divisions having revolvers, in sheer daring running up to the soldiers to ensure a better aim, and thereby preventing the riflemen and other comrades from supporting them. The stockade was ultimately surrounded and those

who still remained taken prisoners and marched off to the camp.

When the soldiers had once tasted blood
they became violent, and had not the officers
used every exertion, the prisoners would have
been murdered on the spot. When it was clearly seen by the officers that no further resistance was offered, they wished no more blood
shed.

Mr. Commissioner Amos is also most favourably spoken of! He saved two lives which else
would have instantly been sacrificed. Mr.
Commissioner Johnstone interfered in a praise-
worthy manner, to preserve property which
had been set on fire, and eventually succeeded
in saving it.

But after giving credit where it is due, I
must protest against the barbarities practised
by the mounted troopers. Those who had
taken the law into their own hands were
punished by the soldiers — those who were
warned and were perfectly innocent of rebellious notions were murdered, fired at, and
horribly mangled by the troopers.

The names of the officers commanding the
troopers on the morning in question should
be inquired about by His Excellency, for their
allowing such barbarities to be carried on
should disqualify them from service under any
civilised government.

Some men were killed outright, others were
dangerously wounded, and a few slightly hurt
from shots and sword marks from the troopers, who, after the fight was all over and all
resistance passed by, kept up firing at such
unfortunates as presented themselves from
the doorways of tents to see what was going
on . . .

The patrols and outposts of the camp have
been called in since sunrise, and for three or
four hours we may expect peace. Most likely
afterwards we will have the Riot Act for the
third time. Tomorrow, I fear me, will prove
a day of sorrow if the affair is not settled
before then.

*Irwin attached this official hand-out to his
report:*

Her Majesty's forces were this morning fired
upon by a large body of evil-disposed persons
of various nations, who had entrenched themselves in a stockade on the Eureka, and some
officers and men killed.

Several of the rioters have paid the penalty
of their crime, and a large number are in
custody.

All well-disposed persons are earnestly
requested to return to their ordinary occupa-
tions, and to abstain from assembling in large
groups, and every protection will be afforded
to them by the authorities.

> Robert Rede
> Resident Commissioner

God Save the Queen.

Irwin continued:

I hear many persons express their determination to go on with their work as usual; it is
nearly time that something was done, as many
of the claims on the Gravel Pits are nearly
ruined, owing to the height which the water
has risen in the shafts.

But is the affair over? I sincerely hope so,
though I fear not. Had I somewhat more
accurate information, I could form an opinion
on the subject, but as we are, no one wishes
to appear more wise than his neighbour regarding the movements of either the insurgents or
of the camp. The principal leaders of the
insurgents are still free, they made their escape
after the Eureka conflict.

*Irwin sent with his dispatch a short note,
signed by J.L., which testified:*

The diggers' encampment is burnt to the
ground. I was over there at 6 o'clock this
morning, the camp was still burning, and the
sight of the dead and wounded was enough to
harrow the soul of the most callous. When
this may end it is impossible to say, no doubt
many versions of the affair will be given in
town; but I have been an eye-witness of
almost the whole of the proceedings, and say
without hesitation, that the authorities here
are wholly to blame, for they seem to have
done everything in their power to provoke the
diggers, who would have remained quiet but
for this provocation. . .

1856   Lola Montes horse-whips an editor, and is herself whipped

UNKNOWN REPORTER AND SAMUEL IRWIN
Ballarat Star and Geelong Advertiser, February 1856

One of the most celebrated pieces of horse-whipping in Australian history occurred on 17 February 1856 at the United States Hotel, Ballarat. The protagonists: the dancer Lola Montes and the newspaper editor Harry Seekamp, both of whom could wield a handy whip.

The lovely Lola, born in Limerick in 1819 of an Irish mother and a Spanish father, was one of the most tempestuous women of her time. She smoked cigars, conducted a number of spirited affairs, and she entranced gold-diggers with her famous, fleshy Spider Dance. In 1855, when she first visited Melbourne, she upset the critic of the Argus *with her Spider Dance; it was, he wrote, 'utterly subversive of all ideas of public morality'.*

She wrote a spirited letter to the Melbourne Herald *defending her dance, and pointing out that 'the symbol of innocence is the statue of Eve'. A few days later a Dr Milton attempted to take out a warrant against all repetition of the performance of Miss Montes, which was 'too disgraceful to be tolerated in a civilised community'. At her last performance an old man was arrested for chasing Miss Montes across the stage at the Theatre Royal.*

Next Lola visited the mining boom town of Ballarat and her opening night at the Victoria Theatre was the most memorable in the town's history. Next morning, on 17 February 1856, a letter in Mr Seekamp's Ballarat Times, *under the fictitious signature of 'Civis', condemned the Spider Dance and claimed that Lola was notorious for her immorality. 'The press should be a moral guide to the people,' wrote the anonymous correspondent. 'How can it discharge that duty when it fosters an un-healthy excitement about one who to say the least has no claim on our respect and whose*
notoriety is of an unenviable kind.'

That night Lola Montes made a speech from the stage of the Victoria Theatre, repudiating the charge of immorality and accusing Henry Seekamp of accepting her hospitality and getting very drunk in her presence. Seekamp's Ballarat Times *did not quote it, but an oppos-ition journal, the* Ballarat Star, *in its issue of 19 February, reported that she had said:*

The great gentleman attacks poor little innocent me. I am called notorious for my immorality. While he was at my house, the sherry and port and champagne were never off the table. You all know Mr. Seekamp is a little fond of drinking. I was a ten-pound note out of pocket by Mr. Seekamp: but I was rather green at the time.

His wife is obliged to do his duty while he goes out drinking . . . a good-for-nothing fellow. Mr. Seekamp told me that the miners were a set of —— hogs. He told me that he was a great man in Ballarat; and could do as he liked. He said, 'I am going to be made a member of the Legislature.'

Mr. Crosby (the theatre manager) thought that the other paper (The Star) was a young, a rising, and a more respectable one, and that this, belonging to a drinking, good-for-nothing fellow, could not do the printing properly. He — this Mr. Seekamp — has said he will write me out of town.

The following afternoon, Lola attended a 'Fancy Bazaar Lottery' at the Star Concert Hall. She bought a ticket and won a riding whip and immediately began to hint gaily that she proposed to use it on the editor who had offended her. The word spread quickly, and very soon Henry Seekamp was told that Lola intended to horse-whip him.

Seekamp was a frail but fiery little man with plenty of courage. He had played a leading part in the Eureka Stockade incident: some claimed that his writings in the Ballarat Times, *which constantly took the miners' side in their running war with authority, had helped provoke it. After the miners had been crushed at Eureka, Seekamp had been arrested on a charge of sedition and chained to one of the rebels. He had served three months' imprisonment after Eureka.*

As soon as he learned that Lola had a horseship and was talking about using it on him, Seekamp reacted characteristically. Like so many of the more vigorous editors of his day, he used to keep a whip of his own always handy. He picked up the whip and strode into the bar of the United States Hotel. The incident was reported racily in the Ballarat Star, *drily (by Samuel Irwin) in the* Geelong Advertiser and Intelligencer, *and briefly (by Henry Seekamp) in the* Ballarat Times.

Here is Seekamp's fairly tight-lipped report:

Madame Lola Montes having so far forgotten herself as to apply her riding-whip to the shoulders of H. Seekamp on Tuesday last, that gentleman so far forgot himself as to return the compliment with interest. What followed, it is not necessary to state, especially as the affair was maintained single-handed against all the bullying on the other side. We had purposed giving a full account of this extraordinary affair, but as the other journals have anticipated us by giving a version most after their own hearts, we content ourselves with a bare statement of the interesting fact. We do not by this notice wish to give greater publicity to the affair than it deserves, but simply to satisfy our readers that the fact really is a fact, and as our old friend Raffaelo (Carboni, one of the Eureka rebels) says, "it comes from the stubborn things store".

In the same issue Seekamp addressed an open letter to Miss Montes, signing it with his own name. Mainly it was a defence against her attack on him from the stage of the theatre, but there was one sentence in it which seemed to invite legal action for defamation: 'You say

I ate with you and drank with you and I wonder you did not go further, but perhaps you could not call on Mr. Crosby to prove it.'

The Ballarat Star *gave more detail, and more dialogue:*

About 5.00 p.m., while Mr. Seekamp and another gentleman were standing at the bar of the United States Hotel, Madame Lola entered from a wide door with a short light whip in her hand, and, walking up to Mr. Seekamp applied it most vigorously to his head and shoulders. Mr. Seekamp, who it seems was not altogether unprepared for something of the sort, as soon as he recovered himself from the rapidity of the attack, used his riding whip in return, and for a short time the combat raged with more than Trojan fury.

The lady varied her performance feminine-like, by asking such questions as "How dare you attack me in your paper?", "Will you abuse me again?", "Will you attack a woman?" Following up each inquiry by sundry sharp and cutting strokes of the switch, that soon imprinted certain facial notes of interrogation on her opponent. Mr. Seekamp, whose whip was heavy, and bore much the same proportion to the other as a claymore to a damascus blade — struck Madame across the shoulders repeatedly, still thinking the game rather unequal he made a blow at her face with his fist and whip. This, however, was parried by someone standing by, who thinking that the affair had gone far enough, took hold of the gentleman and put his head under his arm, in other words, "in chancery".

A considerable crowd had now collected, and the bar, which is large and spacious, was nearly filled. Both had by this time lost their whips, and on Mr. Seekamp being let go, he slipped through the crowd, and again made at his fair opponent; seizing her by the hair and dress; Madame on her part defended herself with great vigour, and seized his hair in return, and a scene ensued which — to the credit of the press, let it be said — falls to the lot of few journalists to record of another. The crowd interfered however, and took off Mr. Seekamp. Immediately Mr. Folland, one of the company who had been at rehearsal in the theatre adjoining, appeared, calling out where is he?, where is he? Mr. Seekamp immediately left the hotel, followed by the other, and the matter now assumed a more melodramatic air, for on Mr. Seekamp's pulling some weapon from his breast which afterwards proved to be a life-preserver, the other pulled out a pistol immediately saying — "Oh, if that's your game, I am ready for you, come on". On Mr. Seekamp stating, however, that he had no pistol, the other wisely put his out of sight. A large crowd had by this time assembled, who began to hoot and hiss Mr. Seekamp, and to throw oranges, apples and other missiles at him. He retaliated by certain gestures of an *a posteriari* character, and by expressions indicative of strong contempt, but which unfortunately were of such a nature as to justify the strongest in return.

Amid the jeers and yells of the crowd, Mr. Seekamp then retired to the Charlie Napier hotel, while Lola from the window of the United States, shook her whip at him in defiance and contempt.

Samuel Irwin, who had covered the Eureka Stockade so well for his Geelong Advertiser and Intelligencer, *wrote this report on the continuing affair:*

The war between Mr. Seekamp of the *Times* and Madame Lola Montes is still carried on with vigor; the lady today swore an information before Mr. Warren Daly from which proceeding it would seem that Madame and her advisors are desirous of making the action in the matter of the alleged libel assume more the character of a criminal than civil shape.

I have had the misfortune within the hour to hear the merits of the pending law case discussed, i.e., solely whether the action should be criminal or civil, and forbear to inflict a similar penance on you, simply stating the fact.

Tonight the Theatres Victoria and Royal, the former especially, are crowded. The Spider Dance at the Victoria was the great attraction, not less than 1500 could have been present; so far as I could hear the opinion of this celebrated dance was that as there performed it was unexceptionable; far, far less so than others which in the old country has never been ob-

Portrait of Lola Montes, aged 29

jected to in places of public amusement.

As if all this were not enough, Lola Montes had another whip battle in Ballarat the following month — this time with Mrs Crosby, the wife of the theatre manager. Lola claimed that she had been underpaid by £80, and Mrs Crosby promptly attacked her with a whip. A couple of days later the manager's wife had a few more lashes at Lola.

Melbourne Punch *observed on 6 March that it was hard to pick up a Ballarat paper without finding some reference to a horse-whip among the dramatic criticisms. 'It must form part of the stage properties at the Victoria Theatre,' said* Punch *drily.*

1858 A sociologist is appalled by the social cesspools of Sydney

WILLIAM JEVONS
Sydney Morning Herald, 7 October 1858

One of the most remarkable of the early colonial journalists was William Stanley Jevons, who came to Australia in June 1854 — at the age of nineteen — to work as an assayer in the new Sydney branch of the Royal Mint.

Jevons, who went on to become one of the greatest English economists, was absorbed with the studies of metallurgy, astronomy, meteorology, sociology, economics and photography. He compiled our first weather reports, and is credited with having taken Australia's first 'news' picture — of the wreckage of the Dunbar, *after it was lost with 122 passengers and crew outside Sydney Harbour on 20 August 1857.*

Jevons' interest in sociology was almost insatiable. He made a house-to-house survey of the dirty, vulgar sprawling town that was Sydney in the 1850s. His Sydney Morning Herald *series on the social cesspools of Sydney were sensitive and well-documented.*

He summed up Durand's Alley as 'that part of the city where the lowest and most vicious classes predominate'. Of the Rocks, he said: 'I am acquainted with most of the notorious parts of London . . . but in none of these places, perhaps, would lower forms of vice and misery be seen. . .'

In this, the first of his fine series of reportage, he reflects on the beauty of the Harbour and 'the wide country which lies open before us', and makes a point with which sociologists and conservationists might agree today: 'One is compelled to acknowledge how much Nature has done for us, how little we have done for ourselves.'

There are some subjects from which even the most scrupulous of readers during his morning glance over the paper, will avert his eyes, and though sincerely seeking instruction, will unconsciously pitch upon something which combines more of the element of amusement. "Sanitary Reform", perhaps, is one of those repelling titles which a judicious writer would not readily adopt, its meaning is too inanimate. But yet it seems to me that he who bears a right feeling towards his fellowmen, should feel a very lively and enticing interest in many subjects, social and sanitary. Will any one confess himself devoid of charity? I mean not that hypocrisy of respectability which measures itself out so accurately in £ s. d. I mean that sentiment which is the most pure and ennobling of sentiments, and is proclaimed to be the highest of virtues. It is a feeling so refined, and so expanded that exact definition is confessedly impossible, but essentially it consists in regarding one's fellow-men with the eye of sympathy. Does a man commit a mean, or dishonest act? most men will reproach him with it, and shun him perhaps; all may be equally severe upon the act itself, but the man of charity will express if it be only by a sigh, the feeling "it is a pity he had not better sense." Is a man addicted to drunkenness, in the sensual self-indulgence of which so many sink not only their money, their comfort, their goods, their health; but also their self-respect, their moral character, their love for wife, children, parents, brothers, sisters, their affection for friends — in short, their regard for everything? Yet who is not conscious of little weaknesses, if it be only in temper, in trifling injurious habits or mannerisms, which might excite at least a sigh for those who appear powerless under the alcoholic thrall of ever increasing strength? Is a man sunk in the depths of wretchedness and weighed down by the ever-accumulating burdens of the career of vice? Is he ruined in health, decrepid, shrivelled, filthy, and repulsive in person, destitute of every possession; the committer, moreover, of crimes and irremediable injuries to his fellow-men — the weak slave of passions so strong that, in the absence of all better influences, even no fear of punishment is sufficient to restrain him, yet will the charitable man seek no revenge, inflict no unnecessary pain, never regard him with unconcern or with unmixed detestation, but rather look on him with interest and pity, because his is a human spirit like his own, reduced as he himself might have been reduced.

To a person of humane feelings, such as I have described, the sight and acquaintance of social ills has the same lively, although painful, interest that a rare and terrible bodily disease has to the devoted physician. He studies the moral deformities and diseases which daily appear in the police court, just as the medical student attends his dissecting-room and his operating-theatre. A great city is to him a thing worthy of deep research and reflection; it is his pleasure to remark, on the one hand, the neat cottage tastefully adorned with the forms of simple vegetable beauty, and to augur therefrom the pure thoughts and sweet emotions which more or less characterise its inmates; to admire those more pretentious mansions, or great public buildings, which, like flowers on a tree, incorporate the character of the common whole. On the opposite hand, to stray among those less agreeable localities, where squalid poverty and hideous vice retire from view, reflecting on the causes which render certain classes apparently so wretched, and on the means by which the total sum of misery may be diminished. That man who can witness all the phases of a city unmoved, and uninterested, is himself a criminal, a slave of pride and evil feelings, which others should hardly pardon.

On such grounds I claim attention to parts of this city, which, like parts of all other cities, may be termed "social cesspools," the habitual resorts of vicious and filthy humanity, from which the malaria of crime and disease incessantly arises and taints the social atmosphere. Of the most remarkable and worst of these places, the "Rocks" I now speak; — most inhabitants of Sydney know where the locality is; — with its interior aspect they are probably unacquainted. To the west of Sydney Cove is a steep rocky range, culminating in Flagstaff Hill. Too elevated and inaccessible for the pursuits of industry and the traffic of business, it was also too near the centre of trade and bustle to afford pleasant residences for the more wealthy classes. Partly from these causes, partly perhaps from mere chance, it was, I believe, from an early date in the history of the city, appropriated as the resort of the poorer, if not the more vicious, classes of the community. Of the condition of "The Rocks" in former and less happy days, when the overflowing crime of England was continually landed within gunshot distance, I cannot and need not speak. Of its present condition I speak from personal inspection; many readers will be already acquainted with it, others I hope will so become.

The "Rocks" are occupied by several so-called streets, running longitudinally like terraces, the names of the more remarkable of which are Harrington, Cambridge, and Gloucester streets. There are also several cross lanes or passages, the ascent of which is something facilitated by steps: these are named on the map Essex-street, Essex-lane, Brown Bear-lane, Globe-street, Cribb-lane, but the more significant name of Gallows Hill yet cleaves, I believe, to one of those. But in reality these streets are at least not roads, being scarcely traversable by vehicles, and destitute of all signs of forming, metalling, guttering, sewering.

The houses which line them are small and comparatively ancient stone cottages, so unevenly and irregularly built that the doorstep of one residence sometimes approximates to the eaves of another. Where the erections are of wood their dilapidated, filthy appearance is all the more striking. The interior of these abodes usually consists of two dirty bare rusty-coloured chambers, of small size, and yet too large for the scanty articles which constitute their furniture. Of the inhabitants I will not say much; in some cases misfortune may have led and may keep them there; but in others the unhappy, debauched, wicked face, and slovenly, dirtily clothed person, tell too plain a tale.

A young intoxicated woman with a black eye and bruised forehead, and a shrivelled old dame with a face of yellow-brown colour, sitting in a poverty-stricken room, enchained my attention — they were striking pictures of the first and last ages of vice.

But what chiefly requires remedy in this ill-favored locality, is the utter absence of all means of drainage or of removing filthy matter, which consequently lies where it is and poisons the ground beneath and the air above. It is a positive fact that in many cases the foul drainings of one cottage trickles down the hill till it encounters, as the case may be, the back or front wall of the house next below; here it accumulates, soaking down into the foundations, or sometimes actually running in at the door. In other houses the occupants have prevented this accumulation by constructing a drain close beneath the floor, and running quite through the house. Certainly, a flowing stream of filth is to be preferred to a stagnant pool. The various rejectaments of more solid nature which lie about the yards and streets where they chance to fall, of course add to the foul appearance and smell. Again, in many cases, the front or back of a house, or in some places of a whole row of houses, stand close to a wall of rock, upon the summit of which are erected the privies of the next higher row of houses, while various channels and shoots discharge incessant streams of drainage. What can be conceived more unwholesome than these moist surfaces of filth exposed to the sun's rays by day, and at night filling the whole surrounding still atmosphere with malaria.

I will also draw attention to a great (for the most part) wooden building, which stands in this neighbourhood, between Charlotte-place and Essex-street, and which is now occupied as a dwelling, although it is only fit to be burned. It was once my fate to enter this place, but I know not how to describe it to others, the filthy appearance of the whole — the wooden partitions covered by rotten, torn canvas, the uneven blackened floor, not free

from human exuviae, the dark miserable rooms let out to different occupants. One small room was the only abode of a family, including several children.

The father, I think, was lying in bed. This building was originally a vinegar works, and was, I suppose, converted into a dwelling-place when manufacture became unprofitable and population at the same time numerous. The front part forms shops of decent appearance, in Lower George-street, nearly opposite the old *Herald* office. The objectionable part is entered from the back. The rents of such a place are indeed filthy lucre.

And, now I will venture to put a few plain questions with a view to remedy this state of things, disgraceful as it is to the community, but especially to the authorities, and to the landlords. If Dr. Aaron is really a City Officer of Health at all, why do "The Rocks" and the "Vinegar Works" find no mention in his reports? Why does he not urge upon the Council to abate these social and sanitary nuisances? What is the City Engineer doing that he paves, drains, and forms streets above, below, and all round this region, while within the very centre of the evil appear no signs of his supposed ability? What are we to think of the Aldermen, especially those representing Gipps' Ward, who meet opposite the Supreme Court to talk, vote other people's money away, and sometimes to quarrel, yet always to neglect the social plague spots and cesspools of the city? Where is the fulfilment of their election vows? It is no great thing to demand of the united deliberative and executive body of the Town Hall that the streets I have mentioned be guttered, formed, and drained on some simple plan. At all events, let the drainage of one house be prevented coursing into another.

. . . standing in many parts of Sydney, noting the bright sky above, the clear blue waters below, the varied form and slope of the land, the solid dry base of sandstone, the wide country which lies open before us, for the free use of all, one is compelled to acknowledge how much Nature has done for us, how little we have done for ourselves.

1860   Burke is cheered as his expedition sets off with horses, camels and fifteen men

UNKNOWN REPORTERS
Melbourne Herald and Age, 21 August 1860

The twentieth of August 1860 was — as the Melbourne Age *said the following day — a memorable day in the annals of Australian history. The largest and best-equipped expedition yet organised in the colonies set out from Melbourne for the purpose of exploring the vast unknown interior; the massive blank.*

The expedition, under the command of a sergeant of police named Robert O'Hara Burke, intended to cross the continent vertically, via the Darling River and Cooper's Creek, to reach the Gulf of Carpentaria. Second in command was G. J. Landells, who quarrelled with Burke before the expedition got past the settled districts, and returned to Melbourne; W. J. Wills, astronomical and meteorological observer, took over as second-in-charge after Landells' return. Twenty-five camels were imported from India for the expedition, for which £12,000 had been raised.

Fifteen men comprised the original party. There were resignations and a few sackings in the early stages, but Burke was able to pick up a couple of extra hands along the way. One of these was a young journalist, William Hodgkinson, who had been a member of the staff of the Melbourne Age. *Hodgkinson later became foreman of the base camp at Menindie; in January 1861, he rode the 400 miles from the Darling to Melbourne, extracted £400 from the organising committee — enough to buy ten extra horses and 150 sheep   . He was one of the few members of the base party to show a sense of urgency and resolve.*

Here is the Herald *reporter's description of the departure from Melbourne, published on 21 August:*

At an early hour crowds of eager holiday folks, pedestrian and equestrian, were to be seen hieing along the dusty ways to the pleasant glades and umbrageous shade (a warm breeze, the first of the season, was blowing from the north-east) of the Royal Park. A busy scene was there presented. Men, horses, camels, drays, and goods were scattered here and there amongst the tents, in the sheds, and on the greensward, in picturesque confusion — everything premised a departure — the caravansery was to be deserted. Hour after hour passed in preparations for starting. By-and-by, however, the drays were loaded — though not before a burden of three hundred-weight for each camel at starting was objected to, and extra vehicles had to be procured — the horses and camels were securely packed.

Artists, reporters and favoured visitors were all the time hurrying and scurrying hither and thither to sketch this, to take note of that, and to ask a question concerning t'other. It is needless to say that occasionally ludicrous replies were given to serious questions, and in the bustle of hurried arrangements, some very amusing contretemps occurred. One of the most laughable was the breaking loose of a cantankerous camel, and the startling and up-setting in the "scatter" of a popular limb of the law. The gentleman referred to is of large mould, and until we saw his tumbling feat yesterday, we had no idea that he was such a sprightly gymnast. His going-down and upris-ing were greeted with shouts of laughter, in which he good-naturedly joined. The erring camel went helter-skelter through the crowd, and was not secured until he showed to admiration how speedily can go "the ship of the desert".

It was exactly a quarter to four o'clock when the expedition got into marching order. A lane was opened through the crowd, and in this the line was formed: Mr. Burke on his pretty little grey at the head.

The Exploration Committee of the Royal Society, together with a distinguished circle of visitors, amongst whom were some of our most respectable colonists and their families, took up a position in front. The Mayor of Melbourne then mounted one of the drays and said: Mr. Burke, I am fully aware that the grand assemblage, this day, while it has impeded your movements in starting, is at the same time a source of much gratification to you. It assures you of the most sincere sympathy of the citizens. (Hear, hear.) I will not detain you; but for this great crowd, and on behalf of the colony at large, I say — God speed you! (Cheers.)

His Worship then called for "three cheers for Mr. Burke", "three cheers for Mr. Landells", and "three cheers for the party itself", which, it is needless to say, were responded to with all the energy and enthusiasm that are characteristic of popular assemblages. He then concluded with again saying, "God speed and bless you!"

Mr. Burke (uncovered) said, in a clear, earnest voice that was heard all over the crowd: Mr. Mayor — On behalf of myself and the Expedition I beg to return to you my most sincere thanks. No expedition has ever started under such favourable circumstances as this. The people, the Government, the Committee — all have done heartily what they could do. It is now our turn; and we shall never do well until we entirely justify what you have done in showing what we can do. (Cheers.)

The party at once got into motion. Following the leader were several pack-horses, led by some of the assistants on foot. Then came Mr. Landells on a camel, next Dr. Becker, similarly mounted, and these were succeeded by two European assistants, riding on camels — one leading the ambulance camel, and the other leading two animals loaded with provisions. Sepoys on foot led the remainder of the camels, four and five in hand, variously loaded, and the caravan was closed by one mounted sepoy.

Altogether twenty-seven camels go with the Expedition. Two new wagons, heavily loaded, followed at a good distance. These were built expressly for the Expedition, and one of them is so constructed that at a very short notice it can be taken off the wheels, and put to all the uses of a river punt, carrying an immense load high and dry on the water. If it be necessary to swim the camels, air bags are provided to be lashed under their jowls, so as to keep their heads clear when crossing deep streams. Two or three hired wagons, and one of the new ones, were detained in the park until nearly dusk, in charge of the astronomer, Mr. W. J. Wills, and the foreman, who had to look to the careful packing of instruments, specimen cases, etc. The hired wagons will proceed as far as Swan Hill only.

Issuing from the south gate of the park, the party went down behind the manure depot, and thence on to the Sydney Road, and the whole camped late last night near the village of Essendon.

The Age *reporter noted that the expedition appeared to be excellently equipped for its arduous undertaking. He wrote, in the issue of 21 August:*

The boots for the men and the greater part of the harness and saddlery for the horses and camels have all been manufactured at Pentridge, under the strictest supervision. Shoes have also been provided for the camels, to protect their feet when travelling over rough and stony ground. The whole of the stores, &c., with the exception of some ten tons of gram, which will be forwarded via the Murray, and which will be delivered to the party at the junction of the Murray and the Darling, the expedition will take with them, in six American waggons, three the property of the party, and three hired ones. These waggons will proceed as far as Swan Hill, when the loading will be transferred to the backs of the camels. Preparations have been made for every emergency; cots for the conveyance of the sick, which can be slung on either side of a camel, have been provided, and a good supply of medicines for both man and beast; and included amongst the list of medical comforts may be mentioned seven hundredweight of Bencraft's colonial oatmeal. Mr. Burke has also taken with him

Robert O'Hara Burke (centre) makes a farewell speech in the presence of the Lord Mayor at Royal Park, Melbourne, before setting out to cross the continent

every thing necessary for making signals in case any of the party should become separated in the bush, or if from any other cause such should be necessary. He has a large Chinese gong, two Union Jacks, and an ample supply of rockets and blue lights. The tents which the party take with them are in every way fitted for the purpose for which they are intended, being made of the best American drill and lined throughout with green baize. We are sorry we cannot speak so favorably regarding the waggons, the pole of one of them broke in attempting to start it, and we have since been informed that two of them broke down between thé Park and Essendon, and will be unable to proceed until they are repaired. It was intended at first to take only five drays, and to place three hundredweight of gram on each camel at starting, but Mr. Landells objected to that arrangement, stating that it would be necessary to husband the strength of the animals as much as possible for the journey between Swan Hill and Coop-er's Creek, when they will have to do the whole of the work. Mr. Landells' represent-ations were listened to, another dray was engaged, and the camels allowed a further respite. Mr. Landells states it will be absolutely necessary for the party to remain some con-siderable time at Cooper's Creek, in order to refresh the camels, since by the time they arrive there their energies will be wholly ex-hausted. Eighty camels he says would not be too many for the purposes of the expedition. We have previously recorded our opinion of the horses that accompany the party, viz., that they are wholly unfit for their work; and a more minute inspection of the team only confirms that judgment, added to which, whe they were yesterday called upon to start, they showed the greatest aversion to the collar, some of them indeed proving themselves "rank jibs". One consolation, however, as regards this matter is, that there is but little doubt that as Mr. Burke proceeds up the country he will be able to exchange these worthless animals for a better description of cattle...

1861   Miners stage a shameful riot at Lambing Flat, on the New South Wales goldfields

UNKNOWN REPORTER
Sydney Morning Herald, 20 July 1861

Australia's second gold revolution erupted late in 1860 — some six years after the Eureka Stockade — on new diggings at Lambing Flat, near the New South Wales town of Young. The white miners objected to the presence of a large number of Chinese, most of whom had gone to the fields as gold-seekers.

The first clash took place in December, when a party of white miners attacked a bunch of Chinese, hacking off their pigtails and some of their scalps with them. Atrocities of this kind continued to occur; the police force in the area, consisting of a few mounted troopers, were unable to cope — and were often assaulted when they attempted to interfere.

Throughout the first half of 1861 the clashes continued, and the degree of brutality mounted. Early in July a mob, estimated at between 2000 and 3000, attacked a tent township of Chinese, burned it to the ground, and rounded up Chinese with whips and bludgeons as if they were cattle. A number were killed, many were beaten, and all their possessions were destroyed.

The Sydney Morning Herald *sent its own special correspondent — unfortunately, unidentified — to Lambing Flat in February of 1861. His reports remain as eloquent, vividly-written testimony to a campaign of steady brutality and callousness which represents one of the most shameful episodes in Australian history.*

This report, which appeared in the Sydney Morning Herald *on 20 July 1861, was based entirely on the reports of the paper's man at Lambing Flat:*

Since the departure of the troops from Lambing Flat it has been evident to many resident there, that the strong feeling against the Chinese that had previously broken out in disorder had anything but subsided; and our Special Correspondent, who had been sent up purposely to watch the course of events, has over and over again pressed upon the public, through our columns, the necessity for largely increasing the police force on the Burrangong goldfields, if it was intended to prevent the recurrence of scenes of brutality and violence, such as it had been his misfortune to have previously recorded. No attention was paid to these warnings, coming from all quarters; and so long as no actual disturbance took place, all was considered to be going on well. This fancied security received its first shock on the 18th of last month, on which date the cry of "Roll-up" was raised for the first time since the departure of the military.

It was successful to but a very small extent, bringing to the "No Chinese" standard some thirty Europeans only. These, however, were well armed with bludgeons and revolvers, the evident nucleus around which it was intended that a larger force should form. Contrary to their expectations, they were not joined by the numbers they anticipated, and their work was consequently carried on upon a comparatively minor scale of destructiveness. They attacked and drove off from the Flat, on which by the authority of the Commissioners they were encamped, a body of forty Chinese, and were about to burn the tents and other property of the Mongolians, when luckily Mr. Henley, the Chinese interpreter, arrived, and by his prompt interference and decided attitude saved the goods, and no doubt prevented scenes of violence and cruelty similar to those which subsequently occurred.

This outbreak was known to all on Lambing Flat, and was made public through the columns of the Press, and yet all those who alone were in a position to nip the evil in the bud, remained wilfully blind to the significant act here perpetrated. Everything was allowed to go on as usual; no attempt was made to strengthen the hands of those in authority on the ground; no step was taken to prepare for the concentration of such a force upon the ground as would have overawed the rioters who had thus shown themselves so persistent in their violence.

At last the storm, which had been so long seen, by all but those who should have been the most attentive in their examination of the social horizon, to be impending, broke with a violence that at once woke up the sleepers from their pleasant dreams. On Sunday, the 30th June, the residents of Tipperary Gully were aroused by the cries of "Roll up," and in the course of a very short time upwards of a thousand men, armed with bludgeons and pickhandles, no firearms as yet appearing, were assembled round the "No Chinese" standard. Forming themselves in a rude kind of order of march, and with a band of music, which appears to have been thoughtfully provided for the occasion by the leaders of the movement, at their head, shouting, yelling, and singing, the crowd of rioters took the road to Lambing Flat, a distance of some four or five miles. Arrived there, every Chinese resident in the township on whom hands could be laid was attacked and maltreated, the chief object of ambition being to secure the long tails of hair with which the Chinese are accustomed to ornament their heads. The main body was here joined by numerous others, who came flocking in from all quarters, until the number assembled amounted to at least 3000 persons. Finding themselves so strong, and being determined to make a clean sweep of the Mongolians now that they were about it, they now turned their attention to the Chinese camp, situated on the spot and within the area allocated to them by the Commissioner in accordance with the regulations previously made, and apparently agreed to by the diggers. This was at once attacked and carried, the Chinese being driven off, under circumstances of great barbarity in some cases, and in all cases without being

permitted to take with them any portion of their property. It has been said also that many of them were robbed of various amounts of gold and cash; and that, mixed up with the crowd of rioters were numbers of women and children all actively engaged in plundering the property of the runaways of everything valuable, or convertible, prior to carrying the remainder to the enormous fires that were kept up with such kind of fuel. In the mean time the band, placed in a conspicuous position, enlivened the scene by playing spirit-stirring airs, to an accompaniment of yells and shouts that would have done credit to a New Zealand war dance. Excited with their triumph, heated with their violence towards unresisting captives, and possibly thirsting for the plunder, of which this last attack had given them a taste, a wild and savage yell of joy was raised, when some one suggested Back Creek as the next spot to visit. Shouting, firing (for guns were now pretty generally produced), singing, laughing, and cheering, the body of rioters moved off towards Back Creek, a locality about six miles from where they then were, and where it was known that there were several hundreds of Chinese at work. Information of the projected attack was, however, taken over to the Chinese in this locality, who, hastily packing up the most valuable and portable portions of their property, hurriedly made off from the spot. The rioters were not long behind them, and on coming up, a savage yell of disappointment rose up from the mob when they found that their prey had escaped. The tents, goods, &c., left behind were fired, after having been carefully looked over for plunder; and such articles as would not burn were destroyed by being broken with axes. Whilst this had been going on, a number of the rioters, who were mounted on horseback, galloped forward on the track of the retreating Mongols, overtook them, not much more than a mile away, headed them, and rounded them up in the same way as a shepherd-dog would do a flock of sheep. Information of the surround was sent off to those behind, who, eager for their prey, were already on the road. Here ensued a scene such as, thank heaven! it seldom falls to the lot of a British journalist to record. Unarmed, defenceless, and unresisting Chinese were struck down in the most brutal manner by bludgeons provided for the occasion, and by pick handles. The previous excitement had done its work, and now the wretched Mongols were openly and unblushingly searched for valuables, and robbery was committed without the slightest attempt at concealment. Very few of the poor creatures here attacked escaped with their pigtails, none of them without injury of some kind, whilst every article of the property they had endeavoured to take with them was plundered of all that was valuable, and then burnt. Some of the acts of barbarism said to have been committed here were such, that Englishmen can scarce be brought to credit that their countrymen could be guilty of them — for who amongst the British people could ever believe that man of their own country — Britons, would take the Chinese pigtails *with the scalp attached*. That this was done in more than one instance there can be no doubt, since the possessors of these trophies made no concealment of them, but rather prided themselves on their possession. . .

So extensive and savage an outbreak could not fail in at once opening the eyes of all to the real position in which the authorities at Lambing Flat were placed, and now at last was done that which should have been done long before. The electric telegraph was set to work, and all the available police from the districts round about were ordered up to Burrangong. Captain Zouch, with the troopers of the mounted patrol, arrived there on the evening of the 6th instant. Several men of the foot police having come up from time to time, until the total number of the force, horse and foot, reached 57.

On the following day, Sunday, the 7th instant, there was a very large assemblage of diggers and others in the township, and though rather boisterous, there was no rioting.

Things remained in a perfect state of quiescence during the week, and it was imagined by some that this outrage, like those which had preceded it, was to be allowed to die quietly out of memory. But in the interim, explicit instructions had been received from the Government to enforce the law by apprehending every one of the ringleaders in the last riot who could be identified. No opportunity of carrying these instructions into execution, occurred until Sunday, the 14th instant, on which day, from the diggers being unemployed in their holes, and, therefore, out and about, and generally assembling in the township, the police identified and arrested three of the ringleaders in the late riot. The news of this arrest spread like wild fire along the diggings, and the cry of "Roll-up!" was quickly raised in Tipperary Gully, which appears by all accounts to be the centre of all disturbance. The alarm thus raised quickly brought up an armed mob, the number in which has been variously estimated at from 500 to 1000 persons, which, under self-constituted leaders, who appeared to start up ready for the occasion at once marched up to the camp. Intelligence of the advance was given to the authorities, who speedily put the camp into a state of defence, and placed their men in such positions as to offer the most effectual resistance in the event of violence being attempted. . . . Captain Zouch's account of the conflict, as forwarded by telegram to the Government, is as follows:

The mob came on the camp at a quarter to eight last night, after sending in four delegates to speak to Commissioner; demanded the release of the prisoners, and gradually moved forward, evidently intending to rush the place. A division of patrol under Mr. M'Lerie was ordered to clear the ground, and was immediately fired upon by the rioters. The patrol charged well, night though it was, and drove numbers over the banks of the creek. The foot patrol firing into the mob, but it was not till three charges had been delivered, and the firing at intervals continued for more than two hours, before the rioters withdrew. Three men of the patrol were wounded — two gunshot wounds in one arm and one contused; one horse which dropped was recovered with four balls in him, and two horses missing wounded. As soon as I can ascertain losses, I will inform you. The darkness prevented our making any prisoners.

After this defeat, the mob sullenly withdrew, with a threat, however, of returning on the following day, better armed and better prepared for their work. On the following morning, Monday, the three men who had been arrested, and for whose release so much blood had been shed, were brought up, examined, and committed for trial, but were subsequently admitted to bail. Of the course that Mr. Zouch afterwards found it necessary to pursue, he thus speaks, in a later telegram to the Government:—

The Camp was attacked for the purpose of rescuing three prisoners for Chinese riots. We fought them for two hours and more. Attack commenced at a quarter to eight o'clock, and by ten o'clock we drove them off, killing and wounding many. Three, we know, are dead, and we have heard of numbers wounded. My report will explain all. Seven special constables came to the camp — two only armed. There was no response to the call made to the respectable part of the community. Position, I found, untenable, against the numbers that were prepared to revenge the defeat of Sunday night. Some three thousand, better prepared and organised, were to attack, and had sworn to destroy the whole of us. I have brought away the whole force, wounded included.

When the police authorities determined upon evacuating their position, our Special Correspondent, whose life had been threatened by the ringleaders in the riot, on account of the too truthful way in which he had dealt with their proceedings, left Lambing Flat, and fell back upon Yass, and thus we are without positive information in regard to the subsequent proceedings of the rioters, or to the number of killed and wounded in the repulse of Sunday night; but this gentleman telegrams from Yass to say that three men killed on that night were buried on Tuesday, 16th, and that at the funeral of one of them, forty men bandaged for wounds were present, and that it was currently reported that over a hundred had been more or less wounded.

Immediately on the receipt of this intelligence by the Government the Commander of the Forces was communicated with, and orders were at once given to forward on to Burrangong, detachments of the 12th Regiment, of the Artillery, of mounted and foot police, and of blue jackets from H.M.S. Fawn (whose services were offered by Captain Kater), the various detachments amounting to 225 men, which, with the police of the district, will give a total effective force of 280 men. Arrangements were made with the mail contractors to carry up to Goulburn in twenty-four hours fifty men per diem for such period as the Government may require. At Goulburn, the inhabitants have nobly come forward, and placed every means of conveyance at the disposal of the Government for the conveyance of troops and police, and no time will consequently be lost in forwarding them on from Goulburn to Lambing Flat.

On Wednesday, a first detachment of infantry, artillery, and police left Sydney by rail, and was followed on the following day by seventy-five blue jackets under Captain Kater.

In the meantime, the Burrangong Gold Fields remain indisputably in the hands of the rioters. All those who have property to lose are leaving them as fast as they possibly can; the managers of the branches of the three banks established there having come into Yass on Wednesday, 17th, for security, bringing with them 4500 ounces of gold. No attack had been made upon the stores, though they had all been searched for arms and ammunition. Nothing else had been taken, as the leaders who now prominently direct every movement declare that they will not allow robbery. Business of every kind is suspended on the ground, and there appears to be a general impression that the rioters have determined upon holding out to the last.

1861 Brahe brings back the news that Burke and Wills are dead

REPORTS BY THE EXPLORERS
Melbourne Argus, November 1861

On 2 November 1861, the news reached Melbourne — via a telegram sent from William Brahe in Bendigo to the Exploration Committee — that the continent had been crossed, that Burke and two members of his party were dead, and that one man, King, was returning to tell the tale. As Alan Moorehead later noted in his book, Cooper's Creek, the commotion was such 'as we might have in our time at the news that just one survivor was returning from the moon'.

What had happened was this: On 11 November 1860, Burke had reached Cooper's Creek with six men and fifteen camels. William Wright, a cattle station manager who had joined the expedition along the way, was sent back to the base camp at Menindie to bring up the remainder of the party.

Burke waited impatiently for six weeks for Wright and the others to return; finally he could stay no longer, and he announced that he intended to 'dash into the interior and cross the continent at all hazards'. He plunged north with Wills, King and Gray, six camels, one horse and twelve weeks' provisions — leaving the others, under Brahe, at Cooper's Creek. Brahe was told to wait three months before leaving on the home journey.

Burke and his three companions crossed the Dividing Range and followed the Flinders River until it widened into an estuary. He noted briefly in his diary: 'At the conclusion of report it would be as well to say that we reached the sea, but we could not obtain a view of the open ocean, although we made every endeavour to do so.' They began their return trip on 21 February, and on 21 April three emaciated figures staggered back into the depot at Cooper's Creek. The fourth man, Gray, had died on the way back. Only seven hours before their arrival, Brahe, who had waited an extra month more than the agreed three, had departed on the home journey, leaving some provisions and a letter. Wright had not come back, he explained in the letter. The natives were troublesome, and provisions almost exhausted. Brahe was only fourteen miles away when the party reached the depot. Burke, instead of following Brahe south, insisted on making for Mount Hopeless, 150 miles away; before he left, he buried a letter in the hole in which Brahe left the provisions. Unfortunately, Burke smoothed the earth over this and when Brahe rode back a few days later to check whether they had returned there was no visible sign that Burke and his two companions had been there.

From then it was a losing struggle for existence. Wills died first, and Burke two days later. King, the only survivor, made himself useful to a native tribe, and was supported until a rescue party from Victoria reached him.

William Brahe arrived at Spencer Street Station early on Sunday 3 November, with the journals and letters which had been dug up by the rescue party from the cache at Cooper's Creek. Poor King arrived back on 22 November, bewildered and confused by the noisy, triumphant reception he received along the way. 'John King,' the Melbourne Herald noted, 'is regarded with feelings similar to those which made the people say of Dante, "There goes the man who has been in Hades".' The Argus published King's narrative, and the last messages from Burke and Wills:

Mr. Burke, Mr. Wills, and I, reached the depôt at Cooper's Creek, on April 21st, about half-past 7 in the evening, with two camels — all that remained of the six Mr. Burke took with him. All the provisions we then had consisted of a pound and a half of dried meat. We found the party had gone the same day, and looking about for any mark they might have left, found the tree with DIG, April 21. Mr. Wills said the party had left for the Darling. We dug, and found the plant of stores. Mr. Burke took the papers out of the bottle, and then asked each of us whether we were able to proceed up the creek in pursuit of the party. We said not; and he then said that he thought it his duty to ask us, but that he himself was unable to do so, but that he had decided upon trying to make Mount Hopeless, as he had been assured by the committee in Melbourne that there was a cattle station within 150 miles of Cooper's Creek. Mr. Wills was not inclined to follow his plan, but wished to go down our old track, but at last gave in to Mr. Burke's wishes. I also wished to go down by our old track.

We remained four or five days to recruit, making preparations to go down the creek by stages of four to five miles a-day, and Mr. Burke placed a paper in the plant, stating what were our plans. Travelling down the creek, we got some fish from the natives, and, some distance down, one of the camels (Landa) got bogged, and although we remained there that day and part of the next trying to dig him out, we found our strength insufficient to do so. The evening of the second day, we shot him as he lay, and, having cut off as much meat as we could, we lived on it while we stayed to dry the remainder. Throwing all the least necessary things away, we made one load for the remaining camel (Rajah), and each of us carried a swag of about 25 lbs. We were then tracing down the branches of the creek running S., but found that they ran out into earthy plains.

We had understood that the creek along Gregory's track was continuous; and finding that all these creeks ran out into plains, Mr. Burke returned, our camel being completely knocked up. We then intended to give the camel a spell for a few days, and to make a new attempt to push on forty or fifty miles to the south, in the hope of striking the creek. During the time that the camel was being rested, Mr. Burke and Mr. Wills went in search of the natives, to endeavour to find out how the nardoo grew. Having found their camp, they obtained as much nardoo cake and fish as they could eat, but could not explain that they wished to be shown how to find the seed themselves. They returned on the third day, bringing some fish and nardoo cake with them. On the following day, the camel Rajah seemed very ill, and I told Mr. Burke I thought he could not linger out more than four days; and as on the same evening the poor brute was on the point of dying, Mr. Burke ordered him to be shot. I did so, and we cut him up with two broken knives and a lancet. We cured the meat, and planted it; and Mr. Burke then made another attempt to find the nardoo, taking me with him.

We went down the creek, expecting to find the natives at the camp where they had been last seen, but found that they had left; and not knowing whether they had gone up or down the creek, we slept in their gunyahs that night, and on the following morning returned to Mr. Wills. The next day Mr. Burke and I started up the creek; but could see nothing of them, and were three days away, when we returned, and remained three days in our camp with Mr. Wills. We then made a plant of all the articles we could not carry with us, leaving 5 lb of rice and a quantity of meat, and then followed up the creek to where there were some good native huts.

We remained at that place a few days, and finding that our provisions were beginning to run short, Mr. Burke said that we ought to do something, and that if we did not find the nardoo, we should starve, and that he intended to save a little dried meat and rice to carry us to Mount Hopeless. The three of us then came to the conclusion that it would be better to make a second attempt to reach Mount Hopeless, as we were then as strong as we were likely to be, our daily allowance being then reduced. Mr. Burke asked each of us whether we were willing to make another attempt to reach the South Australian settlements, and we decided on going. We took with us what remained of the provisions we had planted — two and a-half pounds of oatmeal, a small quantity of flour, and the dried meat —

this, with powder and shot, and other small articles, made up our swag to 30 lb. each, and Mr. Burke carried one billy of water, and I another.

We had not gone far before we had come on a flat, where I saw a plant which I took to be clover, and, on looking closer, I saw the seed, and called out that I had found the nardoo. They were very glad when I found it. We travelled three days and struck a water-course coming South from Cooper's Creek. We traced this, as it branched out and reform-ed on the plains, until we at last lost it in flat country. Sandhills were in front of us, for which we made, and travelled all day but found no water.

We were all greatly fatigued, as our rations now consisted of only one small Johnny cake and three sticks of dried meat daily. We camped that evening about four o'clock, intending to push next day till two o'clock, p.m., and then, should we not find water, to return. We travelled and found no water, and the three of us sat down and rested for an hour, and then turned back. We all felt satis-fied that, had there been a few days' rain, we could have got through. We were then, accord-ing to Mr. Wills' calculations, forty-five miles from the creek.

We travelled on the day we turned back very late, and the following evening reached the nearest water at the creek. We gathered some nardoo, and boiled the seeds, as we were unable to pound them. The following day we reached the main creek; and knowing where there was a fine water-hole and native gunyahs, we went there, intending to save what remained of our flour and dried meat for the purpose of making another attempt to reach Mount Hopeless.

On the following day, Mr. Wills and I went out to gather nardoo, of which we obtained a supply sufficient for three days; and finding a pounding-stone at the gunyahs, Mr. Burke and I pounded the seed, which was such slow work that we were compelled to use half flour and half nardoo. Mr. Burke and Mr. Wills then went down the creek for the remainder of the dried meat which we had planted, and we had now all our things with us, gathering nardoo,

and living the best way we could. Mr. Burke requested Mr. Wills to go up the creek, as far as the depôt, and to place a note in the plant there, stating that we were then living on the creek, the former note having stated that we were on our road to South Australia. He also was to bury there the field-books of the journey to the Gulf. Before starting he got 3 lb. of flour and 4 lb. of pounded nardoo, and about a pound of meat, as he expected to be absent about eight days. . .

During his absence, while Mr. Burke was cooking some fish, during a strong wind, the flames caught the gunyah, and burned so rapidly that we were unable, not only to put it out, but to save any of our things, excepting one revolver and a gun. Mr. Wills being return-ed, it was decided to go up the creek and live with the natives, if possible, as Mr. Wills thought we should have but little difficulty in obtaining provisions from them if we camped on the opposite side of the creek to them. He said he knew where they were gone, so we packed up and started. Coming to the gunyahs, where we expected to have found them, we were disappointed, and seeing a nardoo field close by, halted, intending to make it our camp. For some time we were employed gathering nardoo, and laying up a supply.

Mr. Wills and I used to collect and carry home a bag each day, and Mr. Burke generally pounded sufficient for our dinner during our absence, but Mr. Wills found himself getting very weak, and was shortly unable to go out to gather nardoo as before, nor even strong enough to pound it, so that in a few days he became almost helpless. I still continued gathering; and Mr. Burke now also began to feel very weak, and said he could be of very little use in pounding. I had now to gather and pound for all three of us. I continued to do this for a few days, but finding my strength rapidly failing, my legs being very weak and painful, I was unable to go out for several days, and we were compelled to consume six days' stock which we had laid by. Mr. Burke now proposed that I should gather as much as poss-ible in three days, and that with this supply we should go in search of the natives — a plan

Burke's expedition encamped. Landells is on the far left and Burke is centre with beard, hat and long dark coat

which had been urged upon us by Mr. Wills as the only chance of saving him and ourselves as well, as he clearly saw that I was no longer able to collect sufficient for our wants.

Having collected the seed, as proposed, and having pounded sufficient to last Mr. Wills for eight days, and two days for ourselves, we placed water and firewood within his reach, and started. Before leaving him, however, Mr. Burke asked him whether he still wished it, as under no other circumstances would he leave him; and Mr. Wills again said that he looked upon it as our only chance. He then gave Mr. Burke a letter and his watch for his father, and we buried the remainder of the field books near the gunyah. Mr. Wills said that, in case of my surviving Mr. Burke, he hoped that I would carry out his last wishes, in giving the watch and letter to his father.

In travelling the first day, Mr. Burke seemed very weak, and complained of great pain in his legs and back. On the second day he seemed to be better, and said that he thought he was getting stronger, but, on starting, did not go two miles before he said he could go no further. I persisted in his trying to go on, and managed to get him along several times, until I saw that he was almost knocked up, when he said he could not carry his swag, and threw all he had away. I also reduced mine, taking nothing but a gun and some powder and shot, and a small pouch and some matches. On starting again, we did not go far before Mr. Burke said he would halt for the night, but, as the place was close to a large sheet of water, and exposed to the wind, I prevailed on him to go a little further, to the next reach of water, where we camped. We searched about, and found a few small patches of nardoo, which I collected and pounded, and, with a crow which I shot, made a good evening's meal. From the time we halted Mr. Burke seemed to be getting worse, although he ate his supper. He said he felt convinced he could not last many hours, and gave me his watch, which he said belonged to the committee, and a pocketbook, to give to Sir William Stawell, and in which he wrote some notes. He then said to me, "I hope you will remain with me here till I am quite dead — it

is a comfort to know that some one is by; but when I am dying, it is my wish that you should place the pistol in my right hand, and that you should leave me unburied as I lie." That night he spoke very little, and the following morning I found him speechless, or nearly so; and about eight o'clock he expired. I remained a few hours there, but as I saw there was no use in remaining longer, I went up the creek in search of the natives. I felt very lonely, and at night usually slept in deserted wurleys, belonging to the natives. Two days after leaving the spot where Mr. Burke died, I found some gunyahs, where the natives had deposited a bag of nardoo, sufficient to last me a fortnight, and three bundles containing various articles. I also shot a crow that evening, but was in great dread that the natives would come and deprive me of the nardoo.

I remained there two days, to recover my strength, and then returned to Mr. Wills. I took back three crows; but found him lying dead in his gunyah, and the natives had been there and had taken away some of his clothes. I buried the corpse with sand, and remained there some days; but finding that my stock of nardoo was running short, and being unable to gather it, I tracked the natives who had been to the camp by their footprints in the sand, and went some distance down the creek, shooting crows and hawks on the road. The natives, hearing the report of the gun, came to meet me, and took me with them to their camp, giving me nardoo and fish. . .

Every four or five days the tribe would surround me, and ask whether I intended going up or down the creek; at last I made them understand that if they went up I should go up the creek, and if they went down I should also go down, and from this time they seemed to look upon me as one of themselves, and supplied me with fish and nardoo regularly. They were very anxious, however, to know where Mr. Burke lay; and one day when we were fishing in the waterholes close by I took them to the spot. On seeing his remains the whole party wept bitterly, and covered them with bushes. After this they were much kinder to me than before; and I always told them that the white men would be here before two moons; and in the evenings, when they came with my nardoo and fish, they used to talk about the "whitefellows" coming, at the same time pointing to the moon. I also told them they would receive many presents . . .

From this time to when the relief party arrived — a period of about a month — they treated me with uniform kindness, and looked upon me as one of themselves. The day on which I was released, one of the tribe who had been fishing came and told me that the whitefellows were coming, and the whole of the tribe who were then in camp sallied out in every direction to meet the party, while the man who had brought the news took me across the creek, where I shortly saw the party coming down.

These messages, which include the last dispatch written by Burke, were among the papers dug up at Cooper's Creek by the rescue party:

Depôt No. 2, Cooper's Creek, Camp 65.— The return party from Carpentaria, consisting of myself, Wills, and King (Gray dead), arrived here last night, and found that the depôt party had only started on the same day. We proceed on to-morrow slowly down the creek towards Adelaide by Mount Hopeless, and shall endeavour to follow Gregory's track; but we are very weak. The two camels are done up, and we shall not be able to travel faster than four or five miles a day. Gray died on the road, from exhaustion and fatigue. We have all suffered much from hunger. The provisions left here will, I think, restore our strength. We have discovered a practicable route to Carpentaria, the chief portion of which lies on the 140th deg. of E. longitude. There is some good country between this and the Stony Desert. From there to the tropics the country is dry and stony. Between the tropics and Carpentaria a considerable portion is rangy, but it is well watered and richly grassed. We reached the shores of Carpentaria on February 11, 1861. Greatly disappointed at finding the party here gone.

    (Signed) ROBERT O'HARA BURKE, Leader
April 22, 1861.

William Wills

P.S.— The camels cannot travel, and we cannot walk, or we should follow the other party. We shall move very slowly down the creek.

May 30, 1861.
We have been unable to leave the creek. Both camels are dead, and our provisions are done. Mr. Burke and King are down on the lower part of the creek. I am about to return to them, when we shall all probably come up this way. We are trying to live the best way we can, like the blacks, but find it hard work. Our clothes are going to pieces fast. Send provisions and clothes as soon as possible.

    (Signed) WILLIAM J. WILLS.

The depôt party having left, contrary to instructions, has put us in this fix. I have deposited some of my journals here, for fear of accidents.

    (Signed) W. J. W.

1863   The explorer John McDouall Stuart returns in triumph to Adelaide

UNKNOWN REPORTER
Adelaide Advertiser, 22 January 1863

Probably the most doggedly tenacious of all Australian explorers was John McDouall Stuart. Three times he pushed northward from the centre of the continent, and twice he had to turn back. Finally, on 24 July 1862, he succeeded in reaching the northern shore — and he kept a promise to Governor MacDonnell to dip his feet in the Indian Ocean.

Stuart was a surveyor, an ambitious little man with burning eyes and a dour nature. At twenty-nine he accompanied Captain Charles Sturt's expedition to the centre of Australia; and he obtained valuable experience of exploring methods and of the nature of the country.

In May 1858, with a companion and six horses, Stuart made an expedition into the country west of the Torrens basin; he covered more than 1,000 miles, and made important discoveries in the Lake Torrens region and to the west. He made two more journeys among the lakes, surveying, prospecting and exploring; then, in March 1860, came his first major expedition. He travelled to the centre of the continent, named the MacDonnell Ranges in honor of his governor, and then travelled 150 miles to the north-west, trying to reach the mouth of the Victoria River; shortage of food and water, and scurvy forced him to turn back.

Less than two months after his return to Adelaide the following September, he was off again, this time with a party of twelve men. Again the objective was to get from the Southern Ocean to the Indian Ocean, and there was considerable rivalry in Adelaide towards the Victorian expedition of Burke and Wills, which had set out in the August. This time Stuart traversed his earlier route, and got still further north; but he was blocked by dense scrub, and had to retreat. When he did turn

around, he did not know that Burke had already reached the tidal waters of the Gulf of Carpentaria; when he named a watercourse Burke's Creek 'after my brother explorer', Burke was already dead.

On his third attempt to cross the continent, and his sixth major expedition, Stuart succeeded; it was his best prepared and best disciplined journey of all. He did so at the expense of his health and good eyesight. He reached the coast not far from the present city of Darwin, some nine months after he left Adelaide. The trek back was a great ordeal for Stuart. 'My health is so bad I am no longer able to bear a long day's ride,' he wrote.

Adelaide turned on a great demonstration for Stuart on 21 January 1863. The Advertiser *summed up the spirit of the city that day in its editorial: 'Had Stuart never reached Van Dieman's Gulf he would still have been the greatest of explorers, in as much as he solved the terrible mystery of the interior, telling all other explorers that he had been there, and they might go.' Sir Roderick Murchison, who led the Royal Geographical Society in rewarding explorers and making their discoveries known, said of Stuart's achievements:*

In no time or country has any geographical pioneer more directly advanced the material interests of a colony more than Mr. McDouall Stuart has done those of South Australia; whilst as a geographer we especially recognise the value of the numerous astronomical observations he made under the severest privations, by which the true features of large portions both of the interior and the north coast have been for the first time determined.

This is how Adelaide celebrated one of its greatest days ever:

Wednesday, January 21, 1863, will be one of the memorable days of South Australia. On that day the explorer, JOHN MCDOUALL STUART, accompanied by his gallant band of fellow travellers, made his formal entry into the City of Adelaide, after having crossed the continent from the southern to the northern shore. Stuart had arrived in town sometime previously, with one or two of his companions — but the formal entry of the whole party — as such — was arranged to take place on Wednesday, and the citizens determined to give them a true South Australian welcome home. The feat accomplished by these brave men is unparalleled; many have attempted it, but none — except Stuart and his party — have achieved it. Burke *nearly* effected the object, though not quite; but Stuart succeeded completely. It is not, however, merely the fact that Stuart has crossed from shore to shore, which entitles him to be placed among the heroes of discovery; — of still greater significance is the fact that he, and he alone, wrested from the interior its long hidden secret. What was the map of Australia in our school days? what was it ten years ago? It was a vast blank, having no line traced upon it, no mark, even conjectural, by which an opinion might be formed of the nature of the vast interior. The coast was dotted with settlements, and its principal features were mapped down, but it was a mere fringe of description marking the edges of a vast desolation, as sea-weed marks the margin of the ocean. The interior of Australia was *unknown*. Many were the speculations as to its possible nature. Was it a region of burning mountains, a desert of shifting sands, an unapproachable expanse of rocks and chasms? Was it a sea, or a lake, or a forest, or a fruitful country? Was it a region of eternal solitude; was it the domain of wild beast; was it the home of savage tribes? Did the rains of heaven fall upon it, or was it doomed to eternal sterility and drought? Who could answer these questions? No one; but Stuart said *he would go and see*, and he went and returned to tell us.

We rejoice that this heroism was eventually rewarded by the sight of the Indian Ocean. It would have been a matter of deep regret if this hero, after having so often crossed and recrossed the vast main land of Australia, had been precluded by any physical or other impediment from actually approaching the waters of the opposite sea. But Providence reserved a better fate for Stuart and for his brave companions; and in the demonstration of Wednesday they could not but plainly see and powerfully feel how hearty and genuine was the public sympathy cherished on their behalf.

A Committee, including many members of Parliament, members of the various Corporations, and other citizens and colonists, had been sitting daily for a week or more in arranging the preliminaries for the demonstration and for the banquet with which it was to close. With the breaking of day numerous workmen were engaged at various points in arranging the decorations, and an immense number of citizens gave their free services to aid in carrying out the general design. The streets at an early hour presented a truly gay appearance. The day was brilliantly clear and fine; the water-carts had effectually laid the dust along all the streets in the line of procession, and there was every promise of a successful demonstration. . .

To manage a cavalcade in motion in a street a mile long is not, however, so difficult as to arrange it in order in a confined and limited space. Could the whole of the procession have been formed into a hollow square with the explorers in the centre the effect would have been much better; but to say nothing of there being no space in the city large enough for such evolutions, we fear it would have been necessary to have had two or three previous drills by way of rehearsal. Of course, a little crowding and elbowing at the termination of the march was inevitable, but on the whole there was excellent order kept. The carriages containing members of Parliament, Corporations, members of the Demonstration Committee, &c., were arranged three abreast in front of the Post-Office, and Stuart with the explorers then rode up between the carriages and the platform . . .

After the cheering had partially subsided, His Excellency addressed Mr. Stuart as follows:— Mr. Stuart — I have preferred meeting you upon this platform, because I have desired in the most public manner possible to express to you the admiration I feel for the great qualities you have displayed, the inestimable services you have rendered, and the hardy character that has shone forth in you in your late most glorious achievement. You had undertaken the most difficult and the hitherto deemed impossible task of crossing this continent, and you have accomplished it with a success that sheds honor upon you, and glory on the country you have served. I do not in any way wish to disparage the glorious efforts of others who have gone before you, but who have unhappily sunk under the hardships of the gigantic undertaking they endeavored to accomplish, but which you have successfully encountered. It seemed that by a direct ordination of Divine Providence, the fates of the gallant Burke and your own have so varied. On this very day the colony of Victoria are mourning over those daring men who have gone before you and fallen in the attempt, men who went forth upon the same task as you. They were now assembled to do honour to Mr. Stuart as the first and foremost and most successful of Australian explorers. (Tremendous cheers from the whole multitude.) As he (Mr. Stuart) had now six times crossed the continent, he had made the practicability of the route for the future a matter of course, and he (His Excellency) hoped that immediate benefit would result to this colony from his discoveries. He did not think, from the number of persons assembled and the heat of the sun, that it would be advisable for him to advert in detail to the hardships and trials which were recorded in his journal; and therefore he would not do more than express the gratitude which he knew they all felt to Divine Providence that he (Mr. Stuart) had been preserved to receive the honors which had been prepared for him that day, and he hoped that by the same Divine protection the life in which the colony took such an interest would be long preserved to them. . .

It seems to have been a trying assignment in many ways for the man from the Advertiser. *Often in his report he noted that he had been unable to hear what Stuart was saying in his brief speeches — mainly because his voice was drowned by the cheering and the 'oompah' of the brass band. But in his report of the great dinner that night, he captured some direct quotes from the explorer, and these are worth recording:*

(The Governor had proposed the toast of 'the health of Mr. John McDouall Stuart and his gallant associates'; it had been drunk three times in a row; the band had played 'See The Conquering Hero Comes'; and Stuart had to wait quite a time for the cheering to subside.)

When quiet was restored, he said, "I have received more commendation from you than I deserve. I did the best in my power. For five years, with the assistance of my friends, Mr. Finke and the late Mr. James Chambers, I have been endeavouring to penetrate to the coast. I determined to do or die. (Cheers). When I left the north-west coast I was at death's door. I dared not tell any of my party how ill I was, except Mr. Thring, for fear it should dishearten them. I determined that if the crossing of the continent could be done by man, it should be done by me. (Loud cheers). This is the second time I have met you in this room. On the first occasion I was unsuccessful, but this time I have been perfectly successful in my endeavours. I think you have given me the finest procession ever seen in South Australia. I gloried in it today, and I felt it deeply when I saw such a multitude assembled to cry, 'Welcome, Stuart'. . .

The South Australian Government gratefully paid Stuart £2000 and gave him, in addition, 1000 acres of land rent-free for seven years. A further £1000 was donated to him by the colonists, and the Royal Geographical Society of Great Britain awarded him its gold medal.

In 1863, after suggesting the building of the overland telegraph line, he sailed for England, and died in London three years later.

Assemblage of Premiers at the 1890 National Convention
called by Sir Henry Parkes (centre) then Premier of New South Wales

1863   Australia's first war correspondent accompanies troops into battle against the Maoris

HOWARD WILLOUGHBY
Melbourne Argus, 12 December 1863

Australia's first war correspondent was Howard Willoughby, who emigrated from Birmingham with his family in 1857, at the age of eighteen. His first job was as a clerk with a firm of wine and spirit merchants, but his brother-in-law, J. B. Thompson — a member of the Melbourne Argus *staff, and a cricketer who played against the first 'Gentlemen of England' team to tour Australia — persuaded him to seek a post on the* Age. *A year later he transferred to the* Argus.

Willoughby was a natural; he wrote brilliantly and fast, he was energetic and he had great judgment. When a contingent of Australians was sent to the Maori Wars under General Cameron in 1863, Willoughby was chosen to accompany it. Not long after his return, the Argus *sent him to investigate the convict system in Western Australia. His conclusions: the sending of more convicts would be bad for Australia, and from the British point of view, transportation, housing and guarding of convicts was comparatively useless and wastefully expensive. In 1866 he became a founding member of the staff of Victorian* Hansard, *and he remained with that publication until, in 1869, he became editor of the* Daily Telegraph. *In 1877 he rejoined the* Argus, *as chief of the news department and leader writer. He went on to become editor of the* Argus *in 1898, but ill-health forced his retirement in 1903.*

Howard Willoughby was one of journalism's great characters. His handwriting was so bad that linotype operators were given an extra rate for handling his copy. He used to tell the story how, when he was describing a cricket match and praising the performance of the English slow bowler Tinsley, the expression 'slow bowler' finished up in print as 'steam boiler'. He was also notoriously absent-minded, mainly because he spent much of his time composing copy in his mind; once he arrived at a Government House ball wearing full evening dress with tweed trousers, and he often arrived at the office wearing his wife's muffler instead of his own. He was also adept at picking up the wrong hat, entirely by accident, and walking off in it. Once, on his way to Parliament House, someone bowed to him, and Willoughby, deep in thought, responded with a brief nod; next day Lord Hopetoun (then Governor of Victoria and later, as Marquis of Linlithgow, Governor-General of Australia) told him: 'I don't think you quite recognised me in the street yesterday, Mr. Willoughby.'*

Willoughby was twenty-two when he wrote this characteristically thorough account of the battle against the Maoris, in which the Australians lost 130 men:

The most brilliant engagement of the war took place at Rangariri, on Friday, the 20th inst., with a result which renders the triumph of the British arms secure. General Cameron assaulted the enemy's fortified position, and, after a heavy loss of 130 men killed and wounded, carried the stronghold. The event has taken the public here by surprise; but despite the price paid for it, the victory has been gladly hailed, for the hope is that it may save further effusions of the blood of our countrymen.

After their evacuation of Meremere last month, the hostile Maories retired to Rangariri, where they received such powerful reinforcements that at one time 2,000 men are believed to have been in the place. The difficulty of feeding so large a number was felt, however, and led to several bodies being moved into the country, to the eastward and southward.

Australian mercenaries recruited for the war in New Zealand

General Cameron, receiving private information to this effect, made his attack when the defenders did not muster half the number stated. Profiting by his experience at Meremere, and having the requisite forces at his command, he advanced a strong force with such secrecy and despatch as to take the enemy, well-informed and vigilant as they generally are, by surprise, and, cutting off their retreat by a skilful flank movement, he struck the heaviest blow they have yet experienced. . .

General Cameron's plan of action was to attack the enemy in front from the land, and simultaneously to land a force from the river to take the works at the rear, and cut off all retreat. For some days before troops were congregated at Meremere, and when, on Wednesday, Captain Mercer was ordered to the front with two Armstrong guns it began to be generally known that an assault upon the rebel position was in immediate contemplation. The troops, disappointed with the Meremere affair, and annoyed by the harassing bush duties imposed upon them, were eager to be led where they could meet their foe. As for the tars from the Curacoa and Miranda, who manned the river flotilla, they were absolutely enthusiastic, and were to be seen sharpening their cutlasses, and slashing away at trees for practice, in all directions. Events commenced

early on Friday morning. By nine o'clock 1,145 men and forty-eight commissioned officers were on their way to the scene of action, independent of the marines and sailors, who would muster 250 men more. There were no volunteers engaged in the contest — General Cameron decided to act solely with troops of the line. The corps represented were — the Royal Artillery, under Captain Mercer; the Royal Engineers, under Colonel Mould; the 12th Regiment, under Captain Cole; the 14th, under Colonel Austin; the 40th, under Colonel Leslie; and the 65th, under Colonel Wyatt. Once more the brunt of the action fell upon the gallant 65th, who, after nearly seventeen years' service in the colony, have thus won another laurel. . .

The hundred men of the 65th, with smaller detachments of the 12th and 14th, were told off for the storming party. The 65th advanced in four companies — the right under Captain Gresson, the centre (the ladder party) under Lieutenant Toker, the left under Lieutenant Talbot, and the reserve under Lieutenant Pennefather. From the flotilla the advance of the men could be plainly seen. First came the warning roll of the drums, and then on dashed our gallant soldiers from the thick tea-tree jungle through the scrub and fern, which was breast high, their arms glittering in the sun, and their cheers ringing down the breeze. The rugged ground broke their line, and the enemy's shot caused gaps, which could not always be closed. The men did not reach the work in field day order, but they dashed up to the rifle pits with unbroken spirit; and how can I describe the feelings of the spectators when the gallant band became lost in the white smoke which curled up from the ascent and from the brow of the hill, and when the crackling roll of musketry which followed told that the Maories were pouring in their fire from all their hiding-places? Their firing was better than on any previous occasion.

It was evident that they had secured many rifles, and as they lay securely protected, they could take deliberate aim. Before the first work was reached, Captain Gresson had fallen, but Ensign Spiller was at once at the head of the company, cheering on the men. The first obstacle was a wide ditch, inside the parapet of which were the lines of rifle-pits. The ladder party rushed forward, bridged over the space, and, headed by Lieut. Talbot, who was first man on the parapet, sprang over into the trenches, while Private Gallagher planted the 65th's regimental colours on the work. Now the bayonets would have had full scope, but the Maories shrank from the charge, and fled with such precipitancy that but few met their death by this weapon. Chased impetuously by the storming party into the inner and flanking lines, the foe abandoned these also, numbers springing into the swamp and lake, and others seeking shelter in the inner and heretofore concealed works. Simultaneously with the advance of the land storming party, the 40th were put on shore — not without much difficulty, for the Pioneer seemed hard to manage — carried the unfinished works on the flat, and, sweeping round the base of the hill, joined the 65th in pouring in volleys upon the flying foe.

. . . Many did escape, but the troops lining the edges of the gully, continued pouring in their fire while there was a foe to be seen, and from the space which had to be traversed, the execution done must have been most severe. On the lake there were several canoes, and the flying wretches in their mad terror crowded some of these till they were overturned, while a shell from Captain Mercer's battery smashed one of the most crowded into fragments from stem to stern. . .

The exterior lines thus fell into our hands without any great loss, but it was now that the strength of the inner position was discovered. A regular bastioned redoubt had been constructed, surrounded by a dry ditch nine feet wide, and having a height, as already remarked, of over eighteen feet from the ditch to the parapet. Orders were issued to storm the place, but the scaling-ladders were found to be too short, and the men fell back before the murderous fire of the Maories. The high ground to the left of the works was literally honeycombed with zig-zag rifle-pits, and the Maories, fairly brought to bay, fought with the utmost determination — a determination which rivalled that of our own forces. . .

General Cameron was everywhere inspiriting the men and forming new arrangements. He determined to effect a breach by undermining the parapets of the works, and blowing them up. It was found, however, impossible to do this, the soil being so friable as to fall in whenever a drive was attempted. Still the height of the parapet was materially reduced. Guns were put into position to render the breach perfectly practicable, and a storming party was told off. The men not actually at work lay on their arms, completely surrounding the redoubt. The escape of the Maories was thus rendered impossible. They were conscious of the fact, but seemed defiant and determined to resist to the last. All night long they maintained a howling so hideous at times that it was hard to believe that the sound proceeded from human beings. With daylight, when they saw the preparations made, and how their fate was certain, their spirit failed them, and the white flag was displayed. The general, with a Government interpreter at once communicated with the head chief, and informed him that no terms could be made, and that if the assault were not to be made, there must be an unconditional surrender. Without much consultation this was done, and, amid tumultuous cheering on the part of the troops, the Maories marched out of the place. Thus Rangariri passed into our hands, but at what a price.

An elaborate 'beano' is served as the Duke of Edinburgh visits Melbourne

MARCUS CLARKE
Melbourne Australasian, 30 November 1867

Marcus Clarke, the finest writer of his time in Australia, emigrated from London in 1863 at the age of seventeen. He brought with him an inheritance of £800, a moody tightrope of a temperament, and a taste for bohemian living. When his money ran out, Clarke took a job — found for him by his uncle, a county court judge — as a clerk in the Bank of Australasia. He was not really banking material; he spent most of his time writing satirical verse lampooning the officers and his fellow clerks, and it was said of him that he used to add up columns of figures by guesswork. Finally he applied to the bank for a few weeks' leave of absence; the manager let him know that there was really no objection to his absenting himself from the place indefinitely. Clarke took the hint, and resigned.

Again his uncle came to his aid, and secured a job for him as a jackeroo on a sheep-farming property near Glenorchy on the Wimmera River in western Victoria. He loved the bush, the gallops on horseback, and the unceasing festival conducted by parrots, wild ducks, flocks of turkeys and emus, and for a time he considered a share-farming proposition. But, he later wrote, he had to weigh 'civilised attire, cigars, claret and a subscription to the Union Club balls, Governor's levees and Melbourne life' against 'sheepfarming, cattle-hunting, horsebreaking, duckshooting and a share in twelve thousand sheep'; in 1867 he settled for the cigars and the claret. He took a job writing theatre reviews and leading articles for the Melbourne Argus, *and was an instant success.*

As a journalist, Marcus Clarke was brilliant, extravagant, exuberant and unpredictable. Sometimes, too, he was arrogant. After only three months on the Argus, *he received one of the newspaper's plum assignments; he was asked to cover the Melbourne Cup meeting. He did the job superbly, but spoiled his record by indulging his anti-Semitism. In his color story on the Cup Day crowd, he coarsely assailed the young Jewish women on the course: 'Young ladies, oily as to their hair, pulpy as to their lips, and heavy as to their noses, were alternatively watching the course and casting stolen glances at the magnificent attire of Anonyma. . . Round the judge's corner the ladies mustered and the air was darkened with the shadows of the noses of the daughters of Judah. . .' It was as indefensible as it was unnecessary; there were indignant criticisms in other newspapers, and the* Argus *management apologised for the incident as an oversight of the editor.*

There was, in Marcus Clarke, a basic lack of discipline. He was once assigned to cover a concert; he wrote his piece without bothering to attend the concert, the concert was postponed, and his paper was made to look ridiculous. He lived riotously, borrowed heavily, and failed often to meet his publisher's deadlines. But he was still the most exciting newspaperman of his time, and his novel, For the Term of his Natural Life, *came to be accepted as the one great literary work written in Australia in the whole colonial period. Some of his best journalism was done as 'The Peripatetic Philosopher' for the* Australasian: *his columns were witty, cynical, blasé, provocative. Sometimes the wit was brittle and a little superficial, but there was a total freshness to it.*

The start of the column, in November 1867, coincided with the arrival of His Royal Highness Prince Alfred, Duke of Edinburgh, who was about to make a round of visits to the Australian colonies. The royal visit, like so many royal visits since, spawned a mass of breathless reporting. In contrast to most commentators, though, Clarke affected an air of boredom. The Duke bored him, and so did colonial pompousness and snobbery. When an elaborate beano was turned on to welcome the Duke — with one bullock and twelve sheep barbecued, 900 gallons of colonial wine drunk, and 3452 buns and three hogsheads of ginger beer served up to the children — the function got out of control. It became something of a public scandal. Again, Clarke did not join the popular mood of moral indignation; he settled for gently twitting the critics.

These comments, from the Australasian *of 30 November and 21 December 1867, demonstrate Clarke's use of boredom as a devastating weapon:*

Though a Bohemian I am loyal. I have assisted in the reception of the Prince. I have cheered, and shouted, and screamed my welcome to His Royal Highness with deafening energy. I have climbed up into uncomfortable grand stands. I have baked on the top of verandahs, and I have had my toes desperately trodden on at the corners of streets. I have been choked with dust, deafened with brass bands, cut down by furious volunteers, and chaffed by small boys perched in provokingly secure positions. I have been poisoned with bad brandy, drained to the health of the Prince. I have had my clothes burnt with crackers, my hat crushed by excitable youths, my eyes, limbs, and body in general, anathematised by enraged cab-drivers. I am nearly colour-blind from the variety of tints that my optic nerve has been unwillingly compelled to take notice of. I have got "bunting on the brain," and the prospect of coming insolvency; but I am still loyal, and permit me to suggest that loyalty in a carriage and pair, or with a front seat at a window, is well enough, but loyalty on foot, or in a crowd, with several elbows converging into one's ribs at various angles, has not such an easy time of it. There is some credit in feeling a glow of enthusiasm when a butcher (in boots and spurs) is standing on your favourite corn, the neck of a bottle Hennessy's cognac is impinging on your fifth rib, a crying baby is

close to your ear, a small boy is picking your pocket, your arms are jammed close to your sides, a fly has settled on top of your head (whence all contortions of that organ fail to dislodge him), and you have a shrewd suspicion that Augustus Chassemari is making love to your wife at a window immediately behind you. . .

There has arisen much indignation in the up-country districts against the press. All the publicans are in arms and eager for the fray. They declare that nobody was drunk during the Duke's tour. If we are to believe them, the reporters of the daily journals were mistaken in their unanimously expressed opinions. Perhaps drunkenness up the country is a very different thing from drunkenness in the city, and what would be regarded as bestial intoxication in Melbourne is looked upon merely as decorous jollity in the Western District. Of this I am ignorant; but having once journeyed up the country, I was present at a teetotal meeting, at a little township containing some two hundred souls. After the lecturing and reading was over, the company took the pledge with much grace; but before midnight every male adult, numerous boys, and a few women, had consumed an average of one bottle and a half of Hennessy's anchor brand apiece. I grieve also to say that some ungodly person having put gin into the lecturer's lemonade he drank it off in the excitement of argument, and was prevailed to "try another," until he likewise was somewhat merry, and, after dancing a mysterious dance, fell asleep in the middle of a text, with his head in the fender. But this, perhaps, was an exceptional case. No doubt in many cases the reports have been unintentionally exaggerated. One drunken man is more noticeable than fifty sober ones. Milliners are gradually sinking under their weight of woe. Messrs. Tulle and Sarcenet are coining money. Fancy dresses are talked of as though they were the most important things on earth. Ladies keep their costumes "a secret," — *i.e.,* no more than thirty near and dear friends are told of them. In my peregrinations, however, I have picked up some news. There will be thirteen Hamlets at the ball, three Ladies of Lyons (all over fifty years of age), five Charles the Seconds, eight Cromwells, thirty-two Neapolitan peasants, one hundred and one "pages," seven demons in tights, one hundred and fifty gentlemen of no particular century, and twelve *débardeurs.* All the worn-out dresses that had been peacefully slumbering in the property-room at the Royal will be walking about with figures inside them. The Bishop of Melbourne has signified his intention (privately) of going as Terpsichore. The hon. the Chief Secretary will appear as a thimble-rigger, and from what is known of his financial abilities will doubtless act the character well enough. Mr. Higinbotham will simply turn his coat. One of H.R.H.'s *suite* will be dressed as a gamekeeper; and Mr. Joseph Thompson and a D-st-ng-h-d P-rs-n-ge will represent Cupid and Psyche. I have not a doubt that the affair will be a terrific success. Even now the mayor and councillors are besieged with applicants, and young ladies who have not had an invitation are in lady-like despair. All is preparation and practice:

> "A fat Beau Brummell tries his wit, in trite and wornout platitudes;
> And thirty gawky Graces all are sprawling into attitudes.". . .

I met my friend X., M.L.A., yesterday, at the corner of Collins-street, and asked him how he liked the Parliamentary banquet? He said it was the greatest joke he had assisted at for a long time. I was surprised. "Why so?"

"Why, you see, it was the way in which the thing was done. The Governor knew that the 'people's chosen' must be near to the Prince some time or other. So he chose a banquet; put huge vases of flowers on the tables in order to conceal their appearance as much as possible; would not allow any of them to speak, and took H.R.H. away to the opera at nine o'clock."

"Were there no speeches?"

"The Governor rose solemnly and said, 'The Queen!' I cried 'Hear, hear,' and was instantly hushed down, but as it seemed that His Excellency was not going to say any more, hon. members gave out little echoes of his

Marcus Clarke

toast at intervals, and drank off their bumpers in a shamefaced way, looking very hard at each other. One enthusiastic person added, 'God bless her!' whereat another and serious member pulled up his shirt-collar, and muttered something about 'profane oaths' which I didn't catch. The affair was as gloomy as a mute's funeral until H.R.H. left."

"Oh! then it began to be cheerful?"

"Hon. members sighed relievedly, passed the bottle, and called each other by their Christian names. The dessert melted away with astonishing quickness. You should have seen S——t's face! He thought he was going to make immense profits, and then to have hon. members singing comic songs and drinking his wine until midnight! It was rather hard!"

"I suppose, though, that the ladies didn't stop until that hour?"

"The ladies? Oh! ah! in the gallery. No. Well, you see, they could not have seen much if they had. For in order to give them as good a view as possible, a number of dirty pocket-handkerchiefs and things were hung about on lines, a la washing day in the backyard of a dyehouse, and they could see nothing."

"But they could hear the singing?"

"Well, yes; I'm afraid they could."

"Good-bye, old fellow," said X. and departed. Ministerial dinners are not usually such fun as this.

1872 A great achievement: the two ends of the overland telegraph are linked

UNKNOWN REPORTER
South Australian Register, 23 August 1872

One of the truly great Australian pioneering achievements was the construction of the single-wire Overland Telegraph line, through country that was hazardous and virtually unknown. By the year 1870, all the States except Western Australia were linked telegraphically; meantime submarine cables were snaking around the world, linking countries and continents. There were various proposals from overseas to bring a cable to Australia to connect with the colonial systems. The Australian colonies were ambitious, and, for the most part, jealous of each other. They were all acutely aware of the advantage of having the submarine cable terminating in their territory — and of obtaining the revenue from all on-going telegraphic traffic.

The political rivalry between the States to obtain the overseas terminal led to various proposals for building overland lines terminating on the northern and western coasts of Australia. The keenest rivalry was between Queensland (supported by New South Wales) and South Australia; there was also a proposal to terminate the cable on the Western Australian coast, and to build an east-west line. South Australia, proposing to build a north-south line from Adelaide to Darwin, had two trump cards: the explorer John McDouall Stuart had already shown that the route was possible, and the South Australian Postmaster-General (also Superintendent of Telegraphs and Government Astronomer) was Charles Todd, a man of great repute.

In June 1870, the South Australian Government signed a contract with the British Australian Telegraph Company; the company undertook to extend its cable from Java to Darwin if the South Australian Government would provide a line down to Adelaide. The Government immediately voted £120,000 for the project, and Todd was appointed to take charge. It was a massive undertaking, and Todd tackled it by dividing the construction into three sections: southern, central and northern.

The central section involved five parties of workers, totalling 100 men. They had fifteen horse wagons, eighteen bullock wagons and five buggies, using 165 horses and 210 bullocks in teams, as well as pack horses and riding horses. A string of eighty camels carried supplies. The centre section and the southern section were both completed on time but floods interrupted the northern construction. When the time allowed for the contract had expired, at the end of 1871, there were still 394 miles of line between the King River and Tennant Creek to be completed. The British Australian Telegraph Company pressed for compensatory payment, but on 24 June 1872 the South Australian Government had some luck: the cable to Java broke. No more was heard about compensation, and by the time the cable was repaired (21 October), the two ends of the Overland Telegraph line had met. The final join was made at Frew's Ponds on 22 August.

The opening of the line had tremendous significance for news-gathering in Australia. Until then, newsmen used to meet each incoming ship carrying newspapers from Europe, and telegraph material gleaned from them around Australia. At one stage homing pigeons were used to get the news from ships off the Heads outside Port Phillip Bay to Melbourne newspaper offices. At a Sydney banquet held on 23 November 1872, to celebrate the opening of the Overland Telegraph link with the rest of the world, the then Postmaster General

The first pole of the northern section of the Overland Telegraph is officially placed at Port Darwin

of New South Wales (Mr G. A. Lloyd) said: 'The advantages of this wonder-working wire will not be disputed. We have on our breakfast table on the seventh the re-election of President Grant on the fifth, and on Wednesday we heard of a fire calamity which befell the city of Boston on Sunday. The ashes of that fire are still smouldering, the intelligence of which has come to us over 20,000 miles of wire.'

The South Australian Register, *a paper which competed intensely for the news — to such a degree that it once sent a compositor to the port of Albany (Western Australia) on a steamer, so that he could pick up the European news from the monthly mail steamer and set it in type during his voyage back to Adelaide — welcomed the Overland Telegraph. The paper had been bought in 1853 by a syndicate of seven, which included W. Kyffin Thomas, whose family stayed closely associated with it during its eighty years of existence. Here the* Register *announces the linking of the Overland Telegraph:*

Little more than two years have elapsed since the actual work of constructing the Overland Telegraph was entered upon, and we have now the gratification of announcing the completion of the line. At 1 o'clock on August 22 the Government received a message direct from Port Darwin, intimating that the last length of wire had been stretched, and that uninterrupted communication across the Continent had been established. The message was instantaneous in its transmission, and also announced that the cable still remains silent. Immediately on receipt of the news the red ensign was hoisted on the Victoria Tower, the Town Hall bells were rung, the Press flagstaffs were decked with bunting, and the Consular flags were hoisted. The Public Offices were also ordered to be closed, and the clerks were granted a holiday for the afternoon. . .

The persistent hostility of Queensland was intelligible enough; but not so the conduct of the larger provinces, who, when they saw fit to break through their chilling reserve, only did so to damn us with faint praise. They spoke patronizingly of our youthful ardour, and magnified the difficulties of the work,

not with any view of aiding us, but in order to rebuke our presumption for having undertaken so immense a responsibility. Tasmania from the first has been more generous in her criticism, and it is only fair to Victoria and New South Wales to say that they have for months manifested an increasingly sympathetic and just policy towards South Australia than at one time characterized them. Still, the fact remains that this colony, with a population of 190,000 souls, has, singlehanded and alone, in the face of obstacles and disappointments all the more formidable because unforeseen, brought her grand scheme to a triumphant conclusion. . .

In the course of Thursday afternoon the Chief Secretary forwarded a message to the constructors complimenting them on having stretched between eight and nine miles of wire after nightfall on Wednesday. Later in the day communication was opened up with Mr. Todd, who is on his way from Barrow's Creek southwards, and it will be seen from our telegraphic columns that he was positively inundated with congratulatory messages. Certain it is that the Superintendent of Telegraphs deserves all the commendation that can be bestowed upon him. It is mainly through his warm advocacy of the work in the first instance, and his indomitable energy in carrying it through, that the colony has secured the inestimable boon of telegraph communication with Port Darwin, and consequently with the whole civilized world. He is a man whom South Australia may well delight to honour, and it is to be hoped that a more substantial recompense than mere empty praise will be accorded him for the part he has played in the execution of the grand undertaking which has now become an accomplished fact.

The next day, 24 August 1872, the Register *sent a reporter to watch the working of the Adelaide—Port Darwin telegraphic line. This is his report:*

Through the courtesy of Mr. Cunningham, the Acting Superintendent of Telegraphs, we had on Friday, August 23, an opportunity of observing the wonderful steadiness and precision with which the Adelaide and Port Darwin telegraph line works. Shortly after 3 o'clock we repaired, by Mr. Cunningham's invitation, to the operating-room, where one of Morse's self-registering instruments was placed in direct communication with Port Darwin. The length of the wire is computed at nearly 2,200 miles, so that to complete the circuit of the magnetic current a distance of something like 4,400 miles — more than half the diameter of the globe — had to be traversed. Nevertheless the batteries worked as freely, as powerfully and as instantaneously as if they were simply telegraphing to Port Adelaide.

For upwards of half an hour a lively conversation was maintained with the Port Darwin operator and with most of the leading men of that sparsely-inhabited community, who to the number of nearly half a dozen speedily flocked to the scene of action. The state of the weather was of course the first topic of discussion, but the conversation speedily diverged into such friendly chit-chat as might pass between two persons meeting in the street. We need scarcely add that it was "not intended for publication." In every instance, either of sending or receiving a message, we were gratified to observe that the instrument worked perfectly. From the close of a question from Adelaide to the first preliminary signal of the reply from Port Darwin the interval was scarcely appreciable.

The reader who has seen one of the instruments at work will best appreciate this when we say that the travelling paper slip which receives the impression both of the question and reply showed a blank space, often considerably less than an inch in length, between the last sign of the question and the first indication of the answer. Among other questions, the Port Darwin operator was asked what o'clock it was, and whether he received the time signal dispatched daily at 1 o'clock from the Adelaide office to all the South Australian Stations. He replied that the signal duly reached him, and that the then time was twenty-one minutes past 3. The transmission of the whole of this question and answer occupied from first to last exactly twelve seconds.

Subsequently Mr. Cunningham spoke to

The men who built the telegraph: (from right) J. A. C. Little, R. G. Patterson, Charles Todd, Telegraphs Superintendent and Postmaster General, and A. J. Mitchell

other stations, including Alice Springs, the Peake, and Beltana, when the various styles of manipulation by the different operators were distinctly perceptible even to our untrained ears. A skilled operator can in this way recognise the person who is working the instrument even at a distance of 2,000 miles as easily as he would identify a familiar handwriting. In conclusion, we would remind our readers that the experience we have thus recorded was not at an exceptional time carefully picked out when the line was in unusually good order. It was within twenty-six hours of the first completion of the connection, and we imagine there is no reason to suppose that the line will be found as a rule to work less freely in the future. So satisfactory a result must be eminently gratifying to Mr. Todd as it is equally creditable to the care and skill of those who have so successfully carried out this great work under his instructions.

Although we have on a previous occasion fully described the interior of the Postal and Telegraph Offices, we cannot close this notice without a word in praise of the noble proportions and admirable arrangements of the operating-room. A more perfect development of the value of skilful organization and contrivance it would be difficult to find.

1873   South Sea islanders are kidnapped for forced labour by the notorious brig *Carl*

HENRY BRITTON
Melbourne Argus, 6 September 1873

During four decades of the nineteenth century 60,000 South Sea islanders were brought to the colony of Queensland to work as cheap labour — first on cotton and later on sugar plantations, clearing new ground in a climate that was considered too hot for work by white men. Little ships sailed from Australian ports to scour the almost unknown islands of the Pacific; they were skippered often by ruthless men prepared to kidnap and murder. Natives were lured on board schooners by displays of trade goods, then bundled below to have hatches slammed down on them. Canoes were run down, and the occupants dragged from the water by their hair to be signed on as 'volunteers'. Many who tried to escape were shot. The natives fought back with equal ferocity. Shapely brown girls would lure seamen ashore and into ambushes, where they would be clubbed to death and dragged away, often to be eaten. Warriors would climb aboard moored schooners at night to loot and burn and massacre. It was a savage slave trade — with the principal roles taken by labour-hungry sugar planters, unscrupulous seamen, and untamed islanders, who were called kanakas. The industry was known as 'blackbirding'.

One of the more notorious blackbirding voyages was that of the 256-ton brig Carl, *in which large numbers of a captured cargo of islanders were massacred by the crew. The* Carl *left Melbourne in June 1871, under Dr James Patrick Murray, a disreputable adventurer who had once distinguished himself by getting roaring drunk during an expedition searching for the lost Ludwig Leichhardt, and causing such damage that the expedition had to be abandoned. During August and September of 1871, the* Carl *hunted through the New Hebrides and the Solomons for kanakas. They tried one old ruse of sending men ashore dressed as missionaries to lure the blacks on board; this did not work well, but they were more successful with the tactic of running down native canoes and fishing kanakas out of the water. A brawl broke out between natives in the hold, and crewmen ended it by firing indiscriminately. About fifty natives were killed outright, and another sixteen were badly wounded; all were thrown overboard, some of the wounded with their arms and legs bound. Then the blood was washed from the ship, and all surfaces were whitewashed.*

Reports of the massacre led to a trial in Sydney in November 1872 and two crewmen were sentenced to death and two others to long terms of imprisonment. Dr Murray, the most guilty of the blackbirders — evidence was given that he sang 'Marching through Georgia' while firing at the natives — turned Queen's evidence, and escaped without punishment.

The colony of Victoria, shamed by the exploits of the Carl *and Dr Murray, later offered a large sum for the location and compensation of relatives of the murdered men. It was also decided to repatriate all of the* Carl *survivors who could be located. Towards the end of 1873, the war schooner* Alacrity, *under Captain F. W. Sanders, was assigned to take home twenty-seven of them.*

The Argus, *the most enterprising Australian paper of that time, sent its own reporter on the* Alacrity *— Henry Britton. Britton, born in 1846, became something of a specialist in South Seas reporting during the 1870s. A former parliamentary reporter on the Age, he went to Fiji in 1870 for the* Argus *and his series of letters had a large sale when they* *were published later in booklet form. Next he went to Cape York with the Australian Eclipse Expedition in 1871, and had his account published in* Nature, *the London scientific journal.*

In 1873 the Argus *sent him as its special correspondent to inquire into the Pacific slave trade, and it was during this investigation that he accompanied the* Carl *survivors to their homes. Again in 1874, the* Argus *sent him back to Fiji, at the request of the Governor of New South Wales, Sir Hercules Robinson, to cover the annexation of Fiji. During this assignment he also acted as special correspondent of the London* Times. *He later wrote a novel about cannibal life among the Fijians, and became dramatic critic of the* Australasian.

Britton began his examination of the slave trade on 6 September 1873, in this fashion:

It was apparent from the first that this labour traffic, though not necessarily dishonest in itself, was one which would always be peculiarly liable to abuse unless very strictly watched, and guarded by the most stringent provisions for the protection of the native races. The misfortune is that such measures are only now being adopted, after several years of crime and suffering, the disgrace of which, if ever obliterated, must long cling to the British flag in the Southern Seas. The large profits of the trade speedily attracted many of the most disreputable members of the seafaring class, whose object was simply to make one or two successful labour trips and then leave the country. The traffic was begun honestly enough by persons who were desirous of faithfully fulfilling their engagements, but it was soon found that the most disreputable captains often brought the largest number of "immigrants." Some disclosures were made in Queensland which showed the utter lawlessness of the proceedings of certain shipmasters. Many foreign labourers in Queensland and Fiji who were supposed to have emigrated voluntarily, as soon as they learned to speak a little English or Fijian told their employers that they had been kidnapped or cajoled from their homes, and many circumstances came to light disclosing a state of things existing on the labour

grounds closely resembling, as regards a few vessels, some of the worst features of the African slave trade, while it was made clear that a large proportion of the Polynesians employed in Fiji and Queensland had been obtained by unfair means. The number of labour vessels which sailed away and were never heard of again, and those which came back with the dismal story of a South Sea tragedy, the features of which are unhappily too well known to need repetition, and finally the murder of Bishop Patterson by islanders in revenge for the death of slaughtered friends, all pointed to the fact that the labour trade had to no inconsiderable extent passed into the hands of the most abandoned South Sea ruffians, some of the worst of whom were those engaged in the deportation of labour to Tahiti. . .

Supposing the vessel duly equipped to have arrived upon the labour ground, she will, in honest hands (and this is often the case), have no great difficulty in procuring men, especially if she has brought return labour who speak well of their employers. The ship anchors off an island, probably outside the reef which encircles nearly all the South Sea Islands, and natives come off to barter yams, fruits, shells, &c., for bright-coloured cloths, knives, and other attractive articles. The stores are enticingly displayed; and partly influenced by a desire to possess so many valuable things, and partly persuaded by the romantic description the interpreter gives of their future life as the white man's plantation hand, while some have private reasons for wishing to leave their homes, and others are sold for the term by their chiefs for firearms, a number of islanders agree to come with the ship, having a vague idea that they are going to make a trip to a foreign country and return in a short time to astonish their friends with their wealth of European goods. If the captain of the ship is well-known in the islands and liked by the natives, he has generally no great difficulty in procuring his complement of men.

But often, for various reasons, the natives are unwilling to come, or they say in the evening they will come and change their minds in the morning. In the meantime they continue trading on and around the ship, and the temptation is often too much for the honesty of the master and his co-partners. "Here," they say, "are a lot of people hanging about, and they don't know whether to come with us or not. We cannot wait here, with the expenses of the ship going on at the rate of £20 a week. All these men are worth £15 a head, and it would be absurd to leave them idling about here when nature evidently intended them for plantation hands. We will take them." So the hatches are clapped down when the unsuspecting islanders are examining the trade below, or their canoes are upset so that they cannot return ashore, and perhaps a hundred Polynesians are hurried away, many of them never to see their island homes any more. There is perhaps some lamentation the first day, and then the natural light-heartedness of these childish people prevails, and if a number of the same town are together, they become as full of life and fun as if in their own country, though in nearly every case a strong desire to return home remains. If numbers of hostile tribes, however, are thrown together in a ship, fighting is the inevitable result, and then the white men save their own lives by sacrificing two-thirds of the living freight. While there are many honestly-conducted vessels in the trade, it is now well-known from the statements of natives in the group that others have set out with the deliberate intention of kidnapping, and have remorselessly run down canoes without making any attempt to trade. But men so kidnapped, when on the plantation, and fully understanding that they · are to be returned at the end of three years with £9 worth of trade, are generally quite willing to remain at work until the contract time has been completed. . .

The initial shipment to Fiji was made by the Van Tromp, of Sydney, which in November, 1864, landed 35 New Hebrideans on Messrs. John Campbell's plantation, Vanua Leva, then superintended by Captain Wilson. The demand for the foreign labour increased rapidly, There were soon so many vessels competing that it became necessary to go further afield for the supply. The cost, or passage-money as it is called, also rose proportionately. Up to the

year 1868 men were landed in Fiji to serve for three and five years at from £2 10s. to £4 10s. per head. In 1870 the cost rose to from £10 to £15, which are the rates now current.

Here is Britton's description of the repatriation of the Carl *survivors — an event which, while easing a few consciences in the colonies, was not a spectacular success:*

It seems, that the captives, on their arrival in Fiji, were engaged by different planters for a term of three years on the understanding that they were to receive £9 in goods at the end of that time and be returned home in the ordinary course. They all settled down to their work very composedly. Although some expressed doubt at first at the opportunity of being allowed to return to their homes, all eventually decided to return, after sixteen months' labour on the plantations without receiving a penny of pay.

In order that they should not go home entirely empty-handed, the naval authorities divided £12 worth of goods between the twenty-seven labourers. The Levuka traders deducted a good commission, and eventually each of the labourers got a knife, a small piece of cotton print, a few pipes, and some tobacco, worth in all about 5/-. The poor creatures seemed disappointed when their property was given them, although they were not entitled to anything after breaking their engagements.

They were given comfortable quarters on the *Alacrity*, but they did not seem to have any strong desire to reach their homes. The bulk of the islanders were landed at Taputeuwea, (Tabiteuea) or Drummond Island in the Gilbert group, and at Mille in the Marshall group. The islands in these populous archipelagoes are nearly all atolls, or lagoon islands.

As soon as the *Alacrity* hove in sight of Drummond Island a fleet of canoes came out to meet her and her decks were soon crowded with naked savages who had shells, mats, and other articles to exchange for tobacco. These men were unarmed and did not seem to have the least fear, though they could not have forgotten the outrages committed by the crew of the *Carl*. The fact is, they are easily induced to emigrate, having but few attractions at home,

Many natives died in the holds of 'blackbirders' before they even saw their destination

and it would seem that they do not resent the crime of kidnapping very strongly.

When these islanders came on board, many of the returned captives recognised fellow tribesmen among them, but there was no feeling evinced at the meeting on either side, and the few words that passed between the two sets of long separated people were confined to inquiries about tobacco and fish. When the captives were landed, not the slightest notice of their return was taken, nor did the captives themselves evince any joy on touching their native shore.

These islanders in their own country wear no clothes at all, but those returned by the *Alacrity* were dressed out in a variety of odd garments which had been given to them. The men were mostly stalwart, good looking fellows who were tattooed on the naked chest in chequer work forms. One had on a black bell topper with a deep mourning band. Another wore a pair of thick trousers carefully tied around his neck.

One of the ugliest women was resplendent in a scarlet waistcoat and very little else.

One man, who must have been a suboverseer at least, had a complete, well-fitting, striped cotton suit, while his wife was smothered in an enormous gown and sun hat, both of a favourite flowered bed curtain pattern.

There were three women on board, but a girl of sixteen called Margaret was the only one that attracted any attention. She was a Polynesian beauty with arms and feet like those of a Greek model, perfect teeth of dazzling whiteness, and long, dark hair. Her complexion was a rich olive, and her features were as regular as those of a Spanish Jewess. Her only defect was her gait which was not at all graceful, probably because she was dressed in a long cotton gown which, to her, must have been irksome to wear. At all events, in the warm weather she summarily dispensed with this garment and appeared to be quite satisfied to move around clothed only in 'the armour of her own loveliness.'

Margaret was engaged to be married on her own island, but was too young for the ceremony to be performed at the time she was taken from her home. As soon as she was landed an ugly looking savage took possession of her and she walked away with him, not looking at all pleased.

1876   'The Vagabond' writes about a night in a model Melbourne lodging-house

JULIAN THOMAS
Melbourne Argus, 15 April 1876

One night in 1876, the general manager of the Argus, *Hugh George, heard a disturbance outside his office. The night attendant and a visitor were yelling at each other. George asked the trouble, and was told: 'The man insists on seeing the editor, and I tell him that's impossible without stating his business.' George asked the man what he wanted, and the visitor replied: 'I'm a journalist . . . I want to know if there is a show for any man who is a journalist on this paper.' George wasn't impressed by the man's unkempt appearance, but decided to give him a try. When he said he was staying at the Model Lodging House, George asked him to show how he could write by doing an article on the lodging house and its inmates.*

So began the Australian newspaper career of 'The Vagabond', who was christened John Stanley James; Hugh George later described the engagement as 'the most profitable deal I ever made for the Argus'. *Bearing the by-line 'by the Vagabond', James's piece, 'A Night in the Model Lodging House', was published in the* Argus *on 15 April 1876, and reprinted in the* Australasian *a week later. The Vagabond wrote simply and straightforwardly, almost tersely, and was never sentimental. He concentrated on the life-style of the oppressed and under-privileged — the vagrants, criminals and prostitutes of Melbourne's back-alleys. While there were some scandalous revelations which led to public inquiries, the Vagabond's columns relied mainly on matter-of-fact reportage, written from what he called 'the inside track'. The Vagabond spent 'A Day in the Immigrants' Home', lived as an inmate in the Benevolent Asylum and the Sailors' Home, dined at a sixpenny restaurant, worked as an attendant at the Kew Lunatic Asylum and at Pentridge. His columns quickly became the talk of Melbourne, and for a considerable time his identity remained a secret.*

The Vagabond was in fact something of a mystery man. He was hired as Julian Thomas, and was known by that name throughout his Australian journalistic career. James was born in November 1843, the son of a Wolverhampton (England) solicitor, and was something of a vagabond by the time he reached his teens; he had an unhappy life at home and school, ran away often, and frequented threepenny and sixpenny lodging-houses in villages and market-towns around England. The historian J. B. Cooper says of James's relationship with his father: 'Father and son had a serious and life-long disagreement about a lady, and the son, in consequence, left home.' James was about seventeen or eighteen at the time.

In his early twenties, James earned a living as a freelance crime reporter in London, and later reported the Franco-Prussian war of 1870 for Fleet Street papers. He went to America, adopting the name of Julian Thomas; when he joined the Argus *he claimed to be a native of Richmond, Virginia, and to have been married to 'a rich Southern lady', the widow of a Virginian planter. He was a fairly imaginative liar; in Melbourne he circulated the story that he was a graduate of a southern university, and a former officer in the Confederate army.*

During the fuss caused by his early Vagabond articles, James had some problems. While working as an attendant at Pentridge, he broke regulations by giving some of the prisoners tobacco; he was summoned to appear before Coburg magistrates, but, since the Chief Secretary of the time had helped him get the job at the jail, the case did not proceed. In 1877, he was given a testimonial dinner at the Yorick Club, and presented with a bag of 308 sovereigns. As a practical joke, someone substituted farthings for the sovereigns; he lost his temper, and the party broke up in some disorder. An Argus *historian later noted: 'He did not recover his composure until some time after the sovereigns had been returned to their place.'*

The Vagabond wrote for the Australasian, *the* Argus, *the* Sydney Morning Herald, *the* Victorian Review, Melbourne Punch, *the* Age, *and the* Leader *during an Australian career which spanned twenty years. He travelled about Australia a great deal, and was sent on assignments to London, Fiji, the Solomons, New Caledonia, the New Hebrides and New Guinea; at one stage he took charge of an* Argus *expedition which was trying unsuccessfully to compete in New Guinea with an* Age *exploring party under George 'Chinese' Morrison. But nothing he wrote ever again made the impact of his early Vagabond pieces. He died at the age of fifty-three in a squalid room in the Melbourne suburb of Fitzroy; he was buried at the Melbourne General Cemetery, where a monument simply identifies him as 'Julian Thomas, "The Vagabond"'.*

Here is James's first piece for the Melbourne Argus, *titled: 'A Night in the Model Lodging House'.*

It is a wet, dismal night. I consult a friendly policeman, who informs me that, at the Model Lodging-house in King-street, Melbourne, I can get a bed for sixpence. Rejoiced at the news, I wend my way through the pouring rain and biting wind. The building is a large one, of plain brick, three stories high. On the steps I find three decent-looking men smoking. Entering the hall, on my left I perceive a little window, where I deposit my sixpence, and the official in charge gives me a ticket marked 154, on the back of which he writes my name in chalk. Passing through glass doors, I mount the stairs, and, on the first landing, am received by a courteous warder, who takes my ticket and directs me to my bed. I find that, with the exception of the enclosed staircase, the whole floor is open, the landing being partitioned off by iron screens about six feet high, dividing the floor into two parts. Entering the left hand ward, I see, by the dim gaslight, two long rows of small iron beds; and, passing between these, I find my way to No. 154, each bed being labelled in large characters. The beds are placed very close together, and there is no furniture in the room but these. As I look around I see, by the beds already occupied, that it is customary for the lodgers to place their clothes under their pillows for safety's sake, or because there is nowhere else to put them. I follow the custom of the place, and am soon in bed. The mattresses and pillows are straw, the sheets coarse, but apparently clean, and the blanket and counterpane warm. There is barely room to walk between the beds. Stretching out my arm, I could easily place my hand on the forehead of the man in the next bed. Indeed, I was disturbed in the night by a stroke on the cheek from the hand of my left-hand neighbour, who lashed out wildly, killing mosquitoes in his dreams. About half of the fifty beds in the ward were occupied when I entered, and, sleepless, I watch the new comers, who troop in one by one. I find the general custom is to strip to the buff. Night-shirts, of course, there are none; and the naked figures flitting about the room, as a rule, show a lamentable lack of physique, and would serve as examples that we have sadly degenerated since the days of the mighty men of old . . .

I see that many of the lodgers are old hands, and appear to have their regular beds, to which they make their way as to their home. There has been little talking up to this, those who have gone to bed early being evidently tired out, but now two men at the end of the room nearest me begin an argument . . . This is interrupted by the entrance of a decently-dressed youth, whom they tell not to keep them awake to-night. "I assure you, gentlemen," says the youth as he takes off his coat, "that I went to sleep last night with my finger between my teeth, and this morning it was quite sore, but I'd do anything rather than disturb you." I wonder with what strange malady he can be afflicted that involves such a curious mode of taking rest, till by the conversation I gather that before his time he has taken to gnash and grind his teeth, awaking all his neighbours . . . All these experiences were perfectly novel to me, and I could not sleep. I longed for a pipe which might purify the air around me . . . .

Hour by hour the night passes away, the only disturbance an Irishman in the next ward fighting in his sleep, and cursing his mythical antagonist. I listen with much curiosity for any sign of the Grinder. I should have liked to have heard a specimen of his powers, but he is staunch as steel to his word; his teeth, presumably, are crushed on his finger, for he gives no sign. There is one sound, however, which continues all night, and falls gratingly on my ear. It is the continual coughing — not, as a rule, that caused by a trifling cold or bronchitis, but the dry, hacking cough which physicians know so well. The place sounded like a consumptive hospital, and as an indication of the health of the colony was anything but reassuring. Towards daybreak I fall into a heavy sleep. I am awakened in the morning by a loud call of "Cab," some cabman is being aroused. Many of the inmates call each other and exchange morning greetings. I find that the man I christened "the swell" slipped away early; the Grinder also is gone. I am one of the last to arise, and consequently on going to the lavatory (there is one at each end of the building on each floor) I find it hard to discover a clean bit of towel. I manage to get a good wash at last and make my way down stairs and through a passage into the back yard, where I am told I can clean my boots. On one side of the yard I find a shed where there are brushes and blacking, and where lodgers are allowed to smoke. At the end of the yard is the laundry, and in the centre sheets are hanging out to dry. On the other side is the kitchen, which I enter, and find filled with lodgers, who are evidently old hands . . . Rooms containing only one bed are charged 1s. a night. For a bed four in a room you pay 9d. a night. On the other side of the building is a large room furnished with tables and forms, which is used as a sitting and reading room by the lodgers. A few daily papers are taken in for their use, and draughts and dominoes also provided. Leaving this I pass through the glass doors, and over the ticket window see a framed copy of the rules of the Model Lodging-house

Company (Limited), which appear fairly reasonable. Smoking in any part of the building is strictly prohibited, and no intoxicating drinks are allowed to be brought on the premises.

As I am perusing these rules, the superintendent, Mr. James Watkins, comes from his office, and courteously answers my questions. On the first and second floors there are 200 sixpenny beds, and on the ground floor 96 shilling and ninepenny ones. On Tuesday night there were only two beds vacant in the establishment, and during the winter months scores are nightly turned away. The staff is composed of a superintendent, matron, and three wardsmen, with laundry girls. The institution, although not started by its proprietors with any idea of great pecuniary results, is likely to pay 10 per cent. Mr. Watkins showed me a small library which he has in his office, and from which he lends books to the lodgers . . . Mr. Watkins says that fully five-eighths of the lodgers are studious men. One-fifth he states to be men who have occupied, and may again, good positions. They are ex-army officers, barristers, lawyers, and doctors — men who have either been thoroughly ruined, or are under a temporary cloud. The remainder are generally tradesmen, or good, honest workingmen. Altogether, after my trial of the Model Lodging-house, I left very well pleased with the courtesy of the officials and the cleanliness of the place. One or two reforms I would hint at. There are, I think, too many beds in the wards. Smoking should be allowed in the reading-room at night; on wet, cold nights men will not stay in an open shed in the yard, the only place where they are allowed to enjoy tobacco, but will certainly go to the nearest public house. I think, too, more clean towels and sheets might be provided. In conclusion, I will mention one curious fact which may be of interest to the churches. I particularly watched at night to see if anyone knelt in prayer. Not a soul. In the morning only one boy knelt, and that after everyone else had left the room. Poor lad, I hope he was not ashamed of his devotions.

1880   The Kelly gang is destroyed by police at Glenrowan

JOE MELVIN
Melbourne Argus, 29 June 1880

The final confrontation between Australia's most notorious outlaw band, the Kelly gang, and police took place at Glenrowan on 28 June 1880.

The gang began its legendary career in March 1878, when Ned Kelly wounded a constable named Fitzpatrick who was attempting to arrest Dan Kelly for cattle thieving. Ned, Dan, Steve Hart and Joe Byrne took to the bush, and on 26 October 1878, at Stringyback Creek in the Wombat Ranges, they shot three policemen dead.

After they had committed audacious bank robberies in Euroa and Jerilderie, the governments of Victoria and New South Wales put a price of £8,000 on their heads; the reward offer was enough to tempt Aaron Sherritt, one of the gang's early associates and a former schoolmate of Joe Byrne, to turn informer. On 26 June 1880, the gang executed Sherritt outside his hut near Beechworth.

Deducing correctly that a trainload of police would be heading for Beechworth as soon as news of the murder became known, they forced a group of locals to tear up the railway line between Glenrowan and Beechworth; the idea was that they would destroy the train, then wipe out the police who survived the wreck.

The Sherritt murder occurred on a Saturday. On the Sunday, four newspaper reporters were advised that there would be places for them aboard a special train leaving for Beechworth, via Benalla and Glenrowan, at nine o'clock that night. It would carry a police inspector and several black trackers, and would pick up Superintendent Hare and a squad of troopers, complete with horses, at Benalla. One of the newspapermen invited was Joe Melvin, of the Argus; another was the artist-writer Tom Carrington, who illustrated news events for the Australasian Sketcher. Melvin was one of the boldest, most enterprising reporters of his time.

When the train stopped at Benalla, Superintendent Hare, aware of rumours that the line had been torn up, sent a lone engine ahead to 'scout' the way. Its driver reported that the line had been torn up half a mile beyond Glenrowan station. While Superintendent Hare went ahead along the line, the others waited, expecting an ambush at any moment. Melvin, Carrington later wrote, acted in 'the pluckiest manner possible'. He climbed out of the window of the press carriage, pulled the train's lamp down, returned with it to the carriage. Then the four pressmen barricaded the windows with four big cushions, and waited in silence. Wrote Carrington: 'We had no arms except one little revolver, and the carriage doors were locked, so that if the Kellys had descended on the train at that time they could have shot us all without any chance to escape.'

The ambush did not eventuate, and finally, before daybreak on the Monday, the train edged along to Glenrowan station; the Kellys' last battle was just beginning. When Superintendent Hare was shot, Carrington tended the wound. Melvin's account, published in the Argus the following day, was a masterpiece of eye-witness reportage. He interviewed the gang's sole survivor, Ned Kelly, who admitted that he had intended to kill everyone in the special train.

At last the Kelly gang and the police have come within shooting distance, and the adventure has been the most tragic of any in the bushranging annals of the colony. Most people will say that it is high time, too, for the murders of the police near Mansfield occurred as long ago as the 26th of October, 1878, the Euroa outrage on the 9th December of the same year, and the Jerilderie affair on the 8th and 9th of February, 1879. The lapse of time induced many to believe that the gang was no longer in the colony, but these sceptics must now be silent. The outlaws demonstrated their presence in a brutally effective manner by the murder of the unfortunate Aaron Sherritt at Sebastopol. Immediately on the news being spread the police were in activity. A special train was despatched from Melbourne at 10.15 on Sunday night. At Essendon Sub-inspector O'Connor and his five black trackers were picked up. They had come recently from Benalla, and were *en route* for Queensland again. Mr. O'Connor, however, was fortunately staying with Mrs. O'Connor's friends at Essendon for a few days before his departure. Mrs. O'Connor and her sister came along thinking that they would be able to pay a visit to Beechworth. After leaving Essendon the train travelled at great speed, and before the passengers were aware of any accident having occurred, we had smashed through a gate about a mile beyond Craigieburn. All we noticed was a crack like a bullet striking the carriage. The brake of the engine had, however, been torn away, the footbridge of the carriage shattered, and the lamp on the guard's van destroyed. Guard Bell was looking out of the van at the time, and had a very narrow escape. The train had to be pulled up, but after a few minutes we started again, relying on the brake of the guard's van. Benalla was reached at half-past 1 o'clock, and there Superintendent Hare with eight troopers and their horses were taken on board. We were now about to enter the Kelly country, and caution was necessary. As the moon was shining brightly, a man was tied on upon the front of the engine to keep a look-out for any obstruction of the line. Just before starting, however, it occurred to the authorities that it would be advisable to send a pilot engine in advance, and the man on the front of our engine was relieved. A start was made from Benalla at 2 o'clock, and at 25 minutes to 3, when we were travelling at a rapid pace, we were stopped by the pilot engine. This

stoppage occurred at Playford and Desoyre's paddocks, about a mile and a quarter from Glenrowan. A man had met the pilot and informed the driver that the rails were torn up about a mile and a half beyond Glenrowan, and that the Kellys were waiting for us near at hand. Superintendent Hare at once ordered the carriage doors on each side to be unlocked and his men to be in readiness. His orders were punctually obeyed, and the lights were extinguished. Mr. Hare then mounted the pilot engine, along with a constable, and advanced. After some time he returned, and directions were given for the train to push on. Accordingly, we followed the pilot up to Glenrowan station, and disembarked.

No sooner were we out of the train, than Constable Bracken, the local policeman, rushed into our midst, and stated with an amount of excitement which was excusable under the circumstances, that he had just escaped from the Kellys, and that they were at that moment in possession of Jones's publichouse, about a hundred yards from the station. He called upon the police to surround the house, and his advice was followed without delay. Superintendent Hare with his men, and Sub-inspector O'Connor with his black trackers, at once advanced on the building. They were accompanied by Mr. Rawlins, a volunteer from Benalla, who did good service. Mr. Hare took the lead, and charged right up to the hotel. At the station were the reporters of the Melbourne press, Mr. Carrington, of *The Sketcher*, and the two ladies who had accompanied us. The latter behaved with admirable courage, never betraying a symptom of fear, although bullets were whizzing about the station and striking the building and train. The first brush was exceedingly hot. The police and the gang blazed away at each other in the darkness furiously. It lasted for about a quarter of an hour, and during that time there was nothing but a succession of flashes and reports, the pinging of bullets in the air, and the shrieks of women who had been made prisoners in the hotel. Then there was a lull, but nothing could be seen for a minute or two in consequence of the smoke. In a few minutes Superintendent Hare returned to the railway-

Schoolmaster Curnow stops the special train

station with a shattered wrist. The first shot fired by the gang had passed through his left wrist. He bled profusely from the wound, but Mr. Carrington, artist of *The Sketcher*, tied up the wound with his handkerchief, and checked the hemorrhage. Mr. Hare then set out again for the fray, and cheered his men on as well as he could, but he gradually became so weak from loss of blood that he had reluctantly to retire and was soon afterwards conveyed to Benalla by a special engine. The bullet passed right through his wrist, and it is doubtful if he will ever recover the use of his left hand. On his departure Sub-inspector O'Connor and Senior-constable Kelly took charge, and kept pelting away at the outlaws all the morning. Mr. O'Connor took up a position in a small creek in front of the hotel, and disposed his blackfellows one on each side, and stuck to this post gallantly throughout the whole encounter. The trackers also stood the baptism of fire with fortitude, never flinching for one instant.

At about 5 o'clock in the morning a heart-rending wail of grief ascended from the hotel. The voice was easily distinguished as that of Mrs. Jones, the landlady. Mrs. Jones was lamenting the fate of her son, who had been shot in the back, as she supposed, fatally. She came out from the hotel crying bitterly and wandered into the bush on several occasions, and nature seemed to echo her grief. She always returned, however, to the hotel, until she succeeded, with the assistance of one of the prisoners, in removing her wounded boy from the building, and in sending him on to Wangaratta for medical treatment. The firing continued intermittently, as occasion served, and bullets were continually heard coursing through the air. Several lodged in the station building, and a few struck the train. By this time the hotel was completely surrounded by the police and the black trackers, and a vigilant watch of the hotel was kept up during the dark hours.

At daybreak police reinforcements arrived from Benalla, Beechworth, and Wangaratta. Superintendent Sadlier came from Benalla with nine more men, and Sergeant Steele, of Wangaratta, with six, thus augmenting the besieging force to about 30 men. Before daylight Senior-constable Kelly found a revolving rifle and a cap lying in the bush, about 100 yards from the hotel. The rifle was covered with blood, and a pool of blood lay near it. This was evidently the property of one of the bushrangers, and a suspicion therefore arose that they had escaped. That these articles not only belonged to one of the outlaws but to Ned Kelly himself was soon proved. When day was dawning the women and children who had been made prisoners in the hotel were allowed to depart. They were, however, challenged individually as they approached the police line, for it was thought that the outlaws might attempt to escape under some disguise.

At daylight the gang were expected to make a sally out so as to escape, if possible, to their native ranges, and the police were consequently on the alert. Close attention was paid to the hotel, as it was taken for granted that the whole gang were there. To the surprise of the police, however, they soon found themselves attacked from the rear by a man dressed in a long grey overcoat and wearing an iron mask. The appearance of the man presented an anomaly, but a little scrutiny of his appearance and behaviour soon showed that it was the veritable leader of the gang, Ned Kelly himself. On further observation it was seen that he was only armed with a revolver. He, however, walked coolly from tree to tree, and received the fire of the police with the utmost indifference, returning a shot from his revolver when a good opportunity presented itself. Three men went for him, viz., Sergeant Steele of Wangaratta, Senior-constable Kelly, and a railway guard named Dowsett. The latter, however, was only armed with a revolver. They fired at him persistently, but to their surprise with no effect. He seemed bullet-proof. It then occurred to Sergeant Steele that the fellow was encased in mail, and he then aimed at the outlaw's legs. His first shot of that kind made Ned Kelly stagger, and the second brought him to the ground with the cry, "I am done — I am done." Steele rushed up along with Senior-constable Kelly and others. The outlaw howled like a wild beast brought to bay, and swore at the police. He was first seized by Steele, and as that officer grappled with him he fired off another charge from his revolver. This shot was evidently intended for Steele, but from the smart way in which he secured the murderer the sergeant escaped. Kelly became gradually quiet, and it was soon found that he had been utterly disabled. He had been shot in the left, foot, left leg, right hand, left arm, and twice in the region of the groin. But no bullet had penetrated his armour. Having been divested of his armour he was carried down to the railway station, and placed in a guard's van. Subsequently he was removed to the stationmaster's office, and his wounds were dressed there by Dr. Nicholson, of Benalla. What statements he made are given below. . .

The siege was kept up all the forenoon and till nearly 3 o'clock in the afternoon. Some time before this the shooting from the hotel had ceased, and opinions were divided as to whether Dan Kelly and Hart were reserving their ammunition or were dead. The best part of the day having elapsed, the police, who were now acting under the direction of Superintendent Sadlier, determined that a decisive step should be taken. At 10 minutes to 3 o'clock another the last volley was fired into the hotel, and under cover of the fire Seniorconstable Charles Johnson, of Violet Town, ran up to the house with a bundle of straw which (having set fire to) he placed on the ground at the west side of the building. This was a moment of intense excitement, and all hearts were relieved when Johnson was seen to regain uninjured the shelter he had left. All eyes were now fixed on the silent building, and the circle of besiegers began to close in rapidly on it, some dodging from tree to tree, and many, fully persuaded that everyone in the hotel must be *hors de combat*, coming out boldly into the open. . .

In the meantime the straw, which burned fiercely, had all been consumed, and at first doubts were entertained as to whether Seniorconstable Johnson's exploit had been successful. Not very many minutes elapsed, however, before smoke was seen coming out of the roof, and flames were discerned through the front window on the western side. A light westerly wind was blowing at the time, and this carried the flames from the straw underneath the wall and into the house, and as the building was lined with calico, the fire spread rapidly. Still no sign of life appeared in the building.

When the house was seen to be fairly on fire, Father Gibney, who had previously started for it but had been stopped by the police, walked up to the front door and entered it. By this time the patience of the besiegers was exhausted, and they all, regardless of shelter, rushed to the building. Father Gibney, at much personal risk from the flames, hurried into a room to the left, and there saw two bodies lying side by side on their backs. He touched them, and found life was extinct in each. These were the bodies of Dan Kelly and Hart, and the rev. gentleman expressed the opinion, based on their position, that they must have killed one another. Whether they killed one another or whether both or one committed suicide, or whether both being mortally wounded by the besiegers, they determined to die side by side, will never be known. The priest had barely time to feel their bodies before the fire forced him to make a speedy exit from the room, and the flames had then made such rapid progress on the western side of the house that the few people who followed close on the rev. gentleman's heels dared not attempt to rescue the two bodies. It may be here stated that after the house had been burned down, the two bodies were removed from the embers. They presented a horrible spectacle, nothing but the trunk and skull being left, and these almost burnt to a cinder. Their armour was found near them. About the remains there was apparently nothing to lead to positive identification, but the discovery of the armour near them and other circumstances render it impossible to be doubted that they were those of Dan Kelly and Steve Hart. The latter was a much smaller man than the younger Kelly, and this difference in size was noticeable in their remains. Constable Dwyer, by-the-bye, who followed Father Gibney into the hotel, states that he was near enough to the bodies to recognise Dan Kelly. . .

After the house had been burned Ned Kelly's three sisters and Tom Wright were allowed an interview with him. Tom Wright as well as the sisters kissed the wounded man, and a brief conversation ensued, Ned Kelly being to a certain extent recovered from the exhaustion consequent on his wounds. At times his eyes were quite bright, and, although he was of course excessively weak, his remarkably powerful physique enabled him to talk rather freely. During the interview he stated:— "I was at last surrounded by the police, and only had a revolver, with which I fired four shots. But it was no good. I had half a mind to shoot myself. I loaded my rifle, but could not hold it after I was wounded. I had plenty of ammunition, but it was no good to me. I got shot in the arm, and told Byrne and Dan so. I could have got off, but when I saw them all pounding away, I told Dan I would see it over, and wait until morning."

"What on earth induced you to go to the hotel?" inquired a spectator.

"We could not do it anywhere else," replied Kelly, eyeing the spectators who were strangers to him suspiciously. "I would," he continued, "have fought them in the train, or else upset it if I had the chance. I didn't care a — who was in it, but I knew on Sunday morning there would be no usual passengers. I first tackled the line, and could not pull it up, and then came to Glenrowan station."

"Since the Jerilderie affair," remarked a spectator, "we thought you had gone to Queensland."

"It would not do for everyone to think the same way," was Kelly's reply. "If I were once right again," he continued, "I would go to the barracks, and shoot every one of the — traps, and not give one a chance."

Mrs. Skillion (to her brother) — "It's a wonder you did not keep behind a tree."

Ned Kelly — "I had a chance at several policemen during the night, but declined to fire. My arm was broke the first fire. I got away into the bush, and found my mare, and could have rushed away, but wanted to see the thing out, and remained in the bush."

He is very reserved as to anything connected with his comrades, but answered questions freely when his individual case was alone concerned. He appeared to be suffering from a severe shock and exhaustion, and trembled in every limb. Now and again he fainted, but restoratives brought him round, and in his stronger moments he made the following statements:—

"I was going down to meet the special train with some of my mates, and intended to rake it with shot; but it arrived before I expected, and I then returned to the hotel. I expected the train would go on, and I had the rails pulled up so that these — blacktrackers might be settled. I do not say what brought me to Glenrowan, but it seems much. Anyhow I could have got away last night, for I got into the bush with my grey mare, and lay there all night. But I wanted to see the thing end. In the first volley the police fired I was wounded on the left foot; soon afterwards I was shot through the left arm. I got these wounds in front of the house. I do not care what people say about Sergeant Kennedy's death. I have made my statement of the affair, and if the public don't believe me I can't help it; but I am satisfied it is not true that Scanlan was shot kneeling. He never got off his horse. I fired three or four shots from the front of Jones's hotel, but who I was firing at I do not know. I simply fired where I saw police. I escaped to the bush, and remained there overnight. I could have shot several constables if I liked. Two passed close to me. I could have shot them before they could shoot. I was a good distance away at one time, but came back. Why don't the police use bullets instead of duck-shot? I have got one charge of duck-shot in my leg. One policeman who was firing at me was a splendid shot but I do not know his name. I daresay I would have done well to have ridden away on my grey mare. The bullets that struck my armour felt like blows from a man's fist. I wanted to fire into the carriages, but the police started on us too quickly. I expected the police to come."

Inspector Sadlier — "You wanted, then, to kill the people in the train?"

Kelly — "Yes, of course I did. God help them, but they would have got shot all the same. Would they not have tried to kill me?"

Ned Kelly

1880   Ned Kelly is tried and has an extraordinary dialogue with the judge

EDWARD CUNNINGHAM
Melbourne Age, 30 October 1880

Edward Sheldon Cunningham had the kind of career aspiring journalists dream about. He began as an office boy on a country newspaper; before he finished he possessed an editorship, a knighthood and an honorary doctorate of laws. He was one of an exclusive band of editors of the early 1900s — among them Howard Willoughby (Argus), D. H. Watterson (Argus), G. H. F. Schuler (Age), J. E. Davidson (Melbourne Herald) and Montague Grover (Sydney Sun) — who had all had distinguished reporting careers.

Cunningham was born in Hobart in 1859, and began his newspaper work with the Bendigo Advertiser at fifteen; part of his job was to count and distribute the papers at 4 a.m. each day to messengers who would take them by foot to news stands, and to mail copies of the paper to postal subscribers. After three years in Bendigo he went to the Hobart Mercury as a proof-reader, and attended shorthand classes in his own time.

In 1879 he answered an advertisement seeking a parliamentary reporter for 'a mainland newspaper' and was surprised to receive a letter from David Syme offering him a job on the Age. He worked with the Age's gallery staff, but doubled up as a police rounds and law courts reporter.

He was a particularly enterprising reporter. One legend told of him concerns the days when steamers used to bring the newspapers from London; rival reporters would meet them in launches, pick up the London papers, scan the papers while their launches were heading back to Queenscliff, and file stories by electric telegraph as soon as they disembarked. Often the reporter with the fastest sprint from the wharf got his copy on to the wire first. Once, when Cunningham was assigned to meet

a P & O ship, he used the Bible to ensure that his stories were first; before he left Queenscliff he pasted the first half-dozen pages of Genesis on to telegraph forms, and instructed the operator to start sending the text some twenty minutes before the press launch was due back. When the reporters got back, the operator was busy with Cunningham's biblical copy. While his rival from the Argus cursed, Cunningham substituted new, hurriedly-written text for the unsent Genesis material. There is no record that Cunningham ever resorted to this device again.

He demonstrated his initiative again after the capture of Ned Kelly on 28 June 1880. Joe Byrne, Dan Kelly and Steve Hart had been shot dead, and Kelly had been wounded — some reports say twenty-eight times. On the evening of his capture Kelly was taken from Glenrowan to Benalla, and taken next day by train to Melbourne. Large crowds formed at Spencer Street as the train's arrival time drew near, but Cunningham played a hunch. He reasoned that police would not want too large an audience when they took Kelly from the train; his theory was that the train would stop at North Melbourne before it got to Spencer Street and that Kelly would be taken off there. That was what happened. Only fifty people were waiting at North Melbourne when Kelly arrived in a brake-van, lying on a pile of mattresses and surrounded by a dozen armed policemen. Cunningham was the only reporter on the spot, and was able to write a good atmosphere story about Kelly's progress to Melbourne jail.

Cunningham reported the trial of Kelly — one of the great criminal trials in Australian history. Even apart from its pure dramatic quality, this trial was notable for one of the

*most extraordinary pieces of courtroom
dialogue ever, between Mr Justice Sir
Redmond Barry, a graduate of Trinity College,
Dublin, and the convicted murderer, Kelly. It
was a dialogue which ended with Kelly reminding the learned judge that a day would come
at a bigger court, when they would meet again.*

The trial of Edward Kelly for the murder of
Constable Thomas Lonigan was resumed yesterday morning, at the Central Criminal Court,
before Mr. Justice Barry and a jury of twelve.

Mr. C. A. Smyth, with Mr. Chomley, conducted the case for the Crown; and Mr. Bindon,
instructed by Mr. Gaunson, appeared for the
prisoner.

Frank Beaucroft, draper's assistant, deposed
that he was stuck up by prisoner and his mates
on Younghusband's station. He was locked up
in a room all night along with a number of
other people. During the night prisoner confessed having shot Lonigan in the Wombat
Ranges.

Robert Scott, manager of the National Bank
at Euroa, also gave evidence to the effect that
after the bank was stuck up and robbed of
£2300. The prisoner, in a conversation on the
way to Younghusband's station, said that he
had shot Lonigan.

Constable Henry Richards, stationed in New
South Wales, deposed that he was present
when the Kelly gang stuck up the police station
and bank at Jerilderie. The prisoner said to
witness that he did not go into the Wombat
Ranges to shoot the constables, but to get
their arms and horses and to make a rise.
"But," he added, "there are some members of
the Victorian police whom I will roast when
I catch them."

E. M. Irving, clerk in the Bank of New South
Wales, deposed that he was employed in the
bank at Jerilderie when it was stuck up by the
Kelly gang. The prisoner gave him a document
about his life which he wanted printed. Witness
gave the paper to the police.

J. W. Tarlton deposed that he was manager
of the Jerilderie branch of the Bank of New
South Wales when it was stuck up by the Kelly
gang. The gang stuck up the bank while he was
having a bath. While in the bar of the hotel,
where twenty or thirty people were under
guard of Hart and prisoner, a sort of speech
was made by Ned Kelly. He said: "It is all
very well to say that we shot the police in
cold blood. We had to do it in self-defence."
He also said he had been driven to become an
outlaw. The prisoner further remarked that
he had himself shot Kennedy, Scanlan and
Lonigan.

Senior-constable Kelly deposed that in June
last he was at Glenrowan. He said the prisoner
made his appearance out of the bush. Witness
told him to go back, but prisoner continued
to advance with a revolver in his hand. He fired
upon the police, who returned the fire. After
exchanging several shots, the prisoner staggered, and then Sergeant Steel rushed on him and
seized him by the wrist. The prisoner was encased in armor made of plough shares and
mould boards, which had the brand of Hugh
Lennon.

Sergeant Steel stated that he was present
at Glenrowan, and he described the capture
of the prisoner.

S. Reynolds, medical practitioner, residing
at Mansfield, deposed that he made a *post
mortem* examination of the body of Thomas
Lonigan. There were four gunshot wounds on
the body. The fatal wound was from a bullet
which lodged in the eye, and which penetrated
to the brain. He also made a *post mortem*
examination of Sergeant Kennedy's body. He
thought Kennedy's wound in the chest was
received while he was standing. . .

Mr. Smyth summed up the evidence for the
Crown, and said that as the "motive" of the
prisoner had been referred to, he thought that
when they found one man shooting down
another in cold blood they need not stop to
inquire into his motives. It was one of malig-
nant hatred against the police because the
prisoner had been leading a wild, lawless life,
and was at war with society. He had proved
abundantly, by the witnesses produced for the
Crown, who were practically not cross-examined, that the murder of Lonigan was committed in cold blood. So far as he could gather
anything from the cross-examination, the line
of defence was that the prisoner considered
that in the origin of the Fitzpatrick "case," as

it was called, he and his family were injured, and that the prisoner was therefore justified in going about the country with an armed band to revenge himself upon the police. Another point in the defence was that because Sergeant Kennedy and his men did not surrender themselves to the prisoner's gang this gang was justified in what they called defending themselves and murdering the police. He asked, Would the jury allow this state of affairs to exist? Such a thing was not to be tolerated, and he had almost to apologise to the jury for discussing the matter. The prisoner appeared to glory in his murdering of the police. . .

Mr. Bindon, in addressing the jury for the defence, said it was his intention, in conducting this case, not to refer or introduce a variety of matters which had nothing to do with the present trial, but, unfortunately, his intentions were rendered futile by the Crown, who brought forward a number of things foreign to the present case. The question still remained how far this material was to be used in influencing the jury in arriving at a verdict. According to all principles of fairness and justice, these matters should not have been brought forward, because the only thing that the jury was concerned in was the shooting of Lonigan. With the shooting of Kennedy and the p·oceedings at Glenrowan and at Jerilderie the jury had nothing whatever to do at present, and he therefore requested them to keep these things from their minds. In McIntyre's evidence a long account was given of what took place in the Wombat Ranges, but he would point out that the police had appeared on the scene, not in uniform, but in plain clothes, and armed to the teeth. . .

The Kellys were not assassins. The whole career of the prisoner showed that he was not an assassin, a cold-blooded murderer, or a thief. On the contrary, he had proved himself to have the greatest possible respect for human life. The story of McIntyre was too good to be true. It showed the signs of deliberate and careful preparation, and of being afterwards carefully studied. He asked would the jury convict a man upon the evidence of a single witness, and that a prejudiced witness? If they

had the smallest doubt the jury would give a verdict in the case different from that which the Crown expected.

His Honor, in summing up, said that if two or three men made preparation with malice aforethought to murder a man, even if two out of three did not take part in the murder, all were principals in the first degree and equally guilty of the crime. They aided and abetted, and were as guilty as the man who committed the crime. The fact that the police party were in plain clothes had nothing whatever to do with this case. The murdered men might be regarded as ordinary persons travelling through the country, and they might ask themselves what right had any four men to stop them or ask them to surrender or put up their hands. . .

As to whether the prisoner shot Lonigan or not, that was an immaterial point. The prisoner was engaged with others in an illegal act; he had pointed a gun at McIntyre's breast, and that circumstances was sufficient to establish his guilt. The jury would, however, have to regard the evidence as a whole, and accordingly say whether murder had been committed. It could not be manslaughter. The verdict of the jury must either be guilty of murder or an acquittal.

The jury retired from court at ten minutes past five in the afternoon, and after half an hour's absence, returned with a verdict of guilty.

Upon the judge's associate asking the prisoner whether he had anything to say why sentence should not be passed upon him,

Kelly said: Well, it is rather late for me to speak now. I tried to do so this morning, but I thought afterwards that I had better not. No one understands my case as I do, and I almost wish now that I had spoken; not that I fear death. On the evidence that has been given, no doubt, the jury or any other jury could not give any other verdict. But it is on account of the witnesses, and with their evidence, no different verdict could be given. No one knows anything about my case but myself. Mr. Bindon knows nothing about it at all, and Mr. Gaunson knows nothing, though they have tried to do their best for me. I'm sorry that I did not ask

Ned Kelly is tried at the Central Criminal Court, Melbourne

my counsel to sit down, and examine the witnesses myself. I could have made things look different, I'm sure. No one understands my case.

The crier of the court called for silence while his Honor passed the awful sentence of death upon the prisoner.

His Honor: Edward Kelly, the verdict is one which you must have fully expected.

The prisoner: Under the circumstances, I did expect this verdict.

His Honor: No circumstances that I can conceive could here control the verdict.

The prisoner: Perhaps if you had heard me examine the witness, you might understand. I could do it.

His Honor: I will even give you credit for the skill which you desire to show you possess.

The prisoner: I don't say this out of flashness. I do not recognise myself as a great man; but it is quite possible for me to clear myself of this charge if I liked to do so. If I desired to do it, I could have done so in spite of anything attempted against me.

His Honor: The facts against you are so numerous and so conclusive, not only as regards the offence which you are now charged with, but also for the long series of criminal acts which you have committed during the last eighteen months, that I do not think any rational person could have arrived at any other conclusion. The verdict of the jury was irresistible, and there could not be any doubt about its being a right verdict. I have no right or wish to inflict upon you any personal remarks. It is painful in the extreme to perform the duty which I have now to discharge, and I will confine myself strictly to it. I do not think that anything I could say would aggravate the pain you must now be suffering.

Prisoner: No; I declare before you and my God that my mind is as easy and clear as it possibly can be. (Sensation.)

His Honor: It is blasphemous of you to say so.

Prisoner: I do not fear death, and I am the last man in the world to take a man's life away. I believe that two years ago, before this thing happened, if a man pointed a gun at me to shoot me, I should not have stopped him, so careful was I of taking life. I am not a murderer, but if there is innocent life at stake, then I say I must take some action. If I see innocent life taken, I should certainly shoot if I was forced to do so, but I should first want to know whether this could not be prevented, but I should have to do it if it could not be stopped in any other way.

His Honor: Your statement involves wicked and criminal reflection of untruth upon the witnesses who have given evidence.

Prisoner: I dare say the day will come when we shall all have to go to a bigger court than this. Then we will see who is right and who is wrong. As regards anything about myself, all I care for is that my mother, who is now in prison, shall not have it to say that she reared a son who could not have altered this charge if he had liked to do so.

His Honor: An offence of the kind which you stand accused of is not of an ordinary character. There are many murders which have been discovered and committed in this colony under different circumstances, but none show greater atrocity than those you committed. These crimes proceed from different motives. Some arise from a sordid desire to take from others the property which they acquired or inherited, — some from jealousy, some from a bare desire to thieve, but this crime was an enormity out of all proportion. A party of men took up arms against society, organised as it was for mutual protection and regard for the law.

Prisoner: Yes; that is the way the evidence brought it out.

His Honor: Unfortunately, in a new community, where society was not bound together so closely as it should be, there was a class which looked upon the perpetrators of these crimes as heroes. But these unfortunate, ill-educated, ill-prompted youths must be taught to consider the value of human life. It could hardly be believed that a man would sacrifice the life of his fellow-creatures in this wild manner. The idea was enough to make one shudder in thinking of it. The end of your companions was comparatively a better termination than the miserable death which awaits you. It is remarkable that although New South

Wales had joined Victoria in offering a large reward for the detection of the gang, no person was found to discover it. There seemed to be a spell cast over the people of this particular district, which I can only attribute either to sympathy with crime or dread of the consequences of doing their duty. For months the country has been disturbed by you and your associates, and you have actually had the hardihood to confess to having stolen 200 horses.

Prisoner: Who proves this?

His Honor: That is your own statement.

Prisoner: You have not heard me; if I had examined the witnesses, I could have brought it out differently.

His Honor: I am not accusing you. This statement has been made several times by the witnesses. You confessed it to them and you stand self-accused. It is also proved that you committed several attacks upon the banks, and you seem to have appropriated large sums of money — several thousands of pounds. It has also come within my knowledge that the country has expended about £50,000 in consequence of the acts of which you and your party have been guilty. Although we have had such examples as Clarke, Gardiner, Melville, Morgan and Scott, who have all met ignominious deaths, still the effect has, apparently, not been to hinder others from following in their footsteps. I think that this is much to be deplored, and some steps must be taken to have society protected. Your unfortunate and miserable associates have met with deaths which you might envy. I will forward to the Executive the notes of the evidence which I have taken and all circumstances connected with your case, but I cannot hold out any hope to you that the sentence which I am now about to pass will be remitted. I desire not to give you any further pain or to aggravate the distressing feelings which you must be enduring.

His Honor then passed sentence of death, and concluded with the usual formula, "May the Lord have mercy on your soul."

Prisoner: Yes; I will meet you there.

The prisoner was then removed, and the court adjourned.

Sir Redmond Barry, who presided over the trial of Ned Kelly

Cunningham went on to cover the proceedings of the Royal Commission which later inquired into the whole Kelly affair. In 1882 he joined the Argus *parliamentary team, which at that time included T. Pugh, E. C. Westlake, J. D. Melvin and T. Wells. He accompanied Alfred Deakin to America in 1885, and two years later to the Imperial Conference in London. He became editor of the* Argus *in 1906.*

1883 George Morrison's New Guinea expedition fails when he is speared by natives

GEORGE MORRISON
Melbourne Age, 21 November 1883

George Ernest 'Chinese' Morrison was one of the most adventurous men of his time. He went to Peking in 1897 as correspondent for The Times *of London, became a world authority on China, was a hero of the Boxer rising, and for years was political adviser to Yuan Shih-K'ai, first president of the Chinese Republic.*

Cyril Pearl, in his biography of Morrison, Morrison of Peking, *called him a latter-day Elizabethan who never quite grew up. Certainly he remained from his early years a romantic idealist, obsessed by adventure. Before he went to Peking, he sailed on a blackbirding vessel in the Pacific, walked across Australia from north to south, alone and unarmed, led an exploring party into New Guinea, and travelled on foot and horse from Shanghai to Burma.*

In 1883, New Guinea was the largest unexplored region in the world. The Australian colonies were aware that the French, Russians, Italians and Germans all had designs on the unclaimed areas of the place; the Dutch had held the southern coast since 1828. The general feeling in Australia was that British rule in New Guinea was essential to Australia's security. The Leader *said on 16 June 1883: 'We cannot afford to let the islands of the Pacific pass into the hands of dangerous neighbors; and it is not only the European powers who can be dangerous to us. Settlements of Chinamen or Malays will infallibly be formed . . . If Chinamen enter in, they will be the outpost of a possible Chinese invasion.'*

Around that time, Morrison applied to the proprietor of the Age, *Mr David Syme, for backing to lead an expedition to New Guinea. It was, Morrison later wrote, a role without pay. 'I was young and inexperienced and ardent,' he wrote. 'I cared nothing for money.*

I had a firm belief in my own future.' While Morrison was preparing for the trip — he tried to insure his life, but no Victorian company would give him a policy — the Argus *heard of his plans, and hastily tried to organise its own expedition. New Guinea was suddenly a prize in a contest between two rival newspapers.*

On 2 July 1883, the Age *announced triumphantly that it had 'despatched Mr. George Ernest Morrison to New Guinea for the purpose of exploring that island'. It was extraordinary, it said, that no explorer had yet made any serious attempt to penetrate the interior. 'That Mr. Morrison possesses the stuff of which explorers are made is shown by his various pedestrian travels in Australia, his experience on board a Queensland labor vessel, and his recent trip on foot from the Gulf of Carpentaria to Melbourne,' said the newspaper.*

Arrangements would be made, as far as practicable, to keep up communications with the mainland. His progress reports would be published in the columns of the Age *as soon as they were received.*

Morrison's first dispatch, dated 9 July, reported that he had had a wretched passage from Cooktown to Port Moresby in a little five-ton boat. 'Troops of little boys and girls follow you everywhere,' he wrote. 'The girls especially are so well made and pretty that one wonders what freak of nature ordained that they must develop into the ugliest and most repulsive old hags.' He told of a girl he had fallen 'head over heels in love with . . . a beautiful and graceful girl of 15, with the loveliest bust and figure that woman ever had. She was already bespoke, and would shortly marry a hideous fuzzy-headed savage who bought her cheap when wives were down in

*the market'. He wrote animatedly about
mangrove swamps — 'brilliantly colored crabs,
lizards, snakes, thousands of molluscs, with
quantities of animal and vegetable matter in
rank decay, giving birth to all manner of
slimy and creeping things . . . rioting together
under the hot sun like maggots in carrion . . .
the forests and hanging gardens, and the six-
shafted bird of paradise. The shades of the
breast vary from gold to green and blue;
the feathers on the back of the head gleam
like malachite.'*

Next day the Age *said proudly that Morrison
had already established that he was 'entitled
to be counted among the most expeditious of
explorers'. It added: 'In the event of no unlooked for obstacle arising Mr. Morrison may
be expected to quickly penetrate the great
central mass of the island, of the nature of
which the world is in complete ignorance.'*

*An unlooked for obstacle did arise. On
21 November, the* Age *reported that Morrison
had given up his expedition, after being speared
by natives. Then it published his report, which
had been sent by telegram from Cooktown:*

I have failed in my attempt to cross the
continent of New Guinea, and have returned
to Queensland. Our party had to turn back
when on the point of success. Pursuing a
north-easterly direction from Port Moresby
we had, with much labor and difficulty, taken
horses over the mountains, and where the
diggers turned back from want of grass we, by
keeping a different track, got into country
splendidly grassed right up to the main watershed. Latterly we had kept bearing to the east
to find a place low enough to cross. We had
reached the foot of the dividing range, and a
day later expected to be across it. For a few
hours we were going to camp there. The range
ran into a spur at the top, far less steep than
many we had previously surmounted. Once
across we intended as soon as possible to bend
round to the west, and to strike for the great
land belt.

We could not, however, get on with the
natives. They saw the weakness of our party,
and took advantage of it. The country was
thickly populated, and the natives of each

district resorted to every means but open
violence to prevent our moving further. Our
camp was always more or less surrounded by
natives, waiting an opportunity to make a
raid. By day and night we had to keep watch,
and scarcely a night passed but we had to fire
shots to frighten the natives, who were heard
in the neighborhood of the tents. The work
was most fatiguing, for there were only three
of us to share the watch, as we could not trust
the black boys. In spite of all our vigilance we
had axes and tomahawks stolen, and a native
sneaked off in open daylight with one large
red blanket. We awoke one morning to find
our tea stolen. The natives ultimately regarded
our firearms as harmless instruments of noise,
and crowds of men were in the habit of coming
with spears, clubs and shields, and motioning
to us to go back. They would also run with
their spears and pretend to discharge them at
us. On one occasion a man brought a shield
down to our camp, laid it at our feet, signed
to us that it would be to our advantage to go
back, and immediately ran away.

Our only safety lay in conciliating the
chiefs by a liberal distribution of gifts. Whenever we were going to shift camp a crowd
would come down to oppose our further
passage, and I had then to give each of the
more surly looking men a present, which
pleased them, and before they had lapsed
into their bad humor we had dodged through
their district. Our party was very weak. The
old digger who swore to go with me to death
gave in at the end of 15 miles from the start,
and only one man could be obtained in his
place. This was a worthless half-witted new
chum, who became a constant source of
danger to us. The two black boys could never
be taught to fire a gun. My other man, Lyons,
gave unqualified satisfaction, but when he went
forward to prospect the track I was never
certain but that I might find the camp wrecked
on my return. As we got further inland the
country became densely populated, and the
natives increased in boldness. One came quietly down to where three of us were packing
the last horse, picked up a tomahawk and
darted for the scrub. I could have shot him
easily, but, instead of doing this, one of the

party chased him, caught him, punched his head and let him go, though the savage had turned round half-way and flung the tomahawk at his pursuer. We decided next time to use the guns.

The opportunity came on the 2nd October. On that day I went out with four natives to cut the track, all the others but the new chum being sick with fever. I gave the natives a valuable scrub knife, which we took turn and turn about in using. As we proceeded with our work the natives increased in number till 4 had become 40, most of them carrying spears. When about three miles from the camp, one of them suddenly seized the knife and bolted with it. This stealing was getting a farce, so I waited until the man had got such a distance that a shot would not inflict much injury, and I then gave him one charge in the back. Everyone declares that I made a mistake in not shooting the man dead, as I might then have effectually frightened the natives and given them an idea of our superior power. As it was they inferred that the worst our arms could do was to inflict but a temporary pain.

That afternoon we could hear the news travelling everywhere, and see crowds of men collecting with piles of spears, and intently watching us. In the morning when I loaded up early, intending to shift the camp, warriors with heavy bundles of spears gathered in crowds at some points which we had to pass, until the long grass where they stood fully bristled with spears. Lyons was at this time very ill with fever and could hardly walk. We went on, however, exercising extreme caution. till we reached the last rise we had to go up. I was leading the horse some distance ahead of the rest, and was just taking a steep step from the scrub into the long grass at the top when I was struck by two spears, one in the hollow of the right leg and the other in the stomach. The steep step saved me. I pulled the spears out, and fired a shot from my Winchester. I saw no men, though they must have been within four or five yards when I was struck. I had then to lie down, as blood flowed from me freely, and my stomach gave me great pain.

When Lyons came up he thought I was mortally injured, for I was lying in a pool of blood, vomiting large quantities of blood, and suffering frightful pain. To save my life he resolved to abandon everything and bring me down to the coast. We were then over 100 miles from Port Moresby, but we could not return by the way we had travelled as we knew the natives were waiting for us. Over 50 spears in bundles were picked up near where I was wounded, showing the attack to have been premeditated but badly planned. Lyons, when packing the horses, could get no help from the new chum, who was paralysed with terror, and in consequence we retreated, leaving our stores behind, and escaped from the natives to nearly perish from starvation. For eight days I had not a morsel to eat, but the change of air healed my wounds, which are now quite well. Lyons, by the exercise of extraordinary courage and endurance, brought us safely into port. The first twenty miles of our return journey was through new and very rough country. For nine days Lyons was entirely without food, and but for his marvellous stamina I should now be rotting in the New Guinea bush.

1885   Australian troops arrive in the Sudan to fight the Saracens

JOE MELVIN
Melbourne Argus, 5 May 1885

In February 1885, news was received in Australia of the assassination of General Gordon at Khartoum. Amid the general mood of mourning and patriotism, it was suggested that Australia should send a contingent to the Sudan — not because the English troops fighting the Saracens were in any dire need of assistance, but because such an act would show how keenly Australia had felt the loss of Gordon.

The response was immense and immediate. The New South Wales Cabinet quickly decided to offer the Imperial Government two batteries of field artillery, with ten sixteen-pound guns, and 500 infantrymen. The contingent was composed of volunteers; so great was the rush that the entire force was on its way by sea within sixteen days of the receipt of the cable from England accepting its services. Embarkation day, 3 March, was one of tremendous excitement; the Herald *took nine full columns to describe the day's events, and the* Sydney Mail *published full-page drawings by Julian Ashton of the scenes at Victoria Barracks and Circular Quay.*

The Sydney Morning Herald *decided to send a member of its own reporting staff, William J. Lambie, with the contingent. The Melbourne* Argus *nominated Joe Melvin, the man who covered the destruction of the Kelly gang.*

Lambie was accredited as a correspondent; Melvin was not. Refused a passage on the troopship Iberia, *Melvin signed on as a steward; as soon as the contingent landed at Suakin in the Red Sea on 29 March 1885, he revealed his identity as a newspaperman. After filing this dispatch on the arrival of the Australians, Melvin joined the contingent, remaining with it throughout the remainder of the campaign:*

The New South Wales troopship Iberia arrived in port here at about 1 o'clock on Sunday last, and the troops disembarked during the afternoon. Our run from Adelaide was smooth and rapid, and we arrived among the shoals, coral reefs, and islands off Suakin on Saturday evening. Taking the island of Barr Masa Kebir as a landmark, we hove-to for the night, and lay off the island until about 5 o'clock on Sunday morning, as it was impossible to pass through the dangers of the reefs during the darkness. There are three approaches to Suakin — one from the south, another from the north, and a third in the middle channel from the north-west. The southern one is very dangerous, owing to the presence of shoals and reefs. The northward channel is easily navigated, but as it is enclosed between the mainland and a well-defined reef, with only about half a mile distance from the coast, it was anticipated that we might be fired on by Osman Digna's Arabs, and accordingly the more seaward course was chosen.

At daybreak we heaved ahead, and after carefully threading our way between the coral reefs and shallows we got into the harbour at about noon. Here we were welcomed by the crews of a crowd of men-of-war transports, and the old familiar "coo-ee" came over the water with a startling effect from men who had visited us in Australia, and knew where to touch a home chord in our Australian hearts. Our men replied with the cheers which British brotherhood calls forth all the world over. When we came to anchor Brigadier-General Ewart, of the Guards, and other officers of the staff came on board. Rumours of war awaited us, and orders were received to land at once. . .

The town is under military government, and has guards and sentries at various posts. There are two bazaars, or business streets, which present lively scenes during the busy hours, and several good stores, kept by English and Greek merchants, are to be found in the larger thoroughfares. The place has no plan, and the houses are so much alike that without sharp observation one may easily lose one's way. The British camp lies on a wide sandy plain, with low sandhills stretching away behind the town. It outlies the inner lines of defence, consisting of mud walls with the ditches in front, and extends irregularly for about two miles, with a depth of about half a mile. It is separated from the town by about a quarter of a mile of undulating sandy soil, over which numerous tracks carry the traffic for the lines. Two structures, known as the right and left water forts, stand prominently above the tents. On the front of the former floats a flag which marks the headquarters. There are about 12,000 troops in camp including the English and Indian regiments, and besides these there are crowds of camel drivers, native labourers, camp followers, &c., numbering altogether fully 4,000. Thousands of camels, mules, and donkeys are moving about in all directions with their loads, urged on by their busy drivers, with whom they have sometimes lively and amusing encounters.

A narrow railway from the island helps to supply the troops with water, and the main line from Suakin to Berber runs about two miles into the plain. Preparations are being made to carry on its immediate construction with sufficient protection for the navvies, who are now in town in considerable numbers, including native workmen. The carriage of water absorbs an immense amount of labour, and forms a large item among the huge encumbrances which hang about the movements of an army in such a situation. The advance into the plain depends on the establishment of depots containing a sufficient supply of water. A zareba, or redoubt, has been made about six miles out, and convoys have been making trips with water camels. It is near this place that the fighting of Sunday week took place, and it lies on the road to Tamai, about 10 miles to the south-west, where there are some good wells whence the enemy obtains water.

It was expected that the Australian Contingent would have gone out with water, and also joined in the advance convoy, but many necessary camping arrangements had to be made, and stood in the way of the first proposal, while the retreat of the enemy changed the general's plan. On their march through the camp the English soldiers, the Indian contingent, and the Arab camp followers lined both sides of the route at every turn. We were met with hearty cheering, and the men standing on each side smiled on us as if we were dear old friends. The reception of the Australians was most enthusiastic, and every hour we have spent in Suakin has shown that the Contingent is highly popular with the forces in camp. We hear in all directions expressions of the great uprush of natural spirit and kindly feeling between Great Britain and her colonies which has been created by this movement on the part of Australia.

When the Contingent reached the parade ground, it deployed into line, and was inspected by General Graham and his staff. The flanks then wheeled forward, and the general addressed the Contingent in a speech of welcome and encouragement. The troops heartily cheered in answer to the call of their colonel, as an expression of their intention to do their duty. They then marched off to the quarters allotted to them with the Second Brigade. The following day was occupied in shaking down into something like order, and the men were supplied with khakee clothing in place of their scarlet uniforms. The men are settling down in a satisfactory manner to the regular work of the camp. The appearance and physique of the Contingent has been much admired. The troops are spoken of as a very suitable class of men for the work before them. The horses also have elicited the highest praise. They are, as a rule, larger than the horses in camp, which include the beautiful little animals ridden by the Indian cavalry.

The Australasian came in on Monday, and immediately landed her men and horses in fine condition. She lost only about five horses, and this, considering the heavy weather she had to go through, says much for the endurance of the horses and the care of those

The parade of New South Wales troops embarking for the Sudan provided a magnificent spectacle

in charge of them.

At the time of our arrival everyone was talking about the recent fighting near the zareba and the attack on the convoys, but these attacks had suddenly ceased, and the spies who advanced to Tamai found that the place had been deserted some days previously, except by parties burying the dead. The enemy had not been seen for a day or two, and it is supposed that Osman Digna has withdrawn to Tokar, which is his source of supply. Hasheen was also reconnoitred, and only a few stragglers were found there. This clears the way for the present, and the next step will be to proceed with the construction of the railway. We are now awaiting orders to proceed towards Handub to protect the railway works. The Australian Contingent is brigaded with the Shropshire regiment, second brigade.

The troops already in camp include the Grenadiers, Coldstreams, and Scots Guards, one battalion of each; the Shropshire, Berkshire, and East Surrey regiments Marines and Artillery; one squadron each from the 5th Lancers, and the 20th Hussars; one battery of the Royal Artillery, the 15th Sikh, 17th Native Infantry, Bombay Sappers and Miners, Madras 9th Bengal Cavalry, Hodson's Horse, 17th and 24th Companies of Engineers, Ambulance and Service Corps. The commander-in-chief is General Sir G. Graham; the chief of the staff, Sir Geo. Greaves; the brigadier of infantry, Sir John M'Neill; the brigadier of cavalry, General Ewart; the officer commanding the Indian contingent, General Hobson. Our men are in fine health, and the weather is splendid.

1890   **Carbine wins the Melbourne Cup carrying record weight**

FRANK MYERS AND NAT GOULD
Melbourne Argus and Referee, 5 November 1890

The two greatest Australian racehorses ever have been Carbine and Phar Lap: in their time, both were proclaimed as the finest the world had ever known. Strangely, neither was purely Australian; both were foaled in New Zealand, but Phar Lap did all of his racing in Australia, and Carbine's only starts in New Zealand were as a two-year-old.

There are many who argue that Carbine's win in the 1890 Melbourne Cup was the finest performance that race has seen. In 1889 he had gallantly carried ten stone into second place behind Bravo, and during that run he had split a heel; that injury was the direct cause of the only unplaced run in Carbine's forty-three races — in the Canterbury Plate on the last day of the 1889 Cup meeting.

In 1890 Carbine carried ten stone five pounds — the weight of a welterweight boxer. It was the heaviest weight ever carried by a Melbourne Cup winner; only Archer, in 1862, with ten stone two pounds, and Po it rel in 1920, with ten stone, have approached it. The reception Carbine got that day from the crowd is still believed to have been the most joyous ever; 'Old Jack', as Carbine was known, loved applause and that day Frank Myers wrote in the Argus *that the fans were: 'all shouting and cheering . . . full of jubilation and exultation over the greatest victory ever known on the Australian turf'.*

Frank Myers, who often wrote under the by-line 'Telemachus', was one of a brilliant gang of writers on the Argus *during the eighties and nineties. They included Marcus Clarke, 'the Vagabond' (Julian Thomas), Henry Britton, David Watterson, Howard Willoughby, Joe Melvin, Donald Macdonald, Peter Symmonds, Billy Salter and D. H. Maling. Myers, formerly of New Zealand and Sydney,*

took over the Vagabond's Saturday sketches (under the name of 'Telemachus') when Thomas left the Argus *in 1887. David Watterson later wrote of him: 'He was able, but erratic. He never quite caught on as The Vagabond had done. He had not the human touch, nor had he the Vagabond's large reserve of personal experiences, to draw upon.' It was not a very fair comparison: Myers was a different kind of writer, something of a romanticist who enjoyed writing mostly about the harshness and beauty of the bush. He was an emphatic Bohemian, and he enjoyed friendship with both Clarke and the Vagabond.*

In those days, covering the Melbourne Cup for the Argus *was an assignment of great prestige. (In 1891, the commission was offered to Rudyard Kipling, and another distinguished contributor of the* Argus's *Cup Day piece was George Augustus Sala.) Myers's report, on 5 November, was characteristic of the Cup Day prose of the time. Certainly its sentiments — 'we ought to have Carbine set up in bronze at Flemington, to stand in perpetual commemoration of November the fourth, 1890' — caught the public mood.*

The year has revolved and the day returned, and once more the toys are out for the great play of Australasia. Nature has given us a glad and a prosperous year, and if our own follies have marred it somewhat, we may hope that we have bought wisdom by bitter experience, and effectually cauterised some cancer growths that were threatening to thrid their poisonous way through the whole of our social and political and national being. Therefore, perhaps, having fought, and won as we hope, we are more than usually disposed to make a good time of this particular Cup, to people the flat, and crowd the hill, and make the lawn and the stand all glorious as the king's daughter.

Saturday was a fair and bright and beautiful day, too fair, thought many a watcher for the pageant of the Cup, to be the happy harbinger of an abiding summer, but Sunday came with a fiercer heat, and Monday with all the true summer's ardour, and Tuesday with the grey sky veil again — the frequent morning vesture of our Austral summer — and generally the assurance of a day when all the bunting may be spread, and will surely be bravely blown and lit by a glorious sunshine. . .

Till nine perhaps the sky was mantled with grey, but then it seemed that the hoarse and ragged peals of music from the Salvation Army bands broke up the cloud floor, the sun burst through, the windy halls of heaven were speedily bared, and a full and kindly light fell on the rivers of people all making towards the Flemington sea. Opinions may and will differ as to the gathering there. It seemed to me to be greater on the flat and the outside hills than we have ever seen before, the black human flock spread farther down the rails, and the near hills without the enclosure were more thickly dotted with people than on any previous occasion. And really when the show was complete, say a half-hour before the Cup start, the massed humanity in stands and hill seemed great as we ever remember it, solid massed as a bee swarm, from the rails by the course to the topmost row on the great hill stand. Dark coloured, almost black in the general mass, but brightened with many patches of orange and vivid green and crimson, and lit with flashes from innumerable costumes of simplest white. The lawn lay as a flounce or a braid about the darkness and density of stand and hill, lightly studded with many varied blooms somewhat as the meadow garden lying frequently immediately below, and quite up to the foundation walls, of a huge and dark towered castle.

In the paddock the mass was dense and black again, and, ah me! there was nothing classic, nothing Greek, about that. I do not find any of the books any record of the bawlers of the odds, or of the frantic layers who crowd and jostle, and jam and jar, and

make the pleasant day hideous over those well-trod acres. It is very modern, that show. . .

There was Carbine. Heavens! how can we write of the outward procession of Carbine, jogging along the course with a boy tugging at his bridle reins, and the jockey urging him with but gentle encouragement. Let him wait awhile. Only one description fits him. It is that of the old border reiver —

"Swank and supple, lank and thin,
 Fine for gaun against the win'."

Though maybe the stable boy hit him off better when he said, "Hoss, he aint no hoss, sir; he's a bloomin' steam ingin — that's what he is." There was Cuirassier of the same stock — noblest brute of all the field — his neck clothed on with thunder, verily pawing the ground and rejoicing in his strength. There was Melos, bursting like a tempest along the course. Truly nothing could withstand that rush, if it came at the finish of the race. There was Richelieu, beautiful as Lucifer, and Vengeance and The Admiral, with all the glories of recent victories about them, and rising and setting suns of equine fame by dozens. Two-score racers are they mustered, all sheeny and shiny and sleek as hands could make them, topped with more and gayer colours than ever appeared on a tulip bed, and fired with a desire that seemed in each individual case to be almost an assurance of victory.

They went far away down the straight channel of the course to where the pines close round the foot of the hill, making a dark and beautiful background for the flitting and changing specks of colour. . .Waiting, watching, always watching, till at length the moment came, the flag dropped, and with a roar from a hundred throats, "Laissez aller!" and away they came. The sun half way down streamed full along the course. The field passing the stand was perhaps three chains in length, all the colours showing, all the horses straining, and as the record shows, the pace hot enough for a Maribyrnong or a Newmarket. And where was Carbine then? By no means prominent. Lying along by the rails, well in the rearmost division, wasting not an ounce, losing not an inch, patiently abiding his time, and letting all the flash and flare of the business go lightly by. And yet there were some searchings of heart about Carbine as the mile and the mile and a half post were passed, and the sporting critics, with their glasses always on the field, made no mention of his name. Whimbrel and Gatling, Chaldean and Enuc, all in turn at the head and "Where's Carbine?" "Where's Carbine?" shouted a score of eager backers. It was only when the turn was reached that everybody knew where Carbine was. He shot through his field like a thunderbolt then, he closed in on the rails; he placed himself clear as the pilot fish before the shark clear away from all his frantic pursuers. Ride, Hales and Power and Harris and Egan then Spring from the whistling whalebone and the red steel, Highborn and Correze and Melos and Cuirassier. With the quick, nervous grip of his knees, young Ramage lifts the favourite along, and lands him an easy, as a gallant, winner, with more than two lengths of daylight between him and his next pursuer.

And then the thunder broke from all the clouds of humanity which had settled down on Flemington. The Hill roared to the flat, and flat to stand and lawn. Hats went flying through the air like leaves rent by a September gale. Men leapt and shouted and women by the hundred screamed with delight. Up in the wake of the horses flowed the people like flood waves across a barrier, all shouting, all cheering, all, whether winners or losers, full of jubilation and exultation over the greatest victory ever known on the Australian turf. And out then from the stewards' stand came Mr. Donald Wallace, his face like the rising sun, barred with the silvery line of his white moustache. A happy man. Aye, doubtless. It must be a strange sensation to march down the turf to greet such a friend as the horse Carbine...

Here is a creature that in less than three minutes has won a noble fortune, has covered his owner with glory and honour, has made a name that will live for ever in the sporting annals of Australia...

We ought to have Carbine set up in bronze at Flemington, to stand in perpetual commemoration of November the fourth, 1890...

Also in the press box at Flemington to see Carbine win the 1890 Melbourne Cup was Nat Gould, a fine all-round reporter who went on to write more than 200 novels — most of them about horse-racing. Gould, the son of an English tea merchant, travelled to Australia in 1884, at the age of twenty-seven, and quickly got a job as a general reporter on the Brisbane Telegraph. *He later worked as a turf writer on the Sydney* Referee, *using the byline 'Verax'. He was one of a group of extremely able Sydney racing journalists — among them Rowley Pickering* (Sydney Mail), *Spencer Cornford* (the Star), *Frank Wilkinson* (Evening News), *Tom Power* (Sydney Morning Herald) *and Bob Mostyn* (Daily Telegraph).

Gould spent eighteen months as editor of the Bathurst Times, *where he became a close friend of Charles White, editor of the* Bathurst Free Press *and author of* The History of Australian Bushranging. *He wrote his first novel,* With the Tide, *while he was at Bathurst, and had it published in the* Referee.

Gould attended his first Melbourne Cup while still editor of the Bathurst Times; *he had been commissioned by the* Referee. *That was in 1889, when the race was won by Bravo. The next year he left Bathurst to rejoin the* Referee, *and attended Carbine's Cup as 'Verax'. This is how he described the finish of that race:*

... Such a roar rent the air that it shook like thunder over the hills. One shout — one mighty shout from thousands of sturdy lungs — a shout not to be forgotten, it had the ring of exultant victory about it.

"Carbine! Carbine! Carbine!"

Before the distance was reached Ramage sent Carbine up alongside Melos, on whom Mat Harris had the mount. Seeing it was the champion tackling him Mat rode Melos hard, but it was no use.

Carbine came along like a giant; he might have had 7 stone 5 instead of 10 stone 5 the way he galloped. When it was realised that "Old Jack" had practically won the race at the distance the cheers were deafening. How they screamed and yelled and jumped for joy! Not a man in that vast crowd begrudged the gallant top-weight his chance of success...

1891 The great shearers' strike and the trials of the strikers

JOE MELVIN AND WILLIAM LANE
Melbourne Argus, 23 April 1891 and Brisbane Worker, 30 May 1891

Joe Melvin was the kind of newspaperman legends are woven about. As we have seen, he was on the spot when Ned Kelly's gang was destroyed, and he masqueraded as a steward to reach the Sudan war.

Once, when he was on the staff of the Melbourne Age, *he was assigned to report an important policy speech to be delivered by Sir James Patterson, the Premier. The late Ernest Power, in his unpublished memoirs, tells the story:*

To Joe's horror, the train had departed when he arrived at Spencer Street Station. Joe's brain worked swiftly. He sought the station master and ordered a special train as soon as possible to take him to Benalla. The station master was equal to the occasion, and Joe entered the hall at Benalla just as the Premier rose to deliver his speech. The good report that Joe was always capable of producing reached the *Age* without undue delay. A few days later Joe was called into David Syme's sanctum. The Great Man spoke. 'Melvin, I am told you missed your train when you were sent to Benalla to report the Premier's important speech. I hear also that you went to Benalla by special train. That must have been costly. Let that be a lesson to you. Always catch your train in future. Good morning, Melvin.' Joe was thankful to get out of his trouble so easily. Next day Joe was surprised and delighted when the cashier handed him, in addition to his pay, the full cost of the special train. David Syme appreciated Joe's enterprise in meeting a difficult situation and particularly his readiness to foot the bill without any squealing.

In 1888 the Argus *posted Melvin to the Pacific Islands to investigate the recruiting of 'blackbird' kanaka labour for the Queensland canefields. Then in 1891 he was in Queensland for the great shearers' strike, as special reporter for the* Argus. *Ernest Power wrote that Melvin had to disguise himself as a 'swaggie' as he toured the State, talking with shearers, pastoralists, volunteers in the Mounted Rifles — who had been ordered by Colonel Tom Price to 'fire low and lay them out' — and free non-union shearers who travelled north from Sydney and Melbourne. At times, said Power, the shearers became suspicious of Melvin; he filled his pipe with cut up tobacco, and shearers traditionally used plug tobacco.*

Melvin did his usual superb job of reporting on the shearers' strike; the story published here is characteristic of his thorough, lucid style. Later he joined the Brisbane Evening Telegraph, *and his final job was as a Hansard reporter in the Victorian Parliament. He died a few weeks after giving that up. Power, a close friend, described Melvin as 'quiet in manner, utterly without ostentation'.*

It was discovered early upon the voyage of the *Derwent* from Melbourne that amongst those who had shipped as free labourers were some unionists who were acting simply in the interests of their order, and with the view of sowing dissension amongst those whose interests were more genuine. It now transpires that there were some who adopted the converse of this plan, and pretended to be converted, in order to gain some knowledge of the unionist plans and methods. Amongst those who were engaged in Melbourne were some young fellows, well connected, and not unknown on the block in Collins Street, who jumped at the opportunity of obtaining a new and rare experience of colonial life. Without any preconcerted plan some of these determined to play back upon the unionists the trick which Burgess and his associates from Wagga Wagga played upon the pastoralists.

I have had an interview with one of these, who made his way to a station, yielded apparently with great reluctance to the arguments of the unionists, went to their camp with them, and after spending several days there, is now prepared to resume his engagement as a jackeroo. His experience of the unionists is that, with the exception of the leaders they are in absolute ignorance as to the true state of affairs. They don't know what money is collected, or how it is spent. They obtain each week from the union officer an order for the allowance of rations, which is supplied by the local storekeepers. The ration is not very varied, but it is liberal, and as long as the men obtain this, the bulk of them care for nothing else. . .

With regard to the men who have gone over to the union, my informant states that they are the very poorest class of those engaged. Those who went over at Coreena were from Carlton, and they described themselves as belonging to a certain slang "push". They knew nothing of station work, and their idea of happiness is now achieved, for they are made much of as men who would not take the bread out of another man's mouth. They are fed, and they have nothing to do. The only one who was really impressed by the arguments of the union, repented of his weakness afterwards, and has now gone back to work, but has for his own safety been sent by the pastoralists to another district. . .

The men who were persuaded to go out of the Rodney Downs Station were brought into camp today, and were received with great rejoicing. News has been received that large numbers of unionists are gathering there, but it is thought that all the work men have now been weeded out, and that the remainder may be expected to remain firm. The only danger of further defections arises from the fact that the rain has stopped all work, and that there is a difficulty in keeping the men contented whilst they are idle. They were well protected by the police and military, and have no excuse for leaving, except their own inclinations.

Instructions in a condensed and handy form have been issued by Major Des Voeux to the military. These set forth that the whole and sole object of calling out the defence force is to preserve the peace and prevent breaches of the law. All hands are bidden to bear in mind that forbearance, good temper, and firmness are their chief duty, that recourse to the use of deadly weapons can rarely be justified except in cases of extreme emergency, and that speaking generally it should be borne in mind that life should only be taken to save life.

The officers are reminded that even if a magistrate gives the order to fire the officers in command are not thereby in any way relieved of responsibility. The hope is expressed that a collision will be averted, but before giving the order to fire as a last resort the officer is instructed to obtain from the civil magistrate a written request, the form of which he is supplied with. This last provision is made so that both the civil and the military officers may be fully impressed by the supreme importance of the step which they are taking . . .

On 30 May 1891 the journalist and social reformer William Lane wrote for the Queensland Labor paper, the Worker, *about the Rockhampton conspiracy trials which followed the shearers' strike:*

In the court-room at Rockhampton. A close, drowsy afternoon. A wearied, listless audience, being lulled into greater listlessness by the droning charge of the Judge. For the great conspiracy trial is drawing to its close, and tonight, apparently, the jury will retire and the prisoners will know their fate — or rather, Society will know its fate, for it is evident on the face of it that the prisoners are not on trial at all. A paradox this, is it not? Ah, well, life is full of paradoxes, as you would think if you were sitting here in the Rockhampton court-room and began to ruminate over things as I have just begun to.

This is the court-room and the bushmen are here on trial, the Judge will say; and the

Strike-breakers on their way to Barcaldine Downs with a military escort

Press and the lawyers and the squatters smile cheerily as Judge Harding "rubs it in". But it seems to me, sitting here, that they are not on trial. It is Society which is being tried, and the verdict of this jury will not matter, whatever it is. Society is being tried here as a whole, prisoners and squatters, the Judge and the jury and the lawyers, tried here as it is being tried wherever the opposing elements of society are brought face to face, wherever the up-springing of humanity finds an advocate or meets a foe. . .

In the prisoners' dock are the bushmen, rough-looking men, roughly dressed, with broad, browned hands, with poses that lack the grace of Vere de Vere and the squatter who lounges easily on his bench half a dozen paces away. They wear moleskin pants, mostly, and a few wear vests; one or two who are better dressed, with all the town-bred attachments, are lost in the general effect. I saw them in a dark, windowless, ill-ventilated cell, two hours or so ago, wherein they were awaiting the reopening of the court; and they looked a pretty rough lot. And so would Judge Harding and his associate and young Lilley and Virgil Power and those aristocratic squatters, if they were dressed in nondescript garments and inducted in the same conditions. If you were to see these men out West, as I have seen them, camping under the starry sky and gathering in on horseback to the great bush meetings, free-handed and free-hearted, open as children and true as steel, and simple in their habits as Arabs, you would not have said they were "rough-looking" then. You would have said that they were fitted — but they don't fit here.

For my part I would rather be prisoner at the bar than any of them. Foolish some of these prisoners may have been; not one of them but has sought to aid his mates against the oppressor, not one of them but is being victimised now on general principles for having given that aid. They to-day, us to-morrow, you some other day; under some pretence or other those who love the people are doomed to suffer. And when our time comes, as theirs has come, may we be as they are, patient, courageous, and fearless, ready for the worst that can be done to us, comforting ourselves with the sure and certain knowledge that we prepare the way for those who will triumph in the end. And surely when the People's Jubilee has come, when Labor shakes off its fetters, when Wrong, and Misery and Poverty are rolled away like clouds before the wind, surely then men will give a thought to the martyrs who have made redemption possible, surely here in Australia men will remember those who stood their trial for Labor's sake at Rockhampton in 1891.

1891   The Victorian Parliament's mace is stolen and a scandal ensues

PETER SYMMONDS
Melbourne Argus, 10 October 1891

On Saturday morning, 10 October 1891, the Melbourne Argus *published an exclusive report on 'the most extraordinary robbery ever heard of in the colonies, probably indeed without parallel in the constitutional history of the world'. The Victorian Parliament's mace, a handsome silver-gilt gift from the House of Commons, had been stolen. Its theft, and the scandal which followed, represented the strangest story in the history of any Australian parliament. Certainly it was a classic unsolved crime.*

Parliament had sat late on the Thursday night, and rose at 1.20 the following morning. The Serjeant-at-Arms took the mace and locked it in an oak box in the ante-room abutting the corridor to the north of the Assembly chamber. The mace had been in use since 1866, when it replaced the highly decorated wooden mace which the Legislative Assembly acquired in 1857. At 2 p.m. on the Friday the Clerk of the Assembly discovered that the oak box had been broken open with a chisel and the mace had gone. The police were called, and all employees of the House were told not to say a word to anyone about the theft.

No statement was made that night, by the Speaker, Sir Matthew H. Davies, or the police; but the final edition of the Argus *carried the story of the missing mace. It was written by Peter Symmonds, a brilliant journalist who was described by the great Montague Grover as 'absolutely the best reporter who ever put pen to paper'. Grover wrote a tribute to Symmonds in his serialised reminiscences in the* Lone Hand. *He said of him: 'I once heard a newspaperman say that he would sooner have Peter Symmonds on a staff than any other two reporters ever born. I am inclined to fancy*

that he was right. Symmonds was more than a journalistic genius; he was a freak, like the giant pumpkin or the two-headed calf. His capacity for work was almost supernatural, and his speed in turning out copy was uncanny. To write a column of longhand ready for the printer in an hour is good work for an experienced man, and he can't do it in the second hour. Symmonds could turn out two columns an hour without turning a hair. Even had his work been mediocre this would have made him a great reporter; but its quality was of a high order, generally of as high an order as it is possible to find in any newspaper. He was a master of humour and pathos. Symmonds could write stuff that would make Melbourne laugh for an hour, and talk about for three days. He was a born newsgetter — quick, alert, and possessed of great deductive ability. His weakness was that he despised the stodgy part of press work. He had a profound contempt for politics, and did not disguise his feelings.'

Symmonds got his scoop about the theft of the mace when he called into the Commercial Travellers' Club at 2 a.m. on the Saturday. He met a sub-inspector of police who was off duty and who had been celebrating. 'Aha,' said the officer, as Symmonds lined up for a drink, 'the press thinks it knows a lot, but it doesn't know what happened tonight.' Symmonds was canny. 'Doesn't it?' he said, a little carelessly. 'I've just spent half an hour writing about the matter you're talking about.'

The policeman looked puzzled, then led with his mouth. 'The messengers at Parliament House must have told you,' he said. 'Not a soul else knows about it outside our office.' Symmonds persisted: 'Don't believe it. It's all over Melbourne. We got it from two sources.'

'The Speaker?' asked the sub-inspector. Symmonds shook his head. He waited, and listened, and soon it was clear that the mace was gone. The policeman himself knew no more. Symmonds raced back to the Argus office, and wrote a fine story which contained phrases like: 'More than once some predatory Captain Blood has made attempts upon the Crown jewels, but never until yesterday has an instance been known in which any sacrilegious hand dared to disturb the inviolate sanctity of the emblem of constitutional liberty – the mace.'

No official statements followed, from the Speaker or from police. The Argus continued to publish stories, and rumours concerning the circumstances of the theft accelerated wildly. Said Melbourne Punch: 'It seems there is reason to believe it was taken from its place by a Member of Parliament in a drunken freak. We hope it is not necessary for us to appear before the Bar of the House for stating the possibility of a member having a drunken freak . . . twenty-three members of the assembly have since been racking their brains to think what they did after that last drink on the night the mace disappeared.'

Later Table Talk, edited by Maurice Brodzky, suggested that the mace had been taken to a bawdy house. The Ballarat Courier, published by Mr Robert Clark, announced that 'the mace was not stolen, but was taken from Parliament by some "festive cusses" for a lark, and is even now, so it is freely stated, in a bawdy house in Melbourne where it is freely exhibited to clients, and where it has, so it is said, been used in low travesties of parliamentary procedure'.

Parliament was offended and Robert Clark was called to the Bar of the House, charged with contempt of Parliament. He apologised and received a reprimand; the Courier's editor, Major Williams, who wrote the offending article, had been prepared to assert the truth of what he wrote, and to defy the House – but he was never called to explain his story.

Parliament conducted an open inquiry into the affair of the missing mace, and even called a well known brothel-keeper to give evidence,

but the mystery was never solved.

One strong theory was aired in the early 1930s by George Cockerill, who had fifty-four years' experience as a newspaperman, in his book of reminiscences, Scribblers and Statesmen. In his foreword to the same book, Billy Hughes wrote:

> To smuggle the gaudy symbol of the majesty of Parliament under the very eyes of the clerks, the Hansard staff and the members of the Government party . . . was an exploit that stamped the principals as men of character and resource. I knew them well, but as their chief still lives – and flourishes in the odour of conventional impeccability – I must perforce hold my tongue.

Cockerill's story, which apparently came from Peter Symmonds' close friend and colleague, Billy Salter, was that the stolen mace was taken aboard an American tramp steamer in Port Phillip Bay by a young man who intended to return it to its maker – a highly-skilled metal worker in London, who regarded it as his masterpiece. When the boat reached San Francisco, the mace was hidden until it could be shipped back to England. But, according to the story told to Cockerill, the great fire of San Francisco swept through the area where the mace was hidden, burning the buildings and their contents.

Peter Symmonds, the son of a Church of England clergyman who lived near Dublin, Ireland, came to Australia because his brother had a farm near Corowa, New South Wales. He joined the Corowa Free Press, the paper on which the Boer War correspondent Donald Macdonald served his apprenticeship. Symmonds worked for the Age before he joined the Argus, and served on the Sydney Morning Herald before he died at the age of forty-four.

Here is Symmonds' report of the theft of the mace, written on 10 October:

A confidential report made at the offices of the Criminal Investigation Branch yesterday evening gives the bare details of the most extraordinary robbery ever heard of in the colonies, probably indeed without parallel in the constitutional history of the world. More than once some predatory Captain Blood has made attempts upon the Crown jewels, but never until yesterday has an instance been known in which any sacrilegious hand dared to disturb the inviolate sanctity of the emblem of constitutional liberty — the mace. It has remained for Victoria to add that proud distinction to her laurels, for yesterday morning, in broad daylight, as it would seem, the mace was seized by some daring thief, its case broken open with scant regard for the privileges of the House, and the golden bauble itself spirited clean away.

How it happened and when it happened no one can tell with any certainty. All that is known is, that when the House adjourned after an unusually long sitting after midnight on Thursday — or to be more correct — Friday morning, the mace was carefully taken away, and locked up in its case in the Speaker's anteroom. Theoretically its custody is delegated to the assistant clerk of the Legislative Assembly, Mr. Geo. Upward; but for practical purposes it is looked after by the caretaker, who acts at night as the custodian of the whole building. In the old days, before the new facade had been added, the caretaker and the mace were almost bedfellows, but the improvements of modern times have relegated the caretaker to a more convenient set of apartments in the basement of the new building, while the mace still retains its old home in the Speaker's ante-room. But when the room was entered yesterday morning it was found that the case had been broken open and that the mace·was gone. And that is all the evidence upon which the three detectives engaged in the task have to work.

The mace was made entirely of Victorian gold, and was valued roughly at about £250. It would, of course, prove a most valuable booty, but it is difficult to understand how so cumbrous an article could have been carried away — in daylight presumably — without awakening attention. Still, those familiar with Parliament-house will well comprehend the ease with which a perfect stranger may walk about the building, and gain access to its most private rooms undisturbed.

And on 12 October, Symmonds wrote this:

In spite of all the efforts of the detectives not the slightest clue has been found to the mysterious disappearance of the Speaker's mace from Parliament-house early on Friday morning. The when and the how of the robbery have been fairly well established, but the whereabouts of the booty is so far a secret which neither Detective Ward, nor his colleague, Detective Macmanamy, has been able to unravel. A handsome reward has been offered for the recovery of the mace, and there is just a slight chance that the hope of a cash payment more than five times the intrinsic value of the spoil may prove strong enough to save the emblem of Parliamentary authority from the final indignity of the melting pot. The question, in short, resolves itself into this — has the mace been stolen for its inherent value, or is it being held for reward? In the latter case, a little adroit management of the "no questions asked" order may perhaps restore it to its accustomed place on the table of the Legislative Assembly when the House resumes next Tuesday. . .

The box on which the mace rests at night is of a somewhat peculiar construction. It stands on end at the side of a cupboard to which it is firmly screwed, and it opens exactly as a portmanteau would do if placed in a similar position. In fact, supposing a stranger to have entered the room on the search for whatever property came first to hand, this box is the last thing which he would be likely to examine . . .

An ordinary burglar would not have troubled to carefully close the box lid again, because he would have possessed an easy means of converting the mace into lump silver, and he could therefore have no object in delaying discovery. An ordinary burglar would certainly not have overlooked the more valuable silver plate in the cupboards. He would have cleared out the room. But the man who stole the mace knew that the House would not meet again until Tuesday, and hoped to delay the discovery till then. And from the variety and extent of his other knowledge, he must have known where the plate was kept.

MAURICE BRODZKY
Melbourne Table Talk, 4 December 1891

*Throughout the land boom of the eighties
and nineteen, one Melbourne journal campaigned strenuously and fearlessly, investigating and
exposing the actions of guilty men and guilty
institutions. Its name was* Table Talk; *it was
born in June 1885, and edited and published
by a Prussian Jew called Maurice Brodzky.
Brodzky had emigrated to Australia, after
service with the French army in the Franco-
Prussian war, in the steamship* Sussex; *the
ship was wrecked at Barwon Heads, and
Brodzky and other survivors were rowed ashore
on New Year's Day 1872.*

*He taught Hebrew, French and German at
Melbourne schools, and later worked as a
newspaper reporter in Rockhampton, Queensland, and Sydney. In 1880 he joined the staff
of the Melbourne* Herald, *and soon after
became the Australian correspondent of the
London* Daily Telegraph. *In 1885 he resigned
from the* Herald *and began* Table Talk — *a
racy paper which disoussed politics, commerce,
social news and the arts.*

In his excellent book, The Land Boomers,
*Michael Cannon gives great credit to the per-
formance of Maurice Brodzky. He writes:*

There is no question that most of the frauds
of the boom period would have been successfully covered had it not been for Brodzky's
work. . . *Table Talk*'s publication was awaited impatiently each week by thousands of
small shareholders who suspected they were
being defrauded; and with trepidation by
company directors who were just as likely
to find themselves named in the next issue
as partners in some audacious conspiracy
. . . in comparing the old *Table Talk* files
with official documents which later became available, one is constantly amazed

by the depth and thoroughness of Brodzky's
investigations. His work forms a record of
individual public service which, it is safe to
say, has never been surpassed anywhere in
the world.

*Not once during those years of audacious,
explosive journalism did Brodzky receive a
libel writ, although a parliamentary committee
summoned him once to explain an article
stating that the Speaker's mace was being kept
in a Melbourne brothel.*

*Characteristic of Brodzky's style was this
little item, dropped into the 'Personal' column
of* Table Talk, *concerning the wife of a Mr
George N. Taylor, the manager of the Land
Credit Bank, who stood accused in 1891 of
defrauding his company of £114,000:*

Mrs. G. N. Taylor, the wife of the manager
of the Land Credit Bank, it is asserted,
some time ago succeeded to considerable
property from relatives. She is also supposed to have made a handsome profit out of
her share in the publishing adventure of
Fergus Hume's *Mystery of a Hansom Cab*.
Altogether her property, apart from the
bank overdrafts obtained, is stated to have
amounted to about £50,000. The depositors
in the Land Credit Bank would be glad to
know what became of all the money. The
truth, however, probably is that the legacy
is as imaginative as the plot of the *Mystery
of a Hansom Cab*, and that it was part and
parcel of Taylor's programme to spread
rumours about his wife's wealth in order
not to arouse public suspicion that he was
stealing the bank's money for land-boom-
ing purposes. There ought to be a law that
bank managers should not be allowed to
take part in the game of speculation.

*This hard-hitting piece by Brodzky,
published on 4 December 1891, sums up the
causes and the follies of the land boom with
economy and rare insight:*

The constant readers of TABLE TALK who
have closely followed our campaign against
the iniquitous Land Boom for the last six
years are in a position now to judge whether
we have been right in our persistent attacks on
those individuals and institutions that have
brought about the present deplorable state of
affairs. Six years ago we pointed out, week
after week, that the number of allotments
which it was then reported in the daily papers
had been sold at the Saturday afternoon auction sales, were more than enough to settle a
population double the number of London
round Melbourne. Anyone who knew the very
alphabet of money matters could see at a
glance that a population of one million, all
told, could not produce nine or ten millions
of people quickly enough to make these allotments profitable to their speculative purchas-
ers. Mind, and this in a country where the
people shut up its gates, so to speak, against
the influx of strangers. The country was to
belong to those who either came here before
the land boom era or their native descendants.
There was, of course, no objection to get
money from Great Britain wherewith to carry
on a gamble, under the guise of business, on a
scale hitherto unheard of in the history of
speculation, but the "scum" of the old world
population would not be allowed to come to
Victoria and contaminate the fine gentlemen
who had just made their fortunes by selling
their 360 acres, which they had selected
twenty years ago at £1 per acre on time payment of 1s. per acre per annum. Still the
British capitalist did not mind in those days
to send us large cargoes of softgoods, and all
sorts of finery and articles of luxury for the
principal portion of the various loans made
by public companies. Our credit was excellent,
and for a very good reason. The country is
rich in natural products, which only required
developing. The money thus borrowed in
England was understood, by the lenders, to
be required for developing our resources.

Have the Building Societies which are now
stopping payment developed the natural
resources of Victoria? Let their books be
examined, and what will be found? Loans on
land, loans on houses erected by speculative
builders; in fact loans to everybody except the
persons who really could and would like to
develop the country if they had an opportunity. The cry is always — "The assets are good."
Are they good? Then try and convert them
into ready money. If you can't, and still persist in proclaiming your solvency, then the
first principle of commerce is violated,
namely, that of *barter*...

The fact is, as we pointed out in TABLE
TALK some twelve months ago, the *raison
d'etre* of many of the Melbourne building
societies had ceased once their members did
not require any more houses or other buildings
to be erected for their own use. The majority
of the societies, however, continued to carry
on business by lending money to speculators,
and it may now be judged with what result.
Still, we maintain that although the failures
of several of these institutions are doing a
temporary injury to the public credit of
Australia in England, and must cause a great
deal of individual anxiety to many good men
and women, whose only fault is that they
trusted blindly to the sanguine hopes of
brummagen financiers, the present storm will
not do any great injury to legitimate trade.
The natural resources of Australia are very
great, and the failure of a few building societies cannot cause any permanent injury.

Maurice Brodzky sold Table Talk, *after a
series of misfortunes, in April 1903 and the
magazine continued to publish until early in
World War I. Brodzky took his family to San
Francisco, where he worked on the* Examiner,
and later became editor of a weekly called the
Wasp. *He died in New York in 1919.*

1892 Reporters prove that Frederick Deeming committed a series of mass murders

BILLY SALTER AND SAMUEL LOWE (from London)
Melbourne Argus, 12 to 18 March 1892

*When Montague Grover, one of the ablest
newspaperman of his day, wrote his memoirs
for the* Lone Hand, *he made it plain that as a
youngster he had hero-worshipped a reporter
called Billy Salter. Salter was what they used
to call a 'roundsman' — not a police roundsman or a political roundsman — just a roundsman. 'It was Salter who taught me most of
what I know,' wrote Grover. 'The department
in which he shone was the rounds, which
embraces crime, accident, fire, flood, shipwreck and other things. The roundsman needs
to be something of a psychologist, something
of a lawyer, something of a doctor, something
of a liar, and all of a detective.'*

Salter, a member of the Melbourne Argus
*staff in one of the newspaper's vintage periods,
had the opportunity to demonstrate his talents
as a detective during the Deeming case. But
for Salter, it is unlikely that the world would
ever have known that Frederick Deeming was
a mass murderer who, before he came to
Australia, had committed a series of particularly revolting murders in Rainhill, England.*

*In 1891 the landlord of a cottage in the
Melbourne suburb of Windsor noticed a strange
smell coming from the hearthstone of the house,
which had recently been vacated by an Albert
Williams. The hearthstone was removed, and
the body of Williams' wife, Emily, was uncovered. A man answering Williams' description had bought some cement a few weeks
earlier at a nearby shop, but nobody knew
where he was now. He had occupied the house
for only a few weeks, and had left no forwarding address.*

*The police were making no headway when
Salter located a German named Max Hirsch-
feldt, who had arrived in Australia from
England a month before on a mailboat, Kaiser
Wilhelm II. Hirschfeldt told him of a curious
fellow-passenger on the mailboat — a Baron
Swanson, who had had a wife travelling
second-class (while he travelled first), and who
had paid a lot of attention throughout the
voyage to a girl called Kitty Rounsvelle.
Hirschfeldt told Salter that he had met Baron
Swanson a few weeks earlier in the street in
Windsor where the murder had occurred.
Salter's inquiries proved fairly quickly that
Albert Williams was in fact Baron Swanson,
and the reporter suggested to police that they
should question Kitty Rounsvelle. From Miss
Rounsvelle, it was learned that Baron Swanson
had gone to Western Australia after proposing
marriage to her; he was traced to a mine at
Southern Cross, where he was employed as an
engineer; the 'baron's' correct name was found
to be Frederick Bayley Deeming, and he was
ultimately brought back to Melbourne, tried,
and hanged.*

*In the days following the discovery of the
body at Windsor, a next-door neighbor — a
Carlton footballer called Alf Spedding — found
a barely decipherable invitation card while
fossicking around the cottage vacated by
Albert Williams; the address on it was that of
the Commercial Hotel, Rainhill, England.
It might have belonged to the murderer or any
previous tenant, but Salter acted on a hunch
that the town of Rainhill might provide some
clues to the background of the killer. He persuaded his editor to send a cable to the
*Argus's *London representative, Samuel Lowe,
asking him to make inquiries in Rainhill, a
town near Liverpool. Lowe found the dead
woman's mother, told her what had happened
in Melbourne, and obtained an account of
Emily's courtship by Albert Williams. The
*Argus *by now was not only ahead of every*

*other Australian newspaper in what was
described as the greatest sensation in the
history of the Australian press; it was also
well ahead of the police. Lowe found the
house in Rainhill which had been occupied
by Deeming alias Williams alias Swanson
—after establishing that the murderer had also
posed as Harry Lawson, a wealthy Australian
sheep farmer — and then told local police it
might be a good idea to dig up the hearthstone
there. This they did, and soon found the
bodies of an earlier Mrs Deeming and four
children.*

12 March:
When the detectives engaged in the investigation of the shocking murder at Windsor expressed themselves confident that an arrest
would be effected before more than a week
had passed after the discovery of the crime
they were speaking in view of certain knowledge without which the public was incredul-
ous and disinclined to believe that the police
would achieve such speedy and successful
work. It was held that a man who had displayed so much criminal cunning in hiding his
crime and in disencumbering himself of much
useless and burdensome luggage would scarcely
be so foolish as to remain for any time within
reach of the police of the city in which he had
committed his dreadful murder. It was generally thought most likely that he had put to sea as
soon as he had sold his articles by auction in
Melbourne on the 7th January, and that, therefore, by the time the detectives had got a knowledge of his crime he would be as far away as
nearly two months would permit him to be.
And even when it was well established on the
evidence of Captain Firth, a fellow-passenger
with him on the Kaiser Wilhelm II., that
Williams had not taken the earliest opportunity
afforded him of making his escape, but had
lingered in the colonies until well on to the end
of January, it was still thought that his start
of the detectives would have been sufficient
to have ensured his immunity from arrest, if
not for ever at least for months and perhaps
years. Happily, the detectives were right and
the public wrong, and the news of the arrest
of a man who is believed to be identical with

the murderer, which was effected yesterday,
though sudden and unexpected, will be none
the less welcome.

Yesterday was an eventful day in the history
of the crime. It started the second week of the
connection of the detectives with the case,
and thus forcibly reminded them of their boast
that they would be able to arrest the accused
within a week. By the first post from Sydney
the chief commissioner of police, Mr. Chomley,
received a photograph which has been identified
. . . as that of the murderer Williams.
For a time it was thought that no portraits of
the murderer were in existence, and this impression was strengthened by the knowledge
that though there was an amateur photographer on board the s.s. Kaiser Wilhelm II who
has zealously practised his art, and "taken"
almost everybody on board from the captain
down to the cabin boy, Williams and his wife
were omitted. However, careful inquiry by
the police, persevered in because of the feeling
that mere verbal descriptions would not be of
much use in arresting the accused, was ultimately crowned with success, and yesterday the
Sydney police forwarded to Mr. Chomley, as
stated, the photograph of the man who is
identified with Williams. It is of cabinet size,
and in company with Williams, who is seated,
is a woman who is standing on his right hand.
It is said to be a fairly good likeness, but as it
was taken some years ago there are differences
between the original of to-day and the photograph that require to be allowed for. For
instance, Williams is not only older than he
was when he sat for his picture, but in his
person he shows plainly the results of an easy
life and good living. His face as well as his
body is stouter, his square-cut determined jaw
is squarer still, his large and obtruding ears
are not so marked, and he has no side whiskers.
The photograph was sent by the chief commissioner to Superintendent Kennedy, and by him
it was handed over to Detectives Considine and
Cawsey with instructions to have a number of
copies struck off in readiness for circulation by
the post on Monday.
The photograph had scarcely been handed
over to the photographers when information
of a definite character reached the police

which gave them the hope that it would not be necessary after all to circulate it for the benefit of the police and to aid them in making an arrest. At 25 minutes past 7 o'clock in the evening this belief became a settled conviction, when a telegram delivered to Detective Miller at the office of the criminal investigation police was found to read as follows:—

> "Perth, Western Australia,
> "March 2, 1892.
> "Telegram for the Chief Commissioner of Police, Victoria.
> "Williams, *alias* Swanson, arrested to-day at Southern Cross. Arrive here next week. Send officer to identify, also original warrant and information.
> "(Signed)
> "G. PHILLIPS, Commissioner."

. . .

Complete information as to the investigations of Detectives Considine and Cawsey which have led up to the arrest of Williams is now forthcoming. Hitherto it has been withheld for obvious reasons. The particulars given show that the ingenuity of an exceedingly clever criminal had to be coped with, and that the police officers mentioned have shown marked sagacity and perseverance in their inquiries. Nevertheless they acknowledge that they have received the greatest assistance on all hands — from various members of the police force in Sydney and elsewhere, and the general public — and they are grateful accordingly. Notwithstanding that the alleged murderer has been arrested in a locality so remote from Melbourne, to them belongs the primary credit of bringing about his capture, for on their minute investigations everything has depended. Carefully and diligently they collected every scrap of intelligence regarding the movement in Melbourne of the suspected man, and, forming a substantial stratum of facts to proceed upon, succeeded in tracing him to Sydney, then back to Melbourne, and afterwards on board a vessel which took him to Fremantle. Satisfied that they were on the right trail, they communicated sufficient knowledge to the West Australian police to make the apprehension of the supposed Williams an absolute certainty, and the news of his arrest last night did not surprise them. As has been indicated during the last few days, they have been waiting with a feeling of certainty that the man they believe to be the author of a shocking crime must find himself sooner or later in custody. . .

The narrative of the detective supplies a few links in the story of Williams' latter life in the colonies, which before had to be guessed at. Now it runs thus:— On the 2nd of November last year, Williams and his wife embarked on board the s.s. *Kaiser Wilhelm II*, at Southampton, England, and in the second-class saloon travelled by that vessel to Melbourne, which was reached on the 15th of December. That day the two took lodgings at the Federal Coffee Palace, and on the 16th and 17th, and for portion of the 18th they made the coffee palace their place of abode. On the 16th Williams assumed the name of Drewn, and entered into an arrangement with Mr. Stamford to rent the house at 57 Andrew-street, Windsor, at 18s. per week. He paid one week's rent in advance at that time. On the same day he and his wife superintended the removal of their luggage from the Custom-house store at Jolimont to Wrigley's free store in Queen-street. On the 17th he went again to Windsor, and ordered the cement, sand, trowel, broom, and night-pan at the store of Mr. John Woods, High-street, St. Kilda. On the 18th he visited Mr. Woods and abused him because he had not delivered the goods ordered the previous day. The goods were at once sent to the house, and it would seem that the remainder of the day was employed by Williams or Drewn in digging the grave in the fireplace. That night must have been spent in the house. On the 19th Williams engaged Featherstone, the carrier, to remove his luggage from Wrigley's free store and the Federal Coffee Palace to the house at Windsor, and on the same day he instructed Bueller, the handyman, to call at his address for some "washing." Mrs. Williams was seen at the house on the 20th, but not afterwards, and though she is said by the police in the warrant to have been murdered on or about the 24th, it was probably earlier. Several times from that date to the 30th Williams slept at the Cathedral Hotel in Swanston-street, where he gave the name of Duncan. On the 30th he paid a month's rent in advance for the house in Andrew-street, and next day he left it and took up his residence at the Cathedral Hotel, where he remained until the 9th or the 11th of January. He entered the hotel with a lot of heavy luggage, all of which was by his orders put in his room. When he left he had but one portmanteau, so that he must have removed the remainder parcel by parcel, so as not to attract too much attention. He was quiet in his demeanour, and passed as a gentleman of means at the hotel, and looking back upon his conduct in the light of recent developments, Mrs. Thompson, the licensee, feels it difficult to imagine him the murderer. On the 12th, having completed the arrange-ments of his auction sale, he went to Sydney, when he returned on the 22nd to take his passage by the Albany. Next day he left the colony in that boat.

14 March:

In view of the absorbing interest evinced in regard to the murder of the woman Emily Williams, who was killed by her husband, Albert Williams, on or about December 24, at Andrew-street, Windsor, and considering also that practically nothing was known of the woman's antecedents, she having but recently arrived in Australia, we on Wednesday cabled to our London representative directing him to make full inquiries. It had been ascer-tained that her Christian name was Emily, that her husband's surname, as then known, was Williams, and that her mother kept a stationer's shop at Rainhill, near Liverpool. Her conversations with some of her fellow-passengers on the Kaiser Wilhelm II. revealed the abode of her mother, and the fact that among the partially burnt papers found in the house was a piece of one issue of the *Liverpool Guardian* confirmed the recollection of those persons. . .

17 March:

The request cabled to England by *The Argus* that special inquiries should be made at Rain-hill as to the murderer Williams and his pro-

The grave of Emily Mather, Frederick Deeming's last victim

ceedings there has been fully justified by the result. The identity of the Windsor victim was first discovered, and now we publish news of the disclosure of another awful crime — the murder of the English wife of Williams and her two children. It is evident that in captur-ing Williams the career of the most atrocious criminal of modern days has been at last brought to an end. . .

18 March:

Further particulars have been received from Rainhill respecting the shocking discoveries made by the police in the house lately occup-ied by the man Albert Williams.

    The kitchen was the spot first attacked. The work was at once begun of breaking up the cemented floor of this room, in order to dig beneath. This proved to be a more troublesome task than had been expected, and the digging operations had been continued for fully an hour before any result was obtained. A horrible and sickening smell was then encountered — so strong as to compel the police for a time to desist from their labour.

When the police temporarily left the place it was known that discoveries were at hand, and there was great excitement in the assembled crowd.

The first articles drawn away from the opening were a tablecloth and a woman's apron, and underneath these the first horrible discovery was made. This consisted of the bodies of a woman and two children, all in an advanced stage of decomposition.

The corpses were wrapped in oil-cloth and Turkish towelling. The woman lay upon her back, while the children were turned with their faces downwards, and were lying one on each side of the mother.

The continuance of the strong smell from the floor of itself suggested a further search, and in half an hour two more bodies were dug out of the cement in which they were embedded. One body was that of a baby, and the other that of a little girl, and both were found lying at the mother's feet.

Of the five victims, the mother and one child had been strangled, while the other three children had their throats cut.

So far as could be guessed from an examination of the corpses, the ages of the three elder children were about nine, seven, and five years respectively, while the body of the baby seemed to be that of a child of 18 months. The mother was to all appearance about 35 years of age.

The English police are now satisfied that the Rainhill murderer is identical with Frederick Bayley Deeming. He was born near London, and served for many years as a steward in various sailing ships. He was married in 1881 to Mary James, of Birkenhead. Two female children, Bertha and Mary, were born in Sydney, and a boy named Sidney was born at sea. Deeming and his wife returned to England in 1890, and a baby named Leala was born at Birkenhead.

The bodies found at Rainhill are undoubtedly those of this wife and her children.

A copy-book was found with the bodies, and bears Bertha Deeming's name.

The police are continuing their investigations at Rainhill.

They have found a book supposed to have belonged to Williams, in which the name Deeming is written.

The police believe that the body of another woman is buried in Williams's house at Rainhill, and they are now searching for it.

The Argus *sent over another of its best men, Peter Symmonds, to cover Deeming's journey across the continent under police escort. Deeming did little but play 'ha'penny nap' with Symmonds throughout the trip, and died owing the reporter thirty-five shillings; Symmonds was disappointed when accountants at the* Argus *disallowed the item on his expense account.*

Deeming was defended by Marshal Lyle, a leading Melbourne criminal lawyer; the fee was to have been the royalties from reminiscences Deeming wrote in gaol, but these were destroyed on order of the Crown Law authorities. After his conviction, Deeming told Lyle that he had no fear of death, but did not fancy the drop at Melbourne jail. His observations of it, he claimed, led him to believe that it would not act properly — that his body was likely to catch on a wooden plank. 'All I can say,' Lyle told him, 'is that my last three clients went through pretty well.'

At various times the theory has been advanced that Deeming could have been Jack the Ripper, the Whitechapel murderer whose crimes baffled London police in 1888—89. The method of operation differed; the Ripper used a knife with surgical skill, and left his victims to be found, while Deeming was something of a cement hearth specialist. But the theory is chronologically possible; Deeming was in jail (for fraud) in Sydney in 1887, but absconded after his release and was in England early in 1888. There were two gaps in the Whitechapel murders, four months between the first and second, and eight months between the seventh and eighth; during 1888—89 Deeming left England twice, to visit South Africa and Aden.

1893 A 'doomed city': six feet of rain floods the Brisbane River

C. BRUNSDON FLETCHER
Brisbane Courier, 10 February 1893

The Brisbane floods of 1893 were certainly the worst of the nineteenth century. Two tremendous cloudbursts arrived within a fortnight. The first produced a flood which floated the gunboat Gayundah *from the Brisbane River up into the Botanic Gardens near Government House, and left it high and dry. The second, ten days later, floated her back again — after the Government had accepted a tender for more than £6,000 to provide a slipway.*

Those floods marked the arrival of C. Brunsdon Fletcher in journalism. He had trained as a surveyor and was practising in Queensland when the bursting of the land boom, the breaking of the banks, and finally those floods put him out of business. He decided to look at the rising waters from a vantage-point with a good telescope, sweeping around the city as it became submerged. 'The ocean,' he wrote later, 'seemed to be coming fast to town from Moreton Bay, until even the Pacific itself appeared to be at our feet in one vast sheet of water.' His father-in-law had a property on a hilltop overlooking the city, and he studied the rising flood from the verandahs of the homestead.

Fletcher wrote about what he saw, submitted the article to the editor of the Brisbane Courier, *Charles Buzacott, and had it published. A job on the paper followed, and that year Fletcher began half a century of journalism. He became editor of the* Courier, *and in 1918 was appointed editor of the* Sydney Morning Herald.

Fletcher later wrote of that flood: 'Seventy inches of rain had been recorded until further registration was impossible — six feet of rain and over! It was incredible! the hush over the doomed city was like that before an impending siege, or bombing. . .'

This is Fletcher's report from the Brisbane Courier *of 10 February 1893:*

A bird's-eye view of the flood has been possible for some people from its commencement. On the heights of Upper Paddington an observer at the principal points may sweep from Toowong and Indooroopilly onward to Ipswich on the south-west, thence round the compass southward through east and north-east to the Enoggera Valley on the west. In ordinary times the river peeps out from the Toowong, Milton, and city reaches like a threaded band of grey or blue, according to the shadows. The suburbs of South Brisbane are laid out beyond, from Hill End on one side to River-terrace on the other, with Coorparoo and the country districts behind. In the foreground lie Toowong, Rosalie, Bayswater, Milton and Paddington. The city, Petrie-terrace, and Red Hill fill spaces to the east and south-east. To the right of Eildon Hill is a clear stretch as far as the Bay and Moreton Island, with Enoggera Creek hardly showing in fair weather through a strong binocular. The progress of the flood has been watched from windows that thus command one of the finest views outside the city. As the water encroached, the first suburb to show signs of discomfort was Rosalie, just below. The Redjacket Swamp began to fill up fast, and then the river widened at the visible stretches in its course.

As it rose, the blank spaces filled out one by one into a continuous stream. The main road across the swamp grew narrower till it became a thread, with the Milton Fire Station fastened upon it like a red block. Soon the thread vanished, leaving the station more like a buoy to mark some channel. Then the flood came in earnest and wrung its wet hands till

West End was one with Paddington. The red
buoy was slowly drowned, and its watch-
tower stood sentinel alone. The roofs of the
Bayswater Public School and the Milton
Congregational Church were all that marked
their whereabouts. The Milton Railway Bridge
was then covered, and the Bayswater and
Baroona roads, from just below Fernberg to
the high land on M'Dougall-terrace, became
things of the past. One sea of water stretched
from the public school at West End, where
the water was creeping up the walls, to Glen-
allan House at the foot of Latrobe-terrace.
This waste was dotted here and there with
tree-tops and the roofs of houses, some of
which were very much askew. On Sunday
morning, just before six o'clock, sounds like
a battery of cannon discharging were distinctly
heard and the question was asked with a
tremor, 'What was that?' Before the day was
out it was said that the railway bridge at
Indooroopilly had gone, and just at the time
when the reports were heard.

On looking over the city and down upon
the flood one felt utterly sick at heart. Dozens
of houses could now be counted that had
either collapsed or were aslant. The rate of the
river's race to the sea could be easily gauged
as house after house was seen to float down.
Through a powerful glass one after another
was watched as it struck the bridge, the roofs
being crumpled up like paper in a strong man's
hand. Away to the south-west a great lake
appeared that indicated as never before where
the river ran. From Indooroopilly direction
behind Toowong, down to the Domain, was
one great stretch of water that interested while
it appalled the onlooker. Three days before
the river had been a harmless servant, now it
was a devouring monster.

The rain fiend would blot out the city every
now and again with great drenching mists, as
if it would drown above what it could not
push below. One of the South Brisbane gaso-
meters was seen to topple, and soon it appeared like a signal set askew to mark an opening.
A line of omnibuses in Rosalie that were safe
on Saturday night had vanished at daybreak
on Sunday, and houses that were above water
then were a quarter under by noon. Over at

One of the two ships lifted 36 feet by the flooded river and
stranded in the Brisbane Botanic Gardens

Bishopsbourne boats could be seen landing
people and furniture, and the Bishop's residence
looked like an island. The inland sea at our feet
was dotted with pyramids, so strangely did
the comparatively small number of roofs
appear beside the scores of houses that could
be counted in ordinary times.

At midday on Sunday the rain was pouring
down in a blinding torrent that completely
shut out the view in all directions, and we sat
feeling that a second Deluge was in progress.
Through a rift at last we could see gleaming
for a moment a great sheet of water beyond
Given-terrace that evidently covered the
Paddington flats. Enoggera Creek, away over
towards Kelvin Grove, showed sullenly now
and again like a great river, while the low-lying
spaces between were miniature lakes. On
Sunday afternoon we went to see for ourselves.
The reality was so terrible that what we had
seen from afar compared with the scene now
so near was the difference between a tiger
seen through a telescope and the same animal
ten feet off and ready to spring. To see the
flood at close grips with the city and to realize
the wreck it was making was to also realize
the impotence of language. The horrors of
Sunday the 5th of February, 1893, will lie on
the mind like a horrible dream on first waking
— it may not be true for some, but it is for
others.

1893   William Lane and his followers set off for Paraguay in search of a dream

WILLIAM LANE AND AN UNKNOWN STAFF MEMBER OF THE *SYDNEY MAIL*
Wagga Wagga Hummer, 13 August 1893 and Sydney Mail, 22 July 1893

William Lane, the journalist, set out in search of a dream on 21 July 1893 in company with 200 men, women and children. Their idea was to set up a utopian settlement in Paraguay, a place where they would work and live together in love and trust and unselfishness.

Lane had been born in England in 1861, and had worked in Canada and the United States as a newspaperman when he migrated to Australia in the mid-1880s. He joined the Brisbane Courier *and the Brisbane* Evening Observer, *and later established a Queensland Labor paper, the Brisbane* Worker. *Lane was an extremely competent newspaperman, and an enthusiastic, energetic social reformer. He played a large part in the formation in 1889 of the Australian Labour Federation. He was instrumental in raising £30,000 to assist the London dockers' strike of 1889–90, and was active in the maritime and pastoral strikes of 1890–91. In 1892 he wrote (under the pseudonym of John Miller) a novel,* The Working Man's Paradise, *to assist a fund being raised for men imprisoned as an outcome of the shearers' strike. His decision to found a new society in Paraguay followed the realisation that socialism of the kind he wanted would not be brought about by either political or industrial action.*

The New Australia settlement failed, and Lane left Paraguay in August 1899. Lane's own character was said to have contributed to the failure of the dream. He was completely unselfish and idealistic but he lacked tact, business sense and administrative ability. In 1900 Lane was appointed editor of the Australian Worker, *Sydney, but he clashed with colleagues over the Boer War, in which he supported Britain. He later became editor of the New Zealand* Herald, *and retained that post until his death in 1917.*

Lane wrote about what New Australia meant to him in the Wagga Wagga Hummer *on 13 August 1892:*

For this to me is what New Australia means, to the landless, the homeless, the wifeless, the childless, to those whose hearts are sick and sore, to those who long to be manly, to be true, to be what men should be. Come out from this hateful life, the life that is full of unspoken misery, of heartsickening longing, of evil habits growing with the years, of sin and slavery that lead to nothing but death. Come together, in all unselfishness, to trust each other and to be free! To live simply, to work hardly, to win not the gold that poisons but that home life that saves. To be true husband to one woman, to be happy father to healthy children, to be true friend to every mate who grips hands for the well-being of all, to find contentment in the life that is open to every man whose instincts are satisfied, and happiness in the development of the faculties that divide humanity from the brute! Come to work as free men for each other, to labour on the common land for the common good, and not for self alone or for the selfish greed of another. Come, casting behind us the degrading influences of a society that in its every act outrages the precepts of religion which with its mouth it declares divine. Come to give love and liberty to women as to men, to treat both alike as equals, and to secure to the little ones the rearing that is the right of every little one brought by us into the world! We can do it if we only dare.

Here is the account of the departure of the New Australia settlers by a special reporter of the Sydney Mail:

Emigrants for New Australia on board the *Royal Tar*

The departure of the barque Royal Tar from Sydney marks the first epoch of the New Australia movement. The pioneers, with their wives and children, to the number of some 200 souls, left Sydney on Sunday, and people have been forced, by the evidence of facts, to realise that the scheme, instead of being merely the dream of a visionary, has a tangible existence. Four years ago, New Australia was merely an idea, a vision, which had been formed in the brain of an energetic Brisbane journalist. In those days, which seem in the light of recent events so far away, Lane used to talk hopefully about his plans for a new and ideal commonwealth, but he never anticipated their realisation within such a short time. Curiously enough, by one of those singular coincidences which mark the initiation of many social movements, two great minds, at opposite corners of the globe, were at work upon the same idea. Neither held any communication with the other, yet about the end of 1889, they each elaborated communal constitutions of a similar character. Many of us here have read the work of the great Austrian philanthropist, Dr. Hertzka, who in his "Freeland" detailed the history of an imaginary community established on the highlands of Southern Africa. The book created a great sensation in Europe; its graphically written chapters, though full of romance and adventure, embodied many economic truths, and the lessons which it taught in this interesting manner were by no means thrown away. . . The first copy of a monthly magazine, intended solely to further the work of creating a real Freeland, has just reached Australia.

Whilst all this has been going on in Europe, Lane and a few of his chosen disciples have been quietly at work here, and have actually done more than the many Freeland advocates of the Continent, for they have reached the first stage of their experiment, whilst the others are still but writing and talking about their proposed commonwealth. In one way, of course, the start was made easy for Lane; he had to deal with a body of men already organised into trade unions. The opening of the campaign was therefore much simplified; there was no need of an introduction or recommendation for the lecturer, and wherever Lane went he found an audience ready to listen to his propaganda — in many cases already won over to an idea which promised them a relief from the irksome drudgery of bushlife. As a labour leader, and the founder of a paper devoted to the cause of unionism, Lane's name was known through the length and breadth of the colonies, and he was able to gather in recruits from all parts. Mostly the men who joined were strong unionists; in fact, persons who at any period of their working career have been "black" — that is, unfaithful to the cause of unionism, are purposely excluded from the association. They are put on the same level as Chinamen, or others of coloured race. In this way a collection of men used to working together has been gathered, men who have shorn in the bush, and hammered in the workshops. The thousand members which the association now numbers includes almost every trade and calling. There are, of course, first and foremost, the bushmen, the grizzled men from the back blocks, from remote parts of the Never Never Land; there are small selectors, cockatoo farmers, who have given up their single-handed struggle with nature and decided to try cultivation on a co-operative basis. Then, from the towns, there are carpenters and masons and compositors; the seaports have yielded a few seamen — and, indeed, with the exception of the captain and officers, the Royal Tar is entirely manned by members of the association. A crew of this character, it need hardly be said, is not governed by the same customs as apply to other seafaring men, and during their long stay in port they have earned for themselves a most exemplary character, so much so that the captain jokingly complains that not one of them has got drunk. The same thing might be said about all the other members of the association, for the work is being carried out on strictly teetotal lines, and all who join are required to pledge themselves to temperance, until, at any rate, the initial difficulties of settlement are overcome. Taken as a whole, the adult members of the New Australia are probably as fine a body of men as could be got together, and the pity of it is that they are leaving the

Old Australia, a country which is by no means so effete and worn-out as their action would lead strangers to suppose. In short, it is the best, and not the worst, men of their class who are going. They have been weeded out by a monetary test; every member has had to pay down at least £60 before he could embark. Consequently the lazy or indifferent workers – the habitually unemployed – have had no chance of joining, for in times like the present the possession of £60 by a working man argues that he must be a good and steady tradesman.

In a movement of this kind, however, though it is important that the rank and file should be of sterling quality, everything centres around the leader, the one man who is able to hold his flock together, and by his personal influence, neutralise the seeds of dissension which hardship and disappointment are sure to sow. Probably Mr. William Lane, who has collected these people from all parts of the colonies, is the only man in Australia who could have accomplished the work in such a short space of time. And the peculiar thing about it is that there is nothing special about Lane to account for the wonderful personal magnetism which he possesses. He seems to win sympathy from all; even his very enemies admit his sincerity, and often, after a short conversation, find themselves won over to his cause. He is rather a writer than an orator, he speaks slowly and with great deliberation, taking meanwhile long puffs from the great pipe which he is always smoking. Sprung himself from the working classes, his sympathies are always with the downtrodden and distressed, and most of the years of his life have been devoted to the cause in which he so firmly believes. Born in an English gardener's hut, he saw, during his early years, much of the sordid poverty which prevails amongst the English peasantry, and in the United States, where he went whilst still a boy, he had at an early age to commence the struggle for existence on his own behalf. He was apprenticed to the printing trade, though in later years a marked literary gift enabled him to abandon the composing-stick for the pen, and he became a prominent writer for the Brisbane press. In personal appearance Lane is rugged, his features are irregular, and the malformation of one of his feet has rendered him permanently lame. But behind the spectacles which he always wears there are great, wide, honest blue eyes, which seem to look right through you, and which have a knack of convincing you of their owner's sincerity before he has even spoken. He is still quite a young man, but a little over 30, though his manner and bearing, the gravity of his talk, and his generally serious demeanour give the appearance of much greater age.

All Australians who have the interests of the country at heart will regret that the proposed colony could not have been founded somewhere in this Continent instead of in far away little-known Paraguay. There is plenty of land to be had here, and surely a colonial Government might have made terms as liberal as the Paraguayan did. This is what many think, but the idea is one which has never been entertained by the promoters. Rightly or wrongly, Lane holds that in order to make the colony a success it is necessary to entirely shut the people off from all their old associations, to burn the boats, and thus make retreat difficult. In Australia the half-hearted or dissatisfied would soon drop out of the colony and return to their homes. In Paraguay they can do nothing of the kind. All must stick together, for the country is one in which the white man, depending on his own exertions, cannot readily gain a living; but with the capital the association possesses, it should be easy enough for its members to get at least their bread out of the soil. The land, judging from the accounts which have reached us, is flowing with milk and honey; you have merely to scratch the earth and it laughs back fruit and flowers.

The chief dangers which the emigrants to Paraguay will have to face will probably come from within. Of money there is no lack. Over a thousand members have already joined, and this means at least £60,000 capital to start with. There is no reason to fear that the Paraguayan Government, which is of a very weak and spineless character, will be unduly harsh in its dealings with the wealthy newcomers, and therefore the only thing likely to break up the community will be internal dissension. The constitution is settled on absolutely democratic lines, there is to be no distinction of sex — every member alike is to have an equal share in the general property and equal voting power, whilst the only form of government will be a Director elected by a two-thirds majority, aided by a kind of advisory board chosen in the same way. But the power of the President is supreme. There is practically no control over his actions as long as he has the support of a majority of the community, and therefore everything will depend upon the man who holds this position.

Lane relies largely on the fact that his men, as trades-unionists, have already been trained to habits of discipline and obedience; and believes that their past experiences will teach them to avoid the follies which have done so much to injure the unionist cause, and to exercise, as a free and self-respecting Democracy, the absolute liberty of choice in the wisest possible manner. His enthusiasm is contagious, all his followers are affected by it, and to show what they hope to do and what they expect to gain I cannot do better than quote Lane's own eloquent language:— "The world will be changed if we succeed. And we shall succeed. We cannot help succeeding. For what do we expect? Not mansions, but cottages; not idle luxury, but work-won plenty, for each a home, and marriage — honest, life-long marriage — with sturdy children growing all round to care for us when we are old. We expect that the earth will yield, and that the flocks will increase, and that the axes will fell and the hammers weld, under our own hands, as under the hands of all others who toil. We expect that the song and the dance will come back to us, and that with our human instincts satisfied we shall joy in living. If this is a wild dream, an impossible hope, what hope is there for humanity? Is it so extravagant to expect this, even in a new settlement, when our ranks are steadily drawing in the stoutest hearts and strongest arms in Old Australia? The very difficulties in front of us cow the weak. The very criticisms and abuse heaped on us weed out those who can neither trust themselves nor trust others. How then can we fail, on free land, to do so little?"

The first batch of emigrants for Paraguay,

left on Sunday shortly before noon, when the refitted barque Royal Tar was towed down the harbour. At 10 o'clock on Saturday morning the officials of the Health Emigration Department visited the Royal Tar with the intention of giving a final clearance under the Passengers Act. The officers of the Customs also attended in order that the Customs clearance might also be granted. It was found that the requirements of the Act had been satisfied, and with respect to the Passenger Act all the requirements had been fully met. The crew were mustered, and were found to be in good health and of sufficient strength, as in the ship's articles, numbering in all 27. The passengers were then mustered. It was then found three children named Kempson were suffering from measles. They with their father and mother were placed in the Health Department tender for removal to the hospital.

About half-past 9 o'clock on Sunday morning the emigration officer for Port Jackson, the secretary of the Board of Health, and the medical and marine inspectors of the department attended on the vessel. A further mustering of the crew and passengers took place, and it was found that a child named Kidd had developed measles. The patient, together with the father, mother, and three children, were removed from the vessel. Mr. and Mrs. Kidd elected to allow two of their daughters, aged 14 and 11 years respectively, to proceed with their friends to the new settlement. A clearance was then granted to the vessel, she cast off about 11.15 a.m., and cleared the Heads shortly after noon, no communication with boats being allowed after the final clearance had been granted. This precaution was taken in order to guard against any persons being placed on the vessel over and above the number for which she is provisioned under the Act. The vessel had on board at the time of clearance the following:— A crew (including master) of 27; cabin passengers, the master's family (3), equal to 2½ statute adults; passengers (steerage), members of the association, 209, equal to 163 statute adults, the total being 239 souls, equal to 192½ statute adults. . . . One-third men, one-third women, and one-third children under 12 years of age. . .

1898 Devastating bushfires sweep through Gippsland and towns are wiped out

BILLY SALTER
Melbourne Argus, 25 February 1898

Billy Salter, the Argus *reporter who played a large part in uncovering the record of multiple murderer Frederick Deeming, was one of the most versatile reporters of his time. The diversity of country newspaper work is well-known among journalists but Salter, as a youngster on the Bendigo* Independent, *set a one-day record that would be hard to beat.*

He had been covering an agricultural show at Echuca the day before he was to report the execution of a prosperous farmer called Harrison. It was his first execution — his tally when he quit newspapers was twenty-two men and three women — and he was very tired when he got back to Bendigo from Echuca late at night. After a short sleep, he got to the jail in time to watch Harrison hanged. He returned to the Independent , *wrote a long colour story, then went to Bendigo Court at 10 a.m. and covered several cases. At 11 a.m. he hustled away to cover the annual Hibernian procession, and finished writing the description in time to sit down at an official lunch and take down two columns of Irish oratory. He sent his last slip of copy back to the office as he started to cover the Hibernian sports, which lasted until after five o'clock. Between then and 8 p.m. he had to classify sporting results and write his introduction. Pausing only to eat a sandwich, he hustled to the local theatre as the curtain rose for the first act of Grattan Rigg's production of* The Shaugran. *When the play was over, Salter wrote his dramatic criticism and spent the rest of his working night assisting on the sub-editors' desk, handling telegrams.*

It was his work on the Harrison murder which caused the Melbourne Herald *to entice Salter away from Bendigo. Throughout a varied career, Salter tackled every assignment with total enthusiasm. In the terrible Gippsland fires of 1898 — the fires which inspired John Longstaff's fine painting,* Gippsland, Sunday Night, February 20th — *Salter worked for days without rest to tell the story from the viewpoint of the men and women of the bush. His text in the* Argus *was quoted by community leaders throughout Australia as they appealed for funds to help the homeless. Ballarat Fire Brigade sent men and appliances from the other side of the State to fight the fires, and the relief fund assumed enormous proportions; Montague Grover later wrote that this was a superb example of the manner in which a reporter could influence public opinion.*

Here is one of Salter's reports from inside the devastated area:

Now that Neerim North has ceased to exist, and Neerim East has been terribly stricken, and Neerim South is waiting in a state of painful suspense lest the wind may veer to the north again, and bring the sea of flame down upon the township, there is a short breathing space in which to chronicle a few of the incidents of the desperate fight which the settlers have been carrying on for the last few days against the flames. The catastrophe has, at any rate, served to bring out in the strongest colours the unswerving courage with which the men and women of the bush can face the risk of death in its most horrifying shape, and if the details of the great conflagration disclose many instances of the most painful suffering, they are also characterised by some striking examples of extraordinary resourcefulness in the presence of unusual dangers. The district of Neerim may be conveniently taken as the centre of a great system of bush fires in the neighbourhood of Warragul, but several remarkable incidents may be noted as having marked the isolated hand-to-hand encounters which lonely settlers far back from the township have waged with the flames. . .

At Neerim East, the fire has made almost a clean sweep, damaging the crops and holdings of Messrs. Young, Murphy, Downey, Purcell, R. G. Stephens, and J. Holt. Although the houses of the settlers in each case have been saved, the experience of Mr. Holt was truly strange. All day on Wednesday the fire roared and surged through the forest behind the house, growing nearer with every fresh gust of the strong north wind. The air was full of sparks and burning pieces of timber, and Mr. and Mrs. Holt plied their bags soaked in water and their mops and clothes with frenzied energy to prevent the house from catching. Presently the smoke became so dense that the suffocation of the entire family became imminent, but Mrs. Holt's ingenuity was spurred to fresh inventiveness by the pressing danger, and she devised a plan by which she saved the lives of all her six children. The poor woman was herself in no fit state for such a fearful ordeal, having given birth to a baby as recently as last Christmas, but she carried out a plan which was as ingenious as it was happily successful. She made the younger children lie down on the ground, and covered them over with sacks, which were kept constantly saturated with water, so that they could breathe without inhaling the pungent suffocating smoke. Then the husband dug a small hole in the ground, and in it they placed the baby, covering it over with sacks. The eldest boy was deputed to see that the sacks were kept well watered, and in this strange cradle the sturdy infant of this courageous couple went peacefully to sleep, lulled by the roaring of the conflagration and the thunder of the falling trees. It will be a matter of general satisfaction to know that Mr. and Mrs. Holt succeeded in saving their home, and that the baby is none the worse for its fiery ordeal. . .

A few twisted sheets of corrugated iron, an American stove, and the iron framework that once supported a piano are pretty nearly all

that is left of Neerim North. Mr. J. Woolstencroft, who owned the store, is the greatest sufferer, for he saved absolutely nothing except the clothes which he wore, and his stock, which was valued at £250, was uninsured. The experiences of himself, his wife, and his sisters show that true courage and grit are still to be met with in the bush. For weeks past, according to his story, the fires have raged in the neighbourhood of the now extinct township, approaching and receding according to the changes of the wind. At the beginning of the week it was noticed, however, that the fire was coming nearer, and it was already in an adjoining paddock, owned by Mr. Ross. Monday was an anxious day, and on Tuesday anxiety became alarm. On Wednesday morning, the wind changed, with alternate gusts, from north to south, and back again, and the fire zig-zagged in its course, each zig-zag bringing it perceptibly nearer to the doomed township. The atmosphere became so dark that the people could not see each other more than a few yards away, and the roaring of the fire was so tremendous that they could not hear each other's voices. About a dozen men and half-a-dozen women and girls gathered together to fight the fire at the spot which seemed most open to the first attack, namely, the house occupied by Mr. Andrew Wilson, a wooden structure, with a corrugated iron roof. As they were hastily making their preparations a young man rushed in from an adjoining selection, calling upon them to fly from the place, and loudly declaring that if they persisted in remaining not one of them would escape alive. But they turned a deaf ear to his suggestion, and, having reared ladders against the side of the house, one detachment mounted the roof, while the remainder dipped sacks and mops in water from the tank and handed these implements up to the fire-fighters. Mr. Woolstencroft declares that, in the intense darkness and the blinding smoke, the approaching flames showed bluish in colour as they escaped through the tops of the trees in mighty bounds, covering from 50ft. to 100ft. at a time. As fast as the sparks alighted on the roof the vigilant watchers beat out the flames with their wet sacks, and finally they were overjoyed at finding that they had repulsed the enemy definitely. But the fire was not to be baulked, for, actually leaping across the frail structure upon which it could get no hold, it attacked the little cluster of buildings which formed the nucleus of the township, and the forces of the defenders were hastily brought up to hold the new position. Mr. Woolstencroft's store and dwellinghouse, Mr. J. Barr's home, a butcher's shop owned by Mr. Stephens, and the Mechanics' Institute were speedily involved, and as the store was the first to be attacked the courageous little band of fire-fighters renewed the tactics which had already been successful in saving one house. But this time they undertook an impossible task, and yet they maintained the unequal conflict even after a couple of hair-breadth escapes, both of which were sustained by the ladies of the party. Miss Susan Wool-stencroft was perched upon the roof of the store, which was already burning, and was desperately attempting to beat out the flames when the ladder fell from the side, and the plucky girl was left alone in her perilous position. But she did not hesitate for a moment, and leaping boldly from the burning roof, she escaped without injury. Her sister, Miss Jane Woolstencroft, had an unpleasant experience also, and one which might easily have had a fatal result to a person of less self-possession. While she was standing on the ground, passing up water from the tank to the people on the roof, a piece of burning bark set fire to her clothes, and in a moment she was in a blaze; but, as quick as lightning, she tore off the burning clothes, and fled away in scanty garments to the shelter of the house which still remained standing. In a few moments more the fire-fighters surrendered, and the store sank into ashes. A significant fact explains with telling force how terrible the roaring of the fire must have sounded. Inside the burning store was a case containing 500 loaded cartridges; these must have exploded when the flames reached them, but the sound of the explosion was unnoticed by the group of watchers, whose escape from instant death is truly miraculous...

It is impossible to paint in colours too lurid the state of affairs which exist in the Thorp-dale district as a consequence of the terrible scourge which has swept over it since Monday last. Over 50 homesteads have been literally wiped out, and over 50 persons have neither food nor shelter but what their neighbours care to give them. Hundreds of cattle, pigs, poultry, and many horses have been roasted alive, others terribly maimed, and every piece of crop or blade of grass for half-a-dozen miles around has gone. Along the roads one meets families wending their way into the township, where charity awaits them. Some carry a few remnants of furniture or a bundle of clothes saved from the ruin of their homes, and all tell the same story of devoted heroism and shattered hopes. The savings of a life are gone in many cases; many are blind from the effects of the smoke, or have their faces singed as clean as if they had been scraped. Strong men are found in tears, children cry piteously, and women are worn and exhausted to despair. It is a harrowing sight. In one place is met a Mr. Tom Arthur, a settler of 20 years, leading in a decrepit horse, on which is mounted a family of four children, with scarce a stitch among them. Further on is a little procession of three families, dragging after them as best they can what is left of their belongings. Some of these have just come together after being separated by the fire for days, each believing that the other was dead. Fortunately all those who were missing have turned up, so that no loss of life is reported in this locality...

There is no end to the deeds of self-sacrificing heroism which the last few days have seen. Men got separated from their homes in going to help their neighbours, and did not see their families again for days. The Church of England clergyman, Mr. Cox, a typical bush parson, had to be led in exhausted from many a gallant struggle, and is now almost blind. Mr. J. Gynn had 40 people gathered under his roof at one time, all fighting for their lives. Mrs. Smith, an old lady of 70, had to be carried out of her burning house on a stretcher by her children, and the little relief party were nearly destroyed in making their way to the creek — their only refuge...

1899   A governor reminds Australians of their 'birthstain' and regrets it

ERNEST POWER
Sydney Morning Herald, 10 May 1899

One of the most unsuccessful Australian governors ever was Lord Beauchamp and he owed a large part of his failure to a shipboard interview he gave before he had even taken up his office. Beauchamp was sent out from England in 1899 to govern New South Wales, and on the way his mail steamer touched at Albany, Western Australia.

Ernest·Renton Power, who went on to have a distinguished career in newspapers in Queensland and Victoria, was then a young reporter on the Albany Advertiser. *He also acted as Albany correspondent of the* Sydney Morning Herald. *Power went out to interview the new governor. He later wrote:*

As the tender from the shore approached the liner I saw the noble lord looking down from the passenger deck. On getting aboard I told him my business. He said: "You want to see my private secretary". He rushed along the deck and I followed. His secretary, the Hon. Victor Corkran, appeared. A nice young man, he told me Lord Beauchamp had decided not to be interviewed in Australia. I told him that governors were usually interviewed, and that his Excellency would probably have to change his mind. The secretary said if I chose to put questions through him he would take them and obtain replies. I put several, and got replies. Then I asked if he had a message for the people of Sydney. Off went the secretary and on his return he said his excellency was looking up a message. This is what he came back with a little later, written by Lord Beauchamp on his own notepaper:

Greeting! Your birthstain have you
    turned to good,
Forcing strong wills perverse to
    steadfastness.

The first flush of the tropics in your
    blood,
And at your feet success.

Power's report, as published in the Sydney Morning Herald, *is brief and to the point. But it deserves inclusion in this collection because of its effects. Beauchamp, who had taken the lines from Kipling, had chosen to remind the citizens of New South Wales that many of them were descendants of convicts, who, with tropical blood in their veins, had made good. It was an unfortunate message, with patronising, insulting undertones. Beauchamp was promptly nicknamed 'Birthstain', and the* Bulletin *advised its readers 'for birthstains, take Beauchamp's pills'.*

Another Beauchamp blunder came when his lordship issued invitation cards for his first garden party — blue cards for the elite, and white cards for the also-rans. The Bulletin *quickly dubbed these cards 'Seidlitz Powders'. Unlike Governor Bligh, who had been deported by the colonists, Beauchamp apparently recognised that he was not a success, and resigned his governorship well before his term expired. It was generally conceded that he had never recovered from the handicap imposed by his initial 'birthstain' message.*

Eighteen months after the first interview, Power went out in the pilot launch from Albany to meet Lord Hopetoun (later the Marquis of Linlithgow), who was taking up his job as Australia's first governor-general. Again the reporter asked: 'Could you let me have a message for the people of Australia?' 'Yes,' came the prompt reply. Then Hopetoun added, with a wry smile: 'But I shall not quote Kipling.'

Later, through the Australian writer Henry

Lawson, Lord Beauchamp claimed that the 'birthstain' message had been a reporter's fabrication. Lawson had stayed at his English home as a guest; when he returned to Australia he said, in an interview with the Sydney Daily Telegraph, *that Lord Beauchamp had denied ever sending such a message through any reporter at Albany.*

Luckily, Power had followed a dictum of his trade. He had kept his notes. Not only his notes, but Beauchamp's original message, in his own handwriting. Power promptly wrote to Lawson offering to send him the original. He did not receive a reply. The message is now in the keeping of the Mitchell Library, Sydney. Ernest Power later became chief sub-editor of the Melbourne Age; *three of his sons, Kevin, Laurie and Jim (killed in action as an* RAAF *pilot over the Mediterranean during World War Two) became senior journalists.*

Lord Beauchamp arrived at Albany this morning on board the Himalaya. He is accompanied by his sister, Lady Mary Lygon, Lady Raglan, the Hon. Violet Somerset, Lady Bertha Wilbraham, the Hon. Robert Lindsay, of the Royal Scots Grays, A.D.C., Mr. Wilfred Smith, of the Grenadier Guards, A.D.C., and Mr. Victor Corcoran, private secretary. His Excellency and party enjoyed good health during the voyage, which was a most pleasant one.

When requested to grant an interview Lord Beauchamp informed your representative that he intended refraining from being interviewed, and had decided to have all communications made through his private secretary. Under these circumstances no interview could take place. Lord Beauchamp said that at present he was not in a position to express his views regarding federation. Mr. Corcoran, private secretary, handed the press the following message from Lord Beauchamp to the people of New South Wales. It is in verse, being an adaptation of a verse of Rudyard Kipling's "The Song of the Cities":—

> Greeting ! Your birthstain have you turned
> to good,
> Forcing strong wills perverse to steadfast-
> ness.
> The first flush of the tropics in your blood,

And at your feet success. — Beauchamp.

Lord Beauchamp was met on board the mail steamer by the Government Resident, Mr. J. A. Wright, and welcomed to Australia. On landing he was received by the Premier of New South Wales, Mr. Reid, and the Mayor of Albany. His Excellency, accompanied his private secretary, Mr. Reid, the Mayor, and Government Resident, then drove to the forts, and after inspecting them the party was driven around the marine drive, which commands an extensive view of Princess Royal Harbour, King George's Sound, and the outlying islands. Lord Beauchamp was enthusiastic in his admiration of the picturesqueness of Albany, and was charmed with the views obtained from the marine drive.

Mr. Reid informed your representative that an official interview had taken place between himself and Lord Beauchamp. Mr. Reid will leave the steamer at Melbourne and travel overland, reaching Sydney on the 18th, the day that the Himalaya is expected there.

1900   The siege of Ladysmith reported from the besieged town

DONALD MACDONALD
Melbourne Argus, 2 April 1900

Donald Macdonald excelled in three areas of journalism: as a war correspondent, as a sports-writer and as a commentator on natural history. As a boy near Corowa (Victoria) he spent much of his time in the bush.He had his first newspaper experience on the Corowa Free Press, *a weekly paper, and after about a year he applied for an advertised vacancy as a junior reporter on the* Argus. *For a while he worked on the* Argus' *halfpenny evening sister paper, the* Evening Mail, *mainly covering cricket and football. Later, when the* Evening Mail *folded, he transferred to general work on the* Argus; *his country background and some small knowledge of stock influenced his seniors to send him often to report country shows.*

One of his early cricket reports contained a few personal opinions; the editor of the time, Mr F. W. Haddon, told him to produce a pen-name and the byline, 'Observer', which was to sit above Macdonald's cricket and football reports for many years, was born. Similarly, when he contributed some nature notes for an Argus Saturday *magazine section, Mr Haddon ruled that the personal comments demanded a signature; from then Macdonald's nature stories always carried the initials, D.M. He also wrote a column for the* Australasian *under the name of 'Woomera' (Aboriginal for throwing-stick) and the name was passed from him successively to D. H. Maling, Monty Grover, J. P. Edgar, Adam McCay and Charles Pearce. Oddly, Macdonald never wrote under his own name until he went to South Africa for the Boer War.*

The Argus, *an enterprising newspaper, decided in the spring of 1899 that war between the British and the Boer republics was inevitable; Macdonald was dispatched as a war correspondent before the war was even de-clared. The first real clash of arms occurred in the highlands of Natal the day after he arrived in South Africa. He started for the front, and reached Ladysmith just before the town was surrounded and besieged by the Boers. He tried several times to send messages out of the city, through the Boer lines, with Kaffir runners; each message had to be submitted to censors in Ladysmith, and each, because of the danger that it might fall into the hands of the Boers, was mutilated to a point where it was unintelligible. 'We were not allowed to mention sickness, fever, horse-flesh, or anything that gave the siege its real color,' Macdonald wrote later, 'and what was the use of paying heavy prices to runners to take through skeleton messages? Latterly, the cost of a runner was £10 for the trip, and a few failures soon showed some of the correspondents who attempted it that it was a very costly means of getting through a very lame and insufficient report.'*

Macdonald's despatches from Ladysmith began on 1 November 1899; the first batch of them arrived in Melbourne in the S.S. Damascus on 1 April 1900 – just four months later – and publication began in the Argus *the next day. Repeated dysentery and 'siege sickness' caused Macdonald to lose one and a half stone in the three-month siege; he suffered another health breakdown in Capetown a few weeks later, while he was heading for the western front where Australian troops were in action. He was invalided home long before the end of the war.*

Yesterday our isolation became complete. The wires were cut on Wednesday morning. No train came through from Maritzburg on Thursday, and presumably the rail to southward of us is in the hands of the enemy, and, as at Dundee, we are once more isolated. These letters become for the time the history in brief of a besieged town, and the only purpose in making the story of the siege a daily diary is that one may chance at short notice to get the services of a guide who will seek to get through the enemy's lines after dark, or one of the Kaffirs, who are being leniently treated by the Boers, may undertake the task usually performed by the despatch rider. They have us under their guns now from three points, and nothing that we have been able to mount seems fit to do more than temporarily silence them. At any moment they can make the town un-tenable for civilians, but, though many shells came in during the early part of the week, there was until Friday (November 3) no cause to complain of the conduct of the State Artill-ery, who man the Boer guns. On Friday they pitched many shells right into the heart of the town, with no other idea apparently than that of intimidating and injuring the townspeople, for our guns were not answering at the time. To stick to an illustration I have already used, in which the town of Ladysmith corresponds to the heart of the city of Melbourne, the position is just this. The big gun, which from the base of the shell seems to be a 6in. Krupp, looks straight down the main street, and its position would correspond with the Mount Alexander-road at the crest of Flemington Hill. The townspeople can stand at their doors and see the burst of smoke and flame from its muzzle, then wait anxiously for the scream of the shell and the explosion, the dust from which soon rises high over the tops of the houses. Their second gun is at a point corres-ponding with the high ground in Studley-park, yet so perfectly hidden that few know its exact location, though the tune that it plays is as familiar as the National Anthem. The third gun they have thus far placed would approximately be somewhere about the junct-ion of the Yarra and Saltwater rivers.

To southward of us — that is south of the Yarra — they have not yet placed a gun to do any mischief, but some of the heaviest fighting has taken place in that direction. Although many shells fell in the heart of the town during

the early part of the week, it could not be said that the State Artillery — who manage the big Boer guns — were actually shelling a town filled with women, children, hospitals, and wounded, but on Friday there could no longer be any doubt of it. From midday until dark — when the fire invariably ceases — they came' in at irregular intervals. One of the first pitched just outside the Royal, the largest hotel, while the dining-room was filled. It exploded in a cottage next door in a room usually occupied by Mr. Pearce, the "Morning Post" correspond-ent — who reminds me much of the late Coun-cillor Walstab, of Brighton — carried out the side of the house, and blew everything to frag-ments. Splinters of shell flew upward through the windows of the dining-room, which was filled with shattered glass and dust, yet not a man was hurt. This was generally assumed to be a Transvaal welcome to Dr. Jim and some of the Rhodesia people. It was probably known to the Boers, also, that scores of British offic-ers were accustomed to lunch at the Royal, and they nearly got a bagful. Several houses were destroyed by shell during the afternoon, a number of people wounded, yet not one life lost. It makes one wonder whether the destruction wrought by our field-guns is, after all, as great as they say, even admitting that our shrapnel is so much better timed than theirs. The extraordinary mastery which their guns have secured over us was evidenced yesterday, when there was a sudden hurried movement of our cavalry, mounted infantry, and flying artillery to southward, to meet an attack of Free State Boers, which was develop-ing strongly in that direction. As our troops hurried out the three guns mentioned were shelling them at long range, right over their own camp and town. Fortunately, a high ridge close to the road protected them from the two most dangerous guns, while the sweep of the third did not enable them to come nearer than within 50 yards of the column. They were absolutely marching out through an avenue of bursting shells, which did them no damage. . .

Yesterday our war balloon was twice struck. The Boers have realised the futility of shooting at it with artillery when high in the air. Now they get the exact position, and pour in their shell as the balloon descends. Yesterday we were able to see that a shell from one of our naval guns fell right on the Krupp, apparently killing or wounding nearly every man working it. Instantly their white flag was hoisted, and while they were carrying away their men we fired no more. It was a doubtful use of the flag, especially as they took advantage of it to get the gun into action again, and the flag had barely disappeared when the flame was again burning from its muzzle. We have had losses at our guns. Poor Lieutenant Egerton, of the Powerful, a gallant young sailor, would persist in standing to his gun on the exposed ridge, though his men were ordered to the shelter trench whenever the Krupp's smoke was seen. Finally came a shell which literally burst at his feet, carrying away both his legs, and, though amputation was tried, they could not save him, and with Major Taunton and Lieutenant Knapp, of the Carabineers, who were killed in yesterday's fight, was buried to-day, their only wreaths the little mountain marguerites growing on the rocky hills where they fell. I saw two of the volunteers yesterday turn to help a mate who had fallen, when the rattle of the Mausers was like a mowing-machine in the November hayfields, and strangely both of them were hit through the upper part of the arm. On another occasion a half-dozen Imperial Light Horse patrols simply trotted on to a flat swept by both the rifle and artillery fire of the enemy. We who saw their peril could do nothing to warn them a mile away. The Boers, with that consummate patience which marks them, waited till they were fairly in the open, then the hail of nickel and splinter fell upon them. In a few seconds three of them were wounded, one horse was killed, and another was shot through the upper lip with a splinter of shell. Our cavalry and mounted infantry are continually falling into such death traps. Sometimes they are drawn on in a running fight with the idea that they are being opposed by something like their own number, and are getting the best of it. Then of a sudden they find the rocks in front of them literally swarming with the enemy, and have to beat a retreat, with the Boers just pumping rifle bullets into the dust of the

flying squadron. They can lie as low as quail in summer time, and rise with equal suddenness. Wisdom comes with experience — we are dyeing all the grey horses a khaki colour, and it is quite time. I saw Dr. Buntine, one of the heroes of the campaign, on such a weird mount to-day, and we had a chat of mutual friends in Melbourne to whom he wished to be remembered. He looks fit and well — altogether much more of the light horseman than the physician.

During part of yesterday there was fighting going on all round Ladysmith, the fire covering a circle of about 25 miles. Thus they threaten everywhere, yet so far have not come on in force. We drive them back at every point, yet as soon as we return to camp they re-occupy their ground. Yesterday, when they were retreating from the ridges under stress of our artillery fire at nearly 4,000 yards, they reminded me of the big apes one sees bounding away from the train on the ridges above the Berca of Durban. I use the simile without contempt — our men in dodging amongst the rocks, no doubt, presented to the Boers exactly the same impression. When men are in riding breeches and short tunics they look long-limbed and short-bodied. We fought on somewhat novel lines yesterday. Under cover of our field guns, the 5th Dragoons, 5th Lancers, and 18th and 19th Hussars were rushed up under shelter of the kopjes in the hope of cutting off the enemy, but, though the move often promised to be successful, the Boers were too cute to be cornered. The burgher who has seen his mate run through with a lance, the while he clutches with both hands a death grip, to its shaft, has seen something that will last him through the campaign.

. . . There are no tree tops here, yet yesterday I could see the Boer bullets clipping up the dust all round our men; yet, in constant searching with the glass, failed to exactly locate them. There was not a whiff of smoke anywhere. Nor is it possible, except in absolutely open country, to estimate the loss on either side in these running fights. In the dusk one hears the faint call of a wounded man amongst the rocks . . .

1900 Australians fight the Boxers in the siege of Peking and 'Chinese' Morrison reported dead

GEORGE MORRISON AND J. R. WALLACE

Melbourne Argus, 2 August 1900 and Sydney Morning Herald, 29 December 1900

On 18 July 1900, Australian newspapers published obituaries of the famous correspondent of the London Times, *George Ernest Morrison. Morrison, born in Melbourne, had gone to London in 1884 — the year after his unsuccessful New Guinea expedition for the* Age *— and had graduated in medicine in Edinburgh in 1887; in 1897 he became* The Times *man in Peking.*

The anti-foreign, anti-Christian Boxer movement had erupted violently at the end of the nineteenth century, and for fifty-five days in 1900 the Boxers laid siege to the legations of Peking. Morrison made a number of attempts to get messages through to the outside world. One of his dispatches, written on both sides of very thin paper measuring five inches by less than two and a half, dipped in oil (to waterproof it) and buried in an old dish of gruel, was carried by a young Chinese Christian who was let down over the Peking wall, disguised as a beggar. The boy was stopped and sent back to Peking; Morrison retrieved the message and pasted it in his diary. It survives today, and has been praised as evidence that Morrison was a master of 'lucid and condensed telegraphy'. The message, reproduced by Cyril Pearl in his biography, Morrison of Peking, *asked whoever received it to convey it to the Commissioner of Customs in Tientsin, who was then asked to forward it as a telegram to* The Times *— at urgent rate, if necessary. It read:*

Since January 20 been besieged by Chinese troops all communications cut isolation complete stop for ten days unable communicate even with Peitang cathedral where Monseigneur Favier priests sisters 3000 Christians in one enclosure guarded by 30 French 10 Italians their position great peril enemy encompassing fire starvation stop Enemy daily shelling British Legation which crowded all foreign ministers women children Christian refugees danger extreme position being commanded from city wall also wall Imperial city working day night desperate efforts strengthen defence barricades sandbags loopholes nightly furious fusillade all quarters bullets thousands one marine killed inside legation stop Italian Dutch Belgian Austrian legations burned French legation abandoned but retaken severely bombarded wall opposite American Legation held by 35 Americans British Russians stop princes grounds palace east British legation bravely defended by small number Japanese whom seven killed thirteen wounded British two killed also David Oliphant student interpreter of 414 men and 20 officers besieged area 2 officers killed Japanese Ando French Herbert six wounded including Halliday severely doing well 43 men killed 65 wounded civilians five killed including Wagner Frenchman son consul general six wounded stop ammunition carefully husbanded supplies insufficient great anxiety prolonged delay arrival troops we unprovided field pieces general health good Morrison Peking July sixth.

The erroneous report of Morrison's death caused The Times *— which had never before mentioned Morrison's name — to publish the name of 'our devoted correspondent' in an honoured place, with those of the diplomats Sir Claude MacDonald and Sir Robert Hart, to devote nearly two columns to his obituary, and to praise the Australian extravagantly in an editorial. In Geelong, where Morrison went to school, flags were flown at half-mast in his memory.*

Arthur Adams, a young Australian war correspondent who did some work for the Argus *during this period, was staying with Morrison when the copy of* The Times *arrived containing the premature obituary. 'What do you think of this?' Morrison asked. 'Well,' said Adams, 'after two columns in* The Times *and the cheers they gave you, the only decent thing they can do is double your salary.'*

Morrison wrote 30,000 words on the siege for The Times, *and his account was published on 14 and 15 October 1900.*

The Spectator *said of it: 'Gibbon could not have told the story better. It has been accepted as* the *history of that strange episode.'* The Times, *in an editorial about the report, said of Morrison: 'In only one instance has he been unjust. He has left us to learn from private sources of the manful part he himself played in the defence, and of the severe wound which, we regret to hear, still prevents him from walking save with pain and difficulty.' Morrison received a telegram from* The Times, THANKS SPLENDID NARRATIVE, *and the paper's proprietor, Arthur Walker, sent him an eight-page letter which said in part:*

So far as my knowledge and judgement go no other correspondent of *The Times* ever did so remarkable a piece of work as your description of the siege of Peking, and no other correspondent ever gained so completely the confidence of the Public as you have done . . . The service you have rendered to the paper surpassed any expression of value I can use . . . I am proud . . . to associate the paper with the great reputation you have made for yourself. . .

In his detailed report to The Times, *Morrison wrote that Captain Strouts, the senior British officer, had been shot, and had died an hour after being brought into hospital. He did not mention the fact that he, too, had been shot while accompanying Strouts. The British Ambassador, Sir Claude MacDonald, reported in his dispatches: 'Dr. Morrison acted as lieutenant to Captain Strouts and rendered most valuable assistance. Active, energetic and cool, he volunteered for every service of*

danger and was a pillar of strength when things were going badly. By his severe wound on the 16th July, his valuable services were lost to the defence for the rest of the siege.'

Australian newspapers re-printed Morrison's first cryptic, bare-bones report to The Times *after the siege. These details, published in the* Argus *on 2 August, were the first to come from him following the false report of his death:*

"The Times" this morning publishes a long message from its Peking correspondent, Dr. George Ernest Morrison, of Victoria.

The message is dated July 21, and gives a full account of the siege of the legations by the Chinese.

Dr. Morrison speaks in high terms of the unwavering courage and splendid fortitude shown by the members of the legations. He states that the women and children are well, and that the health of the community is excellent. The foreigners, he says, are contentedly awaiting relief.

"The Times" correspondent reports that hostilities ceased on July 18, the Chinese soldiers being probably short of ammunition. They were, however, continuing to strengthen the barricades that they had erected round the besieged area and the batteries on the top of the wall of the Imperial city. The main body of the Imperial soldiers had left Peking with the view of meeting the relief forces from Peking.

On the date of his message Dr. Morrison says supplies had begun to arrive at the legation buildings. The wounded were progressing favourably, and the arrangements for their treatment were admirable. The number of patients who had passed through the hospital was 150 and no case of septic poisoning had occurred among them.

Continuing his narrative, Dr. Morrison states that the Tsungli Yamen forwarded to Sir Claude Macdonald a copy of an appeal by the Empress Dowager to Her Majesty the Queen, asking her to intervene.

On the previous day an edict had been issued by the Tsungli Yamen, urging the Boxers to continue their loyal and patriotic services in exterminating the Christians and foreigners in China. . .

The forces that besieged the legations were, according to Dr. Morrison, composed entirely of Imperial troops, and they were under the command of the Manchu generals, Yung-la and Tung-fusiang. Imperial decrees were issued applauding the gallantry of the besiegers, although, says "The Times" correspondent, this gallantry consisted in bombarding for a month the defenceless women and children who were cooped up in the legation compound. . .

The greatest peril to which the Europeans were exposed, "The Times" correspondent states, was fire, and he records the fact that in their determination to destroy the British legation, the Chinese burnt one of the most important institutions in Peking, the Hanlin National Academy. The library of the academy, with its unique and priceless collection of Chinese books and records, was reduced to ashes.

According to Dr. Morrison proclamations were posted throughout the city by the Chinese announcing that they would remain neutral. This, however, was only done with the object of inducing a feeling of security among the Europeans, for on the night of the day when these proclamations were posted the Chinese made a general attack on the legation building in the hope of taking the garrison unawares.

It was a time of intense news activity. Each day the main pages of Australian newspapers were filled with reports of the Boer war, the Chinese fighting at Peking and Tientsin, the Dreyfus affair, the final plans for the inauguration of the Commonwealth, and forecasts about Mr Barton's Federal Cabinet.

The China situation was of great interest. As with the Boer War, the Australian Government felt compelled to offer assistance. A naval contingent of 451 men, comprising detachments from New South Wales and Victoria, sailed on 7 August 1900 in the Salamis *for China with J. R. Wallace, of the* Sydney Morning Herald *staff, representing the* Sydney Morning Herald *and the* Argus *as war correspondent. It received commendations from Lieutenant-General Gaselee, commanding the British troops in the China Field Force, and its members returned to a heroes' welcome on 25 April 1901.*

Here is one of Wallace's dispatches, published on 29 December 1900:

Yesterday another sailor's soul passed away, and this morning we gave honored burial to his body. Staff Surgeon J. J. Steel, the first Australian officer to leave his bones in China, was the man, and his death means an irreparable loss, not only to the contingent, but to New South Wales . . . At the funeral the whole of the British regiments in North China were represented. General Gaselee and the head quarters staff officers, the Indian medical staff and the Australian officers and men followed the gun carriage on which the coffin was carried. In front the Sikhs' band played a weird funeral march. He was buried almost within the shadow of the city wall, in a little piece of consecrated ground where, under rude mounds and rough hewn crosses, others before him have found their resting place while serving their Queen and country.

It is pleasing to be able to say that the general health of the contingent is good. Not a single case of serious sickness has occurred since our arrival at Pekin. The much abused military authorities did the right thing for once when they insisted on strict medical examination of all troops on service, and weeded out those who were unfit to face the severity of the Pekin winter. . .

Ting Yung, the bloodthirsty Chinese official hereinbefore referred to, is provincial treasurer of Chi-li, of which Pao-ting-fu is the capital, and is notorious as the instigator of the terrible atrocities which occurred there in July last; too horrible many of them for description. One lady, an American, was driven into the streets, stripped of her clothing and violated, her breasts cut off, driven with whips and stones through the city, and finally torn limb from limb. At Tai-yuin-fu an Englishman and his wife died horrible deaths at the hands of the fiends. . .

1900 'Banjo' Paterson, with the New South Wales Mounted Rifles, chases the Boers

A. B. PATERSON
Sydney Morning Herald, 6 September 1900

Andrew Barton Paterson's fame as a bush balladist (and writer of 'Waltzing Matilda') has tended to overshadow his performance as a newspaperman. 'The Banjo' was born near Orange, New South Wales, in 1864, educated at Sydney Grammar School, and practised as a solicitor for some years. He then began writing verses about Illalong Station (near Yass), where he was brought up; collected as The Man from Snowy River, and other verses *(1895), his ballads achieved immense popularity. The first edition sold out in a fortnight, and one English reviewer claimed that Paterson had a bigger audience than any other English-speaking poet outside Kipling.*

He had some prose and much verse published in the Bulletin, *and in 1899 the* Sydney Morning Herald *sent him, as a correspondent, to the Boer War. In October of that year, war had broken out between Britain and two Dutch South African republics: the Transvaal and the Orange Free State. One of the surprises of the war was the outburst patriotic fervour in Australia and New Zealand. Over 16,000 men (and horses) went to the war from Australia, and more than 6,000 of these came from New South Wales.*

Paterson's war reporting earned him a high international reputation; Reuter's, the news agency, appointed him a correspondent. His dispatches, like the one reprinted here, demonstrated a flair for fast-moving narrative — most of it told at short range.

Back from the war, Paterson returned to a career in journalism. He decided in 1901 to go to China for the Boxer Rebellion; the Sydney Morning Herald *also announced that he would visit Japan, and then 'take the trans-Siberian railway to St. Petersburg'. In Peking he met George Ernest 'Chinese'*

Morrison, the legendary Australian-born correspondent of The Times *of London, but from a newspaper point of view the visit to China was badly timed; Paterson arrived after the fighting had ended. From 1903 until 1906 Paterson was editor of the* Sydney Evening News, *and in 1907–08 edited the* Sydney Mail Weekly. *He later became editor of the* Australian Town and Country Journal *— a weekly, magazine-type publication. He continued throughout this time to write verse, short stories and essays — mainly for the* Bulletin. *His book,* Happy Dispatches, *published in 1934, includes some of his best journalistic pieces; he saw himself, he said in a modest foreword, as a looker-on who was able to see most of the game. It was an apt enough description of the role of the good reporter.*

The army under command of General Hunter left Bethlehem and came down here with a view of capturing the Free Staters under De Wet. It must be explained that by occupying all the towns and roads in the Orange River Colony the Boers were gradually forced down into the mountains at the eastern corner of the Colony, and touching the Basutoland border, and at length they were hemmed inside a circle of rugged mountains, through which only a few passes existed. There are real genuine mountains in this country. The whole place is about four thousand feet above the sea, and these mountain-chains run up another one thousand feet or fifteen hundred feet, and are as steep as the Rock of Gibraltar. Consequently, when we had them penned in a circle of mountains, with the Basutos at their back, it seemed a simple matter of tactics to block all the passes and advance on them from all sides and overwhelm them by numbers.

We moved out from Bethlehem and crossed the Jordan (a dry creek) and advanced on Retief's Nek. The only Australians with the forces were Colonel Williams, P.M.O., of the Division, and Captain Martin, his secretary. The colonel had the largest medical command in the army at the time, as Hunter had two infantry divisions and a lot of Yeomanry and sundries, and when Macdonald joined us with his Highlanders, it brought the strength of the troops under Hunter's command up to a very high figure.

As there were so many passes to hold it was mot possible to concentrate a very large force on any one point for fear of leaving the others unguarded, so we advanced on Retief's Nek with only the Highland Brigade — three regiments, Black Watch, Seaforths, and Highland Light Infantry — supported by the Sussex Regiment, three batteries of field artillery, two "cow" guns, and a lot of irregular mounted men, namely, Lovatt's Highland Gillies and Remington's Guides.

And now a word as to the Highlanders. These are the finest troops I have ever seen. They are much more intelligent-looking men than the ordinary Tommies. They are not particularly big men, but all strong, well-proportioned, and alert-looking, very neatly turned out, and evidently in a high state of discipline. The army people say that the Highlanders have not done as well as the Irish troops in this war, the Munsters and Dublin Fusiliers and the Royal Irish being cited as cases in point. There is no doubt the Highlanders were driven off at Magersfontein, and they failed to carry the Boer trenches at Paardeberg; but no other troops have been asked to do such tasks as were put to these men at those two places. Whatever be the respective merits of the troops, no one could fail to be struck by the bearing and appearance of the Highlanders, or the "Jocks", as they are always called in the army; and in this fight at Retief's Nek they acted up to the best possible standard.

Leaving Bethlehem, we advanced to within five miles of the Nek and camped at a farmhouse. Before us there rose a chain of hills about a thousand feet high, with a narrow gap or passage cleft between two of them. This passage, about a quarter of a mile wide, was the Nek through which we were to force our way. Along to the right-hand side of it the hills stretched for miles in an unbroken chain; on the left there were hills for a few miles, and then a patch of open ground, and then more hills. At the back of all were the mountains of Basutoland — great peaks and crags and fortresses of stone towering to the sky.

It was bitterly cold and windy the night of our camp there, and, behold, when we came out in the morning all the hills by the Nek and all the mountains at the back were white with snow. It was a glorious sight — those miles of snow-covered mountains gleaming in the sun. But we had something else to think about than the scenery. About ten o'clock the tramp of feet and the challenge of the pipes told us that the Highlanders were on the march. Grim and stern, with Fighting Macdonald at their head, the Highland Light Infantry filed out to march up the long valley of death that led to Retief's Nek; the Black Watch moved up parallel with them to attack the little bit of open ground that lay to the left of the hills guarding the Nek; and away on the right the Sussex Regiment advanced along the foot of the hills which converged on the attack of the Highland Light Infantry. The Seaforths were left in camp to guard the huge convoy we had with us. The two Generals, Hunter and Macdonald, took their positions on a big bare hill facing the Nek, and from that height the whole battlefield lay before us like a scene in a theatre. Down on the right hand was a long, clear, grassy valley leading up to the Nek. On the far side of this valley the Sussex Regiment could be seen making its way along the foot of the mountains. On the near side of the valley, and only a stone's throw below us, the Highland Light Infantry opened out into long lines and advanced straight up the frowning hills that guarded the pass; and on the left the Black Watch made a similar advance on the bare ground that lay to the left of the Nek.

This bare ground looked as if it might be easily taken, but it turned out that it simply led to the edge of a precipice some hundred feet deep, and down at the foot of the precipice was a huge plain something like the Hollow described by Boldrewood in *Robbery Under Arms*. It was into this Happy Valley that we wished to get, and the only way was to go through the Nek or down the sides of this precipice. The Black Watch pushed their attack first. They were to go to the edge of this precipice and see if there was any way down. The wailing of the pipes died away, and the men opened out and marched in open order across the brown grass, till suddenly a hot musketry fire broke out from the edge of the precipice itself, showing that the Boers had got up to it from the lower side and were holding it in force; in addition to this, a hot fire was opened from the chain of hills on either side. The men dropped in the grass and advanced, crawling along the ground, and actually seized an outlying hill, driving the Boers off it in confusion; but the price paid was too high, and, when the ambulances began to come in with wounded, and the second in command was fatally hit, the advance was stopped, and the men lay motionless in the grass under fire, while an attack was tried by the Highland Light Infantry and Sussex on the Nek itself. . .

It was a gallant attempt to make, and we could scarcely believe our eyes when we saw what looked like a string of black ants crawling up the rocks into the foot of the hill, while the Boer rifles rattled incessantly from the top. The Highlanders had got some little cover from a gully that ran out of the hill, and had sneaked in single file along this till they were at the foot of the hill. The Sussex had wormed their way along the rocks on the other side of the valley, but as soon as they got near the Nek itself a deafening discharge of rifle fire began, and our cannons were worked as fast as possible to try and keep it down. All along the line of hills there was incessant firing for about two hours, and no efforts of ours could dislodge the Boers from their rocks. Word came back from the Highland Light Infantry that they could not get up the rocks, and reluctantly General Hunter ordered a general withdrawal. Here Macdonald showed better judgement than the colonel in charge of the Sussex. The latter withdrew his

men at once, and they suffered severely in the retirement. Macdonald didn't try to move his men till dark, and they came back safely enough. We had about a hundred killed and wounded in the fight, and it is doubtful if the Boers lost ten. . .

Next morning (25th July) the Seaforths were brought away from the task of convoy guarding, and were sent to take this precipice, or rather to drive the Boers from it, in the hope of finding a way down. It was argued that where the Boers could get up the Highlanders could get down. . .

As soon as the signal was given for them to advance, they came along in a long line of prostrate figures, while a terrific fire was poured on to the edge of the precipice to cover their advance. Slowly they crept on, one or two giving little convulsive struggles and lying still. Suddenly, at some signal that we could not hear, they leapt to their feet, and dashed at the run for the edge of the cliff. One or two bowled over like shot rabbits, but the others held grimly on, and when they got within two hundred yards of the edge we saw the Boers bolting out from beneath the rocks. They had clambered down to the valley and jumped on to their horses, and in twos and threes and half-dozens they began to come out from under the rocks a hundred feet below the Highlanders. They split into small parties and galloped off at full speed. About a hundred came out, and by the time the first of the Highlanders got to the edge of the rocks the Boers could not have been three hundred yards off, and yet they rode away almost unharmed under a regular fusillade.

. . . we hope to be on the road home before long now, and it is just possible I may come home through Basutoland. We don't know at all what is doing anywhere else. There may be fighting at Pretoria or Lyndenberg; our Mounted Rifles may have caught Steyn and De Wet. All we know is that we are here in a little circle of hills, and that the Boers, about three thousand, are cooped up in the same circle of hills. So if they don't get out there is likely to be an end of the Free State army in these parts.

1900 An obscure public servant is claimed to be the bushranger 'Captain Starlight'

LUIGI RAMACIOTTI
Perth Morning Herald, 21 and 24 November 1900

One of the most romantic figures in bush-ranging history was Captain Starlight, who plundered northern New South Wales and Queensland in the late nineteenth century. He was immortalised by Rolf Boldrewood in his classic novel Robbery Under Arms.

A great deal of mystery has always surrounded the identity of the bandit. Some people have claimed that Boldrewood based his character on one man, others have suggested that he was an amalgam of several bushrangers of the day, and still others have said that Starlight was purely a figment of the novelist's imagination. As recently as 1972, a painstakingly researched book — Starlight, The Man and the Myth, *by P. H. McCarthy (The Hawthorn Press) — has been devoted to the subject. One of McCarthy's findings: a 'Starlight' did exist before the first publication of* Robbery Under Arms *(in serial form, in the* Sydney Mail *in 1881). That Starlight was Frank Pearson, alias 'Major' Patrick Pelly, who was tried and sentenced to death at Bathurst in May 1869 for the murder of Constable John McCabe.*

Pearson's sentence was commuted to life imprisonment, the first three years to be served in irons. Later, after another prison term, he drifted west across Australia, through Adelaide and the goldfields.

In December 1899, a public servant in the Western Australia Mines Department called Patrick Pelly died and the notice of his death attracted no special attention. Then, in November the following year, Luigi Ramaciotti, the State government rounds reporter of the Perth Morning Herald, *received some information.*

On 21 and 24 November 1900, the Perth Morning Herald *published the amazing story of the obscure public servant who had been a notorious bushranger, and who was believed to have been the prototype for Boldrewood's spectacular novel. It was one of the great scoops of its time. Ramaciotti, the reporter who discovered Pelly's identity and researched his story, later became chief of staff of the Perth* Morning Herald.

The plain announcement which was published in Perth and to the world at large on the morning of December 23 of last year that Mr. P. F. Pelly, or Major Pelly, as he was known to many in this city, had died from the effects of poison, self-administered, but "taken by mistake," did not cause a sensation. Indeed, the occurrence was treated as many others which come under the same category. Major Pelly was an exclusive character. He made no friends in Perth, but earned the respect of those with whom he came into contact. That circle was mainly limited to the officers of the Geological Survey Department of Perth and a few outsiders, whose business brought them into contact with that office. Therefore, no sensation was occasioned by the announcement of his sudden demise under peculiar circumstances. It is not our intention in this article to investigate the circumstances which led to his death, but to make the startling announcement that Major Pelly was none other than "Starlight," the notorious Australian bushranger of the "sixties", and to prove the statement by facts which have come within our knowledge, and which, beyond all question of doubt, are indisputable. . . Readers of Rolf Boldrewood's "Robbery Under Arms" are familiar with this once notorious personage. When he is introduced in that book he is referred to as an educated man, a man of extraordinary attainments, and "a cattle stealer, A BUSHRANGER, AND A GENTLEMAN."

In Perth it was recognised by those over him that he was a man of no mean attainments. Those who came into contact with him could not understand his strange ways. Only on rare occasions was he known to speak of himself. . .

His death, as stated, occurred on December 22 of last year. He was supposed to have taken cyanide of potassium in mistake for medicine. A copy of "The Morning Herald" containing a report of the inquest reached one Father Pelly, in Ireland, and he communicated with a brother confined in Pentridge Gaol, in Victoria, on the subject. This prisoner then wrote to Dr. Black, the coroner of Perth, what was looked upon as an extraordinary letter, but that document, on being handed over to the police, set them inquiring. The text of this letter might here be given in detail:

Pentridge Prison, April 25, 1900.
Dr. Black — Sir, — A letter I received from my brother, Father Elias C. Pelly, on the 21st inst., and which was dated 'Dublin, March 11,' and which informs me that a copy of the Perth 'Herald' was sent by someone in that city to an aunt of ours, Sister Mary Joseph, of the Convent of Mercy, Portumna, County Galway, Ireland, containing the report of an inquest at which you, sir, officiated as coroner, and where it was deposed by the landlady of the house of the deceased, Major Pelly, that he informed her he had a brother, the Rev. C. P. Pelly, a Roman Catholic priest, at Portumna, Co. Galway, Ireland, and that his friends in Ireland had forsaken him. . .

My people were naturally very much shocked by the newspaper report referred to, because they believed it had reference to me, although in truth, my position is little better.

George Kirkcaldy Pelly, my only brother in Australia, is a stout man, of fair hair and complexion, auburn moustache, about 39 years of age, 5ft. 10in. high, and about 16st. in weight. When last I saw him in 1890 he was clerk in the A.U.S.N. Co. at Brisbane, but I heard that he left there afterwards, and I have not heard from or of him since, except once, when I was told he was in Sydney. . . If the description I have given of my brother does not tally with that of the deceased, I am forced to think that Frank Gordon. . . must have assumed my name of Patrick, and adopted our family name on the strength of the information supplied by the papers and photos. A description of Gordon, as appeared to me in 1889, is as follows: — About 5ft. 7in. high, sallow complexioned, long face, high straight forehead, iron-grey hair (stiff and standing up without a parting), large eyes, strong-jointed hands. He had a jerky way of walking, caused by wounds received in the thigh and hip; was of a passionate and impulsive temperament, fierce when angered and affectionate when quiet.

Gordon was a well-informed man, and a particularly eloquent extempore speaker. . . . A letter addressed to Lady Pelly, Hearnsbrook-hall, Portumna, County Galway, Ireland, was sent to my mother after she had been dead some years by someone in Perth, who subscribed himself 'Your affectionate son, Pat.' I have a copy of this letter, which was an application for money.

God grant that neither my brother nor my friend Gordon may be identical with the deceased Pelly, but in furtherance of the ends of justice, and to allay the anxiety of my people, I trust you will let me know as soon as possible . . .

I remain, etc.,
PATRICK EDWARD PELLY

Without delay the authorities in Perth instituted inquiries. It was not a difficult matter to gain some information concerning Patrick Edward Pelly, of Pentridge. He was sent a photograph of 'Major Pelly' of Perth, deceased, and he immediately recognised it as that of his quondam friend and gaol companion, 'Gordon,' *alias* 'Starlight', the bushranger, who had served sentences in several gaols in New South Wales. . .

Emerging Nation
1901-1910

NE WAS LAID BY
E KING O'MALLEY, M.P.
ATE FOR HOME AFFAIRS.

12TH MARCH 1913.

King O'Malley, Minister for Home
Affairs, and Andrew Fisher, Prime
Minister (left) at the ceremony for
the founding of Canberra in 1913

1901   A nation is born on the first day of the new century

GEORGE COCKERILL
Melbourne Age, 2 January 1901

The first day of the twentieth century dawned brilliantly in Sydney, with high-powered sunlight bathing a city which had decorated itself as never before. There had been rain and thunder and lightning through the night, and the thousands of flags were heavy and sodden. There were flowers everywhere, and the brass bands were out early. It was Australia's first day as a nation, and it is difficult now to comprehend the degree of excitement and pride that radiated everywhere.

It was a day for dreams, even though many of the dreamers knew they would never really know how they all worked out. The first Australian government was being sworn in that day; the word 'colonial', as applied to Australian citizens and Australian goods — usually with a suggestion of inferiority — was about to quit the vocabulary. Many saw it as the real beginning of Australia's history — of a new Australia, with a surer and prouder national consciousness.

The nation's first prime minister was to be Edmund Barton, a successful barrister of five feet ten inches, and a sturdy, seventeen stone, with a placid disposition. He was a down-to-earth man who became embarrassed and visibly uncomfortable when civic dignitaries and newspapers took to calling him 'Australia's noblest son'.

The main reporters covering the heady events of Federation were George Cockerill (the Age*), David H. Maling (the* Argus*), H. W. Peters (Sydney* Daily Telegraph*) and W. R. Pratt (Sydney Morning Herald). Together they reported the formation of Australia's first Federal Government and the Proclamation of the Commonwealth, celebrated by six weeks of ceremonies and rejoicings. On Federation Day, half a million people watched miles of* processions through Sydney's streets to the pavilion in Centennial Park, where the proclamation of Australasian unity, signed by Queen Victoria, was read, and the Ministers of State for the new Commonwealth took the oath of allegiance to throne and country.*

Cockerill had fifty-four years' unbroken service as a newspaperman. He was born in Bendigo, and worked on the Bendigo Independent *and the* Ballarat Star *before he joined the* Age. *He led the Federal Parliament staff of the* Age *through the first years of the Commonwealth, became the paper's leader writer, under the editorship of G. F. H. Schuler, and took on the editorship of the Sydney* Daily Telegraph *in 1926. He spent his last working years as chief leader writer for the Melbourne* Herald.

George Cockerill worked at high speed all day, writing and telegraphing to Melbourne about 6000 words.

The Australian Commonwealth was inaugurated in Sydney today. The old century went out amidst rain and storm; the new one made its advent amidst overhanging clouds and portending thunder. Disunity and parochialism made a tearful exit. Federated Australia was nevertheless ushered into being on a day that was full of sunshine and inspiration of life and hope and the spirit of buoyant youth. The whole of the day's celebrations were a brilliant and complete success. But if the heavens had opened and the streets had been converted into sweeping torrents the Federalists of Sydney would not have been robbed of the fetes and ceremonies of today. Beneath the desire for a high holiday there was a joyous and deep seated sentiment in connection with the proceedings that would have found expression in spite of the convulsions of the elements. . .

During the last week or two, as the decorations have gradually grown in pretentiousness, people have begun to marvel at their extent and infinite variety. This morning, as viewed from the procession, the appearance of the city and its people was sufficient to captivate the senses. The start of it all was in the shady Domain, which the rain had clothed with brighter verdure. It wound out slowly under a grand arch of coal, against which the white pennants and flowers glistened like snow. Along by St. Mary's Cathedral 2000 little girls, all clad in white, shook 2000 little handkerchiefs at the gay Dragoons and Lancers. Grandstands reared to a height of 30 feet and 40 feet, on either hand, and gaily dressed crowds occupied every seat upon them. Every one of the people waved flags, threw flowers or sang or cheered. Arches succeeded arches — many of them had never before been heard of or thought of — in bewildering succession. "United Germany Greets United Australia"; "The United States Welcomes United Australia"; "We Welcome in Unity Our Comrades from Over the Seas" — these were some of the thousand mottoes which breathed the spirit of unity and universal brotherhood. At times, as the two miles of pageant — it took 55 minutes to pass a given point — slowly coiled along to the park, the galleries and grand stands rose on either hand so perpendicularly that the living walls appeared to be like the sides of some great excavation hewn into a mountain of living people, along the depths of which the march was travelling. How bright and how gay were all those happy sightseers!. . .

There was so much of interest and of beauty along that triumphant pageant that human eyesight lamentably lost its range. Attention was arrested within a few yards, and all the piles of people and flags and flowers beyond were comparatively lost to view owing to the attractiveness of the detail near at hand. A mile of waving plumes, of glittering lances, of giant bobbing busbies, of prancing horses, of stately plumed life guardsmen, with flashing helmets and breast plates; of swarthy Maories, sitting great lean horses like statues; of romantic looking Indians in gorgeous Oriental costumes; of thickets of swords and lances — these were the main features of the procession as a spectacle. The sight of those walls of stately troops in all the circumstance of glorious war stirred the hearts of the people until their senses were whirled away with their excess of exuberant feeling. They laughed and cheered and kept on cheering, while some of them wiped away tears which they could not explain, for there was no explanation other than the overwhelming excess of patriotism, of loyalty and of kindly feeling. . .

Nearly up to the very last moment — up to the time, almost, when the official signal was given to "press the button", and so impart life and motion to the day's great pageant, men were in many cases briskly at work in Sydney streets giving here and there a last improving touch to the scheme of decorations. As for all else, everybody had ceased to bustle and look businesslike, and is staring open-mouthed along vast avenues of life and of color. The great day is here, and all that remains is to write its history and to count its cost! But where is the caitiff who talks of cost? The heaviest taxpayer who looks from his seventh story window is now deliriously waving his handkerchief at the brass bands, who pass at every minute playing stirring melodies; at the walls of scarlet clad soldiers; at the giant busby bearers; at the proud and jaunty lancers; at the "death or glory boys" from Victoria, and the torrent of all classes of soldiers, consuls, Cabinet Ministers and civic dignitaries who sweep along through the jostling, buzzing, expectant throngs in wait for the starting of the procession. Prominent amongst the sightseers is a well-known Melbourne man, who takes his stand at the corner of George and Park streets, near the Melbourne arch — good patriot he! — and from a fifth floor window gazes down upon the stirring scene, manifestly enraptured at the spectacle. A hundred cameras are pointing in all directions, and he is included in fifty of their negatives. . .

Incessantly, there arises a loud, unceasing buzz — the conversation of a multitude. Above the buzz, sharp and clear arise the shrill "Commemoration medals" and "Commonwealth programs." Now and again the buzz is overborne by the blaring of a brass band; by ringing voices singing Soldiers of the Queen, and by fusillades of cheering that die away, only to be re-echoed from some neighbouring street.

Look down George Street! The Collins-street of Sydney is bedecked in its gayest apparel as it may never be bedecked again. Multiply Park-street — with its arches, its flags, its pictures and its mottoes — by ten and you will have a faint idea of George-street as its decorations now shimmer in the sunlight. Further away, round in Moor-street, near the General Post Office, if you could possibly see that far, myriad banners flutter round dense thickets of poles, with flashing gilt tops and stems as gay as the highest toned colors splashed abroad with a lavish hand can make them. In Queen's place, where the marble statue of her Majesty the Queen has been crowned and wreathed and ribboned in all conceivable ways with stripes of many colored incandescent lamps, lofty plaster pillars support artistic representations of her Majesty's forces. Down by St. Mary's Cathedral, the clouds of banners are even heavier and denser than they are in Park-street, and they lose nothing of their heaviness through the incessant showers of patriotism.

The city was wreathed and bespangled with garlands as far as Centennial Park, the beautiful grounds of which will be historic as the scene of the proclamation of the Australian Commonwealth. As the procession filed under the towering arch of flowers and greenery at the Park entrance all the heights and hollows of that delightful bit of rolling country began to grow black and white and pink and blue with people. . .

When the ceremonies were in progress, the whole of the park, as far as the eye could reach, was covered with dense crowds of people. One estimate is that the number present equalled a quarter of a million. They rose in tier upon tier on either hand, and to three of the main points of the compass. It was impossible to see beyond them. On one hand was a vast natural gallery that looked from a distance like a field stocked to its utmost capacity with white flowering dahlias. These apparent dahlias were

15,000 school children, 10,000 of them white muslin clad, sweet voiced little girls gathered to sing praises and Federal odes, when the proclamation had been made. To the right of the children were 1500 male choristers. On the outer ring were the great public, but around the pavilion and between that dainty structure and the choirs were large vacant spaces still to be filled. They were not long vacant.

The pealing notes of a bugle rent the air. The next instant gaily caparisoned Imperial soldiers and Australian forces were swinging along in battalions, and with enthusiasm creating precision, forming up in solid sections. Every foot of ground available was soon a solid mass of glittering gold braid, silver helmets, cuirasses and khakee and scarlet. The splendour of these Imperial regiments and the gallant bearing of our soldier boys have frequently been described. Today in the sunlight and in the light of the momentous occasion they all seemed far more resplendent than we had ever previously seen them. While, however, the sunshine was a great feature in the spectacle, those bold British soldiers would have been extremely thankful if it could have been omitted from the programme. More than one has gone down before it, and had sought temporary relief in the ambulance. It was no wonder. Those giant black and hairy busbies which many of them were compelled to swelter under are as high and as heavy as a large sized nailcan. Still, despite all drawbacks in in this or any other direction, they bore themselves like British soldiers always do in the face of difficulty, and marched with an exactitude that would have defied comparison by any other body of troops in the world. . .

1901   Federation is celebrated and Australia's first Prime Minister prepares for elections

T. W. HENEY
Sydney Morning Herald, 9 January 1901

The week of celebration which followed the proclamation of the Commonwealth gave pressmen a strenuous task — and they handled it well. The final ceremony of the week was a banquet, held in honour of the journalists. The following day, on 9 January, the Sydney Morning Herald *commented on the function in a leading article written by T. W. Heney. Heney, a former reporter on the Sydney* Daily Telegraph *and editor of the Wilcannia* Times, *was to become editor of the* Sydney Morning Herald *two years later. His article made the point that Federation represented a triumph for the Australian press, which had campaigned strenuously for the cause:*

It was a good idea on the part of those who arranged the Commonwealth festivities to close the week with an entertainment to the members of the press — visiting or local. During the previous days of this memorable week, the programme had consisted of pageant or banquet, at which the function of the journalist was far less to enjoy himself than to record the enjoyment of others. His duty was to secure a report of every part of the inaugural celebrations, neglecting no salient detail, and omitting no sentence from the lips of a representative man, so that for absentees and for future generations this historic period might possess a complete contemporary picture. This was no light or perfunctory task, and all who know the circumstances in which such records of the day's events are secured for the next day's perusal are well aware that the reporter's part in the inaugural festival has been one of heavy and steady work. . . If it was some spirit of recognition for the hard work of the reporter, both special to this occasion and in general, in which the dinner

of last night was planned, it deserves on the part of the press a cordial acknowledgement. The week has been an exacting one for all concerned in journalism, and if the result of their labours has been gratifying to the community, and not unworthy of the beautiful and historic spectacles presented, the men of the press are repaid for their work by public approbation. . . In the sweep of a long programme, where event treads hard upon event, it is difficult to keep record of all which has been justly and fitly spoken; and it may be that, as is not unusual, at the end of a feast or in the closing hours of the inauguration, something ungrudged, spontaneous, and generous has been said of the aid which journalism has contributed to Federation. But that it is so hard to fix upon anything of this character is in itself an argument.

And yet it is the simple truth that when politicians turned their backs, when Parliament ignored or thwarted the Federal cause, when sections of the community derided Federation as visionary, or condemned it as mischievous, when Federation was in some quarters viewed as disguised separation from the mother country, and when the Federal leaders themselves were all but hopeless and could hardly get a hearing for their ideas, it was the Australian press which never faltered nor turned cold. In the columns of a hundred journals, from the metropolitan dailies to the country weeklies, the hope of a Federated Australia was nourished and kept before the people. . . Perhaps it may be said that in this long advocacy of an unpopular cause the press builded better than it knew. But the journalists will remember with pride, however the currents of political gratulation may flow, that this, too, is one of those causes which, adopted in the days of their uncompromising beginnings, the press has helped to nourish and stimulate into their triumphant maturity... In the darkest hours, when Sir Henry Parkes's Government went out, when Mr. Barton could do nothing, when commercial reverses befell us, when Federation stood still in Parliament and Cabinet from Perth to Sydney, whatever encouragement the leaders had rested upon the press, and we may add the pulpit, upon some who in this country or in England and America were watching us with interest, upon the yet unspoken instincts of the people. Well are they justified in this season of world-wide congratulation who in the past committed themselves and their journals to an unknown cause, and strove through dark years with tireless courage and resource to arouse the public to the issues set before them for acceptance.

Edmund Barton, the nation's first Prime Minister, began to prepare for the first elections soon after he took office. This poll took place on 29 and 30 March 1901, and caused the Barton Ministry to remain in office.

Barton presented his Government's policies at a meeting in the West Maitland Town Hall on 17 January. He promised to select a site for the federal capital as soon as possible, and to create a High Court, an Interstate Commission, and an efficient public service. He said that a Postal Department and a Defence Department would soon join the already-established Customs Department. He proposed to extend conciliation and arbitration beyond the limits of one State, to build railways to Western Australia and Broken Hill, to create a uniform railway gauge between the eastern capitals, to introduce female federal franchise, to establish a federal system of old-age pensions, to introduce legislation to prevent an influx of Asiatic labour, and to prevent any further importation of kanakas.

He also talked about federal-state financial relationships — a subject which was to remain a constant source of conflict in Australian politics. This is how the Maitland Daily Mercury *reported him on that subject on 18 January 1901:*

The power of direct taxation of the Commonwealth I agree is a power not to be lightly or rashly exercised. For you will understand that, as the States will upon the passing of the uniform tariff lose the power to raise revenue by Customs or excise duties, the Commonwealth Parliament would be doing them a wrong by invading that province of taxation wherein alone they can augment their income. We ought not to cripple them by using our power of direct taxation, unless under the stress of some great emergency; we ought to leave them free to enlarge their revenues by direct taxation, seeing that they will have no power to resort to Customs or excise duties if they want additional revenue. The rash exercise of the power of direct taxation would be dangerous to the States. I cannot see why it should be supposed that the policy of the Commonwealth will be one in which the States shall suffer. The claims of the States will have to be considered. I can assure you that it will not be the policy of the Commonwealth Government to cripple or do anything that will militate against the interests of the States. I can assure you that the interests of each State will be considered in the imposition of a fiscal policy. It would in my opinion be an act of insanity to do anything that would militate against the States who have built up industries under the principles of protection. I can assure you that any adjustments made in the tariff will not affect the States to any material extent. I need not point out to you that in this new path we have entered upon in this onward march in legislation, the Commonwealth Government has many changes for which to provide. I can assure you that the aim and object of the Commonwealth Government is to make the increase of taxation upon the people as light as possible. Any change made by the Government will be made with that object clearly in view. Now some of our critics have said that the tariff must be a high one. They have estimated that from direct taxation we must get at least £700,000. They had therefore contended that the Commonwealth tariff must necessarily be a high one. Now I need not say that it will not be the aim of the Government to interfere

Prime Minister Edmund Barton is seated second from the left in this photograph of the first Australian Federal Ministry, with Lord Tennyson, Australia's second Governor-General, in the centre

with the financial arrangements of the various States. No doubt a very large revenue will be required to carry on the government of the Commonwealth, and the arrangements for that purpose have been entrusted to my friend Mr Kingston in whom I have the utmost confidence, and if he fails, I can assure you I do not know who will be likely to succeed (Applause.) In the framing of a tariff for the Commonwealth Government, composed of six States, most of them protectionist, the policy of freetrade is manifestly impracticable. In such circumstances majority rule must prevail, and a policy of freetrade would be impossible and would in any case be insane. . .

You must also recollect that within two years of the inauguration of the Commonwealth, all intercolonial duties will drop. The States will at once get the advantage of intercolonial freetrade. . .

I am a protectionist as are nearly all my colleagues, but in making that admission I do not wish to be misunderstood. I do not wish it to be inferred that that explanation has been forced upon me. (Applause.) The tariff will not be in any sense prohibitive. It will be a moderate tariff. The Government will certainly not do anything that will be likely to cripple industries. We will have to consider the circumstances of each State and the fact

that capital has been invested in various industries. It will be the Government's main object in the formulation of a tariff, to do so with the view of assisting and encouraging those native industries. (Applause.) I am a protectionist and I will endeavour to protect as far as possible the productions of our own soil. (Cheers.) The Government will refrain from legislating in the interests of any one colony, to the detriment of any other. I will not attempt to impose a tariff of a freetrade character such as that which prevails in New South Wales, neither will the Government try to place on a high tariff, such as that which exists in Victoria. . .

Our industries have grown up under protection and the Government will not be a party to a policy that would be their destruction. It will be a tariff that will produce sufficient revenue without discouraging industries. It will be a tariff calculated to maintain employment: in other words a business tariff. . . The first tariff will be thoroughly liberal and at the same time of a purely Australian character. The Ministry will not take any action that will have the effect of destroying State industries, and the Commonwealth will not be ushered in by the pattering of the feet of people driven out of employment.

1901   Australia's senior military reporter is killed in action against the Boers

J. A. CAMERON
Perth West Australian, 12 March 1901

William J. Lambie left for the Boer War with the first Victorian contingent in the troopship Medic *on 28 October 1899. Having covered the Sudan war in 1885, he was the senior military reporter with the Australian forces. He accompanied the Australian relief column which headed for Kimberley; most of the newly-arrived Australians were upset at missing the action of the Boer commando counter-attack. Lambie did not share their mood: 'I regard our absence from Magersfontein as little short of providential in the light of the disastrous events of the day,' he wrote. The British were decimated at dawn; when the Australians arrived, all of them were put in the saddle, even the infantry.*

Lambie, who had been wounded in the Sudan, reported that the Australian slouch hat resembled the campaign hat of 'Johnny Boer', and could attract British bullets; the British helmet was substituted. In February, Lambie was at the Colesburg front. It was flat land dotted with kopjes — low masses of broken rocks which gave the Boers splendid cover. He reported in the Age *and* Sydney Morning Herald *that the Australians were 'riding out in small bodies to draw the fire of the enemy and so locate them'.*

On 9 February, Lambie and another correspondent, A. G. 'Smiler' Hales — a Western Australian from the goldfields who was representing the London Daily News — *accompanied a patrol of thirty Victorians and eighteen Tasmanians. J. A. Cameron, of the* West Australian, *decided not to accompany the other two; he elected to stay close to the Western Australian contingent, which was expected to go into action at any time.*

Hales later wrote: 'Lambie and I dropped behind the Tasmanian troops to compare notes, when 40 Boers suddenly dashed out from a ravine. They demanded that we should surrender. We refused, and tried to gallop through. The Boers, however, fired a volley after us, and Lambie fell dead, with two bullets through his head and one through his heart. A bullet grazed my right temple.' Hales fell to the ground, and when he woke he was among 'rough-looking but extremely kind captors', who chided him for having been dressed in khaki like combatants and for trying to gallop through.

Cameron, whose dispatch told of Lambie's death, was allowed through the Boer lines the following day with Major Reay, of the Melbourne Herald. *They were shown the grave of Lambie, the first member of the Australian contingent to die in action.*

In Melbourne, the premier of Victoria, Mr McLean, addressed the Legislative Assembly:

Mr Speaker, I desire to express my deep regret at the sad intelligence conveyed to us through the papers this day with regard to the first death that has occurred in connection with troops sent from Victoria to South Africa. The gentleman who has been killed was well known to members of this House. He was an able journalist and an excellent authority on military matters, and I am sure his genial face will be very much missed in the chamber. Of course, I need hardly tell you that I refer to Mr. Lambie, the war correspondent of the *Age.*

Here is J. A. Cameron's dispatch:

On the day the West Australians were distinguishing themselves near Slingersfontein the Tasmanians, under Captain Cameron, had a hot time with the Boers on a plain near

Jasfontein, 12 miles further round towards the rear of our position. It is noteworthy in this war that our men almost invariably fight on the plain while the enemy occupies the hills. The peculiarity of South African contour is that it is mingled kopje and veldt, hill and plain. If it were all mountain ranges things would be more equalised; if the Boers took up a position on a range, our men could have their choice of the most convenient adjoining hills, or if it were all plains it would be still better. . .

It was some time during the retirement to Jasfontein that Mr. Lambie was shot and Mr. Hales captured. A prisoner captured by our guides who saw the occurrence, states that the two correspondents were riding together apart from the rest, and that Lambie was killed instantly by a bullet through the head, and that Hales's horse stumbled and threw him, bruising and partially stunning him.

Next day Major Reay, of the "Melbourne Herald," and I rode out to Jasfontein for the purpose of entering the Boer lines under a white flag to definitely ascertain the fate of the missing correspondents before cabling to their relatives in Australia. We found that Captain Cameron was just about to despatch Lieutenant Heritage on the same errand, and to ascertain the fate of the missing Tasmanians. Lieutenant Heritage, who was most civilly treated by the Boers, returned in a few hours with Mr. Lambie's watch and other articles found on his body together with a message from General De La Rey to the effect that if Major Reay and I went out we would be shown the place where he was buried. Lieutenant Heritage was fired on by our own pickets when returning. . .

During the four or five hours we were in the Boer lines we chatted freely on a variety of topics, but they never asked us a question that we had to refrain from answering, or even to parry. Their courtesy was absolutely flawless. Most of them could speak our language, and I heard better English among them than among our own Tommies. I did not hear an oath or single disagreeable expression, though there were over a hundred rough-looking men within hearing distance of us for at least an hour. Than those who acted as our guides I do not expect, speaking as I found them, to ever meet a manlier or more naturally gentlemanly lot of men. . .

The Boer horses were in excellent condition, a small breed, quick and light as cats. Our men with their heavy equipment would break them down in a few days, but the Boer, though an equally big man, rides several stone lighter. The mobility of the Boer horseman is simply marvellous. That is their strong point — not their shooting. Ranges are too long now for accurate marksmanship — it is principally a matter of blazing at a general enemy a mile off, or at men lying down or moving over a plain in extended order, which is much like trying to hit the wires in a wire fence. Captain Cameron and Lieutenant Brown, both cavalry officers accustomed to the agile movements of light Indian cavalry, say that the way the mounted Boers appear and disappear among the kopjes is almost magical. Nothing seems to stop the speed of their movements. They go over and round the boulders as if on the grassy veldt. At times one could almost fancy they went underground, so quickly and invisibly do they move.

Several of the Boers reiterated the statement that our artillery does not do very much harm. They say that our rifle fire at about two thousand yards has been responsible for most of their losses. As for the lance and the bayonet, they think them so useless that they do not carry them themselves.

1902   Two Australian soldiers are shot by a firing squad in South Africa

FRANK FOX
Bulletin, 19 April 1902

During the second World War, two members of the 2/14 Battalion, AIF, Chris Walker and Ken von Bibra, both former Melbourne newspapermen, were reported shot dead by a firing squad of pro-Vichy French Senegalese troops. It was claimed that they had continued to fight on after a cease-fire; comrades of the two men claimed that the fighting had been so confused that Walker and von Bibra had no way of knowing of any cease-fire. But the only Australian soldiers ever to have been shot by a firing squad following a court-martial were Harry 'the Breaker' Morant and P. J. Handcock.

Both were members of the Bushveldt Carabineers, an irregular force fighting against the Boers in South Africa. Morant was a colorful horseman and writer of verse, a contemporary of 'Banjo' Paterson. Born in England, he migrated to Queensland in the 1880s — some said, because of an unpaid gambling debt — and gained a reputation as a dare-devil rider. For ten years he contributed ballads to the Bulletin, *most of them concerned with life in the outback.*

When the Boer War broke out, Morant went to South Africa as a sergeant with the 2nd South Australian Contingent. He was given a commission in the Transvaal Constabulary, but appeared some months later as a lieutenant in the Bushveldt Carabineers. In 1901 a fellow-officer named Hunt, a particularly close friend of Morant, was shot from a Boer farmhouse and his body was mutilated; in revenge for this, Morant and three other officers — P. J. Handcock, G. R. Witton and Lieutenant Picton — apparently decided to shoot any Boer prisoners who fell into their hands. Morant was charged three times with having done so. With Handcock and Witton

he was sentenced to death; Witton's sentence was commuted to life imprisonment, and he was freed within three years. Picton, a brave soldier who had fought previously in Algeria and the Congo with the French Foreign Legion, was found guilty of manslaughter only and was cashiered.

Morant was executed with Handcock outside Pretoria on 25 February 1902. There were eighteen men in the firing party and 'the Breaker' was flamboyant to the end. He refused a blindfold, looked down the muzzles of the battery of rifles, and said, 'Shoot straight. Don't make a mess of it.' The execution caused a great deal of controversy in Australia, partly because of the secrecy which surrounded it. 'Banjo' Paterson claimed later, in reminiscences published in the Sydney Morning Herald, *that Morant had been badly affected by the discovery of the disfigured body of his friend Hunt. He had told his men that he had orders to shoot for various offences, had questioned a man he believed to be a spy, and had then shot him. The victim had turned out to be a Dutch padre. Paterson claimed Morant had been 'drunk with his one day of power'. He wrote: 'He had always been the underdog, and now he was up in the stirrups it went to his head like wine.' Whatever the degree of blame, the Federal Government declared that henceforth no Australian serving abroad would suffer the death penalty before his case was fully investigated in Australia, and only then if duly authorised from Australia.*

One of Morant's last letters, sent to a friend, asked him to 'see the Bulletin *people in Sydney town and tell 'em all the facts'. In the* Bulletin *after news of the execution became known, Frank (later Sir Frank) Fox wrote about 'the Breaker's' death on the* Red Page, *where much* of Morant's own verse had been published. Fox, writing as 'Frank Renar', published Morant's last verse for the first time; it had been written in gaol, and it was called: 'Butchered to Make a Dutchman's Holiday'. Fox wrote that 'the Breaker' would become an Australian bush hero: 'his statue in the Valhalla where the venerated Ned Kelly and Starlight wear their haloes unabashed.'

Fox, born in Adelaide in 1874, held down many editorial jobs on Australian newspapers, then went to England, where he became a correspondent during the Balkan war, and an army officer in World War One.

"He died game." That is the most charitable epitaph which a truthful acquaintance can put over the tomb of "The Breaker" — assuming that his acts were, as alleged, the result of cruelty, and not the result of "orders" which he had no alternative but to obey. It may be said of him as of many another of his kind: There was nothing in his life that so befitted him as his way of going out of it; and in his case, as in the case of others, that graceful exit will atone in many minds for sorry stumblings whilst playing his little part on the world's stage,

> Where every actor must perform with art —
> Or laugh it through, and make a farce of all,
> Or learn to bear with grace his tragic part.

Morant at least bore his tragic end with that air of reckless, courageous *diablerie* which is the most suitable mood of all for buccaneer or bushranger or S'African "irregular", who has come to the end of his tether and must at last stand facing the muzzle instead of holding the stock of the murderous rifle. That grace will at least enroll him among the Jack Shepp-ards, Dick Turpins, and Captain Starlights of history; and the man who wants to live in the hearts of the people — the great, unreasoning, unthinking people — might be in worse company.

Heine, translating into the language of poetry a phrase of Gibbon's philosophy, tells how the Tree of Humanity carries down to its latest years the marks of those who scarred it with sword or axe, but has no memory for the gardeners who watered and sheltered it and tilled its soil. The world, in truth, remembers its soldiers and highwaymen long after it has forgotten its philosophers and teachers. Morant, shooting and being shot, has won a fame which his somewhat respectable verses would never have gained for him. He will certainly be an Australian bush hero of the future, his statue in the Valhalla where the venerated Ned Kelly and Starlight wear their haloes unabashed.

Morant kept up his hearty defiance of fate to the very last. Likewise he kept to the very last his utter incapacity to appreciate the fact that he had done wrong. Picturing himself as a patriotic Robin Hood, as an Empire-builder sacrificed for his zeal, "The Breaker" wrote in gaol these verses . . .

BUTCHERED TO MAKE A DUTCHMAN'S HOLIDAY

> In prison cell I sadly sit,
>   A d——d crest-fallen chappie!
> And own to you I feel a bit —
>   A little bit — unhappy!
>
> It really ain't the place nor time
>   To reel off rhyming diction —
> But yet we'll write a final rhyme
>   Whilst waiting cru-ci-fixion!
>
> No matter what "end" they decide —
>   Quick-lime or "b'iling ile," sir?
> We'll do our best when crucified
>   To finish off in style, sir!
>
> But we bequeath a parting tip
>   For sound advice of such men,
> Who come across in transport ship
>   To polish off the Dutchmen!
>
> If you encounter any Boers
>   You really must not loot 'em!
> And if you wish to leave these shores,
>   For pity's sake, DON'T SHOOT 'EM!!
>
> And if you'd earn a D.S.O.,
>   Why every British sinner
> Should know the proper way to go
>   Is: "ASK THE BOER TO DINNER!"
>
> Let's toss a bumper down our throat,
>   Before we pass to Heaven,
> And toast: "the trim-set petticoat
>   We leave behind in Devon."

. . . The Last Rhyme and Testament of Tony Lumpkin —   THE BREAKER.

1902　William Lane's 'New Australia' dream collapses in Paraguay

MARY GILMORE
Sydney Daily Telegraph, 5 November 1902

One of the people who decided to become part of William Lane's New Australia settlement in Paraguay in the early 1890s was Mary Jean Cameron, a schoolteacher who had ambitions to write. She had been born in Goulburn, New South Wales, in 1865, had met Bulletin *editor A. G. Stephens, poet John Farrell, William Lane — the three people who had most influence on her life, she later wrote — and Henry Lawson in Sydney, and had become a follower of Lane.*

Lane surrendered leadership of the New Australia movement in 1894, and he and his followers set up the new settlement of Cosme, about twenty miles from the New Australia settlement. Mary Cameron was thirty when she arrived in Cosme; she married William Alexander Gilmore there in 1897, and returned to Australia in 1902. Following her return, she published a series of three articles, reporting on what had happened to the New Australia dream, in the Sydney Daily Telegraph *of 5, 6 and 7 November that year.*

In 1907 Mary Gilmore began writing a women's page for the Worker, *Brisbane, and continued to conduct that page for twenty-three years: she wrote poetry and prose, and in 1936 she was created a Dame of the British Empire for her services to literature.*

Her article on Colonia Cosme, a first-class piece of reporting, gave a sad picture of the collapse of a dream. Not all members of the settlement returned to Australia, though. The Sydney journalist Gavin Souter visited Paraguay in 1965, and found descendants of the original settlers.

Colonia Cosme is the outcome of New Australia. It may be remembered that the Paraguayan Government granted the New Aus-

tralians a large tract of land for settlement purposes. But there was never any real unity in New Australia. After William Lane left, first one person was chairman, then another; one arrangement followed another; troubles and dissensions grew, parties formed ready to cut one another's throats, each one petitioning the Government against the other, till at last that most long-suffering of bodies, the Paraguayan Government, interfered, and sent out an official to fix up things and report.

The result was that the colony ceased, in the original sense of the word, to be a colony, the Government giving each settler so many acres of land for his individual use. The Paraguayan and the New Australian live side by side, equal under the law, and equal socially. The Paraguayan gives a dance and the white man attends it. The white man gives one and the Paraguayan comes. A wedding is the signal for an all-round drunk, Paraguayan and Australian drinking out of the same bottle. It is easy to get drunk in Paraguay. Everyone grows his own sugar-cane and makes his own rum. So far, though there are half-caste children, there have been no marriages with the Paraguayans.

When the Cosme people, about 58, left New Australia, William Lane, though he could have made any subdivision of the land and cattle, gave up, with the consent of those with him, and with a Quixotism that we cannot but admire, all claim to everything. The new colonists set out with a small supply of food, the general personal baggage, a few implements and tools, and a few head of cattle. None had the least idea where the ultimate settlement would be, but there was plenty of enthusiasm and great faith, and nobody minded things much, even when, later on, as Nurse Grace said, they "had to go to bed early because they got so hungry sitting up." . . .

They had begun to learn that in a fertile country like Paraguay, with a warm climate and a regular rainfall, a large area of land was a deadweight rather than an advantage. Thanks to friends in Scotland, money was forthcoming, and five and a half leagues of land were bought 13 miles from a railway station, in the fork of two inexhaustible rivers, the Pirapo and the Tibicuari. This was the new home, and here they came in July, 1894.

As they entered into possession the thick rain was pouring down, the loose Paraguayan soil was soft and soaking, and the long wet grass was up to their knees as they tramped through it. "But," said a woman to me long afterwards, "it seemed like heaven. It was our own, and there was peace." Utterances such as this show the condition that had prevailed in New Australia, and the anxious uncertainty of the pioneers of Cosme after they had left that colony and lay camped at Codas. . .

Of course, no money passes current in the Cosme colony in Paraguay, either between members or between the colony and members. All share alike in whatever the public labor produces. As some things are not as plentiful as others, and as many things have to be bought, a general system of fixed allowance is adopted. . .

Among the minor disadvantages of the Cosme colony, in Paraguay, are the sameness of the food and the want of meat. Three times a day the colonist eat corn meal, sweet potatoes, and mandioca in some form or other, making variety by leaving one of them out. These three things are more "same" than one who does not know them can possibly imagine. . . . The insect pests are unimaginable. There are many varieties of mosquitoes, from a little brute that stands on his head, and so gets through all but the best and finest net, to a large kind that you can kill every time he comes near you. But, by the irony of fate, the little fellow stings badly, and the big fellow hardly at all. . .

No wonder people tucked their mosquito nets well in when they went to bed. There were dozens of exciting experiences with the reptiles, but only one woman was bitten.

None of the sickness to which we were subject ended fatally. A malarial fever, with or without ague, was the most prevalent. When neglected it turned to intermittent fever. The poor living gave rise to a kind of boil or abscess, probably a carbuncle, which broke out near the elbows, wrists, knees and spine. Sometimes these left holes you could put your thumb in. Parmidora was another amiable affliction, but there were few cases of it. It was a raw open sore, without pus or scab, eating out skin and flesh. Without seeming to enlarge it travelled all round the patient's thumb, healing behind as it went forward. The treatment was cotton wool cut to the exact size and soaked in carbolic and fitted into the cavity. . .

All the deaths that have occurred in the colony in eight years have been caused by accident, with the exception of two which were due to croup and cancer. The general tone of the colony's health is low. This may be due to the poor food. One cannot tell, not even by the native, for he, too, lives poorly. On the other hand, the food may be the best for the climate, and the climate may be the sole cause of the debility. In early times we held ourselves superior to native ways, but as time went on the question was often put, weren't they, after all, the best for the climate? And, bearing this out, of late years the summer working day has been shortened, and the midday break lengthened, and the siests become almost a universal thing for men. Owing to the necessity of taking care of their clothes, some of the men took to working without their shirts. The effect of the sun was to make the skin as dark as a native's.

In conclusion, I would say, we have lived in the colony for years, my husband having been one of the pioneers from West Australia. We have disagreed with its action in several things, we have not been satisfied with its trend in some. Yet Australia has shown us nothing as good as the colony in its kindliness, its homeliness, its sympathy in times of trouble, its freedom from anxiety, for the woman particularly, and the unit generally.

1903   The famous newspaperman, George 'Chinese' Morrison, returns to Australia

A. B. PATERSON
Sydney Evening News, 21 January 1903

Andrew Barton 'Banjo' Paterson and George Ernest Morrison were two of the best-known newspaperman of their time. They met for the first time in China in September 1901, and Paterson wrote later:

I found Morrison at a watering-place outside Chefoo. I knew his record fairly well; for, as a young man, he had explored New Guinea and northern Australia in the days when the blacks were bad. The blacks put a spear into him. He got his black boy to cut off the shaft of the spear, but never had the head of the spear taken out till he got to Melbourne. A man like that takes some stopping.

In person, he was a tall ungainly man with a dour Scotch face and a curious droop at the corner of his mouth — a characteristic I had noticed in various other freaks, including Olive Schreiner, the gifted authoress of *The Story of an African Farm*. Morrison had with him a China-coast doctor named Molyneux who had acted as a sort of Dr Watson to Morrison's Sherlock Holmes. At first Morrison talked mainly about women, and if there was any unbalance in his mentality it was probably in that direction. I plied Molyneux with questions and thus got Morrison talking. Any answers that Molyneux gave me were annotated and corrected by Morrison, and by the time we had lunch I had got the uncrowned King of China talking freely.

It was an education to listen to him, for he spoke with the self-confidence of genius. With Morrison it was not a case of "I think"; it was a case of "I know". Of the three great men of affairs that I had met up to that time — Morrison, Cecil Rhodes, and Winston Churchill — Morrison had perhaps the best record. Cecil Rhodes, with enormous capital at his back, had battled with Boers and Basutos; Churchill, with his father's prestige and his mother's money to help him, had sailed on life's voyage with the wind strongly behind him; but Morrison had gone into China on a small salary for *The Times* and had outclassed the smartest political agents of the world — men men with untold money at the back of them.

Then in 1903 Morrison returned to Australia. Paterson, who was editing the Sydney Evening News *at the time, told Australians about the legendary Peking correspondent of* The Times *in this report:*

Today there arrives in Sydney one of the most notable Australians of the present day — Dr Morrison, *The Times* correspondent in China.

It is necessary to visit China itself in order to get any clear idea of the responsibilities and difficulties of Dr Morrison's position. The huge Chinese Empire has for years been jealously guarded from outside intrusion; just a few treaty ports have been thrown open, and the fringe of the country has barely been touched; and yet, so quickly has the trade grown, that in 1898 China imported over seven million pounds worth of English goods — almost equal to the New South Wales imports for the same year. Besides the English trade, there is the American, German, French, Russian and Japanese trade of China waiting to be developed; and not only is there trade development to carry on, but there are in China undreamed of sources of wealth — fertile lands that will grow anything, mines of fabulous richness, water rights for irrigation to be snapped up, permits to be obtained to make railways that will soon be carrying their millions of passengers annually; all these prizes lie in China awaiting the hardy adventurer who can get in as "first robber". In every Chinese treaty port there is a restless crowd of adventurers of all nations — English, Russian, American, German and Jew — all scheming and struggling to secure land, to secure railway rights, to secure water rights, or to secure mining rights. There are officials to be bribed or bullied into granting concessions — officials whose oath their dearest friends would not believe, and whose written promise is a mere piece of waste paper. There are political adventurers, pulling all sorts of hidden strings, and producing all sorts of amazing gyrations among the puppets of Chinese politics. There are days when the mere knowledge that an agreement has been signed by a Chinese official may be worth ten thousand pounds in cold cash. There are rumours, lies, threats, open violence to be encountered; and among this tumult and strife there moves one man to whose knowledge all white men — Russian, American, German, and Jew alike — defer, Morrison, the Australian, who represents *The Times* in China.

It is hard to explain the secrets of his success in getting information. It is not the amount of money that he has to spend, because the utmost sum that *The Times* could allow for secret service money would be a mere fleabite to the amount that some of the concessionaries and political agents would give for early and exclusive information. And yet so marvellously does he manage that the full text of the important treaty, signed in 1901 at the conclusion of hostilities, was actually wired by him to his paper, and was being read and discussed in English homes, several days before the document was laid before the representatives of the nations for signature. This is not luck — it's a gift! . . .

Dr Morrison's movements are timed to take him back to China in the spring, when the gentle Chinaman, and the Russian, and the Manchu, awake from their winter sleep, and resume their game of swapping concessions and privileges; when the German once more starts to undersell his English competitor, and the river highways teem with human life, and the fishing junks go out to sea from Swatow in a cluster as thick as sailing boats at a Balmain regatta. China is the theatre of the world's chief performance for the next few years; and we may watch the unfolding of the drama with added interest from the fact that the man who is to tell us most about it is an Australian.

Morrison covered the Russo-Japanese War as a correspondent with the Japanese army. In 1907 he crossed China from Peking to the French border of Tonkin, and in 1910 he rose 3750 miles across Asia in 175 days.

He left The Times *in 1912, after seventeen years with the paper. He summed up his service in a diary note: 'No doubt in my work in the Far East I made many mistakes and my judgment was often faulty, but I can look back on the past and declare that I never sent a line to* The Times *that I did not believe to be the truth as I understood it at the time. Enemies I made — a correspondent if he is to be of any value to his paper must make enemies. . .'*

Morrison was fifty when he moved from newspaper work into the service of the Chinese Government as special adviser to the republic's first president, Yuan Shih-k'ai. It was a job with many frustrations. W. H. Donald, the other great Australian correspondent in China (who represented the New York Herald*), was quoted in the Sydney* Bulletin *some six months after the appointment as saying: 'Dr. Morrison . . . has a hard time of it. Advice is easy to give: the Chairman listens to advice but will do what he thinks he wants to do. Morrison feels that, frequently . . . as* Times *correspondent he had twice the prestige and three times the influence.'*

Morrison helped to float a loan in London of £10,000,000 to help Yuan Shih-k'ai's regime, which had destroyed the Chinese monarchy in the revolution of 1911. He tried to induce China to enter World War One on the side of the Allies, and he was adviser to the Chinese delegation during the Versailles peace conference. He died in May 1920, aged fifty-eight. He had married in 1912, and had three sons; one of them, Ian Morrison, was killed in Korea in 1950, while serving as a war correspondent for The Times.

1905   Japan is victorious over the Russian Fleet and emerges as a threat

WILLIAM HENRY DONALD
Sydney Daily Telegraph, 1905

The two Australians who have had some influence on Chinese history were both journalists: George Ernest 'Chinese' Morrison and William Henry Donald, 'Donald of China'. Morrison was thirteen years the senior. At one time in Peking Morrison was representing The Times *of London and Donald the London* Daily Telegraph *and New York* Herald. *When Morrison was acting as political adviser to Yuan Shih-k'ai, first president of the Chinese Republic, in Peking, Donald was performing a similar service for the Republicans in Shanghai. Donald is credited with having written for Sun Yat-Sen the manifesto of the Chinese Republic — with the aid of a battered typewriter and a bottle of bourbon. He later became adviser to Chiang Kai-Shek and Madame Chiang; Madame Chiang later acknowledged that Donald's intervention had saved her husband's life after he had been captured by Chinese Communists.*

Donald was born in Lithgow, New South Wales, in 1875, and his first newspaper job was as a compositor on the Lithgow Mercury. *He later joined the Bathurst* National Advocate, *where he rose to be editor, and later the Sydney* Daily Telegraph *and the Melbourne* Argus. *Around 1903 he became a reporter on the Hong Kong paper, the* China Mail, *and in 1905 he was made correspondent for the London and New York papers.*

The two major scoops of his career came when, as a correspondent accompanying the Japanese fleet, he reported the defeat of Russia's fleet by the Japanese in 1905, and when he reported the twenty-one demands by which Japan sought in 1915 to fetter China politically and economically. The second dispatch was disbelieved by the London Times, *which he was then representing, and*

not published; it appeared later in the New York Herald Tribune. *Here is his report of the Japanese naval victory:*

When approaching the Korea Straits the main Russian fleet changed its course as if about to return, but at 5 o'clock on the morning of Saturday, steaming at the rate of about 12 knots, the full fleet steered through the Straits in a south-easterly direction towards Sai-shiu-tau, within the waters of Iki-shima.

The Japanese had left at a pre-arranged base a detached squadron to press the Russians towards Iki-shima. The enemy passed to the west, and went full steam ahead, providing an impressive and majestic sight. Meanwhile, the Japanese remained lurking in the neighborhood.

The Russians traversed a strong current, running to the west of Iki-shima, and proceeded due north.

But the Japanese were ready with their auxiliary fleet to the north and headed off the enemy.

Then Admiral Togo's vessels, manoeuvring with precision, quickly got into allotted positions, from which they were able to enfilade the Russians on both flanks and in front.

The scene was superby terrible, the guns of nearly 50 ships being fired, occasionally with a tremendous crash, as numerous loud reports coincided. . .

By 2 o'clock in the afternoon the bombardment was at its zenith, the cannonading being most marked. . .

The Russian fleet became disordered and proceeded in a zigzag course, some of the ships' stems being directed east and others west.

Then the Japanese, with a judgment amounting to inspiration, advanced to closer quarters. The Russian ships came under a fire which was rendered all the more terrible by the shortened range. They no longer existed as a fleet. Severed, un-co-ordinated, and demoralised, they were gradually pressed towards the Nagato Province, in the Japanese mainland.

The fight lasted until 7 o'clock, when the atmosphere became obscured.

Admiral Togo risked nothing, and lost nothing.

The Russians then attempted to steer to the north-west, and heavy fighting continued until sunset. By that time the wind had subsided, the seas were smooth, and the atmosphere transparent.

In the blue blackness of night the ships stood out something more than spectres, something less than fearful citadels.

The Russians continued edging towards the north, but a powerful Japanese fleet lying in a horizontal line across their bows proved an effective barrier, linked with guns.

At about 8 o'clock the Japanese torpedo-boat destroyers and torpedo-boats advanced like a cloud of locusts, the sea being swept the while with the pale tracks of innumerable searchlights. The large warships, with their great cannon, covered the attack...

At dawn on Sunday the Japanese approached, and at closer range pressed the Russians to the north-west of Nagato.

The battle continued to rage fiercely, but the Russians were in no strategical position, and quite unable to effectively resist the onslaughts.

The foregoing message was delayed in transmission – presumably in Japan.

The Russo-Japanese war came five years after the birth of the Commonwealth of Australia, at a time when Australians were beginning to learn that their geographical position might make it necessary for them to have a foreign policy of their own. Britain's own diplomatic policies were fluctuating as she made new treaties. In 1902 Britain and Japan signed a joint naval treaty, and Britain withdrew her ships from the South Pacific. When the war between Russia and Japan broke out, Australians felt no great sense of involvement; Australian public opinion was strongly on the side of the Japanese, mainly because of a general attitude of dislike for Russia. That year, as well as the disasters of the Japanese war, Russia suffered demonstrations, strikes, riots, assassinations, and wholesale murder by troops and police in St Petersburg. President Theodore Roosevelt was compelling recognition of the United States as a great power, reinforcing his case by acting as peacemaker between Russia and Japan.

Soon after the war ended, Australian enthusiasm for Japan ebbed. The great naval victory reported by William Henry Donald took on sinister implications. Japan, flushed with success and with free reign over the seas north of Australia, began to look like a threat and people started to talk about the 'Yellow Peril'. Australia began to look in other directions, and the most logically sensible direction was east across the Pacific. The Prime Minister, Alfred Deakin, said in 1905: 'Next to our British kindred, we place the Americans next in our affections.' And the Melbourne Age acknowledged: 'We desire a better acquaintance with Americans ... The Americans are a people who stand in the forefront of the world's progress. They have dealt with problems that reach to the heart of humanity. They are even now dealing with some of them, in the restrictions they are placing on Chinese and Japanese immigrants ...'

Donald remained in China until 1940, when he set out on a tour of the South Pacific. He was in Manila in 1941, when the Japanese invaded the Philippines; he was interned, but his real identity was never known to the Japanese who captured him. He later travelled to the United States to recover from the rigors of imprisonment; his health declined, and he went to Tahiti, where his illness was diagnosed as cancer of the lungs. At his own request he was taken to Shanghai, where he died in 1946.

1905

The motor-car arrives and twenty-eight take part in a contest

UNKNOWN REPORTER
Sydney Daily Telegraph, November 1905

The motor-car arrived in Australia with the beginning of the new century. The Shearer, the Pioneer, the Thompson and the Ziegler were all early Australian-made vehicles. The Thompson steam car was first shown at the Royal Agricultural Show in Sydney in Easter week 1900, and was later driven to Bathurst, and from there back to Victoria, via Albury. The first petrol-driven motor-car imported to Australia was a Benz, brought out from Germany by a Melbourne company and landed in that city in March 1900. This was quickly followed by a three and a half horse-power De Dion, imported from France to Sydney in May of the same year.

The Dunlop Rubber Company conducted two spectacular events in 1905, which were in fact the nation's first reliability trials. One, involving twenty-three cars, began in February, with a route from Sydney to Melbourne, then to Ballarat and back; the second, with twenty-eight cars and ten motor-cycles, began in the Haymarket, Melbourne, in November 1905. After five days, nineteen cars had reached Sydney — but the organisers could not pick a winner. A motoring gymkhana was held on the Sydney Showground, then the surviving field was sent to Medlow Bath, in the Blue Mountains, and back — 132 miles. This still left six cars with a chance, and by mutual consent the remaining contestants decided to fight out the contest with a return journey to Melbourne. By now the nation was captivated by the feats of the drivers. Newspapers published flash reports from each major centre through which the cars passed: Picton, Mittagong, Goulburn, Gundagai, Germanton (now Holbrook), Albury and on to Melbourne.

'The roads are very bad,' said the Daily Telegraph. *'In parts they are a foot deep in dust. It is impossible to maintain anything like a fast pace without risk of breakdown.' But five of the six cars left after the Medlow Bath run made it to Melbourne within their time allowance.*

When the race ended, the Sydney Daily Telegraph *reported:*

G. Hobbs, in his powerful Mercedes, with Tom Scott of Sydney as observer, created quite a sensation in the districts through which he passed, the car passing through the various townships at a tremendous pace. The first to reach Euroa was Syd. Day, who rattled through the town at 10.32 a.m. Next came Wilkinson at 11.22, Grimwade at 11.24, Tarrant at 11.34, and, finally, Hobbs, at 11.45. The latter caught Tarrant some minutes later, and between that time and 2.16 p.m. he overhauled all the others, the last to give way to him being Day. With improved roads Hobbs put on more pace, and after a performance which has never before been equalled in the Commonwealth he reached the finishing post at Coburg at three o'clock, the journey from Albury being completed in 7 hours 30 minutes or an average of 27 m.p.h. That included 13½ minutes that were lost at closed railway gates. The last sixty miles were covered in 1 hour 40 minutes, which is at the rate of 36 m.p.h. Wilkinson arrived at 3.27, after a journey of 9 hours 53 minutes; Grimwade at 3.49, after a riding time of 9 hours 57 minutes; Day at 3.59, riding time 11 hours 44 minutes; Tarrant at 4.4, riding time 10 hours 9 minutes.

Altogether on the trip from Melbourne to Sydney, Sydney to Medlow Bath and back, and Sydney to Melbourne, the competitors traversed 1276 miles, of which 833 were run under conditions which did not even allow

Speeding around a dusty corner during the Sydney to Melbourne motor race in 1905   *(Photograph by courtesy of the James Flood Charity Trust)*

the engines to be stopped or repairs to be effected. Hobbs's time for the full journey was 49 hours 12 minutes, Wilkinson 61 hours 55 minutes, Grimwade 64 hours 43 minutes, Tarrant 64 hours 59 minutes, and Day 75 hours 23 minutes. . .

One of the best performances of the whole trip was that of Syd. Day, who came right through from Albury to Melbourne with both front springs broken, and with them simply tied up with string. The steering rod of his car was also bent, and he could only steer to the left. One spring was broken during yesterday's stage, but another has been broken for four days. . .

The performances of the five remaining in the contest are regarded as equal to, if not superior to, those reported from other parts of the world.

With the consent of the competitors, it was decided that the first prize, the Dunlop Cup, should be inscribed with the performances of all five cars that finished in Melbourne yesterday, and be handed over to the Automobile Club for twelve months. In the event of the cup being won next year by any of those who have established a claim this year, it will become his property.

Mr George Hobbs, who had no points debit-ed against his Mercedes in Class A, was award-ed the Dunlop blue ribbon for the year, and a special gold medal. Messrs W. Russell, Grimwade, W. B. Wilkinson and H. Tarrant, all of Class B, were given a trophy of equal value, and a medal commemorative of the event. Mr Syd. Day, who put up such a fine performance in his single-cylinder car, won the Hurst trophy, value eighteen guineas, and a medal.

The Daily Telegraph *summed up the feelings of most Australians when it said in an editorial:*

The keen interest taken in the motor contest is something more than a sporting interest. It is the recognition that in the development of the motor lies the solution of many transit problems of the future, and among these the problems of our great 'dry' spaces west and south-west. The fascinations of speed are almost irresistible once they have been tasted, but what is really wanted for outback conditions is a car that will be modestly capable of 20 m.p.h., with engine and tyres warranted to withstand the roughest bush tracks. Any car that could survive fast work on the Victorian 'main' roads north and south of Euroa, as many did in this contest, should be able to handle all the rough station work asked of it.

1905-6 The Prime Minister does some free-lance work on the side

ALFRED DEAKIN
London Morning Post, 20 November, 29 December 1905 and 10 May, 22 June 1906

One of the strangest episodes in the history of Australian journalism involved Alfred Deakin, who was three times Prime Minister of Australia. Deakin had qualified as a barrister, but he earned his living mainly as a journalist on David Syme's Melbourne Age *before he went into politics in 1880.*

From 1900, the year Australia became a federation, he was Australian correspondent of the London Morning Post. *For a payment of £500 a year, he sent a weekly letter on Australian affairs for some eleven years; for three years more, from 1911 until 1914, he wrote his article once every three weeks. While he was Prime Minister he continued to write his frank but anonymous commentaries on Australian politics and politicians.*

Very few people knew the secret of Deakin's other role as a newspaperman. According to his biographer, Professor J. A. La Nauze, only the editor and publishers of the Morning Post, *members of his own family, a handful of friends and a taxation official (Deakin used to declare his income from the* Morning Post) *were in the know. Certainly Deakin seemed to delight in the mystery of it all: 'the situation is fit for fiction rather than real life, and that is one of its attractions though its responsibilities are hazardous in the extreme,' he wrote to Richard Jebb, one of the* Morning Post's *leader writers in 1907.*

It was certainly hazardous. The revelation that the Prime Minister was doing a little free-lance work on the side, appraising his own performance and those of his contemporaries for the English public, would have provided his political rivals with embarrassing ammunition. Why then did he do it? His motives are still unclear, but a factor was almost certainly the payment. When he took the job on,

Deakin had no real savings. Undoubtedly, though, as the years passed, he enjoyed the work increasingly. He regarded himself always as a journalist, and he seemed to see his writing while in office as a means of relaxation.

What degree of impropriety was involved in a prime minister making anonymous published judgments on himself and his opponents? How dispassionate were those judgments? These are questions for the historians to argue. The bizarre nature of the situation is enough to justify inclusion of Deakin's work for the Morning Post *in this book.*

Some of the more piquant of Deakin's letters were those which discussed such subjects as 'The Puzzle of Deakin' and 'Enigmatic Deakin'. Two samples follow:

A short visit to Melbourne does not explain the situation or the meaning of the Prime Minister. Though he has lived all his life in that city, and has been prominent in politics for twenty years, there is no consensus of opinion regarding him or his policy. To some his course of conduct is thought to be taken always on the line of least resistance, while to others he is a bookish theorist recklessly pursuing impossible dreams. His leadership has been imposed upon him rather than sought, just as it has been imposed upon his following rather than desired, unless, perhaps, by his personal friends. The Protectionists would have preferred Sir William Lyne or Mr Isaacs, and the Labour Party also, though they would have reversed the order of those names.

The Conservative Liberals have more confidence in Sir George Turner or Mr McLean, while the Radicals, and particularly the Trades Unionists, have not forgiven and are not likely to forget Mr Deakin's ruthless criticisms of their tactics, doctrines, and organisation. Yet perhaps because he is not identified with any section and has a curious aloofness even from his political intimates he is accepted without question as at present the only possible leader of the conglomerate party, whose main principle is Protection and Preferential Trade. Mr Reid, on the other hand, is heavily handicapped on this [Victorian] side of the Murray by his Free Trade associations. . .

It is unfortunate for both that State jealousies should operate against them continuously, though the Prime Minister suffers most, seeing that he has no friendly newspaper in Sydney, nor, indeed in New South Wales, where even the *Bulletin* mocks at his excessively 'affable' and invariably conciliatory demeanour. Mr Reid, on the other hand, has the Free Trade Press of every State at his back, and the absolute control of the funds raised by the opponents of the Labour Party. As against these forces those of the Protectionist leader are puny and scanty. If a dissolution does come soon the odds are in favour of the Opposition to begin with, while it remains to be seen how Mr Deakin's defiant attitude will be justified by that time in the mixed bodies now behind him.

For reasons only known to himself, which are a perpetual subject of controversy in our Press, Mr Deakin pursues his enigmatic methods of action. . . But in spite of Mr Deakin's persistent elusiveness the pressure brought to bear upon him, from within his own party as much as from without, appears so strong that some unexpected development must be near at hand.

In 1904 the personal question whether Mr Reid or himself should become Prime Minister and head the united parties was settled by his refusal to take office. To-day no one else is even suggested for such a leadership. It has been taken for granted on all sides, and even by the large portion of our Press, always irreconcilably hostile to him, that he and no other must lead any combination, however formed. But of Mr Deakin nothing can be prognosticated with confidence in such matters. We may see 1904 repeated in 1909

without obvious reason, but simply because he so decides. If this should happen it will be remembered everywhere that the consequences of his standing aloof in 1904 were most disastrous to the coalition that followed. The apprehensions revived by that reminiscence will require a great deal of soothing.

Queensland politicians outside the Labour ranks have never been friendly either to Federation or to the Protectionist Party which has been in power almost ever since our union. Yet Mr Deakin's meetings in that State were evidently successful throughout his tour, and whatever the sentiments of his hearers may have been only the Labour element was openly hostile. Perhaps this circumstance is the most significant testimony to the nature of his speeches. Calling special attention to the perpetual references to an early dissolution, in which all the Ministers have been indulging, and to the Labour candidates already in the field challenging his supporters in every Victorian electorate, he dwelt upon the weakness of the financial proposals of Mr Fisher, his omissions of any immigration or preferential trade policy, and the crude character of his proposed land tax, for which his own estimates disclosed no necessity.

Mr Deakin's hits were all at the expense of the Ministry. That they told upon his hearers was evident from the outcry provoked. His allusions to the political situation pointed explicitly to some combination against the Labour Party. But he still insisted from first to last upon the policy he has advocated without ceasing in Tasmania and upon our northern rivers in his preceding tours. Its acceptance as a whole is evidently for him the *sine qua non* of any alliance. This wholesale conversion being impossible, he continues to rally his forces against the Labour Leagues, so that all present indications are that any coalition to be formed which desires his support but does not adopt his complete programme will not include him, though it must depend upon his allegiance.

1908　The Great White Fleet arrives from the United States and a national alliance is born

GEORGE COCKERILL
Melbourne Age, 22 August 1908

It was in the first decade of Australia's nation-hood that the earliest embryonic signs of a special defence relationship between this nation and the United States appeared. At the turn of the century Britain was moving towards new alliances with France and Russia, and in 1902 a joint naval treaty was signed between Britain and Japan. The last British squadrons were leaving the South Pacific, and there was a recognition that Britain was conceding the expanding Japanese power in the oceans above Australia. Australian public opinion was on the side of the Japanese during the Russo-Japanese conflict, and there was some elation when the Russian fleet was defeated in 1905; but it soon became clear that Australia needed America as an effective counter-balance to a Japan which was growing discernibly more aggressive.

'It is likely that the United States of America will be our first line of defence against Asia. . .', said an editorial in the Sydney Morning Herald *in 1908. Australia had been impressed with and attracted to the United States during the Spanish-American war of 1898; on the night of the great United States victory in Manila Bay, crowds gathered in front of newspaper offices to cheer the news bulletins and during the first weeks of the war more than 200 Australians tried to volunteer for service in the United States army. When Prime Minister Alfred Deakin invited the United States Pacific fleet to Australia in 1908, there were two significant reactions. The British Colonial Office was angry, claiming that the invitation should not have been issued directly (it was offered in a letter from Deakin to the United States Ambassador in London) but through the British Government. In Australia, the general mood of the public*

and the newspapers was of total enthusiasm. Deakin himself (doubling up in his capacity of part-time journalist, contributing to the London Morning Post) *wrote: 'We have never seen a single British battleship in these waters, and the prospect of sixteen of them (American) in Port Jackson . . . may well awaken fresh emotions.' The* Argus *gave its opinion: 'The Americans will be a safeguard against an oriental invasion, which is always threatening.'*

If a date had to be isolated when Australia's pre-occupation with American protection, as an alternative to the traditional links with Britain began, it would be 22 August 1908. That was the day when the Great White Fleet reached Sydney.

Deakin talked that day of 'the strength of the invisible ties drawing us together as States united in affection'. The New South Wales Premier said he hoped the visit would lead to 'an indissoluble union of the English-speaking race'. The Age *said: 'The six battleships are veritable forces for the betterment of man.' And the Lord Mayor of Melbourne said more bluntly at a banquet: 'You will be helping us to keep an eye on the yellow man.' And over-seas, the significance of the visit was clearly seen. The* New York Times *commented: 'The manifestations of Australian friendship will not be forgotten. . . The greeting in Sydney may be taken as notification to all the powers that in any future obligations involving the Far East the Commonwealth is to be reckon-ed with.' The* Daily Graphic *in London said: 'The phenonenal festivities in Sydney shows how deeply the Englishman in the Pacific feels in regard to the yellow peril.' That last term was about to become a fashionable one in Australian politics.*

To Sydney for the big event, the Age *sent*

Servicemen from the American Fleet march through the
streets of Sydney

its two senior reporters, George Cockerill (later editor of the Sydney Telegraph) *and L. V. Biggs (later editor of the* Age). *Wireless telegraphy had been introduced to Australia in 1905, and a telephone service between Sydney and Melbourne had opened in 1907. The two men were instructed: 'Give us everything.'*

Here is George Cockerill's report of the arrival of the fleet:

To the thousands of expectant watchers whose eyes were strained across the rolling sea from the glimmering of dawn, the outlines of the American battleships appeared faintly through the morning haze like towers and turrets and minarets of some majestic city that had been miraculously washed up out of the Pacific or grown in a night from the depths of the ocean. Sydney had obtained only forty winks or had not slept at all. Torrents of humanity were sweeping through the streets at daybreak, heading for the cliffs along the outer coast and high grounds that wall the hundred inlets of Sydney's glorious harbor. Everything that went on wheels, trams, cabs, coaches, bicycles, motors tore along, double-weighted with human burdens. . .

The throngs and every craft were twitching with expectancy, gazing with eager eyes to the rugged cliffs of the Heads hours before the great war ships could have been expected . . . They waited long, but the fleet came at last. Over the crests of the rugged hills that almost lock the harbor mouth, the keenest-eyed watcher espied a slight column of smoke. It came nearer, and grew thicker. The fog horns roared; the bands played with renewed strength, and before the enchanted eyes of the many thousands, the Connecticut led the long line of battleships through the Heads. As the gallant vessel sailed gracefully towards the city, the fog horns ceased, the musicians put aside their instruments, and the thickly populated places seemed hushed in perfect silence. It was a thrilling moment — a moment of deep emotions and serious reflections.

Admiration for an unexampled demonstration of the latent power of a mighty hand; swelling pride at Australia's blood relationship with the great white people of the west; overpowering enthusiasm at the fact that the rich aspiring young Commonwealth had attained the dignity of exchanging a national hand grip with her illustrious relative, mingled in every breast. Beneath it all there seemed to be the firm faith of a stern self-reliance, worthy of the illustrious ancestry of Australia's people, while there was pride in America's friendship and a desire to strengthen the ties which bind the two nations together. . .

On came the Connecticut, gliding majestically and apparently without creating as much as a ripple upon the water; her white rigid hull, with its stern letters, glittering in the sunlight. Close behind in a direct, unbroken line, stretching over three or four miles, the other battleships glided silently in her wake. As a spectacle the appearance of these great fighting vessels was one of stateliness, majesty and power rather than of grace and beauty. As the ships glided by the passenger steamers their crews stood on parade upon their decks. The vessels of the fleet dipped the Stars and Stripes at the saluting base, and when well inside the harbor their cannon boomed the salute to Sydney's port. . .

It was said that the Newcastle and Hunter steamers chartered by the Commonwealth Government contained nine out of every ten members of Parliament within the States, and more than a share of official Melbourne. The statement seemed to be true. Aboard the Newcastle were Mr. Deakin, several of his colleagues, representatives of Victoria's State Government, High Court judges and political and official dignitaries and their wives almost without number. Mr. Craven, M.L.A., was there wondering which end of the boat would be in front, in order that he might get a fair view of everything that was going. Messrs. Hutchinson, Elmslie and Duffus, M's.L.A., stood at the prow benignly gazing across the water and calling the battleships a variety of names ranging from "swift shuttles of an empire's loom" to "deadly engines of devilry and death." . . .

1908

A black man beats a white to become heavy-weight champion of the world

JACK LONDON
Melbourne Argus, 28 December 1908

On Boxing Day 1908, Hugh D. McIntosh promoted what was proclaimed to be the prizefight of the century. Jack Johnson, the negro challenger, had caught up with Tommy Burns, the heavyweight champion of the world. The Rushcutters Bay stadium was unroofed then, and the fight took place at 11.00 a.m.; all through Christmas night the crowds moved in, until there were 20,000 in the stadium, and thousands thronged the streets outside.

There had never been a black heavyweight champion of the world before. Tom Molyneux, the American slave, had gone to England a hundred years before to fight Tom Cribb for the title — and had been robbed when one of Cribb's seconds almost bit his thumb off. The Australian Peter Jackson had drawn with James J. Corbett, but John L. Sullivan, the champion, had drawn the colour line against him: 'I'll never fight a negro,' he said — and he never did. Now Johnson had gone halfway around the world to chase the title, and negroes everywhere saw him as the avenger of their race.

To cover the battle, the Melbourne Argus *commissioned one of the great reporter-writers of the day, Jack London. Two years before London had completed one of the great reporting feats of the period; he had written a 2500-word description of the San Francisco earthquake and the great fires which followed it, for* Collier's Weekly.

It was a one-sided fight from the start. Johnson, his hairless ebony head and golden teeth gleaming in the sun, taunted the white man as he chopped him brutally. 'It was not a case,' wrote London, 'of too much Johnson, but of all Johnson.' London called on Jim Jeffries to emerge from his alfalfa farm and remove the golden smile from Johnson's face. 'The White Man must be rescued.' So began the search for the great white hope.

Full credit for the big fight must be given to Mr. McIntosh, who has done the unprecedented, and had the nerve to carry it through. But equal credit must be given to Australia, for without her splendid sport-loving men not a hundred McIntoshes could have pulled off the great contest of Saturday.

The stadium is a magnificent arena: and so was the crowd magnificent. It was managed by that happy aptitude which the English have for handling big crowds. The spirit of the stadium crowd, inside and out, with its fair-minded and sporting squareness, was a joy to behold. It was hard to realise that those fifty or sixty thousand men were descended from the generations that attended the old bare-knuckles fights in England, where partisan crowds swarmed the ringside, slugging each other, smashing the top-hats of the gentlemen promoters and backers, and swatting away with clubs at the heads of the poor devils of fighters whenever they came near to the ropes.

Never in my life have I seen a finer, fairer, and more orderly ringside crowd, and in this connection it must be remembered that the majority were in favour of the man who was losing. That many thousands of men could sit quietly for forty minutes and watch their chosen champion hopelessly and remorselessly beaten down and not make the slightest demonstration is a remarkable display of inhibition. There is no use minimising Johnson's victory in order to soothe Burns's feelings. It is part of the game to take punishment in the ring, and it is just as much part of the game to take unbiassed criticism afterward in the columns of the press. Personally, I was with Burns all the way. He is a white man, and so am I. Naturally I wanted to see the white man win. Put the case to Johnson. Ask him if he were spectator to a fight between a white man and a black man which he would like to see win, and Johnson's black skin will dictate a desire parallel to the one dictated by my white skin.

But now, to come back to the point. There is no foolish sentimental need to gloss over Burns's defeat. Because a white man wishes the white man to win should not prevent him from giving absolute credit to the best man, who did win, even when the best man was black. . .

The fight. The word is a misnomer. There was no fight. No Armenian massacre would compare with the hopeless slaughter that took place in the Stadium. It was not a case of too much Johnson, but of all Johnson. A golden smile tells the story, and the golden smile was Johnson's. The fight, if fight it can be called, was like unto that between a colossus and a toy automaton; it had all the seeming of a playful ethiopian at loggerheads with a small and futile white man, of a grown man cuffing a naughty child; of a monologue by one Johnson, who made a noise with his fists like a lullaby, tucking one Burns into his little crib in sleepy hollow; of a funeral, with Burns for the late deceased, and Johnson for the undertaker, grave-digger, and sexton.

Twenty thousand men were at the ringside, and twice twenty thousand lingered outside. Johnson, first at the ring, showed in magnificent condition. When he smiled a dazzling flash of gold filled the wide aperture between his open lips. And he smiled all the time. He had not a trouble in the world. When asked what he was going to do after the fight, he said he was going to the races. It was a happy prophecy. He was immediately followed into the ring by Burns, who had no smile whatever. He looked pale and sallow, as if he had not slept all night, or as if he had just pulled through a bout with fever. He received a heartier greeting than Johnson, and was the favourite with the crowd.

It promised to be a bitter fight. There was

no chivalry nor goodwill in it, and Johnson, despite his care-free pose, had an eye to the instant need of things. He sent his seconds insistently into Burns's corner to watch the putting on of the gloves, for fear a casual horseshoe might stray in. He examined personally Burns's belt, and announced flatly that he would not fight if Burns did not remove the tape from his skinned elbows.

"Nothin' doin' till he takes 'em off," quoth Johnson. The crowd hooted, but Johnson smiled his happy golden smile, and dreamed with ethiopian stolidity in his corner. Burns took off the offending tapes, and was applauded uproariously. Johnson stood up, and was hooted. He merely smiled. That is the fight epitomised — Johnson's smile.

The gong sounded, and the fight and the monologue began. "All right, Tahmy," said Johnson, with exaggerated English accent, and thereafter he talked throughout the fight when he was not smiling. Scarcely had they mixed, when he caught his antagonist with a fierce upper-cut, turning him completely over in the air, and landing him on his back.

There is no use giving details. There was no doubt from the moment of the opening of the first round — the affair was too one-sided. There was never so one-sided a world's championship fight in the history of the ring. It was not a case of a man being put out by a clever or lucky punch in the first or second round. It was a case of a plucky, determined fighter, who had no chance for a look in at any single instant of the fight.

There was no fraction of a second in all the fourteen rounds that could be called Burns's — so far as damage is concerned. Burns never landed a blow. He never dazed the black man. It was not Burns's fault, however. He tried every moment throughout the fight, except when he was groggy. It was hopeless, preposterous, heroic. He was a glutton for punishment, and he bored in all the time. . .

Not Burns, but Johnson, did the in-fighting. In fact, the major portion of the punishment he delivered was in the clinches. At times he would hold up his arms to show that he was no party to the clinch. . .

One criticism, and only one, can be passed

Tommy Burns, heavyweight champion of the world, was no match for the negro challenger, Jack Johnson

upon Johnson. In the thirteenth round he made the mistake of his life. He should have put Burns out. He could have put him out. It would have been child's play. Instead of which he smiled, and deliberately let Burns live until the gong sounded.

And in the opening of the fourteenth round the police stopped the fight, and Johnson lost the credit of a knock-out.

But one thing remains. Jeffries must emerge from his alfalfa farm and remove that smile from Johnson's face. Jeff, it's up to you. And, McIntosh, it's up to you to get the fight for Australia. Both you and Australia certainly deserve it. . .

1909   Australia enters the field of aviation with its first powered flight

UNKNOWN REPORTER
Sydney Morning Herald, 10 December 1909

Australia appeared to pay little attention to its aviation pioneers. Lawrence Hargrave, the genius who studied the flight of birds and applied his findings to the science of aeronautics, was largely unappreciated until after his death; Colin Defries, the first aviator to fly in Australia, received remarkably little publicity at the time.

Even so, there had long been great interest in the subject of flying, and the massive implications of this form of travel. As early as June 1841, the Sydney Herald *published a remarkable prediction that one day 'mails would be carried through the air at 100 miles per hour'. In June 1846, the same paper announced that, 'upon the whole, we think aerial navigation quite feasible', and in January 1847, it published a leading article which stated: 'The whole intellect of Europe, America and the civilised world has been stirred up by this topic, and mechanical and pneumatic appliances are so numerous that we fairly calculate upon a practical aerial machine, which, although it may not satisfy the most sanguine, may yet prove of his advantage to man.'*

The first powered flight in Australia took place on 9 December 1909. The following day, the Sydney Morning Herald *published this account by an unidentified reporter:*

The first aerial flight in Australasia by a motor-propelled machine was accomplished yesterday afternoon at Victoria Park Racecourse. The machine, handled by Mr Colin Defries, flew about 115 yards, the time of flight being registered as 5½ seconds. The height attained varied from 2 ft to 15 ft, and there was every prospect of the aeroplane soaring aloft had not the engine worked badly.

There was considerable excitement as Mr Defries alighted, and many were the inquiries as to why he did not continue longer in the air. The explanation was that the engine was not working satisfactorily. This, indeed, was apparent to everyone. Whereas on Saturday, when the wind was unfavourable, the propellers were registering fully 600 to 800 revolutions a minute, yesterday, owing to defective sparking plugs, the maximum was about 450 a minute. Yet the machine went up.

Certainly no better day could have been chosen. When the first test was made the breeze, which was a south-easterly, was scarcely felt. The aviator faced the wind, and made several trial runs unsuccessfully. Then he turned to the north, intending to run into the wind at the turn. The result was a success. When travelling at about 35 miles an hour, and handling the machine along, Mr Defries suddenly raised his elevating planes, and at once rose into the air. As he left the ground there was an involuntary cry from about 150 spectators, "He's up!" and he was up. As the machine rushed forward it kept in the air, and rose quickly from 3 ft to fully 15 ft or 20 ft, and then tapered down again to earth, after covering about 115 yards. According to the time taken over the measured distance the aeronaut covered 100 yards in 5 seconds, which will give some idea of his rate of travelling.

Naturally the crowd was delighted with the flight, even though it was a small one. "Should the weather turn out favourable tomorrow afternoon," said Mr Defries, when interviewed, "I will certainly make a really good flight. Today my engine was running badly, owing to defective sparking plugs. Just you see me tomorrow, and I will demonstrate what the Wilbur Wright bi-plane can really accomplish."

Some six years later, on 7 July 1915, the Sydney Morning Herald *ruminated editorially on the death of Hargrave — and the lack of appreciation accorded him in his home country:*

"Sydney will one day be noted, not for its famous harbour, but as being the home of Hargrave, the man who invented the flying machine." Lawrence Hargrave, the man of whom these words were spoken by Professor Threlfall, formerly of the Sydney University, died yesterday at his home in Wunulla Road, Woollahra Point. He was 65 years of age.

The late Mr. Hargrave, whose experiments, carried on at Stanwell Park and in Sydney, did so much to advance the science of aviation, was born in England, but he spent the greater part of his life — 48 years of it — in this country. He was a son of the late Mr. Justice Hargrave. The death of his own son, Geoffrey Hargrave, who was killed at the Dardanelles a few weeks ago, was a great blow to him and undoubtedly hastened the end. Geoffrey Hargrave, like his father, was an engineer by profession, and his death in action has cut short a very promising career. . . The name of Lawrence Hargrave will be remembered in this country — the more as time goes on. He worked for some years as an assistant astronomical observer at Sydney Observatory, under the late Mr. H. C. Russell, and it may have been because he had to do with the things above the earth that his thoughts turned to flying machines. However that was, he gave up his work at the Observatory and thereafter devoted most of his life to the study of aeronautics; and certain it is that the present-day successes in mechanical flight are due largely to the work of this man in Australia. Thirty years ago Lawrence Hargrave was studying the flight of birds, and making working models, embodying the principles of their motions. The success of the models convinced him of the possibility of mechanical flight; and in a paper which he read before the Royal Society on August 6th, 1884, he gave particulars of his discoveries in simple and modest terms. . . Eleven years later — in 1895 — Hargrave conducted a remarkable experiment at Stanwell Park, on the South Coast, utilising his invent-

ion of the cellular or box kites, the forerunner of the modern aeroplane, to lift him from the ground. "It is thought," he said, in another address to the members of the Royal Society, "that this experiment marks an epoch in the series of aeronautical contrivances recorded in our journal." And the principle was adopted by practically every military nation in the world for signalling purposes.

It was Hargrave who lifted human flight from the realm of dreamland into realisation; it was upon his discoveries that other men built, who have become famous in the world of aeronautics — the Wright Brothers and Farman, for instance. For 30 years he worked steadily on the problems of aerial engineering, constructing models, improving on them, and ever reaching higher stages. . . And all the time, whilst his work was unappreciated in this country — by many, indeed, his efforts even had ridicule heaped upon them — aeronauts in other lands were working on his ideas. . . It is a regrettable thing — it is, indeed, something of a disgrace — that when, some years ago, Mr. Hargrave expressed his willingness to hand over all his models to the Government, that they might be housed somewhere where they would be available for inspection by other inventors and the public generally, the Government could not see its way to accept them — there was no room anywhere. They were offered to Governments; they were offered to institutions — there was no room available. The same indifference was shown in England. So Mr. Hargrave presented them to Germany, and to-day they may be seen in the Deutsche Museum at Munich — and it is believed that the Taube aeroplane, which has been so prominent in the great war, is fashioned on one of these Australian models.

1910   Henry Lawson writes about the death of a journalistic colleague

HENRY LAWSON
Bulletin, 16 June 1910

Henry Lawson is far better known as a writer of short stories and sketches than as a journalist, and most of his journalism took the form of social and political comment or pieces of autobiography and reminiscence.

He did indulge in reporting, though — even if it was a very personalised kind of reporting — and was commissioned in 1900 by the Melbourne Age *to send back pieces from South Africa on his way to England. His* Letters to Jack Cornstalk *and other articles for the* Bulletin *from London amounted to very attractive reporting, and he wrote some vivid descriptions about life in Western Australia — on visits in 1890 and 1896 — before and during the gold rush, for the* Albany Observer *and later for the* Worker *and the* Bulletin. *For* Fair Play, *the Pahiatua* Herald *and the New Zealand* Mail, *he wrote colourfully and with discernment about life in New Zealand.*

Lawson's easy style and talent for wry, unsentimental observation are demonstrated well in this report, titled 'Bohemia Buries her Dead', for the Bulletin's *Red Page on the death of a fellow-journalist, Herbert Low:*

We all know about his brilliancy as a journalist. The *Star* last Saturday had the best article on it, by Billy Melville, who knew him as long and as well as any; though I've seen little or nothing in the Great Dailies that profited by that brilliancy more than twenty years ago, just when it was wanted — from the time of the Great Dock Labourers' strike onward. But I remember his work best by the London sketches — something more than Pett Ridge in them — and when an Australian writer will watch out with interest for a contemporary's work, there is something in it.

But I remember him as a *clean* man — a tidy, well-dressed man — whisky or no; a good bohemian, a good pal, a generous man, up in the world or down, a doer of kind and noble deeds on the quiet; and — and he died game, if ever a man died game; and it was a long and terrible death to die. Do you know how Herbert Low died? — But — I remember it well now. — He many a time helped Somebody when Somebody was seemingly down and out: saved a life, so to speak, and more. *We* know what that means, if you don't; so it doesn't matter. We know it all too well.

Besides, I would do almost anything for a Yid, because of a little man, with black, curly, oily hair, and a nose that shamed not Israel, who stuck to me, and barracked for me through many brave hard years of the living unburied past. Herbert Low was a Hebrew, and his name doesn't matter any more than the one I write over does.

There were just ten of us, comprising the same men who were at Victor Daley's and, a year later, at Mrs Daley's funeral. (One was unavoidably absent, on account of his death last year: old Archie Cunningham, the sporting writer, his last legs carried to the funeral of his last benefactor.) We are learning to manage without priests or parsons — we have to sometimes, as you will see later. . . We are growing too old and too few now not to pay a little respect to our dead. There's one of us left to round up the old writers for the funeral; one to go out and comfort the bereaved ones — and he is born to it; one to fix up any hitch that might occur when the papers have to be signed; one to get pars. — and he does it somehow — in unlikely dailies, when none of the others would think of it, or do it in time; one to philosophise cheerfully on the way back;

and always one with a few bob to stand drinks all round, hats off, empty glass on the bar, to the memory of the dead, at the first hotel in the city, when all is said and done.

Herbert Low was buried in the Independent Cemetery at Rookwood, down by the railway line, next to the last of 'em; and being neither Christian, nor orthodox Hebrew, a burial service selected from the Book of Common Prayer was read by Billy Melville, who always turns up in the most unexpected places, whether in speech or print, and just when he's wanted. Then Billy said:

"Brother pressmen, artists and friends and admirers of the bright spirit that has passed away. I am asked, as Herbert Low's oldest journalistic friend, to say a few words in appreciation of his fine talents, robust character, and generous disposition. He was a man and a colleague in the truest and noblest meaning of the terms. He has gone for ever and by us will never be forgotten. He was one of Nature's gentlest and most humane . . . God rest his soul!"

Billy faltered a bit; but it didn't matter. Then we groped for the softest handfuls we could find in hard, lumpy, gritty clay.

We're beginning to book our passages out a bit of late years, we oldsters. Let me see: There was Harry Cargill ("The Dipsomaniac"); Barcroft Boake — who didn't wait to see it through before he went where the dead men lie; Victor Daley, who saw it out — "Now what shall a man remember in the days when he is old, and life is a dying ember, and fame is a story told?" And what shall a man remember? "Sweet, ugly women of the past, who had been kind to me?" And, just a year after, the little woman who had stuck to him so well . . . And Frank Myers — "As happy as Larry in Castlebarry". And Goodge, the swift, cheerful political jingler. And others who went away to die — and Herbert Low. We are going to Waverley and Rookwood overmuch of late, and coming back one short. It will be a rather dull time for the last one on the return journey; but after that it won't matter.

And, speaking of little women who stuck, there's a little woman who stuck to Herbert for many years and was the best of wives and

This photograph of Henry Lawson (left) was taken in 1910 whilst he was staying in Mallacoota with his friend Edwin Brady

mates to him, and a Brick through the last, long, lingering, bitter months of pain, suffering, irritation, and poverty. And she's not too well off now, from a Bohemian point of view. We like to do what we can for those little women who have stuck to our dead. We're mostly hard up ourselves and spend our last bobs on black ties, quick half-soling for them boots, and return tickets for the funeral train. But I think there'll be a concert or something — what would be called, in the regions that Herbert Low wrote so grandly about in the days of his fame, "A Friendly Lead". But you will be notified in due time, either in print, writing, or — if you are a privileged person — personally, by some disreputable journalist.

The Women's Auxiliary Army Corps parading through Melbourne during the early years of World War One

World War One
1914-1918

1914   Australia enters World War One and captures German New Guinea

FRITZ BURNELL
Sydney Morning Herald, 8 October 1914

The first shot fired by Australia during World War One came from a short battery at Queenscliff, Victoria. On 6 August 1914, two days after war broke out, there was one German vessel in the port of Melbourne — the freighter Pfalz. *On that day she emerged from the mouth of the Yarra River, ran down Port Phillip Bay, and reached Queenscliff, where her clearance papers were examined. The* Pfalz *was allowed to proceed; she had just got up speed and was entering the Rip when a shot was fired from the Queenscliff fort. It hit the water fifty yards astern of the freighter, which promptly turned around, headed back up the bay, and was captured.*

The first active Australian participation in the war came the following month, when the Australian Navy, aided by a contingent of Australian troops, captured German New Guinea. The soldiers — the first contingent of the 330,000 who left Australia to fight in the war — sailed to New Guinea in the troopship Berrima.

With them, the Sydney Morning Herald *sent a correspondent, Fritz Burnell. The New Guinea campaign was regarded as something of a sideshow, but it did involve fighting. Four men were killed in action at Rabaul; they were the first of 59,258 Australian servicemen to die in that war.*

Two days after the capture of German New Guinea, the AE1 — one of the two submarines in the Australian Navy — disappeared in the Pacific with the loss of all hands; thirty-five officers and men. Two months later, on 11 November, the cruiser HMAS Sydney engaged the notorious German raider, the Emden, *and drove her ashore, a battered and blazing wreck, on Keeling Island, in the Cocos group, in the Indian Ocean.*

Fritz Burnell was with the Australian force when it captured Rabaul. Here is his report, published in the Sydney Morning Herald *on 8 October 1914:*

The various units of the expedition arrived respectively at Rabaul and Herbertshohe, with its adjoining settlement Kaba Kaul, this morning, and since then a continuous and hard-fought struggle has been progressing for the possession of the wireless station, situated eight miles inland from Kaba Kaul. The details of the day's fighting are as yet less definite than could be desired, but the station still remains uncaptured, though it is understood that the troops have reached a point within a hundred yards of the central position, while, in addition to about 30 of the native police, six German prisoners have been taken, including two officers.

It has now been decided that, unless the station surrenders beforehand, the warships will begin at daylight a bombardment of the ridge upon which the enemy are entrenched, followed by a supreme assault by the entire force. Such is the plan outlined this evening by the Brigadier to those officers still on board the Berrima, concluding with the words: "We've got to get the wireless station by tomorrow night."

Meanwhile, on our side we have lost several officers and two able seamen. These are Lieutenant-Commander Elwell, Captain Pockley, A.A.M.C., Petty-officer Williams, and A.Bs. Moffatt and Courtney, R.N.A.R. The number of wounded on either side is at present not ascertainable.

The stubborn resistance offered by the Germans and their forces at Kaba Kaul has far surpassed the expectations of practically everyone in the expedition. It was, indeed, the general anticipation that no defence whatever was likely to be encountered either at Herbertshohe, the old capital, or Rabaul, the new capital, formerly known as Simpsonshafen, in New Pomerania. The two places lie only a comparatively few miles apart, and the coastline connecting the two may be compared in outline to a gigantic sickle, Herbertshohe being set, so to speak, in the centre of the handle, of which Kaba Kaul, a few miles to the south, forms the butt. In the opposite direction Rabaul, with its deep, well-sheltered harbour and its chain of huge volcanoes — one of which, still active, crouches glowering at the entrance like a monstrous guardian — lies within the inner tip of the sickle-blade.

Following the plan laid down on the previous evening, the Australian warships proceeded straight to Herbertshohe and Kaba Kaul at an early hour this morning, and, lying in the open roadstead which fronts the two places, landed at each a party of 25 Naval Reservists, with instructions to search for the two wireless stations which were understood to exist somewhere in the locality. . .

It was now decided, in view of the fact that the wireless station was still being vigorously defended, and the reports of heavy losses on the Australian side, including two other naval officers, continued to arrive, to return at once to Herbertshohe and land a strong force to take the enemy in flank. Some anxiety was also felt regarding the twenty-five who had landed there from one of the cruisers early in the morning, and who, up to that moment, had not since been heard of. Accordingly four companies of Naval Reserves, together with two machine guns and a twelve-pounder field gun, were landed under Colonel Watson, Infantry O.C., at Herbertshohe, and marched rapidly along the road in the direction of Kaba Kaul.

A strong screen of skirmishers linked by connecting files to the vanguard preceded the main body to obviate any possibility of an ambush, and, despite the intense heat, the parching dust, and the crushing weight of the 83lb kit, together with 200 rounds of ammunition per man, the troops swung down the road between the palm tree stems with an elasticity and precision that did one good to behold, and kept the glasses fixed upon the long khaki column until the last man had threaded his way into the invisible bush.

From then onwards there was nothing to do but wait and speculate, while stores and ammunition were hurried ashore, as to the trend of the battle raging unheard and unseen by us upon the fateful ridge. A message was sent at 4 o'clock by the Admiral to the Governor of Rabaul, threatening to use the stronger measures available if the resistance were not ended immediately. The Deputy-Governor returned an answer to say that it was not in his power — a strange phrase — to surrender Rabaul or Herbertshohe, adding, in deprecation of bombardment, that both were entirely unfortified, and that the harbour was quite clear of mines. Later on a message was received from Commander Beresford, informing the Brigadier that the first line of trenches had been captured, and that the troops were now within 100 yards of the station; he added that he had sent in a flag of truce, demanding surrender.

Hopes rose high. But by 6 o'clock and later the position was, apparently, still unchanged, and at daybreak to-morrow the eight 12-inch guns will scour the ridge with shrapnel, while, under cover of the guns, the entire strength of the expedition is to be hurled in a concentrated attack on the position which, during a long day, has been so gallantly attacked and defended.

RABAUL, Sept. 12.

The news that the wireless station had at length surrendered, and that it had therefore become unnecessary to shell the ridge as previously determined was spread on board the Berrima in the small hours of the morning, and by 9 o'clock the head of a dusky column, debouching from among the palm trees and scrub, announced that Colonel Watson's force was already beginning to arrive on its return march to Herbertshohe. Orders had been given that, should the force not succeed before nightfall in establishing communications with Commander Beresford, it was to return immediately. . .

1915

Two men with an ice-cream cart declare war at Broken Hill

HEDLEY WARD AND CYRIL WHETTERS
Broken Hill Barrier Miner, 1 January 1915 and Barrier Truth, 2 and 4 January 1915

On New Year's Day 1915, a train-load of picnickers, seated in open trucks, pulled out noisily from Broken Hill, bound for a picnic at nearby Silverton. The women wore great bonnets, the men were mostly coatless, and a few people carried umbrellas to ward off the hot sun. Hampers and rugs were packed beneath the long, temporary wooden benches in the trucks. There were 1200 men, women and children in the forty trucks, and the general mood that morning was one of joy, even elation.

As the train had squatted, stationary, at the Railway Town terminal, an ice-cream cart, drawn by a tired old horse, had driven slowly past. The picnickers had waved to the two Mohammedans aboard it. The cart was a familiar sight around Broken Hill; today there was just one thing different about it — it was carrying a flag. The flag was in fact Turkish, with a white crescent and star on a red background, but it doubtful whether many of the residents of Broken Hill would have recognised it as such.

Comically, ridiculously, terribly, the Great War had come to Broken Hill. Mulla Abdulla, camel-driver and butcher, and Gool Mahomed, drifter, who used to smoke Indian hemp together, had hatched a mad, brave plan to attack Australia. In their ice-cream cart they carried a Snider and a Martini-Henry rifle, bandoliers of cartridges, and knives.

The final deathroll in the Battle of Broken Hill was six, including the two Mohammedans, with seven others wounded. As a result of the attack, feeling flared against foreigners in Broken Hill. That night the German club was burnt to the ground, and townspeople tried to storm the camel camp.

Why did it happen? Although they carried the Turkish flag, neither of the men was a Turk. One was an Afghan Afridi and the other a native of north-west India; both were Mohammedans, and recognised the Sultan of Turkey as the head of their church. Gool Mahomed had a pleasant manner, and was generally considered a 'good Afghan'. Mulla Abdulla, an older man, was inclined to moodiness; he had recently been convicted of having killed meat off licensed premises, and had been unable to pay the fine. Abdulla had a strange walk, and was the butt of cruel jokes and insults from local children. Often they threw stones at him. One theory is that the younger Gool, fired with fanatical patriotism, inflamed the older man's smouldering resentment — and so the two resolved to make their attack. Another is that they simply used the war as a vehicle for one last defiant protest against unfair treatment. The people of Broken Hill were severely intolerant of the 'Afghan' group outside the town. There was a widespread ignorance of Moslem custom, and the 'Afghans' were often the object of ridicule.

There were plenty of reporters on the scene from both Broken Hill papers, the Barrier Miner and the Barrier Daily Truth. Both had representatives on the train, commissioned to 'do the picnic'. The Truth claimed that it had half a dozen men on the train, although some of them were off duty. One Truth man, Cyril Whetters, acted as a stretcher-bearer, and helped to carry George Stokes, a young boy who had been wounded in the chest and shoulder, from the train. Another Truth reporter was Hedley Ward, who later became turf editor of the Sydney Morning Herald.

The first report was published the same afternoon, in the Miner:

One of the longest and most crowded picnic trains that has ever left Broken Hill, carried those who set out with light hearts this morning to attend the annual M.U. Picnic at Silverton. The train left the Sulphide-street station at 10 a.m., and the goods station a few minutes later. The train consisted of two break vans and 40 ore trucks of the usual sort used for Barrier picnics, with a freight of some 1200 picnickers on board. When the train was about two miles on the way to Silverton, near the cattle yards, an ice-cream cart, with a flag flying on it was noticed on the northern side of the line, close to the railway fence. The flag was red about 18in. square, with a white crescent and white star — the flag of Turkey. Two men were also seen crouching behind the bank of earth which marks the line of the water main from Umberumberka to Broken Hill. These men attracted the attention of Mr. M. Kenny, who was a passenger on the train. Mr. Kenny, who is engaged on the water supply works in the capacity of electrician, thought at first that there must be something wrong with the main, and that these men were attending to the damage. He then saw that they had rifles in their hands, pointed at the train, and almost simultaneously he saw and heard the rifles fired. The firing continued during the whole time the train was passing the two men, 20 or 30 shots being fired in all. The men being so close to the train could be plainly seen to be either Turks or Afghans. As they were flying the Turkish flag it was assumed that they were Turks, of whom there are several in Broken Hill.

Mr. A. E. Millard was riding along the track beside the railway line as the train was fired on, and he became the target for one shot which killed him on the spot, the bullet going through his head.

The train was stopped, and it being ascertained that a number of the passengers had been seriously injured, if not killed, the train was taken a little further on to the Silverton Tramway Company's reservoir, where there is telephonic communication with Broken Hill. Three of the victims were removed from the train and taken to the pumping station at the reservoir, and medical men were summoned from Broken Hill.

The train with its saddened freight of men, women and children, then returned to Broken Hill, meeting on the way Dr. Moulden and others in motor cars, who had responded to the telephone calls. Some of the injured were taken into these cars, and the others were brought in on the train.

The alarm was telephoned from the railway pumping station to the police, and Inspector Miller at once sent a force of police to the scene. The constable on duty at the explosive magazine, not far from the scene, was early on the spot, and was in a position to give valuable assistance to his comrades. Lieutenant Resch was communicated with by the police, and he dispatched all the available men connected with the military forces whom he could reach.

The Turks, after their attack on the train, moved off towards the west of Broken Hill, and were followed by their armed pursuers.

After shooting another man on their way, they at last took cover in some rocks a few hundred yards west of the Cable Hotel. . . There was a desperate determination to leave no work for the hangman, or to run the risk of the murderers of peaceful citizens being allowed to escape. It was not a long battle. The attacking party was being constantly reinforced by eager men, who arrived in any vehicles they could obtain or on foot. At just about 1 o'clock a rush took place to the Turks' stronghold, and they were found lying on the ground behind their shelter. Both had many wounds. One was dead, and the other expired at the Hospital later. They wore the dress of their people, with turbans on their heads. The police took charge of the bodies. . .

Just before the final rush took place Inspector Miller and Lieutenant Resch, in a motor-car (the latter driving), swept round the hill between the Cable Hotel and the enemy's position. On reaching the front of the firing line the occupants (including a third person, a civilian), all armed with rifles, joined in the advance, and were just in time to reach the fallen foe amongst the first dozen or so. Inspector Miller checked a disposition (that was manifested by some) to fall upon the bodies of the killed or wounded men. On first examination both the Turks seemed to be dead. One had been shot through the head, and the other had several wounds, and was motionless. On being carried down towards the road, by which the ambulance would be able to approach, Inspector Miller noticed a movement in the latter, who, on further examination, was found to be alive. He was removed to the Hospital, and there attended to, but he was evidently mortally wounded, and his death was only a question of a very few hours.

Next day, Saturday 2 January, the Truth *had more facts. Hedley Ward interviewed one of the victims, a Mrs Crabb. She told him:*

I was sitting in the second truck from the engine, with the baby on my shoulder. I had turned so as to protect the child from the wind, and had his head upon my shoulder, above the breast. My husband was beside me, smoking, and leaning forward so that the smoke should not go in my face. That probably saved his life. I saw the red flag on the cart, and said, 'There's the danger signal.' My husband thought it was an ammunition cart, and said, 'It's very careless of them to draw explosives up so close to the line!'

Then we heard the guns go. I said, 'My God! It's the Germans! I'm shot! Get down for your lives!'

The bullet had gone right through my shoulder. . .

Of the Turks' last stand, Ward wrote:

Police and military surrounded the dastards from positions of advantage, leaving as the only means of escape the wide flat plains stretching to the westward. If they had retired in the latter direction they would have presented easy marks for the two score or more men who were determined to avenge the awful crime committed by these dark-skinned aliens who had for so long lived under the protection of the laws of Australia. . .

The Moslems took up what was from the front an immensely strong position, the top of a hill from which rose great columns of quartz. The only disadvantage under which they laboured from this aspect was that they showed in relief against the colour of the rocks whenever they in the least exposed their movements.

There are on these natural buttresses two great, black, powder-burnt splotches, showing where the Moslems held the fort.

That on the right, taken by Abdullah, appeared the more secure of the two, but he was unduly reckless. When he received his first dose of medicine, he dropped further back, as smaller powder marks show, but he did not do a great deal of further shooting. . .

On the Monday morning, 4 January, the Truth *cover continued to reflect the mood of emotionalism and wonder which had invaded the town. It insisted, wrongly, in an editorial headed 'The Terrible Turk', that the attackers were Turks, and cautioned against any attacks on Afghans or Indians at the camel camps.*

'They are not to be despised. They are mostly soldiers trained . . . in the most dangerous of warfare — that FOR ENGLAND against the hill tribes on the borders of the Indian Empire — and, given anything like equal terms, they would make a holy show of untrained whites did the latter interfere with them.'

Under a bright half-moon, the Anzacs land at Gallipoli

ELLIS ASHMEAD-BARTLETT
Melbourne Argus, 8 May 1915

Until he reached Gallipoli, Ellis Ashmead-Bartlett, the war correspondent chosen to represent the British press in the Dardanelles in 1915, knew almost nothing about Australia. 'We hear very little about Australia in England,' he later explained to the Melbourne Argus correspondent C. P. Smith. 'I am sure there are hundreds of thousands at home who think that all Australians are black. I really believe hundreds of thousands of Kitchener's new troops expected to see your troops like Indians. I heard of one young fellow who was astonished to find you spoke the same language as he did. . .'

After he talked with the English correspondent, Smith wrote in some astonishment: 'Mr Ashmead-Bartlett knew practically nothing of our compulsory defence system, of our transcontinental railway, of the Federal capital city, of our social experiments, or even of the natural resources of Australia. He had not even heard of the referendum bills or of Melbourne's cable trams.' The only piece of Australian intelligence Ashmead-Bartlett possessed: a returned traveller had remarked one day at his club that the girls were very pretty.

On 25 April Ellis Ashmead-Bartlett, the man who had never heard of Melbourne's cable trams, qualified as a distinguished recorder of Australian history. Under a bright half-moon, he watched the men of the Australian and New Zealand Army Corps land at Gaba Tepe, on the western shore of the Gallipoli peninsula. His account of the landing, published on 8 May, was the first to reach Australia; it was a classic piece of reporting which has become accepted as a major historical source.

It was as if a rich vein of human ore had been discovered. Afterwards Smith wrote:

If he [Ashmead-Bartlett] had by some mischance watched the Helles landing instead of that at Anzac Cove the astonishing bravery and persistence of the Australians in adverse conditions might still have been unrecognised by the great British public, which loves a vivid pen impression. . . These Australian soldiers were just the rugged pioneers, the farmers, the dairymen, the footballers, the cricketers, the tennis players, the professional and business men, and the factory hands of our six great States — the people we meet in trams and trains, who jostle up in Collins Street and crush us good-humouredly at the Flinders Street station barrier — but we did not know their worth until a London journalist discovered that our fighting men were giants, a new, strange race that had no fear, and who could face almost certain death as if they sought to die. Only then did we understand what splendid fellows these were, and what a proud thing it was to be Australian.

A legend had been born.

Ashmead-Bartlett, who made a lecture tour of Australia early the following year, nourishing the legend, was a member of the staff of the London Daily Telegraph. His Gallipoli report which follows was prefaced by the note that, as representative of the British press, he had 'had the privilege of being on board one of the warships that carried 500 Australians who formed the covering party for the landing'.

It required splendid skill, organisation, and leadership to get the huge armada under way from Mudros Bay, on the south of Lemnos Island, in the Aegean Sea, without accident. The warships and transports were divided into five divisions.

Never before had an attempt been made to land so large a force in the face of a well-prepared enemy.

At 2 o'clock in the afternoon of April 24 the flagship of the division, conveying the Australians and New Zealanders, passed down the long line of slowly moving transports, amid tremendous cheering, and was played out of Mudros Bay by French warships. At 4 o'clock the ship's company and the troops assembled to hear Admiral de Roebeck's proclamation to the combined forces.

This was followed by the last service before battle, in which the chaplain uttered the prayer for victory and called the Divine blessing on the expedition. All stood with uncovered and bowed heads.

At dusk the bugle sounded for 'all lights out', and the troops rested for the ordeal that they were to undergo at dawn next day.

It was a beautiful calm night, with a bright half-moon shining.

By 1 o'clock in the morning the ships had reached the rendezvous, five miles from the appointed landing place, and the soldiers were aroused and served with the last hot meal.

The Australians, who were about to go into action for the first time in trying circumstances, were cheerful, quiet, and confident. There was no sign of nerves nor of excitement.

As the moon waned, the boats were swung out, the Australians received their last instructions, and men who six months ago had been living peaceful civilian lives had begun to disembark on a strange and unknown shore in a strange land to attack an enemy of a different race.

Each boat was in charge of a midshipman, and was loaded with great rapidity. Absolute silence was preserved, and there was not a hitch. A covering force was towed ashore by the ship's pinnaces, and more of the Australian brigade were carried aboard the torpedo-boat destroyers which were to go close in shore as soon as the covering force was landed.

At 3 o'clock, when it was quite dark, a start was made for the shore. There was suppressed excitement. Would the enemy be surprised or on the alert?

At 4 o'clock three battleships in line abreast and four cables apart stood in 2,500 yards from the shore. Their guns were manned and their searchlights got ready.

Very slowly, the boats in tow, like twelve great snakes, moved inshore, each edging towards each other in order to reach the beach four cables apart.

The battleships moved slowly in after them until the water shallowed.

Every eye was fixed on the grim line of hills in the front, menacing in the gloom, and the mysteries of which those in the boats were about to solve.

Not a sound was heard, and when a light was seen it appeared as if the enemy had been surprised. In our nervy state the stars were often mistaken for lights ashore.

When close in at least three boats broke away from their tow and drifted down the coast without control. They were sniped at the whole way, and steadily lost their men.

The work of disembarking proceeded mechanically under a point blank fire. The moment the boats touched the beach the troops jumped ashore and doubled for cover, but the gallant boat crews had to pull in and out under the galling fire from hundreds of points.

All through April 25 this went on during the landing of troops, ammunition, and stores. When it was daylight the warships endeavoured to support the boats by heavy fire from their secondary armaments, but, not knowing the enemy's position, the support was more moral than real.

When the sun had fully risen we could see that the Australasians had actually established themselves on the ridge, trying to work their way northward along it.

The fighting was so confused, and it occurred on such broken ground, that it was difficult to follow exactly what happened on April 25, except that the covering forces carried out their task so splendidly that the disembarkation of the remainder was allowed to proceed uninterruptedly, except for the never-ceasing sniping.

The progress of the boats was slow, and dawn was rapidly breaking.

At 10 minutes to 4 o'clock the enemy

Anzac Cove, with Australian and Indian transport on the beach

showed an alarm light, which flashed for ten minutes, and then disappeared.

Our boats appeared almost as one on the beach, the seven torpedo-boat destroyers glided noiselessly inshore, and at 7 minutes to 4 o'clock came a sharp burst of rifle-fire from the beach.

The sound relieved the prolonged suspense, which had become almost intolerable.

When the fire had lasted a few minutes a faint British cheer came over the waters, telling us that the first position had been won.

At 3 minutes past 5 o'clock the fire became intensified. By the sound we could tell our men were firing. This lasted 25 minutes, and then died down somewhat, and the boats returned.

A pinnace was the first to come alongside.

There were two recumbent figures on the deck, and a small midshipman, cheerful, and waving his hand, with a shot through the stomach.

The three had been wounded in the first burst of musketry.

They related that the boats had almost reached the beach, when a party of Turks, entrenched ashore, opened a terrible fusillade with rifles and a Maxim. Fortunately, the majority of the bullets went high.

The Australians rose to the occasion. Not waiting for orders, or for the boats to reach the beach, they sprang into the sea, and, forming a sort of rough line, rushed at the enemy's trenches.

Their magazines were not charged, so they just went in with cold steel.

It was over in a minute. The Turks in the

first trench were either bayoneted or they ran away, and their Maxim was captured.

Then the Australians found themselves facing an almost perpendicular cliff of loose sandstone, covered with thick shrubbery. Somewhere, about half-way up, the enemy had a second trench, strongly held, from which they poured a terrible fire on the troops below and the boats pulling back to the destroyers for the second landing party.

Here was a tough proposition to tackle in the darkness, but those colonials, practical above all else, went about it in a practical way.

They stopped for a few minutes to pull themselves together, got rid of their packs, and charged their magazines.

Then this race of athletes proceeded to scale the cliffs without responding to the enemy's fire. They lost some men, but did not worry.

In less than a quarter of an hour the Turks were out of their second position, either bayoneted or fleeing.

There has been no finer feat in this war than this sudden landing in the dark and storming the heights, above all holding on whilst the reinforcements were landing. . .

As the daylight came it was seen that our landing was being effected rather farther north of Gaba Tepe than was intended originally; and at a point where the cliffs rise very sheer. The effor was a blessing in disguise, because there were no glacis, down which the enemy could fire; and the broken ground afforded good cover, once our men passed across the 40 yards of flat beach.

The country in the vicinity of the landing is formidable and forbidding. Out to sea it presents a steep front, broken into innumerable ridges, bluffs, valleys, and sand-pits. . .

Rising to a height of several hundred feet, and with a surface of crumbly sandstone, covered with a thick shrubbery about 6 ft. in height, it is ideal for snipers; as the Australians soon found to their cost.

On the other hand, the Australians proved themselves adepts at this kind of warfare.

In the early part of the day heavy casualties were suffered in the boats conveying the troops from the destroyers and in the tugs from the transports. The enemy's sharpshooters were hidden everywhere, and they concentrated their fire on these boats.

But then the Australasians, whose blood was up, instead of entrenching, rushed northwards and eastwards, searching for fresh enemies to bayonet. It was difficult country in which to entrench. Therefore they preferred to advance.

The Turks only had a weak force actually holding the beach. They relied on the difficult ground and the snipers to delay the advance until their reinforcements came up.

Some of the Australasians who pushed inland were counter-attacked, and almost outflanked by the oncoming reserves. They had to fall back after having suffered leavy losses.

Those counter-attacks were continued by the Turks throughout the afternoon, but the Australasians did not yield a foot on the main ridge.

Reinforcements poured up from the beach, but the Turks enfiladed the beach with two field guns from Gaba Tepe. This shrapnel fire was incessant and deadly, and the warships for some hours vainly tried to silence it.

The majority of the heavy casualties during the day were from the shrapnel which swept the beach and the ridge where the Australians established themselves later in the day. Then the enemy's guns were silenced or forced to withdraw, and a cruiser, moving close inshore, plastered Gaba Tepe with a hail of shell.

Towards dusk the attacks became more vigorous. The enemy was supported by powerful artillery inland, which the ship's guns were powerless to deal with. The pressure on the Australians became heavier, and their lines had to be contracted.

General Birdwood and his staff landed in the afternoon, and devoted their energies to securing the position so as to hold it firm until the next morning, when it was hoped to get the field guns into position.

Some idea of the difficulty may be gathered when it is remembered that every round of ammunition and all water and stores had to be landed on a narrow beach and carried up pathless hills and valleys several hundred feet high to the firing line.

The whole mass of our troops was concentrated in a very small area, and was unable to reply when exposed to a relentless and incessant shrapnel fire which swept every yard of ground.

Fortunately much of the enemy's fire was badly aimed, and their shells burst too high.

A serious problem was getting the wounded from the shore. All those unable to hobble had to be carried from the hills on stretchers, and then their wounds hastily dressed and the men carried to the boats.

The boat parties worked unceasingly through the entire day and night.

The courage displayed by these wounded Australians will never be forgotten. Hastily placed in trawlers, lighters, and boats, they were towed to the ships, and, in spite of their sufferings, cheered on reaching the ship from which they had set out in the morning.

In fact, I have never seen anything like these wounded Australians in war before.

Though many were shot to bits, without the hope of recovery, their cheers resounded throughout the night. You could see in the midst of the mass of suffering humanity arms waving in greeting to the crews of the warships.

They were happy because they knew that they had been used for the first time and had not been found wanting.

For fifteen mortal hours our men occupied the heights under an incessant shell fire, without the moral or material support of a single gun ashore, and they were subjected the whole time to the violent counter-attack of a brave enemy, skilfully led, with snipers deliberately picking off every officer who endeavoured to give a command or lead his men.

Ashmead-Bartlett followed up that report with another dispatch on the second day's fighting. 'These colonials,' he wrote, 'are extraordinarily good under fire.' He was amazed to see them bathing in the sea, with shrapnel bursting all around them.

Throughout the night of Monday, April 26, the Turks harassed our lines by creeping up and endeavouring to snipe the Australasian troops in their trenches, which were subjected

Members of the Second Light Horse Regiment in an Australian trench at Anzac. The periscope rifle was invented by an Australian at Gallipoli

to constant shell-fire. But the Turks never dared to press their attack, although they were in overwhelming numbers.

The Turks paid dearly for their temerity. One section of the New Zealanders, with a bayonet charge, drove the enemy off in disorder. It was obvious on the morning of Tuesday, April 27, that the Turks had not recovered from the terrible hammering they received on the previous day, and had no stomach for another big attack.

Our entrenchments were then firmly established, in a semi-circular front along the whole of the foreshore, which was being used for the disembarkation of troops, supplies and ammunition. The position of the colonial troops was also immeasurably improved by the landing of field-guns and of several Indian mountain batteries.

It was evident that the Turks intended on April 26 to drive the Australians into the sea by a great concentration of infantry and by increasing their shrapnel fire.

They expected to find our line thinly held, the men exhausted by their losses and exertion during the landing, and so on. They were disillusioned.

These Australians were determined to die to a man rather than surrender the ground they had so dearly won. Every man knew that his only hope of safety lay in victory, as it was impossible to re-embark the army once the ring of hills commanding the beach had been lost.

Most troops, when under fire for the first time, especially volunteers with only a few months' training, keenly feel losses at the beginning, more especially if these occur before they have had time to settle down, but these colonials are the exception to the rule.

Despite their heavy losses, the survivors were as keen as ever. Throughout Tuesday the enemy resorted to new tactics, in the hope of driving the colonials off the shore and so preventing supplies and reinforcements reaching the beach.

The Turks on Tuesday night brought up many field-guns, with which they opened a tremendous bombardment of the foreshore and the sea, and kept up an incessant rain of shrapnel on the trenches. They could no longer enfilade the beach, as every attempt to place their guns was immediately checkmated by a few well-aimed salvos from the Allied warships.

The Turkish gunners tried to put a great curtain of shrapnel over the sea between the warships and the transports and the shore.

It was an amazing sight. Scores of shells were bursting and churning up the water like a great hailstorm.

Some of the shells fell far out to sea. Others, again, made a great danger zone through which the Allies' boats and trawlers had to pass.

This hail of lead did not make the slightest difference to the gallant crews of the pinnaces, boats, lighters, and tugs. They took as much

notice of it as they would of a tropical thunderstorm. The spectacular effect of the bombardment was magnificent, but the damage practically nil.

The Anglo-French warships throughout Tuesday incessantly fired on any of the enemy's infantry which attempted to advance. Our hydroplanes did excellent work in directing the fire on the Turkish guns inland.

The indirect firing of the warships has become more efficient every day. It is now so accurate that nothing in range can live, provided that the target is accurately spotted. The Turks frequently fire their heavy guns on the other side of the peninsula, hoping to hole the transports, but they have not yet succeeded.

If a Turkish warship in the Straits makes any attempt to attack, a salvo from the Allies' ships speedily forces her to fly up the channel.

The scene ashore is one of the most intense activity. One lands in an avalanche of shrapnel, and finds regiments waiting on the beach before moving to the trenches. Fatigue parties are unloading boats and lighters, and mule trains are endeavouring to drag field guns into position, while the Indians are engaged in conveying mountain guns to the point where they are needed. At the dressing stations all are busy tending the wounded, and the telegraph and telephone units are laying the wires of communication. Meanwhile landing parties from the warships have been busy building bomb-proof shelters.

Thousands of hardy Australians and New Zealanders are concentrated on a narrow shore, each engaged in some occupation, for as soon as a man leaves the front trenches he is required for fatigue duty. Few have had more than a few hours' sleep for days past. The General's staff officers fare no better than the men. . .

These colonials are extraordinarily good under fire, often exposing themselves rather than take the trouble to keep under shelter of the cliff. One of the strangest sights was to see the numbers bathing in the sea with the shrapnel bursting all around them.

1915　Australia's official war correspondent reports on the battle at Lone Pine

C. E. W. BEAN
Melbourne Argus, 28 April 1915

In 1914, not long after the outbreak of war, journalists throughout Australia voted for the post of Australia's official war correspondent. C. E. W. Bean, of the Sydney Morning Herald, *got the job by a narrow margin of votes from Keith Murdoch, the Melbourne representative of the Sydney* Sun. *Bean went on to become Australia's major war historian, compiler of the monumental volume* Official History of Australia in the 1914–18 War, *and Murdoch, as editor-in-chief and later chairman of directors of the Herald and Weekly Times, became one of the most powerful newspaper proprietors the nation has seen. Both men, curiously, were parsons' sons.*

Bean was born at Bathurst in 1879, studied law, and was called to the Bar in 1903. Three years later he joined the literary staff of the Sydney Morning Herald, *and in 1909 was appointed London correspondent of that paper. After his return from London in 1913, he became the* Herald's *leader writer. His selection as official war correspondent gave him the automatic rank of captain with the AIF, but he insisted throughout his service that he he a civilian; he felt, justifiably, that any acknowledgement of military status would mean a loss of freedom. He sailed in one of the first contingents to leave Australia, in October 1914, and remained with the troops throughout the Gallipoli campaign. He was wounded while covering the battle of Lone Pine, his account of which is published here. After the evacuation he went to France and remained with the Australians until the end of the war. He was joined in France by a South Australian journalist, Frederick Cutlack, who later also joined Bean on the* Sydney Morning Herald *staff.*

From the day he left Australia until the end of the war, Bean filled 300 volumes of notes and diaries. Scribbling by the light of a sinking moon, he watched the first battalions land at Gallipoli; his fine account of the assault was not published in Australia until six days after the account by the British reporter Ashmead-Bartlett had been splashed in all papers. Ashmead-Bartlett later described Bean as one of the ablest correspondents in the world.

In one dispatch, Bean compared conditions at Gallipoli with those in Flanders. His verdict: the trenches at Gallipoli were more elaborate, the torrents of shell bombardment in France were worse, the weather conditions more uncomfortable on the French battleground. The real discomfort of Gallipoli, he wrote, was that it was impossible to obtain any relief from the gunfire, the flies, the tunnelling, the water carrying and the shortage of canteen stores. 'The so-called rest camp was often within 100 yards of the firing line, and always under shell fire, and the rest consisted largely of mining and water-carrying, so that units honestly preferred the trenches. Brigades were in the trenches for four, five and six months.'

This is his eye-witness account from Lone Pine, published on 28 August 1915, in the Argus:

An inspection of the Turkish trenches, captured at Lonesome Pine Plateau (across which the centre of the Australian line at Anzac runs) had shown what an extraordinarily formidable obstacle the 1st Australian (N.S.W.) Infantry Brigade was up against when it was ordered to take this position. For month upon month we have seen the Turks piling up colossal parapets. It was because the place was so strong and important, and because we desired to give the Turks a really heavy blow at the southern end of our line, that these trenches were chosen for the attack.

The 3rd (Q., S.A., W.A., and Tas.) Brigade had made the famous assault on landing at Gaba Tepe, the 2nd (Vic.) made the wonderful charge at Cape Helles, and the 1st Brigade, therefore, was chosen for the assault on Lonesome Pine. It was a tremendous job to put before any brigade, but these Australian infantry have never from the first to the last shown the least concern about it.

I was with the 3rd battalion five minutes before the start, behind a parapet, over which, five minutes hence, they knew they would have to scramble in the face of rifle fire, machine guns, and shrapnel. They did not know what might be awaiting them in the deadly space between the trenches, but not one showed the slightest sign of uneasiness. A man would pass along the trench to find his platoon just as a belated spectator might hurry to his seat before the curtain rises at a theatre. As he passed along he would recognise some friend. 'Good-bye, Bill,' he would say. 'Meet you over there.' 'So long, Tom,' was the reply; 'See you again in half an hour.'

'Are you going to get a photograph of me?' they would ask me. 'How do you work it — on sandbags or through a periscope?' 'What sort of a camera is it?' 'My word, what a great chance for a photographer.'

Then the conversation was suddenly cut short by the voice of a little officer, crouching just below the parapet, saying: 'Get ready to go over the parapet.' He glanced down at his wrist watch, and so did I. It was 5.27. The men crouched up a little higher on the recess, preparing to spring. Those in the trench below got a firmer foothold. The little officer unstrapped his whistle from his wrist, and held it between his teeth. He glanced down at the watch again. The man next to me asked what time it was. I looked down. 'Well, I make it 5.30,' I answered.

The bombardment had apparently stopped. There were a few minutes of breathless silence, and then the whistle sounded. Within a second the little officer had blown his whistle, too, There was a scramble of feet over the parapet, a sound of falling earth, and the knocking of accoutrements. The peck-peck of Mauser rifles from the trench opposite, which had already begun, gradually swelled into a rattle.

A man fell past me into the trench, bleeding from a wound in the mouth. Out in the scrub a line of old pea-soup Australian khaki was racing, jumping low bushes and wire, straight for the enemy's trench.

When they got there they experienced what in military phraseology is known as a check. That is to say, instead of an open trench, into which they could jump and bayonet the Turks, they found themselves looking down on a solid roof, made of a line of logs, covered with earth, on which our bombardment had not made any perceptible impression.

This surprise might well enough upset the nerves of some troops, but the behaviour of the 1st Brigade did not give the onlookers the least cause for anxiety. The men clearly were puzzled what to do, but they did not show the least sign of even thinking of retiring. Some ran on to the second or third trench, till they found open trenches, where they could fire down and jump into. Others strung out along the first trench, firing into loopholes, from which the Turks were still shooting. Others jumped down into a few gaps left without head-cover. Still others noticed small man-holes every here and there in the solid roof of the trench, and began to lower themselves into the trench, feet foremost, a feat of daring, which, if it had been a solitary example, would certainly have won the Victoria Cross in any previous war.

Such as could not get in simply waited outside on the parapet firing down the communication trenches until they could think of something else to do. Within a quarter of an hour all were in the trenches.

I saw about ten lines cross during two hours under machine-gun, rifle, and such hail of shrapnel as temporarily shut out all sight of them in places, and every line I saw seemed as eager as that first one.

The Australian infantry has made for itself a wonderful name in Gallipoli. Certainly no finer feat has been accomplished here than this taking of Lonesome Pine and holding it against a counter-attack lasting six solid days. . .

This newly captured front-line trench at Lone Pine was only yards from the enemy lines

1915 A correspondent describes Australians under fire at Anzac Cove

C. P. SMITH
Melbourne Argus, 5 October 1915

Evelyn Waugh, in his satirical novel Scoop, *wrote about a gardening writer who had been sent to cover the Abyssinian war. Charles Patrick Smith, the* Argus *man in the Dardanelles and the Balkans during World War One, had almost as unlikely a background for war reporting as Waugh's fictional hero. For most of his life he had been a linotype operator, with a burning, consistently frustrated ambition to become a journalist. For several years before the war he had filled in as rifle-shooting correspondent for the* Argus *on Saturday afternoons. When the paper decided to send a correspondent to join Australian forces abroad in December 1915, his rifle-shooting background was considered a distinct advantage; war, it was reasoned with a kind of bland, disarming logic, was a place where plenty of rifles were shot.*

The success story of Charles P. Smith contains a fine 'if-at-first' moral and a certain inevitability of plot. Hollywood could have used it well: young boy, having migrated from Canada with his parents, becomes obsessed with the idea of becoming a reporter; applies to various newspapers as soon as he leaves school, but the nearest he can get to journalism is a job as an assistant proof-reader on the Melbourne Sportsman; *teaches himself shorthand, sends little contributions to the* Herald *and* Bulletin, *applies for second time to* Argus *at the age of nineteen; is judged to be unsuitable material, either for the editorial or composing rooms staffs. The following year he tries another application to the paper's printer; it is pointed out that, as an apprentice and a non-member of the Typographical Society, he is ineligible for employment in the printing room. In the next few months he saves £25, buys out his apprenticeship indentures, goes*

to Bendigo, is accepted as member of Bendigo Typographical Society after paying thirteen weeks' contributions. Reapplies to Argus, *is accepted as 'sub-grass hand' — lowliest form of life in composing room. At twenty-one, is laid off during an economy campaign, decides to go to New Zealand; is reinstated, as result of influenza epidemic which had laid out many old hands, just before he is due to sail; spends next eight years working steadily in composing room (to become third in charge of linotypes), nurses old ambition, refuses to become bitter; does rifle-shooting notes on casual basis, but big break comes when, in 1910, explosion occurs in Brunswick Street, Fitzroy, as he is passing on his way home after midnight; he returns to office, not only reports blast, but then goes to linotype machine and sets his own story in type; on next holiday, editor asks him to write series of articles on rebuilding of Sydney, and to report boxing match between Sam Langford and Sam Mc Vea. In 1912, at the age of thirty-four, he is accepted as recruit on reporting staff; transfer from linotype operating to journalism earns him a cut in pay — from £8 to £7.*

Although it took him a long time to demonstrate it, Smith possessed real flair. He quickly distinguished himself as a political reporter, and was at Bacchus Marsh, reporting a visit by Prime Minister Andrew Fisher, when Fisher learned that war had been declared. Smith became a war correspondent attached to the staff of General (later Sir) John Monash, and was with Australian forces at Gallipoli from July until September. Invalided to Egypt, he later covered the war on the Balkan front. Smith was a brilliant exponent of the personal style of war reporting which was exploited one war later by men like Ernie Pyle and Alan

Moorehead; in the first World War it was rare. He left the broad tactical analyses to others, and concentrated on relating the war to the men who fought it. 'There is so much to see, and so little can be focussed, that the eyes become bewildered,' he wrote from Anzac Cove. 'It is like trying to read half a dozen books at once, or endeavoring to take in a three-ring circus at a single glance.'

The boy who had been rejected as a recruit for both the editorial and composing room work had a distinguished career. In January 1916, he became chief of the literary staff of the Argus, *and he accompanied Prime Minister Billy Hughes to the Imperial Conference in London in 1921.*

He went on to become managing editor of West Australian Newspapers, retiring in 1951. He died on 5 August 1963, at the age of eighty-five.

No one feels afraid before battle. The one fear that possesses all ranks is that they might display some sign of fright. A few have presentiments of coming evil, but the great majority are confident that all prospective trouble belongs to someone else. The excitement of the moment is contagious. It runs up and down like a current of electricity, galvanising every individual and unit into that condition of stoic bravery that produces the perfect fighting machine.

"Nervous? Why, I'd sooner meet the Turks than a dentist, any day!" remarked a Melbourne youth who was adjusting his web equipment without a tremor, and half a dozen others picked at random answered the question by asking another, "What of?" One pale-faced lad, who boasted of having enlisted under a false age declaration, was sitting by himself, reading a letter. He seemed troubled. This looked like the one case of obvious 'cold feet'. In response to an inquiry the youthful soldier glanced up with a worried smile. He admitted readily to being disconcerted, and went on to explain. "What I'm reading about," he said, "is that my mates keep on week-end camping at Aspendale when they're wanted so bad out here!" He had not been thinking of the coming fight at all. Then he took a needle from

his "housewife", threaded it with the calm of a fireside mother, and set about mending a hole in his trousers. Next time I saw that boy he was pressing sparks out of a bayonet, on a grindstone, and joking about the grim work ahead. Before the Australian troops marched out that night to the fiercest fight of the Anzac campaign, they disported themselves like schoolboys on the brink of a "break-up" or university men at a commencement. There were no serious faces, no signs of tension. Being in company makes all the difference. My own heart was beating faster than was its custom, the palms of my hands were moist, until the step-off — then there was something else to think about.

First came the smashing detonation of our own big guns. The displacement of the air produced a shock that causes the strongest man to recall the occasions when too demonstrative friends have slapped them on the back. Each big-calibre piece has its peculiarity of greeting. One boxes the ears, another uppercuts to the jaw, so as to rattle the teeth, and a third send half-arm jabs to the stomach. The Indian mountain batteries do their best to paralyse the brain of those who happen to be near. There is nothing in war to compare with the ear-splitting crash of these guns at close quarters. At night it is nerve-racking. When these sensations are being delivered all at the same time by ally arms, and enemy shells begin to drop from the unknown, men wrinkle their foreheads. Even the most robust complain of a feeling of nausea during the first few moments of our own bombardment. After a while, however, the punching of the guns becomes softened by familiarity, and those who have contracted headaches soon forget it. A buoyancy of spirit follows and it is stimulated by the thought that every distant outburst of smoke and soil is reducing the number of enemies to be tackled. The terror of the big guns must be a very real thing for the men who have to stand up against them, but to have them on your side is half the battle. It is almost like having public opinion behind you. One man seems so insignificant in these surroundings. With the guns booming and brigades creeping in even a general is inconspicuous as a speck of sand on the beach.

When a shell bursts near enough to be dangerous, half the troops shrug their shoulders involuntarily and sink their chins. The other 50 per cent look on with an air of superior indifference. Every man makes up his mind not to duck, but the sensation is much the same as when a dog barks suddenly through a fence in a quiet street. It is all a matter of grip, not necessarily of nerve, because very often "jumpy" soldiers have been found to do the most daring feats when the real test comes. The imperturbables are frequently slow to move by comparison. The desire to rush into the open and view the wreck at the point of impact is difficult to conquer, although many hundreds of men have given their lives in satisfying this morbid curiosity. High explosive shells have an unpleasant habit of throwing dirt. This peculiarity has caused many of our troops to rush to the conclusion that they have been wounded, whereas in reality the soft, bulgy mass that suddenly forms around the waist belt is nothing more than grit forced violently through the open shirt front. At least one soldier made certain he had not been disembowelled. . .

After the heavy artillery has played the overture the small arms join in the orchestration. The rifles snap and spit with tiger-cat fierceness, but they do not inspire the awe of the big guns. I have heard men say they would much sooner face enemy bullets than shelter where a friendly 60-pounder is crashing constantly behind their ears. Troops move out to meet a rain of shots without a thought of personal risk. They realise the danger, but with that irrepressible optimism of the Australian, presume that they will win through somehow without a scratch. For a quarter of an hour on one occasion I stood watching the plaster of bullets tearing up the dust on a path across which our men had to pass, and was seized with a gnawing pity. When I thought that men would soon be in that storm of lead — men like me — I began to feel alarmed and very puny. It seemed as if someone should go back and warn these troops of the trap that was awaiting them. I had just decided that there was nothing quite so insignificant

in that battle as myself when the Australians began to arrive. They saw the specks of dirt jumping from the ground, but did not stop. Instead, they cheered, and went across that few yards like an express train. Nothing could have stemmed the rush, although it had seemed a moment before that not a living thing could have passed the zone. Later, aggravated firing was heard to the left, followed by a few screams, and the bullets suddenly stopped dropping on the track. There were a few ghastly relics to show the route by which the line had passed, while here and there a wounded man was applying his first field dressing under a shrub, but our aggregate loss was insignificant in comparison with what had been gained. An irresolute force or a timid one would have hesitated on that path just long enough to tempt destruction, but our men seemed to be spurred to further daring by the sight of enemy activity. Their forceful impetuosity has made them the admiration of friend and foe.

From a bullet, interruption to the soldier's career comes suddenly and from the unknown. He does not see what has hit him and the surroundings are usually not gruesome. When steel begins to flash and bombs to roar at close quarters the situation is quite different. I asked a former public school boy how he felt in a charge as he was sanding some nasty stains from his bayonet. "The waiting is worst," he said. "It is like sitting in a doctor's reception room or walking into an operating theatre. The mystery of the unknown begins to get you if the delay is too long. You look at the men around and wonder how many will get back. Somehow one never seems to realise that he might be among the missing. I have found myself thinking, however, that I should have written home, and that I had omitted to send an old chum the war trophies he had asked for. Then my mind turned somehow to the insufferable cruelty of life. I remember deciding while waiting for one charge that I would never be unkind to any living thing again, and that I would never speak another cross word. Now I look back it seems strange, considering I was on the point of slashing and maiming every man I could come across. I had just

Morale is high as Australian troops arrive at Flanders from Gallipoli in 1916

begun to picture what my people might be doing when the word was given. Subconsciously I got into my stride, and was racing with my teeth set, at the trench ahead. I have run in two 10-mile championships in Victoria, and that first burst down the Caulfield racecourse is the nearest thing to a real charge I can imagine. You hear the stamping feet around you, you see the set faces, and feel the jostling. A few men fall here and there but you never turn and look at them. You don't think of anything at all. Your whole mind is set on racing straight ahead. Suddenly you find yourself face to face with another man with a bayonet. Quick as thought you stab, without realising what you are doing. The first time I put a bayonet into a Turk's chest I came instantly back to my senses. After that everything was a blank — one just fights and pushes and runs without knowing what he is doing. It's just the same as in any closely contested athletic contest. Everything is a blurr; you sweat, and blow, and get angry, and begin to feel all out, but the excitement keeps you going."

When a soldier sees his first dead comrade a lump forms in his throat, and his heart sinks a little, but the emotion is only temporary. Use softens all things, however, and philosophic acceptance of the inevitable, rather than indifference or callousness, soon takes possession of all ranks. Sorrow for the wounded never evaporates. Once a man has been hit, whether friend or enemy, the heart of every Australian soldier goes out to him. I have seen men who had been carefully preserving their last few spoonfuls of water for hours toss their bottles to fallen soldiers with whom, in ordinary circumstances, they would have very little in common, and perhaps a few minutes afterwards they might drop down themselves.

It is the man who has lain for days in the open, undiscovered and unattended, who brings more grief and anxiety into an Australian force than an army corps of enemies. The soldier from the Commonwealth is one of the most courageous and relentless fighters on earth, but inside his broad chest there is a mysterious contradiction to all his exterior bluntness that makes him as sympathetic as a girl.

A few evenings ago I watched a party come out of a front trench to spell. They were dirty, hot, tired, hungry, thirsty, and generally "fed up" with everything. They were carrying the equipment of dead mates back to the depot. One caught a helpless little bird, and for ten minutes all delayed upon the road, each offering the other advice as to what might be best for its comfort.

They laughed and chatted like children. "Had a hard day?" I suggested. "Not too bad," one answered. "I only got two, but my mate hit four." Then he went on trying to give the bird a drink from his lips.

1916   Young Diggers move into line for the first time on the Western Front

KEITH MURDOCH
Melbourne Herald, 12 October 1916

For most of his life, Sir Keith Murdoch was a maker of newspapers and a maker of newspapermen. To be known as one of his bright young men, or, more specifically, to be called 'a Murdoch man', was something of an accolade in Australian journalism. The Murdoch man was a special breed; there were scores of them, and they went on to prominent media posts around Australia and in Fleet Street.

There was a time, of course, when Murdoch himself was a bright young man. That was after he had mastered his stammer, after he had had a stint at the London School of Economics, after he had established himself as a promising political journalist on the Age. *In 1914, he was appointed Melbourne representative of the Sydney* Sun. *In 1915, at the age of twenty-nine, he went overseas, partly to act as a war correspondent. He visited Gallipoli, and became involved in a major controversy. He concerned himself with the conduct of the campaign, carried away a letter from a British war correspondent to the British Prime Minister, and wrote in strong terms to the Australian Prime Minister about conditions on the peninsula.*

These actions brought Murdoch into bitter conflict with General Sir Ian Hamilton, who accused the young Australian of breach of faith, ignorance and inaccuracy. Murdoch insisted that he was justified in what he did, and claimed that his actions had been borne out by the views of both the British and Australian governments. In his book Gallipoli *(1956), Alan Moorehead — who was himself, incidentally, one of Murdoch's bright young men of the thirties — examined Murdoch's role in the controversy. He wrote: 'Things had been mismanaged, and Murdoch was telling the plain truth when he said so. In all*

events, it was the truth as he saw it, and in wartime there is a definite place for the reports of fresh eye-witnesses of this kind. . .'

Murdoch visited the Western Front a number of times during the remainder of the war, and many of his reports to the Melbourne Herald *gave accurate, colorful portraits of the war at close range. 'Picardy,' he wrote once, 'is typically and beautifully French. The deep Somme, wide and somewhat marshy, runs through the front. The slopes are gradual and easy, the little woods stand out dark upon the hills of corn and poppies, the ruined villages, mere dust-heaps, are at every cross road.'*

In this dispatch, he gives a fine picture of the first impressions of war for the young Digger moving into the line:

Nothing impresses one about our Australian troops at the front so much as that they have become soldiers. There is a world of meaning in that term "soldiers".

Our men in the trenches and behind them are strong in the physical and moral strength of the fighting man. Surrounded with accoutrements, tanned and weather-beaten, they look capable of giving and taking a blow, of enduring hardship, of using their weapons with ruthless aim, of showing as little mercy as they expect to get. Those left at home could not see them at their daily duties in the trenches, working cheerfully and industriously as men with a purpose, without feeling that for the time being they are different men.

In a recent wander along our firing line not far from Armentieres, I saw battalions changing — a new battalion fresh from Egypt, moving in — an old battalion of the glorious First Division, moving out to God knows what fate further south. And in the contrast was all the difference between the soldier and the civilian — the man who has endured and the man who has not yet seen blood on the battlefield, nor felt the world throb about him as missiles fall thick, and go back as heavily in reply.

There was one young soldier of our First Division with all the knacks of many generations of soldiers already learnt. His heavy iron hat was set with just a suspicion of jauntiness. His tunic was open to the collar, showing a full, strong neck. His pack and weapons were so well carried as to appear of little weight. Round his waist was a belt covered with the bright brass badges of many British regiments, and he sang as he marched. Doubtless, a real mother's son when at home, but here a campaigner of resource and zest.

Many such I noticed, all clean, for cleanliness is a characteristic of the Australian fighting man, and all self-reliant units skilled in war. British generals on our front say it takes an incredibly short time for a versatile Australian, mother's son though he be, to become a hardened soldier. Certainly they soon look real craftsmen at their new trade.

From Salisbury Plain in green, undulating Hampshire, the road for our new Australian soldiers is going to stretch through all the stages of soldiering to Berlin. . .

But the average draft is more lucky. His battalion is in billets behind the lines, resting, licking its wounds, waiting for these very drafts. Or he belongs to a set formation, a brigade or division, which moves up slowly from the back, learns its way, takes over gradually from those it is relieving, and may have few casualties for a month or so.

In any case the arrival of the first shell is a never-to-be-forgotten incident. It is like a man's marriage or twenty-first birthday, or like the death of his mother or the birth of his son. It is considerably more than the first time he kissed a girl. It startles his very soul.

It may be only shrapnel, with which the Germans rake the roads leading to the trenches. You have been half-expecting it. You have seen great curtains of sacks hung across the road, with just room for you to pass under them, and you have learnt that these are screens to prevent the enemy observers in their sausage balloons from directing hidden artillery upon you. The Germans fire a shell more readily than a rifle bullet, and you are far more likely to be under fire first from artillery. It is a curious sensation. The shriek of the shell is hardly over before the burst comes beside you. For the first few minutes the knees of the best of men knock together, his heart shakes, and his tongue requires careful control. But thereafter, if he be worthy of his race, he is fearless. And even when bombardment is fierce and sustained, "heavies" are bursting around, the earth is shaking, pals are dying, and the awful fumes of German shells are suffocating him, he will pull himself together when the German infantry comes, or he lacks the lusty red spirit of the Australian soldier.

Many of our battalions at Salisbury are "training battalions," and from these drafts continuously go forward to the fighting lines in France. While our losses have been so heavy in the Great Push, we have had to rush forward all the reinforcements ready for warfare. The fighting has not had many points of similarity with the Dardanelles — except in losses and in the sudden need for reinforcements. On the Somme the need has become just as pressing as it was on Gallipoli, and officers at present are busily employed in going backwards and forwards with drafts of 100 men each; but every officer agrees that these reinforcements are ready for anything. Most have been in training for more than six months. We have not had to interfere with the new formations; all requirements have come from the training battalions.

Much is done by senior officers to interest the men in the country. Long route marches are made through the most beautiful tracts of Hants and Devonshire, and amidst the landmarks and ruins of earliest England. All men get their occasional four days' leave in London, or five days in Scotland, with free railway passes. Those who are lucky, and are kept long enough at Salisbury, get a second turn of leave, and most manage to get final leave before going to the front. Yet they are intensely glad when they pack their kits and march out with a few comrades to some mid-station on the Exeter-London railway; for, at last, and in incredibly few hours, they will be at grips with the Germans.

The journey is short, because its organisation has become as smooth and regular as an express passenger service. From London trains go at regular intervals to meet cross-Channel boats at the south-east ports — Dover, Folkestone, sometimes Southampton. The boats are met on the other side by more trains. These trains run to time-table to the inside bases of each army — Munro's First, Plumer's Second, Allenby's Third, Rawlinson's Fourth. The distribution of the men on this fan-shaped area, with its pivot in London itself, is methodical. At the army bases more trains are met, and the drafts again subdivided. They pass on to the rail-heads, and then by motor or on foot to the division they are intended for, and thence to the brigade and battalion and company.

And so the Australian sees little on his passage. The attention of the line of communications officers is concentrated on getting him to his objective. He passes through Calais or Boulogne without knowing the extraordinary efforts being made in these quiet seaports to keep armies supplied with bread and meat and munitions; without noticing that huge remount depots are choked with horses, awaiting the great advance; or that thousands of French and Belgian women are mending the clothes and disinfecting the gas-helmets and linen of his comrades, while a corps of men of his own nationality is making, in gigantic factories, the bread he is to eat to-morrow. He is plunged into the wonderful coloring of rural France, and experiences for a moment the light-hearted joys of the new traveller. He cannot help noticing the beautiful domesticity of the countryside, the industrious, thrifty mothers, the clean and vivacious children; unfailingly, he thinks of another country, as lovely, as sunny, as calm and peaceful. He thinks of some of the people there. . .

After the war, in 1920, Murdoch accompanied the Prince of Wales on his visit to Australia and New Zealand in HMS Renown, *as a repres-*

Sydney women march on 5 May 1918

entative of The Times *and Australian newspapers. When the tour ended, he was invited to return to Melbourne and take over editorial control of the* Herald. *In the following years he built up that newspaper and its family of associated journals into the greatest newspaper network in Australia. He took over the Melbourne* Sun News-Pictorial, *which had been started by the Sydney* Sun, *in June 1925; he extended the company's interests to radio and newspapers in other States. His son Rupert became a successful newspaper proprietor in Britain, Australia and the United States of America.*

At his last annual meeting, in December 1951, he used a phrase in his speech as chairman of directors that seemed to sum up his working life. 'The old journalist dies,' he said, 'still stretching out for better English, better cover of actualities, better comment, better taste, more happiness in his paper's pattern.' Sir Keith Murdoch died on 4 October 1952.

1917   Les Darcy, the great Australian prizefighter, dies of a 'broken heart'

W. F. CORBETT
Sydney Referee, 25 May 1917

Les Darcy, the great Australian prizefighter, enlisted in Brisbane for active service in 1916, at the age of twenty. His mother insisted on his discharge as a minor. Meantime, an urgent demand arrived for him to fight in the United States. That, to Darcy, meant a chance to become the first Australian to hold an undisputed world championship. He was persuaded to travel from Sydney to New York, in contravention of the War Precautions Act. On his arrival in the United States, he received a spectacular reception from Tex Rickard, the man who within a few years was promoting the first million-dollar-gate fights.

Soon after Darcy arrived, a number of United States papers launched a campaign against him, accusing him of being a deserter from the armed forces. He was banned from the prize-ring and had to join a travelling vaudeville troupe. The ban was later lifted, and Darcy was cleared of all charges; he then took out United States naturalisation papers, and joined the Flying Corps. Within a matter of days, though, Darcy, who had allowed himself to become exhausted, contracted pneumonia. He died in hospital at Memphis, Tennessee, on 24 May 1917, at the age of twenty-one. His trainer, Mick Hawkins, who had guided his career from the start, was beside him when he died.

In San Francisco, 500 people marched behind the cortege before Darcy's body was taken on board the steamship Sonoma *for the journey home. His funeral ceremony at West Maitland attracted crowds estimated to be as large as 100,000. Thousands of people filed past the body during the two days it was on view.*

W. F. Corbett, senior, one of Australia's best boxing writers and a member of a family which has distinguished itself in sportswriting, wrote this report about Darcy's death for the Referee:

Les Darcy is dead! Only a few short months ago he was the idol of Australia. And then he left us and it became known that he had taken the first steps towards becoming one of another nation, excuses for him were plentiful though he was roundly condemned in some places. Last Wednesday week I published a letter which Mr. R. L. Baker had received from the Australian boxing wonder, apparently ostracised from his own country. The writing was that of a penitent, and it was so brimful of contrition and earnest desire to make all reparation possible that only a heart of stone could have been deaf to the boy's appeal. I strongly recommended it to the consideration of the responsible authorities, and urged that whatever offence against the laws of the land which might have been committed by him should, and could well be, in the circumstances overlooked. I found a good supporter in Mr. Baker.

A couple of days before we heard of Darcy's serious illness Mr. Baker called for the letter with the intention of forwarding it through the proper channels, attended by as many recommendations as he could collect, to the Minister for Defence.

We — Mr. Baker and myself — knew that all going well and the way being open, Les Darcy would sail from America homeward-bound early next month to fulfil his covenant with the Australian military authorities. And the exact date of his departure was fixed. Now he is mere clay.

"Whom the gods love die young." Heaven gives its favorites early death. . .

Corbett also quoted this report, supplied by the Memphis Press:

Darcy's heart was breaking fast.

Then he met Billy Haack, local boxing promoter. The champion was induced to come to Memphis. Learning of the fighter's arrival in the Bluff City, Mayor Tom Ashcroft issued a proclamation that Darcy could not fight in Memphis. Later, . . . Ashcroft withdrew his statement, and announced that if Darcy would enlist in some branch of Uncle Sam's service he could box here.

The champion was elated. He went to the North Memphis Driving Park, where he enlisted in the U.S. Aviation Corps. He passed all examinations with flying colors, and was promoted to the rank of sergeant.

A change was immediately noticed in his demeanour. He was no longer downcast. Darcy was jubilant. He established training headquarters near the Fair grounds, and was matched with Len Rowlands, of Milwaukee. He was too happy to talk. Darcy again wired his mother that the ban had been lifted, and that he was to be permitted to fight in Memphis.

Then came the breakdown.

Physicians announced that Darcy's teeth were causing the trouble. His friends knew better. The sudden news that he might fight in America had affected his heart. Every treatment known to medical science was given him, but there is no cure for a broken heart. He couldn't forget the 'slacker' part. The greatest fighter of the 20th century continued to grow worse.

Physicians say Darcy put up a fight for life that would be a credit to the bravest French soldier. He was not unconscious until the end. He gasped slightly for breath, then appeared to doze off into a sleep.

Just before he passed into the Great Beyond, Darcy motioned for Mick Hawkins — lifelong friend — to come to his bedside, but he could not speak when Hawkins leaned over the bed.

Darcy's thoughts were always of his mother and brothers and sisters in far-off Australia. . .

Darcy's last letter, to an old friend, Mr M. Stapleton, of Cessnock, was published in the Maitland Mercury. *It was dated 21 April:*

No doubt you have heard by this that the dogs got down on me in this country for not going to the war, and now the States are joined there is no living here. When they had me stopped from showing in three or four States it looked as if the only thing for me to do was to enlist. I offered to enlist if they would give me five fights, and it looks as if they are going to take me up, but I am enlisting on condition that they transfer me to an Australian army. This is a great country, Mick, and you would surely like it. There is money here. But they hand out a tremendous lot of bull — everything they have is a champion of the world or the best in the world. I was matched with McCoy for March 5, then Dillon, then McCoy again, and when in the midst of all the trouble and wrangling among managers, promoters, fighters, etc., the Governor stepped in when all was settled for me to box, two days before the fight, and did me out of £6000 for fighting ten rounds. I expect to get going soon now. I am billed to box George Chip in Youngstown, Ohio, on May 19, and with my enlistment it may go through all right. Once I get started I'll take some stopping. I'll fight every week. Poor old Mick Hawkins is disgusted with the place, and wants to go home. I tell you, it would make anyone homesick the way they mess you around. No wonder Dave Smith couldn't get going here. Dave is too honest. I dare say before you get this I will have had a fight. This is the first Mayor or Governor that has given me a fair deal since my arrival in this country. They all took notice of those wild stories circulated by the dirty grafting newspapers here, but now this fellow has started on the enlisting racket the others will follow. But my troubles about them. I don't know how soon I'll be home, but I expect to be home for Christmas, all being well. If this enlistment comes to anything I'll be home in August and join the army. Give my kind regards to all the boys around Cessnock. Address your next letter to 4927 Washington Boulevard, Chicago, Illinois. Always your pal, LES DARCY.

1917 The Prime Minister is hit by an egg during a bitter conscription campaign

LLOYD DUMAS
Melbourne Argus, 30 November 1917

Of all Australia's prime ministers, Billy Hughes was the smallest. He had the appearance of a lively gnome but he compensated with a giant ego, a nimble mind, a biting, take-on-all-comers wit, and a massive, fighting heart. He was twenty when he came to Australia from Wales, and for ten years he earned a living in diverse ways — mending umbrellas, digging post-holes, scribbling pieces for newspapers, orating from tree-stumps, and organising for the Labor Party. When he was thirty, he was elected to the New South Wales Parliament in the seat of Lang; he held the seat until the opening of the Federal Parliament in 1901, when he launched himself into Federal politics as the member for West Sydney.

He succeeded Andrew Fisher as Prime Minister in October 1915, twenty-one years after having been elected to Parliament. The war had been raging for fifteen months then, and Hughes quickly came to the view that it was imperative for Australia to introduce a policy of conscription of manpower for military service overseas. It was in his pursuit of this objective that he showed a single-mindedness that amounted to a ruthless, dictatorial refusal to allow a fair hearing to any conflicting point of view. 'He could be villainous in the exercise of authority,' Norman Makin once wrote of him.

When his own Parliamentary Labor Party refused to support conscription, Hughes led his supporters from the party room, carried on in government with the support of the non-Labor Opposition, and finally formed a new Nationalist Party with the non-Labor forces to fight the 1917 election. His first referendum on the issue of conscription had been rejected by the people in 1916; re-elected in 1917, he held another referendum on the subject, and gave a public undertaking that he would resign if this was defeated. It was defeated and Hughes duly resigned — but he accepted re-appointment immediately. He used the War Precautions Act to suppress discussion of the conscription campaign by anti-conscriptionists, and he used the wartime restriction on libel action to prevent the anti-conscriptionists defending themselves against wild attacks he made on them.

The conscription campaign was one of the most bitter issues in Australian political history. In the south the anti-conscription forces were led by the Roman Catholic Archbishop of Melbourne, Dr Mannix; in the north Queensland's Premier, Mr Ryan, made his State the most fiercely opposed to conscription of all. It was during a tour of Queensland by Mr Hughes that a hectic incident occurred which led to the formation of the Commonwealth Police Force. The Prime Minister had arrived at Warwick railway station, where a number of his supporters had gathered. About fifty anti-conscriptionists attended, and one of them threw two eggs at the Prime Minister. One of them missed, and the other hit him on the hat; a returned soldier punched the egg-thrower and knocked him down. Supporters and opponents joined the brawl, and Hughes was in the centre of it.

At one stage the Prime Minister asked Senior-Sergeant Kenny, who was in charge of the police, to arrest the egg-thrower. The sergeant refused. The Prime Minister reminded the sergeant that he was Attorney-General of the Commonwealth; the sergeant replied that he was an officer of the Queensland State Government, and recognised no other authority. Afterwards, to ensure that no such impasse occurred again, the Commonwealth Police

Force came into being. For some fifty years
— until a shockingly bad shot was fired at
Opposition Leader Arthur Calwell, lacerating
his chin, during another conscription row —
those two eggs represented the summit of
political violence in Australia. The incident
was recorded solemnly in Australia's history
of World War One, with the historian testify-
ing that the eggs were of 'indubitable
antiquity'.

A reporter from the Melbourne Argus, *Lloyd*
(later Sir Lloyd) Dumas was with Billy Hughes
on the occasion of the great egg attack. Dumas
was one of the most successful Australian
newspapermen of his time; he joined the
Adelaide Advertiser *as a copy boy in 1907,*
represented the Argus *overseas, became editor*
(after Montague Grover) of the Melbourne
Sun News-Pictorial *in 1924, and managing*
editor of his first paper, the Advertiser, *in*
1929. He retired as managing director in 1951
and died, aged eighty-one, in 1973.

Sir Lloyd Dumas used to tell a story about
Billy Hughes' deafness and his ability to ex-
ploit this affliction when he did not want to
answer questions. Once, when Hughes was
Prime Minister, Dumas tried at a press con-
ference to pin him down on a pertinent issue,
the price of sugar. He asked if Cabinet that
day had discussed sugar. 'Yes, Mr Dumas,'
said the Prime Minister, 'it is a beautiful day.
I think we all ought to go out in the open air.'
The Age *reporter then shouted, 'No, Mr*
Hughes, we want to know whether Cabinet
discussed the price of sugar.' Hughes replied,
'No, Mr Austin, we didn't deal with steel at
all.' Then the man from the West Australian,
at the back of the group, said softly to the
others, 'I'll make the little bugger hear.' He
walked around and shouted into Hughes' ear.
Hughes replied, 'The answer to that question
is in two parts. . . One, we did not discuss
sugar, and two, I'm not a little bugger.'

Here is the report Lloyd Dumas sent from
Warwick, Queensland, on 29 November 1917:

An extraordinary and disgraceful riot occurred
at Warwick this afternoon, when the Prime
Minister (Mr. Hughes) alighted from the south-
ward-bound train to address an open-air meeting on the platform. The moment he stepped
from his carriage he was surrounded by a howling mob. The platform had been beflagged,
and a large crowd had gathered in the roadway
below to hear Mr. Hughes's address, but about
50 men, most of them of military age, were
waiting on the platform when the train came
in. The moment they saw the Prime Minister
they commenced hooting and groaning and
hurling vile epithets at him. He had not gone
more than a yard or two before a struggling,
jostling crowd was wedged around him. An
egg thrown from the crowd just missed him,
and broke upon the platform railings. The
odour it gave off quickly cleared a space
about it. A second one, better aimed, broke
upon the Prime Minister's hat and knocked
it off.

There was a howl of jeering laughter, which
drowned the cries of "Shame!" which arose
from the crowd in the street and from a few
women on the platform. But the thrower of
the egg did not enjoy his triumph long. A
returned soldier on the platform hurled himself upon him, and in a second a free fight
was in progress. Friends of Mr. Hughes's
assailant rushed to his assistance, and the
loyal men on the platform gave what help
they could to the returned soldier.

So far as could be judged the loyalists had
the better of the struggle. One of the first to
defend Mr. Hughes's assailant came out of the
fight with blood streaming down his face.
Fists were flying everywhere, and the Prime
Minister was in the thick of it striving to get
at the man who had assaulted him, and who
was one of the biggest men in the crowd. Mr.
Hughes was hustled and jostled by men twice
his size, but when he emerged it was his hand
and not his face that was bleeding. One of the
men in the crowd carried a hammer and another a heavy spanner, but the Prime Minister
was daunted by nothing. He demanded assistance from the police in apprehending the man
who had assaulted him, but it is perfectly safe
to say that their sympathy was not with him.
It was only under the most insistent demands
of the Prime Minister that they could at last
be induced to escort the man off the platform, and then they apparently released him

as soon as they got out of Mr. Hughes's sight, for he appeared on the scene again almost immediately. It was a most flagrant case of flouting the authority of the Prime Minister and the laws of the Commonwealth, and this attitude of the police was persisted in to the end. Although Mr. Hughes demanded in his capacity as Attorney-General of the Commonwealth that they should take action against his assailant, Senior-Sergeant Kenny declined to do so, declaring that he recognised the laws of Queensland, and would act under no other. . . . When the Prime Minister commenced his address he was greeted with mixed cheers and hoots. The sergeant of police stepped to the edge of the platform and asked the crowd in the street to give the Prime Minister a "fair and square deal." This appeal was followed by mingled cheering and hoots.

The Prime Minister, speaking with a ringing voice, said:— "We have just had a demonstration before our eyes, proofs of the real motives of those who oppose the Government's proposals and of the shameful abuse of the rights of free citizenship. . .

I will keep law and order in this country. (Cheers and hoots.) Neither Sinn Fein nor I.W.W. will keep me from it, either." (More cheers and hoots.) . . .

GLEN INNES (N.S.W.), Thursday. — The Prime Minister this evening sent the following telegram to the Premier of Queensland (Mr. Ryan):—

"At Warwick to-day, at 3 p.m., when leaving the train to address a public meeting, I was assaulted by a number of men. There was a great tumult, amounting virtually to a riot. I ordered the police to immediately arrest the two most prominent ringleaders; but, acting under the senior sergeant's direction, they refused to do so. I called the attention of Senior-sergeant Kenny to the fact that a deliberate and violent breach of the laws of the Commonwealth had been committed; that the laws of the Commonwealth override those of the State; and as Attorney-General I directed him to take proceedings to prosecute these men under the Commonwealth law. He replied that he recognised the laws of Queensland only, and would act under no other. I then told him I would take proceedings against him for having broken the Commonwealth law, and that, having issued instructions to the police under his control to do likewise, he had not only connived at the disgraceful proceedings at the meeting, but had broken the Commonwealth law himself. I have to request that you as Premier of the State of Queensland suspend him from duty immediately, and take all such steps as are necessary for his immediate prosecution under the laws of the Commonwealth. Unless this is done forthwith the Commonwealth Government will take steps to enforce its own laws, and will hold you responsible for any breaches of such laws.

"WM. HUGHES, Prime Minister."

BRISBANE, Thursday. — The Premier was asked to-night at Parliament House whether he had received any advices of the incident at Warwick. On being informed that the "Courier" had received a copy of the telegram sent to him by Mr. Hughes, Mr. Ryan said that he had forwarded the following urgent telegram to the Prime Minister, addressed to Sydney:—

"The Hon. W. M. Hughes, Commonwealth Prime Minister, Sydney. — Your telegram of even date received. I regret to hear of the incident, and trust that you suffered no bodily injury. I am having the subject-matter of your complaint immediately inquired into. A preliminary inquiry by telephone from Warwick seems to indicate that the occurrence was not so serious as your telegram represented. I am unable to understand the relevancy of your statement to Sergeant Kenny that the laws of the Commonwealth override the laws of the State. It seems to me that such a statement had no bearing on the matter, as I am not aware of any State law which conflicts with the laws of the Commonwealth in the circumstances which you allege. Your threat with regard to the Commonwealth Government taking steps to enforce its own laws is quite uncalled for, as this Government is enforcing, and will continue to enforce, the laws of the Commonwealth and the State. (Signed) T. J. Ryan, Premier."

Kingsford Smith lands the tri-motor Fokker monoplane *Southern Cross* at Mascot, Sydney, after the great trans-Pacific flight from San Francisco in June 1928

1922   A killer shark strikes and two men show rare courage

UNKNOWN REPORTER
Sydney Referee, 6 February 1922

The first recorded death from a shark attack in Australian waters took place in 1791; the victim was an Aboriginal woman. Since then, more than 300 attacks have taken place, and the death toll has passed the 100 mark.

Although the eastern seaboard of Australia has had more shark-caused deaths than any other strip of coastline in the world, the risk to bathers is comparatively small. At Bondi, possibly the best-known beach in the nation, the number of surf bathers over the years has totalled well over one hundred million; only three have ever been attacked there and there is evidence to suggest that they were all attacked by the same shark.

According to Dr V. M. Coppleston, a well-known Sydney surgeon and authority on the pattern of shark attacks, it was not until 4 February 1922 that Australian surfers became shark-conscious. That was the day a young lifesaver, Milton Coughlan, was killed at Coogee Beach, Sydney. The suddenness and ferocity of the attack, and great courage displayed by two men — one of them an Olympic swimming champion — gripped the nation.

Coughlan, a member of Coogee surf life saving club, was an exceptionally fine swimmer; on the day of the attack he was due to compete in a surf carnival on Coogee Beach — and he was 'cracking some waves' beforehand. He caught one big breaker, stayed with the wave for a long distance, and pulled out of it in a channel about forty yards from the shore. He saw a shark cutting towards a group of bathers, shouted a warning, and then he was hit. The terrific force of the strike lifted him clear out of the water. Onlookers on the beach saw him trying to fight off the shark, saw it wrench off one of his arms. Several lifesavers raced to the rescue with a life-saving reel. One of

them was Jack Chalmers, who, without waiting to don a belt, simply tied the line around his waist and dashed into the water. Frank Beaurepaire also swam out to Coughlan. Beaurepaire was then at the peak of a swimming career in which he represented Australia on six overseas trips, set fourteen world records, and won more than 200 titles.

After he had been brought ashore, Coughlan was taken immediately to hospital but he died shortly after admission. For their courage, Chalmers and Beaurepaire were awarded the Royal Humane Society's highest honors. A public fund was opened to reward their bravery. Beaurepaire received £500, which he used to establish a car-tyre business which developed into a massive industry. He went on to be knighted, and was twice Lord Mayor of Melbourne before his death in 1956. He was the principal benefactor of the great young Australian swimmer John Marshall, who died in a road accident, while working for the Beaurepaire company, in 1957.

Another fatal shark attack took place at Coogee Beach a month later; as a result of these attacks, a huge shark-proof net was laid down off Coogee. Here is the Sydney Referee's *account of the death of Milton Coughlan, and the amazing courage of his rescuers:*

Last Saturday afternoon all Sydney was shocked to learn of the terrible tragedy enacted in the surf at Coogee before the horrified gaze of at least 6000 persons, gathered to watch the swimming carnival there — which, out of respect to the victim, was postponed.

There was promise of excellent sport. A light, sparkling, sunny day, and long rolling breakers that would carry a man in at express speed 150 yards of more.

The rollers were too tempting, anyhow, for Milton Singleton Coughlan, the 16-year-old son of the postmaster of Randwick. This fine, sturdy, bronzed youth, with the physique of a grown man, got down on the rocks near the club house before the carnival was due to start, and took a header into the sea, just as thousands have done before him. He got well out into what is known as the reef, about 30 or 40 yards from the rocks, caught a breaker, and came rushing shorewards. Young Coughlan swam out for another, and yet another. A friend sang out to the lad to look out for sharks in the channel, but Coughlan laughed back fearlessly.

Then the tragedy happened. One minute the swimmer was observed standing about waist deep — on the edge of the channel which runs beyond the reef — and the next a huge something flashed in the sun, clear of the water, and the horrified crowd next saw for some minutes a shark and the swimmer threshing around in a welter of blood-stained water and scarlet flecked foam. The shark seized his victim by the right arm just as he was in the act of signalling to his clubmates for assistance. With one snap of its jaws the brute tore off Coughlan's arm, but the plucky boy, although momentarily dragged under, reappeared above water, and the awe-stricken spectators saw him laying about him with the left arm and trying to beat off his savage assailant. Then the shark got the left arm in its jaws.

Meanwhile those on shore were not altogether idle. The first to act was Jack Chalmers, of Woollahra, a well-known swimmer. Seeing Coughlan's plight, and without an instant's hesitation, he rushed down the rocks near the clubhouse. He had hastily got the line off a disused life-saving reel knotted round his waist, and would not wait for a cork lifebelt. Mr. T. F. Doran, a clubmate, helped to give out the life-line. As Chalmers scrambled over the slippery green rocks he fell heavily, and was for a moment well nigh stunned, and his leg was badly lacerated. Struggling to his feet, he plunged into the water to the rescue.

His time out to Coughlan was pretty nearly a record, say those who, with bated breath, watched the plucky fellow go to face what

Frank Beaurepaire (right) and Jack Chalmers photographed after the rescue for the Sydney *Referee*'s souvenir cover picture

looked like certain death. As Chalmers neared Coughlan, the latter, almost spent with his struggle, turned a tortured, appealing look towards his rescuer, and with wonderful presence of mind turned on his back — in the way life-savers are taught to do, so that Chalmers' rescue might be made easier.

Chalmers is near now, and he makes his supreme effort to grab Coughlan before the shark drags the exhausted, rapidly-weakening lad under. The shark is not of extraordinary size, else it would have succeeded in drowning Coughlan before; but is evidently the advance-guard of other sharks who, attracted by blood, are nosing their way towards the struggling pair.

And now Chalmers has his man. He literally has to tear him from the shark's jaws. "Don't let go of me, Jack!" cries out Coughlan. It is his first cry for aid and is torn from him by terrible torture. Slowly the pair are drawn to the shore, and meanwhile that champion of champions, Frank Beaurepaire, and a Mr. Green, of Coogee, the latter fully clad, have dived in and help in the rescue . . .

As the swimmers get nearer land, helping hands lean down to raise the poor mangled body of Coughlan, and bear him away to the waiting doctor and ambulance men. One arm is snapped off clean at the elbow; the other, mangled and torn, hangs by a shred.

Coughlan, though faint and weak, is conscious, and in a whimsical voice, catching sight of a pal, he says, with the very wraith of a smile, "It's a fair cow, isn't it?" Later, someone puts a towel over his face. "Take it off, please," says he. They were tying up arteries and putting on tourniquets at the time and wanted to spare the poor sufferer all they could.

To Mr. Henderson, the District Superintendent of the Red Cross, who sat by him in the speeding ambulance, Coughlan remarked, with a still bright light in his eye: "I don't think I've much of a show, have I? I expect my number's up; but, by Jove, that shark stopped one or two good ones!"

Those were about his last words. Shortly afterwards he lapsed into unconsciousness and about a quarter of an hour after admission into hospital, this plucky young Australian passed away. . .

The gallant part played by Frank Beaurepaire, champion swimmer of Australia, has been overshadowed by the glory surrounding Jack Chalmers. In calm reflection, after the excitement caused by the thrilling circumstances, the deed of Beaurepaire deserves great recognition.

Beaurepaire was in the surf shed on the rocks when the cry of horror went up and caused him to rush to the balcony of the club house. He could not realise what was happening for the moment. Suddenly the swirl of the blood-flecked water brought home the realisation of the tragedy being enacted. Beaurepaire dropped down the rocks to the water's edge. Not knowing the locality, he had to make through the crashing breakers over the rocks. Three times he was knocked back, but at last, following fast on a receding wave, the champion swimmer was able to dive into deep water. He sped out to where Chalmers was holding Coughlan and making very little progress towards the shore. Gripping Chalmers by the costume with one hand, Beaurepaire, using his free arm and his renowned trudgeon kick, assisted the rescuer and the victim to the rocks, where they were lifted out of the water. Beaurepaire's action was one of the bravest, and when the awards are being considered by the authorities, he, no doubt, will come in for high recognition.

Chalmers himself has the highest praise for Beaurepaire, and expressed himself feelingly at the great help given him by the champion swimmer. "Beaurepaire," he said, "reached me at a time when I needed assistance, and his strong swimming was of great value. I hope that he, too, gets his share of praise from the public."

The management of The Referee has decided to have two diamond-studded gold medals struck to be presented to both Chalmers and Beaurepaire as a memento of their bravery. . .

1923   Melbourne streets are terrorised by mobs during police strike

VARIOUS REPORTERS, EDITED BY MONTAGUE GROVER

Melbourne Evening Sun, 3 November 1923 and Melbourne Herald, 4 November 1923

Australia's only police mutiny took place in Victoria at the beginning of November 1923. The police had three major grievances: their pay was the lowest of any police force in Australia, there was no pension scheme for the men who had joined the force after 1902, and they hated the 'spook' system by which senior constables, without uniform, watched how they patrolled their beats.

On the night of Wednesday 31 October, thirty police at Russell Street barracks refused duty and the city was without night patrol. They were to work the next night unconditionally, or be dismissed. Next evening, the night patrol again refused duty and, by the Friday, 475 police had gone on strike. Police were brought from country towns for emergency city patrols, but many of these refused duty. The mutiny grew, and by Derby Eve, the Friday night, 630 policemen had left their posts; Melbourne, crammed with Melbourne Cup visitors, was without a police force, save for a handful of loyal long-service men.

It was not long before hooligans broke loose, shouting abuse at the few police who tried to keep order, and finally pelting them with stones, eggs and bottles. Next evening a criminal rabble took control of the centre of town: Bourke Street, between Swanston Street and Elizabeth Street. Plate glass windows were shattered by flying bottles, and men and women invaded the window displays, stealing clothing and often leaving their own clothes in their place. They dragged out furs, shoes, rings, gowns and suits, brawling among themselves as they looted. Pockets were picked, decent citizens bashed, and one young man was kicked to death and robbed near Princes Bridge.

Finally a counter-attack, consisting of 300

volunteers armed with batons and pick-handles, was launched against the rioting mobs; in squads of about thirty they smashed their way to the heart of Bourke Street. By midnight, 237 people were in hospital, eighty-five looters were in police wagons, and eighty-eight large windows had become drifts of broken glass on the pavements.

It was a difficult night for reporters. Two Evening Sun *men, Noel Monks and Allan Dawes, finished among the injured; Monks was cut by flying glass, and Dawes was pushed over a verandah rail outside the Royal Mail Hotel. Hugh Buggy and J. D. Brown were in the middle of the battle in Bourke Street, and Chris Walker, later killed while serving with the AIF in the Middle East, had to be dissuaded by colleagues from joining the pick-handle volunteers. Others in the thick of the action were the brothers Dick and George Greenlees, both representing the Sydney* Daily Telegraph *in Melbourne. The* Evening Sun's *report was put together by the editor, Monty Grover, who headed a special edition that Saturday with the six-column banner, 'UNLEASHED SCUM'. The opening sentence, written by Grover, read: 'Anarchy, naked, unashamed — and drunken — ruled in Swanston-street to-night. . .'*

Order was finally restored when a force of volunteers moved into the city on the Sunday, and by Monday Melbourne was peaceful. On Tuesday the favorite, Bitalli, won the 1923 Melbourne Cup in brilliant weather, and that day the Argus *editorial reflected the general mood of shock. 'Few people would have thought that an orderly city could so rapidly be captured by its criminal and semi-criminal elements,' it said. None of the 636 striking police was ever reinstated, and the volunteer*

*force, mainly returned soldiers, remained on
duty until new recruits had been trained.*

*This is the report which appeared in the
late-night special edition of the* Evening Sun
on 3 November:

Anarchy, naked, unashamed — and drunken —
ruled in Swanston-street to-night.

Scenes, unparalleled in the history of Melbourne, were witnessed in Bourke and Swanston streets. Routing the police a savage mob
smashed shop windows, stole valuable stocks,
and committed acts of violence in the streets.

Several bluejackets were injured during the
rioting in Swanston and Bourke streets. When
this was reported to their officers a patrol of
men was instantly despatched, and under
their protection their comrades were rescued.

A cable tram was removed from the line,
its crew and passengers thrown over and
trampled upon.

A dash by the Fire Brigade through the
crowd was only temporarily effective.

The crowd returned at once and bottles,
glass, metal, and other missiles were thrown.

The windows of the Leviathan Store in
Bourke-street were smashed and the contents,
comprising ladies' dummy figures, were flung
into the street, and draperies and material
stolen.

A man was pushed through a plate glass
window in Swanston-street.

His throat was terribly gashed.

A soldier, who appeared with a rifle, was the
signal for a momentary panic, and there was a
cry that troops had been called out; but when
he was seen to be alone he was knocked down
and kicked into insensibility, and his rifle
stolen.

At about 7 p.m. the police received reinforcements. Between sixty and seventy of
them made a raid on the mob, and after a few
moment's sharp fighting gained control.

A corporal of the Citizen Forces appeared
carrying a rifle. A yell of rage went up from
the crowd. The corporal was instantly rushed,
disarmed, knocked down, and cruelly kicked
where he lay.

Then the police began systematically to
clear the streets, stretching from pavement to
pavement, they moved along at a sharp pace,
swinging their batons and keeping everybody
moving.

Meanwhile, at the Town Hall hundreds of
men were enrolling as special constables. They
were given badges and batons, and unostentatiously moved to various parts of the city.

At 8.30 the enrolment of specials was proceeding as fast as five clerks could do it. By
then Russell-street had run out of batons, and
urgent telephone messages were sent to suburban stations to bring batons in. . .

*Next day, Sunday, another special edition
— this time of the Melbourne* Herald — *appeared. This is its front-page report:*

The gravity of the situation is indicated by
the following announcement issued by Brigadier-General J. K. Forsyth, from the Town Hall
this afternoon:—

Ex-Light Horsemen required Melbourne in
civilian capacity assist authorities quelling
disturbances. Good horses supplied on arrival.
Expenses refunded. Large and loyal response
expected immediately. Report General Forsyth, Melbourne Town Hall.

One hundred thousand people rushed in
from the suburbs this morning to view a scene
of wanton destruction unparalleled in the
history of Melbourne.

Never has the city been so densely packed
with surging crowds on a Sunday morning.
They filled the church trains and flocked city-
wards in hundreds of cars, cabs, and every
other kind of vehicle.

Mobs of menacing roughs with their lust
for plunder still unsatiated, were scouring the
streets. Two-up schools were in action on
every corner, and a resumption of hostilities
seemed likely at any moment.

After last night's bitter and disastrous rioting the block bounded by Bourke, Swanston,
Little Collins, and Elizabeth streets appeared
this morning as if it had been sacked by a
ruthless invading army.

Four hundred plate-glass windows have
been shattered. Many thousands of pounds
worth of goods have been looted. . .

It is emphasised, too, that this is no industrial dispute or a class fight. The Government

During the Melbourne police strike of December 1923 special constables clash with rioting mobs on the corner of Russell and Little Collins Streets

declares in the proclamation that the security of rich and poor alike depends on the maintenance of law and order. It pays a tribute to the loyal constables who faced grave danger last night with courage and restraint.

The proclamation states that "Sir John Monash, Brigadier-General Elliott, and other well-known Anzac leaders, are as willing and as anxious to serve in the preservation of decency and order as they were to maintain our civilisation against a foreign foe. They will be in charge of this work at the Town Hall."

More special constables were sworn in at the Town Hall depot this morning. It is expected that 1000 specials will be available to face any further onslaughts of the mob to-night.

There are ominous rumblings of a strike of tramwaymen in support of the police strikers. A large number of cable tram men this morning crowded into a mass meeting of the Tramway Employees' Union at Unity Hall, Bourke-street.

The meeting is still proceeding, but so far no decision has been reached on the question of practical support.

Up to 2 p.m. to-day 1000 men had been enrolled as special constables and volunteers were still pouring in. Throughout last night 500 specials were on duty.

When the rioting was at its height the mob broke into Alcock's Sporting depot and looted rifles, revolvers and hunting knives. It is feared that many of these have got into the hands of the most lawless element.

No trams ran into the city to-day. They were all turned outside the city proper and ran back again. Nevertheless big crowds of people, mostly men, poured into the city all the afternoon. Few women came in.

All to-day shopkeepers hammered away barricading those shops which had not been so protected last night.

1927   **Federal Parliament House is officially opened in Canberra, to critical comment**

JIM DONALD
Sydney Smith's Weekly, 14 May 1927

One of the most uninhibited, irrepressible newspapers ever to exist in Australia was Smith's Weekly. *It was born on 1 March 1919 as the result of a union between Sir James Joynton Smith, a Lord Mayor of Sydney, Claude McKay, a clever journalist and publicist, and Robert Clyde Packer, a sub-editor on the Sydney* Sun *and father of the boy who became Sir Frank Packer. It stayed alive for thirty-two years, and it attracted the talents of some of Australia's finest journalists, black-and-white artists, poets and satirists. Its editors (sometimes called editors-in-chief) included Claude McKay, Frank Marien, Harry Cox, Kenneth Slessor, Reg Moses, George Goddard and Edgar Holt. Among its writers were Kenneth Slessor, Lennie Lower, Adam McKay, Edgar Holt, Hugh Dash, Ross Campbell, Stewart Howard, Bill Rodie, Jim Donald, Cliff Graves, Roy Abbott, Tom Foley, Harry Maddison, Alan Hulls, Norman Ellison, Reg Harris, Eddie Dunstan, Dave Barnes, Alex Macdonald, Warren McIlraith, Doug and George Blaikie. Its artists included Stan Cross, Joe Jonsson, Cec Hartt, Virgil Reilly, George Finey, Emile Mercier, Charlie Hallett, Lance Driffield, Jim Russell, Les Dixon and Eric Jolliffe.*

Jim Donald, a former prizefighter, developed on Smith's *into the nation's most colourful boxing writer. It was characteristic of* Smith's *cheeky viewpoint that it assigned Donald, the paper's boxing scribe, to cover the opening of the first Parliament in Canberra in May 1927.* Smith's *had taken umbrage that Parliament was to be opened by the Duke of York at what it considered to be a private function. On 14 May it prefaced its report by Jim Donald with this message:*

The opening of Canberra was by right a ceremony for the people.

Officialdom made it a private function for the Four Hundred few.

Here, however, is the story of Canberra written for the people by one of the people in the way people will understand. . .

FRIDAY:
The poet who wrote that colours are the smiles of Nature, had never seen the great camouflaged German gun mounted outside Canberra station. Grim and sinister, the multi-coloured monster broods o'er the plain, a frowning silent symbol of wrath. In its shade an aged swagman sat on Matilda and watched the social world whizz by. Poor lone wanderer. Little he recalled of the devastation wrought by that Joseph's-coated engine of destruction. It afforded him rest and shelter.

Those in love with the sweet security of streets would be wise if they gave Canberra a wide berth. The only security there is in the banks. In the main street, Commonwealth Avenue, the citizenry spends a great part of its time disentangling itself from the spurs and shielding its optics from the canes of promenading military dandies. Wild riders rivalling the famed horseman from Snowy River gallop madly along the boulevardes. The young squireens of the squattocracy hog the speed limit, and their mudguards are the enemy of all pedestrians.

I am sure the Capitol will provide some of our future, long-distance jump champions. This week Rus jostled Urbs on the side walk. Bewhiskered cockies, pert city flappers, stately senators, bowyanged bush workers, helmeted ear-flapped airmen, soldiers, sailors, fur-coated city and station dowagers, generals (domestic and military), Besses and Berts of the back block barns, tabbies from the Tableland, and men from Monaro, Manly and

Marrickville form a bewildering cosmopolitan crowd, a human haggis. . .

SATURDAY:

This day there was a full dress rehearsal. The troops marched. Melba sang and reproved the bandmaster for playing a three instead of a two-bar introduction, and Stonehaven personally instructed the flunkeys regarding their duties in connection with his own august person on the great day. Planes swooped and looped and span in dizzy circles.

Canberra is a natural amphitheatre. Seven silent hills stand sentinel around it. There's Capitol Hill, Camp Hill, Cathedral Hill, and Red Hill. The remaining hills are ant hills.

To-day at sunset I stood alone on the summit on Capitol Hill. Beneath my feet were foundation stones laid by Andrew Fisher, King O'Malley, and Sir George Fuller. Alas, these mighty men are no longer layers. A Bloomsbury boarding house is Fisher's domicile to-day. The O'Malley's massive brain struggles with drainage and renovation problems and rent defaulters in connection with his Melbourne properties. Sir George has thrown in the towel to the political dragon, and is now bovrilising at Bowral.

'Twas a noble panorama that met my eye. Below me at the top of Camp Hill is the terraced-minareted House of Parliament, a veritable White House of Moorish architecture. Over to the north-east Duntroon military college nestles on the edge of Mt. Pleasant.

There, on a sunny slope, the Anzac, General Bridges, sleeps his last long sleep. Here, too, is the old homestead of Squire Campbell. Sweeping around the eye rests on the huddled hangars of the aerodrome. Now the old German internment camp comes into view. Beyond the foothills lies that wicked sister of Canberra and Mecca of the thirsty, Queanbeyan.

That building in course of erection is destined to be the capital's first theatre.

Due north from Parliament House rises the spire of that Stoke Poges of the Monaro, the old church erected by Squire Campbell nigh on 100 years ago. To the left of the ancient church is a grassy hillock. One day it will proudly bear Australia's national war memorial, a noble structure of white marble, which will stand for all time, a hall of memories as yet only enshrined in the hearts of the people.

Yonder green grove marks the sacrificial and corroboree grounds of the blacks. Local tradition has it that the bush growth and leafiness of the grass and trees is nurtured by the blood of sacrifice and slain warriors in the days when the Monaro tribes proudly trod the soil, monarchs of all they surveyed. Black Mountain frowns down on the ancient battle ground, a fitting sentry for dark deeds. That wooded knoll is destined to be a centre of parish pomp, an eyrie for the owls of wisdom — the Town Hall is to be erected there. . .

Stonehaven's home, "Yarralumla," cannot be seen, but it is over yonder. That peeping roof is Bruce's £14,000 humpy. Rumour hath it that statues of Dummy and John Taxpayer adorn niches in the wall. Prime Ministers have worshipped less munificent gods.

In a thick belt of scrub directly behind Bruce's residence a one-ring circus has established itself, Canberra's most fashionable two-up school. There is, however, no truth in the rumour that the ringkeeper wears spats or works the oracle in a monocle. . .

So I stand and gaze out over the new-born capitol of a great nation, and a vision rises before me of a fair city, a happy contented people, year to year to increase and multiply until that day when Australia takes precedence of the nations of the world. When that time comes Canberra should be worth revisiting. . .

SUNDAY:

The boom is on the rye in dry Canberra. The local bottle-oh, an ancient mariner with a baleful eye, is trembling on the verge of physical collapse.

Sydney city aldermen are arriving in dribs and drabs; several of them turned turtle on the journey. The Lord Mayor's car travelled the royal road to ditches, and his worship spent all Saturday night bogged in Paddy's River, but, thank heavens, he is here, rabbit skin robes and all. Brought up in Labour's rugged school, the worthy chap pooh-poohs the privations of rough and ready parochial board and lodgment.

Without benefit of mitre or crozier, the

archbishops are installed at the Hotel Canberra. So is the judiciary — excellent Judges all. The cream of the consuls, and a galaxy of Governors are also snatching a crust at the big pub. There, too, is India's Ambassador, a glorified Chunder Loo. . .

Over at the Kurrajong there is a tumult of bleatings. Minor politicians, second string social stipendiaries of gossip, military chappies, whose glory is slightly dimmed, swell the guest line. Perhaps the most illustrious inmate is Alfred O'Shea, our national tenor. Apparently Alf is being held in reserve in case Melba bursts her top C. The tenor is to sing at the police camp to-night. It would be a graceful act to include "The Prisoner's Song" and "The Old Turnkey" in his programme, as an incentive to the more frivolous-minded of the force.

Really there are more constables than civilians here at present. All the local bushrangers are working within the law, entrenched behind shop counters. . .

The Governor-General, his minor satraps, and a whole tribe of squatters and daughters attended. Stan. Bruce was there. His shoes shone sable and comely, his linen was whiter than the soul of St. Anthony.

The Duke and Duchess arrived this bright morning. Several hundred friends and well-wishers welcomed the Royal pair. The most enthusiasm was generated by a bunch of sweet Scots domestics domiciled in Canberra. Dainty Elizabeth caught the familiar accent, and slung them a sunny smile.

My friend the Duke appears slightly more robust than of yore, but the little Duchess is blooming like the rose. . .

To-morrow is the great day. The Four Hundred are eager and ready to bray. To-night, as at Brussels on the eve of Waterloo, the twin gods of Gaiety and Guzzle reign. The carnival spirit is abroad, and many hearts beat high in anticipation of a social triumph to-morrow.

MONDAY:
Picked troops line the avenues leading to the ceremonial square, policemen urbane, inexorable, are everywhere. Soon the public stands are filled. Here are the real hosts for the day.

It will be their privilege to pay the bills.

An ancient abo. gazes curiously on the scene. Eighty-four years ago he was born nigh to this very spot, and in his hot youth had thrown spears at the cattle of the first white settler in these parts. Sole survivor of a powerful and warlike tribe, he dwells in a gunyah on the slope of yonder hill. His kinsmen have vanished from the face of the earth. He alone remains to witness history's tapestry woven by the hands of an invading Royalty. . .

Melba stepped forward and stoutly sang one verse of the National Anthem.

Bruce then spoke his piece in a most refined and gentlemanly manner. The Duke replied. His environment lent him time and the microphone volume. While the Duke was speaking, Bruce stood by with an expression like that of a man who carried a wax impression of St. Peter's keys in his pocket.

The Royal oration over, Bruce stepped forward and handed His Royal Highness a key. With it the Duke opened the door to the accompaniment of loud and prolonged cheering from the Monaroites and polite expressions of approval from the Four Hundred. Several clergymen of various denominations indulged in meditation and prayer. Archbishop Kelly was absent. So was the Chief Rabbi and General Booth's representative.

During the devotional interlude, I noticed the Duke cast several nervous apprehensive glances towards the political gallery. Possibly he had just remembered his ancestor, George the Third's illuminating outburst, "Politics is a trade for scoundrels."

Orisons over, the Duke and Duchess vanished into the bowels of the building and the gallant Four Hundred charged the doorway.

It was a massed attack, helter-skelter, with a frenzied staff of photographers taking the hindmost. Coat-tails swished. Hats were tilted and crumpled in the crush.

When the last frantic social climber had scrambled into the inner temple doors were closed. When just one hour and a half later the Royal couple emerged, still pursued by the Four Hundred, Canberra had given birth to a nation.

The Duke and Duchess of York arrive in New South Wales on 2 May 1927 for the opening of Australia's first Federal Parliament

1927 The notorious criminal, 'Squizzy' Taylor, is shot dead in a duel

CLYDE PALMER AND TOM KELYNAK
Melbourne Sun and Herald, 28 October 1927

Australia's most notorious criminal during the 1920s was a little man who had been christened Theodore Joseph Lestor Taylor. He was known mostly as Squizzy Taylor and sometimes, by intimates and admirers, as 'The Turk'. He was a pick-pocket who graduated, through extortion and blackmail, to the planning of bank robberies and armed hold-ups at bookmakers' homes, shops and factories. He was widely believed to have committed the murder of William Haines in 1916, but no positive identification of him was made, mainly, it was later claimed, because of threats received by key Crown witnesses.

Taylor died in a gun duel with Snowy Cutmore, a younger criminal, in the Melbourne suburb of Carlton. Hugh Buggy, one of the reporters who knew him best, said of him:

His crafty dark eyes leered at you from under a rakish bowler hat. He had a nasty mouth that curled in a perpetual sneer. He was flashy and ostentatious, clad always in the best of suitings, and the most iridescent of shirts and ties. He was just a dapper little braggart, but he wielded amazing influence over gunmen, burglars and pickpockets. They elevated him to the stature of a demi-god. To an assorted crew of morons he became a hero, a legendary figure, an examplar of all forms of criminal derring-do.

Buggy always claimed that the reason for the final gun-battle with Cutmore was a pledge made by Taylor to another criminal. This man, sentenced to six months' gaol for theft, asked Taylor to look after his girl friend, a girl called Edna, during his enforced absence. Edna conducted a fairly exclusive beer-house in St Kilda. In October 1927 Cutmore visited
the establishment, got drunk, refused to pay for beer, smashed bottles and furniture, and finally blacked both Edna's eyes. She told Taylor, and the result was the confrontation in Carlton. Taylor, according to Buggy, took several days to summon the courage to visit Cutmore.

Clyde Palmer, a well-known crime and sports reporter, received a tip-off that 'something' would happen at Cutmore's home. He was not far away when Taylor and Cutmore began blazing away at each other. He wrote this report for the Melbourne Sun *the following morning:*

Two men, both notorious members of the underworld, were shot dead, and a woman wounded, last night in a desperate revolver duel in a house in Barkly-street, Carlton.

The shooting was the outcome of a vendetta, which had existed between the dead men for some years. Although the associates of the men are reticent as to what led up to the shooting, the detectives believe rivalry for the affections of a woman was the immediate incentive.

The Victims are:—

DEAD

Leslie (Squizzy) Taylor, 42, of Darlington-parade, Richmond. Bullet wound in right side over lungs.

John (Snowy) Cutmore, 35, of Barkly-street, Carlton. Bullet wound over heart, and on little finger of right hand.

WOUNDED

Bridget Cutmore, 56, mother of John Cutmore. Shot through right shoulder. Condition not serious.

The police were first notified of the shooting when a hatless man named Roy Treverse, rushed into Carlton police station, at 6.45 p.m., and said that a man had been shot. Treverse requested the police to obtain the services of a doctor. Constables McDonald and Payne hurried to the house, and on the way they picked up Dr. McCutcheon at his surgery, in Rathdown-street.

On reaching the house the police found Cutmore lying on his back in a bedroom at the rear of the house.

Mrs. Cutmore, senior, was staggering about the house, bleeding from a wound in the right shoulder, while the dead man's wife, Mrs. Gladys Cutmore, was weeping and wringing her hands.

The floor of the room, which was in great disorder, was littered with cartridge shells, and the walls perforated with bullet marks, and a lamp and looking glass were shattered.

It was not known until 10 minutes later that Taylor had also been a victim. The first news of his being wounded was received from St. Vincent's Hospital. Fitzroy police were informed that Taylor was driven to the institution in a taxi cab, and on stepping out, collapsed. He was carried into the casualty ward by the driver, John William Hall.

Taylor was then unconscious. It was seen by the doctors that his case was hopeless. He recovered consciousness for a few minutes but did not speak, and shortly afterwards fell back dead on the bed. Senior-Constable Haghland and Senior-Constable Sauter, of Fitzroy, hurried to the hospital, but they were too late.

On searching the body Constable Haghland found an empty automatic revolver in the trousers pocket, while in another pocket he found a package partly filled with bullets. The revolver barrel was slightly warm, an indication that it had been recently fired.

The news of the shooting quickly spread, and when Sub-Inspector Piggott, accompanied by Detectives Greive, Milne, McPhee, and Hogg reached the house, they found Barkly-street thronged with curious onlookers.

In their efforts to clear up the shooting the detectives were hampered by the unwillingness of persons in the house to aid them in the reconstruction of the crime.

However, from a statement made by Hall, the hire-car driver, and the state of the room, the detectives were able to piece together a picture, which portrayed one of the most dramatic and sensational encounters in the history of crime in Melbourne.

They visited several hotels, and Taylor and his associates appeared to be in quest of someone. They had several drinks, and apparently not finding the person whom they sought, Taylor ordered Hall to drive to the house in Barkly-street. Taylor and one of his companions entered the house. The other man remained in the car.

Obviously Taylor found Cutmore in bed. What followed can only be conjectured. Mrs. Cutmore, senior, at the time was in the kitchen preparing the evening meal, while her daughter-in-law was absent from the house, buying milk for the meal.

The police believe that following a short altercation between the men, revolvers were drawn by all parties.

Cutmore, who was suffering from influenza, and who had been in bed since Monday, is believed to have risen to a sitting posture, and drawn a revolver from under his pillow, aimed at Taylor and fired. The latter also fired, and both men were hit.

The shots must have been almost simultaneous, as the detectives state they will be able to prove that a shot fired at Cutmore struck his revolver on the side, disabling the weapon, and then ricochetted inflicting a superficial wound on Cutmore's little finger. To support this theory, the detectives found a bullet which was dented and had minute particles of nickelling adhering to it.

Wild, indiscriminate firing followed the wounding of the two principals, and it is believed that the other man who is now being sought by the police also took part in the affray. Two bullets struck Cutmore, two pierced the wall alongside his bed, another entered the wall above his head, and a sixth shattered a lamp on a washstand alongside the bed, while another bullet shattered a mirror on a dressing table in a corner facing where Cutmore lay.

At the first shot Mrs. Cutmore senior

rushed into the bedroom, but received a bullet through the right shoulder almost immediately after she passed through the doorway. Two shots also struck Taylor, one inflicted a graze about three inches below his fatal wound.

The whole affair lasted only five minutes, according to Hall, the car driver, who was waiting outside.

Taylor suddenly rushed out of the house and staggered into the car with his hands clasped to his right side. "I have been shot," he exclaimed. "Drive me to St. Vincent's Hospital." These were the only words he uttered.

There was no sign of the man who entered the house with him. Hall drove in the direction of St. Vincent's Hospital, while the other man in the car attempted to staunch the flow of blood from Taylor's wounds. However, on reaching the corner of Johnston and Brunswick-streets, Hall was obliged to slow down. Here the man in the car with Taylor got out. He quickly disappeared. Hall did not lose any time, and drove straight to the hospital. . .

Comparisons were made at various times between Squizzy Taylor and Ned Kelly. A big difference concerned their respective degrees of courage. Tom Kelynak, the Melbourne Herald *crime reporter, wrote next day:*

"Squizzy" Taylor was a swaggering, conceited criminal fop, who gloried in the underworld reputation of being a man of courage, whereas in fact, he was a sneak with the cowardice of a sneak.

He was a man who to save his own skin would not hesitate to put the police on the track of criminals with whom he had been co-operating.

He was by no means popular among the underworld people — they distrusted him, and possibly this side of his character was, after all, of service to the community, for without the treachery of Taylor perhaps many desperate ruffians would have escaped punishment.

In the underworld a "shelf," that is a common informer, is a man who is wholeheartedly hated. Taylor was blamed by many who had been sent behind the blue walls of

Pentridge as the man who had "shelfed" them.

So bitter was the hatred of him by two or three ruffians who were pining in Pentridge a few years ago, that on hearing he was likely to be convicted and sent to gaol, one of them sent out a request for poison to be smuggled into Pentridge.

He made no secret of his intention. If the poison could be obtained he was determined to poison Taylor.

"Squizzy" was told of the hostility of the convicts, and he was terror stricken. His fear of going to gaol was not because of an enforced absence from the busy haunts of criminals about the city, but of physical violence.

He was determined that any of the felons whom he had doublecrossed would not have the satisfaction of wreaking vengeance on him.

He was on trial for the murder of Haines, the chauffeur, in 1916. With him was another well-known criminal. Haines had been engaged to drive two men to Heidelberg, where they had arranged, it was thought, to rob a bank manager. The chauffeur was ignorant of their intention and was shot in his car on Bulleen road.

The accused men were acquitted, but the police never faltered in their belief that Taylor was one of the passengers, who had murdered the young man.

Taylor had made arrangements with a woman so that in the event of his conviction for the murder, he would not be executed.

The woman was to visit him after the conviction, and on leaving him was to embrace and kiss him. As the last kiss was to be given, she was to slip from her mouth a capsule containing poison into his mouth.

Taylor later boasted of the sensation which would have been created had such a dramatic incident taken place. He considered it was a clever contingency.

Taylor lived on his wits and on the credulity of others rather than by any bold action of his own. He made capital out of the fear that his reputation as a gunman and gangster inspired, but when anybody showed violence toward

'Squizzy' Taylor (centre) photographed for the front page of the *Sun* minutes after he gave himself up on 22 September 1922

him he wilted and became a cringing sneak, though he frequently tried "to get even" for any affront — usually by inducing someone else to do the dirty work for him.

Bookmakers were systematically blackmailed, but one day he went to the Victorian Club rooms and struck a snag. With a pal more desperate and daring than himself, Squizzy ascended the stairs.

"Hey!" he called to a well-known bookmaker. "Hey! Give us a tenner."

The bookmaker did not recognise either Squizzy or his associate, and laughingly replied, "Are you sure you con't want a pony, young fellow?"

"I said a tenner, and it's a tenner I want, and don't you get funny."

"You young rat," said the bookmaker, as he seized Squizzy. "Get out of this." And he

flung Squizzy down the stairs.

Taylor and his mate ran through the door into Bourke-street, and as they were passing the doorkeeper, threatened to kill him if he stopped them or made a call for the police.

Next morning the bookmaker, whose one great pleasure was his garden, awoke to find that it had been wrecked. Squizzy had induced someone to destroy the valuable plants. That was one of his ways of "getting even."

Taylor never forgave the police for having declared that he was 44 years of age instead of 32 when he was being searched for in 1921-1922. The man was as vain as a woman on this point.

One thing is certain, and that is whatever his age was, he had never put his life to any good or useful purpose.

1928   Bert Hinkler, the bird man from Bundaberg, flies solo from London

UNKNOWN REPORTER
Melbourne Age, 27 February 1928

Bert Hinkler, a short, modest man who used to spend hours as a boy watching the flying technique of the ibis, flew into history in February 1928. That was when he piloted an Avro Avian from London to Darwin in fifteen and a half days, slashing the previous record of twenty-eight days for the journey. It was the longest flight ever made solo.

Hinkler was a plane-crazy youngster who had one unswerving ambition: to spend most of his life flying. He built gliders, modelled on the ibis, and when he was twenty he left his native town of Bundaberg, Queensland, determined to learn to fly. At Richmond common, near Sydney, he made a bargain with a man selling joy-ride flights over Sydney: Hinkler undertook to wash down the plane every night for just one flight. Before he completed the contract his mother arrived in Sydney from Bundaberg and prevented him from having his first flight.

There were no flying schools in Australia at the time, so Hinkler departed a few months later for Europe, working his passage in a German freighter. He was still only twenty; the year was 1912. He made his way from Hamburg to London, and landed a job as a mechanic with the Sopwith aircraft company. When war broke out, he joined the Royal Naval Air Service and was soon flying in combat as an observer. He won the Distinguished Service Medal, gained a commission, and later joined the Royal Flying Corps.

On demobilisation he bought an Avro Baby plane, took it to Australia, assembled it, and on 11 April 1921 established a world's record for a non-stop solo flight by covering 850 miles from Mascot to Bundaberg. Hinkler returned to England soon after, obsessed with the idea of flying to Australia. He tried un-successfully to interest newspapers in the project, and was unable even to raise the £150 required to insure his aircraft for £2000. After a good deal of frustration, he finally secured advertising contracts, and on 7 February 1928 he took off from Croydon airfield, London, for Australia. He carried a handful of tools and an inflatable dinghy.

For a time Australia went Hinkler-crazy. The Government sent a cruiser to stand by when Hinkler flew on his final leg, across the Arafura Sea. Composers wrote songs about him — the nation's hit tune was briefly Hustling Hinkler — small boys wore Hinkler buttons, flappers wore close-fitting Hinkler helmet-type hats, Federal Parliament stopped its business to welcome him, the Queensland Government gave him £500 and the Australian Government awarded him £2000 in cash, plus the Air Force Cross and the honorary rank of squadron leader in the Royal Australian Air Force. Characteristically, Hinkler never used the rank or wore the uniform.

After his arrival in Darwin, Hinkler headed for his home town. The Melbourne Age *sent a special reporter to Bundaberg. This was his story on 27 February 1928:*

Bert Hinkler, who has been accurately described as "the brilliant bird man of Bundaberg," expects to complete to-day his self-imposed task, which will go down in the history of aviation as an epoch-making event. His solo flight from London to his home town has captured the public imagination. Never has airman displayed greater courage, resource and determination. His departure was so unostentatious, and his progress so rapid, that it was not until he had landed on his native soil in the astonishing time of a little more than fifteen days, that the world realised that this Australian "Digger" had outclassed even the great performance of America's wonder air-man, Colonel Lindbergh.

And it is since he landed in Australia, no doubt thoroughly wearied in body and mind by the constant strain of flying, in solitude, vast distances over sea, desert and mountain, that Bert Hinkler — few bother to call him "Lieutenant," though he well deserves a higher title — has been called upon to show his finest qualities. Though longing to greet an anxious, yet confident parent, and his old-time 'pals' in Bundaberg, he delayed a day at Darwin to give his historic machine the overhaul it must have sorely needed. Few people realise that to fly from Darwin to Bundaberg is almost equivalent to a flight from London to Rome and back. Yet, having reached Darwin, one of the most difficult stages yet remained. He had to cross the so-called "Dead Heart" of Australia, which, further south, in other pioneering days had swallowed up other great men of resource, grit and determination — Burke and Wills and Leichhardt — and had proved a temporary obstacle in the path of those brilliant airmen, the Smith Brothers, Parer and Cobham. And so it proved to Hinkler.

When leaving Darwin on Friday morning his destination was Cloncurry, about 800 miles, with a final leap the following day of a similar distance to Bundaberg. The whole Empire became anxious when night closed in on Friday and Hinkler was "missing." Every one was confident that all was well, yet there was just ground for apprehension. The civil aviation resources of North Central Queens-land were requisitioned and many planes went out from Cloncurry and Camooweal to search the "Never Never." They failed to find him. What might have been expected happened — he found them. While the continent was be-coming alarmed this "dynamo of energy" sailed in on the air and landed amidst his searchers.

Where had he been? Well, the story was simply told. He had encountered head winds, dust storms and darkness, so he did what any of the resourceful "diggers", who proved their superiority at Anzac and elsewhere, over the machine-made type of soldiery, would do. He made a safe landing beside a wind mill, 38 miles from Brunette Downs homestead, and slept in a boat he found there. Probably he had a longer and a better sleep than at any time since his departure from London. With dawn, and the need of breakfast, he flew across to Alexandria Station, where, after the warm welcome that he might have expected, he moved on 120 miles to Camooweal, and the whole world knew he was safe. Perhaps the most unconcerned person was the airman himself. His mother waited proudly and con-fidently in her home on the banks of the Burnett. His wife, in England, doubtless had few fears, despite the fact that her husband was reported "missing.". . .

Bundaberg never gave credence to the suggestion that anything serious had happened to Hinkler, for remembrance of earlier intrepid efforts, such as landing on the foundry green, or diving beneath the Burnett traffic bridge, buoyed them up in the hope that he would be discovered safely before long. As proof of this a proclamation was issued by Mr. C. D. O'Brien, police magistrate, announcing that the fire bell would be rung as soon as news was received that Hinkler had been discovered. This action at 11.15 a.m. brought almost the whole of the town population to the main street awaiting further information. A system of flag signalling to indicate the time of arrival was also arranged, and posters explaining the proposal were set out in various points throughout the town.

Early in the afternoon a message was received by the mayor from Hinkler himself, lodged at Camooweal at 1 p.m., as follows:—

Arrived Camooweal after trying time North-ern Territory; extreme contrary winds; landed wind mill Brunette Downs over night; break-fast Alexandria; suggest arrive Bundaberg Monday soon after 5 o'clock. — Hinkler.

Learning that the airman was still at Camoo-weal in the afternoon, the mayor sent the following telegram to the officer in charge of police there:—

Please make personal representations on behalf of citizens of Bundaberg and ask Hinkler what route he will take to Bundaberg;

tell him his wire received; can he reach Bundaberg at 4 o'clock on Monday?

Many distinguished visitors are awaiting the arrival of Hinkler at Bundaberg. The State Premier, Mr. W. McCormack, and Colonel Brinsmead, Director of Civil Aviation, reached here at lunch time yesterday. One of the first actions of the Premier was to make arrangements with Qantas for an aeroplane to escort Hinkler from Longreach to Bundaberg if possible as a tribute from the State Government to his gallant effort.

Rain has fallen almost incessantly, but the ten-acre paddock which is to be utilised as a landing ground for Hinkler's Avian machine is well drained, and no trouble is expected in him getting down on Monday afternoon.

Provided the weather conditions are favorable, it is the intention to effect a simultaneous radio broadcast of Hinkler's arrival at Bundaberg on Monday afternoon. Land lines will carry the description of the historic incident to Brisbane, Sydney and Melbourne, from where it will be broadcast in each instance. Experiments are also to be tried of broadcasting on a short-wave length in an endeavor to describe the scene to English listeners. Tests made with the lines at the week end proved entirely satisfactory.

Hinkler later returned to England and put his money into a company making an aircraft named after the bird whose flight he used to study — the ibis. He later flew across the Atlantic from east to west; this was considered to be the greatest piece of solo navigation in aviation history..

On 7 January 1933, Bert Hinkler took off from London on the last flight of his career. The Sydney Sun *published this report from its London representative on 10 January:*

Captain Lingham, a sky-writer well known in Australia, and Major Savage were probably the last men to see Bert Hinkler, the Australian airman, when he set out on his attempted record-breaking flight to Australia from a private English hangar at 3 o'clock on Saturday morning.

"We were watching at the end of the illuminated stretch 300 yards from the start," Captain Lingham said to a representative of "The Sun." "We heard the engine roaring and caught the faint flicker of the 'plane 25 feet aloft, going strong into the mist and moonlight above. As far as I know, Hinkler has not been seen since." . . .

The Air Ministry stated at 10 o'clock last night that Hinkler was still not reported, and that his friends had begun to speculate because of the lack of news of him from any of the recognised Australian routes. They know that Hinkler was aiming to make a different record, possibly to the Cape, but that is difficult to reconcile with the fact that he accepted from Major Savage messages for Australia. . .

According to Mr. L. J. Gruter, friend of the Hinkler family, at present on holidays in Sydney, there is no need for anxiety.

"Of course, accidents can happen," says Mr. Gruter, "but Bert likes doing things on the quiet, and his thoroughness is such that I cannot imagine that anything has happened to him. I think that when he is reported he will be well on his way to Australia."

Mr. Gruter has known Hinkler since he was a small lad. He used to come to his dental surgery in Bundaberg, and even as a child was a very good patient.

He has watched that small boy grow. First he was interested in the flight of birds. Stunning them with a stone from his catapult, he would measure their wing span and take other details. At 13 he made a glider which was the pride of the district.

Hinkler's body and his plane were found in a remote spot in the Apennines at the end of April. On 1 May the Melbourne Herald *published this description of the aviator's funeral from Lionel Lindsay, a member of the famous family of artists and writers. Lionel, an etcher, wood-engraver, water-colorist, worked as a journalist for a number of years and was a member of the editorial staff of the Sydney* Evening News *under the editorship of A. B. 'Banjo' Paterson; he was art critic for the Melbourne* Herald.

The morning papers of Florence gave no hint that Bert Hinkler was to be buried this afternoon. I had learned from my waiter that his body had been brought down the night before from Strada, and was lying in state at the Aero Club. But for this chance information I might have missed paying my respect to our great airman, and assuring the presence of at least one Australian at the obsequies.

I reached the Via Cavour but ten minutes before the departure of the cortege, and through the courtesy of an aero officer, was admitted to the Capella Ardente.

The coffin, covered by the English and Italian flags, to which some pious hand had pinned a small Australian flag, lay on a catafalque of black and gold before a heavy canopy. About it were placed great wreaths of flowers, and the humbler floral tributes of the little village to which his body had been brought upon discovery.

In front stood the three officiating British chaplains, and the room was filled with officers. On guard by the coffin stood an officer with drawn sword, and in front of him a Fascist bearing a gold standard inscribed with the S.P.Q.R. of Ancient Rome.

At 6.30, borne on the shoulders of airmen, the coffin descended the stairs. I waited until the last, and saw the great candles — extinguished and laid together upon the bier — throw up their column of smoke as from some altar of sacrifice.

A dense crowd thronged the footways behind the lines of steel-hats and bayonets, and from every balcony and window faces looked down upon the hero's passage.

Slowly, to the strains of a dead march, the funeral moved toward the Piazza del Duomo. In front marched a company of Italian Infantry, behind the officiating prelates, followed by officers of the Air Force, the Fascist and Italian Army, and some few casual or resident Englishmen.

The afternoon — so different from the bleak day on which his body had been found — was warm and sunny, a veritable Australian spring day, and when the Ghiberti Gates were reached — those that Michael Angelo judged worthy of Paradise — the late sun lit up the face of the great Cathedral, and transfigured the funeral car into one of triumph.

As the hearse passed the Piazza to the

Bert Hinkler in 1928 starting his Avro Avian

roar of circling planes overhead, men gave it the Roman salute, and in the poorer quarters, once the Arno was crossed, the girls of Tuscany threw flowers from the high windows.

Far up the Via Romana troops still lined the streets, and when the Old Roman Gate had been passed, the cortege halted, the military band played our National Anthem, and the Italian service was finished.

From the Porta Romana the passage by car to the English Cemetery was rapid, but night had closed in before the conclusion of the burial service.

Hinkler was laid by the side of a noble column of cypress, such alone as the Tuscan soil can build and by that dense and solemn wind-screen he may well sleep sound, nor dream of any records still to break.

The Aero Club of Florence at the instigation of the Italian Government gave Hinkler a hero's burial. The gesture is so finely magnanimous that I trust the Australian people will in some way recognise it.

This great country raised again through the genius of one man to faith in herself, paid to Bert Hinkler such tribute as only his own country might have followed when in the high Roman fashion she gave him that last heroic salute of Hail and Farewell.

1928   'Smithy' lands at Brisbane after flying across the Pacific

CLEM LACK
Brisbane Courier-Mail, 11 June 1928

On 31 May 1928, Charles Kingsford Smith, with C. T. P. Ulm as his second pilot and two Americans, Harry Lyon and James Warner, took off on the first flight across the Pacific Ocean. Kingsford Smith, born in 1897, learned to fly with the Royal Flying Corps in the Great War and won the Military Cross for service with a fighter squadron. After the war he spent about a year with flying circuses in California, and flew for a time as a pilot with Western Australian Airways Ltd.

'Smithy', one of the great folk heroes of Australian history, pioneered many air routes inside Australia and overseas. His nagging ambition during the 'twenties was to fly the Pacific; it took him several years to coax enough financial assistance to enable him to buy the airframe of a Fokker monoplane that had been used in the Arctic by Sir Hubert Wilkins. He re-equipped the plane, gave it a new engine, and christened it Southern Cross.

The epic flight across the Pacific was made from east to west in three hops; from San Francisco to Honolulu, to Fiji, to Brisbane. Between Honolulu and Fiji, a stretch of 2740 nautical miles, the longest distance flown non-stop to that time, the Southern Cross was in the air thirty-three hours. The Southern Cross landed in Brisbane on 9 June, after a flight which lasted three days, ten hours, forty-two minutes. The journey, the Melbourne Herald noted, 'makes the steamer trip comparatively an ocean crawl'. The fastest mail boats took nineteen days to cross from San Francisco to Sydney, it pointed out.

One of the pressmen who had most to do with 'Smithy' was Jack Percival (of the Sydney Sun and later the Sydney Morning Herald), who flew with him across the Tasman and in fact remained a leading aviation writer for more than thirty years. Another who was in Brisbane that day was the irrepressible Hugh Buggy. The Brisbane papers were represented by Clem Lack, Ted Jackson and Reg Vickers.

This was Clem Lack's report, published on 11 June 1928 in the Courier-Mail:

With her three 220 h.p. motors roaring above the minor drone of the two diminutive Moths who escorted her, the giant Fokker monoplane Southern Cross loomed out of the ether thirteen minutes after 10 o'clock on Saturday morning on the triumphal completion of her 7000 mile flight over the Pacific, spanning two continents in a hop, step, and jump that heads a new chapter in the history of aviation. More than 10,000 persons shivered in the rawness of the morning at the Eagle Farm aerodrome to see the big 'plane land. They waited for four hours, and then they saw her swoop over, her enormous wing spread of 60 feet dwarfed, at a height of 2000 feet. Then she circled three times like a giant blue hawk, gradually dropping lower, until she shot over the tree tops, and alighted with graceful precision, pulling up to a standstill in a remarkably short distance. Captain Kingsford Smith (pilot), Mr. C. T. P. Ulm (relief pilot), Lieut. Harry Lyon (navigator), and Mr. James Warner (radio expert) received a wonderful ovation when they climbed out, the crowd mobbing them in an ecstasy of enthusiasm, and breaking the barriers. The final hop of the intrepid aviators from Naselai Beach, Fiji, to Brisbane, occupied 21 hours 18 minutes. They left Brisbane again yesterday, arriving safely in Sydney in the early afternoon.

A number of people had gathered at the aerodrome long before daybreak, and by 8 o'clock — the aviators were expected at

8.30 — there were 18,000 eager spectators, and motor cars were still arriving in an endless stream. Until the sun arose in all its winter glory, it was very cold.

By means of a temporary station at the hangar, 4QG, Brisbane, kept in close touch with the airmen. At 8.40 a radio message came through: "Batteries low. Have not been listening for 30 minutes." At 8.45 a.m. six escorting 'planes flew out to see if they could locate the Southern Cross. At 9.45 a.m. Captain L. J. Brain, manager of Qantas, who was the first to take the air, returned to Eagle Farm with a message that he had flown over sea and bay, at a height of 7000ft., and after careful scouting had failed to find it. At 9.30 another radio message arrived, announcing that the giant monoplane had been blown off its course, had sighted the coast at Ballina, New South Wales, and was flying north with all speed to Brisbane.

There was a buzz of excitement when, shortly after 10 o'clock, a message reached 4QG that the big plane was flying over Burleigh Heads. Another moment, and it was over Beenleigh. Then it could be seen, a speck in the distance, coming nearer and nearer, growing larger and larger, flying at terrific speed from the south, in a perfectly cloudless, though somewhat hazy sky, till its blue body and silver wings were clearly discernible, glistening in the glorious morning sunlight. As it flew over the hangar the buzz of its mighty engines could be heard well above the other 'planes, and it appeared like an eagle flying with six gulls. The crowd cheered lustily. Simultaneously the sirens of 5000 motor vehicles of all descriptions shrieked a weird welcome. The cheering and the tooting swelled into a deafening crescendo as the Southern Cross twice circled gracefully over the aerodrome, flying so low that the words "Southern Cross", in white, on the blue background, the famous symbol of the Southern Hemisphere, and the figures "1985", near the tail, could be clearly seen. Still flying low, the great plane, preparatory to landing almost touched the trees at the the northern end of the 'drome, making their top branches tremble as in a storm; then turning, it swooped gracefully and gradually to the ground, and taxied

Charles Kingsford Smith (right) and co-pilot Charles Ulm pose in front of the *Southern Cross* in May 1928 before their famous trans-Pacific flight

to the enclosure, while the escorting 'planes curtsied in salute. . .

The Americans, dressed in ordinary serge suits, modestly stepped back and tried to efface themselves when Captain Kingsford Smith and Mr. Ulm, clad in their flying attire, were being lionised at the moment of landing. But the crowd insisted on them sharing the honours. "Where are the Yanks? Show us the Yanks!" was the cry, and they were immediately carried on stalwart shoulders in the wake of their Australian comrades. Warner with hair tousled, and a dog-weary look in his eyes, kept a firm grip of the log book under his arm, while Captain Lyon, as happy as a schoolboy, cracked jokes and shook hands with the crowd. "This reminds me of the reception to Lindbergh" he said. The enthusiasm increased as the procession advanced. Once more the police had to clear a passage for the aviators. There was a jam. For a moment Kingsford Smith lost sight of his American companions. "Where are my American friends?" he asked and he was pleased to know that they were still alive. The waiting motor car was reached at last, and a triumphal procession to the City Hall commenced. . .

The personalities of the visiting airmen present a wide contrast. Kingsford Smith, the most outstanding figure of the party, is the typical Australian, pictured by the novelist: tall, with a powerful, lean frame, with his thin face, and jutting jaw burnt a brick red. When the "Courier" representative approached him he was sprawling in an easy chair, leisurely slitting envelopes of telegrams and cables, with his long legs extending under the little table. He has an easy frankness of manner, and a dry humour that is refreshing. Mr. C. T. P. Ulm is the business man of the party, with a brusque, direct manner, and he speaks with the curt rapidity of the machine-gun. A suggestion that Captain Kingsford Smith should issue a message of greeting to the people of Queensland, to which the pilot showed some signs of compliance, was instantly vetoed by Mr. Ulm, who vouchsafed the information that the fliers were bound by newspaper contracts not to divulge any information concerning their flight. Lieut. Lyon, the

navigator, speaks with the soft drawl of the American South, which seems foreign to his bulky frame, just as his pleasant manner is in distinct contrast to the dour set of his broad cheek bones and square jaw. He lost his spectacles at Buva, and this omission lends his glance a quizzical peering effect when he speaks. "Jim" Warner, his compatriot, was considerably embarrassed by the publicity in which he found himself a figure. . .

Underlying the sincere welcome, and the recognition of the incomparably great achievement in aviation that these men had brought to a successful conclusion, there could be detected a distinct undercurrent of affection, an unmistakable note of civic pride in the fact that the chief amongst "the big four" claimed Brisbane as his birth-place. That fact — though otherwise the greeting would not have been less spontaneous — gave an additional fillip to the welcoming plaudits of the crowd. Brisbane rejoiced that one of its sons, the leader of a mighty achievement, had established his right to take his place in the foremost ranks of the greatest aviators of the period, and had worthily upheld the prestige of Australia in the sphere of valour and worthwhile endeavour. . .

The Premier (Mr. W. McCormack) said that on behalf of the Government and people of Queensland he congratulated the four brave men who had that day concluded one of the most amazing feats in history. . .
"I welcome, on behalf of the Queensland Government, the two Americans who are here with us . . . Mr. Lyon and Mr. Warner. (Applause.) We in Australia have much in common with Americans. We live on opposite sides of the Pacific: our methods of living, our civilisation, and our language are similar, and, as the Vice-Mayor has already said, this flight has done something very material, I believe, to bring closer together the English-speaking peoples upon whom, after all, civilisation depends. I congratulate our own Queenslander. Naturally we are proud of him, and I hope that the future holds no trouble for him. . ."

1928   A reporter ridicules wrestling and receives his punishment

CLYDE PALMER
Sydney Smith's Weekly, August 1928

One of the few heroic figures in Frank Hardy's powerful, controversial novel Power Without Glory *was a young reporter called Clive Parker. Like almost every other character in the book, which dealt with the life and times of John Wren, Parker had a real-life identity which the author disguised very thinly. Clive Parker was really Clyde Palmer, who worked at various times on the Melbourne* Sun News-Pictorial, *the* Morning Post, Truth *and* Smith's Weekly. *He covered crime and sports, and he was at the centre of two events which Hardy made dramatic high points in his novel. When Squizzy Taylor and Snowy Cutmore shot each other to death, Palmer was on the spot; according to* Power Without Glory, *he was outside the murder house before the shooting began, and invaded Cutmore's bloody bedroom minutes after the duel. And after Palmer had written a number of articles ridiculing professional wrestling and exposing it as a sham, a huge wrestler contrived to fall almost on top of him in the press seats, injuring his face. It was retribution on a primitive scale.*

Clyde Palmer was one of three journalist brothers, all of whom became senior practitioners of their craft. Howard Palmer wrote for the Sun News-Pictorial *and the* Argus, *and became a film and theatre critic as well as federal president of the Australian Journalists' Association. Lindsay Palmer worked for the Sydney* Sun, *and for a time represented that newspaper in London.*

When American wrestling came to Melbourne in the 1920s, with its diverse, freakish band of King Kongs, Killers, Counts and Indian Chiefs, Clyde Palmer conducted a kind of mocking, one-man war on it. He regarded it as an entertainment, not a sport, and he lampooned it

whenever he could. Ted Thye was a wrestler and a businessman, the master-mind of the grunt-and-grapple invaders. Once a wrestling promoter tried to bribe Palmer, and made the mistake of handing him a cheque; Palmer took it straight back to the Sun *office, dumped it on the desk of the editor, George Taylor, and announced, 'That's how they buy reporters.' The* Sun's *proprietor, Sir Keith Murdoch, is said to have kept the cheque in his office for many years. It was never cashed.*

Palmer tried the patience of the wrestling chiefs too far; they tried to arrange for him to be sacked, but Sir Keith Murdoch regarded him too highly to allow that to happen. Finally, at the first wrestle of the 1929 season, Ted Thye resolved to handle the matter in his own fashion. Thye, who was called Ted Tinn in Power Without Glory, *contrived to fall on to the press table at which Clyde Palmer was writing. This is how the book describes what happened next:*

> Clive Parker looked up and two bodies fell onto the table in front of him. Next thing he knew, Tinn's face was close to his. It was dirty and sweating. And its mouth moved and said in a low but violent whisper, 'Cop this, you bastard!' And Ted Tinn's mighty fist crashed into Clive Parker's face. . . The ushers, normally quick and violent in suppressing a melee, were not yet on the scene. Tinn had Clive Parker's unconscious body under the ring, knocking its snowy head on the floor.

Clyde's brother Howard says that the Hardy version of the incident is broadly factual, but that the wrestler kicked Clyde across the bridge of the nose with his heel. For the rest of his life — he died in 1959, aged fifty-one —

Clyde Palmer had difficulty in breathing through his nose.

There was a piquant sequel many years later to that savage little piece of revenge in the press seats at West Melbourne Stadium. Clyde Palmer's son Scot became a journalist, and developed in time into a sportswriter of quality. When news came in March 1966 that Thye had died in the United States at the age of seventy-five, I was editor of the Sun, *and I assigned Scot Palmer to write his obituary. To his credit, Scot Palmer wrote a piece which showed no bitterness.*

This report, from Smith's Weekly, *demonstrates the kind of reporting which finally influenced Ted Thye to get even with Clyde Palmer in his own primitive fashion:*

Sensations, surprises, and shocks. Mix this in equal proportions, with two teaspoonfuls of holts and grips, add a little bad feeling and ruffled temper, and stir gently while pouring in gratings of good showstuff.

Boil gently for eight 10-minute periods, with a minute in between to prevent curdling — and Melbourne is served up with yet another of the wrestling dishes which, to date, have been readily gulped by eager thousands.

But now, however, it is apparent there is something wrong with the cooks, for Melbourne is seemingly not enjoying the dishes with the same relish as before, despite the desperate efforts of those publicity sponsors of the menu to keep the West Melbourne "cafeteria" well in the boom. Although the hungry hundreds still patronise, they continually complain about the dishes of all the cooks except Santel. The fact is, Melbourne did not know what good cooking was until this laddie got a job at the "cafeteria" and showed the other cooks up to such tune that the boys of this village now know the meaning of distinction of diet.

Ted Thye, it would appear, has been completely deposed from the job of chief hashslinger, and the customers' interest in him lies only in the possibility of his engaging Santel in a contest at 12.7 before the season closes and the cooks play Arabs and folding tents.

Perhaps it might be just as well for Ted to study the cookery book a little more before he engages Santel; that is, if his sortie with Clarence Eckland on Saturday is to be taken as full criterion of his cooking ability. Clarence is the boy specially imported to teach local cooks and chefs the various ways to serve lamb, and also to engage Santel and Thye in a world cooking championship contest before the sheep are gone from the pastures to their mountain grazing.

It might be mentioned here that there is a possibility of both Thye and Clarence kicking against Santel having a male help in offsider Brennan. The great value of this one's conspicuous signals to Santel the other night against Kilonis, specialist in Greek delicacies, was not lost upon all other members of the cafeteria staff.

Well, on Saturday, Ted and Clarence spoilt what would otherwise have been a good appetising morsel by using far too much of the first ingredient of the wrestling dish. The whole thing curdled just after half the cooking was done. There were enough surprises and shocks just before the gas was turned off to put into four dishes, and from the fifth round it was, to the fans, like soup with too much salt. At regular intervals between mouthfuls, the hungry horde hooted the hash slingers, counted them out, called sarcastically to both, and generally behaved in a way which indicated that the food was hard to swallow. . .

It was the first sign of the overdose when Clarence adopted a weak defensive ere he fell to a leg scissor and body press. The house would have none of it and cried right loudly as Clarence sat rubbing an arm, looking dazed, sick, woebegone, and miserable, before he was assisted to his corner. The house scented something funny with the food again as Clarrie stood in the corner as before, while Thye dashed in to repeat the dumpling. This time, however, Clarrie had the laugh, for he came to life, rushed Thye backwards to the mat, and banged the head down right heartily ere he too was touched on the back, as indication that he had done something which must have got him a fall. Ted also reeled about the kitchen when he arose, but he was not the only sick one in the cafeteria. . .

LENNIE LOWER
Sydney Labor Daily, 1928

Lennie Lower was, according to many good judges, Australia's greatest humorist. Certainly he kept the city of Sydney laughing for some twenty of his forty-three years, churning out material for the Labor Daily, *the* Daily Guardian, *the* Daily Telegraph, *the* Sunday Telegraph, *the* Australian Women's Weekly, *and finally* Smith's Weekly. *This last appointment came after Lower was sacked by the publishers of the* Daily *and* Sunday Telegraph *for saying something unpleasant in 1940 to the visiting celebrity Mr Noel Coward.*

Lower was at his best attacking pomp and humbug, and there was plenty of that about in 1928, even as Australia was entering its period of greatest hardship ever. At least 80,000 families in New South Wales were on the dole, and several newspapers were engaging in the new cult of 'social reporting', which Cyril Pearl once described as chronicling the activities of people who don't matter for people who don't care.

For the Labor Daily, *Lower indulged in this piece of social reporting entitled 'Let's Peep Inside':*

Imitation is the sincerest form of flattery, and in borrowing this idea from the *Sunday Sun* and *Sunday Telegraph,* we show our appreciation of the new domestic journalism.

The charming home of Mr. and Mrs. John Bowyang, tucked away in Pelican Street, Surry Hills, is a revelation in piquancy. From the backyard one has a view of every other backyard in the street, and the tall chimney-stack of Tooth's Brewery looms majestically in the distance.

An antique casket, known to connoisseurs as a "dirt-tin," stands by the back entrance. It is one of Mrs. Bowyang's great sorrows that the lid has been pinched.

Mrs. Bowyang has an artistic taste and an eye for effect. Two lines have been stretched between long poles at either end of the yard, and when these lines are full of clothes, the sight is bewitching in the extreme.

Empty salmon tins, kindly thrown over the fence by the next-door neighbours, and a worn-out bath and a coil of wire-netting on top of the washhouse roof, complete the picture.

Fascinating though the yard is, it is not until one enters the house itself that one gets a glimpse of the interior. . .

Mr. and Mrs. Bowyang and little Jacky sleep in one double bed, the three youngest girls in the other, and Mr. Bowyang's brother-in-law, who is out of work, sleeps in the stretcher. . . .Business takes Mr. Bowyang away every morning at 6.30, he being engaged in the sewer-digging profession; but he still finds time for his diversions, namely, washing up and placing tins where the rain comes in. The younger children have a magnificent play-ground in Pelican Street, where they have a jolly time daubing themselves with mud, eating stray apple-cores, and escaping being run over by passing lorries.

Viewed from the front, Mrs. Bowyang's home is extremely attractive. It seems to attract all the dust in the streets, and although it has never been renovated since it was built, it is remarkably cheap for 25/- a week, and the brass door-knob takes an excellent polish.

The writer was intrigued by the quaint, old-world, worn-out, bashed-in atmosphere of the locality, and it was with great reluctance that he left. He lingered for a while, hoping to see the owner of Mrs. Bowyang's residence, with the idea of strangling him when he saw him, but realizing the futility of the idea he left.

1929   **The advent of 'Talkies' revolutionises the film industry**

UNKNOWN REPORTERS
Melbourne Argus, 4 January 1911; Everyone's, 2 January 1929; Sydney Morning Herald, 10 June 1929

It was in September 1896 that the first motion pictures were shown in Sydney. The subjects screened included a view of traffic crossing Westminster Bridge, a burlesque of Trilby, and a round of a boxing match, which caused some hissing among the audience.

The Sydney Morning Herald *said of this first exhibition at the Tivoli Theatre:*

> There seemed to be a consensus of opinion on Saturday evening that Mr. Harry Rickards, in his long catering for the public, has never submitted a more startling or interesting novelty than the Cinematographe . . . The busy traffic in a street . . . a scene in a play, or any other subject that has been submitted by rapid photography is repeated with remarkable fidelity, so much so, indeed, that the spectator finds it hard to realise that he is not part and parcel of the moving panorama . . . The enthusiasm was of a most pronounced order, the audience developing an almost insatiable demand for more.

That same month, Sydney's first theatre for film entertainments, the Salon Lumiere, *opened in Pitt Street. It showed twelve films, with such diverse, and slightly mystifying, titles as* The Demolition of a Wall, The Arrival of the Paris Express, *and* A Game of Cards.

The movies increased steadily in popularity, and on 4 January 1911, the Melbourne Argus *was moved to observe:*

It is not difficult to understand the wide appeal made by this ingenious development of the photographic art. The cinematograph bridges distance. It enables scenes and events in the remotest parts of the world to be brought before the eye and mind of people for whom foreign travel is an impossibility.

Nothing of real interest can happen anywhere without a moving picture of it being taken. Boxing matches in California, stately processions in London, scenes of revolutionary violence in the streets of Lisbon, the very flaming of the Vesuvian volcano itself — all are 'snapped' by the whirring machine and exhibited far and wide. In a country so distant from the centres of population as Australia, the educative effect of the cinematograph must be exceptionally great. It enables the people to obtain fairly accurate conception of scenes which a very small minority of them can ever expect to visit, and furnishes many of them, no doubt, with something of that sense of perspective and relativity which travel alone can ever bring to real maturity. With the multitude seeing is believing. Imagine, too, the number of new ideas which a couple of hours in a picture-hall must present to them, and it will not be denied that the cinematograph, allowing for all the banality and frequently the vulgarity of the comic and sentimental films, provides an entertainment which is both instructive and wholesome.

In the world of public entertainment nothing of recent years has been so remarkable as the rise and development of the cinematograph, or moving picture. Invented only about fifteen years ago, it has been growing in favour ever since. It is estimated by a correspondent of 'The Times' that in the United Kingdom alone about 5,000 distinct 'shows' of the kind are open nightly. The London County Council was recently called upon to grant 87 new electric theatre licences at one time, and in the provinces the vogue is equally pronounced. Australians, too, have shown a wonderful predilection for the amusement. Nearly every public hall available in the principal cities and

The King speaks

Hear the Royal Voice of His Majesty in his last public address before his present illness

And the Regent's talkie sensation

The Stars speak their love in "MOTHER KNOWS BEST"

More Celebrity Talkies, Too!

Raquel Meller, the beautiful idol of Paris, in the songs that made her famous.
Bonelli, famed operatic artist, singing the prologue to "Pagliacci."
Robert Benchley, international humorist, in "The Treasurer's Report."
Ruby Keeler, the first

with Madge Bellamy Louise Dresser Barry Norton

An extract from the Sydney *Daily Telegraph*, January 1919, advertising one of the first talking pictures to reach Australia.

towns finds a more or less permanent tenant in a picture entrepreneur, and a considerable number of large buildings have been specially erected for the same purpose. In the metropolitan area of Sydney between 140 and 150 separate institutions of the kind are open during the summer months. Very little capital is required to set up a 'management' in quite a respectable way. Films are manufactured in such amazing quantities that they can be sold or hired out at a moderate rate.

The advent of the 'talkies' revolutionised the production of motion pictures. The first demonstrations of speech from the screen came in March 1927, when 'phonofilms' were shown in Sydney and Melbourne; but the first full-length talking picture was Al Jolson's The Jazz Singer, *first shown in Australia on 29 December 1928, at Sydney's Lyceum and Regent Theatres. It did magnificent business, as this report in* Everyone's, *of 2 January 1929, demonstrates:*

Talkies cracked the Sydney business wide open this week. For the six days the Regent and Lyceum will take between them from £8,000 to £8,500; each house will break its existing week's record; and the Regent's gross will establish an Australian record for cinema takings.

Holiday season saved other city picture theatres from taking the knock; all things considered, their business held up well; but the legitimate houses went through one of the worst Xmas-New Year weeks they have ever experienced.

The talkies put a new kick into the film business. Both the Lyceum and Regent announced 10.30 a.m. sessions for last Saturday. For an hour before, the crowds started to come. By 10 o'clock Regent queues stretched up and down George Street, while the Lyceum's line-up rounded the bend of Market Street. They kept coming all day. On Monday they came faster still; every session filled; but on New Year's Day the opening was slower because the town was empty. Still the day touched nearly record figures, and both houses reported Wednesday as being within a few pounds of the opening Saturday, despite the holiday aftermath. . .

The value of the voice is best demonstrated by Al Jolson in "The Jazz Singer." That picture in silent form has been in Sydney for months; those who saw it without words condemned it; yet a few seconds of dialogue and half-a-dozen songs turned it into a record-breaker. On the other hand, "The Red Dance" contains no dialogue, but it's synchronised with music by the Roxy Theatre orchestra. Actually that orchestration doesn't help at all. By itself, in silent form, "The Red Dance" is strong dramatic entertainment, and as such it will go into special release.

Competent judges predict the future of the new vogue will rest with dialogue, songs and specialties, while mere synchronisation will pass. To date it has been used largely as a makeshift, to enable producers to get in on the sound vogue.

The suddenness of success has caused all sides to look around, to see what will follow the current attractions. Union Theatres expect "The Jazz Singer" to run for three months. With huge overhead expenses Hoyts mention a take-off figure in the neighbourhood of £3,000 for the Regent. . .

On 10 June 1929, the Sydney Morning Herald *reviewed another fine talking picture,* The Wolf of Wall Street. *It said:*

Those who maintain in a spirit of stout conservatism, that the talking films will never entirely supersede silent drama on the screen, but that the multitude will still look with enthusiasm on photoplays which divorce action from speech, should go to see *The Wolf of Wall Street.* Having done so, they may find themselves shaken in their convictions. For the silent screen has offered nothing, can offer nothing, to compare with the dramatic tension in this spoken play. In comparison with its vigour, the technique that involves a continual alternation of actors mouthing and written announcements of what they are supposed to be saying seems futile.

1929 Bruce becomes the only Australian Prime Minister to lose his seat

JOE ALEXANDER AND CHARLES BANFIELD
Melbourne Herald, 14 October 1929 and Melbourne Argus, 18 October 1929

The only Australian Prime Minister ever to have lost his seat at a general election was Stanley Melbourne Bruce — in October 1929. His biographer, Cecil Edwards, has since written that Bruce's government killed itself by trying to abolish the Commonwealth Arbitration Court. Another self-destructive step taken by Bruce was his withdrawal of a prosecution against John Brown, the country's biggest coal owner, who had been charged with locking out his miners.

Bruce was born to wealth and privilege; he had good looks, fine education, impeccable manners and a splendid war record. His big trouble was that he lacked not only the common touch, but any kind of comprehension of people at the other end of the social scale.

Frank Anstey, a political contemporary and foe of Bruce, summed him up:

Nothing was permitted to ruffle the calm of his superiority. No insult could draw from him the slightest protest, only a gaze of curiosity such as an entomologist might give a bug. He had unswerving purpose, serene audacity, and a half-concealed contempt for all around him . . . He delighted the masses with unfulfilled promises, and the wealthy by the fact that he never fulfilled them. He said what he meant, but it was never what his dupes thought he meant.

Joe Alexander, of the Melbourne Herald, *wrote this first report of the Scullin Labor Party's win after thirteen years in the wilderness:*

Mr Bruce, whose Ministry was defeated at the poll on Saturday, will hand in the resignation of his Government on Monday next. His position in his own electorate is still uncertain.

Mr Holloway (Labor) still has a lead of 393 over Mr Bruce. There are about 5000 postal, absentee and declaration votes to be counted before the second preferences of Mr Burch (Liberal), who up to date has polled 2064, are allocated. The result will not be known today.

Today's additional figures of the election count did not alter the position as regards the state of the parties.

The indications are that Labor will have a clear majority of 11 over all parties in the House of Representatives.

The only important changes today were in Robertson (N.S.W.), where the sitting Nationalist (Mr Gardner) took the lead over Mr Fitzgerald (Lab.), and in Calare, where the Minister for Health (Sir Neville Howse), who is still 923 behind, gained 861 on Mr Gibbons (Lab.).

In Victorian constituencies, the outstanding votes are now mainly postal, absent and declared ones.

The Premier (Sir William McPherson) said today that the Victorian Nationalist Government would try to make a success of the efforts of the new Federal Labor Government.

After consultation with the Prime Minister-elect (Mr Scullin), Mr Bruce will hand in the resignation of the Composite Government to the Governor-General on Monday at Canberra. . .

Messages expressing surprise and regret at the result of the elections were received by Mr Bruce today from all parts of Australia.

Mr Bruce is taking the position philosophically, and in the best sporting spirit. . .
He requires a few days to enable him to clear up at Canberra. Mr Scullin probably would like a few days' grace before taking over to enable him to prepare for the change.

Mr Bruce spent most of the morning at the Commonwealth offices clearing up. He occupied the Prime Minister's room in Melbourne for the last time while the incoming Government remains in office. . .

Mr Bruce's seat of Flinders remained in some doubt until five days after the election. Then, in the Argus, *Friday 18 October, Charlie Banfield wrote:*

Whatever doubt there might have been yesterday about the position of the Prime Minister (Mr. Bruce) in Flinders was dispelled by the additional votes received late in the day and a further scrutiny of the second preference votes of Mr. Burch, the Liberal candidate. It is now clear that Mr. Bruce cannot possibly overtake his Labour opponent, Mr. Holloway, because the number of primary votes outstanding is small and the preponderance of secondary votes to be allocated is definitely in favour of Mr. Holloway. The count in Flinders is expected to be completed to-day, and tentative arrangements are being made for the poll to be declared on Monday.

This is the first time in the history of the Commonwealth that a Prime Minister has been defeated while holding office, and the unexpected rejection of Mr. Bruce by his constituency has come as a shock, not only to his constituents and immediate supporters, but to people in every part of Australia. Even his political opponents, though desiring his deposition from the office of Prime Minister and eagerly seeking the downfall of his party, yet recognised the fine public service that he had rendered to the Commonwealth and were not anxious to expel him from the political life of the country. Generous tributes to his character, ability, and zeal have been paid to him by representatives of widely differing schools of political thought.

Mr. Bruce's sincerity and fine sense of public duty are shown by facts that are but little known among members of the general public. His political career has cost him more than he has ever gained from it. All the time in which he was a private member he did not draw any of his Parliamentary salary, because he took the view that his Parliamentary work did not interfere with his own private income. Only when he became a Minister did he accept any payment for his services, and then he sold all his investments except those in the form of Paterson, Laing, and Bruce, which was founded by his father. The proceeds he has invested in Government stock. In this way he left himself free to serve Australia without regard to other interests.

Mr. Bruce and other members of his Ministry have held their last Cabinet meeting. Mr. Bruce will remain in Canberra until Monday, when he will tender his resignation and that of his Cabinet to His Excellency the Governor-General (Lord Stonehaven). . .

From Canberra Mr Bruce issued this statement:

"The result of the election in the Flinders electorate has come to me as a deep disappointment. I have represented that constituency for 11 years, and I had hoped that the degree to which I have established myself in the confidence and good will of the electors would have been sufficient to ensure my return, notwithstanding the general pronouncement against the industrial policy of the Ministry. The electors have, however, decided otherwise. I accept their decision as the fortune of war, and I offer my congratulations to Mr. Holloway upon the success which he has won.

"My principal regret is that the result will involve my exclusion from the Parliament and the public life of Australia at a time when the economic and industrial life of the nation is beset with so many difficulties and dangers. I feel confident, however, that as soon as another opportunity arises the electors of Flinders will reverse their recent decision and choose me again as their representative in Parliament. In the meantime I trust that I may be able to find some other avenue through which I can be of service to the country.

"I am deeply appreciative of and grateful for the help I have received from those willing supporters in Flinders who have stood by me so loyally throughout my Parliamentary career, and particularly those who have worked so enthusiastically and untiringly to secure my return on the present occasion."

Police fire on miners during a riot at Rothbury colliery

HUGH BUGGY
Sydney Sun, 16 December 1929

Rarely in Australian history have men rebelling against authority been fired upon. One such incident occurred at Eureka in 1854; another was during the riot at Rothbury, a colliery in the Maitland district of New South Wales, on 16 December 1929. Police shot at miners in what has become known as 'the battle of Rothbury'; one young miner, Norman Brown, was killed by a bullet, nine others were wounded, and more than forty suffered various injuries. Ten police were injured by stones and pieces of wood.

The clash came after 10,000 miners had received dismissal notices at twenty-seven collieries. They had refused to accept a reduction of twelve and a half per cent in contract rates and one shilling a shift for day wage men. The miners claimed that they had been locked out; the mine-owners claimed that the men were on strike. Early in December the New South Wales Cabinet, under Liberal Premier Bavin, decided to open Rothbury colliery with non-union, volunteer workers. On 16 December 240 volunteers, under police guard, arrived at Rothbury to re-open the pit.

As they moved in, a demonstration was launched by striking miners, some of whom were armed with sticks and stones. Some 300 of them charged down a hill towards thirty-eight policemen who were guarding about 100 yards of boundary fence at the colliery. Hugh Buggy, on the spot for the Sydney Sun, *sent this first report:*

Fierce rioting, in which there was loss of life, occurred at Rothbury this morning at intervals between miners and police.

Police on a number of occasions drew their revolvers and fired fusillades into the ranks of the wildly-charging miners, who kept up a

Hugh Buggy (left) interviewing Prime Minister Stanley Bruce (right)

fusillade of stones. The latest news is that the position has eased, but that it is still menacing.

Police were reinforced from Newcastle early, and later 75 more police arrived from Sydney.

So far only one miner has been officially reported to be dead, but there are many wild and conflicting reports of other deaths.

The estimates of casualties, too, vary. The latest report indicates that in all there are 45 miners injured, but mostly slightly.

Many police were hurt, but no definite estimate can be given yet.

So far as the hospitals are concerned one man has died of wounds in hospital, and two others are suffering from bullet wounds. In Kurri Hospital four bullet wound cases were treated.

Of the police casualties there is equally little known. It has been definitely established, however, that Sergeant Booth, of Cessnock, and Detective-Sergeant Ryan, of Newcastle, were hurt. It is not believed that they are critical.

A remarkable scene followed the first desperate encounter. The police fired into the air and low down into the ground. A disorderly retreat was made by a thousand or more miners.

Then some of the men fell, wounded. In a tumultuous wave the men rushed across the valley. They were stunned by the revolver fire and by the casualties, and there was a thunder of hooting.

The formidable army of miners then reformed and closed their ranks. Tempers were aflame and the younger element gained the mastery. But the next shooting did not come for four hours.

Portion of a crowd of 4000 miners broke through the fence near the colliery gates, and 50 constables were obliged to draw their revolvers in the face of a fusillade of stones.

At 8.3 a.m. 50 miners pushed boulders on to the trainline, to stop trains carrying volunteers and also coal trains.

There was another serious riot about 9.30. Shots were again fired by the police, when an attempt was made by the mob to force their way on to the mine property.

A posse of police dashed out of the scrub near the line and drove the pickets away. Further stone-throwing occurred and the police were obliged to fire four or five shots to drive off the raiders.

All attempts to communicate with the mine from 9.30 a.m. failed. The police stated that the wires had been fired.

All available police have been rushed from Newcastle and Maitland by car.

Fifteen hundred miners crowded into the Strand Theatre in Cessnock on Sunday afternoon, to make plans for the big demonstration before the gate of Rothbury in the early hours.

Mr. Baddeley counselled the men to adopt peaceful means in making their protest against the introduction of non-unionist labor at Rothbury.

Meetings were held at Kurri, Weston and other places, and everything on wheels was pressed into service to carry the demonstrators to the critical centre of the struggle.

Just before the first clash began, Mr. Baddeley made vigorous efforts to prevent bloodshed, but the men were too inflamed to listen.

Mr. Baddeley was slightly wounded in the ensuing riot.

After the first volleys of police fire, Hugh Buggy used his own singlet to apply a tourniquet to the thigh of a wounded miner. 'After that,' he said later, 'I could never do any wrong on the coalfields. The miners were very good to me.' Buggy reported some fifteen mine disputes over the years, and was at Wonthaggi to cover the explosion which killed thirteen men in February 1937. He went down 700 feet in a cage with a rescue gang, and was later accorded the unusual honour of life membership of the Wonthaggi Miners' Club.

The events at Rothbury in December 1929 had two major sequels. They were largely responsible for the overthrow the following year of the Bavin Government; and they were claimed to be the main reason why the Miners' Federation remained under communist control for the next eighteen years.

1930   Amy Johnson becomes the first woman to fly from Britain to Australia

JESSIE LITCHFIELD
Sydney Morning Herald, 26 May 1930

For a while, all the world loved Amy Johnson. When men like Lindbergh, Hinkler and Kingsford Smith were making history, she competed with them and made her own kind of history. Born in Hull in 1904, she decided to learn to fly after she took a five-shilling 'joy-flight' in 1928; she gained her pilot's licence in 1929, and announced the following year that she intended to fly solo to Australia.

She bought a second-hand De Havilland Moth for £700, and budgeted another £100 for petrol. Until she took off on that epic flight, she had never been in the air for more than two hours at a stretch, and had never flown beyond the English Channel. Her first 'hop' was to Vienna, and it lasted ten hours.

On Saturday 24 May 1930, she became the first woman ever to fly solo from Britain to Australia; the largest congregation of people and cars ever seen in Darwin assembled to welcome her. On her return to England, Amy Johnson was met by a crowd of 100,000; the King presented her with the CBE, and the Daily Mail gave her £10,000. She made further solo record flights to Japan and back (1931), and to Capetown and back (1932); on her next trip, which involved crossing the Atlantic, she was accompanied by her flier husband, Jim Mollison, whom she had met in Australia.

In 1934, she broke the air record to India, and in 1936 she made a solo flight from London to Capetown via the west coast of Africa, and made her return along the east coast. She volunteered for active service in World War Two, and spent hundreds of hours in the air ferrying bombers and fighters to combat bases. While flying over the Thames estuary in 1941, her plane developed engine trouble; she bailed out and was drowned.

It was fitting that Amy Johnson's arrival in Australia should have been covered by Jessie Litchfield, who was something of a pioneer for women in the field of hard reporting. Miss Litchfield was for more than thirty years the editor of the Darwin Weekly, *and was Darwin correspondent for the same period from 1930 for the* Sydney Morning Herald, *the Melbourne* Age *and Reuter. She was born in Sydney, was briefly a student of Mary Gilmore, and lived for nearly fifty years in the Northern Territory. This is her report of Miss Johnson's arrival, published in the* Sydney Morning Herald *on 26 May 1930:*

Miss Amy Johnson landed at Darwin at 3.55 this afternoon (Darwin time). She made a graceful landing, amid rousing cheers from an immense crowd.

Thus ended an epic flight from London to Australia, after nineteen days of peril and anxiety, which marks one of the finest achievements of the air.

Miss Johnson set out from Atamboea at dawn on the perilous "hop" across the Timor Sea to Darwin, where she was awaited with anxiety.

Up till half-past 11 o'clock (Darwin time) she had not been sighted.

At 12.25 p.m. (Darwin time), however, the steamer Phorus, midway between Atamboea and Darwin, reported that Miss Johnson had passed over, and later wirelessed it was following in her course.

The successful flight of Miss Amy Johnson from England to Australia has evoked worldwide interest.

As soon as the news was flashed out that the aviatrix had landed safely at Darwin congratulatory messages from the most distinguished aviators and statesmen poured in.

They pay glowing tributes to her skill and determination in accomplishing the epic flight. . .

After circling over the aerodrome, Miss Johnson made a graceful landing amid the cheers of an immense crowd. The 'plane taxied along the ground, and came to rest beside the big Qantas 'plane. After examination by the doctor and waiting until the cameras clicked, the young aviatrix stepped on to Australian soil. Someone called, "Three cheers for Amy," and a ringing response was given. . .

Although obviously weary and sunburned, and showing signs of wear, her ever-ready smile was in evidence.

The mechanics of the other 'planes at once relieved Miss Johnson of any work of covering up and anchoring her 'plane, and she was driven to Darwin in a waiting car. . .

Miss Johnson admits that she left England feeling alarmed at crossing the English Channel in a fog. She left Croydon with a good following wind. The fog suddenly lifted, and she saw a small stream below. At first she thought she had turned around in the fog, and was returning to Croydon. After five minutes she realised she had crossed the Channel without knowing it. Later on she made a forced landing in a desert during a fearful sandstorm. This, she says, was her worst experience of the flight. She lost all control of the 'plane, and the hurricane tossed the machine about like a shuttlecock. As she was dressed in warm clothing, the heat became insufferable. Her sole thoughts were about her mother, who, she knew, would be worrying. She felt some regret at making the flight against all advice. Still later she met with a mishap near Rangoon, where, after landing, the 'plane taxied into a ditch and damaged the propeller and a wing. At Bangkok she found the new propeller was defective, consequently she experienced a delay owing to the necessity for repairs. Then followed the forced landing at Tjomal, between Batavia and Sourabaya, where she spent the night. . .

Leaving Samarang, the 'plane ran into a fearful storm. Everything was black, the rain fell in sheets, and she could see nothing but an immense rainbow. After three hours of veritable nightmare, the 'plane barely missing the waves, she at last ran out of the storm and reached land.

Leaving Sourabaya, she was forced, owing to lack of petrol, to land in the dark in a field full of horses and cattle, 16 miles from Atamboea.

Upon landing she found herself surrounded by natives wearing only loin-cloths and carrying murderous-looking knives and swords. The only word she could catch was "pastor." A native, apparently a chief, caught her by the arm and led her away. Although she was alarmed, she thought she had better submit. After walking two miles, they arrived at a church. She there found that "pastor" meant a benevolent old Dutch priest. She washed, and, after a frugal meal, was grateful to hear the motor of Dutch officers who were searching for her. Soldiers guarded her machine all night, and in the morning she motored to the 'plane and took off for Atamboea.

The flight to Darwin was without incident. She passed the oil-tanker Phorus midway between Atamboea and Darwin. "Sighting Melville Island," she says, "I stood up and cheered myself, and threw overboard the pneumatic pillow which I had carried inflated to act as a buoy in case of a crash into the sea. I had also kept a sheath-knife as protection against sharks."

Miss Johnson could hardly realise that her object had been achieved, and she alternately cried and laughed until she picked up Point Charles lighthouse and turned towards Darwin.

The reception at Darwin, she asserts, was beyond her wildest imaginings. She says she intends to return to England in September to take a position with the "Daily Mail," London, at a salary of £10,000 for seven months as aeronautical correspondent and lecturer.

Miss Johnson says she intends to visit the Sydney newspaper office which classed her intention to fly to Australia as a "girl's bombast," and to ask to see the writer of the article, and then say: "I am here, anyhow."

1930   The effects of the world Depression are felt in Australia

HAROLD BURSTON
Melbourne Herald, June 1930

The world Depression, which began in 1929, brought a condition approaching chaos to the Australian economy. The basic cause was the massive fall in world prices, which made the vast bulk of Australian primary production uneconomic; but the impact of the slump was made more severe by the inability of Australian governments to borrow more money overseas.

Every year for ten years the government had been borrowing some £30 million; the sudden cutting off of what had been a customary loan brought about a fall in living standards. The decline in export prices and the halt on borrowing reduced the real national income by more than ten per cent.

The first impact of the loss fell mainly on the primary producers and those who had been thrown out of work by the cessation of investment, but gradually the whole community was affected. At the worst point of the Depression, one-third of the nation's breadwinners were out of work, subsisting on the dole, and those businesses which were able to carry on could make no profit.

The Depression of 1929–32, like the Depression of the 1890s and the two World Wars, was one of the great traumatic experiences in Australian history. It took almost a generation for the community to forget the dole queues, the begging, the hessian humpies in which hundreds of campers lived, the platoons of 'susso' (sustenance) workers employed on public works projects.

By June 1930 the Australian national income had fallen by about £100 million. Reduced borrowing, reduced prices for exports, and reduced domestic buying had cut the nation's total revenue by nearly one-sixth. In that month, the financial editor of the Mel-bourne Herald, *Harold Burston, wrote a series aimed at demonstrating to the man in the street what had gone wrong, and what might be done if Australia was ever going to achieve prosperity again. This was one of his reports:*

The long run of national prosperity enjoyed by the Commonwealth came to an abrupt end when prices for export produce collapsed early in the past season, and when, concurrently, overseas money markets became unfavorable for loan flotations. The difficulties created are of a magnitude not yet fully appreciated by the community. An examination of some of the problems, and how they must be met, are the purposes of this series of articles.

Prosperous conditions that ruled, with but minor breaks, since wartime conditions inflated prices, were partially real, but, unfortunately, they were to a large measure also artificial.

Real prosperity had been the reward of increased production that secured very favorable average prices; but, at the same time, financial obligations overseas were being met by heavy borrowings, that resulted in abnormal activity when expended within the Commonwealth. In this way, false standards, that had developed in the war years, were permitted to persist throughout a period when other countries were in process of deflation.

Had only one of the factors that contributed to the prosperity become unfavorable, current and prospective difficulties would not be so severe. But their combined influence has weakened and almost wrecked the foundations of the whole superstructure of public and private finance.

An understanding of the causes of the big decline of national income, and of the setback to national advancement, is necessary to appreciate the problems that have to be met by individuals, all corporate bodies and associations, and, more particularly, by every Government.

The public mind has been confused by the involved nature of the problems, particularly when expressed in terms of money, and does not realise the extent and incidence of some of the difficulties. Consequently the actions of a few outstanding leaders, who have endeavored to apply the only possible remedies to avoid catastrophes, are not adequately appreciated.

Australia's big financial problems today are in three divisions. Foremost is the necessity for preserving international solvency. At any sacrifice, we must pay our commitments to the rest of the world, whether they have been incurred as interest on borrowings or by purchases of goods.

An acute position, that has been only partially indicated by the adverse swing of exchange rates, has been developing for some months in London, the clearing centre for our international activities.

The extremely delicate situation there, owing to the accumulation of big commitments, is still not fully understood. Export trade adversity makes it impossible for the Commonwealth to meet the big current indebtedness incurred by interest accruing on loans, and by the excess of purchases of goods over exports, though the latter have included the shipment of nearly 27 millions worth of our gold stocks.

The banks, by rationing overseas credits at high charges, and the Federal Government, by imposing embargoes on imports, have been applying remedies to rectify the position. The extent of their success is not yet visible, but even should more drastic measures become necessary, complete adjustment of the London hiatus, representing some tens of millions, will not be possible for an extended period.

The ultimate restoration of a satisfactory balance of the London account is beyond any doubt. In extreme circumstances we would be compelled to eliminate most imports and live almost entirely on our own resources till the adjustment should be complete.

Other major problems are internal. The heavy decline in receipts from exported production, and the consequent fall of national income, are forcing adjustments in every section of private finance.

A complete revision of Government, or public, finance has become urgent. Swift adjustments to balance accounts are the first requirements. Of no less importance is the necessity for relieving the community of tax burdens it is no longer capable of carrying in its weakened financial condition.

If, by some magic, the prices of all commodities and services, and of wages and other costs, could be lowered within a brief period by, say, 15 per cent., and big economies could be effected in Government activities, general internal financial soundness would be rapidly restored, and a new prosperity would quickly follow. . .

The greatest menace to Australia's welfare in the crisis is the condition of public finance. Throughout long periods there has been lavish spending of borrowed money on developmental projects that have been incapable of earning the big interest charges. It has been accompanied by increasing extravagance of administration, by failure to stem huge leakages of revenue, by heavy recurring deficits, and by participation in costly enterprises and services that are luxuries the tax-paying community, now severely limited in numbers and earning power, can no longer afford.

Public finance in the years of national prosperity was notable for huge growths of public debt, and by tremendous inflations of revenues and expenditures. These two factors are the root troubles of the position with which every Treasury is now faced, and these articles will show that the additional interest burden is only a small portion of the spendings of recent years. . .

The first steps in finding the road back to prosperity necessitate drastic curtailment of all uneconomic Government expenditure and far-reaching reductions in all costs of services and of administration. . .

1931   Dame Nellie Melba makes her last journey — to Lilydale

ALLAN DAWES AND CLIVE TURNBULL
Melbourne Herald, 25 and 26 February 1931

*The outbreak of the Great War in 1914
interrupted the international career of Nellie
Melba. She spent the war years in Australia,
and, for her services in concerts for the Red
Cross and other charities, she was created a
Dame of the British Empire in 1918. She was
then fifty-seven, but her voice retained its
freshness and purity. As she reached her
sixties she began to wind up an illustrious
career that had spanned more than thirty years.
Her departure from the stage, which took the
form of a series of farewell performances, was
hardly sudden. She had a final opera season in
March 1924, made her final Covent Garden
appearance in June 1926, and sang the
national anthem at the opening of Parliament
House, Canberra, in 1927. Her last appearance
in Australia was at a concert at Geelong,
Victoria, in November 1928.*

*She returned to Australia in 1930, because
of failing health, and she died in Sydney in
February 1931, in her seventieth year.*

The Age *recorded on 24 February: 'A little
while before she died, Dame Nellie Melba sang
faintly two bars from Gounod's Ave Maria.
The scene was a most poignant one, as those
present listened to the faint melody of the
wonderful woman who was now on the very
threshold of death.'*

*These two reports, written jointly by Allan
Dawes and Clive Turnbull, described for the
Melbourne* Herald *on 25 and 26 February
some of the scenes as Melba made her last
journey — to Melbourne by rail and finally to
a grave at Lilydale:*

25 February:
Past the shaggy ranges and rolling brown hills
of her native Victoria, with warm sunshine
flooding the countryside, the body of Dame
Nellie Melba was conveyed in a mortuary train
leaving Albury at 8.30 a.m. today and timed
to reach Melbourne six hours later.

The train stopped at most of the stations.
The door of the van was thrown open and
hushed crowds filed past the coffin and laid
wreaths on the catafalque.

Women fell to their knees and offered up
short, silent prayers. Many were in tears.

A huge crowd at Spencer Street awaited
the arrival of the train.

The Premier's secretary (Mr H. T. Vickers)
met the train, on behalf of the Premier (Mr
Hogan), who was engaged at the Premiers'
Conference.

Flags were flown half-mast in the city.

In addition to the mortuary van, the train
consisted of a carriage and a guard's van.

Relatives on board were: Mr George Arm-
strong (son of Dame Nellie) and Mrs Armstrong,
Mrs Lempriere (sister), and Mrs Box (sister),
Mrs Frank Mitchell (sister-in-law), Mr Ernest
Mitchell (brother), Major R. A. Little, D.S.O.,
and Mrs Little. Dr W. O. Doyle, one of Dame
Nellie's physicians, was also on board.

The mortuary arrangements were in charge
of Mr Gordon S. Sleight, of A. A. Sleight and
Sons, who addressed the people on the platform and thanked them on behalf of the
relatives for having attended at such short
notice and so early in the day to do honor to
the illustrious dead.

Flags were flown at half-mast on public
buildings at towns that were passed through
by the train and people stood at the door of
bush cottages bareheaded as long as the train
was in sight.

Wreaths had been brought from Sydney, and
the number was steadily added to at each
stopping place. Some of them were of great

size and beauty, but among them were little bunches of flowers picked from humble bush gardens.

Perhaps these created a greater effect among the later crowd who entered the van than the great masses of exotic flowers.

The Mayor of Albury (Cr. A. Waugh) and the Mayoress were the first to place wreaths on the casket after it had been transferred to the mortuary train. . .

The catafalque and the wall of the van behind it were draped with the Australian flags.

As the train came down the line, the crowds on the platforms increased, until at Seymour hundreds filed into the van.

Relatives were deeply touched by the spontaneous expression of sympathy and regret by so large a number of people, many of whom had probably never heard Dame Nellie sing or had even seen her face to face.

Mr George Armstrong expressed the deep appreciation of the relatives for all the expressions of sympathy. It was the kind of reception, unrehearsed and simple, which Dame Nellie most appreciated in her lifetime.

He also voiced the appreciation of the relatives for the action of the State Government in placing the special train at their disposal, and thanked the railway service for the able manner in which the train had been run.

On the small platform at Locksley the scholars of the little school were drawn up bareheaded.

Right down the line, indeed, school children were prominent in the attendances on the platforms. . .

Many times in her remarkable career has Dame Nellie Melba returned to us from wandering in far countries, and always she has met with a tumultuous welcome from her thousands of admiring countrymen and women. Today she returned to her city in the silence of a sadness which could find no words. . .

26 February:
Dame Nellie Melba was buried this afternoon in a flower-lined grave in the country town of Lilydale, so long associated with the great artist's life.

A sad Melba stands among floral tributes after her last operatic performance in Melbourne in 1928

No comparable funeral has ever been seen in Melbourne.

Melbourne's greatest daughter, who had come and gone triumphantly so many times before, left for the last time — a strangely-stilled city paying silent homage.

How this last act of the drama had seized the imagination of the world was shown in the extraordinary number and beauty of the floral tributes. Flowers were sent to Scots Church, where a service was held, by admirers and friends from all parts of Australia, as well as from overseas. . .

At the War Memorial. Lilydale, the coffin was transferred to a gun carriage. Melba's Own Boy Scouts led the re-formed cortege, followed by the staff of the Cave Hill estate. Then came the gun carriage, the coffin draped in the Australian flag. Immediately after the returned soldiers of Lilydale marched, with the Lilydale Fire Brigade in the rear.

The service at the graveside was conducted by the Moderator-General of the Presbyterian Church of Victoria (the Rev. D. A. Cameron), assisted by the Rev. Hugh Kelly, of Scots Church, and the Rev. J. Robertson, of Lilydale. School children of Lilydale were drawn up on each side of the path to the grave, which had been entirely lined with flowers. . .

1931   A government is brought down and a reporter expelled

JOE ALEXANDER
Melbourne Herald, 16 March 1931

It is a rare event for a pressman anywhere to contribute directly to the downfall of a government, but it has happened more than once in Australian history. One such reporter was J. A. 'Joe' Alexander, who covered Federal politics from 1924 until 1944.

In 1931, the Scullin-led Australian Labor Party had been in power for two years and it was under real strain. Factions within the ALP were fighting over the best methods of dealing with unemployment, which was increasing and even accelerating. The Prime Minister, James Scullin, was in Britain trying to make   arrangements to alleviate Australia's desperate financial plight; back in Australia, James Edward Fenton was acting Prime Minister.

At this stage Joe Alexander produced confidential cables which passed between Scullin and one of his most senior ministers, Joe Lyons — cables which indicated that the Prime Minister was thinking differently about methods of dealing with inflation when he was in London, away from the influence of the Parliamentary Labor Party. Publication of the cables brought into the open a major schism inside the party which was to cause it to fall from government, and to stay out of office for another decade. The Scullin ALP was defeated at the 1931 general elections, and and was replaced by a United Australia Party-Country Party coalition led by Scullin's former minister, Mr Lyons.

When Scullin protested about the publication of confidential cables, Joe Alexander's paper, the Herald, *declared:*

Attempts are being made to argue that the disclosure of these cablegrams was a political offence. In other words, the Government's defenders contend that the public should have been kept in the dark about its own business in order that it might be fooled and dragooned by false representations . . . What honest man can object to the revelation of any statement of his opinions on public affairs at any time or anywhere?

Nevertheless, Alexander became the first journalist ever to be banned from entering the House of Representatives. ALP Speaker, Norman Makin, with the backing of the Government's majority, expelled Alexander from the House and its precincts 'until a satisfactory explanation has been offered [by Alexander] concerning the means whereby the text of the cables in question was obtained'. The ban, which lasted for five months, had a comic sequel. The Senate, which had an anti-ALP majority, refused to follow the lead of the House of Representatives. It refused to debar Alexander from the Senate or any area under its control. For those five months, Alexander used to wander up and down the Senate side of an imaginary line running along the middle of King's Hall, Parliament House, signalling furiously at House of Representatives members with whom he wanted to talk.

Although it was Alexander who learned the contents of the damaging cables, the story first broke in the Sydney Sun. *Alexander and the* Sun's *representative Allan Fraser, who was later a member of the House of Representatives from 1943 until 1972, used to swap information. Alexander received the text of the cables on a Saturday morning and later gave it to Fraser. However, Alexander's paper, the* Herald, *did not publish the story that day and his editor-in-chief, Keith Murdoch, tried to induce the Sydney* Sun's *managing director, Herbert Campbell-Jones, to hold the story. 'I have received this story from my Canberra representative, Mr Fraser,' Campbell-Jones replied. 'It is a story he sent me and I am publishing it now.' The Saturday and Sunday* Sun *both published the text of the cables before the Melbourne* Herald *did so on the Monday, 16 March.*

But it was Alexander's story, and he refused throughout his career, and even in retirement, to reveal his sources.

Events continue to move rapidly toward a crisis in Federal politics involving the downfall of the Scullin Ministry.

Publication of cables which passed between the Prime Minister (Mr Scullin) and Mr Lyons when Mr Scullin was abroad, revealing amazing changes of front by Mr Scullin, have caused a sensation.

They have further lowered the prestige of the Ministry.

The Chairman of Committees in the House of Representatives (Mr D. C. McGrath), who is the Labor member for Ballarat, announced today in Melbourne that he had left the Labor Party and had thrown in his lot with Mr Lyons.

There is a possibility that the metropolitan conference of the Australian Labor Party in Sydney tonight will decide that Mr Beasley and his followers must oppose the Fiduciary Note Issue Bill. Such a decision would bring about the defeat of the Ministry on the Bill.

To discuss the position which has arisen following the publication of the cables between Mr Scullin and Mr Lyons, the leader of the Opposition (Mr Latham) will probably move the adjournment of the House of Representatives tomorrow.

The cables which passed between Mr Scullin and Mr Lyons were received in The Herald Office on Saturday morning for publication, and their importance was at once recognised.

Mr Lyons was in The Herald building being interviewed about his proposed political tour when the messages were being received. He made an urgent request to the Editor that they should not be published.

In deference to Mr Lyons's request the matter of publication was held over. The cables having been sent from Canberra to Sydney and published there we now feel, of course, that there can be no further reason for withholding publication.

CANBERRA, Monday. — Members of all parties in the Federal Parliament admit that the disclosure of the secret cables which passed between the Prime Minister, Mr Scullin, and Mr Lyons, while Mr Scullin was abroad, constitutes an outstanding political sensation.

The first matter mentioned when Cabinet assembled today was the position created by the publication of the cables. Ministers, when they entered the Cabinet room, were gravely perturbed at the political effect of the disclosures, but none of them would comment on the likely developments.

It was stated in the lobbies that the Prime Minister had been advised to make a detailed statement on the matter in Parliament when the House resumed tomorrow. Unofficially it is said that Mr Scullin maintains that "circumstances have materially altered" since his return to Australia, and that in any case the suggested fiduciary note issue "is not really inflation." . . .

"At this critical juncture," Mr Hughes added, "what the people desire above all else is leadership by a strong man at the head of a Government composed of men who have a policy constituted to the present circumstances of Australia, and the courage to give effect to this policy though the heavens fall and the Government with them.

"But these cables show that Mr Scullin is not such a leader. That he is indeed, not a leader at all, but a weak man ready to meekly accept dictation by any section which happens to have a majority."

Below is given the text of the series of cable messages which passed between the Prime Minister (Mr Scullin) and the then Acting Treasurer (Mr Lyons), while Mr Scullin was abroad. . .

The first message was sent by Mr Scullin in London to Mr Lyons in Canberra on November 5, 1930. It read:—

"Banks are expected to carry any shortage in Budget, also to underwrite loan conversions. That, together with responsibility to finance harvest, will be heavy strain on banks. To create credit for £20,000,000 for loan work is unsound, and I expect banks to refuse to do so. Government cannot deliberately coerce administration of banks. Such proposal means permanent inflation, which could not be checked as is implied, and would demand further inflation. All this talk about creating credit and inflation is most damaging and will seriously prejudice conversion maturing loans and Treasury bills. Since inflation was suggested efforts are being made by men here to withdraw their money from Australia, as they would lose by payment in a depreciated currency. Depreciation in currency would decrease values of savings banks deposits. Property would increase in price. There would be a rush to sell bonds for investment in property. Financial panic may result."

On November 7 Mr Lyons informed Mr Scullin of the Caucus decision to suspend interest payments, proceeding:—

"This is absolute repudiation. I immediately notified the party I would not be prepared to carry out their decision, but would communicate with you and ask you, if you approved their action, to relieve me of my position in the Cabinet and appoint a successor to submit the necessary legislation, which will inevitably crash credit of Australia. Pending your decision, I propose to carry out my previous intention to recommend loan to meeting Loan Council Tuesday. During discussion effort was made, and received considerable support, to demand Commonwealth Bank to take up whole £27,000,000, failing which demands should be made that board resign. Fenton informed of this message."

Mr Scullin's reply was:—

"I do not approve and will not support resolution of party, which, I agree, is repudiation, which is dishonest and disastrous. Brennan and Moloney concur. We agree that you are right in recommending to Loan Council issue of loans, as party's resolution has demoralised Australian stocks here, and unless rescinded will render renewal of bills here, as well as conversions in Australia, impossible. Inform Fenton of this message. Will telephone early as possible."

Later Mr Scullin despatched the following message:—

"I appeal to the party to reconsider its resolution, which has demoralised Australian stock here, rendering renewal of Treasury bills impossible. I came to London with the consent of the party. Apart from the Imperial Conference, my most important mission was to restore Australian credit so that we could fund floating debt, and, if possible, raise some new money to relieve our economic position. My efforts would have succeeded had party support been maintained. World depression affecting price of our exports, combined with inability to obtain loans, hits Australia very hard. I found in London a desire to assist, and plans were maturing to approach loan markets when Budgets were balanced. Although there was disappointment in financial circles that our Budget is not quite balanced, the door was not quite closed, and I still had hopes of success until the appalling resolution was passed last Thursday. That proposal was disastrous. It is a reversal of the party's declared policy to honor national obligations, and no self-respecting Government could agree to it.

"Our Government floated loan and guaranteed the public a safe investment. Thousands of people withdrew their savings from the savings bank to assist the Labor Government. To default on this loan would weaken the value of their investments, would destroy public confidence, and would delay for years restoration of economic prosperity. If, however, wiser counsels prevail and Government is given chance to obtain credit, a debacle may yet be avoided. But if we are frustrated by our own supporters, by resolution or statement creating financial panic, our position becomes intolerable and our efforts to govern in the people's interest hopeless. The Government proposal is to ask the bondholders voluntarily to renew their bonds. To enforce renewal by refusing to pay the debts for a year is repudiation. The law would not permit that in private transactions, and no one mindful of his personal honor would do it in private life. I know and share members' feelings regarding the sufferings of the unemployed, but the extension of our credit will spread that suffering tremendously. Brennan and Moloney concur."

Mr Lyons, in another message to Mr Scullin, said:

"Fenton cabling you regarding general political position. After discussing matters with Gibson this morning am afraid little prospect of re-establishing confidence while Anstey and Beasley remain in Government.

"My position made extremely difficult, having met opposition from these two Ministers in party meeting. You will need consider this aspect as situation may develop early calling for drastic action on part yourself and moderate section."

Concerning the proposed appointment of two High Court judges, Mr Scullin cabled Mr Lyons: "See telegram sent to Fenton and Daly regarding appointment of judges for your personal information. I would go out of office if under the circumstances appointments were rushed through during our absence. Attorney-General takes same view. Appeal to you to avoid this."

A message to Mr Fenton from Mr Scullin said:—

"Telegram from Vice-president Executive Council to Attorney-General stating that steps being taken to appoint judges astounds us. It is a reversal of Cabinet decision, and means that Cabinet accepts political direction on appointments to the High Court judiciary. Political interference removing this matter from Cabinet responsibility strikes fatally at the authority of the Court. Attorney-General and I will be no party to that. Number of judges adequate; moreover, long vacation begins. Why rush appointment and deny Prime Minister and Attorney-General to express strongly held views? We have the right to take part in the discussion of this most vital question. We ask you to reconsider the appointments before it is too late."

Another message sent by Mr Lyons to Mr Scullin stated:—

"Cabinet agreed to dictation of party during my absence from Canberra. I learned of Cabinet's final decision from press."

Prime Minister Scullin photographed in London, September 1930, whilst attending the Imperial Conference

1931   Life during the Depression: inside 'Happy Valley'

AN UNKNOWN REPORTER AND SID KING

Sydney Morning Herald, June 1931 and Sydney Daily Telegraph, 20 June 1931

These excerpts from short-range views of the Depression, published in June 1931, give some impression of the plight of the unemployed.

A Sydney Morning Herald *reporter wrote about the humpy town that had emerged at La Perouse:*

They call it 'Happy Valley', that little collection of tents and huts erected at La Perouse [Sydney] by homeless men and women, and it does not belie its name. Waiting till the sun shines through the murk of depression, 350 men, women, and children have gathered in a community that for self-help and orderly conduct must stand alone. There is there complete self-government with an absence of bickering that is a lesson to larger communities; there the persons are bound together by a common misfortune, and determined to make the best of things with a smile and a laugh; there is no bowing down before Fate in spiritless resignation, but a whole-hearted and concerted effort to see that the lot of none of the camp is harder than it should be.

The Governor and Lady Game visited Happy Valley yesterday, and went away greatly impressed with its conduct and the type of men and women composing it. . .

Lady Game said she had seen one little home in which she would not mind living herself. . .

'I have only come here as part of my job, and I don't want any thanks at all,' said Sir Phillip Game, responding to a vote of thanks.
. . .

Campers in 'Happy Valley' . . . were . . . exposed to the full force of the gale. In the afternoon the valley was flooded, and tents and huts were washed away or blown down. A big marquee was also destroyed. The shivering residents found it impossible to remain.

Help was sought, and was soon forthcoming. . .

Dr. Richard Arthur, M.L.A., paid a visit to the camp during the day. He described conditions as appalling. There was hardly a hut fit for habitation, he said. . . Those of the men who still had a roof above them had clung to their dwellings, but others less fortunate had been compelled to go into the city and seek shelter at one of the hostels.

And on 20 June 1931 Sid King reported for the Daily Telegraph *on 'Bloody Friday', when police and anti-evictionists fought a pitched battle in Newtown. Landlords wanted the tenants — most of whom were out of work — evicted for non-payment of rent:*

Yesterday will be remembered in Sydney as a day of unexampled violence, casualties, grim threats, window smashings, and general demonstrations by the more violently disposed members of the "anti-evictionist" factions.

Following a fierce riot in Union Street, Newtown, in the morning, resulting in 14 anti-evictionists and 13 policemen being injured — in some cases critically — there was a wild demonstration in Railway Square last night, and some window smashing. Even the "Labor Daily" newspaper office suffered. . .

Altogether, 22 arrests were made through the day and night, police vigilance being maintained until a late hour. . .

The Newtown trouble began when a 'bus crowded with policemen, under Inspector Farley, swung into Union Street from King Street, to enforce an eviction order.

The pickets at the house immediately sounded the alarm, locked the doors of the house, and took up positions before opening fire from the balcony with full-sized bricks and road metal, which showered down on the police.

During the Depression many such shanties were erected along Sydney's seaside fringes by the unemployed in an attempt to house their families

Realising the seriousness of the position, Inspector Farley ordered his men to draw their revolvers and make the most of what proved to be the most sensational hand-to-hand fight to date.

A volley of shots in the vicinity of the balcony forced the pickets to seek cover inside, while the police began ramming at the barricades at the rear of the house, finally breaking the doors down with axes and hammers and pushing aside the sandbags.

Constable Kelly was the first man to enter, but he was immediately felled with a terrific blow on the head. Then, as fast as the constables surged into the place, they found ready combatants with iron bars, sticks, and batons, and the war extended from room to room.

The battle raged for nearly an hour before the pickets were finally overpowered.

A man who was shot down in the struggle was alleged to have been about to plunge what looked like a bayonet into the back of a policeman who was fighting another picket. . .

Although only one man was arrested when he drew an iron bar in the crowd during the Railway Square demonstration, police know that many groups were similarly armed, and were actually at the point of mob violence.

Fortunately, the crowd was kept moving around the centre park used by the demonstrators.

The speeches were of the usually revolutionary nature, and such statements as, "We are not protesting against the bashers of Bavin, but against the bludgeoners of Lang!" were frequent. . .

1932 Arthur Upfield plots a real-life murder and a killer is revealed

RONALD MONSON
Perth West Australian, 21 March 1932

Arthur Upfield, mystery writer and occasional journalist, found himself in March 1932 in the middle of what has become one of Australia's best-known murder cases. He became an important Crown witness in the trial of Snowy Rowles, alias John Thomas Smith, who was hanged for the murder of a Canadian named Louis Carron.

During the Depression, Upfield, who used to roam the outback in search of material for his books, had taken a job on what has been called the longest fence in the world — 1130 miles of rabbit-proof netting, cutting the State of Western Australia from a point south of Broome to the Great Australian Bight. His job was to patrol 170 miles of the fence, in a dray drawn by two camels. At the time Upfield was starting work on a book called The Sands of Windee, *and he was mapping out a plot by which a human body might be wholly destroyed with materials available at any outback homestead; by camp-fires at the government camel station of Dromedary he would ask for suggestions.*

Once in October 1929, sharing a camp-fire with Snowy Rowles and the man in charge of the station, George Ritchie, Upfield offered £1 if Ritchie could come up with a good, fool-proof scheme. According to Upfield's biographer, Jessica Hawke, the conversation went like this:

'That's not hard,' asserted Ritchie. 'Supposing I wanted to do you in, I'd kid you into the bush a bit and when you were nice and handy to plenty of dry wood, I'd shoot you dead and burn your body. When the ashes were cold I'd go through the lot with a sieve, getting out every burnt bone and all metal things like buttons and boot sprigs.

The metal I'd put into a bottle of sulphuric acid, and at every homestead they keep sulphuric for tin-smithing, and your burnt bones I'd put through a prospector's dolly-pot, and toss out the dust for the wind to scatter. There'd be none of you left.'

'Assuming that scientific examination of the ashes proved that flesh had been consumed, what then, Ritchie?'

'Easy, Arthur, me lad, easy. On the fire site you burn a couple of kangaroo carcases. We always burn carcases around a camp or homestead to keep the flies down. Burning a carcase would also shunt suspicion of why the fire was lit in the first place. Getting away with murder is as easy as falling off a log if only you use your brain. Try it some time and see.'

Upfield finished his novel, Snowy Rowles *moved off, and not long afterwards two associates of Rowles disappeared without trace. Then a third man, Louis Carron, disappeared; this time, in what had been a camp-fire beside the rabbit-proof fence, some charred human remains, including a few teeth, were found. Rowles was generally believed to have murdered all three men, but was charged only with the murder of Carron.* The Sands of Windee *had been widely read by then, and while the case progressed it was in fact being serialised in the Perth newspaper, the* Western Mail. *At that time, it was possible to read the serialised piece of fiction in one newspaper, and accounts of the murder trial which had resulted from the camp-fire discussions, in another. Upfield gave evidence, and Rowles was hanged the following June.*

The case was covered by Ronald Monson, a West Australian reporter who later won con-

siderable fame as a war correspondent for British and Australian newspapers. Monson's own life was colorful enough. He covered the Spanish Civil war, the Sino-Japanese war, the Middle East campaigns, the invasion of France, Dunkirk, the Korean war and the Malayan troubles. He went to London to cover the coronation of King George in 1937 and later, after war correspondent Pembroke Stephens had been machine-gunned to death in China, he took his place in China. He secured a world scoop concerning Japanese atrocities in Nanking, avoiding Japanese censorship by sending a messenger 900 miles to Hong Kong. He once swam 100 yards across the Euphrates River to save the life of a wounded British soldier; for this he was recommended for the DSO but, because he was a non-serviceman, the final award took the form of a mention in despatches. For good measure, he once walked from Capetown to Cairo, and wrote a book about the trek. Monson died in 1973.

After a trial lasting eight days, John Thomas Smith, alias Snowy Rowles (26), a station hand, was found guilty of the wilful murder of Leslie George Brown, also known as Louis J. Carron (27), by a jury in the Criminal Court late on Saturday afternoon, and was sentenced to death by Mr. Justice Draper.

The trial, which was one of the most remarkable in the criminal annals of Western Australia, produced much dramatic evidence. Witnesses were called from as far distant as New Zealand to give evidence. . .

The trial ended when the foreman of the jury in the Criminal Court announced to a hushed court that Smith, alias Rowles, had been found guilty of the wilful murder of Brown. . .

Louis Carron, who arrived in Western Australia from New Zealand in February, 1930, disappeared in the Murchison three months later, after having left the Fountain outcamp on Narndee station to go on a prospecting trip towards Wiluna with the accused. Inquiries for him were not commenced until January of last year. About a month after that charred human remains, believed to be his, were recovered from the ashes of a camp fire on a rabbit reserve south of Paynesville, and near the No. 1 rabbit-proof fence, but it was not until a year later that the police investigations into the matter, which were conducted by Detective-Sergeant Manning, were completed. Rowles, who had in the meantime been arrested on another charge, and sentenced to three years' imprisonment, was charged with the wilful murder of Carron by Detective-Sergeant Manning in the Fremantle Gaol on January 7 this year. Police inquiries in connection with the case were made in the Murchison district, Geraldton, Burracoppin, Perth, South Australia and New Zealand, and three witnesses from New Zealand, including Carron's widow, gave evidence at the trial.

The jury were two hours considering their verdict. Rowles maintained that he had been found guilty of a crime that had never been committed.

The Crown Prosecutor (Mr. C. B. Gibson) handled the prosecution, and Mr. F. Curran appeared for Rowles. . .

In summing up, Mr. Justice Draper said:

"There is a curious thing in this case which may be mentioned for what it is worth. Upfield, who is a budding author, gave evidence that he was in the neighbourhood for some time. He says he remembers a discussion one night in a small room when the accused, among others, was present, in October, 1929. The interesting subject of discussion was how a human body could be destroyed without leaving a trace. It was proposed by Mr. George Ritchie that the best way would be to burn the body, and crush the bones remaining after the ashes of the fire were cold. The bones found in the ashes I have referred to were certainly crushed up." . . .

The first important task confronting the jury, Mr. Justice Draper continued, was to discover if Carron were dead. It was true that the police had advertised for him, but not in Canada. However, Carron's letter to his sister in New Zealand, posted from the Murchison, showed that he had relinquished whatever idea he might have had of going to Canada, and was satisfied with Western Australia. The jury, in deciding whether Carron was alive or dead, would have to be guided principally by the human remains found in the ashes. They would have to consider the possibility of the remains being those of an aboriginal. They would ask themselves if it were probable that aborigines wore gold faceted wedding rings, or had artificial teeth in their upper or lower jaws.

The ring, he continued, had been definitely identified as Carron's by his wife, and by Long, the New Zealand jeweller who sold it to her. "If the ring is not enough to satisfy you that the remains in the ashes were Carron's," said Mr. Justice Draper, "what if other belongings of Carron's were found in the ashes? It would indeed be a strange coincidence. We have the teeth, and it is for you to decide if they are Carron's. If you come to the conclusion that they are you must ask yourselves how they got there, and you must remember the pieces of skull. If you are satisfied that Carron was murdered, you have then to decide by whom." . . .

In concluding, Mr. Justice Draper said that not only must the jury be convinced that the facts brought out in evidence were consistent with the accused being guilty, but that they must be inconsistent with any other conclusion. If they were satisfied that there was no other rational conclusion to be drawn from the evidence except accused's guilt, then they must bring in a verdict accordingly.

There was a tense scene in Court when the jury returned at 6 p.m. after an absence of two hours. All eyes turned on their faces, and most read from their grim expressions what the verdict would be. Rowles, who had borne himself with great fortitude throughout the trial, stood on the steps leading from the dock to the cells below, waiting for Mr. Justice Draper to take his seat. While he waited he strained his head to catch a glimpse of the jurymen but was unable to see above the level of the floor of the dock. Glancing behind him to people in the witnesses's section of the Court he appeared to interpret from their expressions what they had read in the grim looks of the jury. When Mr. Justice Draper took his seat in Court Rowles mounted to the dock and stared at the jury. He was seen to shake his head, as if he knew that he was doomed.

The Judge's associate then asked the foreman of the jury what their verdice was. In a husky voice the foreman replied, "Guilty." For a few seconds there was a deathly silence in Court, and then the Judge's associate asked Rowles if he had anything to say before sentence of death was pronounced. In a clear voice he said, "I have never been guilty of a crime that has never been committed." "Is that all? Is that all you have to say?" asked Mr. Justice Draper. Rowles remained silent. Mr. Justice Draper broke the hush that followed by donning the black cap and pronouncing sentence of death.

1932   The opening ceremony on the Sydney Harbour Bridge is ruined by a man named De Groot

HUGH BUGGY
Melbourne Herald, 19 March 1932

It was to be Sydney's greatest day. The Premier, Jack Lang, was to cut a ribbon with a pair of golden scissors, and the great new bridge — the Sydney Harbour Bridge — was to be declared open. It was 19 March 1932, and King George the Fifth had sent a formal message congratulating the people of New South Wales on 'this magnificent triumph of engineering skill'.

It was Depression time, and there was talk that the right-wing New Guard or the Communists would try to upset the ceremony. But there were hundreds of police about, and hundreds of thousands of people lined the route of the procession and every possible vantage point around the harbour.

Hugh Buggy, the reporter's reporter, had been sent to Sydney by the Melbourne Herald *for the assignment. Buggy was the man who was always close to the action; when detectives first dunked the Pyjama Girl in a bath of ice, when miners fought police on the coalfields, when Squizzy Taylor and Snowy Cutmore shot each other dead, when the steamer* Tahiti *sliced through the Sydney ferry* Greycliffe, *Buggy had been nearby, scribbling in a notebook. He covered 200 murder investigations, attended nine hangings and worked as a court reporter with Melbourne* Truth *until shortly before his death in 1974.*

Also covering the Harbour Bridge ceremony was Wally Hamilton of the Sydney Sun. *He had been marked down in the assignment book simply for 'emergencies'; that meant that he had no speeches to cover. no description of the formal ceremonies to write. He was simply to be ready if something went wrong. On the previous day he had walked down the route of the cavalcade, noted the position of the official dais on the Bradfield Highway, strolled on to the pylons where the white ribbon was to be stretched, and given a publican in Miller's Point, below the pylon, a £1 note for the right to exclusive use of his phone.*

It all seemed to be going well when the Governor-General, Sir Isaac Isaacs, drove up in his open coach, with an escort party of the New South Wales Lancers fore and aft. At the back of the party, though, there was one man who looked out of place. He was on a rough-coated, uncurried horse, a horse which turned out to be a broken-down racehorse, and he was dressed in the unlikely uniform of a British unit, the Royal Hussars. Suddenly he was plunging forward, and the horse was rearing wildly, and the officer had his sword raised. Captain De Groot was about to move into history.

Hamilton got the flash through first. There were no radio commentators, and he dived for the pylon steps before anyone could cut him off from the telephone below. Buggy stayed on the pylon, and filed this report:

Expectations that the New Guard would attempt to prevent the Premier (Mr. Lang) from performing the official ceremony of opening the Sydney Harbor Bridge were fulfilled, to some extent, today. While the preliminary speeches were being made, Capt. F. E. De Groot, dressed in military uniform, and wearing medals, rode forward and slashed the ribbon with his sword, thus technically forestalling Mr. Lang. . .

In his speech at the opening Mr. Lang said: "The Bridge is the fulfilment of a dream entertained by many pioneers who did not live to see it realised. Just as Sydney has completed the Bridge, so will Australia ultimately perfect the bridge of common understanding begun 30 years ago."

In the midst of glittering pageantry, and in spite of the vigilance of cohorts of police and detectives, the Premier was forestalled in the actual cutting of the ribbon across the approach of the Harbor Bridge.

Swinging his sword aloft, a military officer, Capt. F. E. De Groot, mounted on a prancing chestnut horse, slashed the wide blue ribbon in two places 10 minutes before the time appointed for Mr. Lang to cut it with a pair of golden scissors.

First Capt. De Groot sought to break the ribbon by pressing his horse against it. The horse took fright, however, and bounded back from the ribbon. The officer urged the horse forward again, and, under the eyes of 50 policemen, who were taken by surprise, slashed the ribbon with his sword.

"I declare this bridge open in the name of His Majesty the King, and of all decent people," shouted Captain de Groot, as his sword flashed in the sunlight.

Twenty policemen leapt at the horse and its rider. Inspector MacKay, Chief of the Criminal Investigation Branch, was first to reach the captain. He dragged him from his horse amid a tremendous hubbub of mingled hoots and cheers.

Captain de Groot, borne down by the weight of policemen, fell on his back from the saddle in the middle of Bradfield Highway, the Bridge approach.

De Groot was bustled into a car with half-a-dozen detectives, and was driven down the Bridge Highway between great banks of excited faces. There was much vigorous hooting from the benches where Labor members and officials and their wives were sitting in the blistering sun. . .

Strenuous efforts were made by officials to have all newspaper references to the incident suppressed. Then began a feverish heresy hunt by detectives about the bridge approaches for other persons who, it was thought, might slash the ribbon again.

Officials of the Premier's Department hurried hurriedly staged a roll-call among the 30 photographers and 60 or 70 journalists who crowded about the severed strand of silk.

They also sought to form the journalists and photographers into a vigilance force to assist in detecting anyone lurking around with another sword or a pair of scissors. . .

By a clever ruse that baffled the 1400 police and the vast army of celebration officials, De Groot reached a position from which he carried out his daring coup before 20,000 or 30,000 people.

With a glitter of lances and the flash of red and white pennons, the military escort of the Governor-General (Sir Isaac Isaacs) clattered past the dais. At their head rode an officer with a gleaming sword held at the present.

As the cavalcade trotted past and on toward the blue ribbon, about 200 yards away, another officer on horseback brought up the rear. He rode a chestnut horse and also carried his sword at the present.

It struck me as being an unusual position for an officer to take. The escort clattered on almost past the point at which the ribbon was later stretched taut. I noticed the officer in the rear fall farther back and linger near the ribbon, which was then rolled up at the concrete wall of the bridge approach.

Speeches went on and on, bands crashed out anthems; planes roared and storms of cheers swept this way and that.

De Groot, who is a British Hussar officer, was wearing the uniform of a captain. He sat his horse calmly within a few feet of 30 policemen, who were busy checking the tickets of guests and turning back those people without tickets from the stairways by which the southern end of the bridge is approached. . .

The Premier had officially declared the bridge open, and had pressed a button which unveiled a bronze tablet recording the fact. All that remained for him to do to complete the ceremony was to cut the ribbon with the golden scissors.

Then the captain turned his horse, and sought to charge through the silken barrier. The animal shied and reared back on its haunches. A blue cloud of policemen swept across the roadway from the guardroom close by.

Drawing his sword, De Groot first began to saw excitedly at the ribbon.

De Groot is tackled by police after he dramatically cut the ribbon at the official opening of Sydney's Harbour Bridge

He failed to sever it, however, by this method. Then before the police could reach the prancing horse, he waved his sword in the air again and again, all in the space of 10 seconds. He brought it down on the ribbon, which fell apart and fluttered into the dust. . .

De Groot was not available for interview; he was in Sydney's Reception House in Darlinghurst, and this fact implied that the soundness of his mind was in some doubt. On the Monday, a panel of doctors decided that he was perfectly sane, and he was released from the Reception House. Waiting for him were some thirty reporters, all of them wanting to ask him so many questions. Hugh Buggy was among them.

After his release, De Groot refused point-blank to talk to any newsmen. With Colonel Eric Campbell, who was a solicitor and the founder of the New Guard, he hustled into a taxi cab and drove off towards the city. Buggy, who had kept his own cab waiting, was able to deliver a line beloved by B grade movie directors: 'Follow that cab!' Buggy's cab trailed De Groot's to the Australia Hotel, where the two men from the New Guard had lunch. As they came out of the dining room, Buggy stepped forward. 'I'm not talking to newspapers,' said De Groot.'They're too sensational.'

'Captain,' said Buggy, 'I'm not from a Sydney newspaper. My newspaper is the Melbourne Herald, *and it's very responsible.' (Until a few months earlier, Buggy had been working for a Sydney newspaper, the* Sun.)

The captain thought for a moment, then nodded. 'I'll talk to you,' he said, 'but not here.' Buggy suggested that they go 'somewhere quiet', which was a good idea, since some burly men on the other side of the street were starting to throw rocks at De Groot. 'They're Lang's basher gang,' said De Groot. Buggy pushed him into the cab, and told the driver: 'The Botanic Gardens.'

The two men in the cab found a quiet spot near Farm Cove, but when Buggy produced his notebook, De Groot told him: 'I can't talk here. This is State territory controlled by Lang.' Buggy, conscious of the fact that he was close to a major scoop and that at that moment *people all over Australia wanted to know what De Groot had to say, took a gamble. 'Let's go to a foreshore,' he said. 'The foreshores are Federal property, outside Lang's jurisdiction.' (He later described this statement as rather a desperate punt.)*

Mollified, Captain De Groot agreed to go with Buggy to Mrs Macquarie's Chair.

There De Groot told his story, which was published that Monday afternoon exclusively in the Melbourne Herald:

This afternoon I interviewed Captain F. E. De Groot.

He threw light on several phases of his exploit which hitherto had been obscure. . .

Captain de Groot, who received 2500 letters and telegrams of congratulation from all parts of Australia — many were from Melbourne — this morning, said that he was well-known, or should have been, to four senior police officers, from whom he was two or three feet away.

They had all seen him at a deputation to the Governor (Sir Phillip Game), when a petition was presented, asking that Mr. Lang be dismissed from office.

"When I got on to the bridge approach," said Captain De Groot, "I did not want to show discourtesy to the Governor-General. I followed his escort, but I carefully waited until Sir Isaac Isaacs had completed his speech before moving into position near the ribbon." . . .

Captain De Groot said: "For a long time I have been convinced that the intentions of Mr. Lang and his Government have been to sovietise the State of New South Wales in a constitutional manner, as a preliminary step to the general idea of sovietising the rest of Australia, with hopes of the disease spreading into other British communities.

"Having arrived at that conclusion, I, with other members of the New Guard, determined that the Sydney Harbour Bridge would be a symbol of power, and that if Mr. Lang were allowed to cut that ribbon then a lot of our people might become dispirited, might feel that the opposition was too strong, and the unemployed might even drift into the Communist ranks." . . .

1932   Phar Lap has his greatest win and dies two weeks later

BERT WOLFE
Melbourne Herald, 21 March and 6 April 1932

Bert Wolfe was, in the opinion of many journalists and racing fans, the finest turf writer Australia has ever known. He wrote for the Melbourne Herald *under the name of 'Cardigan' — a byline he took from one of the first great horses he ever saw, the 1903 Melbourne Cup winner Lord Cardigan.*

Wolfe was born in 1897 and reared among horses; he was present at the foaling of the 1908 Melbourne Cup winner Lord Nolan, which was owned and bred by his grandfather, John Mayo. At nineteen he was serving in France with the field artillery, and he began his long newspaper career soon after the war ended. By 1923 he was racing editor of the Sydney Referee, *and he spent the next four years as sports editor of the* Argus, Melbourne. *Then he left journalism for three years, to be chairman of stipendiary stewards of the Queensland Turf Club. He worked on the* Daily Guardian, *the* Daily Telegraph *and the* Sunday Sun, *all of Sydney, before Sir Keith Murdoch induced him to join the* Herald.

The greatest horse Wolfe ever saw was Phar Lap. He once wrote of him: 'He could gallop like the wind, and he could stay much too well for any horse that was ever opposed to him over a distance of ground. He was gentle and kind, his intelligence was such that he could be taught almost anything. He was a mountain of a horse. He weighed something like 1200 lbs, his height was a fraction more than 17 hands, and his heart was almost double the size of an ordinary horse's.'

In 1932 Wolfe accompanied Phar Lap to America and Mexico. At Agua Caliente, the racecourse where Phar Lap had the first race of the trip, Wolfe secured permission from the Mexican authorities for a plane to land in the centre of the course and wait for him until after the race. When Phar Lap won, he telephoned the result to San Diego, California, for cabling to Australia. Then he ran across the course to the plane; its engine was turning over. Special customs arrangements had been made and Wolfe was ready, when he arrived at the Western Union telegraph office in San Diego, to write his story in fifty-word 'takes'.

Wolfe combined the best reporting instincts with a gift for lucidity and an unsurpassed knowledge of the turf. One of his great feats was the reporting of the Melbourne Cup. As soon as the horses had passed the post, he would amble down from the press box and pick up a telephone. Before the horses were back in the saddling paddock, he would be dictating the story of the race. He would stay on the phone for an hour, completing an account of 3500 to 4000 words without notes other than a few shorthand jottings in the margin of his racebook. His descriptions were always analytical, accurate and highly readable.

On 21 March 1932 he sent this account of Phar Lap's first race abroad — the Agua Caliente Handicap in Mexico:

Phar Lap made all dreams come true yesterday to the shouts of fifty thousand racing fans when he won the Agua Caliente Handicap. He did more to advertise Australia and New Zealand in the United States and Mexico than a million dollars.

Today he is the "big news." Every newspaper of any consequence in the United States is printing stories of the success of "the Big Train from the Antipodes." They are saying that Phar Lap and his connections made American trainers and jockeys look like "suckers." They are lauding Woodcock to the skies for his cleverness, Elliot is being described as the Tod Sloan of Australia, and owners are being advised to send to Australia for a shipload of trainers and jockeys.

Not only was Phar Lap's win considered sensational, but regarded as even more sensational was the fact that he was having his first run in America, his first race on dirt tracks, his first start from the barrier stalls, and his almost unequalled feat of giving the leaders ten lengths' start from the six furlongs and being in front at the half-mile.

Americans love the unusual. They also love to see freaks in sport, and they almost worship anybody or anything that has some pretensions to world's championship class. So today they are talking about Phar Lap with affection and telling their friends that he is "some hoss — and I don't mean maybe."

It could not have been a better day for the big race. Warm in the forenoon with a breeze from the desert, gradually getting chilly as the afternoon wore on. And the excitement! Thousands of motor cars, hundreds of aeroplanes, scores of movie cameras, everybody shouting, gambling, laughing and drinking.

Arrangements had been made for the candidates for the Caliente Handicap horses to be saddled in field, or on the flat, as we know it. Each horse's name was nailed to a flagpole, on which a flag of its owner's colors waved in the breeze. Phar Lap was brought to the course before the twelfth race — there were fifteen on the card that day — and caused quite a flutter. He walked round the inside paddock as if he could not understand what all the fuss was about. Woodcock looked drawn and tense, Nielsen and Martin were like cats on hot bricks, Mr. D. J. Davis wandered from one roulette table to another as if endeavoring to divert his thoughts, while Mrs. Davis gradually got more nervous as the day wore on, and finally disappeared to watch the race by herself. . .

As the field passed the judge the first time (a mile from home) Phar Lap was in seventh place ten lengths from the leaders. Leaving the straight he was in the middle of the track and holding his place. When the back stretch was reached (six furlongs from home), Elliot

let him go. In a flash his amazing speed was apparent, and the crowd, following his dash with intelligent interest, let forth a mighty cheer. As one writer said afterwards, "He won America in an eighth of a mile."

Of all the famous sprints Phar Lap has ever made that two furlongs from the six furlongs to the half mile was his greatest. He ran the journey in 22 seconds, and when he arrived at the half mile he had left the field astern. At the three furlongs he was two or three lengths in front. At the turn he was a length in front, with Reveille Boy gaining ground fast.

I must confess I could not tell whether Elliot was giving him a breather or not. My field glasses would not remain still. When fairly in the straight Reveille Boy almost seemed to head him, and the thought flashed through my mind that owing to his foot injury the amazing dash from seventh to first had taken its toll. But just when everybody was getting ready to cheer the American horse Phar Lap gave a few terrific bounds and in a twinkling he was lengths in front and Elliot was easing him up passing the post well clear of the field.

It is impossible to describe the scene at the finish of the race. The crowd cheered itself hoarse, the paddock seethed with excitement, and when he returned to the winner's circle pandemonium reigned.

It was a great moment, and the coolest person of all was little Elliot, who, in a quiet voice, said, "When do they want me to weigh in?" The crowds milled round Phar Lap, he was photographed from all angles, his connections were photographed, but the horse steadfastly refused to be decorated with roses.

A fortnight after Phar Lap's Agua Caliente triumph, Bert Wolfe, of the Melbourne Herald, was watching the big horse die. Phar Lap had been taken to a stable outside San Francisco, while a contract was being negotiated with Metro Goldwyn Mayer for a series of short films in which the horse would star; he had gone off his food suddenly, had developed a high temperature, and had died quickly on 5 April. At first the cause of death was reported to be colic, but veterinary surgeons said later that death had been due to an irritant poison.

A whole nation grieved for Phar Lap, the thoroughbred freak who had won thirty-seven times out of fifty-one starts. The horse had been idolised in Australia, and his death caused a great deal of anti-American feeling which was still apparent when American World War Two servicemen came to Australia in 1942. Unreasonably, Phar Lap's demise was linked with Les Darcy's fifteen years earlier – and vaguely, 'the Yanks' were accused of two killings.

Phar Lap's regular jockey, Jimmy Pike, was reported near collapse when he heard the news in Sydney, and around the nation flags flew at half mast. The newspaper placards that day simply carried the words: 'He's Dead.'

Phar Lap remains a legend. His greatness has been celebrated in song and verse; a glass case containing his stuffed hide, in the National Museum in Melbourne, has become a place of pilgrimage, and his heart, more than twice the size of a normal horse's heart, has a position of honor in the Institute of Anatomy in Canberra.

Wolfe's report on the death of Phar Lap was filed from Menlo Park on 6 April:

The sudden collapse and death of Phar Lap, the great Australian racehorse, continues to be the subject of intense public speculation.

Opinion is growing that the horse did not die of acute indigestion, but as the result of some poison which was received in some manner at present a mystery.

Following the autopsy, Dr. Neilsen, the Australian veterinary surgeon, told me frankly that the horse had died as the result of an irritant poison.

"I saw the lining of his stomach, and I know what it means when the lining is eaten away," he said tonight. "I would like to be able to come to some other conclusion, but it is impossible in face of the evidence of my own eyes."

"The horse did not die as the result of acute indigestion," he added. "If nothing else, the result of the autopsy has told me that."

The veterinary surgeon late tonight decided to send the contents of the stomach for analysis to the University of California.

The result of the analyst's report on the contents of Phar Lap's stomach is likely to be known late today.

A close check-up is being made of visitors to Phar Lap's stall at Menlo Park in the 24 hours before the horse was seized with illness.

The practice had been to prevent outsiders seeing the horse except during one hour in the afternoon.

When Phar Lap arrived from Australia a large quantity of fodder was brought with him. Some was taken to Agua Caliente, and the balance was stored at San Francisco. On the horse's arrival at Menlo Park the fodder from San Francisco was moved down and stacked outside the stable-door. It consisted mainly of bags of New Zealand oats.

. . . Mr Joseph Schenk, head of United Artists, at Hollywood, who is a keen racing man, is stated to have made an offer of something like 50,000 dol. (normally £10,000) to Mr Davis for his share of the horse, with the proviso that Mr Schenk should be allowed to map out the campaign of the horse in the eastern States.

Mr Baron Long, vice-president of the Agua Caliente Club, today received a telegram from Colonel Mat Winn, head of Washington Park and Arlington Park clubs, authorising him to confer with Mr Davis at San Francisco on Thursday next regarding special match races on both tracks against first-class horses, the prizes to be not less than 30,000 dol. (£6000) in each race.

Mr Davis said tonight that he had practically completed arrangements last week for a special race at the Tanforan track (San Francisco) this month against moderate horses for a purse of 25,000 dol. (£5000), Phar Lap to carry 5lb. more than his weight in the Agua Caliente Handicap.

Everything that Phar Lap did in America in life was regarded as big news, but in death he was even more important, as he actually pushed the Lindbergh baby case off the front pages...

1932

A governor takes the unprecedented step of sacking the Premier of New South Wales

TED DOWNIE
Sydney Morning Herald, 14 May 1932

J. T. Lang, Labor Premier of New South Wales, was dismissed from office by the Governor, Sir Phillip Game, on 13 May 1932, for a breach of Federal law. It was an extraordinary event; although, constitutionally, the Governor had the power to dismiss the Premier, there were many who felt that governors were simply titular figure-heads who had no right to interfere in domestic political affairs. In fact, the dismissal of a premier for any reason other than loss of his majority in Parliament is a very rare event. Sydney's Labor Daily *called it 'a foul blow . . . the most appalling tragedy since the white race superseded the black'. The Melbourne* Sun, *on the other hand, said that all Australia would heave a great sigh of relief. 'Mr Lang and his Cabinet have done incalculable damage to the Commonwealth,' said the* Sun. *'They have dragged the people of their own State to the brink of the precipice of ruin, and gravely impeded the efforts of all other governments to overcome unemployment by balancing budgets and thus restoring confidence.'*

Lang's long-standing disagreements with the right of the National Parliament to enforce the Financial Agreement of 1927, and with ALP official policy on the correct cure for Australia's economic problems, had caused him to defy the Federal Conference of the ALP, the Commonwealth Government, the Commonwealth Parliament and the High Court of Australia. All of them had declared that Lang's policy of refusing to pay interest due on overseas loans, and refusing to hand over revenues due to the Commonwealth Government, was illegal.

The voters of New South Wales overwhelmingly backed Governor Game. Labor dropped from fifty-five to twenty-four seats, against a government coalition of sixty-six, in the following Legislative Assembly elections. Lang never again took office, but Langism continued to exist, and to cause conflict inside the Labor Party, for many years. Mr Lang continued to edit his own newspaper, the *Century, even in his nineties.*

When the news of his dismissal broke, Mr Lang told the Sydney Morning Herald's *State political writer, Ted Downie, 'Well, I am sacked.' This is Downie's report of that historic event:*

The Premier (Mr. Lang) was dramatically dismissed from office by the State Governor (Sir Phillip Game) shortly before 6 o'clock yesterday afternoon.

His dismissal was brought about by his refusal to withdraw a confidential circular issued on Thursday to heads of Government departments instructing them not to pay money into the Commonwealth.

The leader of the State Opposition (Mr. Stevens) was subsequently sent for by his Excellency, and accepted a commission to form a Ministry. He was sworn in as Premier, and asked the Governor for time to choose his Cabinet.

It is probable that the new Ministry, which may include members of the Country party, will be sworn in on Monday. An executive minute may be issued proroguing Parliament, with a view to a dissolution. It is considered in political circles that the general elections will take place late in June or early in July.

Yesterday the Federal Parliament passed the Financial Emergency (State Legislation) Bill, nullifying the Mortgages Taxation Bill passed by the State Parliament.

It is understood that if Mr. Stevens gives

J. T. Lang, Premier of New South Wales and 'Wild Man' of Australian politics, addresses voters at a rally

the Federal Government an undertaking that the State will meet its interest obligations all the enforcement proclamations will be withdrawn immediately.

The circumstances which led up to the dismissal had their beginning on Thursday morning, when the Governor wrote to Mr. Lang directing attention to the circular, which he regarded as illegal and which he felt could not be sanctioned by the representative of the King.

His Excellency demanded its immediate withdrawal. A number of letters passed between Sir Philip and the Premier on the subject. At 3 o'clock yesterday afternoon Mr. Lang was sent for by the Governor, and an important conference took place. Mr. Lang refused to withdraw the circular, and informed his Excellency that he would consult his Ministers. Late in the afternoon a messenger from the Premier's Department was despatched to Government House, intimating that the Government still refused to withdraw the circular.

The Governor apparently then took the stand that he had no alternative but to notify Mr. Lang that he was dismissed from office. A message to this effect was forwarded to the official head of the Premier's Department (Mr. Hay), who conveyed the information to the Premier. . .

A "Herald" representative was granted an interview, and, on entering the Premier's room, was greeted with the remark, "Well, I am sacked. I am dismissed from office."

Beyond that dramatic admission, Mr. Lang would make no comment for publication.

"Well, I must be going. I am no longer Premier, but a free man," said Mr. Lang. "I have attempted to do my duty. . ."

When Sir Phillip Game had sent his formal dismissal notice to Mr. Lang, he directed the official secretary to communicate with the leader of the Opposition (Mr. Stevens), who was then in his rooms at Parliament House.

Mr. Stevens arrived at Government House shortly after 6 o'clock, and was ushered in to his Excellency. He did not emerge until an hour later.

Interviewed on the steps of Government House when the conference was at last at an end, Mr. Stevens said: "His Excellency has sworn me in as Premier, and has commissioned me to form a Government. I have asked for time, and will see his Excellency later." . . .

It was explained by a constitutional authority last night that the Governor might by executive minute prorogue Parliament, which, in ordinary circumstances, would have met on Tuesday next, to some later date. Parliament could then be dissolved by a further minute.

Until this has been done, the date of the election will not be fixed. It is, however, regarded as certain that the Stevens Ministry will endeavour to bring about a general election at the earliest possible moment.

It is regarded as unlikely that the emergency Government will take the risk of meeting the House, unless it is assured of the support of a section of the Lang party. At the present stage there is no indication that this would be forthcoming. In that event, if Mr. Stevens were to meet Parliament, he would not have control of the House, and an extraordinary position would be created.

The Sydney Morning Herald *reproduced this text of Sir Phillip Game's final letter:*

Government House,
May 13, 1932.

Dear Mr. Lang,
Your letter informing me that Ministers are not prepared to tender their resignations has just reached me. In view of this and of your refusal to withdraw the circular, I feel it my bounden duty to inform you that I cannot retain my present Ministers in office, and that I am seeking other advisers. I must ask you to regard this as final.

(Signed)   Phillip Game,
Governor.

Jack Lang, a huge-framed man known as 'the big feller' to three generations of Australians, founded his own newspaper, the Century; *he was expelled from the Labor Party in 1943 for the* Century's *criticism of New South Wales Labor leader, Bill (later Sir William) McKell. He worked as its editor until his death in 1975.*

1933   Tempers flare and the Cricket Board of Control cables that bodyline must be stopped

CLAUDE CORBETT, A. G. MOYES AND ARTHUR MAILEY
Sydney Sun, February 1933

The most bitter cricket season in the history of the game occurred during the England Test team's tour of Australia in the summer of 1932–33. At one stage a complete break in the cricket relations of the two countries was threatened.

At the core of the controversy were the bowling methods of the England fast bowlers, particularly those of a slightly-built, five-foot eight-inch ex-miner, Harold Larwood, under the captaincy of Douglas Jardine. With two other fast bowlers, Bill Bowes and Bill Voce, Larwood exploited the technique of bowling very fast, short-pitched deliveries on the leg side, to a packed leg field. The England players called it 'leg theory'. The Australians used a blunter term, 'bodyline'. That tour became known as the Bodyline Tour; it inflamed public anger, ruined careers and friendships, and did great harm to the cause of cricket.

The essence of bodyline was that it forced the batsman to defend himself as well as his wicket. The ball flew high around the head and shoulders of the batsman; usually his alternatives were to duck, or to risk being caught by the crowded field on the leg side. Sir Donald Bradman once wrote of this form of bowling: 'Neither defence nor attack could overcome it for long – unless the batsman was particularly lucky. Playing the good length balls and dodging the others may sound all right in theory, but it did not work in practice. The batsman doing this must of necessity be hit. In fact no Australian batsman of any note failed to get hit – some on many occasions.'

In the First Test of the series, in which Bradman was unable to play, Larwood took five wickets for ninety-six, and five wickets

for twenty-eight, to help England win. In the Second Test, Larwood took only two wickets in each innings, and Bradman made 103; Australia won. Then came the Third Test in Adelaide – a game described by Wisden as 'probably the most unpleasant ever played . . . altogether the whole atmosphere was a disgrace to cricket'.

Several incidents occurred during the game which enraged the Australian public, and caused the Australian captain, Bill Woodfull, normally an unruffled, diplomatic man, to tell the English manager, Mr P. F. Warner: 'There are two teams out there. One of them is playing cricket. . .' It was as provocative a statement as it was uncharacteristic of Woodfull, and it demonstrated the sharp edge to which players' tempers had been honed by the bodyline dispute.

Claude Corbett, a member of a famous sportswriting family, was in Adelaide for the Sydney Sun. Here are extracts from his reports on the game, in which Woodfull was hit above the heart by a Larwood delivery, Oldfield received a fractured skull from another Larwood ball and afterwards Woodfull made an apology to Warner:

Sensational incidents marked the start of Australia's innings in the Third Test to-day. After Fingleton had gone for a "duck," a ball from Larwood struck Woodfull under the heart. As the Australian captain dropped his bat and clutched his chest, the crowd hooted the fast bowler. Shortly after, Woodfull was struck on the fingers.

Once again England's speed battery crashed through the Australian defences. Allen got Fingleton, while Larwood claimed Bradman and McCabe. The former was not comfortable, and made only eight. The first three wickets fell for 34.

Woodfull seemed to be settling down, when he was clean bowled by Allen for 22. Four were then out for 51. England made 341, Paynter and Verity figuring in a gallant stand. Wall finished with five wickets.

Again the weather was fine for the third Test, and again two hours before the game began there were thousands of people in attendance. . .

Promptly at noon the game was resumed with Wall bowling to Paynter.

Nearly 40,000 people were present. Paynter had a wild swing at the second ball, but failed to connect. Wall was making the ball fly. The fifth ball went for a leg-bye, while Verity played the last. Grimmett had the ball at the other end. . .

Jardine led his men into the field at 3.20 p.m., and Woodfull took Fingleton in with him to open, the latter taking strike to Larwood, who bowled with a cross wind.

Larwood had three slips fine and another wide. Two balls of the over were played to Jardine, in slips, and he was heckled as he fielded them. The over was a maiden, the last ball flying very fast over the batsman's head.

Allen was the other bowler, and Woodfull turned his first ball to leg for a single.

Fingleton allowed the next to pass on the off, but the next he snicked and was caught behind.

Bradman came to a tremendous ovation.

Fingleton had nibbled just as he had done in Melbourne.

There was a roar as Bradman put the second ball he received away to leg for two. Then Woodfull got Larwood away to leg for a couple, followed by a shot, finer, on the same side. He had to duck under the next ball.

The last ball of the over kicked up and hit Woodfull under the heart. He dropped the bat and clutched his chest while the crowd hooted and counted Larwood out.

It was a perfectly legitimate ball. Woodfull soon recovered, but opened his shirt to examine the spot where he had been hit.

Facing Allen again, Bradman forced the first ball to the on for two and pulled the fifth to the boundary, amid tremendous enthusiasm. The last ball of the over he swished at but missed.

Woodfull was still feeling his chest when he took his stance to Larwood's third over.

The leg theory was now put on, and the crowd hooted lustily as Larwood began his run. The second ball cracked Woodfull on the fingers.

From the third Woodfull got a single and Bradman was then in opposition to Larwood and had to duck under the second he received. He did not touch one of the three he received from Larwood.

Woodfull put a ball in Allen's third over through slips for two and turned the next to leg for a single. Bradman played the other two of the over.

Woodfull, batting very confidently, reached double figures with a single off Larwood's first ball of the fourth over.

Bradman, who had not been at all comfortable against Larwood, got under the next ball, but played the third softly to Allen, who was standing close in at square leg. Two were out for 18 then. . .

Larwood's second ball after "drinks" cracked Oldfield on the forehead. He fell like a pitched ox after staggering a few yards.

The fieldsmen flew from all directions to his assistance, and Allen dashed from the field to return a few seconds later with water and a towel.

There was a nasty contusion on the head, and Woodfull went out to him and Oldfield left the field.

The crowd hooted vigorously for minutes. O'Reilly took the vacant place and as Larwood walked back to bowl, he was again hooted all the way on his run to the wicket. There was a wild demonstration, which recurred for the remainder of the over.

It was one of the wildest demonstrations ever heard on an Australian cricket ground. There has been worse at football matches, but not much. . .

It was thought that the ball flew from Oldfield's bat, but it was later reported that Oldfield did not touch the ball, which hit him after he had finished his stroke. . .

A. G. Moyes, one of the most respected Australian commentators in the game, was also at the match for the Sydney Sun. *This was his reaction to Woodfull's extraordinary statement:*

The dignified protest by Woodfull against the tactics of the English side is perhaps one of the most sensational cricket incidents of all time. Woodfull was doubtless in pain at the time, but even that would not account for his comments.

Behind it all was the genuine dislike to anything which is against the spirit of cricket, for Billy is one of the finest gentlemen that the game has known.

Of course Warner as manager has nothing to do with it, and realising this, Woodfull subsequently made it clear that it was not a personal matter between "Billy" and "Plum" but from Australia's captain to England's manager.

He must have felt the position very keenly. It is known that he was definitely averse from introducing the same tactics into his own attack, and therefore his action has been consistent and not a peevish outburst brought on by bodily injury.

The whole position is disturbing. The cricket stream has not flowed smoothly this season and the undercurrents of feeling were bound sooner or later to come to the surface. Woodfull no doubt is supported by his team mates who dislike present methods as calculated to do the game harm. It is an open secret that the feeling in international circles is not what it should be and the remedy is not easy to find or apply.

As I have written on other occasions, there is nothing illegal about it. A bowler can bowl where he likes, but it is a great pity that it has come into the game. There cannot be any argument that it has affected the game as a spectacle, and that it has caused bitterness. Test Matches now are not a game of cricket but a miniature war, where intimidation is made to do the work of science and skill.

The injuries sustained in the 1933 'Bodyline Test' in Adelaide, plus the rebuke by the

Australian captain, Bill Woodfull, to the English manager, 'Plum' Warner, touched off a violent international argument.

The Australian Cricket Board of Control sent a cable to the Marylebone Cricket Club in London, demanding that bodyline be banned. The word 'bodyline' — believed to have been first coined by the great footballer-cricketer Jack Worrall — gained official status when the Board of Control used it in its cable.

This was the text of the historic message: 'Bodyline bowling has assumed such proportions as to menace the best interests of the game, making protection of the body by the batsman the main consideration, causing intensely bitter feelings between the players, as well as injuries. In our opinion it is unsportsmanlike. Unless stopped at once it is likely to upset friendly relations existing between Australia and England.'

It was an unfortunate cable, particularly in its use of the word 'unsportsmanlike'. The MCC sent back a tight-lipped, equally belligerent reply, deprecating the idea that England's sportsmanship was in question, expressing confidence in its captain, team and manager, and said that if the Board considered it desirable to cancel the remainder of the program, the MCC would consent, but with great reluctance.

While the issue was being debated at every level, a group of prominent British and Australian citizens asked Lloyd Dumas, editor of the Adelaide Advertiser, *to do what he could to bring the matter back to reasonable proportions. Specifically, he was asked to use his influence to stop English commentators from using reports accusing the Australian team of being 'squealers'; these reports were being cabled back and reprinted in Australian newspapers and were fanning the controversy. Dumas cabled the editor of* The Times, *and several other London editors. His cable said in part: 'Quite apart from the ethics of bodyline bowling upon which there may be honest differences of opinion I fear results if incidents similar [to those in] third test occur in Brisbane and Sydney . . . all British newspaper comments being cabled out here some unfortunately tending inflame public feeling. Any friendly comment would greatly help Australian press in efforts to prevent demonstration. Am cabling you personally because confident you equally desirous prevent development bitterness between two peoples.'*

Dumas' efforts undoubtedly had some effect, but up to the eve of the Fourth Test, in Brisbane, it remained doubtful whether the match would be played and there were many suggestions that the Australian tour of England, due the following year, should be abandoned. Larwood took thirty-three wickets in the five Tests on the Australian tour, and hit a great ninety-eight in the final match of the series. He dismissed Don Bradman four times in those Tests; when the tour ended he was a hero in Britain and a villain in Australia. He went home saying he 'never wanted to see this country again'; ironically, he returned as a migrant in 1950.

These reports appeared in the Sydney Sun *during the worst week of the controversy.*

Claude Corbett wrote from Adelaide:

The side issues in the Test Match have become so great that it will take something out of the ordinary to happen for either batsman or bowler to usurp the limelight which has been focussed upon the leg theory, Larwood, and Jardine.

Wherever men gather, there are heated discussions on the matter. Everyone, even those who could not see that leg theory bowling was illegitimate, are distinctly of the opinion that, if permitted in Test cricket, or any other class of cricket, the game will be ruined as a spectacle. . .

Now that the agitation against the leg theory is so pronounced, something is sure to be done about it.

I heard an Australian Eleven player say last night that if leg theory was fair, there was nothing to stop one of our bowlers from rushing down the pitch to within three or four yards of the batsman and letting the ball fly at him with all his strength.

Nothing more could happen than for him to be no-balled, and, to this player's way of thinking, it would be a justifiable method of reprisal. . .

The English team is a divided camp on the vexed subject of leg theory and at least two batsmen are absolutely opposed to it. . .

There has been a rumor current that the Englishmen opposed to leg theory are asking for a full meeting of the team to thresh out the question, but it is not likely to be held until after this Test has finished, when a statement may be looked for.

Arthur Mailey, in Ballarat, said:

One of the most unhysterical body of people in the world is Lord's, or the Marylebone Cricket Club, but when its members receive the Board of Control's cable, I can imagine a slight shudder shaking their frames when their eyes alight on the word "unsportsmanlike."

It is probably the first time in the history of cricket that this word has been used in reference to the tactics of the opposing team.

The Board must have summed up all the courage at its disposal to word the cable. Had the message been sent after the Melbourne Test Match, it would have sounded more like the complaints of an injured man, but, having been sent after Australia was beaten, it savored of an expression of disappointment.

Despite the fact that Woodfull and Oldfield were hit in Adelaide, the attack was not nearly so dangerous as in Melbourne against an Australian team early in the season.

The M.C.C., no doubt, will send a courteous reply, but I feel that they cannot take any action in the matter. . .

Neville Cardus, writing in the Manchester Guardian, *said: '. . . nobody in England seems to realise how badly the Australian public is taking this leg-theory violence.*

'If I were the English captain, I would prefer to lose the rubber rather than win it by methods making the batsman think first of his personal safety, and preventing him from using the technique contributing to the glory of the game. Suppose we have a whole race of leg-theory hooligans where then will be the science and the true stroke of cricket?'

1934   In Melbourne the loss of two great theatres is mourned

CLIVE TURNBULL
Melbourne Herald, November 1933 and February 1934

The death of a theatre can be a very emotional event, particularly for people who have at some stage found it a source of stimulus, or even plain enjoyment. People do not feel that way about television sets, or even television studios; but there is something about the character of an old theatre — maybe the knowledge that other great names have trodden those boards, and other audiences appreciated them — that is especially evocative.

Two historic theatres died in Melbourne within about four months late in 1933 and early in 1934. Clive Turnbull, an author, critic and foreign correspondent, was one who felt deeply about their loss. He wrote for the Herald *with some feeling as the wreckers moved into both the Theatre Royal (in November 1933) and the Bijou Theatre (in February 1934).*

Ghosts today people the Theatre Royal and on Monday even they will be disturbed in their fretful musings by the first crashes of falling masonry as the wreckers begin the work of demolition.

The old theatre died last night in a blaze of triumphant glory. Never even in the heyday of the past can there have been such a night. Once more were the splendors of yesteryear rehearsed in tableau and the audience cheered and cheered again until the last sundering curtain fell between it and all the world of pageantry that has been the Royal.

It was fitting that so popular a production as "The Maid of the Mountains" should be chosen for the last performance, and probably there was never a merrier one.

For the invisible barriers between players and audience were dissolved, and an intense personal sympathy between them made every sally of the old favorites, heard by many present probably a dozen or 20 times, doubly amusing, and every romantic moment more glamorous than before.

Often the action of the show was held up by the demonstrations of the audience. For all the cast, and especially for such favorites as Gladys Moncrieff, Arthur Stigant, and Phil Smith, there was continuous applause.

But it was when "The Maid" was over that the real show began.

The Lord Mayor (Cr. Gengoult Smith), who had been sitting in a box, went upon the stage and recalled the grandeurs of the far past and of more recent years. . .

Now Mr Stigant, in his costume as General Malona, introduced a series of tableaus.

"Tonight," he said, "within this historic theatre the curtain falls for the last time and there will remain but a memory of the many plays and players who have been seen upon the old stage with its historic associations of the past. . ."

So, in tableau, Rignold lived again, and the audience cheered once more.

Player after player they appeared, most represented by some performer of the present day, with a few old favorites in person.

Here they all were — George Rignold, affectionately known as Handsome George, who who first appeared in the theatre in 1878; Marion Dunn, The Daughter of the Regiment of 1864, represented by her daughter; Marion Marcus Clarke, in the dress used in the original production; J. B. Atholwood, the character actor, represented by his son Ronald Atholwood; Julius Knight, "A Royal Divorce" celebrity; Pavlova; Jack Ralston; Harriet Bennett, of "Rose Marie"; Melba; Reuben Fax; Lewis Walker; Maggie Moore; Nellie

Stewart; Tittel Brune as L'Aiglon, recalled by Patricia Wenman; and to the rapture of the audience, Carrie Moore herself, the original Merry Widow; Meta Pelham, at 84 Australia's oldest actress; and smiling Cecil Kellaway himself.

Never can any of the famous in the flesh have had a more tumultuous reception than was given their depictors. When Mr Frank Tait had explained that a new His Majesty's was to arise, the theatre was showered in streamers from circle and gallery and, amid a mass of multi-colored ribbons, Gladys Moncrieff sang "Farewell."

So at midnight the last curtain fell.

The audience streamed away, but not a few people lingered wandering across the huge stage or among the deserted dressing rooms.

What tales indeed could be told by these well-worn walls, these rooms all empty now!

But now the lights were going out. Carrie Moore was saying a last farewell. She stopped to speak to Frank Talbot, who was paying the last tribute of a brother showman to the dying theatre.

The corridors were piled high with theatrical baskets. On the walls hung the wardrobe for the last performance.

Mourners and merrymakers alike took their last look and drifted away.

Workmen began to carry out the furniture.

The exit doors to Bourke Street were closed.

The Theatre Royal was dark for ever.

And in February 1934:

When hansom cabs jingled over the streets of Melbourne, when barmaids were Junoesque and peroxided, when mirrors and moustaches, macassar oil and mashers all mingled in the glorious Victorian scene, then the Bijou Theatre was in its heyday, and nervous young men strolling in from crowded Bourke Street looked askance at the scenes of revelry in the long promenade bar.

Now the Bijou is coming down to make way for yet anothet theatre, and the wrecker's pick is stirring the dust from the masonry of that curious architectural trinity of Victorian Melbourne — the Bijou, the sometime Gaiety, and the Palace Hotel.

Today I wandered over the old building from the roof, from which the waters of the bay may be seen blue in the distance, to the cellars, vast in their extent, dungeon-like in their gloom, sprawling beneath the towering bulk of the building.

In the theatre above Brough and Boucicault gave Melbourne the best of contemporary drama when the Bijou was a centre of the fashionable world; and in the cellars below the renowned Squizzy Taylor hid "in smoke." making an entrance to the dungeons, undignified for a king of the underworld, by means of the coal chute.

The Bijou, once the Academy of Music, was established in 1876, and it has lapsed from glory to decay. It passed from smart French comedy and the tragedy of "Camille" by way of "East Lynne" and "Driving a Girl to Destruction" to the historic Brough-Boucicault productions, experienced variety, and in recent years fell on less prosperous times.

The Palace Hotel — it was the first Hotel in Melbourne to have a lift, so it is said — likewise had its vicissitudes. To younger Melbourne it is but a name. . .

In the cellars there is a well. They say there is water in it, I do not know; I did not care to investigate it. There is certainly a bakehouse with a monumental oven to supply the hungry regions above. And a cellar in the real sense.

It is a cellar such as is seldom seen now. In its serried racks reposed the champagne of other days, and faded labels still indicate the quality of the vintages once stored therein. Huge cobwebs hang from the ceiling, and the adventurer who goes searching among its recesses gathers unto himself a vast cloud of dust and webbing.

In one of the darkest cellars of all Squizzy Taylor lived.

While all Melbourne canvassed the redoubtable Squizzy's whereabouts he spent a safe, if not cheerful, vacation underground, supplied with food by his accomplices.

They tell many stories of the old Bijou and the companies therein. . .

Great days, vivid days! Soon how much of old Melbourne will remain?

1934   Race riots erupt in Kalgoorlie's Golden Mile

JOHN LAURENCE AND ROLEY HOFFMAN
Perth West Australian, 31 January 1934

In January 1934, two men — one a local miner who had been something of a football hero, the other an Italian barman — came to blows over a trifling argument in a Kalgoorlie, Western Australia, hotel. The Italian connected with a punch which sent the miner's head crashing against concrete curbing; he died some hours later, without regaining consciousness. That incident touched off an ugly riot in the gold towns of Kalgoorlie and Boulder. A mob went on the rampage against the Italian and Yugoslav communities as the animosities of several decades erupted. The Italians and Yugoslavs had moved on to the goldfields as young men left the mining industry; they were strong and willing, but not always as experienced as the locals in mining methods, and their presence was for a long time the source of rumbling antagonism. Suddenly, on Australia Day 1934, the hatred was allowed to flow. Resentments which had been harnessed for years were cut loose. A thousand men took it all out on their foreign community, just at a time when gold was leading the nation's recovery from the Depression. It was one of the most disgraceful incidents in Western Australian history.

Said the West Australian:

The affair has taken on a complexion of gravity without parallel in West Australian history. In an attack on the camp where the foreigners were entrenched, a Montenegrin was fatally shot, and others of the two opposing forces were wounded . . . these foreigners have been permitted to throw in their lot with the state, the great majority of them are hard-working, decent and honest, and have accepted Australian citizenship. Their children will be Australians born and bred, and thousands of native-born Australians are not ashamed of such parentage. If there were a great deal of poverty and unemployment at Kalgoorlie, an anti-foreign agitation, while not excusable, might be understandable. But that of course is not the case.

The rioting continued for two days. On the second night a pitched battle was fought in which shot-guns, rifles, jam-tin bombs and dynamite were used on a lease area known as Dingbat Flat. In a mood not unlike that of the Chinese-hating miners of the 'fifties, miners decided to cease work until the mining companies gave an assurance that no unnaturalised person would be given a job in the mines.

The West Australian *published this account of the second day's events, from its own representatives, John Laurence and Roley Hoffman:*

At Boulder last night miners who were concerned in the riot on Monday night came into savage conflict with the foreigners who defended their homes and property with rifles and knives.

As a result of the affray, which was still continuing early this morning, one man, a Montenegrin, was killed . . .

. . . the main street of Kalgoorlie, resembled a shambles, and, with the returning day, the full extent of the previous night's rioting was visible. The concrete pavements were deeply stained with looted wine, while plate-glass, smashed into hundreds of fragments, was scattered over the roadway. Fruit, chocolates, crockery, linen, legs from chairs and tables, ornaments, fish, paper bags, cruets and trays, strewed the footpath or were piled in front of the wrecked shops.

At the western end of Hannan-street, where the rioting broke out, the Home From Home Hotel, the All Nations boarding house — both two-storeyed brick buildings — and the Kalgoorlie Wine Saloon stood gaunt wrecks in the dawn. From the twisted iron-work, galvanised iron, and charred timbers and brickwork, smoke still issued. Bedding, mattresses, iron bedsteads, broken bottles, empty wine and beer casks, covered the roadway, and several foreigners could be detected surreptitiously salvaging what remained of their belongings. Battered cash registers taken from the hotels and the shops were also in evidence, and the marks of violence revealed that the looters had endeavoured to purloin any money that they might have contained. In the garage near the Home From Home Hotel the remains of a sedan motor car were the object of idle curiosity. Fences which had been torn down in the mad rush last night to loot and fire the hotel and boarding house in Kalgoorlie added to the desolation.

In the Rex Cafe and the premises owned by G. Kalafatas two new refrigerators had been wrecked and the electric motors wrenched out of them. In all the shops attacked in Kalgoorlie the interiors were wrecked beyond repair, and the furniture was smashed to splinters. A large plate-glass window in the jewellery shop of Messrs. Randall and Edwards, Hannan-street, near Mr. Kalafatas's shop, was broken by a stone. The window was full of watches and jewellery, including cut glass ware, but the timely arrival of the police prevented any thefts. Outside the Kalgoorlie Wine Saloon lay the remains of an upright piano, while inside the building was a wrecked organ. . .

At 1 o'clock this morning hordes of men and women streamed through Kalgoorlie. Several were laden with goods that they had taken from the destroyed buildings and one man filled a tablecloth with chocolates and fruit which he had taken from a wrecked fruit shop. As the minutes passed the crowd of sightseers, who numbered several thousands in attire which showed they had left their beds to view the wreckage, gradually diminished. In Hannan-street small bands of men wandered for some hours and continued to smash plate glass in the already wrecked shops. This desultory smashing also ceased, and when comparative quietness existed at about 4 o'clock this morning a huge sheet of flame suddenly lit up the central portion of Hannan-street. A crowd quickly collected and it was discovered that a foreign tobacconist shop near the recently renovated York Hotel had been fired. The flames had secured a strong hold, and before the fire brigade, which concentrated on saving the hotel, could master the fire, a bicycle shop owned by R. Foy was totally destroyed, resulting in the loss of about £400 to the owner. An adjoining second-hand dealer's store also suffered slightly.

The Kalgoorlie Fire Brigade, which was quickly on the scene, made an excellent save, as the fire might easily have destroyed two hotels. At one stage the Oriental Hotel, about five doors up from the tobacconist shop, became ignited on its west wall, but the flames were quickly extinguished. Boarders from both hotels made preparations for a hurried departure and appeared in the street with their valuables, but as the firemen kept the fire under control and both hotels received only slight damage to their verandahs, their panic abated. By 5 o'clock all danger was removed of a serious outbreak in one of the main business blocks of the town. No sooner had this blaze been quelled than smoke was seen to be issuing from a building lower down the street. This, however, proved of little consequence, as the sheds at the back of the wine saloon only had caught alight and were easily put out.

Some of the mob still bent on plunder, searched through the debris of the wrecked buildings in Kalgoorlie in the early morning, and it is understood broke open an iron safe in the Kalgoorlie Wine Saloon and removed £50, and carried a large iron safe from the Home From Home Hotel, the contents of which are unknown. Inquiries have revealed that many of the foreigners have lost all they possessed in the fires, and they have taken refuge wherever possible.

It was news to many of the afternoon shift men on the mines when they came into Kalgoorlie after midnight when their shift finished, to discover that rioting had taken place.

Special constables parade at Perth headquarters before leaving by special train to quell the riots at Kalgoorlie

Most of the rioters were young men. Many of them carried their plunder miles from the wrecked houses, and this morning a stove was found abandoned in Wilson-street, nearly one mile away from the Cornwall and Main Reef Hotels. . .

When it became time at 8 o'clock yesterday morning for the day shifts to go on the mines on the Golden Mile, people were wondering what action the miners would take, as about 500 to 600 foreigners are employed by the companies out of the 2,500 men working on the field. The underground shifts went below on several of the mines, but on the Ivanhoe, Chafers, and Horseshoe leases of the Lake View and Star group the men, instead of going below, met to discuss the incidents of the previous night. It was decided to cease work until an assurance was received from the companies that no foreigner who was not naturalised or born in Australia would be allowed to work on the mines. The men on the other companies were informed of this decision, and ceased work.

The Lake View and Star, the Great Boulder Proprietary, the Boulder Perseverance, the South Kalgurli, and the North Kalgurli, and Associated were rendered idle by this decision, and at 10 o'clock this morning a mass meeting numbering well over 1,000 men was held at the corner of Burt and Lane streets, Boulder. The meeting was very orderly and although divergent views were expressed on the outbreak last night, there was no roughness. The meeting decided not to return to work on the mines until all foreigners were dismissed, and a committee of seven men was appointed to interview the Chamber of Mines, representing the major mining companies on the Golden Mile. An immediate telephonic communication with the Chamber of Mines disclosed that the managers would be willing to meet the men this afternoon. About 10.45 o'clock the meeting dispersed, and although large numbers of men waited in the street for some time they had disappeared by noon. It was announced later that the Chamber would give its decision after a full meeting of members on Thursday.

1934   An audacious turf fraud, involving a painted horse, is exposed

BERT WOLFE
Melbourne Herald, 14 August 1934

One of the great scandals of the Australian turf involved the 'ringing-in' of a galloper called Erbie during 1933 and 1934 in three States under various aliases. It was the kind of audacious, imaginative plot that might have occurred in a Nat Gould turf novel; Erbie ran and won under the names of Duke Bombita, Chrybean and Redlock, always in an unlikely disguise.

Race stewards were duped. Bert Wolfe, 'Cardigan' of the Melbourne Herald, *was not. His exposure of Erbie as Redlock was probably the greatest story of his career. After 'Redlock' had won at Murray Bridge, South Australia (with his price tightening from 15/1 to 6/4), and again at Kadina, South Australia, Wolfe looked at pictures of the race and decided that the horse was really Erbie. He knew Erbie well, having clocked him often on training tracks. 'You should know an old friend, no matter what sort of suit he's wearing,' he explained disarmingly later.*

Even equipped with a strong conviction, it took considerable courage and a good deal of research for Bert Wolfe to make the bold statement: 'Redlock is a ring-in.' This he did in the Herald *on 14 August 1934. At the time the* Herald *announced the whereabouts of the real Redlock. The sports editor, Fred Laby, found the horse in a paddock near Malmsbury, Victoria, informed the Victoria Racing Club, and returned the next day with VRC officials who confirmed the horse's identity.*

The Herald *announced its exposure of the fraud in this fashion:*

Redlock, the gelding which won the Trial Stakes at Murray Bridge in such a sensational manner on July 28, and which won a seven-furlong race by 12 lengths at Kadina (S.A.) on Saturday, is a "ring-in."

While these races were being run the real Redlock was grazing in a paddock near Malmsbury, where he was located by the sporting editor of The Herald on Saturday and inspected by officials of the Victoria Racing Club yesterday.

"Cardigan," The Herald's turf writer, who went to Kadina to see the gelding which ran in the name of Redlock, wires from Adelaide today as follows:—

"I am satisfied that the gelding which raced at Kadina on Saturday is not Redlock, but is Erbie. Erbie has been disqualified for life. He is a gelding with many names. Last year he raced at Holbrook (N.S.W.) as Duke Bombita. On November 28, last year, he won in sensational manner at Kilmore as Chrybean, and now he has re-appeared as Redlock."

Below are given the facts which expose one of the most audacious frauds in the history of Australian racing.

'Cardigan' wrote from Adelaide:

I have no hesitation in asserting that the gelding which raced at Kadina on Saturday is our old friend Erbie in a new guise.

I know Erbie well. I have watched him race and win on numerous occasions in Sydney and on the provincial tracks within the metropolitan radius. I have watched Erbie work at Randwick and have timed his gallops frequently. I know his markings and his characteristics, and, after seeing "Redlock" win the trial handicap at the Kadina and Wallaroo meeting on Saturday, I say definitely that "Redlock" is Erbie.

He still has his heavy tail and the half white sock on his near hind leg, with exactly the same jagged edges where the white hairs meet the brown. But this time he hasn't a blaize down his face, and his brands are different. How those changes have come about I cannot tell.

But, despite his new face, the gelding is Erbie, who won many races in Sydney under big weights in good company and who is now a disqualified horse.

In the Handicap Trial Stakes of seven furlongs at Kadina on Saturday, "Redlock" carried 8.7 and won by a dozen lengths in 1.27 on a track which was a red mud-heap.

The going made no difference to "Redlock." He jumped to the front soon after the start and with P. Slattery sitting still on him he cantered round the turn ten lengths in front of the field.

His rider urged him along in the straight, and "Redlock," stretching out in Erbie's best style, increased his lead, winning by 12 lengths.

After the race "Redlock" was put on a float and taken back 100 miles to Adelaide, where he is stabled at Shadrick's, opposite Morphettville Racecourse.

"Redlock" was not backed by his connections on Saturday. The reason for taking him to Kadina to run for a £20 stake is one of the mysteries associated with the horse.

An interesting sidelight on events at Kadina on Saturday was the arrival of a horse called Gold Ray entered for the Copper City Cup in the owner-trainership of C. Prince, owner-trainer of Redlock. The horse Gold Ray was in charge of Rupert Coughlin, who was the nominator of Erbie as Duke Bombita at Holbrook and who is now disqualified for life.

'Cardigan' challenged the trainer of the horse which raced as Redlock, Charles Prince. This is what he wrote in the same issue about the confrontation:

A tense drama of the turf was enacted in the dusk at Morphettville yesterday evening.

While detectives and racing officials were examining the horse which won at Murray Bridge and Kadina as Redlock, and C. Prince, who figures as the trainer of the horse, was standing by, I said to Prince: "The Herald says this horse is a ring-in, and his right name is Erbie."

Prince did not answer for a minute, and then he replied: "The Herald may be right, and may be wrong, but all I know of this horse is that I bought him for £30 from a man in a hotel in Melbourne, and if he is wrong, then I do not know anything about it. I don't know anything about other men who had horses at Sunbury. I am on my own, and that's all about it."

It was not until The Herald's story of the finding of the real Redlock at Malmsbury, and his definite identification became known that South Australian Jockey Club officials decided to take action.

The chairman of the stipendiary stewards (Mr Hogan) was holidaying in the country, and it was not until after 4 o'clock yesterday afternoon that the S.A.J.C. advised him to return to the city.

In the meanwhile, the secretary (Mr Reg. Hynes), and the racecourse detective (Mr Duncan Fraser) went to Morphettville, and after questioning Prince on various aspects of the case, asked him whether he would consent — (this is necessary under the Rules of Racing) — to the horse being taken charge of by the S.A.J.C., and a guard being placed on him.

Prince made no demur, and said that the club could do as it liked. . .

Charles Prince, who had painted Erbie and trained him when he raced under the name of Redlock, was sent to jail for two years, after having been found guilty of 'fraudulent and corrupt practices'. He was also disqualified from Australian racecourses for life, but the disqualification was lifted twenty years later by the South Australian Jockey Club as an amnesty gesture to mark the 1954 visit to Australia of Queen Elizabeth.

Bert Wolfe was commended by the SAJC stewards for his help in exposing the fraud. When he died on 6 April 1968, another turf writer, Bill Casey, of the Sydney Sun, *wrote of him: '"Cardigan" was probably the best-known turf journalist Australia has known, and almost a legend in his own time. He was a dominating personality, a prolific and probing writer, and a fine man.'*

1934 The case of the 'Pyjama Girl' remains unsolved for ten years

RON McKIE
Melbourne Sun News-Pictorial, 3 September 1934

On 1 September 1934, a young farmer, walking along the Albury-Howlong Road, about four miles from the Murray River border town of Albury, saw a woman's legs protruding from a culvert. That find began one of the most famous cases in Australian criminal history — the Pyjama Girl Mystery.

The body, burnt and battered, belonged to a woman aged about twenty-five. It was held in a bath of crushed ice at Albury for some days, and then embalmed and transferred to a formalin bath at Sydney University for six years. Many hundreds of people visited the body at the university; it became one of the city's more bizarre attractions. In the first month of the investigation, detectives found eighteen people who gave 'positive identification' of the body. In New South Wales and Victoria, 3000 files of missing women were sifted. For many weeks, detectives inquired into the background of every woman in the 'pyjama girl's' age group who had not voted in the 1934 general election.

When no real lead was found in Australia, police forces around the world became involved, all of them checking out details of missing women. Police made a film about the mystery, appealing to picture goers around the country for information. The file on the 'pyjama girl' grew into a virtual library and for ten years it was the great unsolved case of Australia. One Hamburg newspaper, commenting on the scope of international inquiries, called it the world's most expensive murder.

After an examination by Professor A. N. Burkett, Sydney University's Professor of Anatomy, police were convinced that the body belonged to an Englishwoman who had been raised in limestone country; the professor had based his opinion on the girl's strong teeth, which he felt had been due to habitual drinking of lime-impregnated water.

Then, in March 1944, Victorian and New South Wales police arrested an Italian waiter, Antonio Agostini, forty-one, and charged him with murder. After an inquest the victim was held to be Linda Agostini, and Agostini, the murdered woman's husband, was committed for trial on a charge of murder. On 30 June 1944, Agostini was found guilty of manslaughter but not guilty of murder. He was sentenced to gaol for six years, and later deported to Italy.

Two reporters who covered the case were Ron McKie, of the Melbourne Sun News-Pictorial, *and Hugh Buggy, of the Melbourne* Herald. *It was after Buggy and photographer Bert Rodda pointed out that the girl in the ice bath was developing some green spots on her cheeks that Detective Sergeant Len Allmond arranged for a quick transfer to the formalin. Ron McKie later became a war correspondent and author of stature; in 1974 he won the Miles Franklin award for the best Australian novel of the year. This was his first report on the 'Pyjama Girl' case:*

Although nearly 48 hours have elapsed since the battered and charred body of a pretty blonde girl was discovered in a culvert on the Howlong Road, four and a half miles west of Albury, the identity of the victim of a brutal assault has not been established.

Police consider the girl was murdered last Tuesday night, and that the attempt to burn the body, after it had been placed in the culvert, was made early on Wednesday morning.

As no girls have been reported missing in

Albury district, police believe the body was carried many miles, either from Victoria, or another district of N.S.W. before the attempt was made to dispose of it. A blood-stained towel with a laundry mark either R.I.W. or R.I.N., which was tied around the girl's head, is one of the most important clues.

The description of the victim issued today is: Between 20 and 30 years of age; 5ft. 2 or 3 in. in height; slim to medium build; blue-grey eyes; ash blonde, might be peroxided, bobbed hair, darker at the roots; neck shaved; plucked eyebrows; pink lacquered, well-manicured finger nails; two teeth missing in rear lower jaw, and one gold filled tooth in back lower jaw right side.

The girl wore no jewellery, and was clothed in expensive canary-colored Canton crepe pyjamas. The coat was edged with white crepe, but the white trousers were edged with yellow. The white bath towel found tied round her head had a double and single red stripe at either end.

The left side of the head had been smashed, and there was a large hole in the forehead, considered to have been caused by some heavy instrument, probably the back of an axe or tomahawk. The post-mortem examination today revealed that death was due to a fractured skull, and that the girl had been dead between four and five days. There was no indication of an illegal operation.

The fingerprints of the dead girl were taken by Sergeant Blackman today and have been forwarded to Melbourne and Sydney.

The body was found on Saturday at 9 a.m. by Thomas Hunter Griffith, son of Mr. and Mrs. Charles Griffith, of Delaware station. . . .

Griffith immediately hurried to his home and notified Albury police. It was found that kerosene had been used in an attempt to burn the body, and the legs were charred.

The girl's hands were clasped behind her head.

The brickwork near the mouth of the pipe, which was 20in. in diameter, was blackened by the flames, and grass near the drain scorched.

After removing the body, the police searched the ground in the vicinity and drained the water from the pipe in the hope that some

The Albury Fire Brigade dragging the Murray River for clues

clue would be found.

Near the southern end of the drain they found that a large quantity of kerosene used to burn the body had been washed through the drain. Heavy rain fell on Tuesday night and up to 9 a.m. on Wednesday, proof that the body must have been placed in the drain either before the rain fell or while it was falling.

As it would be almost impossible to start a fire in the rain, and it rained very heavily after midnight on Tuesday, it is most probable that the body was placed there before midnight on that day.

Detective-Sergeant Allmond, who arrived from Sydney today with Detective McDermott to take charge of investigations, considers that his most important clue is the bath towel.

Residents at a farmhouse about half a mile from the culvert did not see anything suspicious on Tuesday night, but Mr. Griffith said today that late on Friday night he saw car lights shining near where the body was found. The next day deep wheel marks in the grass on the north side of the road were discovered. . .

1934   Scott and Black win the great Centenary Air Race from London to Melbourne

CRAYTON BURNS AND ALLAN DAWES
Melbourne Star, 13 and 23 October 1934

The 1934 Centenary air race, from London to Melbourne, was the most exciting contest the nation had known. 'Even Test match excitement has been easily eclipsed,' wrote the Australian Press Association correspondent in London at the time.

Flying was big news then. Bert Hinkler, Sir Charles Kingsford Smith, C. T. P. Ulm, Jim Mollison, Amy Johnson, Ray Parer and Charles Lindbergh had been making history for a few years, and now twenty-seven machines were flying over 11,323 miles of snow-covered alps, burning desert sands, towns, cities, wheat fields, rice fields and long tracts of ocean. It was enough to make minds boggle, and it was all ending in Melbourne.

Crayton Burns, in Melbourne's Star, *captured the general mood when he wrote on 13 October, one week before the start:*

Picture these machines, double-engined, triple-engined, streamlined with tapering wings, retractable undercarriages, directional wireless, robot pilots, wind drift indicators, and all the other gadgets. Whirring propellors, purring engines . . . pilots in closed sound-proof and wind-proof cockpits, in touch with the world by wireless . . . fussing mechanics . . . the great oil companies of the world interested . . . international rivalry stirred, not in mortal combat, but in homeric sport.

All the world is looking on at this race. In a sense it is a trade conflict between the manufacturers of the world, but to the peoples of the world it arouses not national rivalry so much as good sportsmanship among the nations. For personal reasons I would like to see Ray Parer do well. I know him, and like and admire him, but I do not even expect or hope that he will win. I am merely curious to

see whether an American, an Englishman, an Australian, a Frenchman, a Dane or an Italian wins. Admiration for all of them overwhelms all other thoughts, and this, I am sure, is the feeling of millions of people of all the competing nations, and of other nations also.

Those lovable, capable, navigators and airmen the Dutch say beforehand that they do not expect to win. All they aspire to is to be on the tails of the winners. The Dutch, you see, are flying only their everyday working buses, that carry mails and passengers every day over the Dutch air lines; so to be past the winning line at Flemington on October 23 or 24 with the first ten machines will be a triumph for them, considering that they will be racing machines built specially for speed, and built at a cost of tens of thousands of pounds on purpose to compete in this race. But the Dutch will be hard to beat for the handicap race, which is based solely on commercial utility. . .

We all hope that none of them crashes in the mountains or is lost in the Bay of Bengal, but it would be foolish to deny the possibility that some of those fearless men and women — some of the most daring of the human race — might be flying in the face of death. The Americans, even the British and the Australians — not to mention the Irishman — and certainly the Latin races, are represented by men who will take the risks, despite every effort that has been made to ensure safety. . .

In fact one British plane, a Fairey Fox, did crash in Italy, and both occupants were incinerated. Allan Dawes covered the finish of the big race for the Star, *the new afternoon paper which was fighting hard against the* Herald; *apart from Dawes, the new paper had*

R.A.A.F. men chaired the popular C. J. Melrose after the 1934 England-Australia air race. He was the only Australian contestant and the only solo flier. A proud Mrs Melrose stands at right.

attracted such journalistic notables as Jack Waters (later editor of the Sun *and editor-in-chief of the Herald and Weekly Times), King Watson (later editor of the* Daily Telegraph, Sydney), *Cyril Pearl (later editor of the* Sunday Telegraph, Sydney), *Cecil Edwards (later editor of the* Herald, Melbourne), *Reg Leonard (later managing director of Queensland Newspapers), Dick Hughes (later a renowned foreign correspondent) and Allan Burbury (later manager of the* Sun).

Dawes was a man of rare ingenuity. On the day after Scott and Black won the race, he tried to interview the fliers at Menzies' Hotel. Told that they were not seeing anyone from the Star *because they had sold their stories exclusively elsewhere, Dawes borrowed some clothing material from a friend who worked at the One Price Tailors shop; when he was stopped outside the door, he announced that he had come to measure Mr Scott for a free suit which his tailoring office wanted to present to him. He was quickly recognised, and rebuffed. Next he began arrangements with another friend, who owned a painting company, to be lowered down the front wall of Menzies' on a platform to look and listen while the aviators were dictating their stories*

to the opposition. While these arrangements were still progressing, the young cadet reporter assisting Dawes, R. R. Walker, heard a call in the hotel lounge: 'Is the Herald *copy boy about?' Walker promptly answered the call, and was allowed into the ante-room of the fliers' suite to await the copy which was to go to the* Herald *office. Before he was recognised as a* Star *representative, and summarily thrown out, Walker had some ten minutes listening and watching as Scott dictated and accepted congratulatory cables. He was able to provide Dawes with enough good first-person material for a front-page story.*

This is Allan Dawes' report of the end of the great race:

Like a huge crimson-winged bullet, C. W. A. Scott's Comet, with T. Campbell Black as co-pilot, dipped and swept across the finishing line at Flemington at 3.34 p.m. to-day, winner of the Centenary Air Race.

They had made the flight from England to Melbourne in two days, 23 hours, 18 seconds.

Tumultuous cheering arose from the crowded stands at Flemington when a small speck appeared, developed into the unfamiliar shape of the Comet, and hurtled over the course.

Parmentier, the Hollander, with three other pilots and four passengers, is on his way to Charleville.

Flying on one engine, Scott, who left Darwin at 11.34 p.m. yesterday (Melbourne time) reached Charleville (Queensland) at 8.40 a.m. to-day.

He left Charleville for Melbourne at 11 a.m.

The Dutch machine reached Darwin at 9 a.m. to-day (Melbourne time) and left soon afterwards for Charleville by way of Normanton and Cloncurry.

Following the Hollanders are the Americans, Roscoe Turner and Clyde Pangborn. They left Singapore at 9.5 p.m. yesterday (Melbourne time), seven hours behind the Dutchmen.

Tense and expectant, 30,000 people were gathered at Flemington racecourse by 2 p.m. to-day to witness the dramatic finish of the world's greatest air race. Despite ominous clouds and announcements of an approaching storm, streams of sightseers continued to flow into the racecourse. . .

The 13 Air Force planes wheeling and flying in mass formation lagged behind the Comet's breakneck speed on its arrival at Flemington.

Cheering was renewed when the Comet, after swinging away to the west, swept around and circled the ground again.

"Scott has won the greatest race in the history of aviation," the official announcer declared through the amplifier.

Cheering broke out again.

The official party had risen in excitement from the seats behind the great dais. The Lord Mayor, Sir Macpherson Robertson, waved his hat, and the judge (Wing-Commander Cole) raised his arm.

After its second triumphant progress over the course, the twin-engined Comet thundered away to Laverton.

The excitement in the crowd simmered down and the stands and hill awaited expectantly for the return of Scott and his co-pilot in Air Force planes for their personal reception at the racecourse.

At 3.34 p.m. the signal was flashed through to Laverton that Scott's Comet had crossed the line and won.

Mr. A. O. Edwards, who is the nominator of the machine, was waiting at Laverton.

He was obviously under great emotional stress. "Are they really over the line," he asked. "Thank Heaven!"

Nine minutes later the Comet circled the Laverton aerodrome and made a perfect landing.

It stopped in less than 300 yards, wheeled gracefully round, and taxied into the great Air Force hangar.

The first to greet Scott with a wave of the hand was Mr. Edwards, then Miss Jean Batten congratulated him on his success.

It was almost a minute before Scott and Black could force their way out and climb down into the arms of the crowd of friends awaiting them.

The most dignified officials present shouted themselves hoarse. The din was terrific.

Broadly smiling, the airmen were guided through the crowd to a small control-room in the hangar, where refreshments awaited them.

After about five minutes, Scott, who had a growth of Viking beard, obviously not having shaved since he left London, and Black, who was almost clean shaven, emerged from the hangar office and walked over to the corner where their machine was housed.

Officials, who had linked hands to provide the airmen with some sort of a bodyguard, escorted them.

They made their way to the De Havilland Comet, and posed before the machine for press photographers.

Campbell Black appeared a strange figure in a waterproof golfing jacket, plus fours, and an incongruous pair of huge fur-lined felt slippers.

Scott was in a fawn-coloured waterproof jacket with plus fours and socks to match, and a thick pair of brogues.

Newspaper representatives tried to interview the airmen, but they were temporarily almost stone deaf. . .

"It was a dreadful trip, and that's praising it," Scott said to "The Star" representative after he had checked in and had handed over special pictures, which he had brought for "The Star" from London, Darwin, and Charleville. . .

Egon Kisch breaks a leg jumping into Australia

BRIAN FITZPATRICK
Melbourne Herald, 12 November 1934

One of the most celebrated cases involving Australia's immigration laws concerned the arrival in November 1934 of the Czech communist journalist and novelist Egon Kisch. Kisch sailed from Marseilles in the liner Strathaird *to attend the Anti-War Congress in Melbourne; the congress was organised largely by communists, and its 'anti-war' label was another name for a hate campaign against Hitler and Mussolini. The Australian Government of the time, which had rebuked even H. G. Wells a little earlier for 'insulting' these leaders of 'friendly nations', was in a sensitive mood.*

The Government was determined not to allow Kisch to enter Australia; the methods it adopted quickly transformed the whole affair into a farce. He was refused permission to disembark from his ship at Fremantle, and he attempted to solve his problems in Melbourne by jumping overboard. Kisch succeeded only in breaking a leg, and was hustled back on board; the police who took him back on to the ship were promptly charged by Kisch's friends ashore with kidnapping, arguing that once he had actually set foot on Australian soil he could not be deported without some legal reason.

The Government then decided to use its bizarre but powerful weapon: the dictation test. The first Federal Parliament had armed itself, under the Immigration Restriction Act of 1901, with a language test which was really aimed at giving effect to the popular demand for the exclusion of Asians.

Under this Act, any immigrant might be required to write out at official dictation a passage of fifty words in any European language. It was understood when this test was introduced that European immigrants would not be required to pass it, but it was used from time to time as a sneaky, effective means of prohibiting undesirable persons from landing.

On 16 November, Kisch, carried on a stretcher, officially entered Australia amid loud cheering. His glory was short-lived; he was quickly taken to a police station and submitted to a dictation test. Kisch, a brilliant scholar, could have coped with many European languages, but the test was carried out in Scottish Gaelic. Not surprisingly, since only one in 600 native Scots then spoke the language, Kisch failed.

Kisch was jailed briefly as a result. His crime was to have entered the country as a prohibited immigrant. But later, to the dismay of some local Scottish patriots, the High Court reversed Kisch's conviction, deciding that Scottish Gaelic was not a European language within the meaning of the Act.

Kisch stayed in Australia until 11 March 1935. For most of this time he was a free person. With his right leg in plaster for some of the time, his movements were somewhat restricted, but he still managed to tour Australia and to address meetings from north Queensland to Fremantle. The Commonwealth Government was ordered to pay the costs of his legal proceedings, which amounted to £1,524.

Egon Kisch was finally deported after he had been submitted to another dictation test in another language, the European nature of which could not be disputed. He lived in exile in Mexico for most of the Second World War, and later returned to Czechoslovakia to become Minister for Education in the country's first post-war government. He died in 1948, aged sixty-two.

It was fitting that Kisch's jump should have been covered by Brian Fitzpatrick, of the Melbourne Herald. *Fitzpatrick, a historian as well as a fine journalist, was a great believer in individual liberties; when he died in September 1965, at the age of sixty-two, he was general secretary of the Australian Council for Civil Liberties. He worked on the* Age, *the London* Sunday Express, *the Sydney* Telegraph *and the Sydney* World *as well as the Melbourne* Herald.

Leaping eight feet from the lower after deck of the Strathaird, 10 minutes before the ship sailed for Sydney today, Egon Erwin Kisch, the banned Czechoslovakian novelist and lecturer, who shortly before had lost his appeal to the courts, made a dramatic landing on Station Pier, Port Melbourne.

Catching one foot against a steel cable on the pier as he landed, Kisch sprained his ankle and fell.

As he was assisted to his feet by friends who had gathered on the pier, a policeman approached.

"Hurt yourself?" the constable inquired, and began to assist Kisch along.

The jump for freedom had been observed by only a few people, although hundreds were present to see the ship off. Detectives were on the watch, however, and two of them came up to the injured man.

"This is the man," they said, and proceeded to conduct Kisch toward a gangplank that led amidships.

He protested against being returned to the ship.

"You can arrest me," he said, "but I am on shore now, and you have no right to put me back on the ship."

The plea was not listened to, however.

Half carried by the detectives, Kisch was hurried aboard, under the streamers and waving hands of hundreds of sightseers who, unaware of what had happened, were farewelling friends...

The jump for the shore followed the reception of the news on board the liner that the Court had quashed the move to have Kisch released.

Kisch, although he had assured friends and interviewers that he did not expect to be released in Melbourne, was greatly cast down by the official verdict.

Talking to a representative of The Herald on the deck, he said:—

"To have come 18,000 miles for this!" Going to the rail and looking down a pier, he asked, "Do you think I could jump ashore? They would arrest me but they would not put me back on the ship. They cannot do that."

He was advised against doing that.

Utterly depressed, he bade farewell to a group of University students and other sympathisers.

These went ashore, and joined a party on the pier, who waited near the after-side of the ship for a last word with Kisch.

Some Melbourne Communists were in the group here. When Kisch appeared at the rail above them, some of them shouted, "Why don't you come ashore?"

Kisch indicated the steward who was in more or less close attendance on him. He walked away from the rail, and some of his friends began to move off, thinking that he had gone to his cabin.

A moment later, and quite unexpectedly, he reappeared, scrambled over the ship's side, and jumped.

He had not trod twenty paces on an Australian pier before the first of the police watchers approached him, with the kindly inquiry about his ankle.

Recognised instantly, he was hurried, protesting fluently, back to a gangway. His right ankle had been badly injured.

Detectives stated that as the commander of the Strathaird (Captain Carter) was under a £200 bond for the safe custody of Kisch, and had asked for the man to be returned, they were in order in placing him aboard again.

Suffering from his injured and swollen ankle, and bitterly resentful at having been banned by the Federal authorities, Kisch, before the Strathaird sailed, complained of police interference with conversations he had with visitors on the ship, and of interruptions throughout last night by officials, who rapped on his cabin door to ascertain if he were still present...

1934   The dedication of Melbourne's Shrine of Remembrance is witnessed by thousands

BRIAN FITZPATRICK
Melbourne Herald, 12 November 1934

The building of Melbourne's Shrine of Remembrance, an imposing granite structure on a hill in the Domain, south of the Yarra River, was preceded by considerable public controversy. About three years after the end of the First World War, the decision was taken to provide a fitting memorial for the 60,000 Australians who had lost their lives in the war.

The State Government and the Melbourne City Council each agreed to contribute £50,000 over a period of years for a 'non-utilitarian memorial'. Twenty sites around Melbourne were considered before the Domain was chosen. Then a design contest began, open to all Australian artists, architects and designers. Eighty-three designs were submitted, and after several months' consideration, the first prize was awarded to the Melbourne architects, Hudson and Wardrop. Almost immediately, violent controversy began; some critics favored the second-prize design, others wanted a civic square as a memorial, others wanted a hospital. It was nearly four years before the War Memorial general committee confirmed its original approval of both the site and the winning design.

The dedication of the Shrine, on 11 November 1934, was an immensely moving occasion. It was performed by the Duke of Gloucester during his centenary-year visit to Victoria. Ten thousand pigeons were released, 28,000 ex-servicemen and women marched, and 200,000 watched. The ode to commemorate the occasion, subsequently printed in bronze, was written by Rudyard Kipling.

Brian Fitzpatrick wrote this description of the event for the Melbourne Herald:

Sunday, November 11, 1934, at 9 a.m., of a fine, fitful day. We are standing a few feet from the southern steps leading up to the granite stack of the Shrine of Remembrance, that we prefer not to know by its alternative title, the National War Memorial. From our eminence, 50 feet above St. Kilda Road, where the cars are marching endlessly, and 82 feet above the calm blue of Port Phillip Bay and Albert Park Lake, we look out over the south-eastern and south-western slopes, lawns soft to the pilgrim's feet.

Although the eastern and western margins of our perspective's quadrant are darkening with humanity, the broad south way to the foot of the Shrine is clear. Up this ascent, presently, the old battalions will quickstep again.

Towards this green hill, set in the garden of Melbourne, towards its memorial cap of uniform grey, the people of Victoria — one from every family — are converging. Policemen's white helmets are lost in the hosting of the people. Troopers' groomed mounts are seen, are cloaked, and vanish. Scarlet facings are obliterated from the jackets of the picketing gunners. Their blue jackets are neutralised by the imperceptible chemistry of the multitude. . .

A tiny section of those who now possess the hillside have white tickets to frank them into an enclosure from which they may reach out to touch the Duke of Gloucester when he comes to dedicate the Shrine. Others have red, others blue, tickets — 5000 who today are the musicians, the minstrels, whose voices shall praise.

But there are no tickets in the hands of the majority, the innumerable, hydra-headed, the patient, the voiceless. These, a quarter million of the people of Victoria, come with no colored pasteboard in their hands, nor any expectation of seeing the princely cortege pass. They come for the purpose of the Shrine, the remembrance of the State of Victoria's 18,000 men who died in the war of 1914—18. . .

We stand on the hill, with our white tickets in hand, and look down on those whose day it is, by virtue of the men of the people who died in war sixteen, eighteen years ago. We look up at the people's monument to their dead men. Why, the very granite groups about its base were set in place by the children of the people, whose pennies made £10,000 to set the figures up. Peace here, Justice there!

The bands are playing below to marshal the men, for whom the broad way to the Shrine has been cleared. There is movement beyond the trees. A column swings into view, and wheels to the north towards the Shrine. Another and another and another. They wear no uniform, save the drab of the crowd.

A current of excitement runs through the enclosures badged with the white tickets, the red and the blue. For who of us ever saw, before today, a score of thousands of men, un-uniformed, march up a gentle hill? Saw them from the hilltop so that, so many abreast, wide rank on rank, the whole concourse, steadily advancing, stretched itself before the awed eye. . .

Well, it is 10.45, and a cortege with the Duke of Gloucester and the Governor of Victoria in it, moves up through the old soldiers and round the western terrace of the Shrine to the northern entrance. The Duke has entered the Inner Shrine; on our side the color parties turn about to face south. Black-coated Shrine trustees and khaki officers are in position before them.

Trumpeters blow G, there is a blast of gunfire. Within, the Duke is placing the King's wreath, of poppies and bays, on the Rock of Remembrance. It is 11 a.m., Armistice Hour, and the sun, that shone a moment ago, is dimmed so that the ray of light which only at this hour falls upon the black granite of the Rock illumines but faintly the word LOVE on its inscription, Greater Love Hath No Man. For two minutes the people are utterly silent. The sun re-emerges. . .

"The Old Hundredth" from the slopes and the choirs in the enclosure, the Dedicatory Ode of Rudyard Kipling read by the Premier of Victoria — then, at 11.18, the Duke steps forward to dedicate the Shrine, the flag is drawn aside, the blue jackets thunder a roll of drums and the trumpeters sound a fanfare.

But the people will sing a hymn. They are here to mourn. What says the hymn?
"For frantic boast and foolish word,
Thy mercy on Thy people, Lord!"
What said the Premier in his speech?
"We are here, not in frantic boast of victory. . ."
What says the dedicatory ode he read, of the people whose dead men the Shrine commemorates?
"They, scoffing at all talk of sacrifice,
Gave themselves, without idle words, to death."
Yet (so the ode says, too) the name that the dead men — and these, the living, behind the barriers — blazoned for Australia on the battlefields of the world "shall outlive Troy's tale, when Time is old." . . .

Chopin's Funeral March, through the silence of the multitude, and a Benediction from the Archbishop of Melbourne. After the Benediction the bands — oh, irony of someone's insensibility! — play "Martial Moments." The National Anthem is played, the Duke departs, the Anthem is played again, and the trumpeters blow the Royal Salute.

From the upper gallery of the Shrine a host of pigeons is released, for a symbol of the news of peace. They fly eastward, and wheel in a lovely convolution against the background of a great, dark, low-lying rain cloud. Just before the last rendering of the National Anthem the pigeons are lost in the distance.

And so are the people of Victoria. The slopes show raggedly again the character they had before the multitude possessed them. Again the southern road to the Shrine is clear. The old battalions are broken up, gone, soldiers are men, individuals again. "Troops will disperse independently."

In a generation, there will be no more old soldiers to march up the hill and stand with bowed heads behind the barriers; no more widows and orphans to lay wreaths when the ceremonial is done and the people are given access to their Shrine. . .

200,000 spectators crowded to see the opening of the Shrine

1935   A shark is sick and a fascinating murder mystery is revealed

SID KING
Sydney Daily Telegraph, 14 June 1935

One of the most fascinating Australian crimes ever was the Shark Arm Murder. The story broke on 25 April 1935, at the Sydney seaside suburb of Coogee, as a few people were watching a captured shark circling an aquarium. Suddenly they saw the water lashed to foam, a scum appeared on the surface, and, as the shark quietened, a man's arm lay on the bottom of the pool. Fished out, it was found to have a piece of rope lashed to the wrist. Two boxers were tattooed on the forearm.

The arm was identified from fingerprints as that of James Smith, a billiard marker, who had one conviction for illegal starting-price betting. He had been missing since 8 April, when he told his wife he was going for a week-end's fishing to Port Hacking, a few miles south of Sydney.

Police recalled that Smith had been mixed up in the suspicious destruction of a luxury yacht, the Pathfinder, *which had caught fire and foundered off the coast in April of the previous year. Smith, the only man aboard, had swum ashore. The owner, a wealthy boat-builder named Reginald Holmes, had bought the* Pathfinder *for £11,000 and had insured it for a great deal more. Police who investigated the circumstances surrounding the fire were certain that a big smuggling ring, with Holmes as a member, had been operating in and around Sydney. They could not get enough evidence to bring anyone to court, but the insurance company refused to meet Holmes' claim on the* Pathfinder, *and it was not pressed.*

Police theory on the Shark Arm case was that Smith had either been blackmailing Holmes or had threatened to expose the smuggling ring because he had not received the promised payment for destroying the Pathfinder. *They believed he had been lured to a hut at Port Hacking, murdered, dismembered, packed into a tin trunk and dropped out at sea. The theory was that a small shark had somehow eaten the arm, and that it had in turn been eated by a larger shark which was captured on 18 April when it was entangled in a fisherman's set line at Coogee. An expert said that the temperature of the water could have affected the digestion of the shark so that the arm remained undigested for more than a week.*

Police had a number of interviews with Holmes, who seemed excitable and erratic. In May, police received a report that a motor launch occupied by one man was careering madly around Sydney Harbour. They ran the boat down in a police launch, and found Holmes with blood flowing from a bullet wound in the head. He said he had been fired on by another man, but this story was so inconsistent and incoherent that they believed he had attempted suicide. The wound was superficial, and after a short stay in hospital Holmes was allowed to go home.

A couple of weeks later a well-known forger, Patrick Brady, was arrested and charged with Smith's murder. Police later claimed that he had been seen with a suitcase similar to Smith's, after Smith's murder, and that he had been drinking with Smith on the day of the murder.

The inquest on Smith was set down for 12 June, and Holmes was to be the chief prosecution witness. At 8 p.m. on 11 June, Holmes received a telephone call; he told his wife he had an urgent meeting, and left home in his car. At 1 a.m., police saw a parked car with its headlights burning; they pulled up and shook the driver, who appeared to be asleep. He was Holmes, and he had been shot dead.

The Telegraph

LIGHTEN THE PEOPLE'S BURDENS!

Vol. 5. No. 101   SYDNEY, THURSDAY, JUNE 13, 1935   PRI

CITY FORECAST: Cloudy, With Showers.

LATE CITY EDITION

STARTLING MURDER DEVELO

Previous Attempt On Life Of Victim?

NEW POLICE THEORY IN HOLMES CASE

NEW and vital facts were revealed yesterday following the murder of Reginald William Holmes, boat-builder, whose body, pierced by three bullets, was found in a car in Hickson Road, City, early yesterday morning.

Chief of the new developments was the growing belief that at least one previous attempt had been made on Holmes's life.

On May 20, with a bullet wound in his head, he drove a speed-boat around the Harbor for four hours, until captured by the police.

Mr. Reginald William Holmes, McMahon's Point boatbuilder, who was found murdered in his car in Hickson Road, Dawes Point, early yesterday morning. He was to have been an important witness at the "tattooed arm" case inquest.

King's Again Causi

OFFICIAL BULLETIN IS ISSUED

Has Bronchial Trouble And Must Rest

(SPECIAL BEAM SERVICE)

LONDON, Wednesday.

THE King's health is again causing concern, and the following official bulletin has been issued:

"The King is suffering from bronchial catarrh, which is slow in disappearing, because his Majesty is fatigued by the efforts of the last few weeks.

"At least a fortnight's rest is

THE K

TAXES I STA

INSTALMENT

Front page of the *Telegraph* reporting the murder of Holmes

The reporters on the case included Sid King of the Daily Telegraph, *Vince Kelly of the* Sydney Sun, *Geoff Hawksley of* Truth *and Jack Hatch of the* Daily Telegraph. *Hatch got an exclusive for his paper's final edition that morning on the death of the key witness in the shark-arm inquest. Unfortunately, it referred to Holmes as the 'chief police witness in today's coronial inquiry into the murder of James Smith, the Shark Arm victim'. In his haste, Hatch had used the wrong word — 'murder', rather than 'death'. Brady's counsel, Mr Clive Evatt, promptly had a writ for contempt of court served on the* Daily Telegraph. *It cost the paper £500.*

The police by this time were fairly uncommunicative with reporters. There were large squads of them working on the case, and they had just failed to protect their most important witness in what was being dubbed

Australia's most famous crime. Sid King, a very capable investigator in his own right, clashed with senior police officers, who were understandably a little touchy, and began making his own inquiries.

King later wrote that he had received a tip from Hatch, his colleague, that the police had a man named Oliver Summers smoked away in a cheap little pub not far from where Holmes had been shot.

Sid King's exclusive story on Summers was one of the newspaper coups of the Shark Arm case, and is reprinted here:

Another day of public probing into the murder of Reginald William Holmes, who was found shot dead in his own car in Hickson Road, City, early on Wednesday morning, has established several important points, which reveal:—

The murder was committed at about 9 p.m.

on Tuesday.

One man heard the shots at that time and saw a crouching stranger hurrying away from the car which, even then, was standing at the kerb with the lights shining.

Three men have come forward to state that on Tuesday night they heard shots fired in the vicinity of Hickson Road, and one almost stumbled upon the man who police consider was implicated in the crime.

The statements by these informants have caused the investigators to alter their conclusions of the time of the shooting, as all three agree that they heard the shots at approximately 9 p.m.

This means that police need no longer attempt to trace Holmes's movements from the time he left home until about midnight, when it was first considered he had been slain.

Investigations have extended to country centres and to other states, for it has been learned that Holmes made frequent trips from Sydney in the course of his business.

How near the murderer was to being caught in the act of committing the cold-blooded crime is told in a story related to police by one of the men who heard the shots.

Out for a stroll, he was slowly descending the flight of steps leading from Lower Fort Street to Hickson Road, when there was a volley of staccato reports, close at hand.

"They sound like shots," he thought to himself, pausing, and straining his ears.

He continued to descend, and, when a few steps from the bottom, saw a strange figure slink past. From his elevated position he caught a glimpse of the man's face, but it was his peculiar slinking gait that aroused his curiosity.

It was if the man was trying to restrain himself from appearing to hurry, and at the same time make himself as inconspicuous as possible.

As the watcher reached the street level he saw, about 25 yards away, a sedan car. The headlights were burning and he was immediately reassured.

To him the car explained the reports as backfires, and the fact that the headlights were on suggested a "petting party".

For fear of intruding on a couple of lovers he turned away from the car, and took the direction of the man he had seen, and who was then some 30 yards ahead.

They continued in this manner for about 100 yards, when the man with the peculiar gait became hidden by a bend in the road. On reaching the bend, the stroller was amazed that the man was out of sight.

He was meditating on this when he was startled by a slight noise, and, looking round, saw a man stooping over a fishing basket.

They looked at each other, then the stroller retraced his steps with a feeling that he had had enough mystery for one night.

On Wednesday night the stroller and the fisherman faced each other again, this time under the glare of the electric light at the CIB.

The recognition was mutual, and the stroller, who had been described accurately to the police by the fisherman, was relieved to be able to give an explanation of their meeting.

The police have not definitely established a motive for the murder of Holmes. In their endeavour to do so, they are tracing his past life, both in business and privately, as minutely as possible.

Besides his boat building business, Holmes was known at one stage to have dabbled considerably in real estate.

Holmes, it is understood, was insured for approximately £5000 with a big city company.

The detectives, directed by the chief of the CIB (Mr. Prior) engaged on the case are Detective Sergeants Matthews, Allmond, Baker, Detectives A. W. Burns, Calman and McDermott.

With only a few members of the family and intimate friends present, Rev. C. A. Stubbin (Ryde) yesterday conducted a service when the remains of Reginald William Holmes, who was shot in his car at Dawes Point, were privately cremated at Northern Suburbs crematorium.

Two weeks later, police arrested two of Holmes' closest associates and charged them with his murder. Summers was an important witness, and this time police went to some lengths to protect him. The jury disagreed at the first trial, and at the second the two accused men were acquitted. The Shark Arm Murder remained unsolved.

1935   Wheelbarrow-pushing becomes news in the 'silly season' after the Depression

COLIN BEDNALL
Melbourne Sun News-Pictorial, 24 June 1935

It all began because a publican said to a garage proprietor that the road to Mount Buffalo was dangerous and the garage man replied: 'That's nonsense. I could wheel you there in a barrow.' Suddenly the little town of Beechworth was back on the map for the first time since the goldmining days. For a wager of £20, Mr Tom Parkinson, of the Beechworth garage, undertook to wheel 160 lbs of human freight, in the person of the publican Mr Tony Evans, fifty miles through snow and rain up 4500 feet to the top of Mount Buffalo.

For a while it was the most famous wheelbarrow in the world, and wheelbarrow-pushing was a craze fiercer than pole-sitting or marathon-dancing. Aircraft from Sydney and Melbourne invaded Beechworth, radio commentators broadcast the story around the world, local schoolchildren were given holidays, and champagne flowed along the route. Some newspapers were carrying Mr Parkinson's exclusive story; it was called, logically enough, 'Looking at Life from a Wheelbarrow'.

It was the era between the Depression and the war that ignited Europe, between Lindbergh and Joe Louis — a decade when crimes and nudist colonies and peroxided movie stars and bodyline cricketers made news. It was a silly season that lasted longer than most.

The great wheelbarrow push could hardly have had a more distinguished coverage. Alec Chisholm, the ornithologist who later became chief editor of the Australian Encyclopaedia *and editor of the* Australasian *and the* Argus, *was there for the* Argus; *Alan Moorehead, who was to become an eminent war correspondent and historian, was the* Herald *reporter; Colin Bednall, who went on to a brilliant career in Britain as a war correspondent and later as a newspaper and television executive,* represented the Sun News-Pictorial.

Here is Bednall's report, filed from Mount Buffalo Chalet, on the last stage of the eight-day marathon:

At 12.25 p.m. today Mr. Tom Parkinson wheeled Mr. Evans up to the Mt. Buffalo Chalet door. The nightmare barrow ride ended with just 43 minutes to spare. The pusher had accomplished what Mr. Evans wagered £20 could not be done in eight days and what, during those final days of grim struggle on the slopes of Buffalo, seemed to be an utter impossibility.

Figures tell best the story of this amazing saga of the Beechworth barrow:-

Distance covered 50¾ miles. Actual number of feet climbed about 5000. Time on the road, 56 hours. Actual wheeling time, 33 hours. Number of rests, 688 — ranging from a half-minute to three hours and absorbing 23 hours.

In climbing the last 18½ miles from Porepunkah to the Chalet more than half the travelling time and two thirds of the total number of rests were taken.

There was a remarkable break in the weather for the marathon's finish. In brilliant contrast to the weather of previous days, the sun shone gaily as the barrow trundled the last mile. A few minutes after the barrowmen had entered the chalet in triumph it was snowing again.

Flying barrow pennants, and flaunting barrow mascots, about 230 cars, including several from New South Wales, came to see the barrowmen finish. Six men travelled 300 miles on the back of an open truck. About 1500 cheering men, women and children saw Mr. Evans cut a ribbon to show that the barrow trek was ended.

With one and a quarter miles to cover today,

Mr. Evans did not take his seat in the barrow until 10.26 a.m. Mr. Parkinson even discarded his harness and, in Sunday dress, complete to stiff collar and tie, he ambled along in the wake of the snow plough.

His chief concern was to ensure that he did not arrive before Australia was home from morning church. The Australian Broadcasting Commission had made a special request that he should time his arrival so that it would not disorganise the national network.

Marshalled by a special squad of police in snow boots, a large crowd of followers was soon behind the barrow. A girl from Melbourne begged Mr. Parkinson to surrender one of his black curls, but he referred her to Mr. Evans, who has neither curls nor very much hair.

Just before he began the last stiff pinch of the journey, Mr. Parkinson slipped and tossed his passenger on to, not into, thanks to ice, a creek that ran beside the track.

Skiers formed an arch of triumph with their stocks as the barrow came up to the chalet. Waiting at the ribbon that marked the finish were the barrowmen's families, but they were lost in the crowd that surged forward.

Some started singing There's a Long, Long Trail, as the last dozen yards were covered, but their voices were drowned by cheers and then, as one and all roared it, by They are Jolly Good Fellows.

Three big policemen, forestalling souvenir hunters, took charge of the barrow and the two barrowmen stood smiling with as genuine a pleasure as ever two men smiled with while blue ribbons were hung about their necks.

Inscribed on one was, "Parkie, the Pride of Beechworth" and on the other, "Tony, Still Smiling."

A way was made to the Chalet verandah and there the barrowmen were welcomed by Mr. A. W. Keown, of the Railways Department, the president of Beechworth Shire (Cr. J. A. Humphreys), the president of Bright Shire (Cr. J. Smith) and the engineer of Oxley and Beechworth Shires (Mr. L. H. Sambell).

"You will quite understand that when I say I am pleased to be here I am telling no lie," began Mr. Parkinson in reply. "The last three or four days have been the most trying I can remember.

"My friend has been a true and generous sport during these last few terrible days. He could have made things very nasty for me, but he didn't. He always played the game, often at his own expense.

"Some people have called me a fool for undertaking this marathon," continued Mr. Parkinson. "When I tell you that this barrow has brought the greatest crowds and publicity to Beechworth and Myrtleford that the towns have ever known I hope you will agree with me for saying I am glad I have been a fool."

More cheering burst out when Mr. Evans, having tried to excuse himself from speaking and then thanking them all for their kindness, said he had never parted with £20 more cheerfully.

Next to be brought forward were the two trainers, to whom the barrowmen admit must go a lion's share of the credit for the marathon's successful completion.

"I can tell you I am very pleased to see my man arrive in such good spirits," said Mr. Claude French, who cared for Mr. Parkinson. "Many times coming up the mountain I expected him to go out to it."

"My man has shown wonderful endurance," said Mr. Evans's trainer, Mr. George Dennett. "How he sat it out through the snow I do not know."

After a terrific struggle to make progress in a foot of snow yesterday, Mr. Parkinson collapsed as he was sitting before a fire prepared for him in Berger's cottage.

Struggling on from 10.14 a.m. until 3.25 p.m., he could cover only three miles. The snow was so thick in the morning that it was impossible for cars to get through to the starting point, and the barrowmen had a strenuous journey before they even took up their places at the barrow.

Mr. Parkinson refused to rest longer than 30 minutes for lunch. With the aid of a snow plough he was able in the afternoon to do another mile and a quarter.

Tonight the barrowmen rest here in preparation for a long series of engagements ahead that threatens to be almost as strenuous as the marathon itself. . .

1935 'Smithy' and the *Lady Southern Cross* are lost — 'Thank God this isn't an obituary'

NORMAN ELLISON
Sydney Smith's Weekly, 10 November 1935

Australia's greatest airman, Sir Charles Kingsford Smith, took off on the last journey of his life on 6 November 1935. With Tommy Pethybridge, one of the best aviation mechanics of his time, Kingsford Smith intended to break the England—Australia record set by the winning Comet in the 1934 Centenary air race. He was hoping to establish a trans-Tasman air service, and he wanted to demonstrate the worth of his Lockheed Altair, Lady Southern Cross.

At 2.30 a.m. on 8 November, the youthful Jimmy Melrose, who had set out from Croydon airfield ahead of Kingsford Smith, saw flames from the twin exhaust of the Lady Southern Cross *some 200 feet above him, 200 miles south of Rangoon. That was the last sign of Kingsford Smith; at thirty-eight, he was presumed to have crashed in the Bay of Bengal. When Melrose arrived at Singapore later that day, Kingsford Smith was already missing; Melrose sportingly gave up his own chance of setting a record, refuelled and took off immediately to search the area where he had seen the Altair's twin exhausts. He searched for four days, and finally had to make a forced landing himself.*

While 'Smithy' was missing, but before his death had been confirmed, one of the pressmen who knew him best, Norman Ellison, wrote about him for Smith's Weekly *with great affection:*

'Smithy'

It's hard writing about "Smithy" at this time. From a newspaper angle he is in a No Man's Land. Thank God this isn't an obituary. But the fact that both Hook and Matthews were missing for ten days in the same locality, and Bertram and his mechanic were alive nearly a month after they got off the news track in the Nor'-West, and there was a German landplane that floated for over a week, with personnel intact — these escapes slightly brighten the after-Akyab black-out. . .

And while the Fates are doing things with the news threads they snapped after Jim Melrose saw the Altair over the Bay of Bengal, one's memory goes back.

There was the day "Smithy" arrived in Sydney from Perth, about eight years ago — "Smithy," ex-airmail pilot, Keith Anderson, his partner, and Bob Hitchcock, in two old converted British tourers. They came to the "Daily Guardian" office.

"We are organising to fly the Pacific," said "Smithy," "and we want money. Like to back us for the newspaper articles?" No frills or salesmanship. Just directness.

The old Brisbane aerodrome, when the "Southern Cross" first touched — and so very gently — Australian soil. A dishevelled "Smithy," very tired, but grinning happily. And later in that memorable day, the news, but not for general publication, that the Pacific flight was only the start of the job — he hoped to fly it completely round the world.

"Smithy" turning back the pages and laughing at himself. About the time, for instance, when he was put in irons on a ship. And at his mother's orders. But six-year-olds had to be punished for appropriating the freedom of a ship, outswung anchor included. That was when the Kingsford-Smiths were going to Canada.

And there was the time when "Smithy" was stunting for the movies. Wing-walking and head-down stuff, with the feet slipped in grips under the plane.

That was for bread and butter.

And the time he was an aerial scarecrow in a Californian valley — for so much an acre the pilot had to shoo hungry ducks away from the new rice crop.

"Smithy" wrinkles his nose. "You wouldn't be so keen about mallard duck after you've had 'em wrapped round your struts, or bashed against the cockpit. Ugh!"

Bernt Balchen, Polar pilot de luxe, and one of the highest ranking flyers in U.S.A., speaking — in Sydney: "I can't make out you people in Australia. You seem to regard 'Smithy' as just an ordinary kind of a chap. Why, over in the States, we all take our helmets off to him. Don't you know he's the greatest pilot in the world?" And as "Smithy" joined us, Balchen clapped him on the shoulder, and repeated his rating. "Smithy" grinned

shame-facedly, and said, "Mine's a beer!"

"Smithy," vocalist and instrumentalist. He played a ukulele — in a kind of a way. His baritone carried. He was at his best at a Flying Corps Association smoko.

"Smithy," tight-lipped and hands akimbo, looking on while the word "Anzac" on the fuselage of the Altair was covered with pasted slips of paper. That was after his new Centenary Air Race machine had been landed at Sydney. "Smithy" knew he should not have taken the name. But he knew that of the Australians he had the best chance in the race. And as he himself was an Anzac, he thought he might have been permitted to "carry the colors." No go.

And those ugly black days when he was bucking the I.C.A.N. clauses of the Air Race regulations with regard to tankage. Probably had he been more methodical when taking delivery of the plane in America, there would have been less trouble. But "Smithy" is not so hot when it comes to red tape, and, especially when in the wrong — he lacks the diplomatic touch in handling officials. The world's greatest stunt pilot, and Australia's best advertisement since the War, was having a gruelling time. And when the cracked cowling put him out of the race, and the cranks wrote letters without names and addresses, there was a grim jut to "Smithy's" jaw, and his hands became fists. "I'm no squib!" he declared. There should not have been any need for him to state the obvious. . .

"Smithy," the easiest of "touches" for hard-ups and wild-catters. His business associates got so incensed with his charities and investments, made by heart rather than head, that they coaxed his cheque-book away from him.

But leave it to that stubborn big heart to have his way — he used to get a loose cheque at the bank. He bought a share in a goldmine just before he left.

"Smithy" all smiles. That was the day when the cheques had gone to his Air Race backers. They all had been repaid, and he still had his beloved Altair. He loves that machine.

But where is it? You're giving us some heartaches, "Smithy".

1939 Black Friday: Australia's most disastrous bushfires sweep across an entire State

FRED ALDRIDGE
Melbourne Sun News-Pictorial, 16 January 1939

Australia's worst bushfires ever occurred when fires swept across the State of Victoria in January 1939. A long drought had set the scene and on the worst days of the continuing disaster, conditions of maximum temperature, minimum humidity and maximum wind velocity occurred almost simultaneously.

This extract from Judge L. E. B. Stretton's report of his Royal Commission on the fires summarises what happened:

Seventy-one lives were lost. Sixty-nine mills were burned. Millions of acres of fine forest, of almost incalculable value, were destroyed or badly damaged. Townships were obliterated in a few minutes. Mills, houses, bridges, tramways, machinery, were burned to the ground; men, cattle, horses, sheep were devoured by the fires or asphyxiated by the scorching debilitated air. Generally, the numerous fires which during December, in many parts of Victoria, had been burning separately, as they do in any summer, either "under control" as it is falsely and dangerously called, or entirely unattended, reached the climax of their intensity and joined forces in a devastating confluence of flame on Friday the 13th of January. On that day it appeared that the whole State was alight.

Steel girders and machinery were twisted by heat as if they had been of fine wire. Sleepers of heavy durable timber, set in soil, their upper surfaces flush with the ground, were burnt through. . . Balls of crackling fire sped at a great pace in advance of the fires, consuming with a roaring, explosive noise, all that they touched. Houses of brick were seen and heard to leap into a roar of flames before the fires had reached them. Some men of science hold the view that the fires generated and were preceded by inflammable gases which became alight. Great pieces of burning bark were carried by the wind to set in raging flame regions not yet reached by the fires. Such was the force of the wind that in many places hundreds of trees of great size were blown clear of the earth, tons of soil with embedded masses of rock still adhering to the roots; for mile upon mile the former forest monarchs were laid in confusion, burnt, torn from the earth, and piled upon one another as matches strewn by a giant hand.

For reporters and photographers covering the fires, it was a time of hardship and danger. One Melbourne Herald *man wrote afterwards in that paper:*

It was an unnatural, timeless horror of smoke, fire, no sleep, few meals, long drives interspersed with more or less successful efforts to get telephone calls, and, having got them, to make oneself heard and understood.

One of the outstanding impressions is Erica on Friday, the 13th. As the fires drove down with the 60-mile an hour northerly the town became enveloped in darkness and the air filled with fine dust and carbon particles.

Flames were barely visible through the smoke pall. But the roar as the fire tore along gullies could be heard clearly. Explosions as trees burst and toppled gave the scene the atmosphere of a war-time bombardment.

And so the climax developed.

Only one telephone line remained to Moe. All other lines to Walhalla and outlying places were silent. At this stage representatives of all papers decided to pool resources in order to get through as much as possible in case disaster struck the township. One wire, jointly compiled, was duplicated to all papers.

Meanwhile efforts were being made to evacuate the women and children to a ploughed paddock on the outside of the town. Our car was used for this purpose when the police decided that the danger was so great that it was unsafe for women and children to remain.

When it appeared that the town must burn the wind changed and Erica breathed again. Then our work started. Rumors, dozens of them, said that this mill and that had gone and we got busy to find out the truth.

By various means and with the aid of bushmen and axes we were able to make contact with almost every mill or settlement in the danger zones and give accurate reports of the happenings.

In several instances we were of assistance to men who were blind and ill from the effects of their desperate fight with the fires.

Almost the entire reporting and photographic staffs of Melbourne's newspapers had some part in the coverage of the bushfires. Some of the most tireless work was done by reporters Fred Aldridge, Gerry Whiting, Vic Houldcroft, Alf Brown and Roley Hoffman, of the Herald *and* Sun, *and by photographer Alf Ferguson, of the* Sun.

Aldridge, a cousin of the noted correspondent James Aldridge, later became a war correspondent in the South Pacific. His son David graduated from reporting to become a news executive of the Sun. *Here is some of Fred Aldridge's reporting from the bushfires:*

Somewhere west of Healesville, in the burntout Chum Creek area, a blackened cow and a hen, petrified in motion, stand like statues in a blackened stubble-field. The hen's leg is raised in the act of running. The fire sweeps up, and roasts them.

To me they are a monument to the ferocity of the forest fires which hold the country in their grip, and have hung above the State a smoke pall which extends far out to sea.

Before the flames arrive, a great gust of expanded air comes. It roars like an express train. It tears galvanised iron off and hurls it like scraps of paper above the trees.

Trees crack before it, to explode a few

minutes later like cannon as the sap in them expands with the heat.

In the wind's wake comes the fire, faster than a fast car. A strip of stubble in its path disappears as though a black curtain were being drawn across it.

A vanguard goes before the fire, flying above the untouched trees. When the main front arrives, small outbreaks half a mile or more ahead, ignited by flying embers, are ready to join it.

This vanguard already has trapped a score of people; as they have turned from the new menace ahead, the furnace has engulfed them.

It is wrong to believe that because fire has already passed an area, safety lies ahead. The fires of the past few days have travelled with such incredible speed that the flames often have not had time to consume the overhead.

They have rushed, instead, through the undergrowth, leaving trees burnt and blackened on their boles, but still carrying a mass of foliage above. . .

In all north-east Victoria people weep — some because of lost relatives or homes, most because of smoke, or close encounters with the flames. Many have not breathed fresh air for days. Some, including children, are smoke-sick.

By roadsides and in the smart holiday hotels —where the bath water runs black with fire-dust — men in stained shirts and bedraggled women sit in the luxurious lounges awaiting news.

While middle-aged postmistresses and girl assistants in their teens have outdone previous efforts in juggling the existing lines, communication in many places is still almost impossible.

Through the forests the lines in many places are holding great trees off the roads; others have crashed through, and the vital strands dangle in the ashes.

There is little hysteria noticeable when the fires sweep round a bush town. The cry goes up, "Here she comes!" and, as the wind changes, people begin to battle with the flames.

At Buxton we saw a man sit down and milk his cow while hell raged a mile away. . .

Bushfire devastation at Woods Point, Victoria, 1939

1939   An Australian reporter solves New Zealand's Piha Bones case

RICHARD HUGHES
Sydney Daily Telegraph, 21 March 1939

One of Australia's most outstanding and most colourful reporters of recent years has been Richard Hughes, veteran of more than three decades as an Asian correspondent. He started work as a shunter with the Victorian Railways after leaving school at the age of fourteen; he moved to clerical work, and finally became a junior reporter on the Melbourne Star *in 1934.*

His greatest journalistic triumph was the finding in Moscow of the British diplomat-spies Donald Maclean and Guy Burgess. He covered a good deal of combat in World War Two as a war correspondent, represented the Melbourne Herald, *the London* Sunday Times *and the* Economist *as Far Eastern correspondent from 1948, and wrote two books,* Hong Kong: Borrowed Place, Borrowed Time *and* Foreign Devil. *A legendary 'China Watcher', he died in Hong Kong in 1984, aged 77.*

Hughes achieved some notoriety when he became the second person, after Joe Alexander of the Melbourne Herald, *to be banned from Parliament House, Canberra. The ban was imposed after Hughes had been guilty of having committed a breach of privilege by expressing contempt for the Senate. He wrote these things, among others, about a debate in that chamber:*

The old boys of the Senate pulled down their woollen stomachers . . . weak arthritic wrists and wheezing voices . . . a comfortable home for old men . . . Senator George MacLeay, red-faced and bespectacled, looking like a stern Mr. Pickwick . . . sad, black-haired Philip Albert McBride, with the itchiest nose in the Senate . . . but the real ruler of the Senate is a thin, querulous fellow, with a beaky nose, light, angry eyebrows, and a small wig. He hisses acid instructions to the timid Senators like a bad-tempered stage prompter.

This last reference was to the Clerk of the Senate, Robert Arthur Borinowski. The ban continued for about three months and ended when Frank (later Sir Frank) Packer, proprietor of the Daily Telegraph, *expressed regret and claimed that no contempt was intended. By that time Hughes had gone overseas as a correspondent.*

Richard Hughes used to write crime-book reviews for the Telegraph *under the pseudonym of Dr Watson Junior, using the sometimes pompous style of Sherlock Holmes' famous offsider. It was in his capacity as Dr Watson Junior that the* Telegraph *sent Hughes to New Zealand to cover one of the major mysteries of the late 1930s — the Piha Bones case.*

Gordon Robert McKay, forty-three, a Sydney skin dealer, disappeared after travelling to New Zealand with a companion, James Arthur Talbot. Talbot reported to police McKay had been burnt to death in a shack at the coastal resort of Piha; he claimed that McKay had been smoking in bed just before the fatal fire. A handful of charred bones were recovered. The shack was burned down in February 1939, soon after it was discovered that McKay had been insured a little earlier for £50,000.

Richard Hughes called on all key witnesses, and soon became convinced that the fire had been 'rigged', that the bones concerned had been stolen from a nearby cemetery, and that Gordon McKay was in fact alive. His report, which proved these points conclusively, was published in the Daily Telegraph *on 21 March. On 22 March, after an intensive manhunt in Auckland, McKay, the man who was alleged to have perished, was arrested by police, and charged with having improperly interfered with the remains of another human. McKay claimed steadfastly, even in court, that he was*

*not McKay, but fingerprint tests proved his
identity. It later emerged that the bones concerned belonged to a man who had died a week
before McKay's alleged death.*

*This is Richard Hughes' report, an outstand-
ing piece of investigative journalism which
embarrassed police working on the case:*

This £50,000 bones mystery in New Zealand
is one of the most curious cases that have been
drawn to my notice.

I have myself been to New Zealand, and I
have made exhaustive inquiries on the spot.

I have seen every person who saw or spoke
to Gordon Robert McKay, 43-year-old Sydney
skin dealer, who is alleged to have been burned
to death in a weekend shack at Piha.

I have inspected a handful of charred bones
and have been courteously made privy to the
scientific evidence which the police are collecting on the case.

I must now regretfully testify that I cannot
accept the statement that Mr. McKay perished
in the Piha fire.

Consider the facts.

The Piha shack was destroyed by a blaze
which burned irregularly and fluctuatingly
for from 35 to 60 minutes.

In that time, it is declared, all of Mr. McKay,
from teeth to sacrum, was burned to dust,
except a small section of skull and vertebrae,
two or three knuckles of bone, and a couple
of pounds of charred flesh...

At the outset, therefore, we are asked to
accept the monstrous supposition that Mr.
McKay could leave some of his flesh behind
him in the fire even while all his bones charred
away.

Dr. Gilmour, Auckland pathologist, who
won criminological immortality by his masterly reconstruction of the Bayly burning murder
in New Zealand, snorts derision at the idea...

I think it will be agreed that there is some
support for the doctor's assertion in the fact
that the coffin of Mr. Shine was discovered to
be empty when it was officially exhumed at
Waikumete Cemetery.

A kindly Providence has also assisted Dr.
Gilmour in his investigations by arranging an
extraordinary selectivity in the soils of all the
cemeteries within 50 miles of Auckland...

Dr. Gilmour reports austerely that the soil
which was found on a shovel in the garage
which Mr. McKay rented before his tragic
death is identical with the soil from the Shine
grave in the Waikumete Cemetery...

After profound meditation, I must report
that I personally cannot accept the provisional
police theory on two other questions:—

(a) When was the Shine body raised from
the dead?

(b) Where was it deprived of its handful of
bones and pound of flesh?

The New Zealand police, a fine body of men,
incline to the view that the conspirators exhumed Shine on Saturday evening, the night
of the Piha fire.

That was two days after his burial.

I have calculated distances and times, and
I agree that it would be possible for the corpse
to be dug up; the grave refilled; the corpse
driven away in a car, and rifled of a handful
of bones; the body disposed of (dismembered
or reasonably whole); and the handful of bones
taken 20 miles to Piha, where the fire occurred.

I agree that all this is possible; I submit that
it is highly improbable.

I submit that it is far more likely that the
conspirators committed their body-snatching
on Friday night, and their arson on Saturday
night.

The police view on point (b), when I left
New Zealand, was that the Shine body was
plundered in the garage which had been hired
for the rented car.

I have seen the garage, and been ordered to
leave it by a short-tempered woman who owns
it...

I have had little experience in corpse-mutila-
tion, but I refuse to believe that two men could
park a car in a garage, remove a covered corpse
from the back seat, and proceed to select suitable bones for a fake cremation, while liable
to interruption from a woman who can hear
a cat sneeze in the garage while working in her
kitchen.

In the meantime, I am convinced that the
late Mr. McKay will be recovered alive and un-
burned by the police this week.

Farewelling an AIF advance party, Melbourne, 15 December 1939

1940   Three Federal Ministers die in a plane crash at Canberra

HUGH DASH
Sydney Daily Telegraph, 14 August 1940

Among the first casualties of World War Two were three senior Federal Cabinet Ministers and the Chief of the General Staff. They died when a Royal Australian Air Force plane taking them to a Cabinet meeting from Melbourne crashed in August 1940 near Canberra. All ten occupants of the plane died, including the Minister for the Army, Mr G. A. Street, the Vice-President of the Executive Council, Sir Henry Gullett, the Minister for the Air, Mr J. B. Fairbairn, and Lieutenant-General Sir Brudenell White, Chief of the General Staff. Also killed were Lieutenant-Colonel F. Thornthwaite, staff officer attached to the Chief of the General Staff, and Mr R. E. Elford, a former Melbourne Argus *journalist who had become private secretary to Mr Fairbairn.*

It was a costly, terrible tragedy for a nation which was trying to adjust itself to the condition of war. Mr Street, forty-six, had served in the AIF in the first World War, and had reached the rank of brigadier in the militia; as Minister for Defence and, later, as Minister for the Army, he had worked tirelessly for the reorganisation of Australia's defences. Mr Fairbairn, forty-two, son of a prosperous pastoralist family, had flown with the Royal Flying Corps as a teenager in World War One, and had been taken prisoner after shooting down two German planes; he had had 3000 flying hours as a pilot and in 1936 had flown his own plane from England to Australia. Sir Henry Gullett had been a reporter on the Sydney Morning Herald, *had served as a war correspondent in France and Egypt, and had written Volume VII on the Palestine campaign for the* Official War History. *He became Minister for Customs in November 1928 until the fall of the Bruce Government and later served as a Minister under Mr Joe Lyons. General Sir*

Cyril Brudenell White had served in the Boer War, and had been Chief of Staff of the First Division, AIF, when it landed at Gallipoli.

The crash had a large influence on the career of a later Australian prime minister, Harold Holt. He had joined the army in April 1940 as an artilleryman, rejecting offers of commissions in the army and the RAAF. The Prime Minister, Mr Menzies, pulled him out of the army and made him Minister for Labour and National Service. It was after this entry to Cabinet, at the age of thirty-one, that people began to talk of Harold Holt as 'PM material'.

Hugh Dash, later press secretary to Mr Menzies, sent this report of the crash to the Sydney Daily Telegraph:

Ten people, including three Federal Cabinet Ministers and two high Army officers, were killed when an R.A.A.F. plane crashed at Canberra today.

The Ministers were Mr. Street (Army), Mr. Fairbairn (Air), and the Vice-President of the Executive Council (Sir Henry Gullett). The Chief of the General Staff (Lt.-General Sir Brudenell White) was also killed.

Turning away from the aerodrome after approaching to land, the plane wobbled in the air, then spiral-dived into a hillside two miles from the Canberra aerodrome.

When it hit the ground eyewitnesses more than a mile away saw a vivid flash a fraction before the noise of the crash.

The wrecked machine burst into flames. The victims were incinerated.

R.A.A.F. men who ran across paddocks to the spot were beaten back by the heat. They had to stand by for half an hour until the flames subsided.

Air Chief Marshal Sir Charles Burnett flew

to Canberra at once. An investigation is proceeding. There is no suspicion of sabotage.

An official inquiry into the crash will follow an investigation which is being conducted by the Inspectorate of Air Accidents and a Coroner's inquiry.

An inquiry will also be conducted by the Air Force station from which the plane came.

The Coroner for the Capital Territory (Lieut.-Col. Goodwin) inspected the wreckage tonight.

He will conduct an inquiry at Canberra Court, probably later this week.

The inquest on the victims will be the only public inquiry.

The Inspectorate of Air Accidents was recently established to investigate Air Force accidents. Such accidents were previously investigated by the Air Accidents Investigation Committee.

The official inquiry, the form of which will be determined after the investigation by the Inspectorate of Air Accidents is completed and the Coroner's inquiry held, will consider these points:

1. Possible misjudgment in air speed and landing approach, which is suggested as a cause of the crash.

2. Whether the machine was overloaded.

3. It is suggested that the personnel were not accustomed to landing with a heavy load.

4. The effect of the load may have accentuated by the fact that the air density at 2000ft. above sea-level may have caused a misjudgment in the approach to the drome and the speed to maintain the craft completely airborne.

In these circumstances a stall would be possible, experts say.

It was officially denied on behalf of the Air Department today that the plane was overloaded.

The only comment was: The plane's load was well within its capacity.

Officers of the Prime Minister's Department searched the debris for valuable documents the Ministers were bringing to Canberra.

Some were found, but they were so charred that they would be of no possible use.

Late tonight a check was being made with the Melbourne department to determine precisely what documents were on the plane. . .

The Ministerial party was travelling from Melbourne to Canberra for a meeting of the Federal Cabinet, preparatory to tomorrow's meeting of Parliament.

The party decided to fly in R.A.A.F. plane when it was found there were too many to be accommodated in Mr Fairbairn's Percival Gull. . .

The pilot made a circuit of the drome, apparently to see if landing preparations were complete.

The plane was then seen to turn in a wide sweep towards Queanbeyan. It came into the easterly breeze and began a glide towards the landing field. . .

Suddenly the nose turned towards the ground. It dived almost vertically behind a hill. There was a crash, followed by a sheet of flame and a dense column of smoke.

Three Air Force tenders loaded with men left the station within a few minutes of the crash.

At the R.A.A.F. station a call was made for fire extinguishers and asbestos suits.

However, it was discovered that only asbestos helmets and gloves were available.

Rescuers had to leave the tenders and run through stump-dotted paddocks and scrubbed hillsides to the wreck.

They were guided by a thick column of smoke. The wreckage was found on a cleared spot, nose-first, at an angle of 45 degrees.

A stunted tree nearby was shorn off. The bodies of the victims were imprisoned in the burning cabin. . .

All occupants of the machine are believed to have been killed instantly. . .

The three Ministers killed had gone to Melbourne when Parliament adjourned last week to attend to urgent war matters.

The Prime Minister has taken immediate action to appoint acting-Ministers for the Army and Air.

It is clear, however, that a serious dislocation in defence administration must occur.

The Cabinet meeting, which was to have been held tomorrow, was cancelled. The Loan Council meeting, which was taking place when the plane crashed, adjourned.

1941   Australian soldiers see their first action in World War Two

ROY MACARTNEY
Melbourne Argus, January 1941

The first Australian ground troops to go to the Western Desert in the World War Two were members of the Sixth Division, under Lieutenant-General Sir Thomas Blamey. The Diggers' first major action took place in January 1941, at Bardia, where they killed or captured more than 41,000 Italian troops. Australian losses were 130 dead and 326 wounded.

The next target was the port of Tobruk, which the British Prime Minister, Mr Churchill, saw as the major supply base for the Allied forces in Cyrenaica. The garrison comprised 25,000 Italian troops.

One witness to the assault on Tobruk was Roy Macartney, a former Melbourne Argus *reporter who was a member of an artillery battery. Macartney wrote articles for the* Argus *during the Middle East campaign under the pseudonym of 'Subaltern'. After Tobruk fell to the Australians, he sat on a crest overlooking the port and wrote his piece for the* Argus.

Roy Macartney became one of Australia's best-known journalists. As a major in the Sixth Division, he was posted missing in action on Crete after the retreat from Greece; he escaped from the island in a motor landing craft which drifted without petrol, under a sail made from blankets, for seven days before reaching the North African coast.

He later became a war correspondent in New Guinea, and after the war was bureau chief of Australian Associated Press in Singapore and Tokyo. He covered much of the bitter early fighting in the Korean war. He served later as press attaché with the Australian Embassy in Washington, managed a television station in Brisbane and was editorial manager of the Herald and Weekly Times from 1955 to 1958. In 1965 he became Washington corres-

pondent of the Age, *Melbourne and travelled extensively with Presidents Johnson, Nixon and Ford as a member of the White House press corps; he covered the Watergate revelations leading to President Nixon's resignation. Roy Macartney died in October 1975 aged fifty-seven. Among his most important assignments in the United States was the coverage of one of mankind's greatest journeys — the 1969 trip from Cape Kennedy of the first astronauts to land on the moon.*

Before me lies Tobruk, our goal of yesterday's attack! A lazy pillar of smoke marks the location of still burning dumps, near which the modern buildings of the port nestle on the side of a hill which sweeps down to the picturesque waters of the anchorage. The Derna road is thronged with vehicles, both British and Italian; but here where I write, on top of the Haggiag Chargia, it is peaceful and quiet after the roar of yesterday's battle.

"Haggiag Chargia" is the designation which captured Italian maps give to a stony razorback whose heights dominate the city and the Bardia Road. On this razorback some of the fiercest fighting took place, and our battery is bivouacked along its crest. On either hand are fortifications and strongposts, built in the main with the huge rocks that lie around. The position had all the strategical advantages a defending soldier could desire, but men of the Victorian brigade took it at the point of a bayonet. . .

All around are huddled groups of blue-clad figures who fought bravely and vainly as the dupes of Fascist Italy. Here and there a perpendicular rifle with bayonet plunged in the ground marks the spot where one of our comrades has fallen on the windswept Haggiag

Chargia. The battalions to which the fallen belonged have been notified, and they have arranged for burial this afternoon. . .

But to go back a little. We moved into camp in Egypt after disembarkation from our voyage. Our guns arrived, and soon after we heard of the fall of Bardia. Our jubilation was tinged with disappointment at our apparently being too late, but the disappointment turned to joy when we received movement orders, and we knew we were to be in the next show.

The first day of our journey west passed uneventfully, except for the number of Italian vehicles full of prisoners which passed us on the way back. Each one was crudely marked "Wop —", the number being an aid to the keeping of a tally by the recovery section. We camped that night outside the wire of Mersah Matruh, where our troops had awaited the coming of the Italians before we took the offensive.

Next day we proceeded through the country which had witnessed the first clash. All around were captured vehicles and guns, while the roads were pitted with shell holes, reminders of the Navy's striking co-operation. Our second night was spent outside the crumbled pillars of what had been Sidi Barrani.

We awoke on the morning of the third day to find that a howling duststorm had descended upon us during the night. It was weird, with visibility about nil, the dawn bitterly cold, and with the fantastic touch provided by the empty petrol tins and other objects which came bounding along before the gale to disappear once more into the gloom. That day was hell. We jolted over the half-completed road lined with crushing machines, steam rollers, picks and shovels, and although out path was rough, the manner in which the uncompleted road had been surveyed and graded indicated that Mussolini had intended that his "victory road" would be a good one. We passed through Sollum and went to bed immediately on stopping, under a layer of blankets, in an endeavour to escape the choking dust.

Fort Capuzzo and Bardia fell behind the following day, and the reconnaissance parties arrived outside Tobruk in the early afternoon. There was sporadic shelling on either side, and the air was disturbed by the rumble of guns and the chatter of machine-guns. That night we found just how dark the desert can be before the moon appears; but we got our guns in safely, and when dawn broke were strongly entrenched in pits. The battery was ready for the attack to come, and I felt quite happy with my four guns prepared for the section it had taken us so long to find.

It was still on the gun position. Occasional reports could be heard, as intermittent harassing fire was continued so that this morning of zero day would appear no different from any other. Two minutes to go to zero, when our barrage would open to support the attack on Tobruk! A man cursed excitedly as a round of hostile battery fire burst near by.

"One minute to go. Thirty seconds. Twenty, Ten, Five, Four, Three, Two, One, Fire." I counted the guns in, and the four guns fired the first salvo as one. All around the horizon the dark sky of an hour before dawn lit to the flash of other batteries. The report of guns, the clang of empty cartridge cases as they were ejected to the ground, the click of the breech, the report of "ready" from the layer, and the shout of "fire" from the No.1 combined in a roar of noise for two and a half hours.

Dawn broke while we were still firing, and by the rays of the early morning sun we could see the huge pall of dust and smoke from the area battered by the barrage where our troops were to break through. The barrage completed, we were engaged on observed tasks as reports came back that our infantry were through the perimeter defence and advancing rapidly. Up forward our battery commander lay in a shell-hole as he sought cover from enemy machine-gun fire pinging around. . .

With our initial successes the story of the artillery support of Tobruk was over. We moved forward rapidly behind the quick-moving infantry and occupied positions which soon gave us command of Tobruk. Besides shelling, our greatest worry was the avoidance of the land mines, which we knew honeycombed the area. By nightfall the flare of exploding dumps on the horizon told us that the battle was almost over, and in the morning came the news that Tobruk had fallen. . .

1941   Australian troops push westward and capture Benghazi

JOHN HETHERINGTON
Sydney Daily Telegraph, 7 February 1941

From Tobruk the Australians drove westward, through Derna and into Benghazi. With them was John Hetherington, war correspondent of evening newspapers throughout Australia.

Hetherington, born in 1907, had worked as a reporter and special writer on the Melbourne Sun News-Pictorial *and the Melbourne* Herald. *Like Noel Monks, Alan Moorehead and James Aldridge, all of whom had worked on Sir Keith Murdoch's Melbourne papers, he made a big name internationally during those early days of the war. His despatches were featured in* The Times, *London, and the* Manchester Guardian. *He later reported the Allied invasion of Western Europe for the Melbourne* Herald. *After the war he became editor-in-chief of the Adelaide* News. *He wrote a number of books, including biographies of Dame Nellie Melba, Field Marshal Sir Thomas Blamey and Norman Lindsay. He died in September 1974 aged 66.*

This is his first-hand account of the Australian victory at Benghazi:

The A.I.F.'s 360-mile advance across eastern Libya reached its climax today when the City of Benghasi formally surrendered to an Australian brigadier.

Three Australian machine-gun carriers and one truck carrying three Australian officers, one English officer and 10 Australian soldiers entered Benghasi at 4.45 p.m. yesterday demanding its surrender, and the population, which had been left to its fate by the retreating Italian army, offered no resistance.

These first arrivals found few shops open and civilians lining the street. The civilians were nervous at first, but they waved and cheered when they found the party's intentions were not aggressive. . .

The last lap of the Australians' race to Benghasi began from Barce on Wednesday afternoon. Barce had surrendered about noon on Wednesday. There was an element of comedy about the circumstances. Australian guns went forward to the edge of an escarpment about eight miles from the town and sent over a few shells. The townspeople immediately ran up a white flag on a pole above Barce's highest building, and the gunners ceased firing.

The flag fell down, however, and the gunners, fearing trickery, re-opened fire. The white flag shot up the masthead again, and this time stayed there.

The Italian troops had fled from Barce, but in retreat they had blown up the road leading down an escarpment at several points. The Australian engineers had it open for trucks within a few hours. The Italians had also destroyed military equipment, fuel and ammunition dumps in Barce by firing them. . .

It was a damp army — physically though not in spirit — which moved on yesterday morning. Rain, punctuated by violent bursts of hail, continued almost throughout the day.

Small batches of Italian soldiers gave themselves up along the road. They were wet and miserable, and seemed to welcome the prospect of finding food and shelter.

The vanguard of the army was at Benina by mid-afternoon. The Italian air force had certainly done itself well at this aerodrome. An area of 10 or 12 acres is covered with solid stone buildings in which the officers and men lived. The officers' quarters were fitted up lavishly with built-in baths and expensive wardrobes, beds and other furnishings. Now they're wrecked. The Italians fired some by rolling 40-gallon drums of petrol inside and setting a match to them.

Australians marching into Benghazi after its capture

British armored units were fighting the fiercest battle of the Libyan campaign 70 miles south of Benghasi while the Australians were advancing on the city. They intercepted a 10-mile-long column of Italian soldiers and civilians in buses, trucks and cars fleeing south towards Tripolitani on the Wednesday night.

The column was defended by about 130 cruiser tanks, many light tanks, armored cars and artillery; but the British tanks sailed in and fought it to a standstill. They were heavily outnumbered with only 26 cruiser tanks in fighting trim, and the issue of the battle was in doubt until an hour after dawn on the Friday — a bare hour or two before the Australian brigadier entered Benghasi to accept the city's formal surrender.

It was a complete triumph for Britain's tank fighters, and was rounded off by the capture of General Bergonzoli. . .

The Italians were stronger in guns at the scene of the main battle. They deployed many of them round a knoll by the roadside. It was round here that the battle swirled all day Thursday.

"They should have been able to deal with us, but their shelling was most ineffective," a British officer told me. "I saw one of their positions today, where 60 guns were deployed.

I can't understand why they did not stop us there."

It is impossible yet to tell the story of Thursday's fight in detail. Men who were in the thick of it have only scattered impressions of noise and chaotic tangle. . .

At nightfall the battle was still not won. About 30 enemy tanks managed to break through the British line in the darkness. This was hardly surprising as there were times when only eight British tanks were functioning together.

The armored Brigadier commanding the British striking force told me that the "bag" in the whole battle was at least 86 medium tanks — probably between 120 and 130 — an uncounted number of light tanks, armored cars and other vehicles, and between 12,000 and 20,000 prisoners, including a number of specialists whose loss will be a severe blow to the Italian force in Libya. He instanced the ground staff of Benina aerodrome, which was captured. . .

An Australian infantry battalion was on its way to the battle yesterday when armored headquarters sent a message that help would not be needed. The Australians were not sorry. It gave them a chance for a long night's rest after many days of hard campaigning.

1941   The Allied operation is defeated in Greece but the Anzacs win glory

JOHN HETHERINGTON
Melbourne Herald, 30 April 1941

In February 1941, Winston Churchill decided that the British advance in Cyrenaica should be halted, and that troops should be sent across the Mediterranean from North Africa to Greece. It was clear that a massive German army was about to attack Greece, supported by a strong German air force. As the Germans spread through Albania and Bulgaria towards Yugoslavia and Greece, the Australian War Cabinet agreed to send two divisions to aid the Greeks, and the New Zealand Government consented to the dispatch of the New Zealand Division from the Middle East. At the last moment, the British commander, Field Marshal (later Earl) Wavell, decided to send only one of the Australian divisions — the seasoned Sixth.

Very quickly, it became apparent that the whole Allied operation was hopeless. The Greek troops, under General Papagos, were unrealistically disposed, and the arrival of Allied troops from North Africa was fairly disjointed. General Blamey, the Australian Commander-in-Chief, wrote to the Prime Minister, Mr Menzies, on 5 March 1941: 'The plan is, of course, what I feared . . . piecemeal dispatch to Europe. I am not criticising the higher policy that has required it, but regret that it must take this dangerous form. However, we will give a very good account of ourselves.' The New Zealand commander, General Freyberg, reported to his government that he had never considered the operation a feasible one. While the Australians were making the crossing to Greece, twenty-one German divisions, seven panzers and fourteen infantry, attacked Yugoslavia and Greece.

The Australians found Greece a welcome change after the desert. Captain Charles Green, who was later killed while commanding Australian forces in Korea, summed up their feelings when he wrote: 'What a contrast! Instead of awaking with eyes, ears and noses full of sand we breathed pure crisp air with the scent of flowers. Flowers! We hadn't seen them since leaving Australia.'

It was a punishing expedition. The Australian Sixth Division lost 320 men killed in Greece, with 494 wounded, and 2030 taken prisoner. The New Zealand Division, which fought with it as the Anzac Corps, lost 291 dead, 599 wounded, 1614 captive.

John Hetherington's dispatch was the first Allied account of the Anzacs' stubborn, heroic withdrawal from Greece. The Times of London published it on its main news page. The London Daily Mail, quoting passages from it, said in an editorial:

> The fault does not lie with the Imperial forces. They fought like lions. It was the old story of magnificent heroism against overwhelming odds; machines against men; local German air ascendancy. . .
>
> There are two lessons from Greece. The first is the gross folly of sending infantry into action without adequate air and mechanised support. The second is that we should never again under-estimate the colossal striking power of the German forces.

This is John Hetherington's report from Cairo, as it was published in the Melbourne Herald *on 30 April 1941:*

Although the full story of the Greek campaign cannot yet be told, one thing shines through the fog of uncertainty which at present cloaks it — the Anzacs have never fought harder or met defeat with greater honor.

The line they held was never broken, despite the deadly blows dealt it by the German forces.

It was like a fight between a giant and a pigmy – with the pigmy still on its feet at the finish. Nobody yet knows what casualties the Anzacs suffered, but it is probable that the final figures will show that the Germans suffered several times as many.

It is impossible yet to give even a partly-adequate picture of events since the Australians and New Zealanders landed in the middle of March.

A New South Wales brigade arrived first. This brigade had been the A.I.F.'s advance guard ever since the force left Australia. It landed in Palestine first, and then moved to Egypt first. It went out in the desert first, and led the attack against Bardia.

It was closely followed to Greece by a brigade composed of New South Wales, Victorian and Western Australian battalions.

The A.I.F.'s tail was up. Officers and men knew that heavy German forces were massing in Bulgaria, but they felt confident that they, with the New Zealand, British and Greek forces already in Greece could hold the enemy while reinforcements crossed the Mediterranean.

I first visited the headquarters of the New South Wales brigade on April 4. It was then established a few miles south of Servia (Northern Greece), awaiting a move by the Germans before going to battle positions.

I talked with a Sydney brigade commander, a tough veteran of the last war. He was busy with his staff officers, reconnoitring the surrounding country, which he told me, offered excellent defensive possibilities. The brigade moved forward, north of Haliakmon River, on April 6, when the Germans attacked.

A brigade drawn from New South Wales, Victoria and Western Australia was also forward, and these two brigades were holding the central position on the line of the German attack.

New Zealanders were stretched out to the coast on the right, and the Greeks were holding a line in the mountains on the left.

The natural strength of the positions was tremendous, but the Allied forces seemed dangerously thin.

An Australian press camp near Elasson, in Greece. From left: Reg Glennie, Chester Wilmot, Gavin Long, Captain E. Wilson and John Hetherington

The prospect became more disquieting when it was learned that no substantial reinforcements had been sent to Greece from Egypt with the exception of a Victorian infantry brigade, which had not yet landed.

Little news reached us in the mountains. We heard that the Greeks were falling back in the north, but this had been anticipated, and caused no dismay. However, the knowledge that the Jugoslavs had failed to hold out and had allowed the Germans to enter the Monastir Gap (running from Southern Jugoslavia to Greece) was more disturbing. It meant that the Germans could probably cut off the Greek Army in Albania, and might even outflank the Australian, New Zealand, Greek and British line. . .

The Nazis had, so far, not shown their air strength over the front line, although they had carried out a series of heavy raids on Greek ports, including Piraeus. The troops saw the first dive-bombers in large numbers on April 13, and this was the beginning of an airkrieg, which grew daily more intense, until a journey of even a few miles on the road between Athens and the front line became a perilous adventure.

We saw some R.A.F. planes before the airkrieg opened, but afterward I did not see one flying over this front. This is no criticism of Air Force activity. I know that the British planes and pilots were doing fine work throughout the campaign, attacking the German lines of communication. The trouble was, there were too few aircraft to carry out regular defensive patrols over the Allies' area, and formations of German bombers, from 30 to 50 strong, escorted by numerous fighters, flew over at regular periods, day after day, and strafed our troops and lines of communication.

The men bore up admirably under this strain, but it would be futile to pretend that these deadly visitations did not impair their spirits.

Casualties, especially in men and even in army vehicles, were surprisingly few in these air attacks. The toll they took of morale was infinitely heavier. . .

The withdrawal began on April 16. There was no help for it. German weight of numbers was simply too strong. Two Australian infantry brigades came out of the mountains, bringing only what the men could carry, and other Australian units followed, leaving the New Zealanders to cover the withdrawal.

The Germans were coming up fast, and the Australian artillery fought a heavy engagement, lasting practically thoughout one night. Their gunnery was an important factor in the success with which the backward move was carried out.

Meanwhile, a Victorian infantry brigade had reached Greece, and it made a swift march toward Trikkala, near which it took up positions in order to defend the flank of the retreating force.

This was the beginning of the movement which ended when the Anzacs took up the Thermopylae line, in the rugged mountains clustering about the foot of Mount Parnassus.

The line was about 30 miles long, in contrast with the 150-mile-long Mt. Olympus line, on which the Australian, New Zealand, British and Greek troops originally awaited the enemy.

However, the strength of the force in both men and material had been reduced by the earlier fierce fighting, nor was the new line by any means impregnable. There were several possible lines of attack from the west and the island of Euboea, in the south, was a dangerous "Achilles heel".

It was separated from the mainland by only a narrow strip of water, and it was necessary to place a small mobile force on it to reduce the danger of Germans landing air-borne troops there.

Luck was on our side in withdrawal from the Thermopylae Line. Heavy rainclouds wrapped the mountains throughout April 16 and 17, and the higher passes were hidden by mist.

The murky conditions practically grounded the German planes on both days. There were two or three attacks on road columns, but mass strafing would have been too perilous for the pilots and aircraft.

Units of the Anzac and British force which moved back later were heavily and persistently bombed and machine-gunned from the air. Many trucks were riddled with bullets, and others blown up. Many more crashed when their drivers swung off the road as the strafing planes swooped on them, but the withdrawal continued without confusion, in the face of the worst the Germans could do.

Australian observers, looking down on the plain of Thermopylae from the Bralos Pass, saw heartbreaking evidence of the Nazis' superiority in equipment — field guns being landed from big Junkers planes, and other planes fetching load after load of troops. It was evident that the line could not long be held by the Anzacs, despite its natural strength. . .

I do not know how far these moves have been carried out according to plan. The whole picture is obscure at the moment, because communications have been difficult to maintain.

It was impossible for the Anzacs to hold Bralos Pass. The Germans were gathering in great force nearby, and the men would have sold their lives without cause, if they had attempted to hold the line.

Three grievous blows: the warships *Sydney*, *Perth* and *Yarra* are lost

AN EDITORIAL AND DON WHITINGTON
Perth West Australian, 1 December 1941 and Sydney Daily Telegraph, 14 March 1942

The Royal Australian Navy suffered three grievous blows inside four months. On 19 November 1941, HMAS Sydney *and the German raider* Kormoran *both sank after a gunnery duel off the Western Australian coast; survivors from the* Kormoran *reached the mainland, but the entire complement of 645 on the cruiser* Sydney *was lost. Then, on 13 March, Prime Minister John Curtin announced that both the cruiser* HMAS Perth *and the sloop* HMAS Yarra *had disappeared in action.*

Here the West Australian *commented on the loss of the* Sydney:

Heavy tidings sadden the people of Australia today with the Prime Minister's announcement that H.M.A.S. Sydney must be presumed lost after an action with a heavily-armed merchant raider which she sank by gunfire. There is news only of enemy survivors, and although the search by air and surface craft is being continued, it must be feared that the cruiser has gone down with her complement of 645 officers and men. While we await the details of the last fight of the *Sydney,* the stark facts already disclosed are an assurance, if any assurance can be needed, that the ship's company performed their duty to their country unto death in the selfless and heroic manner which is the tradition of the Royal Australian Navy. All Australians, in extending their deep sympathy to the relatives of the Sydney's men, mourn a gallant band who take their place of honour with those others who have fallen in the grimly relentless struggle of the sea, on the far-flung battlefields of the Middle East and in the combats of the air. The grief which is felt throughout the Commonwealth is supported by fortitude to face the worst hazards of this war, for which we dare envisage no end

but victory; however long the agony or however bitter the cost. The Sydney had a fighting record of which we are justifiably proud. Her fame has echoed round the world. It was not her fate to rust away. The grievous shock of her loss is tempered by the knowledge that she found a glorious end on the high seas in the service of a just cause; victorious in her defeat and defiant of the enemy to the last. It is for us to salute her heroes in final homage and to avenge them. There are doubtless some impatient murmurings at the delay in the official statement which gave rise to much rumour and heart-burning among the public as news of a serious action at sea was bruited about. But it will now be conceded by the fair-minded that Mr Curtin's explanation for withholding temporarily news the premature publication of which might have been of much value to the enemy.

This is how the Sydney Daily Telegraph, *in a dispatch from its Canberra correspondent Don Whitington, reported the loss of the* Perth *and the* Yarra:

The loss of two Australian warships with complements totalling 833 officers and men was announced by the Prime Minister (Mr. Curtin) in Canberra last night.

The ships are:

H.M.A.S. PERTH (7040 tons cruiser), complement 682.

H.M.A.S. YARRA (1060 tons sloop), complement 151.

The ships disappeared while returning to an Australian port from Java and are now presumed lost, said Mr. Curtin.

H.M.A.S. Perth, Australia's most modern cruiser, had fought gallantly earlier in the Java Sea battle and had returned to port unharmed.

In the Java Sea battle an Allied Fleet inflicted heavy loss on a much stronger Japanese invasion fleet in an attempt to prevent the invasion of Java, which took place on February 28.

Mr. Curtin said: "There is no news of survivors from the Perth or Yarra, but it is conceivable that in the narrow waters in which the ships were operating members of their crews managed to get ashore or were picked up by other vessels."

He continued: "An enemy claim that the Perth had been sunk was made some days ago.

"At that time, however, the Naval Board had no information to substantiate this.

"The position then was that the Perth had fought successfully and unharmed in the battle in the Java Sea.

"She had returned to a Javanese port after that battle. From that port she reported to the Naval Board, from her personal observation during the battle, the severe losses inflicted on the enemy by the Allied naval forces.

"Subsequently the Perth and the Yarra sailed from Java for an Australian port. They have not arrived, and nothing has been heard from them. It must, therefore, be presumed that the ships are lost.

"With so much of the area in enemy hands, communication is naturally difficult. It may be some time before additional news, if any, of possible survivors is received.

"Any information that does arrive will be made public immediately.

"The next-of-kin of personnel have been informed.

"My Government and the Naval Board extend to them our sincere sympathy in their anxiety. They know that with it is joined the sympathy of the whole nation." . . .

Loss of the Perth and the Yarra brings Australia's total losses since war began to two cruisers, one destroyer, and two sloops.

An extraordinary feature of the Perth and Yarra losses is that the ships vanished in circumstances almost identical with the mystery disappearance of H.M.A.S. Sydney about four months ago, with all hands off the northwest Australian coast.

The Sydney's loss was announced on December 1.

She disappeared without a word, and the only account of her loss came from survivors from a German raider alleged to have sunk her.

The Sydney's complement was 645 officers and men. . .

The Perth was a cruiser of the Leander type. She was completed in 1936 and was taken over by the R.A.N. from the Royal Navy in 1939.

She was the last cruiser acquired by the Australian Navy before the war began.

Launched at Portsmouth in 1934, she was completed in 1936, as H.M.S. Amphibion. She was commissioned flagship of the cruiser squadron on the African station. . .

She was taken over by the Australian Navy on June 20, 1939, under Captain E. D. Farncomb, having been re-christened H.M.A.S. Perth by the Duchess of Kent.

She left for Australia in July, 1939, sailing via America and Panama, and represented Australia at the New York Fair.

She reached Australia on March 31, 1940.

Meanwhile, she had been on patrol and escort duty in the western Atlantic.

Her 177 days at sea, of which she had steamed 155 days, was then a record. . .

She took part in the evacuation of troops from Greece and Crete. . .

She reached Australia last October, where she was placed under the command of Captain R. M. L. Waller, who had commanded the Stuart at Matapan.

Since then the Perth has been employed in operations in Australian and adjacent waters.

H.M.A.S. Yarra was laid down at Cockatoo Island on May 14, 1934, launched on March 28, 1935, and completed in October, 1935.

She had a speed of 16½ knots.

Her main armament was three four-inch guns.

The Yarra was on duties in Australian waters until August, 1940, when she was attached to naval forces in the Red Sea and the Persian Gulf.

In August, 1941, during the Allied campaign in Iran, the Yarra took part in successful naval operations in the Persian Gulf. . .

1941 **A week before Pearl Harbour, Singapore waits for the war in a mood of unreality**

DOUGLAS WILKIE
Melbourne Herald, 6 and 23 December 1941

In the week before the attack on Pearl Harbour, Singapore was in the grip of a phoney war. There were troops everywhere, and each day there were fresh rumours; but there was a kind of frantic serenity, even gaiety, about the place. In the clubs and hotels people were still talking about cricket and golf and tennis and swimming; parties were being thrown, white tuxedos being worn. Singapore, after all, was a bastion, and the jungles above it were said to be impregnable. In the great docks of the naval base were the ships of the British Eastern Fleet, including the battleship Prince of Wales *and battle-cruiser* Repulse.

Douglas Wilkie, of the Melbourne Herald, *had arrived a few weeks earlier, and he was writing about the sheer unreality of the island with wry humor. Singapore, he wrote, was being called the world's biggest bluff; the naval base, before the arrival of the* Repulse *and the* Prince of Wales, *was the world's biggest naval base without a navy.*

Wilkie had gone to Singapore to cover the activities of the Australian Eighth Division. This was how he described the state of the city in one dispatch. It was published in the Herald *on 6 December 1941 — one day before the Pacific war began:*

Events began to hum when a British major, deputising last week-end, pounced on a radio rumor that Japanese bombers were already blasting the Burma Road. A few minutes later, page boys were calling spruce English officers from their partners in Raffles' ballroom, and military police were scouring the bazaars for English Tommies, who were recalled to barracks.

Urgent messages were tapped from A.I.F. headquarters to steamy jungle outposts, where tough Diggers cursed the mosquitoes, and hoped their chance had come at long last.

Junior clerks left off totting up tin and rubber profits under electric fans, and other clerks hurried out of club lounges to doff immaculate tropical suitings, and don tin hats and gas masks.

Among the crop of rumors was a report that the crack German battleship Von Tirpitz was snooping round Singapore waters, ready to defy any Allied cruiser to sink her or any battleship to catch her, but it was the local Japanese and not the British who showed queasiness.

Those who had not already made tracks for home or got berths on what remained of Japanese shipping began throwing parties, if not to keep up their courage at least to get rid of pocketfuls of local currency. The parties were strictly among themselves.

Glummest were the Chinese traders, especially those in towns in military areas, where prices had jumped to meet the troops, their best customers, who now had to shop at camp canteens. Pouting Singapore taxi-girls complained of lean days and nights.

With news of the Sydney and Parramatta sinkings, Diggers threw off the last vestiges of jocularity and got nearest to praying that the war would come their way. Many had brothers and cobbers in the Sydney. They were most bitterly disappointed when the main crisis melted just as the battleship Prince of Wales and its escorts slid into the naval base and 1000 British tars invaded the city.

Many still wore the dark blue cold-weather kit in which they had joined with Mr Churchill and Mr Roosevelt and the United States sailors in singing "Rock of Ages" after the historic

Iceland meeting.

They were soon joined by A.I.F. men and other soldiers released from barracks as the cables pricked the "war tomorrow" balloon.

Whether it will be war the day after tomorrow only a few know...

How much face did Kurusu lose at Washington? What did the Australian Cabinet discuss at its emergency session? Had the Japanese infiltration to Bangkok Hitler's efficiency? Were the shiploads of British and American materials and American technicians pouring into Rangoon going to make the full length of the Burma Road?

In Chungking, far-sighted Chinese were balancing the unpredictable chances of a quick three months' ABCD blitz against Japan against the equally unpredictable chances of a long war in which China's tattered armies would be cut off from their last trickle of supplies.

Perhaps the most worried man was Chungking's secret police chief, Tai Li, whose name is whispered even more seldom over tea cups these days than the names of his victims. Tai Li has been a very close henchman of Chiang Kai-shek for 15 years since he studied under the Generalissimo at the famous Whampoa Academy, China's West Point...

A Pacific war with the Soviet as an ally or near ally of the ABCD Powers would revive old tensions in the Chinese United Front, and if Tai Li adds more bodyguards to his payroll, it might affront Chinese good taste which is more discriminating these days...

A week later Wilkie was touring the Malayan northern front; the only Australian war correspondent in the area. The Japanese strength, he wrote, lay in the resourcefulness and mobility of their infantry, and their successful application of infiltration tactics in the jungle. 'Many of the Japanese troops advance to the attack dressed in khaki shorts, tennis shoes and singlet, with tin hat or kerchief on their head... The Japanese soldier's powers of endurance and his few bodily requirements assist him greatly.'

On 23 December, as the crunch was coming for the Eighth Division, he wrote that a lot of *nonsense was being talked about bad feeling between Australian and British troops in Malaya:*

There has been talk of bad feeling between Australian and other British troops in Malaya. I heard a little of it in Australia. I heard it in the more expensive and less comfortable Singapore hotels. I have not heard it anywhere else.

A lot of nonsense is talked about friction between Australian and English. Some say it is a subject which should be avoided in wartime. But the talk is there. One does not lay rumors by ignoring them.

One must expose them as stupid and sometimes mischievous lies.

If there are differences between English and Australians they are comparable to differences between Canadians, Americans and all branches of the Anglo-Saxon democracies. It is time a small, irresponsible minority fell in tune with the great majority of English and Australians who are getting on with the job here, without raising their Oxford — or Woolloomooloo — accents in high-pitched argument.

There were one or two cafe fracas when the Australians were newly arrived, and still under the first impact of heat and equatorial thirst. A few of them talked rather more patriotically in the narrow sense than any sassenach should dare in the presence of a rawboned Highlander.

But from all descriptions there have been better — or worse — exchanges at Liverpool and Seymour between rival Australian units.

The free-and-easy A.I.F. have made a name for themselves here as good mixers with the Malays and other native races.

But this is not a prerogative of the A.I.F. There are British civil servants and others who have devoted their lives to the study and promotion of Malay culture and fought the Colonial Office for better conditions for all races here. It is a fight that has gone a long way towards victory in the last two years.

There is closer understanding than ever before between Indian and English officers, and an exchange of ideas by conversation in messrooms and clubs. Big events are shaping in India and the heroism of Indian troops is one factor in a new attitude towards these changes.

The English are naturally more aware of this than the Australians, and recent comments by some of the most respected men in the long tradition of English administration in India, widely published in the Far East Press, indicate that this war is strengthening India's claims for a new deal.

Much that is best in the Kipling spirit may survive in barrackroom and mess. But "East is East" jingoism no longer makes sense.

What, then, provides a basis for the rumors of friction?

They probably have their origin, as well as circulation, in the more expensive hotels. . .

When the A.I.F. landed in Singapore there was some jealousy among British regulars, because the Australian civilians and their friends clubbed together to provide the A.I.F. with better amenities than had ever been given the British Tommies in Singapore.

This jealousy was fanned by that very small percentage of European womenfolk — again habitués of the more expensive hotels — whose conceptions of hospitality, apart from what is organised with help of their Chinese servants, tends to be narrow.

It has disappeared now that the Tommies are frequent guests at the Anzac Club, and now that, thanks to the Australian example, they are getting better amenities themselves. . .

Another friction of different kind, although also exaggerated, is caused by small percentages of planters and merchants. The Australians don't like this faction within a faction. Nor does anyone else. In the local jargon the British military takes a very poor view of these tuan besars — or "bizarre tuans," as we prefer to call them.

The A.I.F. met a sample when making weapon pits in a coastal area. As the Diggers, stripped to the waist, sweated under the midday sun, shovelling piles of sand and rock, an immaculately laundered estate manager told them not to dig across the front lawn of his house, which, although pleasantly sequestered amid miles of plantations, also came within a tactically important area.

After listening to the planter's indignant lecture on an Englishman's house being his castle, the Diggers made a certain unedifying comment — and went on digging.

An English Tommy would have been more respectful. But he would have thought the same.

This type of colonist is dying out. Unhappily, he still has enough influence to be inordinately vocal in the local Press. This is misleading. He is becoming less important every day.

Many things are misleading in Malaya. A.I.F. men who had not been warned sufficiently of this have learnt it by now.

Heaven help the enemy, who has banked on bad feeling to weaken the morale of Empire troops in Malaya.

Heaven help him, any way, say the men of the A.I.F. Only they say it rather differently.

Douglas Wilkie left Singapore on 10 February for Batavia, and soon after headed for Chungking. He worked as a correspondent on the Burma and India fronts, and was later assigned to the European theatre. Wilkie, who had worked on the Straits Times, *Singapore, in the 'thirties, became the Melbourne* Sun News-Pictorial's *foreign affairs commentator in 1946. He was also the* Manchester Guardian's *Australian correspondent for a number of years.*

Wilkie made history of a kind in May 1969, when he was called to the bar of Victoria's Legislative Council — in company with myself, as his editor — charged with a breach of parliamentary privilege over an article in the Melbourne Sun. *It was the first such case in the Victorian Parliament for more than 100 years. Both of us accepted invitations to explain our actions to the Council, but what we said was never debated. Both received short notice; both were found guilty. Nine years later, in December 1978, the same Parliament took the extraordinary step of voting to expunge these judgments from the records. Party leaders conceded that the original hearing had been mishandled.*

1941   A prime minister recognises the new, strong link between Australia and America

JOHN CURTIN
Melbourne Herald, 27 December 1941

Late in 1941, the Far East situation was deteriorating rapidly for the Allied nations, and particularly for Australia. Japan had entered the war with its massive raid on the American fleet in Pearl Harbour on 7 December, and Japanese troops were attacking vigorously in Malaya and the Philippines. The war was going badly for Britain and the United States, and Australia, with most of its fighting men in the Middle East and one division in Malaya, was feeling increasingly unprotected and anxious.

John Curtin, a former journalist who had been editing the Westralian Worker *immediately before his election to Federal Parliament, became Prime Minister two months before Japan entered the war. He quickly assumed a stature that surprised his critics and even many of his supporters; the Australian people turned to him with an enthusiasm and trust which no Australian leader of the previous decade had been able to inspire.*

Don Whitington, in his book Twelfth Man?, *called him the greatest leader the Australian Labor Party produced in its first hundred years. Sir Arthur Fadden, in his autobiography* They Called Me Artie, *said of him: 'The best and fairest I ever opposed in politics is easy to nominate — John Curtin. . . There was no greater figure in Australian public life in my lifetime.' Curtin had dedication, vision and a great sensitivity to public feeling; as Prime Minister he showed another quality, a kind of nobility.*

Curtin, knowing that Britain was thoroughly occupied with the northern hemisphere war, wanted to bring home Australian troops from the Middle East. Winston Churchill resisted this, sending a telegram to the Australian leader in which he assured Curtin that British forces in Malaya would fall back slowly, fighting delaying actions and destroying communications. It would not be wise to take forces from the Middle East, said Churchill, because victory there 'is within our grasp'.

In his telegram to Curtin, Churchill said: 'You may count on my doing everything possible to strengthen the whole front from Rangoon to Port Darwin. I am finding cooperation from our American allies. I shall wire more definitely in a day or two.'

This message did not satisfy John Curtin. Two days after its receipt, he had published in the Melbourne Herald *an article which marked a change in the course of Australian history. 'Without any inhibitions of any kind, I make it quite clear that Australia looks to America, free of any pangs as to our traditional links or kinship with the United Kingdom,' he wrote. It was a highly emotional and critical moment in Australian history. In a way, it represented a cutting of the umbilical cord which had bound Australia to Britain since the earliest colonial days. It was an admission that Australia could no longer rely on Britain; that her immediate future, if not her more lasting future, depended on protection by the United States.*

Despite Churchill's opposition, and even one last-ditch attempt by the British leader to have Australian forces diverted to Burma during the sea journey home, Curtin succeeded in having the bulk of Australian forces in the Middle East returned to Australia within his first twelve months in office.

Curtin's most memorable achievements as Prime Minister were the dramatic change he effected in relationships with Britain and America, his successful conflict with Churchill over the return of Australian soldiers from

Three different Prime Ministers governed Australia during August to October 1941: John Curtin (left), Arthur Fadden (centre) and Robert Menzies (right)

the Middle East to defend their homeland, and his reversal of the Labor Party's anti-conscription policy. Curtin, a World War One anti-conscriptionist himself, had to fight his own party to force it to abandon its traditional opposition to conscription for military service outside Australia. He had the Defence Act changed so that draftees could be used to fight the Japanese in areas north of Australia.

This is the article by John Curtin which the Melbourne Herald *published on 27 December 1941. Strangely, considering its significance as a charter for a fresh course in Australian history, it did not rate the front page. It was published on Page Four.*

"That reddish veil which o'er the face
    Of night-hag East is drawn . . .
Flames new disaster for the race?
    Or can it be the dawn?"

So wrote Bernard O'Dowd. I see 1942 as a year in which we shall know the answer.

I would, however, that we provide the answer. We can and we will. Therefore I see 1942 as a year of immense change in Australian life.

The Australian Government's policy has been grounded on two facts. One is that the war with Japan is not a phase of the struggle with the Axis Powers, but is a new war. The second is that Australia must go on to a war footing.

Those two facts involve two lines of action — one in the direction of external policy as to our dealings with Britain, the United States, Russia, the Netherlands East Indies and China in the higher direction of the war in the Pacific.

The second is the reshaping, in fact the revolutionising, of the Australian way of life until a war footing is attained quickly, efficiently and without question.

As the Australian Government enters 1942, it has behind it a record of realism in respect of foreign affairs. I point to the forthright declaration in respect of Finland, Hungary, and Rumania, which was followed with little delay by a declaration of war against those countries by the Democracies.

We felt that there could be no half-measures in our dealings with the Soviet, when that nation was being assailed by the three countries mentioned.

Similarly, we put forward that a reciprocal agreement between Russia and Britain should be negotiated to meet an event of aggression by Japan. Our suggestion was then regarded, wrongly as time has proved, to be premature.

Now with equal realism, we take the view that, while the determination of military policy is the Soviet's business, we should be able to look forward with reason to aid from Russia against Japan. We look for a solid and impregnable barrier of the Democracies against the three Axis Powers, and we refuse to accept the dictum that the Pacific struggle must be treated as a subordinate segment of the general conflict. By that it is not meant that any one of the other theatres of war is of less importance than the Pacific, but that Australia asks for a concerted plan evoking the greatest strength at the Democracies' disposal, determined upon hurling Japan back.

The Australian Government, therefore, regards the Pacific struggle as primarily one in which the United States and Australia must have the fullest say in the direction of the democracies' fighting plan.

Without any inhibitions of any kind, I make it quite clear that Australia looks to America, free of any pangs as to our traditional links or kinship with the United Kingdom.

We know the problems that the United Kingdom faces. We know the constant threat of invasion. We know the dangers of dispersal of strength, but we know, too, that Australia can go and Britain can still hold on.

We are, therefore, determined that Australia shall not go, and we shall exert all our energies towards the shaping of a plan, with the United States as its keystone, which will give to our country some confidence of being able to hold out until the tide of battle swings against the enemy.

Summing up, Australian external policy will be shaped toward obtaining Russian aid, and working out, with the United States, as the major factor, a plan of Pacific strategy, along with British, Chinese and Dutch forces.

Australian internal policy has undergone striking changes in the past few weeks. These, and those that will inevitably come before 1942 is far advanced, have been prompted by several reasons.

In the first place the Commonwealth Government found it exceedingly difficult to bring the Australian people to a realisation of what, after two years of war, our position had become. Even the entry of Japan, bringing a direct threat in our own waters, was met with a subconscious view that the Americans would deal with the shortsighted, underfed, and fanatical Japanese.

The announcement that no further appeals would be made to the Australian people, and the decisions that followed, were motivated by psychological factors. They had an arresting effect. They awakened, in the somewhat lackadaisical Australian mind, the attitude that was imperative if we were to save ourselves, to enter an 'all-in' effort in the only possible manner.

That experiment in psychology was eminently successful, and we commence 1942 with a better realisation by a greater number of Australians of what the war means than in the whole preceding two years.

The decisions were prompted by other reasons, all related to the necessity of getting on to a war footing, and the results so far achieved have been most heartening, especially in respect of production and conservation of stocks.

I make it clear that the experiment undertaken was never intended as one to awaken Australian patriotism or sense of duty. Those qualities have been ever-present; but the response to leadership and direction had never been requested of the people, and desirable talents and untapped resources had lain dormant.

Our task for 1942 is stern. The Government is under no illusions as to 'something cropping up' in the future.

The nadir of our fortunes in this struggle, as compared with 1914—18, has yet to be reached.

Let there be no mistake about that. The position Australia faces internally far exceeds in potential and sweeping danger anything that confronted us in 1914—18.

The year 1942 will impose supreme tests. These range from resistance to invasion, to deprivation of more and more amenities, not only the amenities of peacetime, but those enjoyed in two years of war.

Australians must realise that to place the nation on a war footing every citizen must place himself, his private and business affairs, his entire mode of living on a war footing. The civilian way of life cannot be any less rigorous, can contribute no less than that which the fighting men have to follow.

I demand that Australians everywhere realise that Australia is now inside the fighting lines. . .

1942 Darwin: more than 250 people die in Australia's first air raid

MERTON WOODS
Bathurst National Advocate, February 1942 and Sydney Daily Telegraph, 29 April 1942

Australia tasted war on her own soil for the first time on 19 February 1942, when 188 Japanese aircraft attacked Darwin. It was a traumatic moment in the history of a nation which was until that time both vulnerable and a little complacent. It was Australia's Pearl Harbour, and it caused wholesale panic. Some Australian airmen, believing that their commander had ordered 'every man for himself', pelted south — into the bush, along roads, along railways. A Royal Commission, which probed the circumstances of the raid and behavior afterwards, reported solemnly that some airmen were found at Batchelor (sixty miles away), others at Adelaide River (seventy-two miles away), one at Daly Waters (400 miles away); one had even reached Melbourne (2500 miles away) in thirteen days.

Three reporters who witnessed the raid were Douglas Lockwood (of the Melbourne Herald), *who was representing evening newspapers throughout Australia, Merton Woods (Sydney* Daily Telegraph) *and Alex Olsen (Sydney* Morning Herald). *Armed with the greatest story of their careers, they had one major problem: there was no way to get it to their newspapers. During the raid, which killed more than 250 people and wounded 400, the post office, the telegraph office and the cable office — the entire communications system which linked Darwin with the rest of Australia and the rest of the world — were blown up. When Lockwood reached the rubble that had been the post office, he was in time to see the bodies of staff members being carried away. Darwin had no telephone link with other States then; it was established later the same year.*

Lockwood, Woods and Olsen decided to head for the nearest telegraph office, which

they believed to be at Adelaide River. They pooled their petrol rations, and drove there in two hours. At Adelaide River they learned that there was no telegraph office, that the nearest such centre was at Katherine (140 miles further on), and that the road to Katherine had been rendered impassable by floods. Next day, at dawn, they caught a train to Katherine. When they lodged their stories, they were thirty hours late. Not that this mattered much, because all their reports were so mutilated by censors in Sydney and Melbourne that they were unrecognisable.

Lockwood later wrote: 'That night I rested on the hotel billiards table with two other men, and tried to sleep against the worry of knowing that I failed to get through to my office in time with the most sensational story ever to come the way of an Australian journalist.'

The trip to Katherine had one ironic sequel. Merton Woods, utterly fatigued but aware that he had been watching history at close quarters, decided that night to write a letter to his wife, telling her all that happened. It was a blunt, unvarnished account of what he had seen and what he had done. He had in fact been in the Darwin post office when the first Japanese bomb had dropped. His wife read the letter, then sent it to his mother, who was living in Maitland. His mother read it, then took it across the road to show it proudly to an old friend, the editor of the Bathurst National Advocate. *He was proud of Merton Woods too; Merton had begun his journalistic career on the* Advocate. *So the next day the Bathurst* National Advocate *published the text of Merton Woods' letter. At a time when censors were preventing all major Australian newspapers from publishing any but the barest*

details of the raid, the Bathurst National
Advocate *had its own completely uncensored
eye-witness story of the raid.*

*Extra piquancy was provided by the fact
that Ben Chifley, a member of the wartime
Cabinet which had decided to keep the facts
of the Darwin raid out of the newspapers,
was at that time a member of the board of
directors of the* Advocate. *Mr Chifley, who
grew up in Bathurst and represented the area
in Parliament, later succeeded John Curtin as
Prime Minister of Australia.*

*This is Merton Woods' unintentional front-
page story on the bombing of Darwin, as
published in the Bathurst* National Advocate.
*It pre-dated the first official publication of
details of what happened in Darwin (the Royal
Commission findings of Mr Justice Lowe) by
thirty years.*

In a letter to his mother at Bathurst, Mr.
Merton Woods, who learned his journalism on
the staff of the National Advocate, and who
represented the Daily Telegraph during the
recent bombing raids on Darwin, tells some of
his thrilling experiences. Merton writes:

Dear Mother, I came through the blitz o.k.
on Thursday with nothing worse than a crushed
finger and sundry cuts and scratches which
don't amount to much. No one knows how
lucky I was. The raiders were already dropping
their bombs before the alarm finished sounding. I ran to the post office to send a wire that
an alarm had started. Just as I had written it
bombs started to explode and anti-aircraft
guns go off and the whole building shook.
With everyone else in the P.O., I ran down a
gully in front of the P.O. and sheltered in the
open. Then a bomb dropped somewhere close
and covered us in rubble. I got up and ran a
few yards nearer the post office and sheltered
under a rocky ledge. Then another bomb
dropped nearby and a piece of rock, about
ten lbs., fell about eight inches on to my head,
raising a bit of a lump, but only a very little
scratch. Then I crawled over and crouched
with my back against a low concrete wall with
my back to the post office. I was there only
a few minutes when a bomb dropped about
15 yards away. Stones and dirt showered down

all over me. I protected my head as best I
could with my hands. Everything went black
for a minute or so and I felt I was buried, but
could not feel anything on me. Then as the
dust cleared I saw the concrete wall had saved
me. Other chaps who had been lying a yard
or so in front of the wall were hit by the flying
debris and injured, though I don't think
seriously. After this one I again crawled down
the gully and sheltered for the rest of the raid,
against another stone wall. From here I had a
bird's eye view of the dive bombing attacks on
shipping in the harbor. Planes often flew over
machine gunning, but, touch wood, nothing
came within 20 yards of me. When the all
clear sounded I crawled along to an old man
who had been sheltering against the wall a bit
further down from me. He was all in and one
leg was hurt. Another chap and I carried him
50 yards up the steep gully. The effort winded
me, but we made it. As I passed the wall
against which I was earlier, I saw a bomb crater
about 20 yards from the wall. The post office
was wrecked and they were carrying out the
people killed. Pieces of galvanised iron were
caught in trees.

I then walked through the town looking
for someone I knew. Suddenly there was
another terrific explosion from the direction
of the waterfront, flames and smoke shot into
the air. I thought the bombardment had re-
started, and was a bit scared this time as I
feared I'd be caught in the open. Fortunately,
however, it was not another bombing. I then
went to the hospital with a stretcher case. The
hospital, too, had been damaged by bombs
and machine gun fire. I jumped into a military
ambulance going back down town and went
down and had another look at the waterfront.
Then I met the Sydney Morning Herald and
Sun representatives who were getting ready to
leave town in an attempt to drive to Katherine
to lodge wires as Darwin communications were
down. . .

Then in the new Chev. we drove 70 miles to
Adelaide River. Just as we got there another
siren went. It made me feel a bit hopeless, and
I was just starting for shelter when told it was
an all-clear after a false alarm. We could not
get past Adelaide River by car nor could we

Burning storage tanks in Darwin after the Japanese air raid
of 19 February 1942

send any messages from there. There was another alert about an hour later and we drove into the bush. There we had some food and whisky and later returned to the railway station, where I had a shower and put on a clean shirt Lockwood loaned me. We spent the night in the car, having about an hour's sleep. Then at dawn an evacuation train came through. I climbed on to a flat top car and we began the 130 mile trip to here. The train averaged only 10 miles per hour. I had no hat and the sun was pretty hot. I was a bit sun-burnt but am otherwise 100 per cent., except for my finger which I have had properly dressed.

A few weeks later, Merton Woods was visiting an American fighter squadron at Darwin when pilots were ordered into the air to intercept seventeen Japanese heavy bombers, escorted by nine fighters. It was the fifteenth raid on Darwin, and the Americans destroyed three of the bombers and three Zero fighters. This time the censors did not interfere with Woods' report. It was published on the front page of the Sydney Telegraph *on 29 April 1942:*

Fighter pilots were taking things easy — reading, writing, and yarning — when the warning of approaching raiders came.

While the ground staff got planes ready for a speedy take-off, pilots nonchalantly finished what they had been doing when the alert was received.

One pilot sealed a letter and said, "See that this is posted if I don't get back."

Another tested his hunting knife, saying it might be handy if he came down in the bush to hunt kangaroos, or if forced down in the sea, to deal with sharks.

Then the signal came through that the raiders were approaching Darwin.

Ground staff rushed out shouting: "All planes up!" as pilots either ran or jumped on cars to take them to their planes.

Within a few minutes all fighters were airborne, and were streaking in rat-tail formation to intercept the Japs.

After they had disappeared I had early lunch with headquarters staff and, as Americans put it, began to sweat it out (wait for the re-

turn of the fighters).

Almost an hour passed, then one fighter roared towards the field. It flashed over us apparently flat out, and at a height of only 300 ft. gave the victory roll.

The pilot was leader of the flight, Lieut. George E. Kiser, 23, of Somerset, Kentucky.

Immediately he brought his fighter to a standstill it was refuelled and re-ammunitioned.

Kiser told me: "I saw the bombers drop their bombs near an R.A.A.F. 'drome and head away into a thundercloud. I manoeuvred and climbed until I was right in the sun and above the bombers. I saw another lot of bombers tangled with a lot of Zeros. I made a pass at the first formation, getting two bombers. I blew the engine out of the first and saw the second burst into flames and reel off.

"I pulled up to make another pass at the bombers when I saw a Zero making for me. I poured a burst into him. I'm not sure if he crashed. Another Zero made for me, so I got away."

This Zero was shot down after a dogfight over Darwin town by Lieut. Donald M. Morse, 22, of Augusta, Maine, who shot down a Zero on Saturday.

Kiser continued: "My bag today are the first Japs I've shot down over Australia, but I got one in the Philippines and three in Java."

Morse said: "Everyone was hollering over the radiophone 'Watch for Zeros'.

"I watched for bombers until a Zero got on Kiser's tail. I chewed bullets into him. He twisted his plane all over the place, trying to dodge bullets, and then, Fooey, the Zero burst to bits in a mass of flames.". . .

On their return the pilots showed more interest in giving combat reports than eating food which was brought out to them in a mess truck.

Jap bombers approached Darwin in formation of four threes and one five. Anti-aircraft fire broke up the formations. One fighter crashed into the sea with guns still blazing, indicating that the pilot had been killed or badly wounded.

1942 American troops pour into Australia and remark on the 'wowserism'

HUGH DASH AND BRIAN PENTON
Sydney Daily Telegraph, 23 March and 13 April 1942

In March 1942, as the Japanese moved closer, the war news for Australia was extremely grim. Australian ports were being raided, British and Australian warships were being sunk, and an Australian Division had just been lost in Malaya. Then it was announced that General MacArthur had arrived in Australia to take supreme command of Allied forces in the South-West Pacific, including the Philippines, and that American troops, planes and equipment were pouring into the country.

In the first flush of the Americans' arrival, some of the reporting in Sydney newspapers was a little naive, even coy. Readers were informed that some Americans liked their whisky straight, with a beer chaser, and that others put salt in their beer. They loved Australian girls, swapped lessons in 'crap' for lessons in two-up, and wondered why the cities did not have more skyscrapers. One earnest reporter who failed to get a grip on his verbs recorded that some Americans were anxious to demonstrate the craft of 'pitch wooing'. The first United States invaders were interviewed enthusiastically, and their every comment was printed with a kind of good-humored awe. Corporal William E. Bounds explained to the Daily Telegraph *that the soldiers called Sydney 'Yankstown', and Private George Huffman said disarmingly: 'I come from God's own country, and I came to this burg expecting to find niggers and kangaroos. I found a bunch of fine people instead.' One* Telegraph *reporter who visited an American camp reported that the Americans did not salute, that the officers made their own beds, that captains ate at the same tables as privates, that the pilots wore Mickey Mouse and Donald Duck cartoons on their jackets, that ace pilots overhauled their own*

engines; he met, he said, a full-blood Indian, a bronco roughrider and a millionaire's son 'with a 20-room luxury apartment in a big American city'.

Hugh Dash, a famous Telegraph *reporter who later became press secretary to Sir Robert Menzies, accompanied MacArthur to Melbourne and wrote about him on 23 March:*

Never bother to suspect General Douglas MacArthur of liking personal publicity. He pleaded guilty to this years ago. He loves it.

His own officers say he has been reared on a diet of underdone meat and camera flashlight bulbs.

He doesn't relish publicity of the ballyhoo type. The MacArthur publicity is simple yet subtle. It is handled by experts.

To the usual routine is added those little touches which transform a formality into an event.

Only hard-bitten observers can detect the trimmings. As on Saturday.

A group of the high-ranking officers of the fighting services waited for the General on Melbourne's Spencer Street platform.

Against the drab station background they sparkled like Sunday beach umbrellas at Bondi.

There were Australian generals in khaki with generous strips of red braid and glistening shoulder pips.

Admirals in blue and immaculate whites with fringed gold epaulets.

U.S. one, two and three star generals in trim dark khaki jackets and puce-colored pants.

Gleaming swords clanked metallically on the stone platform.

General MacArthur, a four-star general, could have matched them all in his full dress uniform.

Few fighting generals of this war can equal

his row of medals and decorations.

But he stepped nonchalantly from the carriage in a loose two-piece tropical outfit cut like an overall. It resembled Mr. Churchill's black-out suit minus the zipper.

There was not a trace of color relief to the light khaki. No decorations either.

It set him apart from the service ceremonial uniforms like a dinner jacket at an artists' costume ball. . .

Cameramen say he is an ideal subject. He unconsciously poses, but the developed print never looks posed. . .

He carries his tall, spare body with an almost conceited air of confidence.

His penetrating resonant voice contrasts a little oddly with his patrician features.

His fingers are long and delicately tapered, but his hand-shake, according to a few M.H.R.'s who met him, is crushing.

Over the heads of the official party he caught a glimpse of war correspondents grouped behind a barricade. He waved to those he knew, and went on with the introductions.

Photographers tried to snap him through the thick glass of the official car before he left the station.

He touched the driver's shoulder with his cane, stepped out of the car, and stood posing, one foot on the running board.

He gave them one full face, one left and one right profile. . .

In General MacArthur's personal staff is his own Press agent, Colonel Diller. In Australia, the General will follow his invariable custom of giving daily Press interviews.

He has only one injunction to Pressmen, "Don't pull your punches."

He has surrounded himself with tall generals and staff officers. Although he is over 6ft. himself, in a group they dwarf him, but only in height.

Several of them were once his superior officers.

Their relationship is one of easy familiarity.

They call him "Chief," he addresses them by their first names or by nick-names.

His closest staff confidant and associate is breezy General Patrick Hurley, once Hoover Secretary of War, and a multi-millionaire.

He wears a leather jerkin, chews the end of long black cigars and, at 63 years, is still active enough to do a hand flip backwards.

He comes from Oklahoma, and speaks several Indian languages fluently.

On Saturday he was asked if General MacArthur would be back at his hotel for lunch.

"Son," he said to the assistant hotel manager, "the General is just like other men. He will ankle back about two p.m. to refuel."

He inquired about the various Australian brands of "hard likker."

General MacArthur's officers are under no restraint in their relations with the Press.

But every syllable they utter has to go before his staff censorship.

So mistakes and indiscretions are going to be very few.

Brian Penton, the editor of the Daily Telegraph, *visited MacArthur's headquarters in Melbourne to assess American attitudes. He found them unhappy about two things — delays and wowserism. He wrote on 13 April:*

I spent last week in Melbourne talking to the Americans.

They're fine. If you talk to them in a group mixed with Australians you might get the impression that the Americans are Australians, keyed up to fight for their country, thinking of not much else than the coming battle, and that the Australians are reluctant draftees from another country asking, "Why should we put ourselves out for this dump?"

You'll often feel ashamed in that mixed group, and you'll come away reflecting that many suns must rise on this continent, many salutary disasters befall it, many ego-busting sticks of adverse fate be broken over its thoughtless heads before its manhood achieves the quiet maturity of these Americans.

Suggest an idea to an Australian official and he looks tired. You have to argue him into a corner before he promises to do something about it. If he remembers, you may get a formal note in three weeks' time, assuring you that the idea has been passed on. That is probably the last you hear of it.

Suggest an idea to an American, and even if he is busy General Brett, second in command of all the Allied Forces in the South-west Pacific, he'll take time off to hear you to the end. More, he'll have aides running, phones buzzing at once, to put you in touch with the man who looks after the department your idea fits into.

Maybe they are just polite. Maybe they've got the red-tape-worm as bad as we have. But I don't think so. A suggestion I carried to an American on Wednesday had borne some fruit in Sydney on Friday. The same suggestion is still mouldering in the brain of one of our own officials, who listened to it a month ago.

I went down to see how Americans and Australians are co-operating to get this country tuned up for war on or near Australian soil. In many minor and some major ways I found they were not co-operating too well.

Two extra bad breaks stand out:—

We're wasting time getting planes and other urgently-needed goods of war out of ships — and that means we're wasting ships — and that means we're knocking back the assistance America is trying to give us.

With W. S. Wassermann, deceptively drawling, slow-moving head of the Lease-Lend, I travelled to a port away from Melbourne where these ships were supposed to be discharging.

What we saw was enough to take your mind right off the races. Even this gentlemanly fellow Wassermann was moved to a loud, profane reverie on the stupidity of human inertia in a sun-drugged land of hitherto unchallenged tomorrows.

Not one ship was unloading.

Somewhere up north Americans were flying Kittyhawks and Fortresses in and out of battle, losing some, wearing out others at a rate which required ten per cent. replacement on front line strength every week. . .

The wharf-laborers were waiting to work, the truckers were waiting to load and carry, but somewhere down the long line of complicated connections between ship and wharf-laborer and trucker and warehouse and railway and workshop and flying-field there was a block. . .

This is the first bad break I noted.

The other you have heard something about.

Our wowserism is making Americans jumping mad, destroying their interest in us, injuring morale.

A deader city than Melbourne after nightfall it is impossible to imagine.

Through the blacked-out streets hundreds of soldiers aimlessly wander. There is just nothing for them to do if the picture shows are packed out, as they generally are.

On Sundays it is worse. Nothing to see. Nowhere to go.

A high officer said to me: "This is dangerous. When you get really large masses of troops in this city you will have highly inflammable material — unless they are entertained properly."

Hotel hours are absurd. You can't take a man to your hotel for a quiet drink after six o'clock, and that often means that you can't discuss urgent business. . .

Hugh Dash, who has spent a lot of time observing Melbourne in the last few weeks, adds: "Soldiers reckon that Sundays in Australian cities are just like Sundays in Philadelphia — the high spot of American sabbatarianism. On that day the 'blue noses' take over.

"Sunday after Sunday in Melbourne I've seen hundreds of U.S. soldiers and airmen sitting on the banks of the Yarra, just looking at the water. They can't even go window shopping, because most of the windows are sandbagged or boarded up. They can't break the monotony by inspecting public air-raid shelters, because on Sundays these are padlocked."

Of course, all this goes for our own men, too.

Radio commentator Dunn, head of the Columbia Broadcasting staff in Australia, reports a pathetic incident he witnessed one Sunday recently.

An A.I.F. soldier, returned from the Middle East, plodding the desert of Collins Street, yelled to an American: "Buddy, where can a man get a meal in this town?"

The American said: "There's no place I know of, but I'll take you to the American hospitality centre."

Are we assembling huge armies in this country to pave the way to Heaven for a wowser?

1942 Australian Wirraways courageously take off at Rabaul and are blasted out of the sky

OSMAR WHITE
Melbourne Sun News-Pictorial, 7 April 1942

Osmar White first went to New Guinea in the 1930s. His first book, Green Armour, *was a minor classic on the subject of warfare in the jungle. After distinguishing himself during the New Guinea campaign, and having both ankles smashed as a result of a Japanese bomb on a Liberty ship in the Solomons, he covered the European war from D-Day. He was with the first Allied forces to enter Buchenwald concentration camp, and his account of its horrors was published in newspapers all over the world. He represented all Australian newspapers at the official surrender of Germany.*

During a long career as a roving reporter, writing for Australian, British and American newspapers and magazines, Osmar White built up a large international reputation. In 1963 he gave up daily newspaper journalism (on the Melbourne Herald) *to concentrate on writing books. He has also been the author of many short stories and radio and television dramas.*

Japan struck swiftly and savagely in the early days of the Pacific, following its occupation of Malaya and Java with the capture of Australian garrisons in Ambon, Koepang and Rabaul.

From Port Moresby, which was itself being threatened by May 1942, Osmar White told in the Melbourne Sun News-Pictorial *of the heroism of the men who were overcome by the Japanese at Rabaul. In one capsule of rare courage, Australian Wirraways (comparatively slow Australian-built planes whose basic wartime use was as trainers) took off against a mass of enemy bombers. White records that they lasted a bare minute:*

The heroism of 1400 Australian soldiers resisting 25,000 Japanese in Rabaul is being revealed by the hundreds who have escaped. Many of these have reached territory held by Australia.

Before the Australian defenders abandoned the town to the onslaught of men, metal and aircraft 2000 Japanese were killed by machine-gun and mortar fire on the beaches.

After the battle almost every survivor of the Australian force took his chance in the bush rather than surrender. The routes and methods by which their escape was made are still secret.

The outline of the Battle for Rabaul has been told by the first five men to reach Port Moresby 37 days after the Japanese captured Rabaul. For weeks they struggled over mountains, through swamps, and jungles drenched by torrential rains.

In those weeks they starved. They walked their feet red raw. They were weak and delirious with fever and exhaustion. . .

The Japanese assault on Rabaul began in earnest at dawn on January 19 with a smashing attack from the air. On that day — a Monday — a lone Australian plane sighted through a gap in the rain clouds a fleet feeling its way through the reefs.

There were at least 25 ships — men-of-war, transports, minesweepers and tankers. It was bitter for the Australian pilots to know that even a modest fleet of bombers could have smashed this armada.

At dawn next day the first blow fell. Tier after tier of heavy bombers swept in from the sea until the sky from horizon to horizon seemed filled with them.

In groups of five they swept across the aerodrome pattern-bombing, blasting everything in sight with tons of explosive. Then the dive bombers hurtled down with shattering blasts of explosion.

Out of the middle of this hell five Australian Wirraways climbed. From the beginning they had no chance. The men in them knew they had no chance. But they went up. The Wirraways lasted a bare minute. Three were literally shot to pieces in the air. Two crash-landed.

Outgunned, slower, falling to pieces, they still managed to claw down two Japanese between them. Anti-aircraft batteries shot down five others.

Soon news came that the transports had disembarked men a few miles out to sea. Next morning the main body of the enemy fleet, immune from Australian air attack, was sheltering behind Watson Island.

The bombers came again — 70 huge machines with a fighter escort. They concentrated on the anti-aircraft batteries and the coastal defence guns. The Australians realised that the enemy pressure was overwhelming. They set about destroying everything likely to be of value to the enemy.

Troops took up new positions. In the early hours of the morning, after a short, ominous silence, three green flares lit up. They showed crowded barges coming ashore.

They were crammed with Japanese infantrymen, clad in black shirts and shorts, their faces and arms smeared with lampblack. Australian machine-guns, mortars and small arms opened up. The Japanese replied with tommy-guns, but the Australian positions were well concealed, and the barges put to sea again. The first landing attempt had failed.

At dawn the defenders saw that the troopships had come into the harbor behind a screen of minesweepers, supported by other warships.

Simultaneously it was realised that the Japanese, armed with light automatic rifles and grenades, had infiltrated behind the Australian positions. Withdrawal began.

Japanese were mowed down by murderous cross-fire. Those who leapt into the water were caught on submerged barbed wire and shot or drowned. But they came on with fanatical courage. Those behind seized the dead bodies of their comrades and made bridges over the barbed wire with them.

More that 1500 Japanese were killed in this sector alone. But wave after wave came on. The Australians waited until the first wave was level with them in the jungle, turned and ran inland with them. At a pre-arranged point they escaped with comparatively few casualties.

Then came the retreat, which for heroic drama overshadowed the fighting. It was the middle of the wet season. Most of them had only the clothes they stood in and a rifle and steel helmet.

Some went down to malaria, raved in delirium, recovered, marched on. Some dropped out, physically unable to march another foot. But the stronger ones trickled steadily onward. They travelled hundreds of miles through some of the most difficult country in the world.

They ate native food raw or cooked what they could in their tin hats. They crossed ravines, swinging on vines from tree to tree. Weeks after the fall of Rabaul they emerged from the jungle and entered a coastal village.

There the five men obtained a pinnace. They undertook their sea journey light-heartedly without a navigator or proper provisions. Storms and high seas followed them the whole way. The constant pitching of the small craft prevented sleep for days.

Their navigation was the hit-or-miss method. They reached an island mission station. A day later they reached the New Guinea mainland after one of the most dramatic episodes of tropical warfare in this century.

1942   Australians are shocked when midget Japanese submarines enter Sydney Harbour

GEOFFREY TEBBUTT AND RICHARD HUGHES
Melbourne Herald, 2 June 1942 and 2 April 1949

The war came to Sydney on 31 May 1942, when three Japanese midget submarines entered the Harbour and attempted to raid shipping. One of them torpedoed a ferry boat, the Kuttabul, *which was being used as a naval depot; nineteen people aboard the* Kuttabul *were killed. One submarine was sunk by depth charges, and another became entangled in the Harbour's anti-submarine boom. The third escaped.*

The raid came as a tremendous shock to a city which was still largely unprepared for close-range war. A Japanese reconnaissance plane, then unidentified, had flown over Sydney Harbour on the night of 29 May, and caused no alarm. Harbour traffic had remained normal, and the floodlights at Garden Island naval dockyard were turned on each night.

The Sydney Morning Herald *warned on 2 June: 'Any lingering popular belief in southern Australia that "it cannot happen here" should now be completely dispelled. The risks under which Australians live belong no more to the realm of theory.'*

Wreckage of two Japanese submarines was recovered from the Harbour and used to make one complete vessel, which then toured Australia raising money for charities. Later it was installed at the Australian War Museum in Canberra.

Geoffrey Tebbutt, who died in September 1973, at the age of sixty-six, served as a war correspondent on many fronts; he was New York editor of Australian Associated Press before joining the Melbourne Herald *as a senior writer. When he died, colleague Frederick Howard said of him: 'It is hard for us now to imagine the* Herald *office without him. One hopes that his qualities, his values, will long have their place there. His lean, alert*
figure, striding a corridor, poised over a galley or copy, seemed to express so much of his high concept of what journalism was all about. Reporting is seeking answers to the important questions. Geoffrey was a magnificently tireless reporter. . .'*

Geoffrey Tebbutt, writing in the Melbourne Herald *on 2 June, said:*

Although the first jolt of surprise has been absorbed, and the Japanese submarine raid is seen as a spectacular failure, several odd features of their ambitious enterprise await explanation.

The cheeky crews of the midgets performed a feat of seamanship even to enter, and deeply to penetrate, the greatest harbor and naval base remaining to the Allies in the South-west Pacific. Let us recognise that for the ingenious stroke it was.

But, having been cunning enough to slip in, it is an anti-climax that the only victim should have been a superannuated Sydney ferry-boat. Perhaps there was not such a wide margin between this result — ludicrous except for the casualties just announced — and the infliction of very grave loss upon our shipping. The defences may have been fooled at the outset, but they went to work with gratifying success in time to prevent serious damage.

It is to be noted that the Axis believes in Anglo-Saxon vulnerability at the week-end. The Royal Oak was torpedoed at anchor in Scapa Flow on a Saturday morning; the Japanese struck at Pearl Harbor on a lazy Sunday morning; the Luftwaffe chose a Sunday night to launch its ferocious fire-bomb raid upon the then locked-up and practically deserted City of London; a Sunday night was thought by the submarine marauders to be the most propitious moment for shocking Sydney.

If the midgets came from a mother-ship — and no other theory has been put forward to account for their operation — it shows that the Japanese must have sent larger craft daringly close in to the New South Wales coast, and that the depot ship or ships eluded the sea and air patrols. It is not Pearl Harbor alone that could be approached unobserved. The possibilities of surprise are not yet exhausted. The enemy finds hiding-places in the waste of waters.

The precise objectives of the midgets we cannot know, nor the degree of information the enemy possessed to induce or to encourage him to make his bid at that moment. The dead men of two or three submarines, and documents or equipment that may be fished up from the harbor bed, could yield a tale to Naval Intelligence. What the event does further emphasise is the imaginativeness, and the boldness, even the suicidal boldness, of the enemy. It did not come off this time, but it was, as Mr Churchill said of the sinking of the Royal Oak, "a remarkable exploit of professional skill and daring".

Scapa Flow provides perhaps the closest parallel in the submarine enterprise of this war to the attack on Sydney — except that the Germans did not use midgets, and they did not miss. There, the surprise factor was so complete that, when the first torpedo hit the Royal Oak, many of her survivors — 800 of the 1200 men aboard died — thought the battleship had been bombed. Twenty minutes later, while the admiral and the captain were investigating the alternative possibility of an internal explosion, a second salvo of torpedoes struck, and the 29,500-ton battleship went down.

The first impression of one of the Sydney ferry survivors also was that it had been a bomb attack.

The submarine — whose commander collected the Knight's Cross of the Iron Cross and promotion to rear-admiral for his exploit — got in and got out undetected.

"The Admiralty," said Mr Churchill (then First Lord), "has resolved to learn from the bitter lesson that nothing must be taken for granted. The immunity of Scapa Flow in the last war had led to a too easy valuation of the dangers, and undue risk was accepted both by the Admiralty and the Fleet." He disclosed that the last block-ship required to protect the anchorage against U-boat attack had reached Scapa Flow only a day after the disaster.

On the incomplete evidence, the defences and the state of watchfulness in Sydney were, at the decisive moment, adequate. We come out of the startling affair with considerable credit. But also, considering the Royal Oak and Pearl Harbor, we have been fortunate.

It might have been another Scapa Flow.

After the war, the correspondent Richard Hughes tracked down the pilot of the plane which had made the reconnaissance flight over Sydney on the night of 29 May. He was Susumo Ito, a former second lieutenant in the Imperial Japanese Navy, who was running a fishing-tackle store in Iwakuni when Hughes found him in April 1949. Hughes wrote in the Melbourne Herald *on 2 April 1949:*

Ito said the first time he flew over Sydney was on the night of May 29-30, 1942, to reconnoitre for the Japanese midget submarine entry into the Harbor the following night.

The second time was on the night of January 25-26, 1943 (during the Solomon Islands fighting) to discover the strength of shipping forces in the Harbor.

Each time his two-seater seaplane was dispatched from a Japanese submarine pack which surfaced at points north-east of North Head. Ito, who was then 27, was specially selected for the flights because he was regarded as the Navy's most skilful night flyer.

It was considered highly improbable that he would return safely from either flight.

On the first occasion a pack of six long-range, 3330-ton Japanese submarines surfaced at a point 35 miles north-east of North Head. Three of the submarines carried a midget, two-man submarine each. The other three each carried a tiny Japanese scouting plane.

Ito and his observer took off from their submarine at 3 a.m., just before moonrise. The sea was choppy with a rising wind and there was a cloud ceiling of 2000 ft.

The plane, which had collapsible wings, was no bigger than a Tiger Moth, was not armed and carried no markings or identification.

"I flew in over North Head at a height of 1500 ft. and descended abruptly to 600 ft. to fly up the Harbor, while my observer sketched the position of the boom and its entrance," Ito told me.

He was using an official Japanese navy map, which, he says, was very accurate on harbor detail but highly inaccurate on suburb markings.

As he approached Garden Island, observing what he believed to be a large cruiser and four destroyers, searchlights swung towards him and he climbed into the clouds.

He came down, flew over Farm Cove, where he observed what "looked like an 'A'-class cruiser" (presumably USS Chicago), skimmed at a height of 450 ft. towards the bridge, climbed again and circled over Cockatoo, where he was low enough to see welding flashes from the dockyards.

Trying to get his bearings, he sought Mascot aerodrome, but his map details here were misleading until, he says with a smile, Mascot heard him, apparently mistook him for a friendly plane and turned on the landing lights.

He flew back towards Farm Cove, evaded more searchlights, observed a ship on the north side of the harbor and flew out over North Head towards the sea. He had been over Sydney for about 10 minutes.

Meantime the wind had strengthened and in the darkness he could not locate his mother-submarine. After circling, he flew back a second time to North Head, turned, and, taking a calculated risk, flashed his lights for two or three seconds as he flew back again towards his rendezvous point.

The watching submarine responded with a five-second flash and Ito came down in the sea beside it.

The sea was now high, however, and the plane capsized. Ito and his observer managed to scramble clear and to swim to the submarine.

The floats of the overturned plane were punctured to sink it and Ito made his report to his captain.

In the hot, cramped quarters of the submarine, all the officers jubilantly toasted Ito with one "bottoms-up" round of sake.

Next night, the three midget submarines entered Sydney Harbor. No one really expected them to return, but it was agreed that the mother-submarine would wait for them until the morning of the 31st.

Actually, the pack waited for two days, although there was a heavy storm on the 31st, in the hope that one or more might have survived the entry into the Harbor.

Then, Ito says, Australian radio was heard to announce, to the surprise of the Japanese, that "six Japanese midget submarines" had been destroyed, and the pack dispersed.

On his second flight, Ito took off from his submarine at midnight from a point about 100 miles north-east of North Head. Again there were six giant submarines in the area.

Under a full moon in a clear sky, the tiny plane came in towards the Heads at a height of 9000 ft., descending to 3000 ft. over Garden Island.

"This time," Ito says, " there were far fewer lights in the city and suburbs than there were on the first flight, but all shipping in the Harbor was clearly visible in the bright moonlight."

He flew over the Bridge again, descending as he turned towards Mascot. There were lights near the aerodrome and Australian planes were in the air.

Ito says some rounds of ack-ack fire were directed at him, so he circled, came down lower and flew back towards the moonlit Harbor, skirting the groping searchlights.

He located his submarine without trouble and made a successful landing beside it to report that there was no heavy concentration of shipping in the Harbor. This time he had been over Sydney for 20 minutes.

His submarine took the plane aboard and continued up the coast to make daylight periscope observations off the mouth of the Brisbane River. . .

One of the three Japanese midget submarines which attacked Sydney Harbour on the night of 31 May 1942 being raised after its destruction by depth charges

1942   In the jungle the Diggers fight a different kind of warfare

GEOFFREY HUTTON
Melbourne Argus, 21 August 1942

The difficulty of fighting in the jungle was summed up very well in this report by Geoffrey Hutton, of the Melbourne Argus. *It was not only Australians versus Japanese, he pointed out; it was Man versus Nature.*

Geoff Hutton had been at the Argus *since his graduation with an arts degree from Melbourne University in 1930. He was a leader writer, and drama and ballet critic, before he was chosen to represent the* Argus *as a war correspondent. After service in New Guinea (with men like Allan Dawes, George Johnston and Osmar White), he went to Europe and took part in the Normandy landings. He was one of the few correspondents to receive a mention in dispatches.*

He transferred to the Melbourne Age *in 1954, and was that newspaper's London correspondent from 1957 to 1959. He continued to write leading articles and theatre criticisms, and to carry out assignments abroad. He retired from daily newspaper work in October 1974. His wife, Nan Hutton, also won a considerable journalistic reputation as a columnist. Geoffrey Hutton died in 1985, aged 76.*

Here is his account of jungle warfare against the Japanese in New Guinea, written for the Argus *on 21 August 1942:*

Up in the mountains and jungles of New Guinea Australia is fighting her secret war. It is not only a war of Australian against Japanese, but a war of man against nature. It is small-scale war too, because New Guinea is probably the world's toughest battle ground. While huge forces of tanks and artillery can be deployed on the open plains of Russia, the jungles and mountains of New Guinea limit fighting to raids, counter-raids, ambushes and infiltration moves by almost self-supporting groups of infantrymen.

It is difficult to give an accurate picture of this war except in the words of men who have come back from the forward areas for leave or medical treatment. I have not seen the fighting around Kokoda, nor has any correspondent. Every pound of supplies is needed for the fighting men. . .

New Guinea has been likened to a series of islands. Today the Japanese hold a string of islands along the north coast, while we hold a large island on the south. Between is a sea of jungle and mountain, a nightmare land of matted vegetation, malarial swamps, thundering waterfalls, and muddy rivers infested with crocodiles. In the wildest areas there are still tribes of primitive headhunters, but the whole area is dotted with administrative posts and criss-crossed with patrols maintained by the army, as they were previously maintained by the civil administration. The law still carries throughout hundreds of miles of remote New Guinea, and if it is possible to say that anyone holds these areas, then we do.

In Malaya and Burma the Japanese taught us the folly of talking about impenetrable areas, and it may be that they will repeat that lesson, but I do not think so. The one danger point in New Guinea, if we except the possibility of a seaborne invasion, is along the track southward from Kokoda. I believe that we can hold this track, and that we must hold it. Not only is it the backdoor to Port Moresby, but it is the direct route into a rubber producing area, which today is more important than ever before in history. I have seen some of New Guinea's rubber plantations, and watched the sturdy well-built natives singing at their work, as they tap the precious white fluid from the trees, and carry the buckets strung in pairs on a stick, down the earth tracks. New Guinea's rubber yield has declined in recent months because so many natives are urgently needed for porterage, for loading and unloading supplies, and for road repairs. One of our most urgent tasks is to increase the yield to its maximum and to safeguard the plantations which produce it.

Progress of the fighting has so far given our troops increasing confidence that they can hold the Japanese, even in the jungle country that they like to fight in. New Guinea is a tougher proposition than Malaya, where jungle tracks make infiltration easy, and the Japanese could disguise themselves as Malayans. At Oivi the Japanese showed skill in cutting their way through the jungle to outflank our troops, but they were successful only because they had greatly superior numbers. It is a fact that in the jungle clashes in the last two months our men, normal army units and natives of Papuan forces, have killed several Japanese for every casualty they have suffered. In our retirement from Buna the ledger showed a substantial balance on our side. At Salamaua our jungle troops have done more; they have cowed the Japanese by their superior toughness and bushcraft.

Japanese tactics so far have followed familiar lines. The infantry wear green overalls and face nets, which make it difficult to see them in the shadowy undergrowth. They carry light automatic guns and travel very fast on foot. To intimidate the defenders they shout and squeal before rushing a position. At Oivi a party of five Japanese advancing in the dark tried the old trick of calling to our troops. "Corporal White! Corporal White! Come forward," they shouted. Then pretending they were Papuans: "I help you, Taubada." Our party waited — waited until they were well in range, and then shot all five. We had no Corporal White. . .

The men who have been in action so far have proved that with the right training they can meet the Japanese and stand up to them at their own game. The issue at stake is not only the defence of Port Moresby and the northern approaches to Queensland. . .

A Papuan leads a wounded Australian after fierce fighting at Buna, New Guinea, 1942

1942 Black days for Port Moresby as it waits for the Japanese invasion

GEORGE JOHNSTON
Melbourne Argus, 3 November 1942

George Johnston was a reporter who wanted to be a novelist. So great was this urge that, at a high point in his journalistic career, as London bureau chief of the Sydney Sun, *he turned his back on the newspaper world and went off to the Greek island of Hydra. He and his writer wife, Charmian Clift, stayed for ten years on Hydra and produced about a dozen books in that time. One of them was George Johnston's* My Brother Jack, *the semi-autobiographical novel in which he evoked powerfully the atmosphere of lower middle-class suburbia between the wars.*

George Johnston was born, the son of a tramwayman, in 1912. He grew up in Caulfield, Melbourne, attended a state school and later the Brighton Technical College, took a job as a printer's assistant, and went to art classes at night.

He gained his start in journalism on the Melbourne Argus *with a series of imaginative articles about sailing ships, which he had only ever seen tied up at Victoria Docks. During World War Two he established an international reputation with his dispatches from battle zones for American magazines and Australian newspapers. He was a newspaperman for twenty-two years, and wrote several novels — one of them,* High Valley, *in collaboration with his wife, Charmian Clift — during this period.* My Brother Jack, *which won the Miles Franklin award as the best Australian novel of 1964, was the first of a trilogy; it was followed by* Clean Straw for Nothing *and* A Cartload of Hay, *on which he was working until a few days before his death in 1970. His wife, who wrote newspaper columns for the* Sydney Morning Herald *and the Melbourne* Herald *after their return from Hydra in 1964, died in 1969; she was forty-four.*

In the following report published in the Melbourne Argus, *Johnston wrote about the blackest days of Port Moresby, as it waited for a Japanese invasion. It was datelined 'Somewhere in New Guinea':*

On the night of Tuesday, February 3, 6 4-engined Kawanisi flying-boats dropped bombs on Australian soil for the first time during Port Moresby's first air raid.

Last night 2 twin-engined Japanese bombers dropped a few bombs harmlessly in the scrub near a Moresby airfield. It was the garrison's 85th air raid. . . A lot of things have happened between these 2 attacks.

This morning as I marked the entry in my diary concerning this piffling little raid (none of us knew bombs had fallen until this morning!) I thumbed back through the grubby pages that have recorded something of the day-by-day march of events in this dusty, quite untropical, outpost 9½ degrees of latitude below the Equator. Many of the entries were made in New Guinea, many were made in other operational areas or while at GHQ, but all of them concern one thing only — the "Tropic sideshow" of New Guinea that developed into a full-scale battle for the protection of Australia and the Allied supply line in the South-West Pacific.

The contrast between the diary entries of 8 months ago and the diary entries of today affords an astonishing commentary on the changed spirit and the changed strength of this vital garrison — a change that is evident through every feature, from the morale of troops and behaviour of the natives to air support and the spirit of aggression. Here are extracts of some of the entries written in the Moresby of yesterday and the Moresby of today, placed in juxtaposition for the purposes of comparison and contrast:

FEBRUARY 8: Moresby's first raid is over, and the natives have "gone bush" in a body. The road from Moresby to Porebada Village is black with an endless line of native refugees heading out of town with such speed that a pall of dust hangs constantly over the road. . .

OCTOBER 8: Sergeant Katue, a Papuan native, has come in after 73 days in the jungle, bringing a Japanese prisoner with him. In a private jungle war, which he organised inside the Japanese lines, he killed 26 enemy soldiers and marines and sewed their stripes and regimental insignia to his tunic to prove it!

FEBRUARY 10: The Japanese made a new landing today at Gasmata. A big bombing force of 5 RAAF Hudsons went out and sank 2 enemy merchant ships in an attack from masthead height. One Zero was shot down, but 2 Hudsons went down in flames.

OCTOBER 9: The heaviest bombing raid ever undertaken in the South-West Pacific was carried out on Rabaul before dawn today by Flying Fortresses and other planes. More than 60 tons of bombs were dropped at the rate of one every 12 seconds for 95 minutes, and Rabaul town was left a mass of flames. All our planes came back without a single casualty.

FEBRUARY 14: The civilian evacuation has almost ended. Many of these miners and traders have been forced to sacrifice a life-time's bitter work. A few spoke of defying a hail of Japanese bombs in the "grim hell of Moresby" — bombs, they say, which were filled with old razor blades and hacksaws! . . .

OCTOBER 13: Bitter fighting today in the Owen Stanleys, where the Japanese are entrenched on the high ground and are hammering our troops with mortars and machineguns. In blinding rain our troops are fighting their way round greasy cliffs, clinging by aching finger-tips, never giving up in their hammering of the enemy, who is now completely on the defensive. On this hellish battlefield, by comparison with which Moresby is a tourist paradise, we have recaptured 2 more Japanese strongposts in the worst fighting conditions this war has seen. . .

FEBRUARY 28: Our first Zero fighter shot down in today's raid. The pilot baled out and was captured — our first prisoner. . .

OCTOBER 5: As our troops move north-toward Efogi they see the graves of many Japanese, and the jungle near by conceals the bodies of scores of unburied Japanese dead. The enemy's Papuan invasion has cost him dearly — betweeen 1,000 and 2,000 Japanese killed in the Owen Stanleys, another 700 killed at Milne Bay, several ships sunk, and more than 100 aircraft destroyed. And so far he has very little to show for all this sacrifice.

MARCH 6: Japanese ships have been reported leaving Rabaul, rumours are spreading everywhere. Some say that the long-expected invasion of Port Moresby will come inside the next 48 hours. Panic has gripped the natives, who are streaming towards the bush, their few belongings carried Dick Whittington fashion on sticks across their shoulders. . .

SEPTEMBER 29: While Japanese shipping concentrations are building up in the Solomons and Rabaul I have never seen such perfect morale or complete confidence as there is in Moresby today. A great pall of dust hangs on the roads over the uncountable convoys of military trucks. Tough, sunburnt, determined soldiers are everywhere. The air is pulsing with the throb of our planes. One lorry has just gone by. On its dusty side is chalked: "Buna or Bust —Rabaul for Christmas!" And the troops are singing, "Hirohito, Here We Come!"

MARCH 5: The Japs have reverted to night raids again . . . two attacks last night. They have had so little opposition in their daylight raids that everyone is amazed at their reversion to night raids. . .

OCTOBER 22: Two Japanese bombers raided tonight under cover of darkness. They won't come in daylight now, because against our fighters daylight raiding has proved too costly. It's now 46 days since a Japanese plane has been over Moresby in daylight!

MARCH 20: Everybody with memories of Singapore, Greece, and Rabaul in mind is wondering when we'll get air support. We haven't a single plane left in Moresby. Nobody dares think what would happen to us if it weren't for our anti-aircraft gunners. . . There's a rumour that a squadron of Tommyhawk fighters is coming up, but they've been so long coming that they are now universally referred to as "Tomorrowhawks." Today some of the troops saw fighters coming in. They rushed across to welcome them, tossing their hats in the air and cheering. Next moment they were dodging cannon shells and machinegun bullets. The fighters were Zeros!

OCTOBER 24: For more than 3 months now our aircraft have held undisputed command of the air throughout Papua. Heavy bombers, medium bombers, attack planes, and fighters have smashed Japanese concentrations and supply lines on the north coast. Just for a change the Japanese have been fighting for months without any air support! In the 24 days of this month we have carried out more than 50 heavy attacking missions by air against the Japanese. They have made 3 small-scale attacks against us!

FEBRUARY 16: Our anti-aircraft guns opened up for the first time today against an enemy — a single reconnaissance plane, which was hit on the starboard wing, with the second shot, at 21,000 feet. . .

OCTOBER 13: Called today on the original AA battery that has seen all of Moresby's 83 raids. They are now just a small part of the bristling AA defences of the garrison, but this battery alone claims 43 Japanese victims — not bad when one considers that most of the Japanese bombing has been carried out from 20,000 feet or more.

MARCH 27: Listening to Tokio Radio tonight we were amazed to hear that "the vital battle for New Guinea" had begun in the Owen Stanley Range between "heavy Japanese and Australian forces." Tokio added: "Our troops are marching on Port Moresby, which has been completely devastated by our bombers, and victory is certain." It's all news to us. Moresby has never been more sleepy nor the Owen Stanleys more peaceful!

OCTOBER 29: Having remarshalled and rested, the Australians have begun their advance into the Owen Stanleys, have smashed and taken the Japanese positions at Ioribaiwa, and are moving on toward Menari. The Japan-

ese have left many dead and much equipment behind them, and their threat to Port Moresby has failed.

FEBRUARY 22: Australian flying-boats and US Flying Fortresses left for Rabaul — the first mission of the American Air Force in this area. Bad weather over the target, and the Fortresses couldn't find a ceiling at 20,000ft. . .

OCTOBER 23: A powerful force of Flying Fortresses, some bombing at masthead height, hammered Rabaul for 50 minutes this morning, sinking or seriously damaging 10 Japanese ships. Among the ships sent to the bottom were a cruiser, a destroyer, and 2 large transports. Enemy ship losses totalled 50,000 tons. Everybody is delighted . . . except the Japs, of course!

Well, these few entries should be sufficient — unedited and unaltered entires from an ordinary diary — to paint some picture of both ends of a 9-months' campaign in the skies and jungles of the most advanced outpost of the United Nations in the South-West Pacific. The story is not yet ended, but even at its darkest the picture today is very much brighter than it was in those days of February and March, when Moresby was given a short time to hold out — and when everybody thought the Japanese could "walk in and take the place by sneezing!" Let them try it now! . . .

1942   The Germans leave a trail of destruction as they retreat before the Eighth Army

KENNETH SLESSOR
Sydney Daily Telegraph, 20 November 1942

As the survivors of the Australian Sixth Division were escaping from Greece and Crete, their comrades of the Ninth Division, under Lieutenant-General Morshead, were resisting the Germans at Tobruk. The Seventh Division was preparing to march into Vichy-French Syria; the Eighth was to fight in Malaya.

Kenneth Slessor, an outstanding journalist and poet, covered the campaigns in Greece, Palestine, Syria and Egypt as an official war correspondent and he later reported the New Guinea fighting. Slessor, born in 1901, published several books of verse; he had four years as editor-in-chief of Smith's Weekly, *and for a number of years before his death in 1971 he was a leader writer and book reviewer for the Sydney* Daily Telegraph.

Slessor was thirty-eight years old when he was chosen as official war correspondent with the Second AIF, on a salary of £750 a year. Nearly fifty journalists applied for the job; the final selection was made by Federal Cabinet on recommendations from a committee which included the First AIF's official war correspondent, Dr Bean, and the president of the Australian Journalists' Association, Mr Geoff Sparrow.

From Alexandria on 20 November 1942, Slessor sent to Australian newspapers this powerful picture of the trail of destruction — 'the road to ruin' — along which the Eighth Army was advancing:

The road to ruin runs from Alamein to Gambut and points west. It is ruin, literal and absolute, a corridor of dusty death, lined with ruin, leading to ruin. But, although this endless avenue of dead and wrecked things is littered with the material ruin of guns and vehicles and war-machines, more than a mess

Mr Churchill emerges from a mess tent with Lieutenant-General Morshead at Australian tactical headquarters in Egypt

of German steel lies ruined here. A dream has been smashed as well.

It is, indeed, difficult to realize in its full three dimensions what the disintegration of an army means until you have travelled (as I have done for the past two days) through hundreds of miles in the wake of the German retreat. For hour after hour, mile after mile, the coast road is flanked at every twenty yards by the gutted wreckage of motor transport or the holes into which the dead have been thrust. From El Alamein to Gambut, for 200 miles, I drove past this continuous mortuary of burnt metal and buried men. Now in the rain which has come up from the sea it is beginning to smell sour and acrid. The track of a defeated army is always one of horror, yet this retreat is different from most.

There were no houses or homes to wreck because there are no houses or homes in this abominable waste, except in such battered villages as Mersa Matruh or Sollum, where they have been pounded five campaigns ago to roofless walls. Nor is there a civil population here to massacre or stampede. It has been a battle in a vacuum, a campaign of mechanized destruction, full of the fury and humiliation of machines. . .

The dead are buried in all degrees of graves. There are lonely cairns of stones hastily thrown together where the earth has been too hard and time too short for ceremony. A mile further on you come to the precise geometry of a German war cemetery with its pedantic straight lines and heavy Gothic crosses. But the crosses are everywhere – some made of packing-case sides, some only broken propellor-blades or splinters of rough wood, or helmets on sticks.

They are outnumbered only by the black-ened ribs and vertebrae of ruined vehicles. . .

You pass a truck snapped in half with a gush of sootblack tins spilling from its middle. Once they held food. At the side of almost every ruined vehicle there is an indescribable trampled litter of clothing and papers on the ground, as if its entrails were pouring out. Many of these trucks bear Italian markings but the documents scattered around them are written in German. Italian vehicles carry a squat painted oblong of red, white and green. German vehicles are marked with a black and white cross or the feathery palmtree and swastika of the Afrika Korps. . .

But outside, amongst the wrecks of trans-port, there is grimmer evidence. Hasty burrow-ings and scoopings and ramparts of shallow stones show where the enemy tried to hide in his agony. Nothing escaped the fury of our air squadrons. Even a steamroller lay capsized near Bug Bug, where badly needed roadwork had been in progress and the labourers had fled, leaving their hats, picks, shovels and heaps of stone.

Around the airfields of Daba, Sidi Barrani

and Gambut, the gaunt cartilages of Junkers and Messerschmitts lay rusting like the bones of prehistoric monsters. For 200 miles the trail of ruin led to the west. Wrecked tanks made landmarks in the distance, breaking the flat emptiness of the plain like the black hulls of derelict ships. Field guns and anti-aircraft guns, smashed and shattered, lay with their snouts buried in the sand. The roadside was scattered with their shell-cases squashed flat like tubes of toothpaste. Piles of unsown mines waited by the wire, looking like giant rusty rissoles. Near Mersa Matruh I saw a captured Australian truck lying forlornly on its back, still painted with the kangaroo and boomerang of the Sixth Division. . .

I spent my first night at the cookhouse of a prisoner-of-war camp which resounded like an aviary with the chatter of Italians. The next night I slept in an abandoned German hospital at the top of the Sollum pass. The shelves in the ward were stacked with thousands of tubes of specially prepared Afrika Korps eye-salve and foot-salve, another hint of the thorough-ness of German war equipment.

What I have written can give only a scattered impression of this incredible trail of destruction along which the Eighth Army is advancing. It is the road to ruin. But few of the British troops who pass its dreadful evidence of air-borne death and annihilation can feel any pity for the victims. I, too, had seen our men dying in ditches on the bloody road from Thermopylae and felt no pity.

As darkness fell suddenly over the escarp-ments, I picked up a scrap of paper from a flutter of Italian documents blowing across the sand. Its message was written in spidery purple ink and the writing was that of an old woman. "*Mio carissimo figlio*", it began, and there was much news of Cousin Maria and Uncle Vincenzo, and the last words were, "Oh, come quickly, day of victory and universal peace, and put an end to all our suffering."

1943   Despite opposition from Japanese, the Ninth Division lands at Lae

ALLAN DAWES
Melbourne Herald, 7 and 29 September 1943

On 1 September 1943, soldiers of the Ninth Division were preparing to make the first opposed landing from the sea by an Australian force since the Anzacs disembarked at Gallipoli twenty-eight years earlier. They were steaming in massive convoy through the Solomon Sea to fight the Japanese at Lae.

Allan Dawes, the Melbourne Herald*'s large and amiable war correspondent, accompanied the troops. In these dispatches, published in diary form in the* Herald *on 7 September, he told of the last hours in which the AIF veterans prayed to God to 'give us victory', and of the landing:*

2 September
Despite customary daily cloudburst and sloppy tropical humidity as they trudged laden through the ever-present mud the troops embarged for the sealine to their objective in an atmosphere almost of carnival.

They had been feeling the tautness of the leash for weeks. Trained to the last tendon, fighting fit and spoiling for slaughter, they had been gulping the news of the Komiatum Ridge fighting for days, waiting for their own turn.

This was it — at last.

Roads and tracks were swarming with green-shirts. They resembled nothing so much as the long lines of chlorophyll-colored ants that march up and round the jungle trees of New Guinea and North Australia.

Packs that bristled with jungle knives, axes and spades, M.T. bashing the mud under loads of ammo, and H.E., guns and gear — all combined to make a picture of battle eve.

Troops poured into the yawning bows of the beach landing craft like crusaders passing over medieval drawbridges. Papuans naked to the G String, stared wide-eyed at this new activity of the mad white man.

Aircraft circled overhead. From one of these I saw the biggest concentration of shipping I have ever seen in these islands. Landing craft of all shapes and sizes, some of them stacked one in another and another in that, like a conjuror's nest of boxes or the big fleas in the rhyme — big fleas have little fleas upon their backs to bite 'em and little fleas have little fleas, and so on ad infinitum — were flanked by warships and lesser craft.

Bubbling over with high spirits, Australians who had done the job a score of times before in odd craft and four hemispheres more or less, who didn't know where they were bound, but knew it was to a blue somewhere, trooped to their places, found their berths, stowed their gear, and waited.

They had a trial run and a trial landing on a near island. It was a routine show. But waiting is never a routine. Once a soldier has a job to do he's not happy until he's in it.

There were smiles of relief when the decks suddenly throbbed into life, and, with a rasp of chains and a swirl of muddying blue water, we were under way.

That was yesterday. This morning was like any other day on board any other transport. Men sleeping on deck were washed in a downpour, and the men who had preferred the sweltering heat under cover had the laugh of them. . .

We are the flagship. Our halliards flutter signals that to our sisters must mean something. They mean nothing to the troops who lie on their backs along the decks. Nothing has any meaning until they're "in it."

Not even a two-up school. It's surely a peaceful war.

3 September
Warfare disregards no weapon. This morning under a tropical sun in the blue Mediterranean of the South Seas I saw Australian soldiers on the eve of battle, already armed with fortitude, put on the buckler of faith.

Uncovered in the near equatorial sun they stood in a half-circle six deep, while the padre led them in prayers of intercession – prayers to God to bless "our strength, our wisdom and our equipment, that all of these might be used to give us the victory," and prayers "for peace for the remainder of our days."

The service was held in no dim religious light, and the atmosphere was by no means that of cathedral or cloister, but there was no question as to the sincerity of either celebrant or worshippers.

From the masthead a spotter with binoculars searched the heavens for enemy aircraft. Behind the padre a naked anti-aircraft gun, whose gun crew, still bare to the waist from cleaning it, joined in, lifted its snout.

From the bridge fluttered a colorful signal to the convoy behind, and from an improvised ropeline in the foreground the socks and shirts of a Digger's washing. In the shadow a poker game was in progress.

The troops, fresh from a submarine warning exercise, for the most part wore life-jackets or pneumatic belts. . .

4 September
A note of tragedy struck by what was probably the fluke shot of a Japanese bomb-aimer heightened by contrast the still almost carnival atmosphere on the beaches where Australian troops made their happiest landing today in all this New Guinea war.

Swinging by a stanchion, burning hot, over the huddled body of an Australian soldier whose clenched hand still held the Bren gun he was taking ashore when he was struck down – the same blast which killed him had played skittles with a case of mortar bombs in whose broken remnants his body lay – I plunged into the hold of a still smoking landing craft to retreat hastily before the stench of smoke and high explosive.

The beach on the other hand was throbbing with business like a market-place. The red landing sign was reminiscent of a country land sale. Bulldozer and caterpillar tractor rolled out of the great holds of a long line of ships, straight into the work of making roads, laying steel-mesh strips over soft earth, and transporting supplies.

Dumps of crates and cases and boxes, and dumps and cans mounted like the great Pyramid. An advanced dressing station – further in, a hospital – sprang into being. Ack-ack gun emplacements reared into being. . .

The landing craft moved in. Suddenly, there was a flurry of shellbursts in the sky, again the noise of bombs, a burst of smoke and flame, the flash of passing wings.

Now our own bombers were overhead, looming out of the mountains, heading for Lae and for the rest of the morning at intervals the crash of bombs echoed from the valleys, and here and there the skyline was broken with pillars of smoke.

The smaller craft were unloaded and away in a matter of minutes, the largest delivering huge cargoes of men and machinery in anything up to two hours.

Except for the feeble protest of his little formation of bombers the enemy was silent.

Lae seemed stunned. The air was empty, there were no guns, no soldiers, no booby traps along the beach. No sound of firing came from the jungle into which the first troops had already penetrated a few miles.

Days it took us to get here. Getting back is a matter of hours, and that in spite of a submarine alarm and a hostile aircraft alarm.

Tomorrow we will be back – with more.

The betting is that the enemy will try to recoil from the ruins of his strength. Whether he does or not, this trick is with us. . .

While the Australians were lost in admiration for the skilful handling of the landing craft under bombing and in a difficult operation by U.S. Navy personnel, the Americans returned the compliment by congratulating the Australians on their guts.

"These Australians – you can't rock 'em," Lieut. Edward G. Taylor, engineer officer of one of the landing craft exclaimed.

Lieut. Taylor, who comes from Dallas,

Texas, told me this was the first time he and the other officers and men of the ship had been under fire, and he was as interested in his own reactions as in those of the men.

"I was satisfied," he said. "I am proud of the men, proud of the way they acted. I won't say I wasn't a little excited a moment or two, and that they weren't, but we got round to it — and those Australians — they didn't turn a hair.". . .

The assault on Lae occurred when the major Allied offensive of the New Guinea campaign was at its strongest. South of Lae the Fifth Division, AMF, was closing in on Salamaua; the Ninth Division, which made the landing from the sea, was moving in on the Japanese; west of Lae a mixed force of paratroops, pioneers, artillerymen, engineers and Papuans was in occupation of Nadzab and awaiting the main body of the Seventh Division. In the centre was the 51st Japanese Division, and it was smashed.

The total number of Japanese in the Lae-Salamaua area early in September 1943 was about 11,000. The Australian Seventh and Ninth Divisions killed more than 2000 of them. The Ninth, in a savage introduction to jungle fighting, lost seventy-seven killed, 397 wounded and seventy-seven missing; the Seventh lost thirty-eight killed and 104 wounded.

Allan Dawes entered Lae behind the assault troops. One of the dispatches for which journalists remember him affectionately was written about his own arrival in Lae. It was at the time when some war correspondents saw themselves as awfully intrepid; there was a school of World War Two correspondents which delighted in writing articles beginning, 'I was the first man into . . . . .' Dawes sent them up wryly and briefly with one short report, published in the Melbourne Herald *on 29 September 1943. It announced that he was the last war correspondent to enter Lae, and then it explained what a problem correspondents could be.*

I was the last war correspondent to enter Lae — or what was Lae.

This is saying a mouthful; the war corres-

pondents were an army of occupation in themselves. There were correspondents with Major-General Vasey's force; there were correspondents with Major-General Wootten's force; there were correspondents with General MacArthur, and there were correspondents who climbed into a P.T. boat and came over from Salamaua.

The London press was represented, the American press, the Australian press, Australian Broadcasting Commission, Military History and Information, the Army Press of America, and the Australian Army Public Relations Directorate.

We correspondents constitute a perpetual problem to the army now. We have to be fed, clothed and housed when there is housing, clothing and food; we have to be transported (in the military if not the penal sense); we have to be censored; and finally we have to be tolerated.

Moreover, we insist on writing pieces which require to be despatched. This last is the real problem. In the course of the war newspaper messages have been carried by every means from a cleft stick to radio transmission from a hovering helicopter.

Messages from correspondents in this theatre have been carried by hand, jeep, truck, barges, large and small naval vessels, aeroplanes, staff cars, motor cycles, radio and telegraph. They have taken everything from hours to weeks to deliver.

This message is going to be unique. It will be the first message posted from Lae.

Allan Dawes was not only one of Australia's best war correspondents. He was a columnist, political writer, crime reporter, poet and author. He went into battle, armed with a typewriter, with the AIF in New Guinea, Borneo, Java and the West Pacific islands. He began his career with the Melbourne Age *in 1918, and later worked on the Sydney* Sun, *the Sydney* Daily Telegraph, *the Melbourne* Argus, *the Melbourne* Star *and the Melbourne* Herald. *He died in 1969, aged sixty-nine.*

1944   A newspaper defies the government over censorship and suffers the consequences

BRIAN PENTON
Sydney Daily Telegraph, 17 April 1944

The Australian Government and some of the nation's largest newspapers came into sharp conflict in April 1944, on the vexed issue of censorship. The newspapers claimed that, although censorship of war information had been relaxed in the United States, it had been tightened in Australia, and that this had been done for political rather than security reasons. The Curtin Government's Minister for Information, Arthur Calwell, claimed that many newspapers were publishing biased editorials which had caused mischief in the United States. 'The writers of these diatribes,' he said, 'are little better than fifth columnists.'

The Sydney Daily Telegraph *and the* Sydney Morning Herald *reported that some American war correspondents had quit Australia because of the harsh censorship, and that this was one reason why the United States was not properly informed on Australian policies. Mr Calwell insisted that all reports referring to censorship in any way had to be submitted to the authorities for censorship. This meant, in fact, that it was virtually impossible for the papers to criticise censorship.*

On the night of Friday 14 April, the Daily Telegraph *published the text of an attack by Mr Calwell on the newspapers, but left a blank space for the reply of the chairman of the Australian Newspaper Proprietors' Association, Rupert Henderson, on the ground that Mr Henderson's statement had been censored.*

Next morning, the Saturday, Mr Calwell served an order on Cyril Pearl, the editor of the next day's paper, the Sunday Telegraph, *insisting that he submit all matter intended for publication to the Chief Censor, not only that which mentioned censorship. On the same day Mr Henderson issued a statement*

explaining that the Chief Censor had mutilated his reply to Mr Calwell, and protesting at what he called gross misuse of the powers of censorship.

Cyril Pearl submitted Mr Henderson's statement, plus an editorial commenting on the situation, for censorship. The censor's office 'killed' the whole of Mr Henderson's statement, and hacked the proposed editorial heavily.

For the first edition of the Sunday Telegraph, *Pearl published a blank space on the front page, where he had intended to publish his editorial, and another blank space where he had intended to place Mr Henderson's statement. In the next edition, on the front page, he published photographs of Mr Henderson and Mr Calwell, side by side, and these words:*

A FREE PRESS – ?
The great American democrat, Thomas Jefferson, said: 'Where the Press is free and every man able to read, all is safe.'

Before the printing presses had started, a large force of Commonwealth police arrived at the editor's office; they seized all copies of the Sunday Telegraph.

The conflict quickly escalated as other newspapers gave support to the Daily *and* Sunday Telegraph. *On Monday 16 April, all copies of the* Telegraph *and the* Sydney Morning Herald, *of which Mr Henderson was general manager, were seized. So were both Sydney afternoon papers, the* Sun *and the* Mirror; *so were the Melbourne* Herald *and the Adelaide* News. *At the* Telegraph *and the* Mirror, *policemen produced guns and threatened truck drivers.*

Brian Penton wrote the following report on

Commonwealth Police attempt to prevent newspaper delivery; however, soon after this photograph was taken the van was driven off at high speed by staff members.

the events of the weekend for an emergency issue of the Daily Telegraph, *which was printed on the plant of the then-defunct* Labor Daily. *The next day, the papers won their battle. On application from the newspapers, the High Court granted an injunction to restrain the Chief Censor from continuing to prevent publication of the articles. Very quickly, the Government was compelled to amend its censorship regulations.*

The Sunday Telegraph was yesterday suppressed by the Censor.

This action was the culmination of a conflict of opinion between the Minister for Information (Mr. Calwell), who controls censorship, and Mr. R. A. Henderson (chairman of the Australian Newspaper Proprietors' Association).

At 11.20 on Saturday night, Commonwealth security officers served on the editor of the Sunday Telegraph an order empowering them to seize all copies of the Sunday Telegraph. As a result, all except a few thousand copies of an early edition of the paper were confiscated.

On Wednesday Mr. Calwell defended his department by attacking newspapers. He said: "The hue and cry, by some sections of the Sydney Press in particular, against the Department of Information and Censorship, is being carried to absurd lengths.

"Because an extract from a statement by the Minister for the Army was torn from its context by some Australian correspondents and cabled overseas, where it created momentary misunderstanding, the Department of Information is blamed for not having kept the American people better informed.

"If the American people have not been kept accurately advised of events in this area, the metropolitan newspapers, with some few exceptions, must accept a large share of the responsibility, for a great many very mischievous messages to the United States have been based on partisan and inaccurate editorials published in the eastern States and Adelaide.

"If it had not been for the commonsense restraint imposed by censorship, the volume of anti-Australian propaganda would have been ten times as great.

"Many examples of unwise, if not vicious, propaganda have come under my notice, but they cannot be quoted at this stage for security reasons.

"The writers of some of these diatribes are little better than fifth columnists."

On Friday, Mr. Calwell attacked Mr. Henderson, who had stated that the Minister was diverting public attention from his own failures by making baseless charges against other people.

Mr. Calwell accused Mr. Henderson of untruthfulness and inaccuracy.

"Mr. Henderson," he said, "makes a most inaccurate statement when he says that, because of censorship, most correspondents of American papers have been withdrawn from Australia . . . Mr. Henderson's additional statement that Australian correspondents have not been able to inform their papers truly of Australia's effort is also untrue."

Mr. Calwell ended his attack by threatening to have Mr. Henderson called before the Parliamentary Censorship Inquiry Committee, "where," said the Minister, "his and other wild, exaggerated statements will have to stand the test of cross-examination."

To these accusations, reflecting on his personal integrity, Mr. Henderson replied. His statement covered five typewritten sheets. The Daily Telegraph desired to publish both Mr. Calwell's and Mr. Henderson's statements in full, but this intention was frustrated by the State Publicity Censorship.

In an accompanying editorial, Penton wrote:

Mr. Calwell turned a page in Australian history by using this power to suppress a newspaper which had dared to criticise his tinpot dictatorship.

We publish the simple facts of the crisis which now endangers the freedom of all the Press — and your freedom to think, write, read, and express your opinion as you wish within the limits of security — because we want the people to judge for themselves.

We are prepared to face any retaliation a spiteful Minister can invent — even suppression — because we believe the issue is far greater than any particular newspaper.

1944   Two soldier poets concoct Australia's greatest literary hoax

TESS VAN SOMMERS AND COLIN SIMPSON
Sydney Sunday Sun, 2 July 1944

Australia's most celebrated literary hoax occurred in 1944, when two soldier poets, Lieutenant James McAuley and Corporal Harold Stewart, concocted a fairly meaningless brew of words and dressed it up as poetry. Their aim: to debunk what was the current vogue of surrealism and obscurantism in verse. Their success was devastating.

Angry Penguins, an avant-garde magazine devoted to the publication of subjective, surrealist and experimental writing, was the target of the hoax. It was published by a group which was headed by the writer Max Harris and which included the artist Sidney Nolan.

Angry Penguins received in the mail a letter from an Ethel Malley enclosing her brother's poems for consideration. She told how her brother, an uneducated Melbournian, had died at the age of twenty-five. He had worked from the age of fifteen as a motor mechanic, insurance salesman and watch repairer. He had been cremated on 23 July 1943, at Rookwood. There were sixteen poems.

Max Harris was profoundly impressed by these poems, and decided, with co-editor John Reed and Sidney Nolan, to devote an entire edition of Angry Penguins *to Malley. Nolan illustrated a Malley poem for the cover, and Harris wrote a eulogistic introduction in which he described Malley as a giant of Australian contemporary poetry. 'Unlike the moderns from Dylan Thomas onwards, Malley is never carried along violently within the personal,' wrote Harris. 'With him image can be obscure, but never experienced.'*

One person who knew about the conspiracy was a Sydney girl, Tess Van Sommers, who was studying Arts at Sydney University and waiting to take up a journalism cadetship on the Sydney Sun. *Harold Stewart, a close friend of hers, had told her about it some months before, but had begged her: 'Don't say anything about it to anyone, until the magazine comes out.' When the magazine went on sale in Australian bookshops at five shillings a copy, Tess Van Sommers considered she had been absolved from her undertaking of silence. Besides, she wanted that cadetship badly. She went into the Sydney* Sun *office, she said later, 'like a dog with a bone'.*

The hoax became world news. Max Harris later wrote: 'The hoaxers had the ear not only of the entire Australian press which delighted that modernism in poetry had been dealt a resounding blow, but the distant newspapers of the United Kingdom, America and Europe.'

Branding the spirit which motivated McAuley and Stewart as destructive, Harris continued to claim that the poems did have great literary merit. Later Adelaide police charged Harris with having published offensive material. After a hearing in which the judge stated that he found several of the poems unintelligible, Harris was fined £5 with £21 costs. Angry Penguins *folded three issues and two years later. Experimental poetry in Australia did not recover from the wound for a long time.*

Colin Simpson, who phoned Harris at three o'clock one morning to inform him that the poems were a hoax, wrote the story for Fact, *a supplement of the Sunday* Sun. *But Tess Van Sommers, who provided much of the information which enabled the story to be broken, was the essential collaborator. Both had successful careers on Sydney newspapers, and Colin Simpson became a noted author of travel books (*Adam in Ochre, The Country Upstairs, *etc.).*

Last week FACT said it would clear up the "mystery," motives and merit of the "Poems of Ern Malley". This week it does so.

The works of Ern Malley were deliberately concocted, without intention of poetic meaning or merit, as an experiment to debunk what was regarded as a pretentious kind of modern verse-writing.

[The writings were published in a special "Ern Malley" commemorative issue of Adelaide literary journal *Angry Penguins*, which ranked fictitious Ern Malley as "one of the two giants of contemporary Australian poetry," devoted 30 pages to an allegedly posthumous poet who had never lived.]

The 'Works of Ern Malley' were written, in collaboration, by two Australian poets, James McAuley and Harold Stewart.

Stewart, who lived at Croydon, is a corporal at present in a military hospital. He is 27.

Lieut. McAuley, AIF, lived at Homebush. He is 26.

Both are from Sydney, where they were educated at Fort-street High School, attended Sydney University. They are attached to the same Army unit, stationed at Melbourne.

Co-authors McAuley and Stewart this week made, to FACT exclusively, the following joint statement and explanation:

"We decided to carry out a serious literary experiment. There was no feeling of personal malice directed against Mr. Max Harris (co-editor of *Angry Penguins*).

"Nor was there any intention of having the matter publicised in the Press. It became known to FACT in an unforeseen manner. Some public statement is therefore necessary.

"For some years now we have observed with distaste the gradual decay of meaning and craftsmanship in poetry.

"Mr. Max Harris and other *Angry Penguins* writers represent an Australian outcrop of a literary fashion which has become prominent in England and America. The distinctive feature of the fashion, it seemed to us, was that it rendered its devotees insensible of absurdity and incapable of ordinary discrimination.

"Our feeling was that by processes of critical self-delusion and mutual admiration, the perpetrators of this humorless nonsense had managed to pass it off on would-be intellectuals and Bohemians here and abroad as great poetry. . .

"However, it was possible that we had simply failed to penetrate to the inward substance of these productions. The only way of settling the matter was by experiment. It was, after all, fair enough. If Mr. Harris proved to have sufficient discrimination to reject the poems then the tables would have been turned.

"What we wished to find out was: Can those who write, and those who praise so lavishly, this kind of writing tell the real product from consciously and deliberately concocted nonsense?

"We gave birth to Ern Malley. We represented Ern through his equally fictitious sister Ethel Malley as having been a garage mechanic, an insurance salesmen, who wrote but never published, the 'poems' found after his tragic end, at the age of 25, by his sister, who sent them to *Angry Penguins* for an opinion on their worth.

"We produced the whole of Ern Malley's tragic life-work in one afternoon, with the aid of a chance collection of books which happened to be on our desk, the Concise Oxford Dictionary, a Collected Shakespeare, Dictionary of Quotations, &c. . .

"Our rules of composition were not difficult:

"1 — There must be no coherent theme, at most, only confused and inconsistent hints at a meaning held out as a bait to the reader.

"2 — No care was taken with verse technique, except occasionally to accentuate its general sloppiness by deliberate crudities.

"3 — In style, the poems were to imitate, not Mr. Harris in particular, but the whole literary fashion as we knew it from the works of Dylan Thomas, Henry Treece and others.

"It proves that a literary fashion can become so hypnotically powerful that it can suspend the operation of critical intelligence in quite a large number of people. . .

"And as we have already explained conclusively, the 'Writings of Ern Malley' are utterly devoid of literary merit as poetry.
"— JAMES McAULEY
   HAROLD STEWART."

1944   In a suicide bid to overthrow a prison camp, 232 Japanese die

NEIL MOODY
Sydney Daily Telegraph, 5 August 1944

Not many violent battles have occurred on Australian soil. The most terrible took place outside the New South Wales town of Cowra in the early morning of 5 August 1944, when 1104 Japanese soldiers, sailors and airmen tried to break out of their prison camp. They burst from their huts, armed with table knives, and baseball clubs and sharpened garden tools, and they threw themselves against the concertina rolls of barbed wire which surrounded them. Their purpose, in a military sense, was to overthrow the garrison — but mostly, they simply wanted to die. They believed they had lost honor by allowing themselves to become prisoners, and they wanted to make amends.

During the outbreak and the days which followed, 232 Japanese prisoners were killed, and 107 were wounded. Four Australian soldiers were either stabbed or bludgeoned to death, and four suffered wounds. Of the Japanese who took part in what must have been the most hopeless banzai charge in the history of the Imperial Japanese Army, 334 actual escaped confinement. Within the next nine days, twenty-five of these were dead, and the remainder recaptured by posses of soldiers, police and local farmers.

On the morning of the massacre, a number of accredited war correspondents, among them Neil Moody, of the Sydney Telegraph, *and George Hawkes, of the Sydney* Mirror, *visited the camp at Cowra and learned the whole awful story. They wrote it, but censorship regulations prevented the mention of all but the barest details. The authorities felt that if the facts — and particularly the heavy Japanese casualty lists — were made public, reprisals would be taken by Japanese authorities against Australian prisoners in Japanese camps.*

Neil Moody had the satisfaction of seeing his report in printed form, but only in galley proofs. These were sent to the censor's office, and blue-pencilled. He kept the proofs, and has made them available for this book. Later, and undoubtedly more authoritative, accounts of the outbreak have been published; but Moody's was fresh when he wrote it and based on personal interviews. It was marked 'set and hold' — which is a newspaper way of saying, 'Let's get the thing in type, and hold it until we get a release.' In this case, it was held a long, long time:

More than 1000 fanatical Japanese prisoners of war revolted and attacked guards at Cowra compound early last Saturday morning (August 5).

Three Australian guards were killed, and seven wounded in fierce hand-to-hand fighting.

Japanese casualties total 350, including more than 200 dead.

Many of the dead had committed suicide.

Hundreds of the Japanese succeeded in escaping from the compound. They terrorised the Cowra-Blaney district for three days.

The night after they escaped some of them stabbed and stoned to death an Army lieutenant who attempted to make an arrest at Boyd's Hill, eight miles from Cowra.

Many of the Japanese, after succeeding in their escape, took their own lives in painful and peculiar ways.

One Japanese stabbed himself to death through the face.

Two lay on a train-line, stomachs upward, and allowed a train to run over them.

Another removed his tunic and disembowelled himself within sight of the prisoner compound.

Others burned themselves to death, hanged, drowned, and stabbed themselves, or cut their throats.

More than 1000 troops and a number of R.A.A.F. planes were used to hunt out and recapture escapees.

Civilians throughout the district formed posses and protected their homes with armed patrols.

Announcement of the mass escape and revolt had been held up while the Japanese Government was notified by the Swiss Consul (M. Hedinger), whose duty is to watch Japanese interests in Australia.

The prisoner of war camp authorities first received information several weeks ago that an escape attempt might be made.

The number of guards was increased, and they were given automatic arms.

Arrangements were made by the camp to send up Verey light signals to call for assistance from another military camp if a major escape attempt were made.

At that time there were about 1080 Japanese prisoners of war in the Cowra camp.

There was also a large number of Italian prisoners in a separate compound.

About 1.45 on Saturday morning (August 5) a revolt by all prisoners suddenly began.

Screaming and yelling Japanese attacked in three carefully organised forces.

The main attack was directed towards the capture of a heavy machine-gun near the northern fence of their compound.

This machine-gun was in the direct line of fire from guns in the towers.

Apparently the Japanese believed the guns in the towers could not open fire on them without killing the machine-gun crew.

Simultaneously two other forces rushed the barbed-wire at either end of the northern fence.

While these attacks were taking place, 16 of the 19 Japanese huts were set on fire.

The alarm was given almost immediately, and shots were fired over the heads of the Japanese. These had not the slightest effect.

The Japanese who rushed the wire threw blankets and clothing over it, and began to escape.

The other force attacking the machine-gun crew succeeded in reaching the gun only after heavy losses.

The gun crew was killed.

But with great gallantry members of the crew had held the machine-gun long enough to throw away vital parts.

This prevented the Japanese from using the gun against the Australians, although they attempted to bring it into action.

By this time a pitched battle was taking place between guards and Japanese.

The guards were using rifles and automatic weapons, the Japanese baseball bats and dinner knives.

In heat of the battle, all lights inside the camp, and the surrounding countryside, suddenly went out.

This may have been due to installations being struck by bullets, or may have been caused deliberately.

Many Japanese were killed while breaking through the barbed-wire. . .

Italian prisoners of war in the adjoining enclosure did not try to join in the revolt. They jeered at the Japanese and cheered when they committed suicide.

A large number of Japanese escaped. They divided into small parties and ran for open country. . .

Residents throughout the district were warned that the Japs were loose. Men were told to stay at home with their women and to arm themselves.

Where no men were available to protect women and children, soldiers were detailed by the Commonwealth Director of Security to guard them.

By dawn 1000 soldiers and a number of aeroplanes were searching for the escapees. . .

Some escapees travelled 15 miles before they were recaptured.

Most prisoners were retaken in groups of two to 20. Some were captured singly.

Many of the Japanese were recaptured by armed civilians. Women and even boys retook some. . .

Burial of the Japanese began on Tuesday night (August 8).

The Swiss Consul (Mr. Hedinger) attended

The bodies of three Japanese escapees lie decapitated on the railway line after prisoners-of-war lay down before an oncoming train

part of the burial.

It is believed that Japanese officer-prisoners were present during the burials.

Many prisoners were recaptured near Woodstock.

Armed searchers found four buried in a haystack. Another was found sitting beside a road eating a cake.

About 30 were rounded up in the rough country at Boyd's Hill, about eight miles from Cowra.

It was in this district that Lieutenant Doncaster was killed by Japanese.

No Japanese officers took part in the revolt.

Officers are separated from the men, and have special privileges not given to the rank and file.

They are most insistent on these rights, although, as Japan is not a signatory to the Geneva agreement on the treatment of war prisoners, they are not strictly entitled to them.

The officers demand that they have sheets on their beds, although Australian officers in the camp are not entitled to them.

The officers do not have batmen. They have to make their own beds and keep their quarters clean.

Guards say that both rank and file and officer prisoners are insolent.

They take no notice when instructed at gun-point to do certain work and invite the guards to shoot them.

Sometimes they spit into the guards' faces.

Mostly they refuse to do any work other than that necessary to keep their quarters clean.

They play baseball from morning until dark. Many of them made their own baseball bats. It was these bats they used during the revolt.

The prisoners included men from the Japanese Army, Navy, and Air Force.

Most were thin and in poor health when they arrived. But they rapidly put on weight, and became physically fit.

The Japanese had their own cooks, and were given food, such as fish and rice, to which they are normally accustomed.

Many of the escapees had rice in their pockets when recaptured.

All shops and businesses in Cowra closed for three hours on Monday (August 7) and Tuesday (August 8) during the burial of the Australian soldiers killed in the riot.

On Monday (August 7) the burial of Private Benjamin Gower Hardy, Private Ralph Jones, and Private Charles Henry Sheppard took place.

Lieutenant Harry Doncaster was buried on Tuesday (August 8).

Hundreds crowded Cowra streets on both days as the flag-draped coffins, on Army lorries, were taken two miles to the Cowra war cemetery.

Each time about 80 cars and several buses with local residents followed the funeral. . .

Neil Moody, who covered that dramatic moment in Australian history but never had the satisfaction of seeing it published in his newspaper, died in 1977, aged 62. He had been editor of Your Garden *magazine for four years.*

1945   Curtin's health causes concern: 'How long can the Prime Minister carry this burden?'

CRAYTON BURNS
Melbourne Argus, 6 March 1945

John Curtin, who led the nation during World War Two, died in office in July 1945. He was in fact a war casualty, having accepted the risk of burdens beyond his strength. The anxieties of three of the most critical years in Australian history punished him massively; not only was the leadership of the nation a strain, but Curtin insisted on accepting personally every responsibility that his government incurred.

He suffered a heart attack in November 1944, at the age of fifty-nine, but refused to lighten his burden. Dame Edith Lyons, whose own husband, Joseph Lyons, died while he was Prime Minister, warned him not long before he died that he should leave the job before it was too late. He told her he appreciated the advice, but felt he had a duty to remain.

Crayton Burns, the Argus *correspondent in Canberra, was another who could see the dangerous amount of punishment the Prime Minister was taking. On 6 March 1945, he wrote that Curtin's health, and the strain imposed on it, were causing concern.*

Burns, like most other Canberra newspapermen, met John Curtin on common ground. The Prime Minister had begun as a copy boy, first on the Melbourne journal the Rambler *and later on the* Age, *and he always styled himself a journalist. He had been president of the Western Australian district of the Australian Journalists' Association, and he remained a member of the AJA throughout his parliamentary career. Burns was a highly respected journalist who worked on the Melbourne* Sun News-Pictorial *and* Star, *as well as the* Argus; *he was the father of Creighton Burns, who became a Rhodes Scholar, correspondent in South-East Asia and Washington for the* Age, *and editor of that newspaper in 1981.*

Though not much discussed except in private, the problem of Mr Curtin's health, his political future, and ability to endure to the end, either of the Japanese war or of the Labour Government, the heavy burdens and little irritations inseparable from office, is again assuming importance.

There is an inherent association between his health and problems of the nation. Most people will agree that Mr Curtin's health and capacity to carry on as in past years are much more than his private and domestic concern; it is the nation's affair, too. He probably realises it more than anybody. No man, not even his closest associates, can claim to know Mr Curtin's innermost thoughts. From time to time he thinks aloud, and he often makes considered statements, but there is always the sense of restraint, and there are some unspoken indications which he cannot conceal.

He is visibly not as well as when he returned to Canberra from the rest upon which nature and his doctor insisted. A sense of duty brought him back to office too soon, and it is a physical impossibility in the present setting for him to follow medical injunctions to "take things easy."

The impending departure of Mr Forde and Dr Evatt on most important missions overseas, and now Mr Makin's injury in a motor accident, will increase Mr Curtin's task of leadership, unless an adjustment unprecedented in Australia, but recognised by practice in England, is made. Mr Curtin could remain leader of the nation and appoint a trusted leader of the Government in Parliament who would also preside at Cabinet and party meetings in his absence. This would entail not only delegation of duties, but of responsibilities. In Australia at present almost every problem, no matter how relatively trifling, reacts sooner or later upon the Prime Minister personally.

Even the advertising propaganda against Government policy is levelled against him personally, accompanied by his photograph. That would be hard enough were he a dictatorial arbiter of policy, but in fact he is not. As democracy connotes collective authority, so there should be the substance, as well as the theory, of collective responsibility. As it is, individual Ministers, unable to obtain appointments for individual discussions with him on their respective administrative problems, are prone to open up Cabinet discussions upon them, or worse, to make wrong decisions. . .

A Prime Minister in time of war entrusted with important problems of international relationships, strategy, manpower, food supply, and national economies should not be pestered with trifles. This gives rise to doubts whether the time has not come for Mr Curtin to ask the Parliamentary Labour Party for power to make substantial changes in the Cabinet team. Clearly he is not as strongly supported as he should be.

There are even grave doubts about Cabinet loyalty. Last week Mr Curtin was obliged to apologise in Parliament to Mr McKell, Premier of NSW, and to the NSW Government because some undisclosed Minister had handed to a Sydney evening paper a secret state document which was passed to the Commonwealth Government for its information.

Looking back, it must be admitted that lack of Cabinet and party loyalty contributed to the downfall of the Menzies' administration. Either Mr Menzies or Mr Fadden had authority to change the Cabinet team at will. Mr Curtin has not; he may rearrange the allotment of portfolios, but Caucus decides by secret ballot who is to be Prime Minister and who are to be his colleagues. If he is to exercise any right in his present difficulties to choose the team on the basis of ability and suitability alone, without respect of personal ambitions, Caucus would have to surrender him that right voluntarily. It is not likely to do so.

There would be some aggrieved men if it did; and to put himself and all the team back into the ballot would be risky; he might still

John Curtin photographed soon after he became Prime Minister in October 1941

get some whom he would prefer to drop and lose some he could not afford to lose.

So Mr Curtin does what he is asking every soldier and citizen to do; he carries on to the best of his ability with conditions as they are, and is thankful that the war is going as well as it is. The unpredictable element is how long he can do so? He must long for the day when he will be able to represent Australia at the peace conference, and then get back to his books and his writing. It is to be hoped that he is spared enough years after the war to give posterity the history of Australia and the Japanese war, which nobody else will be able to write as well as he should.

1945 People live in 'Happy Valleys' amid Tokyo's devastation

JIM VINE
Brisbane Courier-Mail, 3 September 1945

*One of the first Australian correspondents
into Tokyo as World War Two ended was Jim
Vine, of the Brisbane* Courier-Mail. *Vine, who
afterwards became turf editor of the* Courier-
Mail, *was representing Australian morning
newspapers. His son Terry was, much later, to
become sports editor of the Melbourne* Herald.
Jim Vine died in Brisbane in 1984, aged 74.

*Here are his impressions of the Japanese
capital, and the damage done to it by United
States bombers:*

Tokyo, once the world's third greatest metropolis, is a dead city with vegetable plots laid
out amidst the refuse of burned-out blocks.

Although the magnificent modern buildings
in the heart of the business centre escaped
extensive destruction, U.S. fire raids have
done terrible damage in the industrial suburbs.

Tokyo's heavy industries now don't exist
and for mile on mile whole blocks of factories
are missing.

Today I made a 60-mile drive in a command-
eered Japanese lorry through Tokyo's "industrial" and "built-up" areas.

Only the foundations of most factories
remain, and gaunt industrial chimneys point
up to the sky.

Great heaps of rusted tin, broken bricks
and tiles have been piled up, and the gaps
filled with crops of sweet potatoes and other
vegetables.

Even footpaths have been ploughed into
vegetable plots.

Australia's "Happy Valleys" of the Depression years can be seen everywhere.

The Japanese have laboriously straightened
out mangled sheet iron and built themselves
humpies among the ruins. Many of these have
black tarred paper walls, and there is no
visible evidence of sanitary services.

Once first-class paved roads have been
allowed to fall into neglect, and neat potholes
have formed on the main highways.

Tokyo was written off as a worthwhile
target by the Super-Fortress command many
weeks ago, but the present covering of weeds
and vegetable crops has hidden its scars. . .

Pyjama-clad women, many with babies
tied to their backs, and men, all semi-uniform-
ed, waited apathetically at every stop, sheltering from the rain beneath big umbrellas.

I saw no evidence of privations from shortage of food. All adults seemed in good condition, and the children looked plump and
well-fed.

Condition of the Japanese contrasted
sharply with that of the war prisoners I saw
on American hospital ships.

Some distance out we waited for another
truck to join us.

Unarmed, we wandered unmolested up and
down the streets.

Girls walked past us with eyes averted. But
when we looked back we always found they
had turned to stare.

Back at the truck, shaven-headed little
boys and doll-like little girls were first to
break the ice, and gradually edged in close.

When the time came to get started, the
Japanese truck had other ideas, and the driver's
efforts to make it go attracted quite a crowd.

The crowd raised a cheer as the engine
finally came to life.

As we moved off they waved and smiled,
and involuntarily some of us started to wave
back.

Then we remembered official instructions
— and the men on the hospital ships.

1945   An eye-witness report from inside the dead city of Hiroshima

WILFRED BURCHETT
Sydney Daily Telegraph, 6 September 1945

When the first American troops landed at Atsugi airfield, Japan, in August 1945, most of the scores of war correspondents accompanying them made a dash for Tokyo. One exception was a young Australian — Wilfred Burchett. With a satchel of rations and an umbrella as his only equipment, Burchett bought a ticket at Yokohama station and boarded the first south-bound train. His objective: the last real scoop of the war.

The train Burchett joined was a troop-train, and there were risks that some of the men on board might have been prepared to cut his throat. Unconcerned, he shared his rations with the Japanese soldiers; at night they made room on the floor of the carriage for him.

Burchett's report was datelined Hiroshima. It was splashed across the front pages of papers around the world, including the Daily Express *in London and the* Daily Telegraph *in Sydney. It was not only the first eye-witness report from inside Hiroshima, the city which had been devastated by the atom bomb; it was easily the best account published until John Hersey, many months later, produced his magnificent, heavily documented report for the* New Yorker.

Burchett, a Victorian, had had a varied life before the war, as a house-painter, a guide-book author and a conductor of European tours. He joined the Daily Express *in Chungking, and covered many phases of the war for British and Australian newspapers. Afterwards he became a controversial figure, reporting the Korean war from the communist side for papers and agencies like* Ce Soir, *Paris, the* London Daily Worker, *the New China News Agency and Peking Radio.*

He was alleged to have interrogated British,

Australian and American prisoners during the Korean war. As a result of his pro-Communist activities, he was stripped of his Australian citizenship and the passport that went with it; this was later restored — in 1972, in one of Gough Whitlam's first acts as Prime Minister. Burchett wrote some 40 books, and reported the Vietnam war from the North Vietnam side. He lived for some years in Kampuchea, where he worked closely with Prince Norodom Sihanouk, then settled in Paris. In 1982 he moved to Sofia, Bulgaria, with his Bulgarian-born wife, and he died there in 1983, aged 72.

This is Burchett's report from Hiroshima on the effects of the air raid which virtually ended the war. It was published in the Sydney Daily Telegraph *on 6 September 1945:*

Hiroshima, which was atomic bombed on August 6, looks as though a monster steam-roller had passed over and squashed it out of existence.

In this first testing ground of the atomic bomb I have seen the most terrible and frightening desolation of four years of war reporting.

Thirty days after the atomic bomb destroyed the city and shook the world people are still dying mysteriously and horribly from its effects.

People who were not injured in the explosion are dying from something unknown which could only be described as the atomic plague.

Hiroshima does not look like a normally bombed city at all.

The damage is far greater than any photographs can show.

After you find what was Hiroshima, you can look around for about 25 square miles, and there is hardly a building standing.

It gives you an empty feeling in the pit of

your stomach to see such man-made devastation.

I picked my way to a shack used as a temporary police headquarters in the centre of the vanished city.

Looking south, I could see about three miles of reddish rubble.

This is all that the bomb left of dozens of blocks of city buildings, homes, factories, and human beings.

Nothing stands except about 20 factory chimneys without factories.

Looking west, there are half a dozen gutted ruins, then nothing for miles.

The Bank of Japan is the only building intact in the entire city, which had a population of 310,000.

I saw people in hospitals who apparently suffered no injury, but are dying uncannily from the effects of the bombing.

For no obvious reason their health seems to fail.

They lost their appetites, their hair fell out, and bluish spots appeared on their bodies.

They then began bleeding from the ears, nose and mouth.

Doctors first diagnosed them as sufferers from general debility, and gave them vitamin injections.

The results were horrible.

Their flesh began rotting away from their bones, and in every case the victim died.

Minor insect bites developed into great swellings, which would not heal.

Slight cuts from falling brick or steel splinters caused acute sickness.

The victims began bleeding from the gums, then they vomited blood, and died.

Nearly every scientist in Japan has visited the city to try to relieve the people's sufferings, but they themselves became victims.

A fortnight after the bomb was dropped they found that they could not stay long and suffered from dizziness and headaches.

In the day I stayed in Hiroshima — nearly a month after the bombing — 100 people died.

They were some of the 13,000 seriously wounded who are dying at the rate of 100 daily, and will probably all die.

Forty thousand people were slightly injured.

Counted dead number 53,000 and another 30,000 are missing, which means they are certainly dead.

That is one of the effects of the first atomic bomb man ever dropped and I don't want to see any more.

While walking through this wilderness of rubble I detected a peculiar odor unlike anything I have ever smelled before.

It is something like sulphur, but not quite.

I could smell it where fires were still smouldering or bodies were being recovered from wreckage.

I could also smell it where everything is still deserted.

Japanese say it is given off by gas still issuing from the earth soaked with radio-activity released by the split uranium atom.

The people of Hiroshima are still bewildered and afraid.

They walk forlornly through the desolation of their city with gauze masks over their mouths and noses.

From the moment this devastation was loosed on Hiroshima the people who survived it have hated the white man.

The intensity of their hatred is almost as frightening as the bomb itself.

Japanese authorities thought that the Super-Fortress which dropped the bomb was leading in a normal attack.

When the plane passed out of sight thousands came out of shelters and watched the bomb descend by parachute.

It exploded when nearly everyone in Hiroshima was in the streets.

Hundreds and hundreds of people were so badly burned in the terrific heat generated by the bomb that it was impossible to distinguish their sex.

There is no trace of thousands who were near the centre of the explosion.

The theory in Hiroshima is that they were burned to ashes instantly by atomic heat.

The water in the city has been poisoned by chemical reaction.

The Imperial Palace at Hiroshima, once an imposing building, is a heap of rubble three feet high.

The remains of Hiroshima after an atomic bomb was dropped on 6 August 1945

1945   After Hiroshima, Wilfred Burchett liberates prison camps

JIM VINE
Brisbane Courier-Mail, 11 September 1945

Once in a while, a reporter becomes a figure of news himself. Such reporters included Ernest Morrison, William Donald, Banjo Paterson; and much later, for various reasons, Douglas Wilkie and Alan Ramsey.

There is justification, occasionally, for one journalist to take a published look at another — as Paterson once did at Morrison. Here Jim Vine, the Courier-Mail *war correspondent, wrote about Wilfred Burchett.*

Burchett had a flair for making news even in 1945 when he became the first newspaperman to enter Hiroshima, and later 'liberated' five prison camps. Years later, reporting the Korean and Vietnam wars from the communist side, he made news again. And again, in his long and finally successful battle to win back his Australian passport.

Jim Vine's report was published in Australian newspapers on 11 September 1945:

A pocket handkerchief-sized Australian, Wilfred Burchett, left all other correspondents standing in covering the occupation of Japan.

Armed with a typewriter, seven packets of K. rations, a Colt revolver, and incredible hope, he made a one-man penetration of Japan, was the first correspondent into atomic bomb-blasted Hiroshima, and "liberated" five prison camps.

Burchett, a Sydney Daily Telegraph correspondent, was told by his office to get to Hiroshima somehow, but quickly.

The quickest and only way was by train, a 21-hour journey, but he got there, after standing all the way, six hours before a special batch of correspondents landed in a Super-Fortress.

For those six hours he was the only white man in Hiroshima, which had had a quarter of its population wiped out in a single bomb raid. The Japs did not exactly strew his path with flowers, and the situation at times was tense.

Before leaving Tokio, Burchett had arranged with the Japanese news agency, Domei, to receive his copy, which was to be transmitted on the Japanese telegraph, but the plans came unstuck when MacArthur placed the capital out of bounds.

With the roads blocked, Henry Keys, of the Daily Express, London, also an Australian, who was teamed with Burchett, tried three times in a day to get to Tokio from Yokohama by train, but was thrown off each time by provosts.

Burchett and Keys solved the problem by hiring an English-speaking Japanese to act as runner between Tokio and Yokohama, but the delay cost Burchett his scoop.

As it was, he broke even with the Super-Fortress group, who had flown their stories back.

After Hiroshima, Burchett embarked on his one-man liberation tour of prison camps, visiting two on the West Honshu coast and three on the Inland Sea, before official rescue parties reached them.

At Tsuruga camp he sprang a masterly piece of bluff which caused hundreds of Japanese to lay down their arms and gave the inmates their first steak dinner in three and a half years.

Here the inmates were alarmed at the increasing concentration of Japanese soldiers, all fully armed. Burchett sent for the camp commandant, known as "The Pig," refused to answer his salute and bow, and, with delighted American Marines for an audience, upbraided him soundly for not seeing that the surrender terms were carried out...

1945   The massacre of army nurses and the sufferings of Eighth Army prisoners

A. E. DUNSTAN
Sydney Daily Telegraph, 17 September 1945

Of 126 Australian nursing sisters who served in the Malayan campaign, only eighty-five survived. The last members of the Australian Army Nursing Service to leave Singapore embarked in the Vyner Brooke, *which was bombed by aircraft and sank in Banka Strait.*

Twelve sisters were lost at sea, and twenty-two who surrendered to the Japanese were lined up on a beach on Banka Island and ordered to walk into the sea. These nurses were machine-gunned in the water and all but one of them were killed. The thirty-two surviving nurses from the Vyner Brooke *became prisoners of war in the Netherlands East Indies. They suffered greatly in captivity, and eight more of them died before the war ended.*

The story of the massacre on the Banka Strait beach was not told until the war ended. The Sydney Daily Telegraph *sent a war correspondent, A. E. Dunstan, to Singapore to interview the survivors of the lost Eighth Division: there Dunstan met the only survivor of the massacre, Sister Vivian Bullwinkel.*

Eddie Dunstan, born in Perth, was an executive on the Sydney Telegraph *before his accreditation as a war correspondent. His sister, Rita, was also a war correspondent. After the war he went to Singapore to help rehabilitate the* Straits Times, *a British-owned newspaper whose presses had been taken over by the Japanese during the occupation of Singapore; he worked for some years as chief sub-editor of the* Straits Times. *He later became a senior news executive of the* News, *Adelaide, and was South Australian president of the Australian Journalists' Association for a number of years. He died in 1984, aged 74.*

Twenty-four Australian nurses, only survivors of a party of 65 whom the Japanese captured in February, 1942, were found alive this morning.

Twenty-one were massacred on a beach on Banka Island on February 19, 1942, 12 are missing, believed drowned, and eight died in prison.

The survivors were found 100 miles west of Palembang, on Sumatra, and were flown to Singapore this afternoon in a R.A.A.F. Dakota transport.

Those killed on Banka Island were bayoneted and machine-gunned.

The 12 nursing sisters murdered by the Japs on Banka Island, off southern Sumatra, were lined up on the beach with their faces to the sea and mown down in cold blood.

The tragic story was told today with the dramatic rescue of the survivors from a foul prison camp in the heart of Sumatra. Nurses located by a war correspondent and an Air Force officer after a night-long search.

They were brought out by special R.A.A.F. aircraft, which flew in to the dangerous airfield of Lahat, where the party had been assembled.

The party included Sister Vivien Bullwinkel, of Adelaide, who was lone survivor of the nurses machine-gunned by the Japs.

Sister Bullwinkel was shot through the thigh and fell into the sea and was washed out 30 yards.

She was left by the Japs for dead.

She staggered to the shore in the midst of the bodies of her comrades and wandered in the jungle for two weeks before giving herself up through hunger and exhaustion.

The whole story of the massacre has since been kept the closest secret, for fear that the Japs would murder her as an eye-witness of their shocking atrocity.

Another survivor of the massacre was Stoker Ernest Lloyd, of the Prince of Wales.

He said the Japs told him and his companions to turn round and face the sea.

A Jap with a tommy-gun lay down on the beach, gun aimed.

The men turned round and a rating next to Lloyd said, "Here's where we get it in the back."

Lloyd replied, "Well, I'm going to give it a go."

He, with another rating, rushed into the sea.

He landed farther down the coast, and after 10 days was captured and taken to Muntok labor station.

He found the bodies of the nurses and others bearing bullet and bayonet wounds.

Dunstan also secured some of the first reports of the horrors suffered by Australian Eighth Division prisoners who worked on the Burma-Siam railway:

Australian and British prisoners sent by the Japanese to Siam and Burma in April, 1943, to work on the Bangkok-Moulmein railway, were flogged with bamboo strips and beaten with rifle butts.

Many prisoners died from repeated beatings.

Those responsible for this appalling brutality were members of a Japanese engineering unit, known as the "Black Triangle Guards," because they wore a black triangular patch on their sleeves.

The story of the sufferings of these Australian prisoners of war was told to me today by NX2589 Private Maurie Ferry, 24 Anzac Parade, Kensington, a former Sydney newspaper man.

When Singapore fell in February, 1942, Ferry was a member of a force known as "F" force, consisting of 3662 Australian and 3336 British troops.

These men were sent to Burma and Siam in April, 1943.

After a five-day railway journey from Singapore, in which the prisoners were crowded 33 to a rice truck, the men were forced to march 200 miles along old elephent trails, through the monsoon.

They marched at night, and tried to get rest during the day.

They plodded wearily through the mud and the darkness of the hot, dripping jungle, covering 17 miles at a stretch.

They walked up to their knees in water, and during the day fell back exhausted, to gain what rest they could.

It was during this march that the prisoners frequently passed through camps of the "Black Triangle Guards," who flogged and bludgeoned them.

Ferry, who was in the march, told me today: "When the prisoners reached their camp, they found other Australians already there.

"One was suffering from cholera, which spread quickly and caused many deaths.

"The Japanese refused to allow us to install any kind of camp hygiene, and when our officers asked that we should be allowed to do so, they were beaten.

"The Japanese, who were immune from cholera because of innoculation, claimed that the sick men were malingering, and reduced the food ration from 15 ounces of rice a day to six ounces.

"The Japanese refused to allow labor to be drawn from among the prisoners to put roofs on the huts.

"We worked 14 hours a day, starting at 5 a.m.

"We returned to the camp always in darkness, and tried to sleep with our groundsheets as the only protection against the teeming rain.

"In September the Japanese decided to take the sick and others unable to work to a camp at Tanabaya, in southern Burma.

"In this camp there were about 1900 men, including 600 Australians.

"We made the journey to the camp in open railway trucks, and by the time we arrived many were lying dead in the trucks. In my truck, six men out of 25 died during the four-day journey.

"On the way we passed through several prisoner-of-war camps, where we saw piles of charred bodies. They were mostly English.

"At the Tanabaya camp about 900 men

Selerang Barracks Square, Changi, photographed secretly by an Australian prisoner-of-war when 15,400 prisoners were herded into the intense heat and four hospital patients shot to force the Australians to agree not to try to escape

died in about a month. Each morning the bodies of the dead were stacked outside the huts.

"These men had suffered from beri-beri, typhus, dysentery, malaria, and tropical ulcers.

"Doctors at the camp carried out operations with common handsaws.

"The camp was no more than a collection of roofless, filthy, native huts, and the hospital was an assortment of tents on the side of a hill.

"Later we were evacuated to Kandury, an old French walled city in southern Siam, and 180 more men died before the remnants of 'F' force were shifted back to Singapore in December, 1943."

Of the 3662 Australians originally in "F" force, 1004 died in Burma and Siam, 32 died after the return to Singapore, and 14 were missing. Of the 3336 British members of the force, 2000 died.

This means that of an original force of 6998, only 3948 were alive nine months later.

"It was an unforgettable nightmare," Ferry added.

"On that railway we worked with elephants, and 10 men were expected to do the work of one elephent.

"If a man lost his shovel, all of us were starved for the next 24 hours.

"The sun rarely penetrated the white jungle mist which hung over the area in which the prisoners built the permanent way.

"The men were made to drag tree trunks and carry logs to buttress the line and provide sleepers."

Ferry, who is well known in Sydney journalism, is fit and well again. He is brown and clear-eyed, and shows little outward sign of his experiences.

When greeting friends among Australian war correspondents, he said he had put on a stone and a half in weight in six weeks.

Changing Face of
Australia
1946–1968

Marchers spread across Collins Street, Melbourne,
during the Peace Moratorium in September 1970

1946 The miraculous flight of a twelve-year-old Javanese stowaway

DOUGLAS LOCKWOOD
Melbourne Herald, 8 August 1946 and Melbourne Sun, 21 May 1957

*On 8 August 1946, the strange story of a
Javanese boy who survived a stowaway trip
in the engine nacelle of a Dakota plane, across
the Timor Sea, was published in Australian
newspapers. The details were sparse; the boy
was twelve, and his presence in the aircraft
had not been discovered until a mechanic at
Darwin airport discovered him twined around
the lowering mechanism of the undercarriage.*

At the time, the Melbourne Herald's *veteran
Darwin correspondent, Douglas Lockwood,
wrote:*

RAAF officers here are amazed that anyone
could have lived for three hours unprotected
at 9000 feet from the cold blasts fanned by
an airscrew only a few feet in front while
the plane was travelling at more than 150
mph. . .

What has everyone most surprised, however, is that the boy, who by this time was
unconscious, did not fall out when the
wheels were lowered. . .

*Lockwood became a close friend of the
boy, Bas Wie. He did not write the full story
of the flight until May 1957, after Bas Wie
had become an Australian. When he did, it
won first prize of £1000 in a contest conducted by the London* Evening News *for the
world's strangest story. Here is that report, as
published in the Melbourne* Sun *on 21 May
1957:*

If the mangled body of a 12-year-old colored
boy had been found somewhere in the bush
near the Darwin airport in August, 1946, the
world's criminal investigation force would
have been faced with an insoluble problem.

The boy's body was not found for the
sufficient reason that he wasn't killed.

Why he was not killed is an inexplicable
fact which can never be answered, least of all
by the boy himself.

Bas Wie, now 21, is very much alive today.

There is no mystery about his arrival in
Darwin. He is normal and happy.

But the story of his extraordinary arrival
in Australia ranks as one of the most incredible incidents of the air since the Wright
brothers first proved that man could fly.

It could just as easily have made the headlines as one of the 20th century's greatest
mysteries.

On the night of August 7, 1946, Bas Wie
was sitting disconsolately on the concrete
floor of a native kitchen at Koepang, in Dutch
Timor.

He was unhappy because he was a waif. His
parents had died while he was still a baby. . .

His friends were Australian soldiers who
had come down from the hills or been
released from prison camps. . .

When the cook kicked him, Bas decided
that it was time for action.

From the kitchen floor he could see a Dutch
Air Force C47 standing on the tarmac.

He knew the plane was going to Australia,
and he knew the captain and crew were in the
dining room having a meal before they took
off. . .

The door of the C47 was locked, and he
couldn't get in. He had intended hiding under
a chair or in a rear compartment until the
plane was airborne, but when he was balked
in this he soon found an alternative.

Bas walked over to one of the huge wheels,
looked up, and saw the vacant engine nacelle
— the cavity into which the wheels retract
when a plane is in flight.

It did not occur to him that once they were

in the air this cavity would be almost completely occupied by the wheel.

He climbed up a wheel, hauled himself into the nacelle — and waited.

He did not have long to wait.

Lieutenant Jan Sjouw, of the Dutch Air Force, had been told that his plane was ready, so he went aboard with his crew and started the engine.

Bas Wie, crouched among the struts at the top of the nacelle, felt the blast of air fanned by the propellor a few feet in front of him.

The exhaust pipe from the engine, only inches away, was already becoming hot when the motors roared and Sjouw began his take-off run.

At this moment of his extreme discomfort the plane was airborne, climbed sharply and the captain selected his "wheels up" control.

The hydraulic mechanism went into action, retracting the wheels into the nacelles, in one of which the 12 year old boy was crouching...

Bas looked down and in the moonlight saw the outline of the Timor coast.

But he also saw the big wheel coming up to meet him, and he saw that it was revolving at terrific speed after leaving the ground.

What happened then is not clear, even to Bas Wie, but it is certain that he tried to squeeze himself into an impossibly small space (thus getting nearer to the exhaust) in order to escape the advancing wheel.

Perhaps he turned on to his back to get his legs out of the way, or perhaps he slipped.

In any case, the revolving rubber caught him and laid bare his shoulder blade before retraction ceased.

The scars of this wound are still visible and Bas will carry them for life.

The wheel, fully retracted, pressed him towards the heat of the exhaust and Bas, wounded and covered in blood, was unable to move.

He was a most unhappy lad when unconsciousness finally overtook him.

The C47 stayed at 9300 feet for its 3-hour crossing of the Timor Sea.

Lieutenant Sjouw flew over the Darwin airport, took his landing instructions from the R.A.A.F. control tower, and then "undid" his wheels...

The wheels dropped into position below the bottom of the nacelle.

The cavity into which Bas Wie had crawled at Koepang reappeared while the plane was still 1500 feet in the air.

Why didn't he fall out? That question can never be answered.

It can only be assumed that Bas, who was still unconscious, was entwined in the structure and was shaken loose by the impact when the plane touched down, for when he was found a few minutes later he was "just hanging there."

He was clad only in a thin shirt and a pair of shorts. There were horrible burns on his body, the ugly wound where his shoulder blade was bare was angry and sore, and he was suffering from exposure.

Bas regained consciousness at the airport...

Bas was in Darwin hospital for three months and on the second day he confided his name to the medical superintendent, Dr. L. W. Alderman, and said that he had run away.

He was interviewed by Immigration and Customs officials, but he had nothing to declare and nothing to say to Immigration except that he didn't want to return to Timor.

When this department, Keeper of the White Australia Policy, let it be known that Bas would be sent back, there were plenty of protests, and finally the Minister for Immigration, Mr. A. A. Calwell, relented.

He was inclined to agree, he said, that a lad with "all that guts" should not be penalised.

A few days later the Government Administrator of the Northern Territory, Mr. A. R. Driver, announced that he would take Bas to Government House when he left hospital.

He was as good as his word. Bas went straight to the big white house on the cliffs overlooking Darwin harbour, was given his own room, treated as a member of the family, sent to school and taught English and how to fight and play football...

When Mr. Driver left Darwin in 1951, a local carpenter named Norman Ballard began a long fight to adopt Bas as a son.

Adoption papers were finally granted and Bas is now an Australian with legal parents. He wants to stay in Australia all his life...

1948   Bradman, the man they either loved or hated, bows out

ARTHUR MAILEY
Sydney Daily Telegraph, 5 December 1948

Sir Donald Bradman's career as an active cricketer ended in a Test match at The Oval in 1948. He was the most famous Australian sportsman of his time and later, as chairman of the Board of Control, he became the nation's top cricket administrator.

His record is formidable. He played 669 innings and scored 50,731 runs in a career that spanned twenty-one years. He had eighty Test innings, hitting an average of 99.9 runs in each of them. And through it all he seemed to occupy the centre stage position. His teammate, the professional journalist Jack Fingleton, observed: 'At one period it almost seemed that the game of cricket was subservient to the individual Bradman. His colleagues frequently felt that they were mere lay figures or items of scenery to be arranged to provide a background for the principal actor.'

The formal end to Bradman's career came in December 1948, when he played in a testimonial match in Melbourne. That weekend a man who had known him closely from his shyest, earliest days, wrote about Bradman. The writer was the versatile Arthur Mailey, cartoonist, journalist, wit, and one of the great slow bowlers. Mailey, who died on the last day of 1967, aged 80, played in 21 Tests himself, taking 99 wickets at an average of 34 runs; he once, in 1921, took nine wickets in a single Test innings against England. In his farewell article for the Sydney Telegraph, *Mailey pointed up the paradox of Bradman, and tried to explain it:*

Don Bradman will be remembered as one of the most remarkable sportsmen who ever graced the sporting stage of any country.

Bradman, playing in his testimonial in Melbourne this weekend, is an enigma, a paradox; an idol of millions of people, yet, with a few, the most unpopular cricketer I have ever met.

People close to Bradman either like or dislike him; there is no half-way. To those who dislike him there is no compromise. There are at least two major reasons: jealousy and this great cricketer's independence.

I have watched Bradman's career since he left Bowral, since he wore black braces on the Sydney Cricket Ground (he still swears he was never guilty of such sacrilege), have seen every innings he has played in Tests against any country, have seen him during moment of rich success and in his moments of embarrassment and frustration; have seen him pleased and annoyed, have seen him grin and sob almost in the one moment, but never have I seen him deviate very far from that line which was intended to lead him to power and success.

Unlike many people who attain power, Bradman has never, to my knowledge, resorted to political intrigue or compromise. His personal success on the cricket field has provided him with a passport which he never hesitates to use.

His intuition, tenacity, and calculative mind have given him an individualism which demands attention and, in most cases, support.

Bradman has a very acute brain. But there are some aspects in his mental outlook which lack the benefit of finer thinking. He is dogmatic on subjects or opinions which even an expert, or a master, would treat with great care and discretion.

That he can express a more sensible opinion than most cricketers on any set of subjects, there is no doubt, and in this particular connection I would mention speechmaking. Bradman has surprised many listeners with his ability to make an after-dinner speech. His complete coverage of interesting points and somewhat unorthodox point of view have given him a reputation that a more efficient orator would be proud of.

But cricketers are not supposed to be good speakers, any more than are wrestlers, boxers, or jockeys, and when one is able to utter a few intelligible sentences people are as surprised as if Bob Menzies had walked out in a Test match and broken his "duck." And, in this instance, the comparison, I feel, is consistent with respective performances.

During his career Bradman has fallen foul of many factions directly or indirectly connected with the game. The Board of Control fined him £50 for breaking the player-writer rule. Other players were disqualified for a similar breach, but Bradman was considered greater than the game, and certainly greater than the administration.

And, as a team-mate, I have always found Bradman dependable, a good sportsman. As an interviewer, I have found him reliable, fearless and fair, but most unsatisfactory; unsatisfactory because he appears to be suspicious of the Press generally. Nobody handles his own publicity as well as Bradman himself. . .

Bradman is a law within himself. This has been proved over and over again, and it is his amazing success as a cricketer, plus his perfect timing and tremendous respect and faith in his own judgment, that have demanded attention where others have been ignored — in some cases ridiculed.

When I asked him if it were true that he had been offered a knighthood, he replied, "I know nothing about it."

"Would you accept it if it were offered?" I persisted.

"I cannot answer a question which, to my knowledge, has no foundation," said Don.

The dialogue was similar when I asked him if he intended to stand for Parliament. . .

The ambitious Master Bradman climbed right over the heads of his contemporaries, some of whom felt that priority entitled them to the plums of captaincy.

Donald Bradman

Many of these men had accepted the captaincy of Australia or their States in similar circumstances, but consoled themselves with the thought that, in their cases, it was a reward for efficiency.

Bradman was brought up the hard way, the lonely way. That's why he practised as a boy by hitting a ball up against a brick wall, and when he felt the cold draught of antagonism within the ranks he kept his counsel, remained unperturbed, and knew his greatest weapon was centuries and more centuries.

Apart from that, his tremendous successes on the field and his value as a box-office attraction made him a valuable asset to those who regard big gates as a proof of efficient administration. Bradman never made the mistake, common to many, of thinking that personal popularity is more potent than success.

Bradman's humor is not particularly subtle, although there is a cynicism about it which makes it more acceptable than the red-nose stage type of wit. Don is more alert than most people in repartee.

I believe that he is quite ready to "swap" wisecracks with Bernard Shaw or any other professional creator of smart sentences, not because he can out-Shaw Shaw, but simply because he refuses to be silenced by greater personalities. . .

1949   Chifley sends soldiers to the mines in Australia's worst coal strike

ELLIS GLOVER
Sydney Daily Mirror, 2 August 1949

The Australian Labor Party Government, which had led the nation well for most of the war, was in trouble soon afterwards. The death of John Curtin had been a major blow. In Ben Chifley, the Government had a leader of great ability, with a remarkable knowledge of the complexities of economic problems, but there were many who said that he lacked Curtin's intellect, his vision, and his understanding of world affairs. He had lost some of his most senior lieutenants in Messrs Forde, Makin and Beasley; Dr Evatt was a capable and loyal deputy, but Mr Calwell, after initiating and administering a fine immigration program, had lost some public support by his dogmatic, unimaginative refusal to make exceptions to a 'White Australia' policy which was giving some offence to Asian neighbours.

Under Chifley, Labor followed a policy of gradual socialisation. Pursuing its policy of acquiring control of all airlines, it bought all the shares in Qantas, Australia's only international airline. It attempted to nationalise the banks with the 1947 Bank Act; this Bill failed after the High Court handed down a judgment declaring vital sections of it invalid, and it was finally repealed. It attempted to give the Commonwealth power to control rents and prices, but this move was rejected strenuously in every State by referendum.

The crunch came in mid-1949, when coal miners claimed a thirty-five-hour week, wage increases, long-service leave, nationalisation of the industry and amenities for mining towns. The Government called a conference of Federal and State Government representatives, colliery owners, the Miners' Federation and the Joint Coal Board to discuss the claims; the conference collapsed. On 16 June the miners held stop-work meetings which decided in favour of a general strike. The strike, beginning on 27 June, operated in all States except Western Australia. It developed into the worst the nation had known.

It was clear then that the Prime Minister had to deal strongly with communism — in the form of the communist-led Miners' Federation. Ben Chifley had always argued that Labor could handle the communists; in that election year of 1949, he had to prove it. It was an agonising time for the man who had been victimised himself for his part in the 1919 New South Wales rail strike. He appealed to miners to defy their union leadership, and return to work. Mostly, they refused and finally the Prime Minister took the unprecedented step of ordering the Army to work the open-cut mines. On 2 August, the troops began work. It was a tense and bitter time; many people felt that clashes of the kind that had occurred between police and miners at Rothbury in 1927 would be repeated. In fact, there was no significant violence, and the strike ended on 15 August. Following the debacle on bank nationalisation, Chifley's handling of the coal strike was a last desperate gamble to win the 1949 Federal Election.

The movement of troops into the coalfields, for the first time in Australia's history, was watched by many newspapermen — including Merton Woods (Sydney Telegraph*), Harry Standish (Melbourne* Herald*), Ellis Glover (Sydney* Daily Mirror*), Brian Hogben (Sydney* Sun) *and Fred Coleman-Browne (Sydney* Morning Herald*). This is Ellis Glover's report, published in the* Mirror *on 2 August 1949:*

The Federal Government's great open cut mining operation is now in full swing with hundreds of soldiers and airmen winning coal on the northern and western fields.

At midnight the well-planned operation slipped into gear with barely a hitch.

Great steam shovels and bulldozers moved into the open cuts and soon an avalanche of coal was on its way to the crushers.

Troops and police maintained a close watch on the roads leading to the mines, but there were no incidents during the night.

By 10 a.m. this morning, when the first shift of soldiers had finished work in the Muswellbrook open cut, 1500 tons of coal had been won, loaded on to trains and sent on its way to Sydney gasworks.

This remarkable achievement by 100 soldiers was carried out despite breakdowns in equipment and a shortage of motor trucks.

Pressmen, Army personnel and police shivered on the brink of the 250ft. deep Muswellbrook open cut at midnight and waited for zero hour.

At one minute past midnight Lieut.-Col. J. Kelly started the Army's greatest post-war venture by sounding the horn on his jeep.

Immediately other vehicles sounded the signal and the gigantic diesel-shovel in the cut below roared into action, blowing clouds of blue smoke through the searchlight beams illuminating the coal face.

Floodlights on the top of the cut were flicked off and on as a signal and the giant machines bit into the coal and swung back awaiting the trucks.

At this stage the trucks, led by a jeep, were snaking their way down the tortuous roads into the cut.

As each pulled in, it was loaded by the shovel and despatched to the crushers.

As each vehicle tipped its load it was driven under the hoppers at the crushing plant, was loaded with the crushed coal, and then driven to the railhead, where the coal was tipped into bins and loaded into railway trucks.

A shortage of motor trucks broke down the operations last night. The Army could only prepare 17 of the impressed vehicles for the road in time. Normally, 40 trucks are employed in the mine carting coal.

The soldiers worked silently throughout the night.

The three Thiess brothers, contractors at the mine, were enthusiastic about the ability of the troops. . .

Early last night at Marrangaroo military camp police, Army and Air Force officers built up a road convoy of 250 heavy earth-moving lorries, utility trucks, buses and motor cycles which proceeded to the open cuts at Ben Bullen, Commonwealth No. 2, Johnsdale, Western Main, Huon, Cullen Main East and Cullen Main West.

At midnight every open cut went into production simultaneously.

Half an hour after the coal winning operations began a continuous stream of heavy lorries was crowding into the crushers at Lidsdale and Ben Bullen.

The Minister for the Army (Mr. Chambers) said this morning that preliminary reports on production in the open cuts were very satisfactory. Mr. Chambers said that he felt confident the troops would make a success of their work, and that the planned production for the northern and western fields would be achieved.

Industrial unrest on the coalfields was an issue at the 1949 election, but not a dominant one. The major issue was banking, and socialism generally played a part. The Opposition Leader, Robert Gordon Menzies, declared in his policy speech: 'The Government misrepresented the vote as an instruction, not to preserve the liberties of the subject, but to curtail them! Not to set up the restoration of normal competitive enterprise, but to set up the Socialist State.' Ben Chifley asked voters to 'judge us on our record, and on our ability to go on with the job of building Australia into the nation we all want it to be.'

Labor was beaten overwhelmingly. It emerged from the election in December 1949 with forty-eight representatives, against a combined total of seventy-four non-Labor representatives. Twenty-three years of Liberal-Country Party coalition rule began.

1950   Australians invade North Korea with United States forces and a C.O. dies

LAWSON GLASSOP AND RONALD MONSON
Sydney Morning Herald and Sydney Daily Telegraph, 1 November 1950

On 25 June 1950, soldiers of the North Korean Army crossed the 38th Parallel into South Korea. The United States Government, claiming that this was a breach of the peace and an act of aggression within the United Nations Charter, requested the United Nations Secretary-General, Mr Trygve Lie, to call an immediate meeting of the Security Council.

In Australia that weekend, the northern rivers of New South Wales, swollen by cyclonic storms, were flooding badly, causing millions of pounds worth of damage. Korea, a country which many Australians would have had trouble in pinpointing on a map, seemed light years away.

On 26 June, as North Korean tanks nudged at the unprotected outskirts of the South Korean capital of Seoul, President Harry Truman ordered American air and naval forces to support the South Koreans. Next day the United Nations Security Council recommended that member nations help South Korea to repel North Korea. On 29 June the Australian Prime Minister, Mr Menzies, announced that two Royal Australian Navy ships in Japanese waters had been placed 'at the disposal of the United Nations through the United States authorities in support of the Republic of Korea'. Next day he advised that the Australian fighter squadron in Japan, 77 Squadron, had been offered for service with the United Nations forces under General Douglas MacArthur.

United States ground forces went into action in Korea on 1 July, and on 26 July it was announced that Australia would be sending an expeditionary force of ground troops to help the United Nations forces. The Australian Third Battalion, under the command of Lieutenant-Colonel C. H. Green, DSO, a

thirty-year-old veteran of World War Two, arrived in Korea on 28 September. With the first battalions of the Middlesex Regiment and the Argyll and Sutherland Highlanders, the Australians made up the 27th British Commonwealth Brigade. They were soon involved in heavy fighting, as the United Nations forces pushed the North Koreans back, through Seoul, across the 38th Parallel, and up the main highway towards the North Korean capital of Pyongyang. From Pyongyang they continued to lunge north. The Australians fought several actions during the advance, in which they reached a town within forty miles of the Yalu River, and in the headlong retreat which followed the entry of Chinese forces into the war.

During the war, which lasted until 27 July 1953, military units from Australia, Belgium, Canada, Colombia, Ethiopia, France, Greece, Luxembourg, the Netherlands, New Zealand, the Philippines, Thailand, Turkey, South Africa, the United Kingdom and the United States fought on the United Nations side. Denmark, India, Italy, Norway and Sweden sent medical units. The United Nations casualties totalled 73,500 men killed. Of these, 45,000 were South Koreans and 25,600 Americans. Australia lost 281 killed and missing; total casualties, including killed, wounded and missing, were 1538.

With the first Australian battalion to fight in Korea went four war correspondents, representing the entire Australian press. They were Ronald Monson, whose parent paper was the Sydney Daily Telegraph, *Alan Dower (Melbourne* Herald), *Lawson Glassop (Sydney* Morning Herald) *and myself (Melbourne* Sun). *Australian reporters who covered the earliest fighting included Denis Warner (Mel-*

Australian correspondents in Korea. From left: Lawson Glassop, Ronald Monson and Harry Gordon

bourne Herald) *and Roy Macartney (Australian Associated Press). The four correspondents with the Third Battalion were all within yards of the commander, Lieutenant-Colonel Green, when he was mortally wounded by a shell fragment. It happened just after a hard-fought battle at Chonju, south of the Yalu; six high velocity shells landed in the battalion headquarters area. The colonel was asleep on his stretcher. Many other people were moving about the area close to his tent, but nobody else received a scratch.*

Here is a report of the incident from Lawson Glassop of the Sydney Morning Herald:

Chonju, October 31. — A shell splinter seriously wounded Lieut. Col. C. H. Green, DSO, in the stomach last night while he was asleep in his tent.

Colonel Green is commanding officer of the Third Battalion, Royal Australian Regiment.

He had been up all the previous night directing the Australian troops in their fierce action only 40 minutes from the Manchurian border.

His batman, Private Jack Redman, of Melbourne, was standing next to him, 10 people were within 20 yards, and about 100 people were on the same hillside; but there were no other casualties.

Major Ian Ferguson, of Manly, Sydney, who took over the command, said: "It was one of the most freakish accidents I have ever seen in a war.

"Theoretically, he was in one of the safest places in the area. No matter how the enemy fired it was a thousand to one against them hitting him."

Major Ferguson served under Colonel Green when they were in the Second Battalion in the last war.

Capt. B. S. O'Dowd, of Perth, said: "People were all around him, walking everywhere. It is incredible."

Capt. Laurie Watts, of Randwick, Sydney, the signals officer, said: "I said to him only a few hours ago that it was all over and we had come through all right. He replied, 'Yes, we're unlikely to be in any more big battles, and we've made it.'

"He is a most considerate leader. He's often said, 'Spread out a bit, boys. We don't want one shell to get you all.'

"Four shells hit the crest of the hill and did no damage. One came over and hit a tree about 30 feet up. A splinter went through Colonel Green's tent. It was shocking luck."

Ronald Monson reported that during the action in which Colonel Green had been dangerously wounded, eight of his men had been killed and thirty others wounded.

He said that shortly after the shellburst, the colonel's headquarters received this message to him from General Hobart Gay, commanding the U.S. First Cavalry Division:

'Congratulations on your splendid and sensational drive into enemy territory. I know it is a proud day in your brigade's record and one which deserves the envy of all soldiers.

'It is a great pleasure to have such a unit as yours associated with the First Cavalry. Men of your unit are true fighting soldiers.

'I send my sincerest congratulations to you and all officers and men of the Argyll and Sutherland Highlanders, the Middlesex Battalion, and the Third Battalion of the Royal Australian Regiment, who marched 31 miles in 12 hours to deal the enemy this disastrous blow.'

Monson reported Australian troops had inflicted a crushing defeat on the enemy in the fierce battle for Chongju.

'They killed 100 North Koreans, wounded many more, and knocked out nine enemy tanks and several self-propelled guns,' he wrote. . .

Monson said that the enemy numbered between 700 and 800, with tanks and infantry, at the beginning of the battle, but were later reinforced by more tanks and infantry.

'The Australians were suffering casualties,' he said, 'but were inflicting 10 times as many

on the enemy.'

Monson said that as darkness fell, with the fortunes of battle still swaying, the North Koreans massed, and, shouting 'Mansai, Mansai,' charged against Australian tanks and infantry.

He went on:

Enemy tanks came up to support this fresh attack, but with two well-aimed bazooka shots, Private L. A. Simpson, of Burwood, Sydney, knocked out two enemy tanks.

Another man destroyed a third enemy tank with a lucky shot from his Owen gun, which struck an outside petrol tank on the enemy tank, ignited it, and blew up the tank's ammunition.

As the crew tried to escape from the blazing tank the Australian Bren gunners mowed them down. . .

The enemy couldn't stand up against the pounding our men were giving them. As the night wore on they drew back, and fought it out at longer range with their tanks and guns.

By this time the pine-covered ridges were blazing in many places.

Several Korean huts were also afire, and the air was thick with choking clouds of acrid smoke.

By daylight the battle had developed into exchanges of artillery fire, the enemy having gone back to the hills beyond Chongju.

Yesterday the Australians provided cover for the Argylls as they crossed the river and entered the blazing town without any real opposition.

But at dusk, while the Australians were resting from their 36 hours of battle, four enemy shells dropped on to the battalion headquarters area, which was located on the other side of the hill.

Lawson Glassop was author of the controversial World War Two novel We Were the Rats, *which was banned after a NSW court in 1946 ruled it obscene and blasphemous. Glassop died in 1966, aged 53; at the time he was revising a 450 000-word novel based on the life of Captain Cook. Ronald Monson, whose career has been discussed earlier in this book, died in 1973. Their colleague Alan Dower died in 1985, aged 70.*

1951   The death of Ben Chifley is announced at a Jubilee ball

ELWYN JONES
Sydney Morning Herald, 13 June 1951

The Labor Party leader, Mr Ben Chifley, died in Canberra on 13 June 1951, while MPs and their wives were celebrating at a grand Jubilee Ball. Many wept as the Prime Minister, Mr Menzies, announced his death, and the ball was abandoned. Mr Chifley had served as Prime Minister after the death of John Curtin; he had been an engine-driver in the railways, and had become involved in politics after being sacked in the New South Wales rail strike of 1917. He was one of three national Labor leaders who died while at the head of their party. The others: John Curtin and Frank Tudor.

Elwyn Jones, of the Sydney Morning Herald, *reported his death. An extract from his report follows:*

The Leader of the Opposition, Mr. J. B. Chifley, died on the way to the Canberra Community Hospital soon after 11 o'clock to-night.

Mr. Chifley had a heart seizure and collapsed in his bedroom at the Hotel Kurrajong at 10.15 p.m., while the Jubilee Ball was in progress in King's Hall, Parliament House.

The Prime Minister, Mr. Menzies, announced the news to the hushed guests at the Jubilee Hall just before midnight and dancing was abandoned.

Mr. Menzies referred to Mr. Chifley as a "fine Australian," and added, "He served this country magnificently for many years. The sorrow of his own people is shared equally by myself and members of the Government."

Many women wept as they listened to Mr. Menzies's announcement and couples left for their homes instead of going to supper.

Mr. Chifley, who was 65, will be given a State funeral. . .

The Deputy Leader of the Opposition, Dr. H. V. Evatt, and the Leader of the Opposition in the Senate, Senator N. E. McKenna, were called from the Jubilee Hall to Mr. Chifley's side.

The Prime Minister was informed of Mr. Chifley's illness soon after his collapse.

He told Mr. Chifley's medical advisers that every facility at the Commonwealth's disposal was to be utilised to try to save Mr. Chifley's life.

When news of Mr. Chifley's collapse spread among the dancers in the King's Hall, a hush descended.

Then, when reports of his death circulated, the floor rapidly cleared.

Just before midnight Mr. Menzies announced:

"It is my sorrowful duty to tell you that to-night, during this celebration, Mr. Chifley, former Prime Minister and Leader of the Opposition, has died.

"I do not want to try even to talk about him, because, although we were political opponents, he was a great friend of mine and yours, and a fine Australian.

"You will agree that it is appropriate on this sorrowful occasion that the festivities of to-night should end, and, therefore, in the circumstances there will be no more music.

"I do suggest that you have supper and that we then leave quietly, having in our minds very great sorrow for the passing of a fine Australian.

"It does not matter about party politics in a case like this. Oddly enough, in Parliament we get to know each other very well, and we sometimes find we have a warmest friendship among people whose politics are not our own.

"Mr. Chifley served this country magnificently for many years. . . ."

A reporter unearths evidence which frees a man serving a life sentence

TOM FARRELL
Sydney Daily Telegraph, 31 July 1951

Frederick Lincoln McDermott made history in 1947 by becoming the first Australian to be convicted of murder without the discovery of a body. After he had served five years and ninety-three days of a life sentence, he made history again by being proved innocent. A Royal Commission found that he had been wrongly convicted, after a great deal of investigative work by Sydney Daily Telegraph *reporter Tom Farrell unearthed new and vital evidence.*

McDermott was sentenced to death at Bathurst on 26 February 1947 on a charge of having murdered William Henry Lavers in September 1936. He left the court, sobbing: 'I am innocent of this dreadful charge.' He maintained his innocence throughout his time in jail, and his frankness convinced many people, including his lawyer, that he was innocent. At the trial, Mr Justice Herron told the jury that they had to consider three major points: whether the alleged victim was in fact dead; whether a certain car was used in the murder; and whether McDermott was associated with that car.

After a number of reports, including one from a Moree priest, that Lavers had been seen alive, it became evident that the case against McDermott rested almost solely on the car. After inquiries which convinced him that McDermott had been wrongly convicted, Tom Farrell set out to prove that the car which police claimed the murderer used was in no way connected with McDermott. In the roof of an old garage at Forbes, New South Wales, he tracked down documents which showed this.

After the Daily Telegraph *published Farrell's reports about the new evidence, it was announced that a Royal Commission would*
be set up to inquire into it; it lasted six weeks, with Mr J. W. Shand, KC, appearing for McDermott on behalf of the Public Solicitor. The Royal Commission canvassed the entire matter of Lavers' disappearance, and the police investigations, which began in 1936 and ended with the arrest of McDermott. The commissioner, Mr Justice Kinsella, said in finding that there had been a miscarriage of justice: 'The fresh evidence placed before me throws a great deal of light on the identity of the car. It proves conclusively that the car which drove to Lavers' store and left tracks . . . could not have been Parker's car.' (The police case had depended on McDermott's association with a car owned by John Frederick Parker.)*

Tom Farrell began his journalistic career on the weekly Murray Valley Standard, *then joined the Adelaide* News. *After war service he joined the reporting staffs of the Melbourne* Argus, *the Melbourne* Sun News-Pictorial *and the Sydney* Daily Telegraph. *In 1954 he flew to Samoa to secure a world scoop interview with the Pacific raft traveller William Willis. He joined the* Sydney Morning Herald *in 1957, and from Adelaide wrote the first reports on the case of the convicted murderer Rupert Max Stuart; a Royal Commission followed, and Stuart's death sentence, for the rape and murder of a nine-year-old girl, was commuted. Farrell was London editor and manager of the* Sydney Morning Herald *from 1962 to 1965, and since then has occupied senior editorial and managerial posts with that paper.*

Here is his report about the new evidence which eventually cleared Frederick McDermott of a murder charge:

Discovery here today of a 17-years-old document proves almost beyond doubt that Frederick Lincoln McDermott was wrongly convicted of the Lavers murder.

The document concerns a car which police said was used to carry Lavers' body away.

It shows that this car could not have made the tracks found in front of Lavers' store.

Nor could the car police produced in court have been the one they claim was used for the murder.

William Henry Lavers disappeared from his store near Grenfell on September 5, 1936.

His body was never found.

McDermott was tried, convicted, and sentenced to death for murder in 1947.

He is now in Goulburn Jail.

He was convicted on a long chain of circumstantial evidence.

At his trial police produced two parts of the body of a car which they said belonged to Jack Parker, a shearer whom McDermott knew.

Police alleged McDermott and another man drove to Lavers' store in this car — a 1925 or 1926 model Essex tourer — got four gallons of petrol, murdered Lavers and took the body away.

The case hung almost entirely on McDermott's association with Parker's car.

Parker and other witnesses said they thought the body parts produced were a different color from Parker's car, but the jury accepted the Crown evidence.

At the trial Detective-Sergeant (now Detective-Inspector) C. S. Jardine said that tracks he had measured outside Lavers' store were 56 inches from centre to centre of the tyre marks.

Jardine said he was a member of the police Scientific Bureau and was a draughtsman.

Inquiries in Forbes and Sydney now reveal that the body parts produced in court could have come only from a 1927 model Essex.

Proof of this is that the body the police produced had a bead stamped into the metal about two inches below the top, running the length of the body and around the back.

The 1926 and earlier model Essex had no such bead.

Another body part produced was the rear part of the engine cover — on which the windscreen was mounted.

This part showed that the car had a rounded radiator and bonnet top.

The earliest Essex to have a rounded bonnet and radiator top was the 1927 model.

N.R.M.A. and other car experts have testified to this and there is ample proof in motor manuals.

At the trial no evidence was called to identify the year in which the car produced was manufactured, nor were the differences between 1926 and 1927 models mentioned.

If this evidence had been produced at the trial, McDermott probably would never have been convicted. . .

Today, with the permission of Mr. F. Peasley, I searched old records under the roof of his garage.

I found a ledger entry showing that J. E. Flood sold Mr. Peasley a 1926 Essex which Parker later bought.

In a dust-covered sack of old papers I found a contract note, written in Mr. Peasley's hand, showing the sale to Parker on October 4, 1934, of a 1926 Essex.

The contract bore the signatures of Peasley, Parker and Flood.

It showed an engine number which confirmed the year of the Essex as 1926.

The 1926 and earlier models had an inverted "V"-shaped radiator.

1952   Britain explodes her first atom bomb at Monte Bello

DAN O'SULLIVAN
Perth West Australian, 4 October 1952

On 3 October 1952, Britain exploded an atomic weapon in the Monte Bello islands, off the north-west coast of Australia. The explosion, which made Britain the third atomic power in the world, came seven years after the first American A-bomb test, and three years after Russia's first such blast. The long delay in the development of the British bomb was due not to lack of knowledge, but to lack of facilities.

During the second World War Britain and the United States pooled their efforts to produce the atom bomb which caused the defeat of Japan. America built plants at a cost of two million dollars, and Britain contributed some of her finest scientists to the project. Soon after the war, though, it was discovered that scientists and other workers, both British and American, employed on atomic projects, had been spying for Russia and had handed to the Soviet Union vital information about the production of the bombs. As a result, access to some of the most secret processes was restricted to Americans; Britain's requests for information that would enable her to produce an atom bomb were rejected. Later the American Congress passed laws barring the disclosure of classified information on the atom to any country. As a result, Britain went ahead on her own; she was a long way behind, but she possessed men of great scientific genius.

In 1951 Britain announced that she had made an atomic weapon, and not long after it was revealed that the weapon would be tested in Australia. The site of the test was to be the sprawling, desolate, uninhabited Monte Bello islands, and the British Government barred representatives of the press from the area.

The Monte Bello islands are forty-five miles from the Australian coast, and the nearest town is Onslow, eighty-five miles to the south-east. The mainland area nearest the islands is rugged, barren, waterless and virtually uninhabited. For Perth's two daily newspapers, the West Australian *and the* Daily News, *the coverage of the test represented a very great challenge. They decided to set up an observation post on the mainland, about sixty miles from the islands and 140 miles from Onslow.*

A road party, consisting of expedition leader J. L. Nicoll, three reporters, three photographers, a mechanic and a driver, left Perth on 16 August 1952, with a convoy consisting of a six-ton truck, a jeep, a Land Rover and trailer, and a sedan car. Five days later they reached the pre-determined camp site, in desolate ironstone and spinifex country with a range of low hills about five miles from the coast. They carried two tons of equipment, including the component parts of a photographic darkroom, up the chosen observation hill, which was christened, after expedition leader Nicoll, as Nick's Nob. The photographic team, headed by Daily News *chief photographer Doug Burton, took some 300 pictures in seven minutes. The pictures were developed in the hilltop darkroom, and the negatives were rushed by jeep to an airstrip twenty-six miles away, where they were put aboard a waiting charter plane. Eight hours later they were in Perth and being grammed to newspapers all over the world. The reporting team consisted of Dan O'Sullivan, J. E. Coulter (*Daily News*), J. W. Cruthers, N. F. Milne and Peter Barnett (West Australian). The first news of the explosion was in Perth within three minutes — one minute and fifteen seconds before the blast of the explosion was felt on the observation hill.*

Britain explodes an atom bomb at Monte Bello islands

Wrote one correspondent, a little effusively, in the mass-circulation London Daily Mirror: *'It [the blast] signalled the undisputed return of Britain to her historic position as one of the world's great Powers. . . To the Commonwealth countries it means that the Mother Country is once more able to deter their enemies, in any part of the world. . . Britain is once again GREAT Britain.'*

Certainly it was a major journalistic triumph. British and American newspaper executives voted it one of the major stories of 1952 – a year which saw the death of King George VI, the accession of Queen Elizabeth, the eruption of violence in Africa, the election of General Eisenhower and the saga of Kurt Carlsen and the ship he refused to leave, the Flying Enterprise. *All of the newsmen involved showed tremendous determination and enterprise. Dan O'Sullivan, who later became editor-in-chief of West Australian Newspapers, wrote the main report of the explosion:*

With a brief lightning-like flash, Britain's first atomic weapon was exploded at 8 a.m. today in the Monte Bello Islands, off the north-west coast of Western Australia.

The flash was followed by a huge expanding cloud which reached a height of 12,000ft. within about three minutes of the explosion. By that time it was about a mile across at its widest part.

Although no official announcement has been made, it is believed that the explosion was from a tower either at Flag Island or at Hermite Island – the largest in the Monte Bello group.

The Press observation point is on the highest point in Rough Range, north of the Fortescue River, and is only 55 miles from the Monte Bello Islands.

Observers here did not feel a ground shock, but a heavy air-pressure pulse hit the mainland four minutes and 15 seconds after the flash of the explosion, which occurred on the tick of 8 o'clock.

At the same time pressmen heard a report like a clap of thunder, followed by a prolonged rumble like that of a train going through a tunnel.

The air and ground shocks were sufficiently intense to cause slight pain in the ears.

The immediate flash resembled the top quarter of a setting sun.

A dense and magnificently turbulent cloud almost immediately shot to a height of 2,000ft.

At first deep pink, it quickly changed to mauve in the centre, with pink towards the outside and brilliantly white turbulent edges.

Within two minutes the cloud, which still was like a giant cauliflower, was 10,000ft. high. A small pure-white milling ball rested on top.

Though the day's wind was strong south-easterly, it changed to west for a brief moment as the shock went inland. By this time, the cloud was being torn about by winds at 2,000 ft. and 10,000ft., but the intensely turbulent ball still rested on top. . .

Unfavourable weather conditions in the sub-stratosphere held up the tests for three days.

The test was originally listed for Wednesday but, since the scientists were ready, it was decided to explode a day early, on Tuesday.

However, though it was a fine, clear day and all ships and scientists had taken test stations, it was found that an unfavourable wind was blowing in the sub-stratosphere and it was decided to postpone the test for a day.

On the following two days, however, conditions were again unfavourable.

Second only in importance to the actual explosion was the task of following the highly dangerous cloud of radioactive dust to find out where it finished.

This role was primarily allotted to a squadron of R.A.A.F. Lincoln bombers, specially flown to Broome from Amberley (Queensland).

It is believed that they were assisted, probably at low level, by Seafuries and Fireflies from the carrier Sydney.

There has been no official indication that today's test completed Britain's atomic programme along this coastline, and there is conjecture on what any future tests may hold in store.

It is known that Hastings aircraft will be standing by from next Monday to take Britain's scientists from Onslow, so that any more tests involving atomic detonations would need to be within the next week.

DAME ENID LYONS
Melbourne Sun News-Pictorial, 28 October 1952

William Morris 'Billy' Hughes, probably the most colourful and tempestuous politician Australia has ever seen, died on 27 October 1952. He had been denounced as a dictator, applauded as a statesman, and had become something of a folk hero. There were many who said that by his single-mindedness he had distorted Australian political life. He certainly had durability: he entered the New South Wales Legislative Assembly in 1894, and he was still in Parliament (in the House of Representatives, representing the blue-ribbon seat of Bradfield) when he died fifty-six years later.

One who remembered him with affection was Dame Enid Lyons, a columnist on the Melbourne Sun. *Billy Hughes had served in her husband's Cabinet. She said this about his death:*

"And so my friend is dead," we say. So many times in life we say it, sometimes in loneliness for one almost unknown beyond our own fireside, sometimes sharing our grief with many.

Occasionally, as with the man we mourn today, a whole people is touched with a sense of common loss.

William Morris Hughes was the friend of many Australians of his time, the benefactor of all among the generations yet unborn who will cherish Australia, and strive as he did to preserve her institutions and her national integrity.

I met him first early in 1915. He was yet to reach the dazzling fame which made him a world figure so short a time afterward, and I was very young and naive.

The small, deaf man, who was one of the party at tea that Sunday afternoon, was completely overshadowed for me by the presence of the Prime Minister, the handsome and courtly Andrew Fisher.

My husband was disappointed, and reproached me gently.

"You were next to the greatest political mind in Australia and did not recognise it," he said.

Years later, when Mr. Hughes was a member of Cabinet during my husband's term of office, I came to know him well, and, during the years of my own Parliamentary service, he and Dame Mary honored me with their close and intimate friendship.

How he enriched the life of Canberra with his force of character, his wisdom and his wit.

Humor flowed from him like water from a spring, and touched even the most serious of his utterances.

His memories, his comments on men and affairs, his knowledge of history, his love of literature, his histrionics and his warm, human sentiment spread a varied and vivid tapestry before us that entranced us always.

It is hard to believe that all the wealth and charm of personality we knew has passed for ever from the scene.

Inevitably, in the course of so long and eventful a public life, there were occasions when the action he took or the policies he espoused aroused bitter and sometimes violent opposition.

There are those who can find neither sympathy nor understanding for any deviation from established custom; those who mistake a party for a principle, people to whom men like Mr. Hughes remain always a mystery.

But this can be said of him with absolute assurance:

As time and circumstances demanded he changed his mind, but he never changed his heart . . .

1954 Mrs Petrov's enforced flight to Darwin climaxes a political scandal

DOUGLAS LOCKWOOD
Melbourne Herald, 20 April 1954

On 3 April 1954, a Russian diplomat, Vladimir Petrov, forty-seven, defected from the Russian Embassy in Canberra. Ten days later the Australian Prime Minister, Mr Menzies, announced that he had been granted political asylum. These moves led to a major international spying scandal, the withdrawal of the Soviet Embassy from Canberra, the expulsion of the Australian Embassy from Moscow, a large political upheaval in Canberra, and an intensive inquiry into Soviet espionage in Australia.

Vladimir Mikailovich Petrov had the post of third secretary at the Soviet Embassy, and was head of the consular department of the Embassy. On his defection he revealed that he had been in charge of Soviet espionage in Australia, and had the rank of lieutenant-colonel in the MVD, which controlled Russia's secret police organisation. He claimed that he preferred the Australian way of life to Russia's, and also that, as supporter of the 'Beria faction', he could be imprisoned on his return to Russia. He gave a large number of documents to members of the Australian Security Service, made a number of statements naming many people as conscious or unconscious agents of the Soviet in Australia, and wrote a series of newspaper articles, commissioned by the Melbourne Herald group. The Australian Security Service paid him £5000 for his loss of position and savings.

Petrov's wife, Mrs Evdokia Petrov, was employed at the Embassy as an accountant and secretary, but she was also revealed to be an MVD officer, with the rank of captain. Mrs Petrov claimed that she was unaware of her husband's intention to defect. Embassy officials announced that Petrov had been kidnapped, ordered Mrs Petrov from her home to live at the Embassy, and placed her under guard. The Embassy also claimed that Petrov had embezzled funds.

On 19 April, before arrangements could be made to withdraw their large diplomatic staff from Canberra, the Russians decided to get Mrs Petrov out of the country. She was booked on a BOAC plane due to leave Sydney that same night, along with two guards and an official secretary. During the day the Russians drove four decoy cars in and out of the Embassy in Canberra, often with a woman in the front seat, apparently to confuse reporters about Mrs Petrov's movements.

Early in the afternoon, Evdokia Petrov was led from the Embassy to a black Cadillac standing in the drive way. She was hustled into a black seat, and sat between two guards, Valery Karpinsky and Fedor Zharvok. The second secretary at the Embassy, F. V. Kislitsin, a close friend of the Petrovs, sat in front with the chauffeur. They travelled through Canberra streets at sixty mph, and headed for Sydney, 190 miles away.

At Sydney airport a crowd of 3000 had gathered. Hundreds surged around the car as the Russians hustled her from the car, and she was weeping hysterically as she was dragged on to the tarmac. 'Help me, save me,' cried Mrs Petrov in English — then, 'I do not want to go,' in Russian. Suddenly the whole scene of excitement and curiosity ignited into an ugly near-riot, as spectators fought, punched and kicked in their efforts to tear at the Russians who were propelling Mrs Petrov towards the plane. She lost a shoe, and asked one of the guards to recover it; but he either could not or would not. Hundreds who had broken through the tarmac barriers crowded around the gangway steps as Mrs Petrov was dragged up.

Mrs Petrov is dragged, crying, on to a plane at Sydney airport by two Soviet officials

The major sequel to the Petrov defection was a Royal Commission into Soviet espionage in Australia; it sat from 17 May 1954 until 31 March 1955, and examined 119 witnesses, plus a mass of documentary evidence. It was found that the Petrov documents were authentic, that the Petrovs were truthful witnesses, that large-scale spying had occurred in Australia, that there had been leakages of information from the Australian Department of External Affairs between 1945 and 1948. The Petrovs became naturalised Australians in 1956. Diplomatic relations between Australia and Russia were not resumed until 1959.

Douglas Lockwood, whose story of the Darwin drama occupied front pages around Australia and the world that day, first went to Darwin in 1941. After service in the AIF in New Guinea and the Solomons, and later as a war correspondent in Borneo, he returned to Darwin. He served in London as a correspondent for the Melbourne Herald group and was later managing director of the Papua New Guinea Post-Courier, based in Port Moresby, for three years. He was subsequently a newspaper executive in Queensland and in Bendigo, Victoria, before his death in 1980 at the age of 62.

Lockwood had arranged for his office to phone him at the airport every half-hour; this was a wise precaution, because in the next few hours priority government calls jammed all the telephone traffic out of Darwin:

Mrs Petrov decided today to stay in Australia.

She did so after a sensational scene at Darwin airport and a dramatic last-minute long-distance telephone talk with her husband.

She is now safe and sound at Government

House, Darwin, heavily guarded by armed police, and will be brought back to rejoin her husband in his secret hiding place as soon as possible.

Vladimir Petrov is the former Soviet spy chief in Australia who was granted asylum here last week.

The plane with Mrs Petrov and her Soviet guards had arrived at Darwin early this morning from Sydney, where there were wild scenes last night as the party left.

They alighted at Darwin — all passengers on overseas planes must alight here while their planes refuel.

As Mrs Petrov walked down the gangway, the Northern Territory Government Secretary, Mr R. S. Leydin, approached her.

The two Soviet couriers taking Mrs Petrov back to Moscow, V. Karpinsky and F. Zharkov, tried to intervene.

Police forcibly restrained the Russians while others searched them. Both were found to be carrying two automatic pistols in shoulder holsters, which were removed.

Karpinsky struggled violently, and a police sergeant held him in a headlock while his pistols were taken from him.

Mrs Petrov — who is 32 — had an hour-long talk with Mr Leydin at the airport.

On behalf of the Federal Government, he told her that she could stay here and rejoin her husband.

While Mrs Petrov and Mr Leydin were talking, Mr F. V. Kislitsin, Second Secretary at the Soviet Embassy in Canberra, who was also travelling with Mrs Petrov, protested to reporters that the diplomatic rights of the Russians had been infringed.

Mr Kislitsin shouted: "What is your freedom — a lot of police and gunmen."

He then vehemently protested to Mr Leydin.

After Mrs Petrov's hour's talk with Mr Leydin, she sat for a quarter of an hour between the two Soviet couriers, looking composed despite the tremendous emotional strain she had gone through.

Then, only a few minutes before the plane left for Europe, Mr Leydin arranged for her to speak to her husband by telephone. At that stage she had no idea where her husband was.

She was invited to climb the stairs to the top of the airport hangar, where she could talk privately to her husband by long-distance telephone. But Mr Kislitsin objected to this, and instead she took the call in the Customs office.

She spoke to her husband in Russian while the two couriers and Mr Kislitsin listened. She talked to him for about three minutes, as about 50 people, mainly police, local residents and Government officials, looked on.

Eventually, according to a local resident, who knew a little Russian, she said: "No, No," and hung up the telephone.

She was immediately approached by Mr Leydin, who began asking her questions. Mrs Petrov looked blankly ahead of her, and shook her head.

She then returned to her seat with the couriers.

At the last minute, as other passengers were arriving at the airport to rejoin the plane, she said she would speak to Mr Leydin again.

She went to the airport office, while Mr Kislitsin stayed outside.

A few minutes she came out with Mr Leydin, and was taken immediately to a car driven by Police Superintendent W. C. Littlejohn.

She was taken to Government House and immediately placed under the protection of a guard of security officers and police. Soon after she entered Government House she resumed talks with Mr Leydin.

Her decision — made 3½ hours after her arrival — obviously came as a shock to the Russians, who had seemed confident that she would re-board the plane with them.

Mr Kislitsin shouted angrily: "Why don't you let me talk to her? She is being kidnapped."

After Mrs Petrov had gone, Mr Kislitsin turned to those about him and said, "This is a comedy. My Embassy is going to hear about it."

He then telephoned to Canberra.

Mr Kislitsin and the two Russian couriers left in the plane for Jakarta — without Mrs Petrov. . .

1954   The Labor Party is split again and Santamaria is named

ALAN REID
Sydney Sun, 21 September 1954

The Labor Party, which first appeared as an Australian political force in the 'eighties and 'nineties of the nineteenth century, has endured three great crises. The first of these occurred on the issue of conscription during the first World War (when the nation's population was less than six million, and when 60,000 Australian volunteers lost their lives in Europe and the Middle East); the party split over Prime Minister William Hughes' proposals for compulsory military service, but he continued in government with the aid of the non-Labor opposition, and finally formed the new Nationalist Party.

Labor did not regain government after that schism until 1929, and another split occurred in its ranks in the early 'thirties, mainly as a result of the world economic crisis, violent differences on how to combat it, and the refusal of the New South Wales branch of the party, led by Premier John Thomas Lang, to accept decisions made by the Scullin Government.

The third, and greatest, split occurred in 1955 — outwardly on the issue of combating communism in the trade unions. Even before Mr Chifley died in 1951 (to be succeeded as leader by Dr H. V. Evatt) a dissident force, largely Roman Catholic, was developing inside the Labor Party. This group was known early by various names, but it became the Democratic Labor Party. It had opposed the Chifley Government's bid to nationalise the banks, but its real quarrel with the Party was over the handling of communism.

Through much of Australian history the Roman Catholic Church had been sympathetically disposed to the Labor Party. This was natural enough. A large number of Labor's rank and file had always consisted of Irish

Catholics and their sympathisers. The Irish Catholics had figured prominently in every rebellious or reformist movement since the convict days, and their link with the party which stood for freedom of the workers was distinct.

Now, inside the party, a strongly Catholic sub-party was emerging and the ideological conflict was violent. A secret organisation, known as 'The Movement', was organising resistance among the industrial groups to the communist leaders. It was led by Bartholomew Augustine Santamaria, a man of intellect, ability and total dedication. As the tension within the Party mounted, and attacks on Dr Evatt in the parliamentary wing of the party became more frequent, the name of Santamaria was being whispered a great deal.

On 21 September 1954, the Sydney Sun published an article by Alan Reid, one of the best-informed reporters in the Canberra press gallery. It was the first time Santamaria's name had been mentioned, in connection with the industrial groups within the Labor Party, in any newspaper.

This is what Reid wrote:

In the tense melodrama of politics, there are mysterious figures who stand virtually unnoticed in the wings, invisible to all but a few of the audience, as they cue, Svengali-like, individuals among the actors out on the stage.

Such a figure appears to be Bartholomew Augustine Michael Santamaria, of politics but not in them, a man dedicated to an unrelenting crusade against communism, reputed by his enemies (who include some powerful men) to exercise a major influence on the course of Australian politics, yet out of the public eye, and seemingly a casual bystander

When his name is mentioned, as it is frequently, by politicians, it is usually in a guarded whisper behind a hand muffling the mouth, for they appear to fear speaking aloud of him, just as medieval men feared to speak aloud of bogies.

Only Sydney's Ned Ward, still possessed of the powerful figure of an ex-boxer and the non-drinking, non-smoking habits of a now ageing Spartan, has departed openly from this pattern of furtiveness.

In the semi-publicity of the Labor Party room Ward accused Melbourne's Stan Keon, communist-hating, young, with a tongue barbed like a fish-hook, of being under the influence of Santamaria, particularly where foreign policy was concerned. . .

Despite the fact that Santamaria has mattered in politics now for years, he does not appear in the latest (1950) Who's Who in Australia, nor, as far as I am aware, in any published work on Australian politics.

Yet he is credited with being one of the best-informed men in Australia on communists and communism.

He seems to have contacts within every Commonwealth Department and most State ones and in all parties.

But if there is some intelligence service which operates on his behalf, there is also apparently one which operates against him.

Periodically, through the post, anonymously, to nearly all parliamentarians comes what purports to be a Santamaria speech with usually a laconic, unsigned tag, "Address by Santamaria to his boys on such-and-such a date."

They may not be Santamaria speeches, as they so claim.

But internally they show evidence of having been prepared by a man with a strong, vigorous and original mind, with an inflexible anti-communist bias and a firm viewpoint which is derived from this fervent anti-communism and with a fervent belief in the family as the basic unit of Western culture. . .

But for many parliamentarians outside Victoria, which is his headquarters, Santamaria is a wraith, a will-of-the-wisp.

They hear of him one day addressing a luncheon club in a NSW country district, another calling on trade union secretaries in Sydney, the next visiting a former Country Party member, still a power in CP councils, in his rural home, then in Canberra unostentatiously and reputed to be holding academic discussions on leadership with those susceptible to his influence, and hobnobbing with a few Liberals.

Only in the pages of the Catholic Directory does he come to life for those to whom he is only a name.

There he is listed as "lay member of Catholic Action in Australia" and "national secretary of the Catholic Rural Movement".

It is from these comparatively minor posts that he draws his influence.

Australian-born, of Southern European descent, he is a brilliant legalist, a fluent, powerful and convincing speaker, with an agile though disciplined mind.

Even his enemies, who are far from few, do not question the intellectual brilliancy that has brought him offers of lucrative and prominent positions which he has turned down preferring to dedicate himself to anti-communist activities.

He is credited with being the driving force behind News Weekly, a trenchantly written pungent weekly, produced in Melbourne, and usually regarded in the Labor movement as the mouthpiece of the political, as distinct from the religious, wing of Catholic Action.

News Weekly exercises an influence out of all proportion to its circulation. . .

Its pet hates are Senator Pat Kennelly, one time an ALP Federal secretary and Victorian ALP secretary, Deputy Opposition Leader Arthur Calwell, Ned Ward, and Clyde Cameron, of S.A., probably in that order. . .

And, offstage, out of the public eye stands Santamaria, already a legendary figure in the folklore of politics, as a man whose influence reaches across the political stage to the men in all three parties who, perhaps unconsciously, perhaps because they are in sympathy with his views anyway, reflect to the public aspects of his keen and anti-communist mind.

1954   Dr Evatt brings the Labor fight out into the open

ALAN REID
Sydney Sun, 6 October 1954

The great, traumatic conflict inside the Labor Party was brought into the open when its Federal leader, Dr Evatt, suddenly and publicly attacked the Victorian right-wing members of the party in October 1954. He branded them as disloyal to the Labor movement and to Labor leadership, and charged them with being directed largely from sources outside the Labor movement. The Victorian right-wingers had been attacking Dr Evatt since he involved himself in the Petrov Royal Commission hearings, without party approval, apparently to the benefit of the communists.

In the first week of October 1954, Dr Evatt drafted a momentous press statement. He consulted Senator Ormonde and Leslie Haylen, both parliamentarians who had been journalists, about the content; he was encouraged by an assurance from Ormonde that many Catholics inside the party were opposed to 'The Movement'.

The statement was reported in newspapers around Australia on 6 October 1954. Alan Reid, of the Sydney Sun, *called it a 'hydrogen bomb'. It caused the battle lines of the great split to be drawn, and it unleashed such passion that the party was contorted.*

The statement said in part:

At the recent Federal elections on May 29 we put forward a policy of development and we polled a majority of the people of Australia.

We made gains in every State except Victoria.

All this was achieved by the self-sacrifice of tens of thousands of voluntary workers for Labor.

But in the elections one factor told heavily against us — the attitude of a small minority group of Labor members, located particularly in Victoria, which has, since 1949, become increasingly disloyal to the Labor movement and to Labor leadership.

Adopting methods which strikingly resemble both Communist and Fascist infiltration of larger groups, some of these groups have created an almost intolerable situation — calculated to deflect the Labor movement from the pursuit of established Labor objectives and ideals.

Whenever it suits their real aims, one or more of them never hesitates to attack or subvert Labor policy or Labor leadership.

A striking example of this at the elections was the attack upon Labor's proposal to abolish the means test.

That proposal had been approved, not only by myself but by the authorised representatives of the Federal executive, the A.C.T.U., the A.W.U., and the leaders of the Parliamentary Labor party in both Houses.

In spite of that, there were further attacks on the agreed policy.

These attacks were eagerly seized on by anti-Labor parties as though by a preconceived plan and advertised from one end of the country to the other.

Since the elections nothing has been done officially to deal with those responsible for the disloyal and subversive actions to which I refer.

In addition, it is my clear belief that in crucial constituencies members of the same small group, whether members of the Federal Parliamentary Labor party or not, deliberately attempted to undermine a number of Labor's selected and endorsed candidates with the inevitable and intended result of assisting the Menzies Government. . .

They are almost all to the effect that this planned and somewhat desperate attempt to disrupt and injure Labor leadership is really intended to assist the Menzies Government, especially in its attempt to initiate in Australia, some of the un-British and un-Australian methods of the totalitarian police state.

Having in view the absolute necessity for real, and not sham, solidarity and unity within the movement, I am bringing this matter before the next meeting of the Federal executive with a view to appropriate action being taken by the Federal Labor conference in January.

Ninety-five per cent of the rank and file of the Parliamentary Labor party are absolutely loyal to the movement. There is not the slightest reason why their efforts should be undermined by a tiny minority.

Alan Reid reported in that day's Sydney Sun *that a showdown was coming:*

Dr. Evatt's outburst last night, when he accused a small minority of Labor members of "disloyal and subversive actions", was undoubtedly aimed against Messrs. Keon, Mullens and William Bourke, all from Victoria.

But they are merely symbols.

In Dr. Evatt's eyes, Mr. Santamaria is the master puppeteer who is the real power, pulling the strings that sent Stan Keon, Jack Mullens and others into their anti-Evatt performances of recent months.

Dr. Evatt, with his bitter onslaught, has precipitated a showdown.

Powerful forces behind him, including leading men in the ACTU and AWU, have advised him to fight to the limit for the expulsion of at least Messrs. Keon and Mullens.

This group is prepared to have the entire Victorian Labor Party, if it backs its two representatives — superseded by a Federal machine — as the Lang group was during the depression years.

Mr. William Bourke, a consistent Evatt critic, is in a slightly different position from Messrs. Keon and Mullens.

Though a devout Catholic, he is known to be anti-Catholic Action, the zealot group that Mr. Santamaria personifies.

To enforce the harsh discipline it was building up within the Victorian ALP this group was prepared at one stage to assassinate politic-

ally anyone who stepped out of line on its anti-communist program.

Hitherto Dr. Evatt had been restrained from taking action because, though he loathed the CA supporters, he was oddly in sympathy with much of their social doctrine.

Senator Pat Kennelly, former Federal secretary of the ALP, who alleges that he lost his post through Mr. Santamaria's influence, is probably the most bitter anti-CA member of caucus, though himself a devout Catholic.

Dr. Evatt is understood to have mustered powerful allies, including Mr. Vic Stout, chief of the Melbourne Trades Hall, who is alleged to be guided by a former Sydney Church of England clergyman on the course he should follow.

Those close to Dr. Evatt claim that what touched off the explosion last night arose out of a gathering in Sydney for the Six-hour Day celebrations.

Mr. Albert Monk, ACTU chief, attacked the conception of the trade unions becoming the vassals of any Labor government, or "alleged" Labor government, because certain persons aimed at establishing a corporate State.

This was construed by the more discerning listeners as an attack upon Mr. Santamaria, and the parliamentarians associated with him — and a direct invitation to Dr. Evatt to take action in the knowledge that he would have union backing. . .

If the Victorian executive, group-dominated and with elements close to Mr. Santamaria, including the powerful assistant secretary Mr. Frank McManus, does not bow to the inevitable, the next move will be to suspend and reconstitute the entire Victorian ALP. . .

For Labor the next few months are going to be difficult. The attitude of the Victorian executive will probably be the key as to whether there will be a major split. . .

It was, of course, a major split. The open break came at the Federal ALP conference in Hobart in March 1955. On 17 March, the Hobart Mercury *reported:*

Both armies in Labour's civil war yesterday committed themselves irrevocably to a long and bitter struggle for control of the Federal

Dr Evatt was a brilliant High Court judge, Foreign Minister and one-time President of the United Nations General Assembly

party machine.

Any prospect of an early armistice vanished when:

— The 17 breakaway delegates decided to main their boycott of the Federal A.L.P. conference in Hobart;
— The Federal Leader (Dr Evatt) plunged into the battle with a furious denunciation of the "rebels";
— The conference outlawed the "old" Victorian Executive.

After Dr Evatt's bitter declaration at the conference in the afternoon several delegates forecast that Federal caucus would split in two when Parliament meets next month and the anti-Evatt group would move to the cross benches.

After announcing the conference's decision to outlaw the "old" Victorian Executive, the Federal president (Mr Eric Reece) said: "We are being accused of many things, but all we are doing is putting the Labour Party back on its feet."

Delegates stood and cheered when Dr Evatt, accompanied by the Opposition Leader in the Senate (Senator McKenna), walked to the official conference platform in Trinity Hall. . .

"I believe this conference by showing steadfastness and courage in the face of open force and attempted blackmail will bring to an end this coalition between monopoly capitalism, anti-Labour politicians and secret anti-Labour groups posing as Labour.

"The object of the coalition is to divide the workers of Australia" . . .

He added that the overwhelming majority of Labour people had supported the Federal Executive's decisions in Victoria.

Any secret organisation trying to capture the Labour movement must, in the long run, assist Communism just as McCarthy had assisted it in the United States.

"The Santamaria movement's members have the right to be as anti-Communist as they want to be.

"The Labour Party is anti-Communist, but it is anti-Fascist, too. . .

"Both totalitarian doctrines, left and right, are foreign to Labour, which is based on the principles of social democracy or gradual democratic socialism, achieved by Parliament or constitutional methods approved by a free vote of the people."

1956   At a time of world crisis Australia holds the Olympic Games

GAVIN SOUTER
Sydney Morning Herald, 21 November 1956

Melbourne was the host city for the 1956 Olympic Games, which opened on 22 November. It was the first time they had been held south of the equator, and there were some signs that they would not go well. Some wrangling over sites marred the early planning, and at one stage the president of the International Olympic Committee, Avery Brundage, suggested that it might be best if Melbourne abandoned its claim to hold the Games. A great deal of international tension existed just before the Games, with a Middle East crisis involving many nations; then the Russians invaded Hungary, and emotions and sympathies became so sharply jagged that many observers felt that the Olympics should not take place. Holland, which had strong chances of winning gold medals, was one of several nations which withdrew from the Games because of the international tension.

Despite all the forebodings, the 1956 Olympics were a wonderful success. A writer on the Melbourne Sun *summed up the general mood of relief when he wrote on the day after the opening:*

A lot of us thought it would never happen.

A lot more of us thought that if it did happen, something would go wrong.

Yesterday, on the sun-drenched basin of the Melbourne Cricket Ground, more than 103,000 of us watched it happen. And nothing went wrong.

Four thousand Olympic athletes from 68 nations turned on the most fabulous, colourful procession Australia has ever seen — and Melbourne's Olympic Games opened perfectly.

Sir Robert Menzies later wrote that the Games would live as 'a green and pleasant memory'. He added: 'In the course of my own life I have seen many magnificent sights. I have seen nothing more stirring than the opening and closing days at the main stadium.'

What was particularly impressive was the great goodwill which was evident throughout the Games.

During the Games Russia won thirty-seven gold medals, and America thirty-two. Australia, which had never won more than six gold medals before, emerged with thirteen gold medals; third, behind the rival giants, on the 'unofficial' point-score list. The Australian swimmers, headed by Murray Rose and Dawn Fraser, did exceptionally well. John Landy, in the last race of a magnificent career, finished third in the 1500 metres race which was won by Ireland's Ron Delaney; the Australian ran with injured tendons, and had considered himself unlikely to reach the final. Other Australians who distinguished themselves included the girl athletes Betty Cuthbert and Shirley Strickland.

But the undoubted hero of the Games was Russia's Vladimir Kuts, winner of the 5000 and 10,000 metres runs. The Sydney Morning Herald's *Gavin Souter, whose series of articles on New Guinea in 1960 won him a Walkley Journalism Award, covered the Games. Souter has written books on New Guinea and the history of William Lane's Utopian socialist colonies in Paraguay.*

Trite as the subject may be, let us consider the Russians.

Far too much has already been written about poor Nina Ponomareva, the Gruzia and the missing stewardess. And most spectators at the Games have been revolted by Soviet brutality in Hungary. Yet the Russians, like

Vladimir Kuts crosses the line after a sensational win in the 5000 metres run during the Melbourne Olympics.

sin, are still fascinating.

The enamelled red flag is the most highly prized of the team lapel badges which everyone at the Olympic Village collects; the American team has a Soviet pennant hanging in its administrative building; and a blue "C.C.C.P." track suit will draw six times as many autograph hunters as any other colour.

Why? First, the Russians look their part. All 400 of them wear the bright blue track suit with baggy trousers, and a long grey jacket and cowl. The cowl may be tossed back, but at night it is usually worn over the head. It looks positively Siberian.

Secondly, and most important, the Russians have shown themselves to be good losers and, so far as the language barrier permits, good fellows.

Melbourne has by no means embraced the Russians. But it certainly feels a little warmer towards them than it did before the Games began. By the same token the Russians, who have by no means embraced Australia, feel less wary of their hosts.

The catalyst in this reaction is the most remarkable Russian athlete of them all —Vladimir Kuts, who has almost certainly become the outstanding athlete of the 1956 Games.

This formidable 29-year-old navy lieutenant delighted the Melbourne Stadium by his almost naive exuberance after winning the 5,000 and 10,000 metres. He also delighted Melbourne by letting the Australian Alan Lawrence win a heat of the 5,000 metres. Kuts qualified for the final, but was content to stay well behind the Australian.

"I don't know what Kuts said to me when we were running together," said Lawrence after the race. "But I think it was Russian for 'You can have it, mate!'" And as far as Melbourne is concerned, that is just what Kuts did say.

Kuts has influenced the Russians, too. Before his victory in the 10,000 metres, it was very difficult to obtain an interview, at least a satisfactory interview, with a Russian athlete. Now it is easy.

"They have won," explained an interpreter. "Now everything is fine."

Kuts and his coach, Grigorii Nikiforov, were down on the oval when I called at the Village this week. I am sure Nikiforov speaks some English, but he disclaims all knowledge of the language.

He answers questions through an interpreter, but the gleam in his eye, and the half-formed word before the question has been fully translated, leave little doubt that he knows what has been asked in English. . .

Kuts is tough. He has a long, lean face; his cheeks are hollow, and his light-grey eyes are set deep beneath craggy, sandy brows. His mouth is wide and tight, and there was a ginger stubble on his chin. Above and below his track suit, he was wearing a green woollen cap with the word "Australia" sewn in yellow wool, and brown socks and sandshoes.

I asked where he had found the cap. "Stephens gave it to me." Had he given Stephens a cap? "I will give him one when he comes to the students' festival in Russia."

How did his legs feel after the 10,000 metres? "Good or bad, it doesn't matter. They have to go!" . . .

There were more smiles and a little clapping. Kuts is a good fellow. At least, you feel that he is.

Vladimir Kuts had his brightest taste of glory in Melbourne that November. He took his two gold medals home to Moscow, framed them on a wall, retired from running, became a coach and got steadily fatter. He was seventeen stone and only forty-eight years old when he died of a heart attack in Moscow in August 1975 — nearly nineteen years after his triumphant laps of honour in Melbourne.

JOHN MONKS AND GEOFFREY WRIGHT
Melbourne Herald, 28 October 1958

Australia's greatest aviation mystery concerned the disappearance of the three-engined Avro-Fokker airliner Southern Cloud, *which disappeared without trace on a routine flight between Sydney and Melbourne. It involved the loss of eight lives, and it was the nation's first big civil airline disaster.*

The largest and most thorough air search ever carried out in Australia failed to find any clues about the whereabouts of the plane. When the wreckage was discovered accidentally twenty-seven years later, the Southern Cloud *was one of the few airliners in the world on a scheduled run on a regular route still posted as missing.*

Some of Australia's greatest fliers, Sir Charles Kingsford Smith, Charles Ulm and Jimmy Mollison, took part in the massive search. The captain, Australian National Airways' senior pilot, T. W. Shortridge, had had 4600 flying hours, and was familiar with the route. The plane disappeared on 12 March 1931 and the search through eastern Victoria and south-east New South Wales continued for three weeks. After that, most experts concluded that the Southern Cloud *had overshot Melbourne in heavy cloud, and plunged into either Port Phillip Bay or Bass Strait.*

E. H. Cox, who covered the search for the Melbourne Herald, *flew as observer with Kingsford Smith, Mollison and Scotty Allan. He later wrote: 'Mollison was perhaps the most indefatigable of all the searchers. His Fokker lumbered into the air before dawn most days of the week. It never made fewer than three sorties to the limits of its fuel.'*

When the first reports of the finding of the Southern Cloud *arrived in October 1958, the* Herald *sent two reporters, John Monks and Geoffrey Wright, to the scene in the*

The wreckage of the *Southern Cloud* was discovered in rugged Snowy Mountain country

Snowy Mountains and John Monks wrote:

The airliner wreckage found in the Alps is the Southern Cloud.

Civil Aviation Department officials today identified as the airliner which disappeared 27 years ago on a flight from Sydney to Melbourne — and gave Australia its biggest civil aviation mystery.

I saw the wreckage at 7 a.m. today, on the steep side of World's End, a 5000 ft. mountain in the Toolong Range overlooking the Tooma River gorge. The plane's nose was buried deep in the ground.

Big trees had grown up through the twisted engines, which took the full force of the impact when the plane crashed on March 21, 1931.

Immediately they arrived at the spot today, the search party I was with began digging among the wreckage.

Within minutes they found fragments of bones, which were taken as evidence that none of the two crewmen and six passangers survived the crash.

Three shattered wrist watches were found. One was a gold watch with its hands at 1.15, suggesting that the airliner crashed at that time.

The Southern Cloud left Sydney at 8.15 a.m. on a flight scheduled to take about eight hours. It flew into a storm, but had no radio and could not be warned.

The searchers also found a vacuum flask still holding liquid.

There was evidence of fire, but the searchers don't think the plane caught fire when it crashed.

It is believed that a bushfire swept through the area about 1938.

Mr A. H. Green, senior inspector of air safety, was among today's search party with other Civil Aviation officials and police.

Tomorrow, plates containing engine numbers and other details of the Southern Cloud will be taken to Melbourne.

One mystery cleared up today is the story of the "gold bullion" supposed to have been lost in the wreck. A thorough search showed no sign of it.

Mr Green said the Southern Cloud was apparently on its correct course when it crashed.

It had apparently flown into the mountainside, and it was most unlikely that any of those aboard could have survived, he said.

What made the Southern Cloud crash? One theory is that it was caught in a blizzard. . .

Geoffrey Wright wrote:

For half-an-hour today I circled in a plane over the most rugged and inhospitable country in Australia.

We were above the Alps a few miles south of Cabramurra, near the Victorian border.

Somewhere below, in those green, manacing mountains, a search party had reached the wreckage of the Southern Cloud down in the great gum forests.

It is terrible country for flying men.

There is no hope for a disabled aircraft — nothing even remotely resembling a landing place. . .

The searchers hoped to light a fire to guide us to the spot where the Cloud's wreckage is, but we did not see it. In that overwhelming country they would have had to start a bushfire to attract our attention.

We came low hoping to see them moving through the trees.

But the fierce updraughts of the mountains buffeted us, and our pilot, Captain John Williams, of TAA, pulled the nose up and rose to a more comfortable height.

Whether it was those deadly air currents that caught the distressed Southern Cloud and sucked it into the mountains will never be known. Those silent mountains are good at keeping secrets.

1962 New riches, in the form of uranium, are found at Rum Jungle

ALAN MOOREHEAD AND KEN BLANCH
Melbourne Herald, 2 July 1962 and Brisbane Courier-Mail, 15 April 1983.

One of Australia's best-known reporters is Alan Moorehead. He abandoned a law course at Melbourne University to take on newspaper work on the Melbourne Herald, *and in 1937, at the age of twenty-seven, he sailed in the liner* Ormonde *to try his luck abroad.*

He became a specialist in watching battles. He began with the Spanish Civil War, then covered World War Two fighting in Tunisia, Sicily, Italy, north-west Europe and the Far East. He was twice mentioned in dispatches, and awarded the OBE. Throughout this period he worked primarily for the Daily Express, *although his reports were published in Australian newspapers. His books,* African Trilogy *and* Eclipse, *were recognised as some of the best reporting to emerge from the war.*

Moorehead has had a distinguished career as an author. He wrote two biographies, Montgomery *and* The Traitors, *two novels,* The Race of the Vulture *and* A Summer Night, *three African books,* The White Nile, The Blue Nile *and* No Room in the Ark. *His books* Gallipoli, The Russian Revolution *and* Cooper's Creek *were judged to be masterpieces of historical reconstruction.* Gallipoli *won him two of the most distinguished of British literary awards — the* Sunday Times *£1000 prize for the best book of the year (1956) and the Duff Cooper Prize for Literature. Another book,* The Fatal Impact, *dealt with the sad sequels to the white man's intrusion into Tahiti, Australia and the Antarctic.*

When he died in 1983, aged 73, an obituary in The Times *described Moorehead as one of the most celebrated reporters in the language. It added: 'Perhaps because he was an Australian he brought to his work an alien fascination, a separateness, which became more apparent as the years passed.'*

Moorehead returned to Australia, after sixteen years away, in 1962 to examine the country afresh. One place which fascinated him was the uranium-mine settlement of Rum Jungle. This was his report on it, published in the Melbourne Herald *on 5 July 1962:*

Fifty-four miles south of Darwin you turn right from the main road to the Batchelor airstrip and from there a gravelled track leads on for half a dozen miles into the bush. Then you are at Rum Jungle.

There is nothing very remarkable in the scene: it looks more like one of those early colored prints of the gold diggings than anything else.

There is a fettlers' camp on the lonely narrow-gauge railway, and beyond that Rum Jungle station, which is nothing more than a siding with a line of trucks waiting there; no building of any kind.

But there is a jungle of a sort, just a patch of green mangoes and other tropical shrubs among the gum trees: and this was the spot where the prospectors came out looking for tin last century.

They called the place The Jungle and for a time they did get tin out of the ground. Presently a storekeeper came out from Darwin and put up a shanty where he sold food and alcoholic liquor and other odds-and-ends to the miners. No doubt they found uranium as well as tin, but nobody wanted uranium at that time so they left it in the ground.

Things seem to have gone reasonably well for a time and the miners bought their liquor from the storekeeper with straight tin. But then the tin gave out and when the storekeeper refused to allow credit the miners broke in one night and smashed open a cask of rum.

As they drank, the rum poured down the slope into a spring close by and made a convenient mixture with the water in the pool there. In the morning the miners were still to be found lapping up the rum and water from the pool; and that is one version of how Rum Jungle got its name.

The present camp lies a little above the railway line and about half a mile away. You can see the whole thing in five minutes. The mess is a rectangular iron shed which was used as a detention barracks by the army in the war; crossed-bars and barbed wire are still fixed to the windows. . .

The rock in which the men are working is so soft that it has to be timbered — and, indeed, Jack White, the original discoverer of the mine, was nearly buried when the timbers came astray over his head in one of his experimental shafts.

White still lives and works at Rum Jungle. He has a tent set a little apart from the others, with an iron roof above it. In his spare time he goes off prospecting again since, like gambling, there is no end to prospecting; one can never have enough.

All through the Northern Territory there is a story that White has not been rewarded by the Commonwealth Government for this fabulous discovery at Rum Jungle, which may well alter the history of Australia before the 1960s are done.

But this is not true. The Commonwealth has contracted to pay £1000 to any man who finds uranium in workable quantity, and thereafter to pay him an additional £1000 for every 25 tons of ore extracted up to a maximum of £25,000. This is being done with White.

There seems to be every reason to believe that White will get his £25,000. Uranium lies about you everywhere at Rum Jungle. It juts out of the ground under your feet as you walk about; you can pick up a rock anywhere and see signs of it; and no one yet can say how far this field will reach or how rich it will be.

The first discovery was made in October, 1949. Then the rains intervened and the foll-owing year was swallowed up in the preliminary surveys. . .

It is only when you visit Rum Jungle that you realise how unbelievably fortunate Australia has been with this discovery, and how cheaply it is being developed. Uranium of this quality and quantity might easily have been found in the wilds of Arnhem Land or in the vast, uninhabited interior.

But the luck was to get it here — a quarter of a mile from a railway line connecting with the deep water port at Darwin, six miles from an airstrip and a made road. . .

What is needed now is more money — and quickly. Rum Jungle is a safe bet. That is beyond all doubt.

The field is now about to become a restricted area, but they will have a difficult security problem here. You might perhaps put up a road block to check the car traffic, but you cannot ring so large an area with barbed wire, and it would not be very effective if you did.

There is, perhaps, no great secret about the actual method of mining uranium, and it will be difficult to disguise the means by which the ore is transported from the field.

Two secrets, however, have got to be kept if possible — the quantity of uranium in the field and its quality. As the mine expands and more men are employed, it will be hard to prevent these facts from getting about.

What Alan Moorehead saw at Rum Jungle. was a taste of the mineral riches which turned Australia in the 1960s, quite suddenly and spectacularly, into a booming continent. There were many such new riches — iron ore, bauxite (and with it, aluminium), copper, phosphate, oil and natural gas. Together with the lead, zinc and silver which had long been the basis of the Australian mining industry, these finds represented a bonanza of almost incalculable proportions.

The discoveries led to a frantic mood of mine share buying during the seventies and finally, under pressure of intensive speculation, the market buckled. But there was no doubt that the mineral finds were of huge long-term value to Australia. Key fuels which became available for export were liquified natural gas, coal and uranium. Uranium — which Alan Moorehead observed 'juts out of the ground under your feet . . .' — was in larger and richer supplies than anywhere else; because of it, Australia began to emerge as an influential force in the world nuclear fuel market. The uranium mining industry remained fairly buoyant in the 1970s and 1980s, if at times the subject of bitter political conflict. There were casualties, though. . .townships which prospered for a time, like the old goldfields towns, and then died. They died mainly because they ran out of ore, or because they became uneconomic. One such town was Rum Jungle itself. Another was Mary Kathleen, whose promise had been so great when the mine was commissioned in 1976 that the Whitlam Government bought a 41.6 per cent equity in it. It was named after Mary Kathleen McConachy, wife of one of the discoverers of the uranium deposits. By 1983, Mary Kathleen Uranium Ltd, based near Mount Isa in Queensland, was the oldest surviving uranium producer in Australia. . . and it had run its race.

Mining ended in September 1982, and the last load of ore blasted from the rocky walls of the mine was processed the following month. When the town ceased to exist in April 1983, Ken Blanch of the Courier-Mail, *Brisbane, was there to record the death.*

Watching a town disappear, lock, stock and barrel, is a melancholy experience.

As some bush bard might have written, there's nothing so lonesome, morbid or drear than to stand in the street of a town that's not here.

The town of Mary Kathleen, scarcely out of its teens — it was built only 26 years ago — was moving out, house by house, on the backs of semi-trailers yesterday.

Seventy of the uranium township's 200 homes have gone already. The rest will have disappeared to new locations many kilometres away by the end of June.

As the great, lumbering trucks disappeared down the bitumen towards Mount Isa or Cloncurry yesterday, the hopes and aspirations of the people of Mary Kathleen seemed to go with them.

People had begun their married lives in some of those loads of timber and asbestos cement, planned their futures in them, conceived and begun to raise families in them.

Now the people had gone, and so had their homes.

The Mary Kathleen population of 1000 is down to 33, and soon will be reduced to six, the tailenders who will remain behind to oversee the final dismantling of the huge mine and its township and the restoration of the sites to as near as possible their natural state.

Tonight the town's only watering hole, its wet canteen, will close for the last time when the licensee calls "Time gentlemen please" at 10 o'clock.

Tomorrow its public buildings — a post office, stores, town administration centre, the community centre, fire station and single men's quarters and mess — will go under the auctioneer's hammer.

On Sunday, Mary Kathleen's last public amenity, its swimming pool, will be emptied, never to be filled again.

In its short history, the town in the red mineral hills and spinifex of arid north-west Queensland has had two lives.

It prospered from 1957 until 1963 to fill uranium orders for atomic powerhouses in Britain and then closed until new orders were received from Europe and Japan in 1976.

Uranium production at the mine ceased last October when those orders were filled and its ore body almost exhausted, and there were grandiose schemes for preservation of the town.

Suggestions included a study centre for Aboriginals, a camel farm and a Greek community centre, but all were found to be not viable.

The township cost its owners, Mary Kathleen Uranium, $3 million a year to maintain and was due for expenditure of about $7 million on capital works to update its accommodation and services.

So the company decided reluctantly to sell it off. It was determined Mary Kathleen, the oasis it had created in the desert, should not

be left as a ghost town to decay with time as
so many other mining towns in Queensland
have.

The big sale began last Monday. Office
furniture and equipment, mining machinery,
a fleet of vehicles, tools, spare parts, workshop equipment, even the power station —
all have gone under the hammer since then.

Today the mine buildings are on the block,
and tomorrow it is the turn of what is left of
the town itself.

When it has all been dismantled and carted
away, the enormous job of rehabilitating the
area will begin. Costing between $10 million
and $20 million, it will take at least until the
end of 1984.

And the area will be monitored for any
radioactive contamination for years after that,
although engineers are confident it will be
safer than many of the high natural radiation
uranium bearing areas around it.

The only traces of Mary Kathleen for future
generations to see will be its huge water-filled
open-cut — the water is expected to be 50 m
deep eventually — the remains of its bitumen
roads and the concrete slabs on which its
buildings once stood.

Even the exotic poincianas, bauhinias and
oleanders that flourished with tender care in
the desert will wither and die.

1964   The aircraft carrier *Melbourne* cuts the destroyer *Voyager* in two

ALAN STEWART AND JACK STANAWAY
Melbourne Herald, 11 and 12 February 1964

*The worst peace-time disaster in the history
of the Australian services occurred on 10 February 1964, when the aircraft carrier HMAS
Melbourne cut in half the destroyer HMAS
Voyager. Eighty-two men, all of them members of the crew of the Voyager, died in the
collision, which occurred off Jervis Bay on
the New South Wales coast. The dead included
the captain of the Voyager, Captain Duncan
Stevens.*

*It took the Melbourne only three seconds
to carve through the $14 million destroyer.
'The impact is hard to describe,' the Melbourne's captain, Captain R. J. Robertson,
said later. 'When you get 20,000 tons going
at near top speed — about 22 knots — there
is a lot of momentum there.' In another interview, re-published here, the captain said: 'We
cut through the Voyager like a knife through
cake. She split clean in halves.' These awful
seconds echoed through Australian history
for years, through endless allegations, rumors
of scandal, political debates and judicial
inquiries.*

*A Royal Commission, under Sir John Spicer,
sat for fifty-five days and found that the
Voyager had made a turn beyond 020 degrees
when the Melbourne had ordered a rigid course
of 020 degrees. The Commission criticised
Captain Robertson for 'hesitation', and the
captain felt obliged to resign his commission.
In Parliament, the debates and questions
dragged on; finally, following a campaign by
back-benchers, a second Royal Commission
was held in 1968 under Sir Stanley Burbury.
This inquiry lasted eighty-five days, heard 143
witnesses and cost $650,000. The drinking
habits of the Voyager's commander were
investigated; Captain Stevens was found not
to have been a chronic drunkard or an*
*alcoholic — but the Commissioners found that
he had been a sick man at the time of the crash.*

*The collision occured during manoeuvres,
at 9 p.m., and the first sketchy reports of it
reached newspaper and radio stations late
that night. Major afternoon newspapers
immediately dispatched reporters to Jervis
Bay. The Melbourne Herald sent Alan Stewart
from Melbourne and Jack Stanaway from its
Canberra bureau. These are some of their
reports the next day:*

Alan Stewart wrote:

Eighty-five officers and men are missing from
the destroyer HMAS Voyager which was cut
in half at 9 o'clock last night by HMAS
Melbourne.

They include the Voyager's captain, Capt.
Duncan Stevens, 43, who is reported to have
been on his bridge when the collision occurred.
The Voyager carried 324 officers and men.

The Prime Minister, Sir Robert Menzies,
said in Canberra today: "It is a shocking
disaster, unparalleled in the peace-time history
of Australia." . . .

The Voyager, a 3500-ton Daring class
destroyer, sank at midnight in at least 100
fathoms (600 ft.), 19 miles east-south-east of
Jervis Bay. Jervis Bay is 120 miles south of
Sydney.

Many of her crew were below decks — some
of them playing the traditional Navy game
tombola (housey-housey) in the forward
section. Suddenly, the call "Collision Stations!"
was sounded.

There was a crash. Survivors' stories of what
part of the Voyager was hit by the Melbourne
vary. Some men were trapped. Others got out
by luck. Some were thrown into the sea.
Others stood in orderly lines and waited for

their chance to use the life rafts.

One crew member said at Jervis Bay today: "It's hard to think of your mates as heroes, but that's what they were last night. No-one got upset."

The Melbourne — 19,930-ton aircraft-carrier and flagship of the Australian fleet — stood by the Voyager until she sank and helped to pick up survivors. Now she is steaming slowly to Sydney with damaged bows. She is not expected to reach there until noon tomorrow.

Jack Stanaway wrote:

Two navy crash boats stationed at Jervis Bay picked up 70 men from the sea after the destroyer Voyager went down last night.

Both boats resumed the search early today after landing the survivors, but they found no more men.

Gloom spread through Jervis Bay Station at 10.30 a.m. when the station's two crash boats returned without any more survivors.

The captain of one boat, the Air Nymph, Lieut. Kerry Stephen, 25, said: "It was a terrible business. There was just nothing more when we got to the scene."

Bleary-eyed and covered in salt, Lieut. Stephen said: "We've been out since 9 o'clock last night.

"When we got out there it was a mass of oil and we found the rafts clustered together.

"We came back at 12.30 a.m. with 34 on board, including four injured, and went straight back again after refuelling. . .

"On our second trip out we could not find survivors or bodies. We brought back a buoyancy tank and the two stands used on the Voyager to mount her ceremonial lifebuoys when she was in port."

Lieut. Stephen's crash boat brought back a battered stretcher and one empty life raft from the Voyager.

Capt. D. H. D. Smyth, Officer-in-Charge of Jervis Bay Naval Station, said search and rescue craft got under way within 60 seconds. . .

"Wessex helicopters took off from HMAS Albatross at Nowra with special crews equipped to make winch rescues." . . .

The helicopters, the only ones in Australia allowed to hover at night, ran a shuttle service between the Melbourne and the Nowra naval college with the Voyager's survivors.

The shuttle flights were still operating at 7 a.m. today as the Melbourne moved up the coast towards Sydney.

Next day the Melbourne's *skipper, Captain Robertson, gave an interview. This is how the* Herald *reported it on 12 February:*

Captain Ronald James Robertson, 47-year-old captain of the aircraft carrier Melbourne, stood in the hangar of his battered ship in Sydney today and told of the moment the carrier chopped into the destroyer Voyager on Monday night. . .

"We had been engaged in night flying exercises which require the carrier to move as fast as possible," he said.

"Both ships were moving at near top speed.

"Both were blacked out, except for port and starboard and red masthead lights.

"Then it happened.

"The Melbourne hit the Voyager amidships, and cut through her like a knife through cake.

"There was a crunching noise. It reminded me of those collision noises you hear on TV or the movies.

"The Voyager split clean in halves, and the halves slid along our side.

"The Melbourne actually pushed the Voyager sideways — it was 20,000 tons hitting 3500 tons — and this served to help the Melbourne to stop.

"I ordered our engines astern, and I suppose the Melbourne stopped in not much more than one length, with the two halves of the Voyager still not back to our stern.

"In a case like that you don't have any emotional reaction. The first thing you think about is, 'What's to be done to clean up the mess?'

"So we went about that job." . . .

Shortly after the first Royal Commission Captain Robertson resigned his commission, forfeiting his retirement benefits. The second Royal Commission cleared him of any blame or criticism for the disaster, and the federal government paid him $60,000 compensation. He died on 17 July, 1980, aged 63.

A great career ends as Dawn Fraser is expelled from swimming

JUDY JOY DAVIES
Melbourne Sun News-Pictorial, 1 March 1965

Dawn Fraser was a rare champion. She was the only person, male or female, ever to win gold medals for one swimming event at three consecutive Olympic Games. But it was not only her performance in the water that caused her to achieve a kind of folk-heroine status in Australia. She was one of the most exuberant, controversial, refreshing characters in the fairly grim business that is international sport; she sometimes showed a likeable larrikin quality that delighted most Australians, but dismayed swimming officials. Her trouble was that, even though she loved swimming and could churn through the water faster than all women and most men, she did not regard the sport with total seriousness. She was prepared to devote great quantities of time, effort and dedication to it; but she still wanted to enjoy it. She shared with the great erratic boxers Young Griffo and Harry Greb one unlikely quality: she could break all the accepted rules, and still win.

She won the 100 metres freestyle event at the 1956 (Melbourne), 1960 (Rome) and 1964 (Tokyo) Olympics, and in October 1962 she achieved one of the great ambitions of her life by becoming the first woman ever to break one minute for the 100 metres. She broke her first world record at the age of nineteen, in 1956 (the 100 metres freestyle mark, which had stood for twenty years), and she set another thirty-five individual world records during the next eight years.

She was fifteen when Harry Gallagher, a part-time teacher then, but later one of Australia's top coaches, saw her, liked her rough style and tomboyish hatred of being beaten, and took over her coaching. Because her parents could not afford to pay for lessons, he did not charge. Gallagher took her from Syd-

ney to Adelaide at the age of seventeen, and she stayed there for several years — living beside a swimming pool, working as a shop-girl, swimming around ten miles a day. Under Gallagher's tuition, she was transformed from an unruly, gangling, potential delinquent into a world-beating athlete.

Dawn Fraser was suspended for eighteen months by the Amateur Swimming Union of Australia after the Rome Olympics, because she refused a manager's instruction to swim in a medley relay heat. But her troubles really came in Tokyo, where she was arrested on the morning of the closing ceremony by Japanese police after an attempt to steal a flag from the gardens of Emperor Hirohito's palace. That day, in the final ceremony, she carried Australia's flag, limping from an injury sustained during the chase by police through the Emperor's gardens. On her return to Australia (in a wheelchair, with her injured leg in plaster) she was accorded a heroine's reception. On the day of the Melbourne Cup, she was driven along Flemington racetrack in an open car while 90,000 people cheered. A swimming pool in Sydney was named after her, the Australia Day council named her 'Australian of the Year' for 1964, and about a million people ranged across the continent watched the live televising of the ceremony in which she married a young man called Gary Ware.

The reporter who covered Dawn Fraser's expulsion for the Melbourne Sun *was another former great woman swimmer, Judy Joy Davies. She started breaking records at the age of nine, and went on to hold every women's Victorian and Australian freestyle, backstroke and medley championship; she represented Australia at the London (1948) and Helsinki (1952) Olympic Games and the Christchurch*

(1950) Commonwealth Games. She finished third in the Olympic 100 metres backstroke in 1948, and won the Commonwealth backstroke title in 1950. As a career journalist, Judy Joy Davies worked first for the Melbourne Argus, *and, from the death of that newspaper in 1957, for the Melbourne* Sun *When she stopped attending Olympics as a competitor, she began attending them as a correspondent. She attended all the Olympics from Rome (1960) to Los Angeles (1984) as a correspondent for the Melbourne* Sun News Pictorial *and* Herald.

Dawn Fraser, triple Olympic champion, and the world's No. 1 swimmer, has been virtually banned for life by the Amateur Swimming Union of Australia.

Expelled with her from the ASUA and all affiliated bodies for lesser periods are three other girls who swam for Australia at last year's Tokyo Olympics.

Charges against the girls were not given. There is no appeal.

It is known, however, that they included marching — or attempting to march — at the opening ceremony in Tokyo against orders.

An additional charge against Dawn Fraser was that she did not wear a regulation swimsuit.

Dawn, 27, now Mrs. Gary Ware, was expelled for 10 years.

Linda McGill, 19, of NSW, last year's Australian breaststroke and medley champion, was expelled for four years.

Marlene Dayman, 15, of Victoria, Australia's No. 1 junior champion, was expelled for three years.

Nan Duncan, 17, who won a title at the National swimming championships which ended in Hobart yesterday, was expelled for three years.

Marlene Dayman's mother announced immediately that her daughter would never swim competitively again.

In the strongest words, she alleged "personal prejudice" against Marlene.

Linda McGill's father, Sgt. First Class M. K. Gill, said: "My daughter has been convicted without a trial."

Linda is at present in Italy on a world pleasure tour with former Olympic swimmers Ilsa Konrads and Ruth Everuss.

From Tokyo, AAP reported the Olympic organising committee chairman, Mr Daigora Yasukawa, as commenting:—

"We, in Japan, do not recall any incident in which Australian swimmers were involved which could have led to such drastic action."

The two younger girls are expelled until after the Commonwealth Games in Kingston, Jamaica, next year.

Linda McGill is expelled until after the next Olympic Games.

Dawn Fraser has a life sentence because she will be 37 before she can apply for readmission to amateur swimming.

The expulsion means that the girls cannot swim in any club event, State or Australian championships or compete overseas until they are readmitted to the ASUA. . .

The official ASUA statement on the expulsion was:

"The reports of the manager, Mr W. H. Slade, and the manageress, Miss Anne Hatton, of the Australian Olympic swimming team, have been discussed at length and given deep and earnest consideration by the delegates at the annual conference of the Amateur Swimming Union of Australia.

"The union is very jealous of its good name and of the reputation of the members of its teams, both in and out of the water.

"It is conscious of its responsibility to parents to entrust their children to its care and the young men and women who have built up such a fine reputation for Australia over the years throughout the world.

"The union has decided to take steps in an endeavor to prevent a recurrence of incidents such as those which have been reported to it.

"It is determined that it will maintain a strong discipline especially among the members of its teams who represent Australia overseas.

"It is with deep regret that the union finds it necessary to take strong action arising out of incidents which occurred in Tokyo."

The sentences were then given.

1965   Australia follows the United States into a punishing war in Vietnam

DAVID MATHEW AND DON PETERSEN
Australian Associated Press, 10 June 1965 and Melbourne Sun News-Pictorial, June 1965

For Australians as well as Americans, the Vietnam war was a traumatic, nationally divisive experience. It began as an unpleasant little affray, with the United States propping up a weak, sometimes corrupt South Vietnam Government in 1961 in its battle against the communist forces of North Vietnam and the Viet Cong. It escalated, and as it did so it became more brutal, most costly, more frustrating, more complex. It seemed for a time as if it would never end.

President Lyndon Johnson, of the United States, summed up his justification for the war in July 1965, when he stepped up the American troop commitment in Vietnam from 75,000 to 125,000, and raised the monthly draft intake to 35,000:

Three times in my lifetime — in two world wars and in Korea — Americans have gone to far lands to fight for freedom. We have learned at a terrible and brutal cost that retreat does not bring safety, and weakness does not bring peace. . . This is a different kind of war. There are no marching armies or solemn declarations. . . But we must really not let this mask the central fact that this is really war. It is guided by North Vietnam and it is spurred by Communist China. Its goal is to conquer the South, to defeat American power and to extend the Asiatic dominion of communism. Most of the non-Communist nations of Asia cannot, by themselves alone, resist the growing might and the grasping power of Asian communism. Our power therefore is a very vital shield. If we are driven from the fields in Vietnam, then no nation can ever again have the same confidence in American promise or in American protection. We did not choose to be the guardians at the gate, but there is no one else. . .

The Australian Liberal Government, under Sir Robert Menzies, took the same view: that the war in Vietnam was part of the downward thrust of Chinese communism. A small training team of army advisers had been assisting the South Vietnamese since July 1962, but in April 1965 the Australian Cabinet announced that a combat force would be sent. The first force, mainly infantrymen with a support unit, numbered 1100. National servicemen went to Vietnam the following year, and the build-up continued until more than 8000 Australian servicemen were fighting in Vietnam.

The controversial war divided Australian political opinion under five prime ministers: Sir Robert Menzies, Harold Holt, Sir John McEwen, John Gorton and William McMahon. It did not end until January 1973. Between 1961 and 1973, 56,227 United States servicemen died in Vietnam. From 1962, when thirty army advisers began Australia's involvement, until the end of the war, 41,000 Australian soldiers and 6000 air force and navy men served in Vietnam. Of them, 474 died and more than 3000 were wounded. Four Victoria Crosses and 600 other decorations were won by Australian servicemen.

On 10 June 1965, Australian newspapers published this Australian Associated Press report by David Mathew from Washington, following talks between Sir Robert Menzies and President Johnson:

Australian troops in Vietnam will fight alongside South Vietnamese and American forces.

The Prime Minister, Sir Robert Menzies, announced this today.

He warned that the next two or three months in Vietnam would be "crucial" during the monsoon season.

Sir Robert's statement came at a Press conference after two days of talks with President Johnson and U.S. officials.

Yesterday, the U.S. State Department announced that American troops in future would fight alongside South Vietnamese units, if the Saigon Government sought combat support.

The U.S. Commander in South Vietnam, General Westmoreland, already has authority to commit American troops to battle.

Sir Robert said he could not predict whether more Australian troops might eventually go to Vietnam.

Australia was "fully stretched" at the moment in regard to manpower and to its budget, he said.

Even so, the defence budget would be increased by £80 to £90 million for the next year.

Sir Robert, who saw President Johnson on Monday, said he had been summoned to a surprise breakfast meeting with the President again this morning.

He also was interrupted during his Press conference to take a telephone call from the President.

Sir Robert yesterday also conferred with the U.S. Defence Secretary, Mr McNamara, and the Secretary of Commerce, Mr Connor.

It was believed that the session at the Commerce Department dealt chiefly with the effect on Australia of the U.S. restrictions on private capital investment overseas.

From Mr McNamara, Sir Robert received a report on the progress of the F-111A fighter bomber. Australia, with 24 of the planes on order, is due to take its first delivery in 1968.

In Sydney last night, the Defence Minister, Senator Paltridge, said that Australian troops had a "static defence role" in Vietnam at present.

Asked if President Johnson's authorisation of the use of American troops in Vietnam in offensive operations would alter the role of Australian troops, he replied: "Although the Australian troops are in a defensive role, they may undertake patrols."

Asked the exact role of the Australian troops, Senator Paltridge, ending his short interview, said: "They have a static defence role."

The Acting Prime Minister, Mr McEwen, said said that Cabinet had discussed Vietnam, but he declined to give details.

The Australians sailed in the troopship HMAS Sydney *late in May 1965, and in mid-June were in action against the Viet Cong. Don Petersen, of the Melbourne* Sun, *sent these early dispatches from the Australian base at Bien Hoa:*

BIEN HOA, Tues. — There were four of us beneath a small sloping patch of dull green nylon which troops call a "hutchie".

Rain poured in, soaking bodies which had not been dry all day, and around us 20 ft. high scrub rustled with the mass movements of countless millions of insects.

Although it was only 8 o'clock, the night was dark.

The dull glow of a cigarette showed briefly as one or the other of us swiped half-heartedly at squadrons of mosquitoes now assuming the harassment which ants had enjoyed all day.

The talk, in the soft tones of men who are listening for something else, was of home. . .

"At least the pubs are still open in Sydney," said Company Sergeant-Major Frank Cramp.

"There's one I know that's got the best beer in all Australia, but what the heck, we're too far away to start thinking of it."

The company was on a 24-hour security patrol some distance from the First Battalion's perimeter at Bien Hoa.

All day the three platoons had been bush-bashing through secondary jungle which at first sight defied any penetration at all.

The company's assignment, like several before it, was to search the area for signs of Viet Cong.

Just beyond the patrol area is the Song Dong Nai River and across it is the jungle stronghold of an estimated division of Communist regulars.

Troops look at that river and at the jungle

Two Australian soldiers crouch in the jungle of South Vietnam during a battle with Viet Cong across the Dong Nai River

beyond and itch for action.

This sort of emu bob close to base is frustrating.

The First Battalion's acclimatisation period ended today and the battalion became officially a fully operational unit, ready for combat at a moment's notice.

But patrols like this one have to be done and at least they are better than garrison duty at Bien Hoa. . .

From 11 p.m. on the war rumbled and flashed around us.

To the north, USAF Skyraiders pounded a flare-lit target less than five miles away.

Australian mortars and American artillery fired over our heads at jungle slopes across the Song Dong Nai, and an American patrol on our left flank sent up phosphorous flares several times during the night.

Drifting off to his own hutchie, Jack Cramp observed: "We haven't fired a shot or sent up one flare yet.

"The Americans think we're mad. Seems to me, though, that all they're doing is letting the VCs know where they are.

"I guess we have a bit to teach them."

The first brew was made at 6.15 a.m. today.

From 1.30 on there had been only the distant sounds of war and one strangled yell from a young Digger guarding patrol headquarters.

His rain-filled hutchie had collapsed, spilling a gallon or two of water down his neck.

Few of us ate breakfast.

Four more hours of bush-bashing and John Healy signals the platoons to return home. BIEN HOA, Wed. — At exactly 11.10 last night the first 60mm mortar bomb whistled in, the crunch of its explosion almost drowned in an American salvo.

It was the opening shot in a brief, but furious attack that blooded the Australian 1st Battalion.

The attack, directed at a company field headquarters, wounded three Australians and knocked out all communications.

Digger infantry, held to a defensive role, could not counter-attack. But Australian mortars fired back.

The action occurred at an abandoned hamlet deep in the strongly Viet Cong War Zone "D", about 15 miles from Bien Hoa air base.

The Diggers, flown in by helicopter as part of a big search-and-destroy operation, expected to be hit, and their platoons dug into a tight, interlocking defence perimeter designed to repulse the strongest attack.

But until 11.10 p.m. the only sound in the night was the crash and thunder of American 105s and Australian mortars a few yards behind us. They were firing at distant targets which could have been Communist staging areas or supply depots.

And then came that first mortar bomb. The second landed closer and in our deafened hutchie Pte. Mick Jones, 20, of Sydney, who was on my left, jerked up with a grunt of surprise.

There were still three bombs in the air, marching towards us.

The headquarters platoon, with one exception, was diving into its trenches.

Pte. Neville Riddock, 20, of Melbourne, the company's medical orderly and a boy whom I said last week had no love for the jungle, was moving towards the last explosion.

Cpl. Dick Kennedy, a mortar fire controller from Brisbane, had been hit in the leg by shrapnel and "Doc" Riddock had heard him cry out.

The third blast wounded Kennedy again in the back and Pte. Kevin Grey, a West Australian, collected a shrapnel bolt in his ankle while tumbling head first into his pit.

With young "Doc" Riddock already working on Kennedy, an extraordinary calm voice — the company commander, Major John Healy, of Melbourne — began calling for the casualty position and communications.

The fourth explosion, some distance away, cut him short but did no damage. . .

The Australians greeted the dawn with some funny grins. Most of them had been under fire for the first time and they had discovered something that they had badly needed to know. . .

1966   Prime Minister Menzies steps down after seventeen years in office

GRAHAM PERKIN
Melbourne Age, 21 January 1966

*Before he stepped down from the job in
January 1966, Sir Robert Menzies had been
Australia's Prime Minister for a record
unbroken term of seventeen years. He was,
that January, the only Prime Minister many
young Australians could remember — an
institution who had been in power before
bikinis and sputniks and drip-dry shirts,
before the mini-skirt and the pill, before John
Fitzgerald Kennedy had become even a junior
senator. Menzies, who died in 1978, aged 83,
was regarded by many as perhaps the most
commanding figure in Australian history;
a magnificent orator, a world statesman, and
a leader under whom the nation had achieved
a rare degree of prosperity.*

*He was an autocratic man who was never
challenged as leader of his Liberal party after
it took office in 1949. (He had one earlier,
brief and ill-fated spell as Prime Minister
after the death of Mr Lyons, and was replaced,
first by the Country Party's Arthur Fadden,
and then by the Curtin-led Labor Government.) Menzies had flaws; his critics claimed
that he took no real interest in Australia's
Asian neighbours, that he was too pre-
occupied with England and the fading
Empire, that he manipulated some election
issues, that he regarded parliament as a
rubber stamp for decisions already made in
the Cabinet room, that his foreign policy was
based on the 'great and powerful friends'
alliance with the United States and Britain
rather than any sense of national independence.
But he possessed great stature, and his regime
was characterised by good management.*

*When Sir Robert Menzies resigned, at the
age of seventy-one, he made a statement on
television and radio. Graham Perkin, of the
Age, watched that historic moment on tele-*
*vision, and wrote about it. Perkin, one of
Australia's finest modern journalists, was
assistant editor of the* Age *at that time, and
had won a Walkley Award seven years before.
He became editor of the* Age *later in 1966
and steered it with brilliance, flair and a
maximum of integrity until his sudden death
in October 1975. At his funeral service,* Age
*associate editor Creighton Burns summed him
up well: 'We will remember him in his shirt-
sleeves laying out the display of the newspaper and anguishing over the words. . . He
enjoyed himself and his work as a newspaperman hugely, and swept others along with his
enthusiasm.'*

I don't suppose there was anyone in Australia
who heard the news for the first time when
the familiar face came up on the television
screen at 8 o'clock last night.

For years and years and years (and generally
in prime listening and viewing time) the same
face has lifted its great eyebrows and said
things we expected, or sometimes didn't
expect, from a Prime Minister.

Last night we expected to hear he had
resigned. He came into the picture, made two
small jokes and confirmed our expectations
in 30 seconds.

At once, it was one of those times when
you watch a piece of history and wish the
action would stop while the mind absorbs
the moment that just flicked past.

It could have been an uncomfortably
maudlin night if the principal character had
been different.

There was, after all, a fairly sentimental
atmosphere abroad, which a less sensitive man
might not have been able to control.

But he controlled it. Not only that, he made

Although political enemies for many years, Sir Robert Menzies (centre) and Mr Arthur Calwell enjoyed a mutual respect. Sir Robert was Chancellor of Melbourne University when this photograph was taken and Mr Calwell had just received an honorary doctorate of Laws

us laugh for the right reasons and at the right times.

As Prime Ministerial press conferences have gone for the past 16 years (and not too many have gone, of course) it was a night of kindness.

He showed an uncharacteristic readiness to answer questions he at other times might have scorned. No one was left bleeding in the press seats.

As always, the wit sometimes dispersed the dignity.

He had gone to see the Governor-General and produced a document "in such English as I could command."

As he said this, he looked up and that creeping smile began to creep from his mouth to his eyes.

He knew that his English in this document was impeccable and he knew that everyone else would know it too.

It was, indeed, a night for the history book. Whether things change for the better or for the worse, they will surely be different.

Even that much change can hurt a little.

1966   Vietnam brings the first death of an Australian conscript on service abroad

E. H. COX
Melbourne Herald, 25 May 1966

On 8 March 1966, the first day of the sitting of the 25th Parliament, Prime Minister Holt announced that Australia would be sending conscripts to fight in Vietnam. It was a decision of considerable historical importance. In two World Wars, Australia had sent only volunteer troops overseas to fight, although in World War Two conscripts were called on to serve in New Guinea and nearby islands, in what was considered to be the defence of Australia.

The first national servicemen to be sent to a battle zone arrived in Vietnam on 5 May 1966. The first of them to be killed in action died within three weeks. He was Private Errol Noack, twenty-one years old. Nationally it was an emotional moment.

'It would be wrong to bring this or any other death in action into political argument,' said an editorial in the Melbourne Herald *on the day after the announcement of Noack's death. 'The debate on whether we should be fighting in Vietnam can only be confused and degraded by any attempt to separate our dead into groups of those who were drafted and those who took up arms by choice.'*

Even so, controversy flared. The Labor Opposition Leader, Arthur Calwell, who branded the Vietnam conflict as a 'cruel, filthy, unwinnable war', said: 'Every member of the Liberal and Country Parties and the DLP in Parliament who supported the Government in its policy of sending 20-year-old voteless youths to Vietnam shares with the Government a terrible responsibility.'

This was the report E. H. Cox sent to the Melbourne Herald *on Private Noack's death:*

The first National Serviceman ever to die on foreign soil has been killed in an operation against the Viet Cong in Vietnam.

The Army Department announced early this afternoon that he was Pte. Errol Wayne Noack, 21, single, of the Adelaide suburb of Gilberton.

A report to Army headquarters this morning said that he died of gunshot wounds.

Pte. Noack went into the Army in July last year. He was one of the first draft of about 2100 National Service trainees to be called into the Army.

When the news of his death reached Canberra early today, the Prime Minister, Mr Holt, and the Minister for the Army, Mr Fraser, were immediately informed.

However, for nearly three hours the Army Department declined to confirm the report or to give any information.

Australian forces in South Vietnam are currently engaged in a major operation which so far has been kept secret for security reasons, and Pte. Noack is believed to have been killed during this operation.

Full details of his death are not yet known in Australia, but the commanding officer of the Australian forces in Vietnam, Major-General Kenneth Mackay, has been asked to send details to Australia as soon as possible...

Pte. Noack's death is the first indication that the first members of the new task force of nearly 4500 soldiers at present being mustered in Vietnam have begun operations.

The unit in which he was serving has not yet been disclosed but a big proportion of the South Australians from his draft went to the 5th Battalion or its ancillary services and he is believed to have been with these...

This afternoon it was announced that so far as is known in Canberra, Pte. Noack is the only casualty suffered by the new drafts...

1967

A little town called Snug burns in Tasmania's catastrophic bushfires

JOHN HAMILTON
Melbourne Age, 8 February 1967

On 7 February 1967, catastrophic bushfires swept across Tasmania. They killed more than fifty people, destroyed 1200 homes, and caused more than $3 million worth of damage to buildings, as well as huge losses to livestock and crops. Excepting the Victorian bushfires of 1939, they were the worst fires in Australian history.

Squads of reporters from the Hobart Mercury and the Launceston Examiner covered the fires. Also, reporters from Melbourne, including John Soreil (Herald), Michael Ryan (Age), John Hamilton (Age), Geoff Jones (Sun) and Alan Dearn (Herald), flew across Bass Strait within an hour or two of the first reports of the tragedy.

John Hamilton had just arrived home, having finished his daily column 'Briefing' when someone from his office telephoned to say: 'The bushfires in Tasmania are really bad. We're chartering a plane to get down there fast. You've got ten minutes to get on your way to the airport. . .'

The chartered plane could not land at Hobart because dense smoke from the fires ruined visibility. The plane finally landed at Launceston around 11 p.m. Hamilton had little sleep that night; after he and the Age party reached Launceston, he worked for a couple of hours helping to send pictures back to the mainland on a picturegram transmitter, and at 6 a.m. the following day he hired a car and drove to Hobart.

He toured relief centres which had been set up for the homeless, and found scenes of total confusion. At one of these centres, he met two people from a town called Snug; they told him that things were particularly bad there, and that many people had been killed. Hamilton reacted with characteristic profess-ionalism. 'The name Snug struck me as ironic,' he said later, ' and in all the confusion it seemed to me that a story on what had happened in one small town would sum up what was happening right through Tasmania.'

He drove to what was left of the little township of Snug, and spent three hours walking around the ruins, talking and observing. Then he drove back to Hobart, where most of the communications were jammed. He managed to persuade a post official to let him use a phone long enough to dictate his story. His report of one small capsule of the horror that existed that day in Tasmania won him a Walkley Award for the best piece of newspaper reporting of the year of 1967.

A massive nation-wide effort — involving governments at every level, the services, charities, churches and private industry — was launched to provide disaster relief. The Herald and the Sun in Melbourne demonstrated the positive power of the press by raising $600,000 by public appeal to help bushfire victims; this amount was matched dollar for dollar by the Federal Government.

Inevitably, there were inquiries into what had caused the disaster. The extremely high temperatures and gusty northerly winds had proved a terrible combination; but other factors had contributed. These included a general lack of fire protection, public unawareness about the dangers of bushfires, obsolescence of much fire-fighting equipment, isolation of many townships in deep forest areas, plus a certain lack of co-ordination between fire authorities.

This is John Hamilton's report from Snug:

The town of Snug met death bravely yesterday afternoon.

The holiday visitors who came to this little town on the seaside, 19 miles from the heart of Hobart, used to write on their postcards that they were "snug as a bug at Snug."

The town had been the butt of jokes like these ever since a sea captain, 100 years or so ago, anchored in the little bay with six sick sailors aboard his ship. The sailors recovered in the restful surroundings and the captain called the place Snug.

But, yesterday, all hell broke loose in Snug.

At about 1 p.m. the sky went black and a roaring holocaust of flame engulfed the town, killing, maiming and blinding people.

Houses exploded, cars melted into twisted piles of junk and the apples in the orchards baked on the trees.

Mrs. Mavis Hughes is the post mistress at Snug. When I arrived in the town yesterday, following the Red Cross relief trucks, she was still on duty at the little weatherboard post office — incredibly one of the few remaining buildings in the town.

"It was hot yesterday and the first news of a fire we heard was about a small fire some way from Snug at 10.30 in the morning," she said.

"Then I started to get deluged by phone calls for help, and all the available men went off to fight the fire."

But the men went to fight a fire burning south of the town. The fire that destroyed Snug roared in from the north.

"It seemed like the air exploded — the whole air seemed alight and there was a terrible wind," Mrs. Hughes went on.

Opposite the post office, the brick classrooms of the local school caught fire.

Alongside the classrooms is a brick school hall. When the teachers realised that fire was engulfing the town, they shepherded more than 100 children quietly into the hall.

Kaylene Barrett, 13, was one of those children.

"Mr. Hawsley, our music teacher, sat down at the piano and said that we should all join in and sing a few songs," she recalled. . .

Near the seaside, Mrs. Lavinia Millhouse, with her four children aged from seven to four, was visiting her mother who was running the Millhouse corner shop while her husband was away fire fighting.

Mrs. Millhouse, senior, is an invalid, and when the fire suddenly came, her daughter realised she couldn't save both her mother and the children.

"We ran into a wall of flame, and I was dragging the kids behind me. I went back for mum but I couldn't get through the fire.

"I didn't know till later that my uncle, thank God, arrived just after I left and was able to get mum out before the shop and all the houses in the street went up."

Mrs. Millhouse dragged her children 200 yards until she reached the beach.

"I got all the kids into the water, and we went out as deep as we could," she said.

"There were other people who had arrived, and they drove their cars through the sand right to the water's edge, and then they got into the sea as far as they could.

"We all cuddled a child apiece."

Perhaps 40 adults and children stayed in the sea for over two hours. In the words of another of them: "The waves were pretty heavy, and outside the water it was jet black, just like night. All you could see were red sparks flying through the air with the wind."

Mrs. Millhouse said simply: "If the water hadn't been there, nobody would have lived.".

They were all shocked but very calm. They told their stories quietly. There were very few tears.

One even managed to joke: "I suppose this fire will put Tasmania on the map of Australia.".

Seven confirmed dead, another man who had collapsed and died after the fire. And eleven others — missing. And there were probably more; had anybody heard anything about the couple with six children who lived a mile or so away from Snug? Nobody had.

About 70 houses totally destroyed. The carbide factory, Snug's only industry which employed 300 men, destroyed. The churches gone, the school gone, the farms, all gone.

I cried as I left Snug today, as it lay in ruins under a grey shroud of smoke, the earth around a black and smoking pall.

It is Ash Wednesday. Pray for Snug and Tasmania.

1967   Prime Minister Harold Holt disappears into the Portsea surf

JACK DARMODY, MIKE RYAN, ALLAN BARNES, PETER BLAZEY AND JOHN HAMILTON
Melbourne Age, 18 and 23 December 1967 and Australian, 18 December 1967

Harold Holt became Prime Minister of Australia on 20 January 1966, after ten years as the patient understudy of Sir Robert Menzies. His reaction to his unopposed election by parliamentary colleagues after the resignation of Menzies was characteristic of the man. 'It was wonderful,' he told his wife by phone as soon as the election meeting broke up. 'Quick, calm . . . and I walked over nobody.' Mrs Zara Holt recalled later that same day: 'He's a nice man, he truly is. In his big moment, he wanted to let me know that he hadn't hurt someone to get the job.'

Some of his colleagues considered Harold Holt too nice. Unlike Menzies — a man who rarely sought advice, acted on intuitions, and sometimes refused to take Cabinet or Parliament into his confidence — he was a team man who sought advice often and allowed himself to be guided by it. Under him, Cabinet took on the appearance of a board of directors, motivated by an attitude of collective responsibility.

When he took over as Australia's 18th Prime Minister, Harold Holt was fifty-seven years old, trim, affable and extraordinarily energetic. He settled for four hours' sleep a night, held his breath under water when he took a bath, did calisthenics every morning, and went skin-diving and spear-fishing whenever he had the chance. His philosophy, he let it be known, was not to waste a moment — and he certainly wasted few after he took over the prime ministership. Before the end of 1966, he trebled Australia's military commitment to the Vietnam war; took the politically touchy decision to send conscripts to the war; visited Australian and American troops on the Vietnam front; toured South-East Asia; called on President Johnson twice; had the President

call on him once; pledged that he would go 'all the way with LBJ'; personally rebuked Britain's Prime Minister, Harold Wilson, for his dissociation of Britain from the bombing of oil installations in North Vietnam and his lack of understanding of Asia; attended a Commonwealth Prime Ministers' conference at which he rebuked the other leaders for spending too much time discussing Rhodesia's problems and not enough on Asian affairs; handled a number of domestic problems ranging from drought relief to immigration — and fought and won an election.

The big issue of the November 1966 Federal Election was the Vietnam war. The Holt Government claimed that Australia had to be involved; that containment of communism was even more vital to Australia than it was to the United States. The Labor Opposition, led by Arthur Calwell, called the Vietnam conflict a war which had no legal or moral justification. One of the Labor Party promises was that all draftees would be brought home from Vietnam immediately after the election. Harold Holt won that election sweepingly, with a record majority.

On Sunday 17 December 1967, after he had returned to his Portsea (Victoria) holiday home from the last Cabinet meeting of 1966, Harold Holt went swimming in the ocean beach off Portsea. He swam strongly for a time, then disappeared in boiling surf. A witness, Mrs Winton Gillespie, said later: 'It was like a leaf being taken out. It was so quick, so final.' A great sea and air search was mounted, but Harold Holt's body was never found. He had been Prime Minister for just 692 days.

Published here are the Age's first report, written jointly by Jack Darmody, Mike Ryan (from Portsea) and Allan Barnes (from Can-

berra), and a poignant description of Mr Holt's disappearance, given by his friend and neighbour, Mrs Winton Gillespie. The second report was filed by Peter Blazey for the Australian.

Harold Holt was a keen sportsman and a strong swimmer

The Prime Minister (Mr. Holt) is missing believed drowned. He disappeared in heavy surf off Portsea's ocean beach just before noon yesterday and early today had not been found.

Mr. Holt, 59, was swimming with a friend in about 40 feet of water at his favorite spot in Cheviot Bay when he disappeared.

He was a strong swimmer, but it was disclosed last night that he had been under medical treatment for a back complaint.

A massive sea and air search will resume at first light this morning. All of Melbourne's police, army, naval and air force resources were thrown into yesterday's hunt.

At 8.30 last night the Prime Minister's press secretary (Mr. Tony Eggleton) said at Portsea that the searchers still retained a slim hope of finding Mr. Holt alive.

"This is the opinion of the Government at the present moment and will remain so until an official statement is issued from Canberra."

Mrs. Holt, who was spending the weekend in Canberra, was flown to Melbourne yesterday afternoon and driven to the Holt holiday home at Portsea.

Last night Mrs. Holt was joined at the holiday home by her three sons and their wives.

Several close family friends joined them.

Mr. Eggleton said Mrs. Holt was being "extremely brave."

"I don't think I know any woman who could show equal courage and composure in these circumstances," he said.

The Deputy Prime Minister (Mr. McEwen) flew to Canberra from his Stanhope property last night and informed the Governor-General (Lord Casey) of the situation.

No administrative action will be taken to appoint a new Prime Minister until either Mr. Holt's body is found or all hope is abandoned...

In this event, Mr. McEwen is expected to be sworn in as Prime Minister until the Government parties elect a successor.

He was swimming with a friend, Mr. Alan Stewart, director of the Port Quarantine Station at Portsea, when he disappeared.

The two men swam out from the shore in a heavy surf. They became separated in strong currents.

Mr. Stewart raised the alarm about 12.40.

A full-scale search and rescue operation was immediately mounted.

Mrs Winton Gillespie, a neighbor and friend of the Holt family at Portsea, watched from the beach as Mr Holt swam out and disappeared.

Mr A. Eggleton, Press secretary to Mr Holt, obtained a statement from Mrs Gillespie at the request of reporters.

At a Press conference yesterday afternoon he handed a copy of the statement to an ABC television reporter, Brian Peck, and said: "Perhaps you would like to read it."

Before a national television audience, Mr Peck read the statement.

His voice faltered as he reached key points in the text. Mr Eggleton, sitting grimly behind him, was obviously under stress.

This is what Mrs Gillespie's statement said:

We went slowly, wondering where we would go. It was not a good morning and there was no question of snorkelling.

We were just going for a little swim or sunbathe. We went right to the very end to see the yachtsman, Rose.

We all got out of the car and watched for a moment.

Then we returned, thinking it might be better on Geyser Beach, which is on the bay-side.

But Harold said: "Oh, let's go to Cheviot", which he always goes to, because it's more fun.

So we pulled in to the usual corner and ran down the beach.

It's a long walk right to the end of the beach. It was very high tide, with masses of floating wood.

I had never seen it like that before. Usually, when he is snorkelling, it is low.

We all dropped back very quickly, stumbling down with the wood and the waves. Harold went on ahead.

Alan Stewart said to me: "The Prime Minister must be a lot fitter than we are. There he goes, striding along like Marco Polo."
. . .

I think he thought he would go for a quick plunge where there weren't any rocks.

I took one look at it and wasn't interested to put more than my toe in. However, he plunged in.

I just watched a moment and then went on up towards where our things were.

When I looked back, I could see that he was swimming in this broad stretch of swirly sort of water.

I think he must have got to the stage where he tried to stand up and there was nothing.

He seemed to be going out fairly rapidly and yet he was still swimming happily.

I ran down to where Alan was standing on the edge of the water, not really wanting to go in.

He said to me: "If Mr Holt can take it, I'd better go in too," and he went into the water.

But Harold was getting further and further away.

Suddenly I had the most terrible feeling and said: "Come back, come back."

By then he was too far out to see or hear. We could still see his head — he was swimming.

Alan said: "Does he often stay in this long?"

I knew it wasn't right, but there was nothing Alan or anybody could do at this stage.

As we watched, the waves became violent and boiled up into a fury. . .

I knew then there was nothing anyone could do, even if you had all the lifesavers there. It was too late then.

He did swim for quite some time, it seemed to me. But I suppose it was only a couple of minutes.

He seemed to be swimming with his head above the water quite well — I suppose desperately trying, thinking at this stage that if he swam he might catch a wave back.

But, after this boiling up, it all subsided. There wasn't a sign.

Alan and I went and stood on a rock and I don't think Alan realised.

But nobody could have done a thing. It was like a leaf being taken out; it was so quick and so final.

A memorial service for Prime Minister Harold Holt was held at St Paul's Cathedral, Melbourne, on 22 December 1967. President Johnson, with whom Mr Holt had established an unusual degree of rapport, flew from Washington for the service. Prince Charles made the trip from London, and so did the British Prime Minister, Harold Wilson. From Korea, the Philippines, South Vietnam, Taiwan, New Zealand, Western Samoa, Thailand, Singapore, Fiji, Malaysia, Canada, Laos, Indonesia, Cambodia, India and Japan they came — prime ministers and presidents and senior ministers.

John Hamilton, columnist of the Melbourne Age, had been writing about the Holt tragedy all that week. The service was the culmination of it all, and great publicity had been given to the VIPs who were attending the service. Hamilton was given a pass to allow him into the cathedral, but he decided not to use it. He felt that the ordinary people who came to mourn and pay their tributes would provide better material than the celebrities. Accordingly, he got up early that morning and stationed himself on the tram tracks opposite the cathedral door for three and a half hours.

The Age featured John Hamilton's report, decorating it with sketches by cartoonist Leslie Tanner. 'The story,' said Hamilton later, 'wrote itself.' The judges in the Walkley Award that year did not agree. They gave

President Johnson, Prince Charles and Lord and Lady Casey (seen in the right foreground) were among the dignitaries who attended the funeral of Prime Minister Harold Holt

Hamilton credit for writing it, and gave him his second Walkley Award. He later joined the Melbourne Herald, *and became its Washington correspondent in 1976.*

We were the people who came to mourn.

Not the Presidents and the Prime Ministers and the Ambassadors in their big black shiny cars. Not the security men with their walkie-talkie sets and their binoculars. Not the motor cycle escorts or the mounted police on their grey horses.

But the general public.

We stood and waited behind the barricades and we didn't talk much except to ask somebody up front to take his or her hat off or perhaps to ask people to make way for a child or old lady so that they could get a better view. . .

Two policemen kept smoothing down the red carpet opposite as it was ruffled by the breeze, and then the black cars and the motor cycle escorts began arriving and the world's statesmen began to walk into the church.

We didn't understand protocol and we couldn't understand why they arrived in such a seemingly odd order. We tried to guess who some of them were in the black top hats and the caps heavy with gold braid. We kept asking each other: "Where's Charles? Where's Johnson? Was that man with the grey hair Mr. Heath?"

We couldn't hear the commentary through the silver loud speakers mounted on the tram poles because the great peal of bells clanged over all.

And then they'd all arrived and the great wooden doors had been closed and the bells were silent.

"I am the resurrection and the life, saith the Lord . . ."

Some of us took off our hats, some of us clasped our hands in prayer, some of us just stood and listened.

Some of us cried.

Then it was over. The great doors opened and down the red carpet came Mrs. Holt with courage and bravery.

We all stood and — there is no other word for it — felt for her.

And she knew it. As she drove off, leading that great galaxy of people who had come to pay tribute to her husband, her tiny white gloved hand was waving to us from the window, gently.

We didn't wave back. We knew that she was just saying "Thank you."

Gough Whitlam on the steps of Parliament House after his dismissal as Prime Minister of Australia.

Loss of Innocence
1969-1988

1969   Police corruption is exposed and high-ranking officers are jailed

EVAN WHITTON
Melbourne Truth, 13 December 1969

On 13 December 1969, Melbourne's Truth *newspaper published what it called some of the most serious allegations ever made against members of the Victoria Police Force. The charges were that hundreds of thousands of dollars in 'protection money' had been paid to high-ranking police officers to enable abortion practices to be carried out without police intervention. They took the form of affidavits sworn by three doctors and three other people.*

The report brought into the open a campaign which had been waged throughout that year by a little-known Scottish doctor, Dr Bertram Wainer, alleging bullying and graft by members of the police force. It also began one of the most powerful scandals, involving corruption at high levels, in Australian police history.

The allegations were far too damaging and documented to be ignored. A month after they were published, Victoria's Chief Secretary, Sir Arthur Rylah, announced that a government-appointed board of inquiry would be set up to probe the bribery allegations. The inquiry sat for eighty days and heard 140 witnesses, whose evidence ran to 7000 pages of typewritten transcript involving well over two million words. As a result of it, four policemen (one of them an inspector who had been in charge of the Homicide Squad, and another an ex-superintendent) were charged on eleven counts of conspiracy. The trial began on 3 February 1971, and on 8 April a jury found that three of the men were guilty. John Edward Matthews, sixty, a former police superintendent, Jack Ralph Ford, fifty-four, a former police inspector, were sentenced to five years' jail; Martin Robert Jacobson, forty, a former detective, received a three-year sentence. Mr Justice Starke found that the convicted men had

used their positions as members of the Homicide Squad to conduct an extortion racket and that they had, by their actions, seriously shaken public confidence in the police force, as well as morale inside that force.

Evan Whitton, the reporter who broke the story of the affidavits, later received a Walkley Award for the best piece of Australian news reporting of the year. It was his second such award.

Six people, including three Melbourne doctors, have lodged sworn affidavits with the Solicitor-General naming senior police officers alleged to have been running an Abortion "Protection" Racket.

The affidavits, lodged with the Solicitor-General Mr. B. L. Murray, on Friday, allege that payments totalling hundreds of thousands of dollars have been made to some of the top men in the Victoria Police Force.

The police officers named in the affidavits are among the highest ranking and best known in Victoria. Their names and photographs have frequently been published in newspapers in connection with their work on major cases.

One of the doctors has sworn that he paid a high-ranking police officer $600 a month "to cover every eventuality including possible fatality" (of a patient).

Another doctor has sworn that he paid lump sums ranging from $200 to $1200.

The third doctor states in his affidavit that he "set up" a police officer to test stories of the officer's corruption. The doctor alleges that the officer readily agreed to join him in setting up an abortion extortion racket.

Two of the other affidavits have been sworn by doctors' receptionists who say that they have either handed over money to senior police officers or have seen it being handed over.

The sixth affidavit has been sworn by a man who alleges that he paid a police officer between $200 and $300 a week to ensure that an abortion practice could continue without police intervention.

All six affidavits contain the names and ranks of the police officers alleged to be involved.

The documents were all sworn before a Commissioner of the Supreme Court of Victoria for taking Affidavits.

Three were sworn before Commissioner M. M. Gorman and three before Commissioner H. A. Greening.

They were prepared by solicitors acting under the Evidence Act of 1958.

Truth has copies of all six affidavits, and publishes them in detail today.

Because of the serious nature of the charges and the laws of libel, Truth does not at this stage publish the names of the police officers said to be involved, or the names of the six people whose allegations are contained in the affidavits.

It is emphasised that this information is contained in the affidavits handed to the Solicitor General.

Truth refers to the four men who swore affidavits as Doctor A, Doctor B, Doctor C and Mr. D. The two women who swore affidavits are referred to as Miss E and Mrs. F.

Although the police officers named are of various ranks, they are referred to here only as Officer W, Officer X, Officer Y and Officer Z.

None of the initials so used corresponds with the initial letter of the person's surname.

To avoid confusion, the names of all other people in the affidavits are deleted entirely and are not referred to by any initial.

This is the affidavit of Dr. A:

In the matter of the Evidence Act 1958.

I (Doctor A), of Melbourne in the State of Victoria medical practitioner, make oath and say as follows:—

1. When now (Officer W) became — (a higher rank) ex-detective Mr. —— arranged for Mrs. F to meet Officer W at her residence (full address).

2. Two appointments were made and nobody turned up. On the third occasion I saw Officer W and Mr. —— arrive at (full address). I remained outside for approximately two hours.

3. Mrs. F subsequently told me:—

(i) that they demanded $600 per month in order that Doctor —— practice and mine might continue;

(ii) that the money was essential and Officer W commented that it is not what you say that counts, it's what we say you say;

(iii) that if these payments were made every eventuality would be covered including possible fatality;

(iv) that if the money was not paid, we would be put out of business.

4. Subsequently $600 was paid each month following phone calls from Officer W to arrange site for payment. I would listen to these phone calls on my extension phone and came to know his voice very well.

5. The venues of payment were usually Mrs. F's then residence.

6. Money was frequently paid in my presence and I always observed Officer W's arrival at these venues.

7. When Officer W was transferred . . . he still demanded these payments for a further year. He stated that to discontinue these payments would mean that my practice would be shut down, it was therefore obligatory that they be made.

8. At the end of this year he demanded $100 per month and this continued to be met until my arrest.

Sworn at Melbourne in the State of Victoria this 5th day of December, One thousand nine hundred and sixty-nine.
(Signed)
H. A. Greening,
A Commissioner of the Supreme Court of Victoria for taking Affidavits.

This is the affidavit of Doctor B:—

In the matter of the Evidence Act 1958.

I (Doctor B) of . . . Melbourne, in the State of Victoria, Medical Practitioner, make oath and say as follows:—

1. That at lunchtime on Wednesday 20th August 1969 I received a telephone call from Mr — advising me that I was due to be visited by Officer X at four o'clock that afternoon and that I should sit quiet and not take any notice since the visit was only to make an impression on the police force.

2. That I was visited by Officer X at four o'clock that afternoon during which time Officer X threatened that I would be prosecuted if I continued to carry out abortions.

3. That for some years past I have received messages from Sister — that I would be raided by police unless money was sent to the — (a section of the police force).

4. That in the early 1950s I paid Officer X and to an intermediary $1200 following a raid of Sister — private hospital in — and consequent threatened police prosecution.

5. That on receiving these calls I would send amounts of between $200 and $600 through Sister — to the — (a section of the police force).

Sworn at Melbourne in the said State this 5th day of December, 1969 by the said deponent.

(Signed)

H. A. Greening,

A Commissioner of the Supreme Court of Victoria for taking Affidavits.

This is the affidavit of Doctor C:—

In the matter of the Evidence Act of 1958.

I (Doctor C), of (full address), in the State of Victoria, Medical Practitioner, make oath and say as follows:—

1. I am a duly qualified medical practitioner.

2. I first became acquainted with Officer X's name as a result of my having met Mrs. F in the course of my attempts to have Abortion Law reformed in Victoria.

I had a conversation with him on one occasion when he was in the process of beating up Mrs. F.

Mrs. F rang me during this scene and was obviously mentally distressed and crying.

I could hear blows being struck on what sounded like her body and a man's voice raised in the background.

Officer X then took the phone from Mrs. F apparently not being aware of who I was.

He asked who I was and what business it was of mine, that they were having a domestic argument.

I said I was Dr. C and that I found it to be amazing that a senior police officer should be beating up a woman. He then hung up without further ado.

3. I have met Officer X on a number of occasions when I have laid complaints at Russell Street about abortionists and backyard abortions. . .

I did not at this stage name Officer X as the officer.

4. Mr. D who was arrested on backyard abortion charges as a result of my activities contacted me when he was released from Pentridge Gaol where he had been serving 14 weeks' sentence on another matter.

Mr. D said in this conversation that he wanted to give me complete details of police corruption because he had paid large sums of money to the police and was charged on 14 counts of abortion.

He also stated that the police officers informed him every time I set a trap to catch him.

5. I met Mr. D and in my presence he rang Officer W and engaged in a pleasant conversation, initially asking about the officer's wife and remarking on how good a cook she was.

I could hear all the conversation.

He then asked Officer W how he was charged on 14 counts when he had been paying Officer X and Officer W $600 a week for protection.

Officer W said not to worry as the trial would not be for two years and that he would have everything fixed up and quietened down by that time.

Mr. D then asked him how Officer W had allowed Mr. D to stay in Officer W's house when Mr. D was in hiding from the police.

Officer W replied, because we are good friends.

Mr. D then asked him how Officer W had rung him in Queensland and told him to come back and get into the backyard racket again, because everything was all right.

Officer W said that at that time he had believed it was all right, but Dr. C made things too hot. . .

1971 A reporter is involved in the events which brought down John Gorton

ALAN RAMSEY
Australian, 4 March 1971

In 1931, material published by a journalist, the Melbourne Herald's *Joe Alexander, helped to topple Prime Minister Scullin. Forty years later, material published by another journalist, Alan Ramsey, began a series of events which led to the fall of John Gorton as Prime Minister.*

The affair began when Ramsey wrote a report in the Australian *saying that the Chief of the Army General Staff, Lieutenant-General Sir Thomas Daly, had accused the Defence Minister, Malcolm Fraser, of disloyalty to the army and its minister, Andrew Peacock. John Gorton promptly denied the report and was supported by General Daly. Ramsey then claimed that the Prime Minister had had the opportunity to repudiate the report, which had been submitted to him before publication. Another well-known political journalist, Maximilian Walsh, of the* Financial Review, *suggested that Ramsey had been 'given the nod' by the Prime Minister to publish his report.*

Suddenly, the credibility of the Prime Minister was being challenged. Mr Fraser forced the crisis into the open by resigning as Minister for Defence. Mr Fraser told Parliament on 9 March that Mr Gorton was 'not fit to hold the great office of Prime Minister'. He accused the Prime Minister of disloyalty, and said, 'I cannot serve in his government.' He added: 'This man, because of his unreasoned drive to get his own way, his obstinacy, his impetuous and emotional reactions, has imposed strains on the Liberal Party, the Government and the Public Service.'

John Gorton defended himself in Parliament with dignity and without rancor against the charges. When he talked of his discussion with Alan Ramsey, Ramsey interjected from the press gallery, 'You liar.' *The Speaker, Sir William Aston, ordered Ramsey's removal from the House of Representatives. Ramsey later apologised and said there was no question of the Prime Minister being a liar.*

Next day the Parliamentary Liberal Party held a vote of confidence on the leadership of John Gorton. When the vote was tied, Mr Gorton used his casting vote to put himself out of office. William McMahon, sixty-three, became Prime Minister of Australia.

That vote ended one of the most hectic and turbulent periods in Australian politics. John Gorton came to power after the death of Harold Holt and, ironically, his strongest backer then was the man who caused his downfall, Malcolm Fraser. The Melbourne Sun *said of him on 10 March:*

> Mr Gorton has been guilty at times of clumsiness, arrogance and single-mindedness which amounts at times to a rejection of advice. Most of all, he has shown an almost obsessive inclination to cut down talented aides . . . men who might be regarded by Mr Gorton as future rivals.

The Age *said of Mr Gorton's defence in Parliament:*

> He as much as admitted that Mr. Fraser had reason to feel aggrieved. He acknowledged that on March 3 he might have circumvented publication of the devastating account of his talk with . . . Daly by uttering a few cautionary words. The impression remains that publication suited Mr. Gorton's wishes at the time. Mr. Gorton conceded that his failure to utter these cautionary words may have been "a mistake". It is rather too mild a word for something

which reflects so sadly on his loyalty, judgment and credibility. . .

Mr Gorton became deputy Prime Minister (to McMahon) and Defence Minister. In August that year, after criticism of him in Alan Reid's book, The Gorton Experiment, *John Gorton wrote a series of articles for the* Australian *called* I Did It My Way. *Prime Minister McMahon, explaining that the articles had breached basic principles of Cabinet solidarity, sacked him from the ministry. Malcolm Fraser himself later became Prime Minister after the fall of the Labor Government in December 1975.*

Here is the report by Alan Ramsey which ignited the fuse:

The Chief of the Army General Staff, Lieutenant-General Sir Thomas Daly, has accused the Defence Minister, Mr Fraser, of extreme disloyalty to the army and its junior minister, Mr Peacock.

He has told the Prime Minister, Mr Gorton, he believes the army, its department and its minister are being discredited by Defence sources as part of a political campaign against Mr Peacock.

He is also known to have given Mr Gorton examples of what he sees as Mr Peacock and the army's having been deliberately and wrongly blamed for "mistakes" embarrassing to Mr Fraser as Defence Minister.

These include the recent controversies over the ceremonial military guard for the Governor of Victoria, Sir Rohan Delacombe, and the army's civic action programme in Vietnam.

In each case, General Daly claimed, statements attributed to Mr Fraser and Defence "sources" had made the Army Department and, by ministerial responsibility, Mr Peacock, appear at fault when this was known officially to be incorrect.

The outspokenness of General Daly underlines the extent of the antagonism between the military and the Defence Department since Mr Fraser became Defence Minister.

Defence (or, at least, certain senior officials) claim the military resents Mr Fraser because of what has been described as his brusque, no-nonsense style.

They also defend him as certainly the most active, the most involved and the best Defence Minister Australia has had for many years.

Mr Fraser's detractors say that as well as running the military like office boys he also "stands over" his service ministers, particularly the Minister for Air, Senator Drake-Brockman.

The real point is that Mr Gorton not only has to deal with what apparently is a rift in his ministry, he also faces a situation in which one of the Government's three most senior military advisers has lost confidence in the Defence Minister to the point where he denounces him to the Prime Minister.

General Daly made his allegations in a private interview with the Prime Minister in Canberra on Monday.

Mr Gorton had called him to his Parliament House office to discuss increasing reports of worsening relations between the army and the Department of Defence.

These reports mentioned private briefings critical of the army having been given to some correspondents by Defence sources.

Mr Gorton is known to have referred specifically to rumors making certain allegations against the army and identifying General Daly by name.

The Prime Minister told General Daly he knew the reports to be wrong and that he would not allow them to go unchallenged.

He said he would see they were officially refuted if they appeared in print.

On Tuesday, a front-page story was published in a Sydney newspaper claiming that the Joint Intelligence Organisation had been ordered to report on Australian army activities in Vietnam. . .

The statement denied not only that the JIO had been ordered to report on the army in Vietnam but also that the army had engaged in military activity "outside the area covered by its directives." It had never done this, he said.

Mr Fraser admitted that the JIO did "assist in assessing and interpreting information from military, political and diplomatic sources in Vietnam." . . .

In fact, the JIO has been "making assessments" on Vietnam since it started operations in February last year.

1972 After twenty-three years, Labor sweeps into power

ALLAN BARNES AND BEN HILLS
Melbourne Age, 3 December 1972

After twenty-three years of government under a Liberal-Country Party coalition, Australia voted Labor into power on 2 December 1972. During those twenty-three years the Labor Party had suffered its most traumatic split, as a result of which the Democratic Labor Party was formed. For Gough Whitlam, who had taken over leadership of the party from Arthur Calwell, the victory was a huge personal triumph. He became Australia's seventh Labor Prime Minister (not counting Frank Forde's seven-day interregnum in 1945) after J. C. Watson, Andrew Fisher, William Morris Hughes, James Scullin, John Curtin and Ben Chifley. Until Mr Whitlam's win, the Labor Party had had only seventeen years of rule in the seventy-one years since Federation.

The last Labor Prime Minister, Mr Chifley, had been beaten in 1949 by a revitalised Liberal Party (built by Mr Robert Menzies from the wreckage of the old United Australia Party). After Mr Chifley died in 1951, the Labor leadership had passed into the hands of the brilliant but eccentric Dr H. V. Evatt. After Dr Evatt came Mr Calwell, a Labor traditionalist who brought the party close to electoral victory in 1961; he was replaced after two more election defeats by Mr Whitlam. It was largely he who managed to control the disparate elements in the ALP, gave it a fresh outlook and a forward-looking policy, and restored public confidence in what had become a divided and dispirited party.

This was how Allan Barnes (in Canberra) and Ben Hills (in Sydney) reported Labor's victory for a special Sunday edition of the Melbourne Age on 3 December:

The Australian Labor Party yesterday won a clear victory in the election for the House of Representatives.

Labor will become the new Federal Government with a majority of at least seven seats and possibly 15 or 17.

It has won nine Government seats firmly and has a chance of winning another 13.

Labor seems likely to lose two seats. It could drop another two in Western Australia.

Labor gained a swing of 3.5 per cent. across the nation. Its biggest gains were in Victoria and New South Wales. . .

In Victoria Labor's vote rose by 6.4 per cent. on the last election in 1969, while the Labor vote in NSW was up 5 per cent.

Edward Gough Whitlam, 56, will be Australia's eighth Labor Prime Minister since Federation. He will fly to Canberra from his home in Sydney today.

He is expected to be sworn in by the Governor-General (Sir Paul Hasluck) early this week.

The outgoing Prime Minister (Mr. McMahon) conceded defeat about 11.30 last night.

He said: "The vote has shown a decisive majority for Mr. Whitlam. I congratulate him and members of the Labor Party.

"For my own part I accept the verdict of the people."

Mr. Whitlam said the voters had given Labor a very good mandate to carry out its policies.

"We are very much reassured by the response the public gave our programme," he said.

"We are very much aware of the responsibilities with which the people have now entrusted us." . . .

Mr. Whitlam said that Australia's first Labor Government in twenty-three years would be "damn busy".

He said that the top priority would be to

repeal conscription within hours of taking office.

Mr. Whitlam gave the economy as Australia's number one problem and said: "We have unemployment and inflation together. Both must be tackled urgently."

He also named the establishment of a prices justification tribunal, and a Commonwealth grants commission as two high priorities on his legislative programme.

Asked what the key issue in the election had been, he said: "The great significance of the victory has been that the people now have greater expectations of their Federal Government.

"A Government which has no plans, which makes no innovations, which has nothing to offer in the whole range of things which concern the people loses support.

"In very many things we have a programme which would not really be fulfilled for two Parliaments."

Mr. Whitlam slammed the door on reconciliation with the Democratic Labor Party by saying: "It was a contemptible campaign and the public showed its contempt for it." . . .
The first champagne corks cracked in Mr. Whitlam's election night hide-away at 9.30 p.m. "We're in," he told a dozen top staff and advisers.

The hide-out was room seven at the Sunnybrook Motel on the Hume Highway about 20 miles west of Sydney. Super confident, Mr. Whitlam booked out the entire motel two weeks ago for his victory celebration.

While about 300 people cheered, drank, sang and celebrated at his home in Albert Street, Cabramatta, the Prime Minister-elect was hidden away for two hours.

The war-room where he watched the results was an ordinary motel suite filled with four simultaneously "live" television sets and seven white hot-line telephones which rang continually.

Mr. Whitlam emerged at 10.30 p.m. and poured a glass of Australian champagne while his wife joked as she posed with him: "Do you want me to be all coy and feminine?"

Meanwhile, only 200 yards up the road revellers at a garden party chanted: "We want Gough" as the figures flooded in on five television sets set up around the lawn.

Beer kegs whistled in the night, a panel van full of salad on cardboard plates was emptied, and at midnight two men were seen staggering into the house carrying a crate of Hawkesbury oysters.

The Press, the Party faithful, and the neighbors saw out 23 years of Liberal Government in style.

Five plain-clothed Commonwealth policemen patrolled the fuchsia bushes and guarded the front gate against at least 1000 people who tried to "crash" the party.

The crowd warmed up as the results came in . . . cheers when Len Reid lost his seat . . . cheers for Oldmeadow . . .

When Mr. Whitlam returned to the party about 10.45 there were wild scenes as the crowd stampeded around him, crushing the Whitlams and knocking over several women.

There were two fights between jostling TV and radio men. A camera was smashed. The Whitlam's eldest son, Tony, 6 ft. 6 in. and 16 stone, tore in to break up one scuffle.

About 30 media men crammed into the Whitlam's book-lined lounge for a press conference which had to be abandoned because of the crush.

Mrs. Margaret Whitlam pushed her way into the arena first, claiming "I'm a sturdy older woman", and told an interviewer she was not terribly excited about becoming Australia's first lady.

"How do you feel about Sonia?" she was asked.

"She has young children . . . I expect she is looking forward to a bit of a rest," Mrs. Whitlam said.

And then Mr. Whitlam, sweat on his face, his careful grey hair tousled, shouldering his way through the crowd for a quick televised comment . . .

Before leaving he climbed a 10-foot scaffold and stood under three television arc lights in his garden to tell the crowd: "Tomorrow is the first Sunday in Advent — the advent of the first Labor Government in 23 years." . . .

Mr Bob Hawke and Mr Clyde Cameron (left, background) watch as a supporter kisses the hand of Gough Whitlam after Labor's sweep to power in 1972

1973 Sydney gets its Opera House after nineteen years of wrangling

CLAUDIA WRIGHT AND GERALDINE PASCALL
Melbourne Herald, 20 October 1973 and Australian, 22 October 1973

It took nineteen years and more than $100 million to build. It was financed by lotteries and plagued by so much controversy that it became something of a national joke. The Sydney Opera House, a great soaring structure which dominates Sydney Harbour, was conceived by Joern Utzon, a Danish architect whose design won an international contest organised by the New South Wales Government. The steadily escalating cost of the structure — estimated in 1957 at seven million dollars — caused so much political conflict that in March 1966 Utzon resigned from the project. He would not even return to see the opening, on 20 October 1973.

Three hundred million people around the world watched that opening, via television satellite, and three-quarters of a million Sydneysiders turned out for it. The Queen performed the ceremony, and as she did it 60,000 gas-filled balloons, simulating champagne bubbles, burst from the surface of the harbor. The man who arranged it all was a former newspaper reporter, Sir Asher Joel, veteran organiser of such extravaganzas as the receptions to Pope Paul and President Johnson, and the Captain Cook bi-centenary celebrations.

Two reporters who watched were Claudia Wright, of the Melbourne Herald, *and Geraldine Pascall of the* Australian. *This is Claudia Wright's report for that day's paper:*

I have just seen the million-dollar opening of the Sydney Opera House . . . and it looked as if the world had come to Sydney.

The city's people . . . and visitors . . . abandoned their life for 15 minutes to see the Queen — the eternal never-changing little Queen — put her blessing on the Opera House.

I have never seen so many people at any gathering in Australia. From one end of the Sydney Harbor Bridge to the other they were lined three deep.

There were 15,000 guests at the Opera House. All around the Harbor about 750,000 people sheltered under sun-hats, umbrellas, yacht sails and trees.

It was hot in Sydney and with every sweep of your eye there was Hollywood technicolor.

In fact, the whole thing was a sort of Aussie Ben Hur. There were fanfares of trumpets, bands playing, people marching, pennants — that looked like Pucci bath towels — fluttering like the colors of Roman legionnaires.

Organisers had so many police around the Opera House it would have been a great day to miss a big crime. We were told not to move because they had snipers all around.

They were prepared for an assassination, too . . . of whom they won't say.

Timing was spot on. The Governor, Sir Roden Cutler, arrived. The Prime Minister, Mr Whitlam, and Mrs Whitlam were dead-on. Then came the Premier, Sir Robert Askin, and finally to a fanfare of naval trumpeters, the Queen came.

In her aqua silk dress and typical Queen's felt beret, she didn't look much different from all those other times she came here.

But the occasion was a bit different this time and with the greatest respect to the Queen, the Opera House was just too gargantuan to officially open in the old true and tried method.

I must say the old cockles of the heart were stirred when nine F-111s zoomed over the Opera House as they played good old "God Save The Queen" and all the while the Queen held on to her hat because the wind was strong and playful.

And then, suddenly, thousands of heads turned to the pinnacle of one of the Opera House shells. High up there like a Red Indian on a mountain in a cowboy movie, there was Ben Blakeney, an aboriginal actor who was playing the role of Bennelong, that famous aboriginal who was captured at Manly in 1790.

"I am Bennelong," he said . . . and spread out his arms.

"Two hundred years ago fires burned on this point. The fires of my people and into the light of the flames from the shadows all about, our warriors danced.

"Here my people chanted . . . on this point my people laughed and then came the great canoes floating . . ."

One of the dozens of big ships moored in the harbor blasted its whistle. The Queen gave her oration and though she came 10,000 miles to do it, the wind whipped away just about every word she spoke, so that only her final words, "I have much pleasure in declaring the Opera House open," were audible. . .

In her speech, she said that the Sydney Opera House had captured the imagination of the world, "though I understand that its construction has not been totally without problems, but every great imaginative venture has had to be tended by the fire of controversy.". .

The real fun started at 3.20 when four tugs dragged 400 ft. pink nylon streamers from the pinnacles of the points of the shells out to sea. It was a symbolic launching of the Opera House. . .

From a secret signal from the Opera House organiser, Sir Asher Joel, white pigeons flew into the sky and 30,000 helium balloons drifted skywards over the Opera House.

There were Maoris and New Guineans and national groups and pensioners and 1000 men and their wives who had worked on the site and there were nine helicopters that did something that their pilots had possibly longed to a all their life — they flew in formation UNDER the Sydney Harbor Bridge.

Do you know the only thing that was missing today? . . . a modern-day Captain de Groot.

Fireworks light up the Sydney Opera House on opening night

Geraldine Pascall, in the Australian, *said:*

Don't be modest, Sir Asher Joel, you beat Cecil B. de Mille hands down. His spectaculars were celluloid make-believe; yours are for real.

On Saturday at Bennelong Point you brought off the Opera House opening live in front of millions on a worldwide TV hookup with metronome precision.

The planning was sheer logistic genius. Everything happened to the second it was supposed to happen, and what happened is exactly as it was described months ago.

The inner city was successfully blocked to traffic, the special trains and buses ran on time, the crowds came, and enjoyed and behaved themselves in the special crowd assembly areas, or took to sea in their boats, and the entertainers entertained.

The helicopters flew past at their appointed times (the security ones hovering like special deliveries from SMERSH), the fire-floats spurted, the tugs broke their streamers, the gaily costumed folk groups marched and danced. . .

The nine F-111s actually did swing-wing past at a low-gear 480 mph — $127 million saluting $100,000,000 on the ground.

Only the wind was unprogrammed, whipping by at up to 40 knots, knocking over chairs and microphones, playing hell with TV sound and all the pretty hats — the cheeky poltergeist of the great white shells, just letting us know. . .

1974   A river spreads across Brisbane in its worst floods this century

HERBERT G. TURNER
Brisbane Sunday Mail, 3 February 1974

Brisbane suffered its worst floods of the century at the end of January 1974. The floods, which came in the wake of Cyclone Wanda, claimed fifteen lives, cost an estimated $200 million, and left thousands homeless. When they were over, both Brisbane and nearby Ipswich were cities of mud.

There was about these floods a certain inevitability. Between 1840 and 1900 three floods worse than that of 1974 had hit Brisbane, and another three at least equalling it had gushed through the city. Residents had been lulled into a false sense of security, because until 1974 they had experienced nothing of real note except the 1931 flood, when the water in the Brisbane River registered about fourteen and a half feet above sea level. Homes were built closer and closer to the river and its creeks; the only restriction by authorities was to prevent building below the 1931 level.

Hugh Lunn, who won a Walkley Award reporting the floods for the Australian, *wrote on 29 January 1974:*

The river is a swollen torrent. You can hear it from 100 yards away rushing past, tossing 44-gallon drums up and down like tiny corks and ripping giant ships from their moorings.

Even the traditional Queensland 'homes on stilts' have found their extra height no protection. The muddy water is in the 10th row of seats at the famous Milton tennis courts, has made elegant towering home units on the river at St. Lucia part of the river, and has flooded the basements and the first floors of at least a third of the city centre. . . Businessmen in swimming togs have swum into city basements and offices

and moved safes and computers to higher floors as the river slowly spread out into the city yesterday.

In the Brisbane Sunday Mail, *editor Herbert G. Turner, writing anonymously as 'one of the flood victims', reflected the personal experiences of thousands. Here are some extracts:*

It all starts with the familiar comment: "Cripes! Listen to the rain coming down! That's really heavy."

A little later you look out of the window at the unfamiliar sight of the drains overflowing and the street that has never before been flooded, running a banker from fence to fence. It's quite a joke, really.

The next time you get up from the TV, the lawn of the house down the street is under water, and the man you've never even spoken to is at his front door watching the rising water in puzzled wonderment.

Half-an-hour later he's knocking at your front door asking can you help him lift a few things in case the water comes into his house.

He feels a bit silly asking you. You, and the other neighbours rallying around, feel a bit self-conscious about going into a strange house, putting the dining-room table in the middle of the room and piling everything moveable on it.

In fact, it's downright embarrassing going into the bedroom, grabbing his wife's things and piling them on the bed, the dressing-table, anywhere out of harm's way.

After all, you don't know these people, only nodded to them when driving past. Matter of fact, you don't even know their name.

Before the job's completed, the water's coming in through the side door. At first it crawls in, a sluggish dirty trickle bringing an empty match-box and other debris of the street.

You all look in astonishment as the water grows to a quickly rising stream, then runs across the room, out into the corridor, into the bathroom, the kitchen, the bedrooms . . . in minutes this slimy intruder has taken possession of the house. . .

Your place is on a rise and it's high-set — typical "New Brisbane-style" architecture with garages and playroom under and living-area upstairs. Everything nice and high . . . and dry. Everyone decides to play it safe and move in there. . .

From everywhere come people carrying chairs, record players, suitcases stuffed with clothing, the best blankets, a baby's cot, two mattresses balanced crazily on a head.

A laundry-trolley is trundled past, laden with salvaged tin foods, a baby's potty, and on top of the lot, a carton of beer that, sodden, suddenly spills open.

And TV sets, TV sets seemingly by the hundred so that you think most people would sacrifice themselves before parting with their electronic ogre.

Into your basement they flow, and into every basement or doorway that offers the refuge of a few feet of high ground.

For the lucky ones who have been warned by others' tragedies there is time to disconnect washing-machines, dryers, other valued appliances. Refrigerators go past you up the street to be lined up on front-verandas as if for a huge bargain sale. . .

It's an unearthly 3 a.m. when you get up for the eleventh time to check the staircase and find the water is now waist-high in the basement.

It's time for the toughest decision you've ever made — to gamble to stay because the water cannot do the impossible and reach your upper storey or get out while all those willing helpers can carry your things to safety.

You stake everything you own on a certainty; the flood won't — can't — reach your refuge.

It's the most expensive, heart-breaking, losing bet you'll ever make.

"Just in case," a small army throws most of your clothing into bags and disappears with it . . . and bed clothes, two mattresses, all the meat and butter from the fridge because there'll be a few extra mouths to feed at breakfast, the spare torch batteries that later will help save a life when a rescuer's torch drops in the water at a critical moment.

Your wife trails behind you, carrying the special food-mixer you gave her for Christmas, and that ugly damned vase you've always hated.

Soon after, as you look out of a window into the teeming, miserable dawn, marvelling that only the ridge of Red's roof shows above water, the lights go out. The water has reached your fuse box. . .

It suddenly hits you; every single possession you have is about to be ruined. Already those wall-to-wall carpets, paid for with hours of exhausting overtime, are ruined. The kitchen tidy goes floating past, spilling garbage under the bed. You open a door to see what you can grab, and a precious crystal goblet floats away in the stream. . .

You begin to panic. You are trapped. But miraculously, when you slosh your way to the window, there is a boat coming up the street. You recognise it; it belongs to that fellow three streets away you criticised for his boat, and swimming-pool and two cars.

Within an hour you're going to discover he's the most generous, unpretentious, sympathetic, helpful bloke you've ever known; that his wife is Peg; that the brother-in-law who arrived to "give a hand for an hour" and stayed five days or so working ceaselessly, is likely to become a life-long friend. Yet even now, you still don't know their surnames.

As you clamber out of the window into that welcome boat carrying only your brief-case stuffed with a few hastily gathered papers — bank books, income tax receipts, insurance policies (does your policy cover flood?) a whole lifetime ends.

You are abandoning to the waters everything you have worked for. . .

1974   The Prime Minister offers an ambassadorship to a bitter political rival

LAURIE OAKES
Melbourne Sun News-Pictorial, 2 April 1974

Vincent Clair Gair, a former clerk with the Queensland Railways, became the centre of one of the nation's greatest political controversies when he was appointed Australia's Ambassador to the Irish Republic in April 1974. He had been Labor Premier of Queensland from 1952 until 1957; his reign had ended when he was expelled from the party. In 1965 he became a senator representing the Democratic Labor Party; he tossed a coin with another DLP senator, Victoria's Frank McManus — and thus won the leadership.

Senator Gair, a short, tubby man with an owlish expression and vast reserves of political shrewdness, had exerted great pressure over the Liberal-Country Party government at times during the late 'sixties and early 'seventies because his DLP held the balance of power in the Senate. Even after Labor was elected in December 1972, the DLP's three-man representation in the Upper House meant that Government Bills could be rejected. Senator Gair had performed badly, particularly on television, in the 1972 election campaign, and afterwards was forced to relinquish the party's leadership in favour of Senator McManus. He was angry about this, and his anger was no secret.

The Prime Minister's offer of an ambassadorship to Senator Gair was one of the daring gambles in Australian political history. If he accepted, the Labor Government's chances of gaining control of the Senate would be greatly increased. If it won control, it would be able to pass legislation which had been blocked by the Senate; it would also be able to make changes in electoral redistribution which would considerably improve its chances of winning the next election.

Senator Gair accepted the offer. The Parlia-

mentary Democratic Labor Party, outraged, promptly expelled him. Opposition leader Bill Snedden, suddenly faced with the prospect of losing power in the Senate, decided to force a snap general election. In Parliament he branded the Gair appointment 'the most shameful political act in Australia's history'. Mr Snedden's intention was to have the Senate refuse money bills on which the Government depended to continue to operate; this would have the effect of forcing an election. In fact, it was the Prime Minister, Mr Whitlam, who finally took the initiative by asking the Governor-General, Sir Paul Hasluck, for a double dissolution of Parliament.

The story of the offer of an ambassadorship to Senator Gair — the first link in a chain of events which sent the country to the polls — was broken by the Melbourne Sun's *chief political correspondent, Laurie Oakes. It was one of the great political scoops, not only because of its significance, but also because of the very bizarreness of the offer. Senator Gair and the Labor Party had been bitter enemies for seventeen years. In ALP parlance, the senator was a 'rat' who had betrayed the party. The first tip that an important diplomatic appointment was to be made had come in the form of a phone call to Oakes's colleague, John Lombard, on the morning of 1 April. The pair had checked sources throughout the day, and had found several people who knew what was brewing, but none who would talk about it in any detail. 'It's big, big, big,' said one man. 'I only wish it was half as big.' Oakes picked up hints which indicated that the appointment could give Labor a chance of winning the coming May half-Senate elections; some of the hints pointed to Queensland, and Senator Gair represented Queensland. Oakes*

*decided that Gair had to be the man, and —
from various conversations — that the appointment would have to be to a Roman Catholic
capital.*

*Finally he took a punt. He telephoned
Senator Gair's home. The senator was out,
but his wife Nell asked what the call was
about. Oakes said that he understood that
the senator had been offered an important
government appointment, and offered his
congratulations. Mrs Gair said, 'Thank you,'
Oakes had his story. Before he filed it, he took
one more precaution. He telephoned another
important contact and told him what he was
writing. 'Will I have to start worrying about
how to feed my wife and kids if I write it?'
he asked. The answer was no. The report was
correct on all but one point; it suggested that
the appointment might be to the Vatican City.*

*The election took place, and Mr Whitlam's
government was returned with a working
majority in the House of Representatives.
DLP Senators McManus and Kane lost their
seats, but Labor failed to win control of the
Senate. Ex-Senator Gair took up residence in
Dublin.*

The Federal Government has offered the
former DLP leader, Senator Gair, a diplomatic
post.

The Prime Minister, Mr Whitlam, is understood to have approved the proposed appointment last month.

If Senator Gair accepts, a political sensation
is certain.

The Foreign Minister, Senator Willesee, is
strongly against the plan and has argued
angrily to stop it.

Government sources said last night there
could be an announcement today or tomorrow.

The shock move would create an extra
vacancy in the Senate.

It would greatly increase the Government's
chances of winning control of the Senate in
the May 18 Senate election.

If Senator Gair resigned from the Senate,
there would be six vacancies instead of five to
be filled in Queensland.

At present, Labor can win only two Senate
places in Queensland, but an extra vacancy

could enable it to win three.

The move will infuriate many Labor MPs
who have never forgiven Senator Gair for
joining the DLP.

Senator Gair, 72, is a former Queensland
Labor Premier.

He resigned as leader of the DLP late last
year and was succeeded by Senator McManus,
of Victoria.

But Senator Gair's Senate term is not due
to expire for another three years.

The Government has kept the proposed
appointment a tight secret.

It obviously feared that an outcry from
Labor MPs and DLP senators could upset the
plan.

Mr Whitlam is understood to have decided
on the appointment while Senator Willesee
was overseas last month.

Mr Whitlam was Acting Foreign Minister. . .

Two of Mr Whitlam's staff members are
believed to have visited Senator Gair in Queensland recently.

One of them is believed to have been Mr
M. J. Young, a former federal ALP secretary,
and a key figure in Labor's federal victory
16 months ago. . .

It is not known what post Senator Gair has
been offered, but there was some speculation
last night that he could become Australian
ambassador to the Vatican.

*Senator Gair enjoyed being in Ireland until
1976. One of the first decisions of the new
Fraser government in 1975 was to recall its
Ambassador to Dublin. He arrived home in
Brisbane in March 1976; Canberra shunned
him, and he claimed he was not even called
upon for a debriefing. He died on 11 November
1980, aged 78, and was given a State funeral.*

*On 17 August 1980, Laurie Oakes came up
with another astonishing scoop. Two nights
before the federal Treasurer, John Howard,
was due to bring down the 1980-81 Budget
in the House of Representatives, Oakes gave
full details of it on television. It was one of
the most comprehensive leaks of its kind in
Australian political history, and it provoked
an immediate inquiry by federal police.
Laurie Oakes refused to reveal his source.*

Cyclone Tracy devastates Darwin and forty-nine die

BRUCE STANNARD AND DENNIS MINOGUE
Australian, 4 January 1975 and Melbourne Age, 27 December 1974

Darwin is a city with a great capacity for survival. It has been devastated four times: by cyclones on 7 January 1897 and 10 March 1937, by Japanese bombers on 19 February 1942, and by another cyclone in the first hours of Christmas Day 1974. The last piece of destruction resulted from Cyclone Tracy, a ball of meteorological fury that developed into one of the worst of its kind in recorded history. During it, people sheltered in cocoons — in bathtubs, cars, laundries and cupboards; and when daybreak came and they emerged, they saw a city that had virtually ceased to exist. It was the greatest natural disaster in Australian history.

On Christmas Eve, Darwin had a population of some 47,000. Thirty-five thousand, including most of the women and children, were flown out over the next few days, in the largest peacetime airlift the nation has ever known. The city resembled Hiroshima after the bomb, that first morning after Tracy hit. Communications with the outside world had gone, and most of the suburbs had been stripped bare. The official death toll reached forty-nine, and there were claims that others were unaccounted for.

An ironic facet of the tragedy concerned a young reporter, Kim Lockwood. As has been noted earlier in this book, when Japanese bombs flattened Darwin, correspondent Douglas Lockwood was faced with the biggest story of his life — and no way to get it out. Lockwood's son Kim, from the Perth Daily News, *later took over the representation of the Melbourne* Herald *group in Darwin, just as his father had done for twenty-three years. After Tracy hit, Kim faced an almost identical problem: a massive story, with no way to communicate it. All telephone lines were down, as were the local radio transmitter masts and the bigger masts of the Overseas Telecommunications Commission. Every light aircraft in Darwin had been destroyed and larger planes had been flipped over like plastic toys. Lockwood's car had been flattened under a collapsed garage; if he had been able to obtain a mobile vehicle, he would have been unable to use it because Darwin's streets and the only road link to the south (the Stuart Highway) were heavily blocked by fallen power poles and trees. The railway line south to Katherine (which his father had used in 1942) had been washed away.*

Lockwood later wrote, in an emotional report published in the Perth Daily News *and other group newspapers: 'I am weeping for Darwin today. My home town, the place where I grew up and have lived most of my life, has been obliterated. I am weeping for friends dead or injured or homeless. I am weeping for their homes — now mountains of debris scattered for miles through the city and suburbs. I am weeping for Darwin's future.'*

Many reporters, flown north soon after news of the disaster reached southern cities, missed Christmas with their families. Photographer Lloyd Brown, who teamed with reporter Ron Holdsworth from the Melbourne Sun, *had the compensation of seeing his superb sweeping picture of the flattened, apparently pulseless city, published around the world. Some of the finest reporting came from the* Australian's *Bruce Stannard (who a few months earlier had covered the America's Cup, as a yachting expert) and Dennis Minogue, of the* Age.

These are extracts from Stannard's reconstruction of what had happened, titled Anatomy of a Catastrophe:

Like the rest of Australia on Christmas Eve there were parties to attend, gifts to exchange and toasts to be drunk in Darwin.

At dusk the Harbor Master, Captain Carl Allridge, and his assistant, Captain Colin Wood, noticed a three-masted schooner putting to sea. Two teenage girls had joined the crew for what they called a "moonlighter."

But the moon had long since been hidden by thick, threatening black clouds and Captain Allridge urged them not to go. They laughed and waved goodbye. Neither the schooner nor her crew has been seen since.

The West Australian Government freighter Nyanda was due at first light on Christmas Day. Captain Allridge checked her berth and went home leaving Captain Wood to make a final check. At 6 pm Mrs. Wood arrived with a billycan full of thick stew for her husband. It was the last time Captain Wood saw her alive. While he stayed at the wharf she returned to their northern suburban home which would soon be smashed to pieces by the cyclone. . .

By 10 pm Christmas Eve there was rain with the wind and the combination set up an eerie wailing roar as it lashed the monotonous suburban acres of fibro-and-iron houses perched high on their concrete stilts.

The very substance of the houses would soon become part of the cacophony — tearing metal, crashing masonry, splitting fibro and creaking nails. Glass louvres were the first to go, shattering in deadly shards under the tremendous pressure of the wind.

Many of the early casualties slashed by flying glass huddled in pools of their own blood wondering if they would be crushed before they bled to death.

The people of Darwin began to crawl into kitchen cupboards, hide under beds, tables, cars, in bath tubs, lavatories and laundries. They took shelter in anything that might be haven from the crashing wreckage. The gallery of photographed corpses in Darwin police headquarters testifies to the fact that both the very old and the very young simply weren't able to find the right cocoons in time. . .

By 11 pm it was obvious, even to the most cock-eyed optimist, that Tracy was not going to fade away like her sister Selma. By mid-night, Tracy's tight vortex was halfway down Clarence Strait and headed directly for the city already softened by a three-hour pounding from gale-force winds.

The first cyclone-force winds hit the northern suburbs at 1 am and blew the ABC radio transmitter off the air. The power station was knocked out. Communications with the outside world were cut.

Within three hours the suburbs Casuarina, Rapid Creek, Nightcliff and Fannie Bay were in ruins.

At the airport light planes were back-flipped into crazy, crumpled piles: wreckage worth $100 million. Entire hangars were stripped of their iron. Huge 6 x 4 steel beams were twisted like soft wire. Traffic lights, steel power poles and radio towers bent flat to the ground. And down at the harbor 20ft containers were sent flying through the air like matchboxes.

Two ratings who struggled ashore from the stricken patrol boat HMAS Arrow were struck by flying drums and tossed back into the sea.

People prayed for their lives; there was almost nothing else they could do. For many of them survival became a miracle. Some were given tremendous strength through a faith they never knew they had.

Harry Rowntree says he has never been a religious man but he swears a faith in some greater power helped him survive. Through a combination of prayer, incredible courage and superhuman strength he used his broad shoulders and his back to help support a tottering wall which threatened to crash down on his wife and their two children. He braced the wall with his back for three hours.

When the cyclone faded he collapsed with the flesh stripped raw from his shoulders. Harry Rowntree, his wife and their children survived. So too did Jack Degan, his wife and their twin six-year-old daughters.

The Degans were sucked out of the bedroom of their Nightcliff home when it disintegrated about 2 am.

All four landed uninjured on their front lawn. Mr. and Mrs. Degan crouched over their babies until it was safe to move. Jack Degan, a big and almost completely bald man, will bear the physical as well as the mental scars of the ordeal for the rest of his life; his scalp was blasted to pulp by windborne sand, glass fragments and rocks.

By 2 am Tracy had damaged every building in the city.

Moving along a path 20 miles wide, the cyclone's power made a mockery of even the most secure city buildings. At the airport, the new $2 million terminal was wrecked and flooded. Large plate-glass windows at first resisted the wind by curving inwards like sails. They exploded about 2.30 when the wind gauge on the control tower registered 170 km/h and blew up.

At Darwin base hospital doctors and nurses were working almost normally. They were among the few who had taken any precautions. A wire mesh fence had been strung up to protect the glass front doors from flying debris. Windows were taped with adhesive plaster and draped on the inside with heavy curtains.

At 2.45 a baby was born — the first newcomer to the disaster area (it would be some 17 hours before Major-General Stretton, Dr. Rex Patterson and a team of RAAF and Canberra doctors and nurses could fly in). The eye of the cyclone arrived at 3 am. It lasted in most areas from 10 to 20 minutes.

It brought with it a sudden eerie calm. The wind ceased, the rain stopped and out of the awful devastation the people of Darwin began to move. They came out of their cupboards and bath tubs, their laundries and their lavatories and looked out into the face of their own personal apocalypse.

Some tried to clean up, but those who had experienced cyclones before knew that once the cyclone had passed the wind would come again, with even more power and in a completely different direction. They scrambled back into their holes and resumed their prayers. . .

At 5 am Tracy was finished. So was the city of Darwin.

People emerged into something like the devastated landscape of Hiroshima or Flanders' no-man's-land. With the first light of dawn they saw that not one house, not one single, solitary structure was intact. The roads were choked with debris.

Police turned Darwin High School and Casuarina High into refugee camps; the courthouse and the post office became temporary morgues.

General Stretton's arrival at 10.20 pm on Christmas night signalled the beginning of the greatest relief and evacuation operation in Australia's history.

Officially the toll stands at 49 but police expect to recover more bodies as they search the ruins.

And this short report from Dennis Minogue in the Age *of 31 December gave a picture of Darwin as the first signs of normality began to invade the city. They came in the form of a bird and a Test cricket score:*

Odd things are happening now in Darwin, odd normal things that help the blood seep back into the crippled arteries. The first bird returned. The damning, tweetless, silence ended.

And someone asked the cricket score, first time in near a week, or lifetime. "England six for 160", someone said, and was thanked.

It did not matter really, no-one knows what happened early in the game. It was simply normal to ask.

Early in the morning, two hours pre-dawn, the mosquitoes came, flown back 1000 miles perhaps and nothing to eat since Christmas Day. Big, they sounded as if four could carry off a man, and Darwin had not missed them.

In the city an Aboriginal art shop opened its doors, third shop in the town after the Smith Street chemist, and Yankee Al's, which offers shooting to all looters, by the way.

The girl in the Aboriginal shop: "Yes, please, can I help". But few needed painted boomerangs and awful mulga ashtrays. Tourists are thin on the ground.

Mayor Tiger Brennan, pith-helmeted, took time from shooting dogs to talk of the future Darwin.

And the bird came, just a lone biggish finch. It flitted through the botanical gardens in which all trees are snapped, palms that would not bend enough for Tracy.

And suddenly it seemed strange that we had no birds. That Darwin's birds are somewhere in the desert.

This photograph depicts poignantly the hopelessness of those who lost almost everything in the violence of Cyclone Tracy

The mosquitoes had to be the first ones back, of course, to join flying cockroaches who never left. Ten million years defying evolution and cyclones, too.

The Carba iceworks at Winnellie are back in action and the census could be done each day in the queue that stretches out a mile and in the mad race against the melting lumps to make it home.

All Darwin goes there.

Or to Stretton's showers on the Stuart Highway — Major General Alan Stretton's contribution to the place.

And there are those warnings, so solemn, so severe, that taking nude showers on the Stuart Highway is against the law.

Yesterday, with its ice and its boomerang shop, Yankee Al's cigars and cigarettes, and with the mozzies and lone, welcome, bird, Darwin started coming back.

The dogs are still being shot and punched-down houses searched for dead, people still look for one another, and divers comb the shallow harbor for bodies they know they will find.

These things are still there and ready to depress, but better things are happening.

The water is on, or mostly on, and open air lavatories are gone and bodies cease to smell of sweat and dirt, at least for half an hour after showers.

And in the streets a noisy miracle is trying to happen as bulldozers plough away the wreckage of Darwin and trucks pick up the rubbish.

Buildings may still be wrecks, the people may be gone, but the streets will be spotless when the Australian fleet arrives tomorrow.

And the airport refugees now get, for their long exodus, apple pie and lemon drink — a breakfast for a king.

But it was the bird that made my day.

1975   Report of loan deal triggers an election

PETER GAME
Melbourne Herald, 8 October 1975

Tirath Hassaram Khemlani, a pocket-sized Hindu who seemed to circle the world constantly and who lived mostly on a diet of high protein nuts, potato crisps and packets of savory rice pieces, was not the kind of man who might be expected to take a major role in Australian politics. Few people in the nation had heard of him early in 1975; by the end of that year, though, he appeared to have played a considerable part in the downfall of the Whitlam Labor Government.

He was the central figure in the Loans Affair, a bizarre exercise in international borrowing through unlikely channels for unlikely purposes on an unlikely scale. The Loans Affair caused two senior Ministers, Dr Jim Cairns and Rex Connor — each in turn Deputy Prime Minister — to lose their portfolios; it also gave the Opposition leader, Malcolm Fraser, an excuse to use his majority in the Senate to reject a Labor Budget, thus forcing an election; at that election it made Labor vulnerable to charges of economic irresponsibility — and the election was fought largely on the issue of management of the economy.

In a way, it was Australia's abundance of energy resources which caused the Loans Affair. At first Mr Whitlam was reluctant to disclose why he and some senior Ministers attempted to raise $US.4 billion, without Loan Council approval or Treasury awareness, through fringe-area dealers who stood to gain large commissions, but it later emerged that the intention was to buy back minerals and energy equity from overseas, establish transcontinental pipelines and chemical complexes to convert coal to oil and gas to gasoline, and enter the field of uranium enrichment. It was also later learned that the plan, which would

have a heavily detrimental effect on Australia's balance of payments, had not been subject to any feasibility test.

For months after the first revelations of backdoor multi-million-dollar loans, reporters had tried without success to interview Mr Khemlani. He was known to be the central, totally mysterious figure in the whole affair. Then Peter Game, of the Melbourne Herald, *stumbled on to his trail while on another assignment. Game, on loan to the London* Daily Express, *had been covering the journey from Australia of the runaway House of Commons member John Stonehouse, who was returning to Britain to face charges of fraud. Game's commitment to the London newspaper ended in Hong Kong; while he was in that city the news editor of the South China* Morning Post, *Kevin Sinclair, suggested that Game might be interested in chatting to a Sindhi businessman who had been involved in the Australian Loans Affair. The businessman, a Mr Bhojwani, told Game that Tirath Khemlani had a mandate to raise eight billion American dollars for the Australian Government; it was the first time mention of such a sum had been made.*

On his way home from Hong Kong, Game called at Singapore, where Mr Khemlani's first wife lived. She gave him the address of Shanti, the twenty-five-year-old daughter of that marriage. He met Shanti, got on well with her, and later sent her a note to pass to her father; the note simply told Mr Khemlani that if he would talk to Peter Game, his story would be told fairly and accurately.

Mr Khemlani later called Game from Singapore to arrange a meeting; the call caught the reporter at Mt Isa airport, on his way south from covering the Timor revolution.

The pair met next day in Sydney, then a few days later in London. Their interview in London lasted four weeks, punctuated by flights by Mr Khemlani to Beirut and Accra, Ghana. Game flew with him then to Hong Kong, spent eight hours with him there, then accompanied him back to London. During this strange interview-on-the-run, Game saw many hundreds of documents and accumulated many tapes. The little commodities dealer made it clear always that he would speak only to Game. He claimed that he had been offered first $500,000 and later $1 million for his loans file, but he neither sought nor was offered any money by Game or the Melbourne Herald. *He claimed he wanted to tell his side of the story because it had been distorted, and that he had suffered from slurs and innuendoes during the political debate in Australia.*

Finally, on 8 October 1975, the Herald *published the first of a series of articles based on Game's interviews with Tirath Khemlani. In his first report, Game quoted Mr Khemlani as saying that he still had authority from Mr Connor, Minister for Minerals and Energy, to raise $US 8 billion for the Australian Government, and that about $US 200 million commission would be payable on the deal. Immediately Mr Connor sued the paper for alleged libel. After a number of conferences involving Lyle Turnbull (Herald and Weekly Times managing editor), John Fitzgerald (Herald editor), Peter Game and lawyers, the* Herald *decided — at its peril — to continue publishing the articles. It claimed that they were in the national interest.*

Mr Connor claimed that he had had no dealings involving loan-raising with Mr Khemlani since his authority to pursue the question of loan raising had been revoked on 20 May. Mr Khemlani promptly signed a statutory declaration stating that this was not true. The Herald *published copies of telex messages supporting this declaration. On 14 October the Prime Minister, Mr Whitlam, accepted the resignation from Cabinet of Mr Connor, and on 14 October the Opposition parties decided to force an election by rejecting the Budget in the Senate. (Mr Fraser had*

earlier stated that he would take such action in 'exceptional and reprehensible circumstances'.)

Publication of Peter Game's report led in turn to the libel writ, the resignation of Mr Connor and the decision by the Opposition to force an election. Some might argue that, because of the events it triggered, it caused the fall of the Government.

This is an extract from one of Game's articles, in which he gave the first close-up view of Mr Khemlani, the man in the middle of the political storm:

Tirath Hassaram Khemlani squats on the floor of his room in a Hongkong hotel, his legs tucked beneath him in the manner of a Yogi.

He is a devout Hindu, and all his life has been interested in forsaking the materialistic world for the contemplative spiritualism of his religion.

But circumstances, and his own dynamic, restless energy have projected him into the hurly burly of the world's market places.

Today, instead of sheltering in the quiet sanctuary of some Hindu monastery as a monk — a vocation he has three times tried to follow — he heads a London commodity trading company which last financial year did 1.6 billion U.S. dollars of business.

In his luggage is the Hindu bible which he reads each morning, along with documents relating to contracts worth hundreds of millions of dollars.

One case with a combination lock, and measuring 30 cm. deep, 20 cm. wide and 45 cm. long, never leaves him — it contains the bulging file of documents which record the remarkable details of the Australian Government's loan negotiations.

As we sit now in the Hongkong hotel, the brass tumblers have been operated and the contents of this case are spread tantalisingly over the carpet around Mr Khemlani.

But first, he talks about the past as he pulls on one of the 80 cigarettes he puffs impatiently on every day but never inhales.

Tirath Khemlani was born on September 12, 1920, in Hyderabadsindh near Karachi.

Like most Sindh people, his father was in

the import-export business, managing a trading company.

Tirath Khemlani won a scholarship to a local Hindu school and passed the equivalent of higher school certificate before he left.

His ambition was to enter a monastery and become a Yogi, but he was an only son, and his parents did not look on this career with serenity.

To please them he went to Singapore to join an uncle's import-export business. His uncle also had a dress design and manufacturing business. . .

About 18 months ago he joined the world-wide firm of Dalamal and Sons as manager of their commodities division which is called Dalamal and Sons (Commodities) Ltd.

The arrangement on which he joined the firm was that he would receive 20 per cent of the division's net profit.

It is as manager for Dalamal that he has been trying to arrange a huge loan for the Australian Government.

He says he will receive no direct commission for his role: he will get 20 per cent of what is left after expenses of the minimum 15 million US dollars which Dalamal expects if the loan goes through.

Dalamal was founded 90 years ago by a Mr Dalamal, now dead. It is carried on by his sons and grandsons and has branches all over the world, including Australia, the United States, Singapore, Hongkong, the Philippines, Japan and India.

Mr Khemlani estimates that the company would be worth from £10 to £15 million. It has its head office in Ibex House in the City of London, Britain's financial centre.

Dalamal invested £50,000 in the new venture and gave Mr Khemlani a free hand to make money.

He set up headquarters in a basement office rented at £4000 a year in a terrace block in the expensive Sloane Square area of South-West London.

It stands in West Eaton Place almost opposite a similar terrace in which a blue plaque proclaims that Chopin played his first London concert in 1848.

But Mr Khemlani was after a different sort of keyboard when he took the basement premises — they already had Telex facilities — an essential tool in the hands of today's middlemen.

It is on this Telex, in between snatches of sleep when he is in London, that he does deals worth hundreds of millions of dollars with people with similar keyboards around the world.

He punches up his own Telex tapes for transmission. As we talked on many nights in London in the early hours of the morning a timer on his desk would ring, reminding him to get up and send a message.

Dalamal and Sons (Commodities) Ltd. quickly prospered. Within four months it had made a profit of 400,000 U.S. dollars.

Altogether in the past 15 months the value of commodities handled has totalled about 1.6 billion U.S. dollars, resulting in commissions of 136 million U.S. dollars gross — out of which must come taxes and expenses.

Mr Khemlani estimates that profit is currently running at around three to five million U.S. dollars net a year. . .

His personal travelling bill is £100,000 a year (his only concession to comfort is to travel first class). His hotel bills cost £30,000 a year, the same amount as his Telex messages.

Mr Khemlani carries a passport which is really four passports stapled together and representing four years of countless stampings by immigration officers around the world.

He keeps his case packed in the office where he mostly sleeps, doing his drip-dry washing in the bathroom attached. He snatches what sleep he can — sometimes while talking to you.

His food in London consists mostly of high protein nuts and potato crisps and packets of savory pieces made from rice.

Only when he is in a hotel in some faraway place does he indulge in a plate of vegetables.

It is his peripatetic existence which earned him the scornful tag of "carpetbagger" during the loan controversy in Australia.

But he points out that it is only by travelling about that he can maintain the personal contact, and build up the trust which is so essential to the business he does. . .

1975 The Governor-General sacks a Prime Minister

PETER BOWERS
Sydney Morning Herald, 11 November 1975

On 11 November 1975, the Governor-General of Australia, Sir John Kerr, took the unprecedented step of dismissing the Prime Minister, Mr Whitlam. Within an hour he swore in the Opposition Leader, Mr Malcolm Fraser, as Prime Minister, pending a federal election. He did so, he said, to allow the people of Australia to decide as soon as possible what should be the outcome of the deadlock over Supply between the two Houses of Parliament and the Government and Opposition parties.

The decision came after a great deal of sparring between the two leaders over the issue of the rejection of Supply. The Opposition had decided not to pass the vital money Bills and thus to force an election, following the resignation of Mr Connor from Mr Whitlam's Cabinet. On the morning of 11 November the two leaders discussed the situation. Mr Whitlam told Mr Fraser that if he did not get an assurance that the Opposition parties would pass the Budget Appropriation Bills through the Senate, he would advise the Governor-General that there should be a half-Senate election on 13 December. Mr Fraser rejected this, saying that the Opposition would continue to block the Budget Bills (which it had been blocking for four weeks) until a House of Representatives election was called. Sir John Kerr a few hours later made his shock announcement that 'if a Prime Minister refuses to resign or to advise an election, and this is the case with Mr Whitlam, my constitutional authority and duty require me to do what I have now done — to withdraw his commission and to invite the leader of the Opposition to form a caretaker government'.

The Whitlam dismissal stunned the nation. Brawls broke out at pro-Labor demonstrations in capital cities around the nation, and the president of the Australian Labor Party and the Australian Council of Trade Unions, Mr Hawke, was moved to warn against violence by Labor supporters. As Mr Whitlam greeted his advisers after the interview with Sir John Kerr, he told them: 'I've been sacked.' The initial reaction of each was that he was joking. The Melbourne Age said next day: 'Yesterday was the most extraordinary in the political life of this nation. It was also one of the most regrettable. The decision . . . to dismiss the Whitlam Government was, we believe, a triumph of narrow legalism over commonsense and popular feeling.' Lawyers, academics and newspaper commentators argued the rights and wrongs of Sir John's action for a long time afterwards, and it seemed likely that future historians would continue to do so. For a time the Labor Party made the sacking of Mr Whitlam the central issue of its campaign for the 13 December election. Later, sensing that many Australians were more concerned with the economy than interpretations of the Constitution, it switched its focus to issues like social welfare and economic affairs.

Some piquancy was given to the historic decision by the fact that Sir John Kerr was appointed to the position of Governor-General on the advice of Mr Whitlam. At the time of his appointment Sir John had told reporters: 'I believe the office is a worthwhile one, otherwise I would not have accepted it. It provides the opportunity to play a non-controversial part but an important one in the nation's affairs.' It did not prove to be a totally accurate assessment.

In the election which followed, Mr Whitlam's party suffered a devastating *defeat — the worst inflicted on Labor since the Scullin Government was swept out in 1931. Mr Fraser became the nation's twenty-second Prime Minister.*

The Sydney Morning Herald's *reporter Peter Bowers wrote this report at the end of a day in which the Prime Minister had been sacked, both Houses of Parliament had been dissolved, and Mr Whitlam had bitterly attacked Sir John Kerr, accusing him of acting unconstitutionally:*

Prime Minister in the morning . . . the Honorable Member for Werriwa in the afternoon. No one was more astonished by the Prime Minister's dismissal than Mr Whitlam himself.

To the last he was supremely confident that the Governor-General would move against the Senate, if he moved at all. He was convinced the Governor-General would act only on his advice and typically scorned any other view. His over-confidence led to his overreaching himself yesterday, providing the opening for Sir John Kerr to dismiss him.

Mr Whitlam was so confident that Sir John would accept his advice to call a half-Senate election on December 13 that he telephoned the Governor-General at 10 am yesterday to forewarn him of his decision.

Mr Whitlam is reported to have told Sir John he would be announcing his decision in a few minutes to a meeting of the Parliamentary Labor Party and would then call on Sir John before making the announcement to Parliament in the afternoon.

Mr Whitlam apparently got no hint of his impending dismissal because he plunged on merrily. The man loves to live dangerously, but surely even he would have pulled back if he had suspected his fate.

Mr Whitlam did not get a chance to call on Sir John and proffer advice on any early Senate election.

Sir John took the initiative, summoned Mr Whitlam to Government House at 1.30 pm and unceremoniously dismissed him.

The savagery of Mr Whitlam's subsequent attack on Sir John Kerr — "Well may we say

God save the Queen because nothing will save the Governor-General" — is indicative of Mr Whitlam's total dismay at his dismissal.

It is as if he regards his dismissal as an act of betrayal.

It is Mr Whitlam's nature to make sweeping character assessments and to gamble heavily on his own judgment.

Mr Whitlam appointed Sir John Governor-General and, consequently, he seems to have made the mistake of regarding Sir John as "his man," only to discover that when the crunch came the Governor-General proved to be his own man.

The 3½-page statement in which Sir John set out his reasons for dismissing Mr Whitlam bears the mark of careful and long consideration. Clearly Sir John had made up his mind days ago and was only biding his time to intervene.

Both the Government and Opposition expected Sir John to intervene this week. It was on the cards last Thursday after his fourth round of interviews with Mr Whitlam and Mr Fraser. But few, apart from Mr Fraser and his advisers, believed he would move against Mr Whitlam.

Sir John's statement is a complete vindication of the constitutional propriety of Mr Fraser's — and the Senate's — action in blocking Supply to force the Government to the polls.

Mr Fraser's justification may be found in three sentences, in Sir John's statement:

"Because of the Federal nature of our Constitution and because of its provisions, the Senate undoubtedly has the constitutional power to refuse or defer Supply to the Government.

"Because of the principles of responsible government, a Prime Minister who cannot obtain Supply, including money for carrying on the ordinary services of government, must either advise a general election or resign.

"If he refuses to do this, I have the authority and indeed the duty under the Constitution to withdraw his commission as Prime Minister."

Sir John's statement indicated that he did

not give Mr Whitlam the opportunity formally to request an early election for the half-Senate. He had called him to Government House to dismiss him, and having made up his mind, Sir John was not interested in further advice.

In seeking the advice on Monday of the Chief Justice, Sir Garfield Barwick, Sir John probably was doing no more than exploring the possibility of an alternative view to the one he had already reached.

Now to the campaign, and it promises to be bitter if the demonstration against Mr Fraser by ANU students milling in Parliament's Kings Hall yesterday is any indication. Any violence will play into Mr Fraser's hands, as did the anti-Vietnam demonstrations in the 1966 campaign which gave Mr Holt a huge majority.

The sudden reversal of their political roles will give Mr Fraser an authority he could never hope for as Opposition Leader.

He will be seeking electoral confirmation of his appointment as Prime Minister, rather than as an Opposition Leader trying to unseat Mr Whitlam. Suddenly Mr Whitlam is the underdog, if bulldogs are capable of such a role.

Mr Fraser will try to get the campaign back to the Whitlam Government's sorry record — realities which have been smothered by the emotional backlash sparked by the blocking of the Budget bills.

Mr Whitlam will campaign on the right of the party with the majority in the House of Representatives to govern for a full three-year term.

The Labor Party has gained more than sympathy from the political deadlock, because it will enter the campaign totally united and, perhaps, rejuvenated by a crusading cause.

Now Mr Whitlam joins another formidable Labor figure, Mr Jack Lang, in having been dismissed by Vice-Regal decree.

Mr Whitlam seems certain to attract huge sympathetic crowds during the forthcoming campaign. So did Lang, but that was not enough to save him.

Sacked Prime Minister Whitlam on the steps of Parliament House immediately after the shocking announcement of his government's dismissal.

After his humiliating defeat in the election of December 1975, Gough Whitlam served one term as Leader of the Opposition. Two years later the Labor Party was again trounced by the coalition team led by Mr Fraser. Mr Whitlam, Australia's only Labor Prime Minister in twenty-eight years, resigned the leadership immediately, and Bill Hayden became the new Leader of the Opposition.

In October, 1980, another federal election was held. Opinion polls during the campaign indicated a swing against the government of such dimensions that Labor would be put into power. This did not eventuate, and Malcolm Fraser won his third election as Prime Minister — with a comfortable majority in House of Representatives. The coalition parties did, however, lose control of the Senate from July 1981; the Australian Democrats, a party formed by the disaffected former Liberal Minister, Don Chipp, effectively held the balance of power in the new Senate. Before the election the 'Chippocrats' vowed never to use such Senate power to block Supply — as Mr Fraser had threatened to do in 1975.

1979 A new wave of settlers, the boat people, arrive in Australia

MARGARET JONES
Sydney Morning Herald, 20 June 1979

Australia, the most sparsely-populated continent in the world, has known many waves of immigration. The people we call Aboriginals, who had had the place to themselves for some 25,000 years before the white man came, were themselves the survivors of three distinct migration movements. In the first forty years of settlement after the arrival of the First Fleet in 1788, three-quarters of the immigrants were convicts — half of them from the growing industrial areas of London and Birmingham. Then came rural settlers, then gold-seekers, then immigrants attracted by an unsound land boom. It was the gold which created the basis for a substantial Australian population; in one gold-rush decade — the 1850s — the Australian population was trebled to 1,200,000, largely by a huge influx of immigrants which would not be matched until the 1950s. Among the non-British were Germans, Italians, Americans and, largest of all, Chinese.

After the 1939-45 war, Australia embarked on a vigorous policy of large-scale, financially-assisted European immigration. Australia was suffering an acute labour shortage — mainly because of the needs of post-war reconstruction and development, but partly because of the very low birth rates of the 1928-36 depression period. Migrants came from Poland and the smaller Baltic countries crushed by the Nazis and the Russians; Australia became the largest receiver of people in the camps of the International Refugee Organisation. Large numbers of Britons, Dutch, Germans, Greeks, Italians, Maltese and Yugoslavs arrived during the '50s and '60s. Turks and Lebanese arrived in smaller numbers in the '70s, and a steady, if limited, intake of

Asians continued as restrictions against them were liberalised in the '50s and '60s. By 1965 the old slogan of 'White Australia', with its racist overtones, had been eliminated from the constitution of every major organisation in Australia; the Australian Labor Party was the last political party to abandon it (in 1965), and it was followed soon after by the Returned Servicemen's League.

In the late 1970s, in the wake of the savage Vietnam war, a new wave of immigrants began to arrive in Australia . . . the boat people. These were refugees — many of them of Chinese origin — who fled their homeland after the communist victory. They headed for Thailand, Malaysia, Singapore, Hongkong, Manila, Indonesia and Australia; sometimes only fifty per cent of those who set sail ever made landfall, and many of those who did received hostile receptions. It was, as Tony Walker and Michael Gordon wrote in the Age, *a human tidal wave of misery and despair. By June 1979, Australia had received just on 22,000 Indo-Chinese refugees. In that month Margaret Jones, foreign editor of the* Sydney Morning Herald, *flew with 170 Vietnamese on the last stage of their journey to a new life in Australia. This is her story of the flight:*

As they board the plane in Singapore, they do not look in the least like refugees: 50 men, 64 women and 56 children from the Indonesian island camp of Tandjung Pinang.

They are slender, healthy people with glossy hair and excellent teeth, and the graceful good looks of southern Asia.

If they seem healthy, it is because they are, despite the boat voyage and the refugee camps. Probably only the fit survive. . .

Everybody is in best clothes: either pains-takingly preserved through months of wandering on the flight from Ho Chi Minh City, or bought in Singapore with what funds they have left . . .

These are, in any case, not peasants, but urban people, used, in many cases, to a soft, middle-class life. This makes the risks they undergo to escape from Vietnam all the more astonishing . . .

A couple of stories are worth telling:

Ho Thi Duoi is a pretty woman of 32 in a trendy blue pants suit. She is the wife of La Quoc Hue, 31, formerly owner of an electrical goods store in Cholon, the Chinese twin city of Saigon.

The family made four attempts to leave Vietnam over a period of three years, and during one of them, this slender, middle-class housewife was separated from her husband and spent the night in the forest with her four children, the oldest now only six . . .

On the boat voyages, one of the worst things that happened was when the crew of a patrol boat that pushed them off the Malaysian coast took all their cooking utensils.

'We could not cook anything, so we had to eat raw cabbage and dry noodles,' Ho Thi Duoi said. After a while, even this food ran out, and the children were very sick and hungry. It was a relief to beach in Indonesia, and be sent to the camp at Tandjung Pinang, where they spent five months.

La Quoc Hue, racially Chinese but a second-generation Vietnamese who has never lived anywhere but in Vietnam, gave a run-down on the family's four escape attempts.

Like the others we heard of, they seemed to be a Kafkaesque mixture of danger, frustration, double-crossing, and the sort of sheer inefficiency one might expect of middle-class people organising illicit activities for the first time.

La Quoc Hue paid 35 taels (thin leaves of gold worth about $337 each on the black market) to a friend for the first escape, but it fell through because the family couldn't find the meeting place.

The second attempt cost only six taels, and Ho Thi Duoi and the children went while La

stayed behind. The five of them couldn't get on the boat, because it was too overcrowded, so that was the night Ho and the children spent in the forest.

The third attempt cost six taels — but the boat left without them.

By this time, the Chinese were being encouraged to leave by the Government in Hanoi, and the family could have gone in reasonable comfort on a freighter.

But La Quoc Hue no longer had the asking price, so it had to be the lower-priced (15 taels) illicit attempt again. On the fourth try, the family succeeded.

The boat was only 15 metres long and three metres wide, and with 200 people aboard, there was no room to lie down. But it took them to Malaysia, then to Indonesia, and eventually they arrived at Melbourne's Tulla-marine Airport, on a cold winter's night this week . . .

Do Gia Tuyen and his wife, Duoi, are better off. They have no children yet, and Tuyen, 30, is a graduate in electrical engineering from Canterbury University, and speaks fluent English.

Tuyen said he was not trusted by the authorities in Saigon because his father had been a police lieutenant under the Thieu regime, and had been sent to prison. So Tuyen was downgraded to a clerical job in the post office . . .

Once again, the familiar story of mishaps and bungling: the first attempt failed because a plan to drug guards did not go to schedule. On the second try, the weather was so bad that some of the passengers abandoned the boat — among them, Tuyen, who swam ashore. His brother-in-law stayed on board, and was caught and sent to prison after the boat ran aground.

On the third attempt, Do Gia Tuyen and his wife paid $560 for places on a boat but when they went to the meeting place, there was no boat.

The fourth try was successful, though there were 160 people on a 15-metre boat, and in less than five days, the refugees were in Indonesia . . .

So the refugee trade goes on.

1982   The dingo and the baby: a murder case begins at Ayers Rock, and lasts for six years

BILL HITCHINGS, LINDSAY MURDOCH AND KEN BLANCH
Melbourne Sun News-Pictorial, 30 October 1982, Melbourne Age, 30 April 1983 and Brisbane Courier-Mail, 8 February 1986

It was without doubt the most bizarre murder mystery in Australian history. It occurred in the ancient heart of Australia, in a camp site beside Ayers Rock. Primarily it involved a Seventh Day Adventist couple, their infant daughter and a dingo — but later it came to embrace a huge team of investigators, witnesses and advocates, an eminent British forensic scientist, two coronial inquests, two judges of the Supreme Court of the Northern Territory, 12 jurors, the Full Bench of the Federal Court, five judges of the High Court, and finally a judicial inquiry. Along the way the drama of the Azaria Chamberlain case captured the attention and imagination of the entire nation.

It began on the night of 17 August 1980, minutes after a young mother had tucked her baby daughter into her bassinet in the family tent in the Ayers Rock camping ground. Suddenly a cry was heard: 'My God, a dingo's got my baby.' The baby was 10-week-old Azaria Chamberlain. Next day newspapers around Australia carried interviews with Azaria's father Michael, 36. He explained that the couple were cooking a barbecue about 20 metres from their tent. 'We had put our second child, Reagan, down to bed as well in the tent, but Aidan, our six-year-old son, was still at the barbecue,' he said. 'Then Lindy (his wife) heard a whimper. . .only a small cry. We spun around and saw a shape, just like a dingo, slinking out of the tent. It had something in its mouth, but at that stage, in the darkness, we could not see what it was. We all ran for the tent and looked inside, and baby Azaria was gone.'

That, basically, was the story Pastor Michael Chamberlain, of the Seventh Day Adventist Church, and his wife Lindy con-
tinued to tell as the Azaria case followed its dramatic, controversial course through the machinery of the Australian legal system. Seven days after the infant vanished, a Victorian tourist, Wallace Goodwin, was walking a narrow track through tangled spinifex and shrubs when he found a blood-stained jumpsuit, singlet, napkin and bootees scattered at the foot of a huge boulder. The clothing was later found by a forensic dentist not to have suffered the kind of damage consistent with it being caused by a dog or dingo. Despite a massive search by police and trackers, no body was found.

In December 1980, the Alice Springs Coroner, Mr Denis Barritt, SM, opened an inquest into the disappearance and presumed death of Azaria Chamberlain. His finding, delivered on 20 February 1981, was that a dingo had taken Azaria, but that someone unknown had disposed of the body; he exonerated the parents from any involvement in the death of Azaria, and noted that they had been subjected to 'months of innuendoes, suspicion and probably the most malicious gossip ever witnessed in this country.' His finding was broadcast live to millions of television viewers around Australia; it was the only live TV broadcast of court proceedings in the nation's history.

His finding that, despite the actions of a dingo there had been 'human intervention', served to deepen the mystery. The police file remained open. The investigations continued, as did the speculation and rumors. A few months later Dr Kenneth Brown, a forensic orthodontist, obtained permission from police to take the clothing worn by Azaria to London, where special tests were conducted on it by one of the world's leading forensic teams at the London Hospital Medical College. The team, headed by Professor James Cameron, conducted special tests involving ultra-violet photography; later, in September 1981, Professor Cameron flew from London to Brisbane for meetings with police and the Northern Territory Chief Minister, Doug Everingham.

On 19 September, after consultation with the Territory's police Commissioner and solicitor-general and the leading Brisbane barrister Des Sturgess, the Chief Minister announced that new evidence had emerged. He applied to the Northern Territory Supreme Court for an order quashing the findings of Mr Barritt's inquest. On 20 November, Mr Justice Toohey granted that request, ordered a new inquest and announced that fresh evidence, if accepted, would prove that a dingo did not take Azaria. The second inquest was held before the NT Coroner, Mr Gerry Galvin, CSM, and on 2 February 1982, he formally charged that Alice Lynne (Lindy) Chamberlain had murdered Azaria Chamberlain and that Michael Leigh Chamberlain had been an accessory after the fact.

The murder trial began in Darwin, before the Northern Territory Supreme Court, on 13 September 1982, and lasted seven weeks. By this time Mrs Chamberlain, who was also the daughter of a Seventh Day Adventist country minister, was pregnant with her fourth child. The prosecution case amounted to this: On the night of the barbecue, after spending some time there, Mrs Chamberlain carried Azaria, who was asleep, towards the family tent and car. Her son Aidan followed. She went to the car, sat in the front passenger seat, and cut the baby's throat. The baby shed a great deal of blood. Precisely how she killed the baby was unclear. Apparently she entered the tent soon after the killing, and small areas of blood were left on items inside the tent. She and Aidan returned to the barbecue area. Precisely where the body was at this stage could not be proved. In all probability it was inside the car, possibly in Mr Chamberlain's camera bag. Later a noise was heard. It was impossible that it was the baby, because the baby was already dead. Mrs Chamberlain cried out that a dingo had taken the baby. She did her utmost to convey to everybody present and later to police that she saw a dingo coming out of the tent. Mr Chamberlain became aware of the murder soon after. At least for part of the time while 300 people searched, the body was in the car. Later that night, after the Chamberlains had been driven to a motel, Azaria's jumpsuit was cut with scissors. Her clothes were buried, probably with the body still in them. Later the clothes were dug up, the body removed from them. The clothes were left about four metres away, at the base of Ayers Rock.

The case for the defence, as given by Mrs Chamberlain, was this: Azaria was asleep in her arms at the barbecue shelter. She walked to the tent with Aidan, unzipped it and crawled in. Aidan took off his parka and hopped into his sleeping bag while she was tucking Azaria in, but then he said he was still hungry; she went to the car to get some baked beans. He decided to eat them at the barbecue area, so he went back with her. As she was about to open the can, 'Michael said that he heard Azaria crying or something to that effect.' She decided to go and check on the baby, and was about halfway back to the tent when she saw a dingo. 'It just had its shoulders and head sort of half in, half out of the tent and was shaking very vigorously at something. I thought it had a shoe or something and I yelled at it to get out of the tent. I did not see anything in its mouth, the tip of its nose was in the shadow from the scrub and railing.' At first she simply called for it to get out, but a few seconds later, when she realised that Azaria had at least been disturbed, 'I started to run to the tent and called out, "Michael, a dingo has got my baby," or "A dog has got my . . . ".' She dived into the tent and felt under all the blankets and in the carry basket, and gave Reagan a kick to see if he was all right. She called again that a dingo had the baby, and chased in the direction she thought the dingo had gone.

On the night of 29 October 1982, after six hours' deliberation, a jury found that Lindy Chamberlain had murdered Azaria and that her husband Michael had been an accessory after the fact of murder. The Acting Chief Justice of the Northern Territory, Mr Justice Muirhead, sentenced her to life imprisonment with hard *labor, and imposed a suspended sentence of 18 months' jail on her husband.*

For three and a half years after that judgment, the Lindy Chamberlain drama continued. On 19 November 1982 she was released on bail pending an appeal to the Federal Court; she learned of her release in Darwin Hospital, where she had given birth to another daughter, Kahlia. On 29 April 1983 the Federal Court unanimously rejected the appeal, and she went back to jail; she was transferred from the Mulawah Detention Centre in Sydney to Darwin's Berrimah Jail a week later. She appealed to the High Court, but the plea was rejected, by a three-to-two majority, on 22 February 1984.

On 12 November 1985 the Northern Territory Government refused to hold a judicial inquiry into the case. A report compiled by the Territory's Solicitor-General, Mr Brian Martin, rejected reasons advanced to free Lindy Chamberlain as 'of dubious value' and based on 'vague and unscientific generalisations.' When, on 25 November 1985, the Northern Territory Government rejected an application for release on licence, it seemed that all the legal avenues available to her had been exhausted.

Then, on 2 February 1986, came a development which Mrs Chamberlain's supporters called the kind of miracle for which they had been praying. During a search for a missing tourist (who in fact had fallen from the Rock to his death), a baby's white matinee jacket was found, about 150 metres from the place where Azaria's clothing had been found in 1980. A white matinee jacket which her mother claimed Azaria was wearing at the time of the tragedy had never been recovered.

Three days afterwards, on 5 February, Mrs Chamberlain inspected the jacket and identified it as the one worn by Azaria at the time of her disappearance. Then, on 7 February, the NT Attorney-General, Mr Marshall Perron, made the dramatic announcement that the balance of Mrs Chamberlain's life sentence would be remitted, that she would be released from Darwin Prison, and that the NT Government would set up a judicial inquiry to investigate new evidence. Whatever the outcome, Mrs Chamberlain would not return to custody, he

added. Australia's most famous prisoner was freed that same afternoon, at 3.45 Darwin time. It was three years and four months since her conviction for the murder of her baby in August 1980.

The judicial inquiry took the form of a Royal Commission, headed by Mr Justice Trevor Morling of the Federal Court. It began on 8 May 1986, cost an estimated seven million dollars, heard 144 witnesses and shifted base from Darwin to Ayers Rock, Melbourne, Sydney and back to Darwin. It ended on 2 June 1987 with the finding that new evidence not available at the trial would have caused the judge to direct the jury to acquit the Chamberlains. Morling criticised much of the scientific evidence which led to the original conviction. The Morling finding led to the granting of a pardon to Lindy and Michael Chamberlain by the Northern Territory Government, but not to the quashing of their convictions. The Attorney-General, Daryl Manzie, told the Northern Territory Parliament that the Morling finding did not exonerate the Chamberlains, and was not a proclamation of their innocence.

A submission by the Chamberlains asking the Northern Territory Government to quash the convictions was rejected in September 1987. But the Government, recognising that all legal avenues had been exhausted by the Chamberlains, passed special legislation enabling an application to be made to the Northern Territory Court of Criminal Appeal for the quashing of the convictions. This action began on 29 February 1988. Counsel for the Chamberlains indicated that if the couple were exonerated, application for a large compensation payment would follow.

The Chamberlains had by then been the subject of a best-selling book and a major motion picture project. Evil Angels, by John Bryson, was published in October 1985. It became the basis for a film starring the Academy Award-winning actress Meryl Streep as Lindy Chamberlain and Sam Neill as Michael. The twenty-three million dollar film, shot in part in Darwin and Mt Isa, was directed by the Australian Fred Schepisi.

Three reports, written at vital moments along the way, are reproduced here. Bill Hitchings, working for the Melbourne Sun News-Pictorial *and* Herald, *who covered much of the story, wrote the first report for the* Sun News-Pictorial *(on 30 October 1982) of the result of the murder trial in Darwin:*

Lindy Chamberlain was found guilty last night of murdering her baby daughter Azaria.

She was sentenced to life in jail with hard labor.

Mrs Chamberlain, expecting her fourth child next week, was taken from the courthouse to the local Berrimah jail.

The prison, opened in late 1979, can house 150 inmates and has provision for 10 women.

At 8.40 p.m. (9.10 p.m. Melbourne time) the jury returned after just over six hours' deliberation and the foreman announced the unanimous decision.

One of the jurors wept as the verdict was announced.

Mrs Chamberlain and her husband, Seventh Day Adventist Pastor Michael, sat in the dock and heard as the trial judge, Mr Justice Muirhead, sombrely asked the foreman to stand.

"Have you reached your unanimous verdict?" he asked.

The foreman replied: "Yes."

The judge then asked: "Do you find the accused, Alice Lynne Chamberlain, guilty or not guilty of murder?"

The jury foreman replied in an almost inaudible voice: "Guilty."

The judge: "And that is the verdict of you all?"

The foreman: "Yes."

The judge then asked: "Do you find the accused, Michael Leigh Chamberlain, guilty or not guilty of having been an accessory after the fact, of that murder?"

The foreman again replied: "Guilty."

The judge: "And is that the verdict of you all?"

The foreman: "Yes."

The judge then turned to Mr John Phillips, QC, who rose haltingly to his feet and told him that Michael Chamberlain would be remanded on bail for sentence on Monday. He later corrected this to mean today.

But, he said, there was only one sentence he could pass on Mrs Chamberlain.

As Mrs Chamberlain stared at the 12 members of the jury, her face blank with shock, he said: "Alice Lynne Chamberlain, you have been found guilty.

"Only one sentence can be passed upon you.

"The sentence of this court is that you be imprisoned with hard labor for life."

During the brief, but shattering announcement each member of the jury sat with his or her head bowed.

Women wept in the courtroom.

No one spoke for several minutes.

Even the Crown Prosecutor, Mr Ian Barker, QC, shook his head as he walked past me.

He, too, appeared shocked.

As Mrs Chamberlain was driven away one woman shouted "you'll be right love," and another man shouted "appeal."

A large crowd gathered outside the courthouse as the news spread throughout the town.

Mrs Chamberlain, whose fourth baby is due in just over a week, was taken to the cells in the basement of the courthouse.

Lindy Chamberlain, then pregnant with her fourth child, during the Supreme Court trial at which she was found guilty of the murder of Azaria.

A woman officer from the Corrective Services Department accompanied her.

As I stood near the basement outside the court I heard noises coming from inside.

They appeared to be of a woman crying. Exactly half an hour after sentence was passed, Michael Chamberlain came out through a back door.

He was ashen and had to be helped as he walked zombie-like to a car.

He had obviously been crying.

Five minutes later a station wagon backed into a garage behind the courthouse basement.

I saw officers lead Mrs Chamberlain from a side door and put her into the station wagon.

The roll-up doors of the garage were opened and the car drove out with a police car, with its blue lights flashing, ahead of it.

Mrs Chamberlain looked directly ahead but her face was puffy and she, too, had obviously been weeping.

Mrs Chamberlain, 34, denied having murdered her nine-week-old baby, and Michael Chamberlain, 38, denied having been an accessory after the fact of murder.

The prosecution case was that Mrs Chamberlain cut her baby's throat while sitting in the front seat of the family's car which was parked alongside their tent at Ayers Rock on the night of August 17, 1980.

The Chamberlains said a dingo took their child as it slept in its bassinet inside the tent.

After the Full Bench of the Federal Court unanimously dismissed the Chamberlains' appeal, Lindsay Murdoch, of the Age, *wrote on 30 April 1983:*

Azaria Chamberlain would be nearly three years old were she still alive. Since she disappeared at Ayers Rock on 17 August 1980, aged 10 weeks, there have been two inquests in Alice Springs, a Supreme Court trial in Darwin and a Federal Court appeal in Sydney, which ended yesterday.

It remains a remarkable case.

A Melbourne barrister, Mr John Phillips, QC, said at the Darwin trial of the parents of Azaria last year: "There has never been a case in Australian legal history where the jury trying the accused has heard so many words that the accused have uttered before the trial began."

Unlike the New York mafia boss who told police: "Boys, I don't know nothing about nothing", the Chamberlains, he said, had talked.

But Mr Phillips told the jury during his final address that the most important allegation had never been put to Alice Lynne Chamberlain. It was: "I put it to you that the reason you cut your baby's throat was . . ."

Mr Phillips said the allegation was never put because the Crown was stone, motherless broke on motive.

"There's no other way to look at it," he said.

But the absence of a motive is not the only reason the case remains remarkable.

One of the accused at the trial, Michael Leigh Chamberlain, the baby's father, was a Christian clergyman. He was not believed on his oath.

A Crown witness, Mrs Sally Lowe, of Hobart, provided alibi evidence for both accused. She was not accepted.

The Chamberlains' defence that a dingo took the baby could not be challenged as a recent invention, for the claim was made at the scene.

Instead, the Crown presented this defence as evidence of guilt.

A Melbourne barrister, Mr John Bryson, who is writing a book about the case, says the trial was even more remarkable because at the inquests and the trial, the witnesses who seemed most convinced that a dingo could take a baby were Ayers Rock rangers, members of the Dingo Foundation and desert tribes-people.

Mr Bryson says the trial was not the first at which a prosecution had been successful without production of a body, a weapon, eyewitnesses or a motive.

"But at the trial the prosecution was without every one of those evidentiary advantages," he says.

Mr Bryson says that the most imporant exhibit was invisible. This was the molecular structure of certain particles of haemoglobin. Blood discovered in the Chamberlain family car was said to contain foetal haemoglobin, a finding inconsistent with the defence that a dingo had taken Azaria.

In the end, the jury believed the Crown. Mrs Chamberlain cut Azaria's throat while sitting in the front seat of the family car. Mr Chamberlain helped her to cover up the crime.

It has been a traumatic two and a half years for the Chamberlains. At the first inquest, which cleared them, they were friendly and co-operative to local and national media representatives, many of whom were filing the story around the world.

And the Brisbane Courier-Mail *published this report from its reporter Ken Blanch in Darwin on 8 February 1986, the day after Lindy Chamberlain was set free:*

Lindy Chamberlain went into hiding immediately after her release from Berrimah Jail in Darwin yesterday.

She is not expected to emerge into the public spotlight until she is out of the Northern Territory, the place she feels has treated her so badly.

But in a phone call last night to her mother, an excited Mrs Chamberlain, 37, said she was "grateful to be out and looking forward to coming home".

At the jail yesterday an elaborate deception shielded Mrs Chamberlain from the media as she was released just before 4 p.m., Brisbane time.

Three cars, the first two with tinted windows, were driven rapidly from the gates of the women's compound up the road to the main jail gates.

A police motorcycle escort ensured they did not have to pause as they ran the gauntlet of television and press cameras at the gate.

At the first junction on the Stuart Highway, about 300 m from the jail gates, police set up a road block to delay pursuing media cars.

A female figure could be seen dimly through the tinted glass of the leading car.

But it could not be identified as Mrs Chamberlain, and it probably was not her.

She is believed to have left the jail later in a fourth vehicle.

The decision to release Mrs Chamberlain came suddenly and unexpectedly yesterday afternoon as pressure built up on the Northern

Lindy Chamberlain, after her release from prison, visits Melbourne in April 1986 with her husband Michael for consultation with their counsel, John Winneke QC, before the judicial inquiry into Azaria's disappearance.

Territory Government after the discovery at Ayers Rock last weekend of a matinee jacket she said was Azaria's.

Mrs Chamberlain had always maintained that Azaria was taken by a dingo from a tent in which she and her husband, Mount Isa Seventh Day Adventist pastor Michael Chamberlain, their two young sons and the baby were camped near Ayers Rock on the night of 17 August 1980.

But she was convicted of having murdered Azaria and sentenced to life imprisonment after the Crown told a jury her story was a fanciful fabrication.

The Crown alleged she had cut Azaria's throat in the family car for unknown reasons and then hidden the body.

The jacket found last weekend was one she said Azaria had been wearing over a singlet, napkin and jumpsuit when she was taken from the tent.

The Crown described as a lie her story of the jacket, which was not recovered, even though the other clothing was.

In a sudden about-face, the NT Attorney-General, Mr Marshall Perron, told an astonished press conference that Mrs Chamberlain was to go free.

The Government had decided to remit the rest of her sentence and set her free with no strings attached, he said.

"The decision follows advice received from the Solicitor-General and the Police Commissioner on what they regard as significant new evidence," he said.

"They have advised me that the discovery of a baby's matinee jacket near the base of Ayers Rock and its subsequent identification by Mrs Chamberlain may have a bearing on the case.

"The Government proposes to take whatever steps are necessary, including the possible introduction of legislation at the forthcoming sittings of the Legislative Assembly, to set up the inquiry.

"At this stage, terms of reference have not been drawn up, nor has the composition of the inquiry body been decided. This is not an immediate consideration, given the amount of time it will take to assemble forensic data.

"I can also advise that a short time ago His Honor The Administrator, accepted the advice of Executive Council that the balance of Mrs Chamberlain's life sentence be remitted, and that she be released from Darwin prison.

"The decision to so recommend was made in the light of Mrs Chamberlain's need for unrestricted access to legal advisers to prepare for the inquiry.

"Although Mrs Chamberlain's remission is subject to the usual condition of good behavior, it is not my intention that she be taken back into custody, regardless of the outcome of the inquiry."

Mr Perron released a letter sent by the Police Commissioner, Mr Peter McAulay, to the Northern Territory Chief Minister, Mr Ian Tuxworth, yesterday morning.

Mr McAulay referred to the discovery of the matinee jacket "in relatively close proximity to a point where some articles of clothing of Azaria Chamberlain were found in 1980".

"Since that time, I have consulted with the Solicitor-General, and certain NT police officers, at one time or another being involved in the investigation of this case, and I note that the garment in question fits the description of the matinee jacket described by Mrs Chamberlain on previous occasions," he wrote.

"I now believe that the discovery of the garment and particularly the condition in which the garment now is, are matters which may prove to be significant new evidence in the case. I must point out that the significance of the find will not be fully comprehensible until the garment has been subjected to extensive forensic examination.

"I must emphasise that at this stage I am not aware of any facts connected to this piece of evidence which affect the veracity of the prosecution's original case, but that does not alter the fact that the garment, its condition, and the circumstances connected with its discovery, are all significant matters which ought to be tested as evidence against the totality of other relevant evidence."

Mrs Chamberlain was having her lunch break from prison duties when she was told she was to be released.

She was allowed to change from her blue prison dress into civilian clothes while the formalities of her release were finalised.

1983   On Ash Wednesday, 73 die in bushfires

RICHARD YALLOP
Melbourne Age, 18 February 1983

Ash Wednesday, 16 February 1983, was the day south-eastern Australia burned. Separate fires, fuelled by the dry debris of the worst drought in living memory and fanned by strong winds, broke out in the Adelaide hills and in patches across Victoria.

Between them they produced Australia's worst natural disaster since Cyclone Tracy ravaged Darwin on Christmas Day, 1974. It devastated huge tracts of forest and pasture, destroyed more than 2000 homes and claimed 72 human lives.

John Hamilton, one of the reporters who covered Ash Wednesday, later wrote for a book produced by The Herald and Weekly Times to help the State Disaster Appeal:

'The temperature was 43 degrees. The strong wind forced the fires along. Soon they were rolling, gathering momentum, creating their own mighty rushing wind. Walls of flame a hundred metres high roared out of control. Gum trees erupted upwards like giant Roman candles. And soon giant fireballs were leaping ahead of the main fires, landing haphazardly and starting yet more fires.

'Chunks of burning bark battered against the window panes of houses, and soon the panes grew too hot to touch and houses began igniting spontaneously, tile roofs blowing upwards, walls blasting sidewards.

'Priceless collections of paintings and antiques were lost as mansions burned. In humbler homes family photo albums vaporised and toys melted to puddles of metal and plastic. The heat was so intense that in one service station, a car became welded to a hoist and glass insulators, falling from telegraph poles, melted like giant tears.'

On Black Friday, 1939, 71 persons died in the Victorian fires and one died in South Australia. The 1983 toll was 46 dead in Victoria and 26 in South Australia. These two bushfires, the worst of the century, both occurred in searing temperatures combined with low relative humidity, and both followed long droughts.

The heroes of Ash Wednesday were the volunteer firefighters of the Country Fire Authority and the Forests Commission, supported by police, ambulance drivers, the State Emergency Services and many hundreds of volunteers from the St John Ambulance, the Red Cross, the Salvation Army, church groups and CFA women's auxiliaries.

Thirteen volunteer firefighters died, 11 of them together in Upper Beaconsfield, Victoria. They were two crews — one from Panton Hill, the other from Narre Warren — who were caught along the road on a slope of a wooded gully. They went to defend a hilltop house. They parked their trucks and made their stand. . .and were engulfed as the flames leapt up the slope and enveloped the trucks.

Afterwards, Richard Yallop of the Age *visited the scene of that horror. Here is his report.*

The smoke was still drifting across the heights of Beaconsfield yesterday afternoon as the police Disaster Victim Identification Team moved in to recover the bodies of the 12 firefighters who died by their trucks on Wednesday night.

The unit's job is to identify unrecognisable bodies, aided by the skills of forensic science.

The firefighters had been caught in a death trap, after their bravery had carried them into a wooded slope in defence of a house at the top of the hill. They parked the trucks on the track running along the side of the hill and

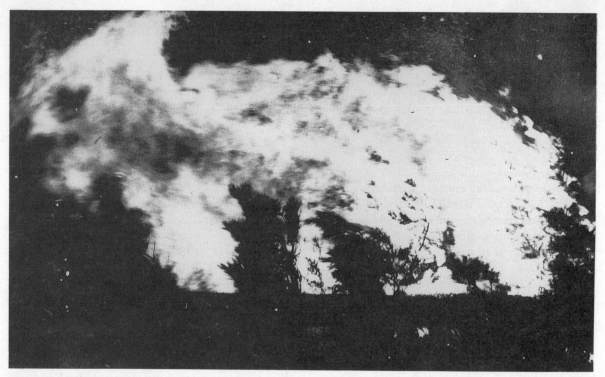

Flames rage through a state forest in the Otway Ranges, south-west Victoria, during the Ash Wednesday bushfires.

made their stand.

The flames leapt up the slope and enveloped the trucks. Some men died seeking shelter beneath the vehicles, some huddled against the bank of the hill. The house on the hill was also taken by the fire.

For one police officer from St. Kilda yesterday was the worst day of 12 years' service, which have included being chased out of a Brunswick bank by a man with a shotgun. "Something like this has a more devastating effect. It is bloody heartbreaking," he said. A home-made mask to keep out the stench, fashioned from a folded handkerchief hung around his neck.

He walked back up the hillside to the road where three undertakers waited to remove the bodies in a hearse. In its desolation, with charred trees on every side, the site at the end of St George's Road seemed a cross between a cemetery and a battlefield.

The officer's day had begun when he found two bodies at a farm on the Emerald-Beaconsfield Road. The husband lay on his

back outside the house still clutching a hose across his chest. His wife lay face down two metres away.

As the officer took stock, the dead couple's daughter walked up the drive. She had come to check that her parents were all right. The police took her to a neighbour's house.

The fire spread through the Dandenongs like an invading army on a scorched-earth campaign. It started at Belgrave, was swept south as far as Officer by the northerly, and then veered north-east as the cool change came at 8.40 pm.

The whole triangular area yesterday seemed like a war zone. Helicopters and spotter planes criss-crossed the skies, and vans, utes, trucks, fire engines, and ambulances were the only traffic on restricted roads.

The police blocked the road into Cockatoo, which suffered the greatest damage (together with Upper Beaconsfield) and just after 10 am refugees could be seen leaving the township, walking with whatever belongings they could fit into cardboard boxes, or in cars with cases loaded up in the back seat.

"Most people lost their houses, mate," said a man walking out of Cockatoo in shorts and thongs. The Scots Church was razed, and on both sides of the main road houses were destroyed, with only smouldering timber stumps and twisted steel remaining . . .

Isolated fires were still flaring at midmorning yesterday, but the major fronts had been contained, and the emergency services gathered outside Cockatoo fire station for their first respite in twelve, and some cases, 18 hours. Morale was upheld by cheery ladies and Rotary volunteers providing tea, steak and sausages.

Two volunteer firefighters sat outside the fire station, at the end of their resources. Bill Goodwin, an unemployed 18-year-old from Upwey, had been fighting his first fire, and it had left a mark. His face was smeared with ash and every word seemed an effort.

He started at 6 pm, and only just stopped. "It was pretty bloody awful," he said. What was the worst thing? "We found a body up there. It was revolting. You don't get time to think about it. You have to look and see if there is anyone else."

The battle had thrown him into comradeship with John Williamson, a 33-year-old volunteer from Emerald, who was in the same firefighting team. Mr Williamson had been in other fires, but none like this. His eyes were red with exhaustion, and he said little because he felt so much.

"It was frightening – the speed of the fire. There was nothing you could do," he said. "We didn't know where it was going, we just had to evacuate everyone. Up here there was no way of stopping it.

"I feel shock for the people. They've lost everything. We've all got friends here, or relations, and they've got nothing."

The fire continued its trail of devastation along the road from Cockatoo to Beaconsfield. Three cars were abandoned on the outskirts of Cockatoo, and are now burned-out wrecks.

Mr Michael Richardson, whose house stands on the edge of Upper Beaconsfield, had almost no warning of the advance of the fire. "I was on the top of the house hosing the gutters, and you couldn't see the fire. The next thing we knew it was across the road.

"I've never been so scared. There was fire on all sides and I didn't know where to go. People were sheltering at the State Equestrian Centre so I drove there, through the flames. The seats were all scorched.

"The panic hit the drivers. People didn't know whether to go on or turn round."

His house was surrounded, but it survived. The fire stopped two feet from the back door and 30 feet from the front door . . .

Up at Belgrave Heights, where the fire started, Mr and Mrs Rayment and their three children have also lost everything. They went out at 1 pm on Wednesday afternoon to see the doctor in Ringwood, and when they returned at 4.30 pm, the two-storey house was a blazing heap of rubble. The only untouched part of the property was the tiled swimming pool.

The Rayments spent the night scattered around friends and family and returned to the ruins at 9.30 am yesterday. On the way to the house their daughter Ruth asked if the guinea pigs, birds, ducks and fish would be all right.

"She wanted to know if the animals would be safe," Mr Rayment said. "We had to tell her they had no chance in the fire." Ruth sobbed, fossicking through the ashes of her bedroom, while her parents and elder brothers maintained an air of stoic resignation.

The family are prominent members of a local church, and Mrs Rayment is State president of the Women's Christian Temperance Union. "People who haven't got faith in God, I don't know how they survive at a time like this," Mr Rayment said. "There were a few tears, but we know the Lord is looking after us."

"My first reaction was thankfulness to the Lord that we were still alive. Then we thought 'What do we do next?' But we can start again, I'm sure." Mrs. Rayment said, "It's got to be. Today is the first day of our lives."

JOHN LARKIN
Melbourne Age, 7 March 1983

When he assumed the leadership of the federal parliamentary Labor Party in February 1983, Bob Hawke was one of the few Australians who had reached the status of political folk hero. Billy Hughes had become one; another was John Curtin, who happened to be Hawke's personal political idol. Of the three, Hawke had of course the biggest personal electorate. Not only had the nation grown, but he was also a creature of the age of television. There is not much doubt that he was Australia's most successful public communicator during the 1970s and 1980s, and that achievement related largely to his skill as a TV performer.

He was a politician long before he entered formal politics. He was president of the Australian Council of Trade Unions from 1970 until 1980, and federal president of the Australian Labor Party from 1973 until 1978. In 1971 the former Opposition Leader, Arthur Calwell, predicted that Hawke would enter politics 'within three or four years', and that he would become Prime Minister before 1981. When, in September 1979, Bob Hawke did announce his candidature for Parliament — an event which the chief political correspondent of the Australian, *Malcolm Colless, described as 'the most important development on the Australian political scene since the dismissal of the Whitlam government' — there was little doubt on anyone's part that he intended to become Prime Minster.*

Bob Hawke was the son of a Perth clergyman, nephew of a former Labor Premier of Western Australia, a Bachelor of Arts, a Rhodes Scholar and Bachelor of Literature at Oxford, a member of the Reserve Bank board from 1973, a member of the International Labor Organisation governing body in Geneva from 1972 until 1980, and one-time

holder of the world beer-drinking record (two and a half pints in 12 seconds). A staunch supporter of Israel, he had a forest of 10,000 trees named after him on the hills of Mt Carmel in northern Israel. One of his more innovative moves as president of the ACTU was to take that body into partnership in the Melbourne department store, Bourke's.

An engaging, generous, emotional man with more than a touch of the larrikin about him, he combined an unswerving belief in his own destiny with a genuine desire to improve the lives of ordinary Australians. Although he was a much more flamboyant, gregarious character than John Curtin, the similarities between the two were interesting. Both came from Western Australia, both were accomplished advocates and communicators in the media of their time, both became agnostics after losing religious faith, both had experience with the ILO, both had a passionate commitment to their own vision of Australia, and both fought and won tough battles against alcohol addiction.

Bob Hawke stopped drinking in May 1980. He later recalled that on the eve of a trip to Geneva, 'I said to myself: "Well, bugger it. You'd be better off not drinking. Why don't you give up?" So I went and washed my hands and that was it.' He had given up alcohol two years earlier for a time, because he realised it was affecting his capacity to perform; he had taken up moderate drinking again, but the 1980 decision was final.

Hawke was 51 years old when he entered Federal Parliament in October 1980. Not long before that happened he was, according to the opinion polls, the most popular man in Australia, with ratings a long way ahead of the Prime Minister, Malcolm Fraser, and the Opposition Leader, Bill Hayden. In July 1982

Hawke challenged Hayden for the Labor leadership, and was narrowly beaten. Less than seven months later, in February 1983, Hayden was persuaded, very much against his will, to relinquish the job; Hawke was unopposed as the new leader. The Labor Party did something then of which most of its opponents believed it incapable: it switched leaders with ruthless efficiency and a total lack of bloodshed. It did so without any show of disunity, and yet with a certain emotion. It did so for one reason only: because it believed Bob Hawke to be a winner, and it badly wanted to win the next election.

If 11 November, 1975, the day of the Whitlam sacking, was the most drama-filled day in the history of Australian politics, then 3 February 1983, the day of the Hawke ascendancy, wasn't far behind. As the power brokers of the Labor Party were seeking to replace Hayden with Hawke, Malcolm Fraser was attempting to exploit Labor's leadership crisis by calling an election. Most significant of the architects of Hayden's demise was Senator John Button. He had been a supporter of Hayden during Hawke's 1982 challenge and was a close personal friend, but by the end of the year he had come to the view that Labor could not win the next election under Hayden. He wrote to Hayden, urging him to resign the leadership in favor of Hawke, stressing his own consistent loyalty in the past to Hayden, but pointing out that his ultimate loyalty was to the ALP. Hayden later revealed that it was this letter, which he described as 'brutal but fair', which did most to convince him to stand down.

On the morning of 3 February Fraser received reliable advice that Hayden's demise was close . . . that the Labor leader might even be dumped at that day's meeting in Brisbane of the ALP Executive. He rang members of his Cabinet and told them he intended calling an immediate election. It was his belief that, if a leadership crisis did eventuate that day, it would be a bloody affair which might continue for some time. He had often told colleagues: 'When Hayden's cornered, he'll fight like a cat.'

Fraser left Parliament House at 12.15 pm with a letter to the Governor-General requesting a double dissolution of Parliament and an election on 5 March. The Governor-General, Sir Ninian Stephen, was lunching with the Polish Ambassador, and was not prepared to be hurried into giving his assent. Fraser left the Governor-General's residence, Yarralumla, empty-handed, about 15 minutes before a tearful Hayden, in Brisbane, rose to tell the party executive that he had decided to resign. While the Prime Minister waited around Parliament House for most of the afternoon for approval from the Governor-General, the Labor Party was already off and running. Hawke met the press and had actually begun Labor's election campaign – pledging a Labor Government to 'national reconciliation' – before Fraser even received the Governor-General's consent to hold the election.

Although Fraser denied strenuously that the Hawke-Hayden switch had caught him with his pants down – 'It makes no difference who the leader is . . . the policies of the Labor Party remain the same' – the impression remained with many that the man who had dealt with Gough Whitlam so convincingly in 1975 had been outsmarted in 1983. Certainly he would have preferred to campaign against Hayden rather than Hawke. His request for a double dissolution had been put together in some haste, and was unaccompanied by any legal opinions from either the Solicitor-General or Attorney-General. Whether this apparent oversight contributed to the delay in giving consent is academic, really. What mattered was that Hawke and the Labor Party had moved quickly and with uncharacteristic unison. In doing so, they took a psychological advantage, and retained it.

After a four-week campaign hinged largely to the notion of consensus – and with it, an economic policy built largely around agreement by the trade unions to a prices-incomes agreement – Bob Hawke and his team won the election convincingly. John Larkin, of the Age, Melbourne, wrote this report on the 14 hours in which Bob Hawke became the nation's leader.

There was a moment, in the almighty rush of events around the election, when Bob Hawke stopped. The pause was for reflection. It came in the aloneness that just preceded sleep.

That was late Friday. The campaigning was over. A dinner for everybody involved had been held in Fitzroy, an evening which was moving for Mr Hawke and the others. Now he was back in his city hotel.

He would sleep well that night, and before he did, he took a last chance at introspection.

Asked whether his feelings on that last night had been in any way religious, he said: "I haven't continued a formal adherence to the church, but I think there's a sense in which certainly the things I believe in have been moulded by my involvement in it. The concept of commitment to people has been shaped by that, and it will always be so."

"There is a sense in which, as things have unfolded, you try to look beyond yourself. I can't in my mind intellectually identify what that is. But so many people identified with you and they have said that they are praying for you . . . there's obviously some strength outside yourself."

He was speaking in his car on Saturday, going to Melbourne airport on his way to Canberra and destiny. He spoke evenly, in a manner that would be seen as common over the next 24 hours. There was no stridency, no fanfare, no aggression.

Instead, there was something akin to acceptance and tenderness. It was consistent with the more female aspects of the election, the dwelling on reconciliation, trust, intuition, the language of the heart. Later, he would be merciful towards Fraser.

Saturday started at the hotel with a small crowd which even then had a wandering American tourist caught up in it saying: "I don't belive this." She should have seen the crescendo at the end.

Mr Hawke initially looked a little tired, though he picked up quickly once among people. He wore blue and seemed reasonably buoyant, making up jokes quickly, catching cues, showing he was in present time.

Mr Hawke senior, Clem, 85 on Saturday, and as upright as principle, came along and so did Hazel and the two girls. They dropped off later as Mr Hawke did a lightning run through many polling stations in his electorate of Wills, a bright start in the cool, grey and kind morning.

At his electorate office in a steamy room decorated with a Birds of Australia tea towel, he was presented with a large cake decorated by a map of Australia.

When asked to cut it, Mr Hawke, in fun, asked where Mr Fraser's electorate, Wannon, was, and stuck the knife into it. Soon afterwards, as if in retribution, some of the cake came away on his coat.

He was impressed that the local Liberal candidate against him had wished him good luck. He considered that not a bad sign. When we heard that just down the street a woman had given birth, in a car, there was talk of an omen.

More pictures, and a wisecrack. Asked to pose with a pile of books, Mr Hawke saw the title of the first one and remarked: "Just what I need to be doing today, reading 'Utopia'."

He and his father had some tea and he announced Clem's occasion and everybody sang happy birthday. "It's hard to keep remembering birthdays today," Mr Hawke said half apologetically to his father, whom he often called Pop.

As we hurtled on through the curious and cheering Saturday morning shoppers, Mr Hawke continued to liven up. He gave his regular wave, the Aussie salute with the curved finger.

As he drove off finally for the airport, the people gathered around the car window and he spoke as if to himself, quietly: "Oh, aren't they great. Great."

In the car he was asked if, for a person who had had so many highs and lows in his life, he was feeling anything extra in the range of emotions.

"I feel as though you're on the verge of something that in a way your whole life has been building up to. You can't help having the feeling that all that life experience has now led you up to that point. In the thoughts that I had before I went off to sleep I just hoped that I had the intelligence and good sense to draw from all that experience to make sure that I do the job to the utmost of my capacity."

Before sleeping, he also considered he had

got the best out of himself, with the people around him.

Talking about the mood of people, he said: "The contrast to 72 had been the lack of hysteria, the thoughtful enthusiasm, and that's been marvellous, plus the way that people have responded to a positive campaign. They understand what we are trying to do."

It was true that there was little uproar among the winners on Saturday, which Mr Hawke spent in his Canberra hotel all afternoon and evening until the result was sure.

Monitoring the figures on TV, computer and interstate telephone, the 20 people in the suite were generally quiet, almost subdued. The family supported Mr Hawke and made a few jokes.

He said yesterday he thought from the first figures that they were going to win. Others in the room had that confidence, but the sense of success came slowly.

Finally, near 11 o'clock, probably one of the best guides, the face of Bob Hogg, the Victorian ALP State secretary, key campaigner and a figures expert, suddenly stopped being taut. About the same time, ABC television gave it to Labor. Then the relaxation that had been in the room previously was out in the open. They knew.

Mr Hawke's understated emotion was evident as soon as he came downstairs, except when he gave Hazel a kiss for the cameras. He did it once, then twice. The second time was something that had nothing to do with publicity.

The subtle spirit in which the Labor people were both happy and serious at once stayed with them.

In the ABC studio where Mr Hawke acknowledged his victory there was stillness. He had no gleam in his eyes as he addressed the country, speaking with measured authority on his favorite theme of healing the society's fractures.

People commented later on his soothing style.

He said yesterday he had an overwhelming sense at that time of responsibility, of the trust that had been given him.

He and Hazel survived the great crush of people, paraphernalia and questions at the tally room, a mayhem adding its heat to the already intense night.

Mr Hawke went back to the hotel where there was a small party. He went to bed at 3 am.

He slept for three hours, no more, awakened by the heat of the room more than anything else.

Mr Hawke was ready yesterday to go for his first TV interview, downstairs, and grew a little restless while waiting several minutes to be cued, having joked about it being his "nice-to-TV day". While being made up, he sat still, with his eyes closed. As he was being interviewed, Hazel sat nearby, and had her eyes closed.

The corridors outside the suite yesterday were awash with the comings and goings of power in transit. Labor people were serious about the business ahead, as they had been the previous night, having considered the prospect of the work ahead.

Between interviews and business, Mr Hawke suddenly asked where his father was. Had anybody seen him?

Sometime later, Clem came along the corridor, and spoke freely, happy to talk, treating us to homely observations.

"It all worked out pretty well, considering," he said.

Asked whether the scripture lessons he used to give the young Bob might still have their effect on him, the father smiled and quoted the mother of Augustine who said, when people were worried about her son: "Oh well, the child of so many prayers will never go astray."

1983   Fraser goes, after a rare display of emotion

MICHELLE GRATTAN
Melbourne Age, 28 March 1983

To several of the coalition Cabinet ministers he telephoned on the fateful morning of 3 February 1983 — to advise them that he intended to call an immediate election — Malcolm Fraser cracked his own rather stony version of a joke. 'Have you had a bath yet?' he asked. Generally the response, a little puzzled, was to the effect that the Minister concerned had not been long out of the shower. 'That doesn't really matter,' said Fraser. 'I'm going to pull the plug anyway.'

It took some time for him to realise it, but what he was certainly not doing that morning was pulling the plug on the federal Opposition, led at that time by Bill Hayden. Hayden had already agreed to surrender his leadership within a couple of hours to Bob Hawke. What Malcolm Fraser was doing was pulling the plug on himself, his party and his government.

He was a shrewd political animal, and he sensed that by calling an election he would catch the Opposition off balance, embroiled in the turmoil of a leadership crisis. He miscalculated, and was beaten devastatingly. Conceding the election early on the morning of 6 March, he accepted absolutely the blame for what had happened. 'I want to say that from this moment I resign the leadership of the Liberal Party. I will not contest the leadership of the Liberal Party. I. . .I want to make it plain that I take total responsibility for the timing of the federal election. I take total responsibility for the conduct of that election. I therefore take total responsibility for the defeat of the Government.'

Remarkably, after 28 years in public life, Fraser gave his first public display of genuine emotion as he spoke that morning. On television screens around the nation, his bottom lip and chin were seen to quaver and

his eyes to be moist; momentarily his voice faltered, but he was quickly back in control again. It was a poignant farewell for a durable, at times ruthless politician who carried with him an air of awkward aloofness.

He was an MP at 25, a Minister at 36, Opposition Leader and Prime Minister at 45, and an ex-Prime Minister at 52. On 26 February 1983 he surpassed the record of Billy Hughes and became the nation's second longest serving Prime Minister (to Sir Robert Menzies). Seven years and four months elapsed between his dramatic assumption of power in November 1975 and Labor's return to office, under Bob Hawke, in March 1983.

Malcolm Fraser was an enigma: a rather lonely, patrician figure who managed to combine an instinct for attacking the jugular in his unswerving pursuit of power with a sense of high moral purpose. To some critics, the means by which he achieved power would always overshadow what he did with it.

As Minister for Defence in the Gorton Government in 1971, he bought down his leader and Prime Minister. Four years later, in Opposition, he led a coup against another Liberal leader, Mr (later Sir Billy) Snedden. In 1975 he orchestrated events which led to the Governor-General, Sir John Kerr, dismissing the Whitlam Government.

Against all this, he maintained a deep sense of parliamentary and ministerial propriety. He was both a radical and a traditionalist. He showed great sympathy for the problems of the Third World and took a brave stand against apartheid, but was often seen to be insensitive to the plight of the victims of economic and racial misfortune in Australia. He was respected among Commonwealth leaders as a negotiator and conciliator, especially in the creation of Zimbabwe, but at home he seemed to thrive on confrontation. He was a protectionist who finally came to see the damage caused by his protection of domestic industry. He had trouble at times reconciling his commitment to the preservation of the environment with his respect for state's rights.

In his book The Hawke Ascendancy, *Paul Kelly noted that Australia was in a deeper crisis in March 1983, when Fraser lost office, than in November 1975, when he assumed it. Kelly asked the questions: What fundamental change did Fraser bring? Or, to what purpose did he use the power which he acquired in 1975 so ruthlessly, with such righteous justification? He answered them this way: 'Fraser, for all his radicalism, was a conventional politician . . . too clever a political animal, too shrewd a judge of the electorate and too smart to alienate the voters. The first major weakness in Fraser as Prime Minister was his caution. At first this claim seems absurd, since Fraser appeared the companion to audacity and sometimes the cousin to recklessness. Fraser's caution was integral to his political success. But the gap between what he did and what he could have done is a yawning chasm on the political landscape. Fraser had a political mandate in 1975 so comprehensive it is not likely to be reproduced in Australia for decades.'*

On 27 March, Malcolm Fraser announced his decision to quit Parliament. In the Age *the following day, that paper's chief political correspondent, Michelle Grattan, wrote:*

It is almost impossible to imagine Malcolm Fraser stripped of power. He was determined that we should not see him so.

It was a sad decision, Mr Fraser observed yesterday, to leave Wannon, but to stay in Parliament would make it difficult for the party and the new leadership. No doubt that was partly his motive: equally it was a matter of pride. The former leader could not be, and had no interest in becoming, another man's follower: that would pile humiliation upon humiliation.

In the weeks since the election, Mr Fraser

has seemed bemused and confused by the situation in which he finds himself. He wanted just to get out of it all.

John Malcolm Fraser entered Parliament for the seat of Wannon in 1955, when he was 25. He leaves it at the comparatively young age of 52, in that dreadful position that confronts

An emotional Malcom Fraser concedes defeat in the 1983 federal election, won by Bob Hawke's Labor Party.

leaders tossed out well before normal retirement age: where to from here?

Of course he has plenty of money, the farm, the opportunity to take up business directorships. But politics and political power have been his existence for more than a quarter of a century. He is a man who has used politics as the medium through which to relate to other people, and, at another level, to reassure himself. In just two months, he has lost all.

The fall of Malcolm Fraser came with amazing speed. In late January he seemed – however deceptive that perception was (and we can't know how he would have gone against Bill Hayden) – to have the next election at least within his grasp.

But really that fall started soon after he inflicted on Gough Whitlam, for the second time, the sort of devastating humiliation he suffered on 5 March. The last five years of his Prime Ministership were a continuing struggle to hold on to the railings as his Government went inexorably down the slide.

In the last days of his Government, his party looked to him as some sort of miracle worker: he had received the scars of so many battles, and survived, that he seemed indestructible.

But when he lost, the Liberals wanted to turn away as quickly as possible from Fraserism, or at least from the harsh style of it. If he had remained within Parliament they would have been embarrassed. He was respected because he was strong and successful. He was never loved.

What of his achievements?

It is much too early to judge how history will regard Malcolm Fraser and the Fraser years. The honeymoon days of the new Government hardly provide an objective vantage point for judgment.

Just now, people are recoiling from the Fraser period, especially from its divisiveness. Mr Fraser won power by an act of political violence and that colored his whole reign.

He took Prime Ministerial government to its ultimate, dominating and often exhausting his Cabinet. He was obsessive and frenetic in the manner he ran his administration. He based many decisions on what would patch up particular situations here and now, and ultimately the electorate doubted that he stood for a consistent or coherent programme.

Mr Fraser came into power in 1975 promising to bring down inflation and unemployment and restore economic growth. It would, he said, take a full three years.

He was relentless about the Whitlam Government's failures. Ultimately he fell victim to many of the same problems that brought down Mr Whitlam: mounting unemployment, a weak economy, the ramifications of economic troubles abroad, Ministerial scandals.

He left the economy as bad as he found it.

But to leave it at that is to ignore an important point: that Australia's problems in the decade have been only partly within the abilities of government to solve.

Mr Fraser broke promises and failed to stick to his rhetoric.

He was judged the more harshly for that because of the standards he himself had claimed a Government had to meet. In power, he muddled through, and that turned out not to be good enough.

1983   An Australian yacht with a strange keel takes home the America's Cup . . . after 132 years

BOB MACDONALD AND PETER CAMPBELL
Melbourne Herald, 27 September 1983

The longest winning streak in the history of world sport ended off Newport, Rhode Island, on 27 September, 1983, when the Australian yacht Australia II *wrenched the America's Cup away from the tenacious grip of the New York Yacht Club.*

America won the trophy 132 years earlier — when the schooner America *whipped a 14-strong British fleet off the Isle of Wight on 22 August, 1851 — in a result which was seen to symbolise the end of British commercial and political supremacy. It had never been surrendered in 24 expensive challenges since then. . .until the arrival of an Australian craft with a controversial winged keel and a battle pennant in the form of a big green flag emblazoned with a gold kangaroo wearing bright red boxing gloves.*

The America's Cup and the New York Yacht Club represented a bastion of American society and a dynasty of American business. It was J Pierpont Morgan who gave the club the land on which to build its lavish New York premises, and Harold Vanderbilt who confronted the tea merchant Sir Thomas Lipton in the last of Lipton's five rather gentlemanly attempts in 31 years to win the America's Cup for Britain. Even Newport, the venue of the contest since 1930, was seen as a symbol of American class-consciousness; it was a fine old town with 17th century roots, a place where the super-rich, like the Valderbilts and the Morgans, built their holiday mansions overlooking Long Island Sound.

Into this commune of high society and gold-plated yachting arrived, in 1983, a distinctly unusual team of challengers, headed by Australia II's *wildly extrovert owner, the Perth businessman Alan Bond. The skipper was John Bertrand, a deceptively placid*

sailmaker with a killer instinct on the water. The designer, and the man behind the delta-wing keel (which was kept shrouded in green canvas when it was out of the water) was an eccentric genius called Ben Lexcen. And behind them came an astonishing caravan of Australian supporters.

Peter Cole-Adams, of the Age, *sent this slightly shocked report from the scene: 'Let me begin with the bad news: there is a person in a koala suit bouncing up and down outside a shop in Newport's Thames Street (the locals, unforgivably, pronounce it Thaymes Street). He or she — I was unable to sex the beast during a muffled interview — is only the most blatant sign that, on the eve of the America's Cup challenge races, the yachting capital of North America has been almost entirely taken over by Australians. Every bar in town is packed with thirsty citizens from Sydney, Melbourne and Perth with Australian flags emblazoned on their T-shirts, and with bemused ladies from Brisbane who want to know what to do when they get mugged.'*

Bruce Stannard, a competitive yachtsman who had been covering America's Cup racing at Newport for 13 years, wrote of the scene each day at Australia II's *dock: 'At precisely 9.30 am, the hi-fi aboard the Australian tender,* Black Swan, *blasts the gallery with Men at Work's "Down Under", the theme song of this, the seventh Australian attempt to lift the cup in 21 years. No matter how many times he hears it, the song, like a hyponist's psychic cue, sends* Australia II's *executive director Warren Jones into a combination Irish jig and soft-shoe shuffle. But down on the racing boat the crew maintain a laconic, almost stoic pose. This is just one more boat race in a summer of endless boat races. . .Down at the blunt end,*

1983 was a triumphant year for Bob Hawke. In his first year as the nation's leader he led the celebration from the Royal Perth Yacht Club – in a gaudy jacket which became drenched with champagne – on the morning of *Australia II's* America's Cup win.

Australia II crosses the finish line 41 seconds ahead of the American yacht *Liberty* in the final race of the America's Cup series at Newport.

with his arms folded and a look of supreme self-confidence on his face, sits John Bertrand, the 36-year old sailmaker on whose shoulders rests the fate of this $4 million Australian campaign. Bertrand's nickname is "Aero", short for aerodynamics. He holds a master's degree from MIT, and is without doubt the most thoughtful and calmest skipper Australia has ever had in Newport.'

The Australians beat Britain for the right to take on the United States in the final show-down. For a time the New York Yacht Club sought to have Australia II *disqualified without even racing, because of the delta-winged keel, but the attempt was finally dropped. In the final best-of-seven series, Australia II* came from being down 1-3 to beat the American defender, Liberty, *in the deciding race.*

Millions of Australians stayed up through the early hours of 27 September to watch Australia II *and the 11 sailors aboard her make history. The day that followed was one of national euphoria. The Prime Minister, Bob Hawke, who presided via the TV screen over a*

nation-wide pre-breakfast party from the Royal Perth Club, called the victory 'Australia's greatest sporting achievement'. Doused in champagne after his all-night vigil, he laughingly declared the day a national holiday, and then added: "We'd be a nation of zombies, anyway." Town hall bells rang in Australian cities, and in Sydney a giant Australian flag was draped across the Harbor Bridge as ferries below honked their horns and sirens in triumph. It was one of the most joyful days in the nation's history.

In Newport for the Melbourne Herald, Bob MacDonald and Peter Campbell wrote this report:

The America's Cup, that most glittering and elusive prize, was captured today by Australia II in a heart-stopping 'grand final' of yachting.

And Australian skipper John Bertrand and his magnificent Australian crew won the treasured trophy in true Aussie battler style — once more coming from behind.

Down 0-2, they fought back, down 3-1

they fought back to three-all, and today they did it again, making up almost a minute on the second-to-last leg.

The margin of victory was 47 seconds. . .and after 132 years the America's Cup finally had been wrenched from the New York Yacht Club.

Australia II began the race well, and crossed Liberty ahead for the first two tacks, then Bertrand failed to cover Liberty.

The American sailing genius Dennis Conner took Liberty far out to one side of the course, picked up a wind shift and came back in the lead.

Australia II could do nothing to break through, and rounded the mark 29 precious seconds behind Liberty.

Down the second leg, Conner's grip only tightened, as the heavier Liberty stretched out to lead by 45 seconds.

But Australia II's ability to run fast before the wind came into play on the third leg, and it was a sign of the American's problems to come.

The Australians almost halved the lead to 23 seconds.

It was enough for Conner to keep a loose cover over Australia going upwind again where he carried the lead out to almost a minute.

Then on the fifth leg, Conner paid the same price as Bertrand for failing to cover. The difference was that it cost the race.

The Australian boat headed far out to the right hand side of the course by themselves, perhaps seeing a better breeze, perhaps in desperation.

Liberty stuck to a more conventional path down to the fifth mark, and hit a brief hole in the breeze.

It wasn't held up long, but it was enough. It was just enough.

Australia II came back with a better breeze, and when Liberty jibed across, it jibed behind.

With the wind blowing in his face on the sixth leg, Conner tried desperately to regain the lead. He repeatedly resorted to tacks, zig-zag manoeuvres, but Bertrand covered those moves to stretch his lead on Rhode Island Sound.

Conner, who successfully defended the cup aboard Freedom in 1980, is the first American

skipper to lose sailing's most hallowed prize. And he did it after squandering a 3-1 lead in the first cup series to go a full seven races.

For Alan Bond, head of the Australia II syndicate, the victory ends a decade of frustration. Starting in 1974, he had mounted three cup campaigns and won just a single race in 13 tries against the Americans.

Bond had said he would abandon his pursuit of the cup if he lost this time.

The Australian victory means the cup competition will leave this seaside resort for the first time since 1930, when it was relocated here from Sandy Hook, New Jersey.

The Aussies said that if they beat Liberty they would defend the cup in 1986 in Perth, located on the Western Australia coast.

And what a day it was to be an Australian in Newport, or anywhere else for that matter where Australians were glued to their TV sets with bated breath.

People in Newport, with their Cup tradition, know just how hard and long the Australians worked to win their triumph.

They know how hard and long the New York Yacht Club fought to stop it happening.

Today's loss could cost many of them money, those of them in the tourist trade who may never see another summer like the incredible one just past.

But they shared a sense with the Australians crowded into their town of having seen history made today.

"Congratulations," they said, and meant it, to Australians in the street, in bars, in restaurants, on the docks where the mobs were gathering just minutes after the race ended to watch the boats sail home against a silver sunset.

"Australia II, Australia II," a voice which could be from the Bronx has shouted over the marine radio from the fleet riotously escorting the two yachts back to port. "Well done, mates."

And a woman's voice, also American, seconded the motion: "That's a positive. That's an absolute positive."

The Coast Guard warned the incoming fleet that two of the front runners, speeding back to port have collided near Fort Adams, a landmark at the entrance of the harbor within sight of the Australia II and Liberty docks.

"There is debris in the water," the Coast Guard warned.

There will doubtless be more collisions and debris ashore during the celebrations which will stretch long into the night ahead and probably through it.

But right now, in the exhilaration of having seen his (or her) countrymen strive, succeed and be saluted, Newport is a great place for Australians to be.

On the night Conner sailed the fifth race, leading 3-1 and so confident of winning that the champagne was already on his dock, his wife and other women supporters wore star-spangled shorts of red, white and blue.

Patriotism was on the line today. So was 132 years of history. So was Newport's tourist economy, the town's principal industry, which is healthy enough to survive the loss of the Cup but will surely feel a blow.

In the same issue of the Herald, *Bob MacDonald wrote about the reaction in Newport* . . .

The Yanks lost it like the Aussies won it – in style.

As Australia II crossed the finish line, breaking the New York Yacht Club's grip on the America's Cup, Americans saluted the little white boat and its crew as worthy champions.

Cheers went up around television sets all over Newport – not just from Australians but from Americans who respected the Aussie crew's guts and refusal to quit.

Some people were crying, from the sheer emotion of a race which captured the world's attention like no other boat race has.

"Let's hear it for the Aussies," the shout went up in the waterfront bar closest to Dennis Conner's dock, where Americans outnumbered Australians by probably 50 to one.

The three cheers rang out and the supporters from the losing country sought out the supporters from the winner to shake their hands.

"Three cheers for the Americans," an Australian voice shouted back over the din.

And everyone cheered themselves, each other, and most of all the men whom the television sets showed dancing, waving and delirious with joy.

In the end 132 years of America's Cup history came down to 22 desperate kilometres.

That was the distance John Bertrand and his mighty men on Australia II had to catch Dennis Conner and Liberty after letting the lead slip away on the first leg of their historic final race for the cup.

And the whole of Newport virtually came to a standstill to watch, listen and hold its breath.

Even some of the Liberty team members had virtually given up when Australia II sailed most of the first leg in front after crossing the start line eight seconds behind.

As the leg neared completion, two of the Conner team who had been out at the course taking wind readings were already back at their dock by speedboat and headed for the car park.

1985 The crusader and the Godfather... an awful network of crime unfolds

JOHN STEVENS, JENNY CONLEY AND BRUCE WILSON
Melbourne Age, 28 March 1985, 17 April 1986 and Herald 19 May 1987

Donald Bruce Mackay was the owner of a successful furniture business in the New South Wales Riverina town of Griffith. In the mid-1970s he came to know that vast plantations of Indian hemp were being grown in the Riverina district, and that a multi-million dollar drug racket was headquartered in his home town. He was a decent man, an aspiring politician (as endorsed Liberal Party candidate for Griffith), and he hated the drug invasion. For several years he campaigned, almost single-handedly, against the cultivation and distribution of drugs in the area. He publicised the drug connection in the media, and, when he had information about specific drug crops, he passed it to police. Two of the reporters to whom he gave details — in April 1977 — were the Melbourne Herald's *Antony Cheesewright and Richard Willis, who were investigating the drug trade. In 1975 he passed to the drug squad of the NSW Police Force information which enabled the squad to raid various farms. One such raid led to the discovery of ten hectares of marijuana at Coleambally, 60 kilometres south of Griffith. Worth $15 million on the streets, it was the largest 'dope' plantation found in Australia.*

The drug racket was operated — it was subsequently established at Royal Commissions and in various courts — by three Griffith families who belonged to a sect of the Mafia active in both Calabria, southern Italy, and Australia. It was variously called 'N'Dranghita' (Calabrian dialect for the Honored Society) or 'La Famiglia'. Mackay's activities nagged at the Griffith branch of the Mafia, and a NSW Royal Commission into drugs, headed by Mr Justice Sir Edward Woodward, later found that Mackay's name had been passed to the Mafia group as a police informant. The group's

profitability was seen to be under threat, and it was decided in 1977 that he would have to be eliminated. It was the report of the Woodward Commission, released in November 1979, which gave first details of the plot to execute Mackay, but full elaboration did not emerge until the Mafia code of silence was broken by one of its members in 1982.

On 15 July 1977, Mackay, 43, walked out of a hotel bar in Griffith. . .and simply disappeared. The following day his blood-stained mini-van was found in the car park of the hotel, where he had stopped to buy a wine cask. A huge search took place through vineyards and farms in the irrigation area for five months, but it yielded no clues. Mackay's body was never found, but he was officially declared dead just one year, minus a day, after he left the hotel bar. Mackay's death symbolised disturbing new elements in Australian crime: the intrusion of drug-trading on a vast scale, and the introduction of a new dimension of violence which involved 'hit men' and took crime across what had been its conventional boundaries. Mackay was an admirable and brave crusader; but it is fair to say that he achieved much more after his death to expose the drug menace than he could ever have alive. First, through the Woodward Commission, the Mafia connection came to be known and the families involved were identified. Later, through the activities of a man known to the Griffith sect as 'the Godfather', and particularly his graduation from the marijuana trade (which Mackay had done much to wreck) to international heroin smuggling, even more sinister facts surfaced. That man was Robert Trimbole.

The Woodward Commission established that Mackay's execution was set for 12 July 1977.

He received a phone call on 6 or 7 July from a 'Mr Adams', who said he had won a lottery and wanted to buy a house full of furniture for his son. Mackay arranged to meet him on 12 July outside a motor inn at Jerilderie, 150 kilometres south of Griffith. He was prevented from keeping the appointment by the death of a close friend in Griffith. Mackay sent instead one of his senior salesmen, Bruce Pursehouse; Pursehouse drove Mackay's gold-coloured Fairlane to the motor inn at Jerilderie for the appointment and waited for two hours. Nobody met him, but he noticed nearby a man he later said had been 'acting strangely.' When Mackay disappeared three days afterwards, Pursehouse gave police details of his false errand to Jerilderie and a description of the man he had seen: a man of dark complexion, with a dark, droopy moustache and collar-length hair. That description, the only eyewitness account which might have given any real clue to the identity of Mackay's killer, was described by a Victorian Supreme Court judge in April 1986 as 'direct testimony' and 'very important evidence'; but police investigating the Mackay murder at the time did not issue it publicly and did not publish any identikit picture. More seriously, the description was deleted from Pursehouse's evidence at the inquest into Mackay's death in 1984.

This unlikely omission led to reports in April 1986 in the Age *and the* Sydney Morning Herald *suggesting that the police handling of the Mackay investigation had been bungled; this criticism in turn caused the NSW Premier, Neville Wran, to order an inquiry into the conduct of the police inquiries after Mackay's disappearance.*

Robert Trimbole once ran a not-so-successful spray-painting and panel-beating business in Griffith, and was declared bankrupt in 1968. Within eight years of bankruptcy he was a millionaire. He attributed his sudden wealth to phenomenal horse-punting luck, but it was subsequently attributed to the profits he harnessed from the growing and distribution of marijuana in the Griffith district. In his Royal Commission report into drug trafficking, Mr Justice Woodward identified Trimbole as 'the practical leader' of the secret Honored Society. By 1983 police from Victoria and

NSW, backed with a large body of intelligence by two Royal Commissions, had eventually turned up evidence that it was Trimbole who had ordered the execution of Donald Mackay.

After the exposure and finally the collapse of Trimbole's marijuana industry, Trimbole moved into the international heroin-smuggling syndicate, the 'Mr Asia' organisation. In 1983, in his 908-page report as Royal Commissioner into the 'Mr Asia' syndicate, Mr Justice Donald Stewart, concluded: 'It is clear that Robert Trimbole was an active member, if not principal (of the gang)...both in Australia and the United Kingdom.' By that time, Trimbole had fled Australia. He left on 7 May 1981 — tipped off, allegedly, by corrupt NSW police officers that Mr Justice Stewart's 'Mr Asia' inquiries were soon to begin.

The 'Mr Asia' gang was run by Terrence Clark; it was based in Sydney, it was worth an estimated $85 million, and its tentacles spread through Australia, South East Asia, Europe and the Pacific region. Clark, who died in 1983 after serving two years of a life sentence for murder, was known personally to have killed four members of his own gang. Two others, drug couriers Douglas and Isabel Wilson, were shot to death not long after they had given police in Brisbane information about the syndicate. Their bodies were found in a shallow grave at Rye on the Mornington Peninsula in Victoria. Police alleged they had evidence that Trimbole, who acted as caretaker leader of the syndicate for Clark, organised their execution. In August 1980, Trimbole was ordered to give evidence at the Wilsons' inquest; but the Victorian Supreme Court ruled soon after the inquest began that Trimbole did not have to appear before it on the ground that he might incriminate himself. A witness, a courier called 'Miss X', told the inquest she heard Trimbole and Clark discussing the murders, and said she believed Trimbole had arranged the killings. Trimbole was again named as a co-conspirator with Clark during the 'Mr Asia' trial at which Clark was found guilty of murder.

With Trimbole absent from Australia, the evidence continued to mount. In March 1982 came the most important development of all. Victorian police arrested a Melbourne business-

man, *Gianfranco Tizzoni, and charged him
with conspiracy, trafficking and possession of
marijuana. Tizzoni elected to break the Mafia
code of silence, Omerta, and tell all he knew
about 'La Famiglia.' Senior police called him
the most important informer in Australian
history. He made a deal under which he was to
be given a new identity, a new background
which would enable him to live in anonymity
overseas, and indemnity from further
prosecution. What he told investigators was that
Trimbole had ordered all three murders – those
of Mackay and the Wilsons – and that the
actual shooting had been carried out by James
Frederick Bazley. In each case Tizzoni himself
had been the middle-man who had made the
contract with Bazley. Tizzoni pleaded guilty to a
charge of having conspired to murder Mackay,
and was convicted on 20 November 1984.
Sentenced to eight years' jail on two counts of
conspiracy, he was paroled on 7 February 1986,
and placed immediately under police protection.
Bazley was sentenced on 16 April 1986 to life
imprisonment for the murders of the Wilsons and
to nine years' jail for conspiracy to murder
Mackay; the lesser charge relating to Mackay's
death, the Supreme Court was told, resulted from
the killing having taken place outside the
jurisdiction of the Victorian police.*

*Meantime, Trimbole – accused of organising
murders, trafficking in marijuana and heroin,
corruption of police and public servants,
laundering of money and fixing of horseraces –
remained free. After he fled Australia he was
reported to have been in hiding in Italy, France
and Switzerland . . . and was finally tracked
down in Ireland, masquerading as a retired
businessman called Michael Pius Hanbury. He
was arrested on the outskirts of Dublin after
booking out of a hospital following tests for
cancer. A legal battle began immediately for his
extradition to Australia. It lasted five months,
and was at times intense. At one stage, in October
1984, he was freed by the High Court in Dublin
of a 'holding' charge of carrying firearms, only to
be re-arrested immediately on 13 new charges,
including the murder of Donald Mackay. On 7
February 1985, after a great deal of wrangling
through Ireland's legal system, the Irish Supreme
Court freed Trimbole. He vanished again, and
the following month, on 16 March, the full*

*bench of the Irish Supreme Court upheld the
decision to free him. Loopholes were found to
exist in Australia's extradition arrangements,
and Trimbole's original arrest in Dublin was
judged to be 'a violation of his constitutional
rights'. The Attorney-General, Lionel Bowen,
who was acting Prime Minister at the time,
vowed that Trimbole would be 'followed to the
ends of the earth' – but the Godfather from
Griffith was gone.*

*Trimbole's whereabouts remained a mystery until
his death near the Spanish resort town of Alicante
in May 1987. Australian police, who described him
as 'the most wanted man in Australian criminal
history', had flown to Europe twice in 1985
following reports that he was living in Spain – but
were unable to trace him.*

*From Dublin, after the man who had arranged
three murders had been set free, John Stevens wrote
a report for the Melbourne Age. Here is an extract:*

Had you listened very carefully, you might
have heard a ghostly peal of mocking
laughter echoing over the spires and grey
tenement roofs of this comfortable old city
yesterday. It would have come a little before
midday, when five bewigged judges of the
highest court in the land were solemnly
confirming that Robert Trimbole walked out
of Mountjoy Prison nearly six weeks ago with
the full sanction of the Irish law.

Their honors threw out the state's attempt
to have the Australian crime boss and
alleged murderer rearrested, not that the
effect of their deliberations mattered two
hoots to the said Robert T.

Nobody imagined Mr Trimbole would have
been fool enough to wait around in Ireland to
oblige the police should the result go against
him. Assuredly the bird had flown and the
laughter came wafting in on far-off breezes.

So ended the five-month farce of the
attempt to extradite Australia's most wanted
man. Now what?

Prospecting for information is a futile and
confusing exercise in this city, where those
who don't know anything are prepared to tell
you everything – "Another pint? Don't mind
if I do" – while those who should be saying
things work on the principle that a soft, waffly
answer turneth away the wrath of public

curiosity, and at the same time keeps everyone out of trouble. You can find any number of people with Trimbole theories: he took his family out in a private plane to Spain; no, he's in Italy; the daughter and girlfriend left by normal commercial aircraft and Mr Trimbole joined them in Switzerland; no, I happen to know he's still in Dublin.

But yesterday attempts to put questions to the Irish Minister for Justice and the Attorney-General met with the same amazing response – it would not be proper to comment. This is after all legal processes have been exhausted.

The Australian ambassador, Sir Peter Lawler, would not comment on the judgment. The Irish police will say little. The Australian detective who followed Mr Trimbole to Dublin does not give information to the press and the legal representative of the Australian Attorney-General's Department has been advised to button his lip following his attempts to be helpful and candid when Mr Trimbole was released.

And on 17 April 1986, the day after Bazley had been sentenced to life imprisonment for the murders of the Wilsons and conspiracy to murder Mackay, Jenny Conley wrote for the Age*:*

The 60-year-old former painter and docker yesterday heard a jury pronounce him guilty of conspiring to murder the anti-drugs crusader Donald Mackay in 1977, and guilty of the contract murders of the heroin couriers Isabel and Douglas Wilson in 1979. He was also convicted of stealing about $260,000 from Downards Security in 1978.

The man who was paid $10,000 for his part in the conspiracy to murder Donald Mackay, and $20,000 for the Wilson murders, sat impassive.

Bazley is a loner, a lover of poodles. He admits he has "not led a good life" and has no friends. But, telling the jury he hoped they would "pardon the way I speak, as I have not had much education", Bazley pleaded not guilty to the Wilson killings and the Mackay murder conspiracy. He says he is a Christian who treasures "the sanctity of human life".

Donald Mackay

He was first married in 1944, at the age of 19, when he had just become involved in crime. They had a son, Barry. After seven years they separated and Bazley moved in with his present wife, Lillian.

At 22, Bazley had his first encounter with the law while working as a bouncer for an illegal baccarat game on the corner of Lonsdale and Elizabeth streets in the city. He carried an unregistered pistol.

Bazley's 39-year criminal history is studded with bizarre events. He is a veteran of union violence on the waterfront and has changed his appearance several times. He was dubbed the "Maxwell Smart" of bank robbers after his getaway in a 1975 armed hold-up was foiled by a one-legged butcher.

Just before Christmas 1964 Bazley was charged over the robbery under arms of £1437 from a Collingwood ANZ bank and was remanded in custody. Pentridge officers said no holding warrants were sent to the jail, apart from a warrant for detention over a small debt. The debt was paid and Bazley was released.

Soon after his recapture in early 1965, Bazley escaped from the Carlton watchhouse. He was again recaptured, this time after a struggle in Toorak Road, South Yarra. He had been spotted window-shopping with a woman in South Yarra's exclusive stores.

In 1969 he was released from Pentridge and

went back to work on the wharves. By 1972 Bazley had become involved in waterfront union elections, standing as a candidate for vigilance officer.

The year was described by Mr Frank Costigan, in the final report of his Royal Commission on the Painters and Dockers, as one of "mayhem" on the wharves. It was marked by car bombings, house bombings, hit-and-run "accidents", shootings and murder.

Bazley, who says he was then breeding poodles, spent September of that year recovering in the Royal Melbourne Hospital after being shot twice in Station Street, North Carlton, only yards from his home in MacPherson Street. Police said Bazley had "some bad enemies", but he had survived two ambushes in four months. They said he did not scare easily.

Bazley had earlier been defeated in the election for vigilance officer. Mr Costigan reported that another union member, Jack Nicholls, who later became secretary of the union, had asserted that Bazley had attempted to frame him over certain crimes. The husband of Bazley's sister had his kneecap destroyed by a gunshot fired by an unidentified assailant. Bazley, who was a member of the William Longley faction, was shot at by occupants of passing cars.

Bill "the Texan" Longley was convicted in October 1973 of the murder of Patrick Shannon, secretary of the union.

During his trial, Bazley said he left the wharves because "I was getting too old for the work".

His reappearance in police files was in February 1975 when he robbed the ANZ Bank in Gardiner of $10,000. His escape was thwarted by a one-legged butcher from the shop next door.

He was granted bail despite strenuous objections from the police prosecutor who claimed Bazley could pay his $4000 surety out of the unrecovered proceeds of an armed robbery earlier that year. Bazley absconded, and yet another search was launched.

In 1979, while still a fugitive, he was made heir to three deceased estates which, according to police, would have made him a wealthy man. The publicity did not tempt him out of hiding, however, and it was not until 1980 that he resurfaced. Sydney police had

arrested him in possession of a stolen car.

Police did not immediately recognise him; his nose had been altered and his hair changed. But a fingerprint check identified him.

Bazley pleaded guilty in the Criminal Court to the 1975 Gardiner armed robbery, and in February 1982 was sentenced to nine years' jail with a minimum non-parole term of six-and-a-half years.

He was still serving that sentence yesterday when, stony-faced, he heard Mr Justice Gray sentence him to life imprisonment.

After Trimbole's death, Bruce Wilson reported from Alfaz del Fi in Spain that Australian police had arrived to identify the body of Trimbole, 'a person they were totally incapable of finding when he was alive'. A press conference by a Spanish magistrate signalled the last ignoble episode in the career of Robert Trimbole. In the Melbourne Herald, *19 May 1987, Wilson wrote about the bizarre events of the day:*

Judge Jose Louis Buiz, a bright man of 29 in sneakers and an open-necked shirt, said that so far as he was concerned the case of Robert Trimbole had ended. No autopsy, no blocking of moving the cadaver back to Australia. As they say in Spanish, no problemos.

Much of the day was high farce. To get into the room where the body of Trimbole was lying they had to whistle up the grave-diggers at the local cemetery in Villa Joyosa.

They were expecting company. Instead of the usual dungarees they were wearing identical tracksuits as if they were about to compete in an undertakers' athletic event. Orders, one said.

The door swung open to reveal the corpse of Robert Trimbole.

He was no longer naked but covered in a sheet. The breeze-block upon which his head rested was covered in a tasteful plastic shopping bag.

The suit in which his son, Mr Craig Trimbole, had him dressed was still missing.

Also missing was Mr Craig Trimbole, but it seems pretty sure he was in Madrid organising the transportation of his father's yellowing body back to Australia for burial.

Certainly Robert Trimbole's mistress's daughter, Melanie Wittig, was in Madrid. She telephoned former school mates here today and said she was going to Australia by way of England.

Melanie is thought to be with Craig Trimbole and her mother, Marie Ann Presland, Robert Trimbole's longtime de facto wife.

The step-daughter in this godfather saga is the most tragic figure of all. Melanie's teachers at the international school here said she was a sad and lonely girl. But she also was well known in nearby Benidorm, one of Spain's major beach resorts and a mecca for expatriates from all around Europe seeking sun and anonymity.

The girl who had trouble with her lessons at school was the same girl who cruised the bars in Benidorm with a handful of 1000-peseta notes buying drinks for her classmates. Melanie is 17, but some of her drinking companions were 12.

One of these she called tonight and said she thought she would never see any of her friends again. She said that once again her life was changing and that she did not know where she was going and when she would arrive but she thought her next stop would be London and then Sydney.

In the meantime, Judge Buiz, of the First Instruction of the Civil and Criminal Court of Benidorm, said he considered the identification of Robert Trimbole to be positive.

He said that no charges were outstanding against Trimbole in Spanish law and no charges were outstanding against any members of Trimbole's family.

He said he had ruled out the possibility that Trimbole was poisoned because of what he described as convincing medical evidence that Trimbole had died of a heart attack. He said that Trimbole had been admitted to hospital "in a proper manner" and had been in intensive care for eight hours before dying.

Trimbole's house today was being manned by its owner, Senor Antonio Moreno, who said Trimbole had been his close friend and that he did not believe one word of the allegations against Trimbole.

He said he was deeply distressed about the entire affair and had been at the hospital when Trimbole died. He also said that if we did not leave the premises he would get his shotgun and blow our heads off.

Senor Moreno said that Mr Trimbole was up to date with his rent, but then said that he paid no rent. He said he considered Mr Trimbole to be "family" and said he was deeply disturbed to hear that Mr Trimbole might have had mafia connections.

Senor Moreno said that he did not want to lose his good name through being associated with mafiosi.

He said he would call the police and when it was pointed out to him that he might not have to call them, rather they would be calling on him, he once again mentioned the shotgun.

Some Australian television crews arrived and Senor Moreno tried his best to stir into action a large but sleepy German shepherd dog to deter the cameramen. The dog, however, woke only long enough to wag its tail and yawn. Clearly it was as fond of the sun in southern Spain as was Mr Trimbole.

Senor Moreno then resorted to a club which he swung about his head with great vigor. However it was difficult to take it seriously.

A large cameraman from one commercial network said in fluent Australian: "Come near me with that mate and I'll throw you over the bloody fence." This was then translated to Senor Moreno and when last seen he was alone with his thoughts.

Apart from the spending money given to Melanie there is no sign that Robert Trimbole lived a life of luxury.

Spanish authorities on this strip of coastline known generically as the Costa Blanca said privately that there could be two, 200 or 2000 Robert Trimboles living here. They said that their main aim was to prohibit their entry, but once in, it was almost impossible to track them down.

1985 A newspaper publishes reports of taped phone calls...
and later a High Court judge is charged before a jury

EVAN WHITTON, JANET HAWLEY AND PRUE INNES
Sydney Morning Herald, 6 and 8 July 1985 and Melbourne Age, 29 April 1986

*In February 1984 Bob Bottom, a former
adviser on organised crime to the NSW Government, handed to the* Age *newspaper a great
deal of material. . .the result of illegal tapping
of telephone conversations by members of the
NSW Police Force. These tapes embraced the
entire spectrum of organised crime, from
shop-lifting through race-fixing to drug
trafficking, and if authentic, they indicated
a degree of corruption in high places. They
came to be known as 'the Age tapes', although
an earlier, far less complete version, had been
published in the* National Times *in November
1983.*

As Bottom wrote later in his book
Connections, *disclosure of some of the phone
tap material in the* Age *resulted in a plethora
of inquiries and charges against various people.
He went on : 'No newspaper could have published all of the material, anyway. Apart from
any limitations due to restrictive libel laws,
the tap material encompassed 524 foolscap
pages of typed transcripts and police reports
covering 3980 tapped conversations, as well as
voice cassettes recording 11 more conversations.
In print form, they would fill two to three
ordinary-sized novels. Moreover, the material
as a whole represented but a miniscule sample
of material gathered by NSW police from
tapping operations over seven years.'*

The Age *began publication of a series of
reports, based on the tapes and written by the
investigative team of Lindsay Murdoch and
David Wilson, early that February. The tapes
had been taken in 1979 and 1980, certainly in
breach of the law. Editorially, the* Age *suggested a possible motive: that certain members
of the NSW police force had become thoroughly
frustrated and disillusioned by the failure of
their senior officers over a number of years to*

*pursue cases against politically well-connected
members of the NSW criminal community, and
the frequency with which known criminals
were alerted to impending prosecutions. The
paper argued that, in their frustration, and in
the belief that nothing was being done to clean
up corruption in the NSW force, the police
might well have resorted to illegal telephone
taps to obtain evidence which could not be
ignored by their superiors. It added that it did
not condone such illegal actions, but had
sympathy for honest police whose best efforts
might have been foiled by corrupt superiors.*

*The first article in the series — headlined
'Secret tapes of judge' — linked a senior judge
to a network of influence involving politicians,
police, public servants and businessmen. Its
publication began an extraordinary trail of
events, culminating in the unparalleled prosecution and conviction of the third-ranking
judge of the highest court in the nation.
Justice Lionel Murphy, a former Federal
Attorney-General in the Whitlam Government
and a justice of the High Court of Australia,
was found guilty in September 1985 of having
attempted to pervent the course of justice. He
was sentenced to 18 months' jail. That conviction was later quashed by five judges of the
NSW Court of Appeal, and a retrial was
ordered. At the second trial before the NSW
Supreme Court, in April 1986, Justice Murphy,
63, was found not guilty. Afterwards he
described the action as a 'political trial'. His
ordeal had lasted two years, and it constituted
one of the nation's great legal sagas.*

*In February 1984, soon after publication of
the phone-tap reports, the* Age *handed to the
Federal and NSW Attorneys-General copies of
tapes and transcripts. The Commonwealth's
special prosecutor, Ian Temby QC, was re-*

quested to examine the authenticity of the material, the illegality of the phone-tapping, and any breaches of the law that might have been shown by their content. On 28 February, the day Temby's task was announced in Parliament, the leader of the National Party, Ian Sinclair, named the Sydney solicitor Morgan Ryan as a central figure in the affair. No public mention of Justice Murphy's name was made until March 6 . . . and then it was not in Federal Parliament, but in the Queensland Parliament – by that state's Minister for Transport, Don Lane.

The judge's name was later mentioned in the House of Representatives, when the Opposition Leader, Andrew Peacock, referred to the gravity of allegations against Lionel Murphy and others. The next day the combined forces of the Opposition set in train a Senate select committee whose charge it was to inquire whether the tapes were genuine, and, if so, whether they revealed misbehaviour by the judge which could have justified his removal from office. It was the first of two Senate inquiries, and at both of them evidence was given alleging that Lionel Murphy had attempted to influence the outcome of a case in which Morgan Ryan was facing committal proceedings. One piece of evidence which became the subject of great argument, then and later, was a reference by the Chief Magistrate of NSW, Clarrie Briese, to a phone call from Lionel Murphy. In it the judge was alleged to have asked the chief magistrate: 'Now what about my little mate?' The little mate was claimed to be Morgan Ryan, and various interpretations were put on the significance of the alleged remark. Morgan Ryan had been in trouble in 1981-82 in relation to charges of conspiracy involving an alleged South Korean immigration racket.

The report of the first Senate committee, delivered on 24 August 1984, was inconclusive, and split along party lines. Three Labor senators found evidence against Briese insufficient for a prima facie case against Murphy, two Liberals found it sufficient, and one Democrat was undecided. The committee made no finding on the authenticity of the tapes. On 6 September 1984 the Senate appointed a second committee, assisted by commissioners, to probe the allegations made by

Briese. Justice Murphy declined to appear before the Senate committee. His counsel, Tom Hughes QC, made a statement that the proceedings were being conducted in a 'highly politicised environment', and it would be inappropriate for the judge to appear because he 'could become a political football.' On the day the second Senate committee made its report, Lionel Murphy went on leave from the High Court. The majority finding of the committee was that the judge could be guilty of misbehaviour which could justify his removal from the court, because of a possibility of an attempt to influence the Ryan case. It was stressed before the Senate (by the president of the Law Council of Australia, C. W. Pincus QC) that 'proved misbehaviour' – not necessarily a specific criminal offence – would be enough to justify the judge's removal from office by Parliament under Section 72 of the Constitution.

On 13 December 1984, the issue became something more than one involving Parliament and the Constitution. Ian Temby QC laid two charges alleging that Lionel Murphy had attempted to pervert the course of justice. A High Court judge was now, for the first time in Australia's history, charged with a criminal offence. The committal proceedings began in March 1985 before a Sydney magistrate, Arthur Riedel; they culminated in his decision to send Lionel Murphy to trial. The trial went before Justice Henry Cantor, of the NSW Supreme Court, and a jury the following June; and resulted in a verdict of guilty on one of the two charges, and a sentence of 18 months' jail.

On 28 November 1985, five judges of the NSW Court of Appeal quashed the conviction of attempting to pervert the course of justice and ordered a retrial for Lionel Murphy. Twenty-one questions of law had been referred to the Full Bench by Justice Cantor at the request of Murphy's defence after the jury had found him guilty on the charge involving Briese. The Full Bench, comprising the Chief Justice of NSW, Sir Laurence Street, and Justices Hope, Glass, Samuels and Priestly, found that the trial judge had erred on four points of law, and that was enough to conclude that the trial had miscarried. Afterwards Lionel Murphy told a crowd outside the court:

'I have every confidence I will be cleared at a retrial.'

That confidence proved to be justified on 18 April 1986, when a jury consisting of six men and six women in the NSW Supreme Court found him not guilty of the charge of having attempted to pervert the course of justice. The court ordeal ended when Justice Murphy heard the trial judge, Justice David Hunt, announce: 'Lionel Keith Murphy, you are discharged.' Murphy had taken the unexpected step of making an unsworn statement, which meant that he would not be subject to cross-examination. Speaking directly to the 12 jurors, he had said: 'I at no time whatever had any intention to pervert the course of justice, and I made no attempt to do so. I never asked in any shape or way or form that Jones (a magistrate) be spoken to, let alone be asked to pervert the course of justice, to act contrary to his duty.'

Within days, Mr Temby disclosed that he had rejected advice to prosecute the judge on other allegations against him.

On 7 May, the federal Government announced a commission of three retired judges to inquire into Lionel Murphy's conduct. Its task would be to address the question of possible misbehaviour under Section 72 of the Constitution. On 6 July, before the inquiry was completed, it was revealed that Murphy had inoperable cancer. Against the wishes of the Chief Justice, Sir Harry Gibbs, Murphy decided to resume his seat on the High Court Bench on 1 August.

The Hawke Government decided that Murphy's illness was sufficient reason to end the judicial commission inquiring into his conduct. Legislation enabling its dissolution was introduced into Parliament in late August.

Lionel Murphy left the High Court of Australia on 7 August 1986. He died in October that year, aged 64. In Time Australia *I wrote of him: 'He was . . . one of the great reformists of our age, and many of his judgments show him to have been a champion of the rights of the accused, a man who based his opinions on an individual view of justice rather than a web of precedents. He was an idealist who combined a nobility of purpose with a compulsive larrikinism. He offended many because he defied a number of conventions that went with his high post, and because he generally behaved in too knockabout a fashion. He was Don Quixote with a little mate. On his way to windmills, he sometimes took short cuts.'*

Some of the best reporting of the first trial came from Evan Whitton, of the Sydney Morning Herald. *After the night verdict, he wrote in the issue of 6 July:*

The impact of the historic verdict in the Murphy case came twice: with the sharp inhalation that met the foreman's announcement of Justice Murphy's guilt at 9.29 pm, and again 11 minutes later when Justice Henry Cantor referred to him as "the prisoner".

Murphy himself revealed little of what he was feeling. He looked quite wretched, with baggy eyes, as he waited for the verdict, but when it came he blinked, looked down and then up, and briefly at the jury, but his expression did not change.

Nor did that of the heavy-lidded Crown Prosecutor, Mr Ian Callinan, QC, of Queensland, who has developed influenza.

Counsel for Murphy, Mr Alex Shand, QC, has not been in the court since Thursday.

Most of the overt emotion came from the jury, who had been deliberating for some 21 hours over a period of elapsed time of 34 hours. Two women appeared to be fighting back tears, and the foreman, a heavy-set man in early middle age with butter-coloured hair, seemed to have developed a habit of biting his knuckles. He shook his head and permitted himself a small wry grin when the judge advised them they could sit on other juries if they were called.

The previous night, Thursday, there had been, in the way of these things, rumours that the jury had reached an early verdict on one charge, and that when the judge wanted to lock them up at 9 pm that night, they had felt a little more time would produce a verdict.

Certainly, a police officer and a prison officer appeared in court that night, but, in the event, the jury was locked up at 9.30.

They proposed to resume their deliberations at 9 am yesterday, and Murphy arrived a minute ahead of time, only to find the doors of the old Banco Court still closed, and he was obliged to wait in St James Road, with television cameras so pressing in on him that one of his solicitors, Sir Clarence Harders, remonstrated sharply with the crews.

As was his wont throughout the trial, Murphy presented a cheery face when the court business was not proceeding, and after this ordeal by camera, he greeted his old friend, Mr Jack Dwyer, 73, formerly of the Miscellaneous Workers' Union, who has attended every day except one at some risk to a heart condition. Murphy said: "I don't mind pictures, but not when they start hassling. They've got zoom lenses."

With Mr Shand elsewhere, Murphy began to write furiously late in the morning when Justice Cantor was answering some questions the jury had put. After the jury left, Mr Linton Morris, QC, for Murphy, was making a submission to the judge and was holding the piece of paper from Murphy in his hand.

Mr Morris, however, appeared to have difficulty in deciphering the writing and finally begged leave to have a five-minute adjournment, during which Murphy, referred to unkindly by some thereafter, as "the learned accused", explained the point he wanted made.

The NSW Solicitor-General, Miss Mary Gaudron, was in court with the Murphy entourage for a short time in the evening, but left after what appeared to be a second false alarm. The barristers sat in the court from 8 pm to 8.30 pm and then walked out. Asked what was happening, Mr Callinan said: "You tell me and we'll both know."

At 9.20 a court official kindly suggested to those who were outside having a smoke that it might be in their interest to move inside, among the 100 or so people, including some lawyers a little fatigued from the admission ceremonies for solicitors and barristers that had proceeded earlier in the Banco Court.

At 9.26 Justice Cantor returned to the court with the fateful words: "I've been informed there is a verdict," and there then ensued an extraordinary period of some three minutes of absolute quiet in the court, while the jury were being fetched, until Justice Cantor's associate put it to the jury: "How say ye . . .?", and the

remarkable career of Justice Murphy was, it must be assumed, over.

Two days later, on 8 July, he wrote again about Murphy's ordeal in court:

Three aspects of the personality of Justice Lionel Murphy stood out during his 21-day ordeal in Sydney's old Banco Court.

First, in the witness box Justice Murphy revealed the supple and agile mind of a great advocate and jurist. His answers suggested that, to such a mind, very few questions were susceptible to simple answers, that questions carried nuances that needed to be elaborated to give a fair answer.

The risk in this was that members of the jury, lacking such agility of mind, might have interpreted, or misinterpreted, such an approach as perhaps indicative of a mind not so much subtle as slippery, and a general desire to answer any question but the one asked.

It would be quite in line with the evidence brought on behalf of Justice Murphy that his devotion to the law was such that this risk, if it was a risk, would have to be taken in the interests of answering fully, properly and appropriately.

Second, there was the Murphy of the adjournments. Here, his attitude may be compared, for example, with that of Mr Robert Trimbole in the Dublin courts.

Trimbole, thought to be facing death by incarceration or cancer, or both, was pretty glum until a solicitor from an English firm with a large criminal practice was brought over to Dublin. At each break, he maintained a constant flow of babble at Trimbole, and eventually managed to extract a smile that revealed for the first time the famous gap in the teeth.

I asked the English lawyer if his role was to cheer up the accused. "Pretty much," he said.

In the Murphy case, this useful role seemed at times to have been taken on by the accused himself. Here, he was the little mate (if that phrase can ever again be used without a wince) of all the world, in particular with a small group of supporters.

Among these were:

• Gnarled old Jack Dwyer, 73, formerly of the Miscellaneous Workers' Union, who found a front row seat near the well of the court every day bar one in mute encouragement for the man he called "the best mate I ever had".

• Ingrid, Murphy's wife of 16 years, a trim woman with a small face vaguely reminiscent of Nefertiti, a mouth often set in a quizzical expression, a retrousse nose and brown hair swept aloft bouffant style. After she gave evidence, Mrs Murphy appeared in a range of tailored suits, grey, white, terra cotta, cream.

(By contrast, Justice Murphy stuck throughout to a blue pinstripe, except for one day when he turned up in that sort of electric silver suit Mr Hawke favoured before he became a statesman and which Max Gillies still persists, perversely, in using to portray the great helmsman.)

• His brother, Bill Murphy, formerly a plastics engineer and now a refurbisher of vintage cars. He is a man with something of the look of an Old Testament prophet with his white beard, bald pate and long grey-white hair over his neck.

• Frances Murphy, wife of Bill Murphy, whose sharp, olive face is topped by silver hair tied at the back in a bun.

To raise the spirits of all these, Justice Murphy offered at the breaks an abundance of chatter and jests.

The third Murphy was the man sitting, during the long hours of examination of other witnesses, counsel's addresses and Justice Cantor's summing up, on the arc of red leather behind the barristers.

This was a harder man to read. In the early part of the case, he had a cold and looked pretty wretched. Later, although the cold was cured, he still looked pretty depressed – who would not? – as he sat, one leg over the other, hands clasped and resting on a thigh, his face immobile for hours on end.

It was thus difficult to tell whether this or that piece of evidence, or comment by the judge, suggested to him that the case was running his way, or the reverse.

This is how Janet Hawley, of the Melbourne Age, described the emotional scenes which followed the acquittal at the second trial . . .

As the packed court emptied on to the street, shouting the verdict "Not guilty", Lionel Murphy remained inside, tenderly hugging his sobbing wife Ingrid.

His two young sons, who sat in court for the last three days of the trial, patted their father's back, flushed faces smiling, then running with tears.

The High Court judge's brother, and his wife, and the small devoted band of followers who've sat in court every day of this and the previous trial, joined the group, hugging, kissing, smiling, eyes glistening with tears.

Perhaps Mr Justice Murphy was crying with relief too, but all we could see was his hunched back, and the tears of others dropping on to his shoulders.

This extraordinary, costly, two-year saga, with highly learned tedious, flamboyant, and sometimes shouting-match arguments over the alleged use of seven words – "And now, what about my little mate?" – was finally over.

After the ponderous length every foregoing procedure in the trial had taken, the final scene was remarkably swift.

Mr Justice Hunt had sent the jury of six men and six women out at 10.30 am, to "consider your verdict".

An army of media clustered around the courthouse, waiting. It was anyone's guess how long the jury would deliberate. Veterans remembered waiting until 9.30 pm for the

Justice Lionel Murphy, photographed outside Sydney's Banco Court after being sentenced to 18 months for conspiracy to pervert the course of justice. His wife is beside him. The sentence was later quashed.

verdict at the previous Murphy trial.

At 2.10 pm, court resumed. The jury filed into their seats, all looking very solemn. Not one glanced at Mr Justice Murphy.

While jury watchers were analysing what this body language signified, the foreman (a woman) rose, and with an absence of dramatic pauses delivered the verdict: "Not guilty."

A loud burst of shouting and cheering erupted from the Murphy camp, and at 2.13 pm Mr Justice Murphy was a wholly free man.

Mr Justice Murphy's counsel, Mr Ian Barker QC, left the court looking suitably pleased, another win notched up.

Some moments later, Mr Justice Murphy, surrounded by his family, stood in the spitting rain on the steps outside the courthouse, speaking to the media.

Mrs Murphy, who had remained so composed during the trial, clutched one son's shoulder, her chin trembling with emotion.

Asked how she and the family had coped, she replied: "Just. It was very trying for us all."

The expression on Mr Justice Murphy's face was one of gentle relief when he began to talk, saying he was glad it was all over. "It's been a horrible ordeal for my family and my friends."

It changed to one of warmth, as he thanked "those many tens of thousands of people who sent messages to me throughout this ordeal, those who wanted to assist in some way by subscribing small amounts and large amounts. One of the things I'm going to do is see those who are unknown to me are repaid for what they've done."

His facial expression then switched to anger, as he loudly declared:

"This has been a political trial and I hope there are not going to be more political show trials like this."

The anger, tinged with a triumph, continued, as he answered the question, did he think the reputation of the High Court had been damaged in any way?

"I think the fact a person has been charged and cleared has in no way any effect on the High Court.

"Everyone in this country is able to be charged by private prosecutors, by others, by scalp hunters, by people who wish to advance their own careers – it can happen to you or anyone else. We're all open to be charged, and it's right that a member of the High Court or Parliament or anyone else in the community can be charged. But it's also good we have a jury system to declare their innocence if they are innocent."

Asked what he was going to do now, Mr Justice Murphy hugged his sons and responded with a proud fatherly beam: "The first thing I'm going to do is take these children, and if I can get in, to see 'Crocodile Dundee'."

That unique endorsement spoken, the High Court judge strode off with his family.

In the same newspaper, Age *court reporter Prue Innes, wrote about the 'gamble' Murphy and his legal counsel, Ian Barker QC, had taken.*

On Monday last week, in keeping with what had been a noticeably more relaxed defence, Mr Ian Barker QC, announced that there would be no opening of the defence, and his client was going to make an unsworn statement.

The High Court judge then stood immediately in front of the jurors, asked them directly to be his judges, and for about 30 minutes, told them his side of the story.

What a gamble it was. It was either going to be a very successful move – a simple, direct appeal to the jury, keeping the dispute to a very narrow focus and allowing no cross-examination – or it was going to be seen as an extraordinary thing for the third most senior judge in the land to do.

It was very different at the first trial.

Ten months earlier, Mr Justice Murphy went into the witness box, gave an affirmation, and went through his evidence, first questioned by his own counsel, Mr Alex Shand, QC, then rigorously cross-examined by Mr Ian Callinan, QC. He spent almost four days in the stand.

Altogether Mr Justice Murphy called seven witnesses as well as himself at the first trial. They included his wife, Ingrid, who gave evidence supporting his own that another two couples had been at the Briese dinner on the night of 6 January 1982 – and referred to by the Crown as the "phantom guests". There was no such evidence or suggestion the second time around, and the Brieses were adamant that there were no guests other than the Murphys.

There were great similarities, of course. The backdrop was the same, the decorative but rather small and extremely uncomfortable court, the Crown team was the same, led by Queensland silk Ian Callinan, with Mr Nick Cowdery, a Sydney barrister, and Mr Peter Clarke – now back at the Melbourne bar, but at the time on the staff of the federal director of public prosecutions.

Mr Justice Murphy's team had changed. Ian Barker, QC, who was to have appeared at the first trial but caught hepatitis, was there this time. Alec Shand, QC, stepped in at the last moment last year and ran a very different trial. Ian Barker became known, when he prosecuted Lindy Chamberlain, for his relaxed approach, and his style is very different from Alex Shand's rather frenetic one.

Ian Barker was leisurely, almost chatty, where Alex Shand had been intense, involved, quite keyed up.

But both proved to be gruelling cross-examiners when Mr Clarrie Briese was in the witness box, trying to land as many blows as they could to dent his credibility and suggest to the jury that his evidence should not be accepted uncritically. This time he spent one-and-a-half days in the witness box, most of it under sustained attack.

Mr Briese was virtually the only witness to be cross-examined, except for minor and short points.

Neverthless, some interesting points arose from Mr Briese in the second trial, when for the first time he told the court hearing the charge that he had been persuaded to go public about the doubts he had harbored when the Senate committee investigating the NSW police tapes and Mr Justice Murphy's conduct contacted him. There were a few references to "every little breeze" in the taped conversations.

And the rest, as the saying goes, is history, literally, with the unprecedented trial of one of the most senior judges in the Western world accused of trying to fix a case for a friend.

As Mr Briese gave his evidence of the dinner where he first met Mr Justice Murphy (at Morgan Ryan's house in May 1979 – it was also his first meeting with Morgan Ryan) it was like a few more pieces being fitted into a jigsaw puzzle. The other two guests were Murray Farquhar – about to retire as chief magistrate, with Mr Briese about to take over and the then NSW police commissioner, Merv Wood, who resigned suddenly a month later on the day that Mr Briese was asked to investigate how Mr Farquhar came to deal personally with the highly controversial Cessna-Milner drug case, a prosecution of two men accused of importing 110,000 buddha sticks.

Had the case been sent to trial by a judge and jury, the offence could have earned 15 years in jail. Mr Farquhar, sitting on his last case, gave one man a bond and the other a short jail sentence, and had been asked by the police prosecutor, at Mr Wood's request, to hear the case.

Mr Briese said Mr Farquhar phoned him and asked him not to mention the dinner in his report to the Attorney-General, because, he said, people might misunderstand. Mr Briese kept the dinner out, but did so, he said, because he did not want to drag in Mr Justice Murphy and subject him to guilt by association.

The other small but fascinating fact is that the magistrate whom the Crown says Mr Justice Murphy intended Mr Briese to lean on to benefit Morgan Ryan was Mr Kevin Jones, now dead: the same magistrate who heard the Kevin Humphreys case which eventually led to the Street Royal Commission in 1983 because of concern that the rugby official had not been sent to trial on misappropriation charges.

A sequel to the publication of the 'Age tapes' came in December 1984, when the editor of the Age, *Creighton Burns, was named the Graham Perkin journalist of the year. Sir Theodor Bray, chairman of the judging panel which made the award – which honors the memory of a former distinguished editor of the* Age – *praised Burns' 'courageous and sustained leadership' in bringing organised crime into the public arena.*

1987   Echoes of 1929 as world stock markets tumble

PETER SMARK
Melbourne Herald, 20 October 1987

On 19 October 1987, Black Monday, the stock markets of the world collapsed and, in the week of disaster which followed, the percentage loss on Australian stock exchanges was even worse than those experienced overseas.

The free-fall, and the panic, began when trading opened on that first day in New York; it was a collapse on a scale never seen before, not even in 1929. Prices dropped, dropped, dropped, wiping out an entire year's spectacular gains. By the time the 4 p.m. closing bell rang at the New York Stock Exchange, the Dow Jones index had plunged 508 points, or an incredible 22.6 per cent. Some U.S. 500 billion dollars in paper value, a sum equal to the entire gross national product of France, had vanished. With the losses came fears that a global depression, of the kind ushered in by the Crash of 1929, was on the way. Certainly, in the frenzy of selling which followed Black Monday, stock exchanges in Tokyo, London, Paris, Zurich, Frankfurt, Amsterdam, Hong Kong and New Zealand set records for one-day losses.

That Monday in Australia, which came earlier than the collapse on Wall Street, saw investors' funds worth nine billion dollars disappear from the Australian share market, as the all ordinaries index crashed by a record 80 points. On Tuesday, after the events in New York, Australia's dealers were braced for disaster. It came in a bloodbath which wiped 25 per cent off the value of Australian industrial and resource stocks. Even gold miners were mauled. Wave after wave of selling slashed an unprecedented fifty-five billion dollars off the value of stocks. It was by far the worst day in Australian share market history.

Much blame for what happened on Wall Street was attributed to the United States trade deficit of 156 billion dollars (against a surplus of exports over imports of three billion dollars in 1975), and the resultant United States foreign debt of 250 billion dollars. Computer program trading was judged by many to be a contributor to the panic.

But why did Australia suffer proportionately worse? Apart from the obvious domino effect, Australian economists fixed much blame on the nation's high level of foreign debt and its dependence on commodity exports. But regional factors intruded, too. British and United States based companies which specialised in Pacific Basin investment were forced to unload stocks heavily in Australia after the over-heated Hong Kong Stock Exchange suspended trading after Black Monday.

In the Melbourne Age, economics editor Kenneth Davidson offered some solace: 'The fact that $3.2 billion was wiped off the value of BHP's shares in a day has nothing to do with the price BHP will get for its iron ore, coal or steel tomorrow or the cost of producing them. The dividend BHP pays to its shareholders or what it pays to its suppliers and workers is not determined by the stock exchanges. More generally, the overall movement in share prices has not affected the real worth of the country, only the valuation of that wealth as determined by those who are prepared to buy or sell shares on the day.'

And on 20 October, the day the worst happened on Australian stock exchanges, Peter Smark of the Melbourne Herald submitted that one result of it all might even be a return to investor sanity.

I would draw the attention of all stock market investors today to the latest American Express gift catalogue. Your Wakizashi will set you back only $299.94 or your estate may choose to opt for the six monthly payments, each of $49.99.

The Wakizashi, of course, is the ritual sword used for committing Seppuku (hara-kiri, if you will) and comes in a magnolia wood scabbard to add even more style to the occasion. The quick dash to the window is, well, just a mite vulgar these days, don't you agree?

Is it just possible that we could see this week an outbreak of investor sanity? A rediscovery of things like asset backing, prudent price earnings ratios, "gearing" described more honestly as debt and some of the wide boys doing the splits?

It's bizarre that, at the Melbourne Stock Exchange yesterday, lots of the brokers, bright young men and women, confessed they hadn't experienced a real downer before. Five years the bull market has run and most of them haven't been working that long.

The experts, naturally, are divided about how dodgy the next couple of weeks will be. But it takes a special sort of faith, or blindness, to think yesterday and today have seen the worst of the "technical correction", or bust to you and me.

It's being stressed that the institutions haven't started to sell off yet to large amounts. The finger is pointed at investment pillars like the AMP.

But it's the enormous growth in unit trusts which has funded a large part of that five-year boom. Many of the unit trust managers weren't around in the last bear market. And many of the trusts will have to become big sellers now as financial advisers tell their retirement-planning clients to cash in at least part of their holdings.

Large-scale redemptions are a factor to test the nerve of even veteran investment fund managers. We'll see now what some of them are made of. Many are like the kids on the floor; they've never had a storm to weather.

That small print in the unit trust advertisements about investment records being no guide to the future? This week is an explanation of why they are compelled to insert that.

For quite some time now, Australian shares have been run by the rules of Japanomics without the Yen; investment without regard for prudence . . .

Sensible people have been expecting a bust for some time and have got out of the market. But still banks have gone on lending money to the foolhardy to buy shares. Now, the borrowers will be saddled with the cost of the loans and the sight of a drop in the value of their security.

Well, of their evident security. The real security is the second mortgage on their houses, and this week bricks and mortar are looking pretty good, even if stocks aren't . . .

As a nation, and as individuals, we have fallen into the fool's gold habit of substituting debt for equity, becoming jugglers all in the process. This week, our arms are becoming tired and that's no bad thing.

In the past five years, market valuations of shares have increased several hundred per cent. If the market now falls back 25 per cent overall, as some shrewd people are forecasting, we will have escaped cheaply. Some paper profits may be burned in the process, but one hopes we'll learn a bit, too.

In the huge unit trust industry, investors will learn that one-year and two-year performances mean little, despite the colorful ads with the huge "last year, we made 120%" headlines. Five-year performance through a slump is what matters.

In specific stocks, gearing does matter, despite the "Look Mum, No Hands" operators. And so does asset backing. John Spalvins has been criticised for being a pessimist; in fact, he was just an early realist.

All of this, of course, is written in the expectation that the New York and Tokyo exchanges won't continue to career downwards. If they do, the "correction" could be very severe in its impact on world trade, and our trading position could become even tougher.

Still, let's not be too gloomy. If we're lucky, and we usually are, we'll just realise that the game of Pass the Parcel is over.

If we're unlucky, it's no more Zegna suits for Paul Keating. It's Yakka overalls for the whole lot of us.

1987　A pattern of crime and corruption is revealed in Queensland

PHIL DICKIE
Brisbane Courier-Mail, 8 November 1987

*Early in 1987 a Brisbane journalist, Phil
Dickie, of the* Courier-Mail, *embarked on an
investigation into organised crime in
Queensland. From January to April he wrote a
series of stories, the overall thrust of which was
that organised crime was rife in the northern
capital, and that police condoned this situation.
One of his conclusions was that two groups
controlled prostitution, illegal gambling and
pornography; another, implicit in his assertion
that both groups received police protection, was
that corruption existed, possibly at senior levels,
in the Queensland Police Force.*

*To gather his material, Dickie kept watch on
a large number of brothels and illegal casinos,
thereby managing to acquire the nickname
'Raincoat' from colleagues. He noted and later
checked the registration numbers of cars seen
outside these places, and followed some around.
He trailed some of the people he named as vice
bosses, and he spent a large amount of time
going through documents held by the Valuer-
General, the Lands Office, the Titles Office, the
City Court and the Magistrates' Courts, as well
as the 1985 report by Des Sturgess QC into
prostitution.*

*His articles were met generally with denials
from police and politicians, as well as six writs
alleging defamation. After some stories had been
published, Dickie received a supportive letter
from a former Licensing Branch Officer, Nigel
Powell. The pair met, and became an
investigative team.*

While Dickie's stories were surfacing in the
Courier-Mail, *a television team from the
Australian Broadcasting Corporation's 'Four
Corners' program was also investigating crime
and police bribery in Queensland. It was headed
by Chris Masters, who had won acclaim for his
earlier TV programs on corruption in New*
*South Wales and the bombing of the Greenpeace
yacht* Rainbow Warrior *in New Zealand. His
first leads on the Queensland situation had
come from what he described as an informal,
nation-wide network of honest police.*

*One story he heard was that a senior officer
in north Queensland had bribed his subordinate
to cover up for drug traffickers. He received
information about syndicates involved in
prostitution, drugs and illegal gambling, and at
one stage learned that a regional police
superintendent had advised an illegal casino
operator to close down for a while because the
'Four Corners' team was in town. In May the
TV program called 'The Moonlight State' went
to air; in it Masters supported Dickie's claims,
and made further charges of police graft and
corruption.*

*On 13 May the Queensland Government
announced that a judicial inquiry would be held
into allegations by Dickie and Masters. Tony
Fitzgerald QC, a former Federal Court judge,
was appointed to take charge of the inquiry. The
acting Premier Bill Gunn, who announced the
probe into police corruption and organised
crime, expected it to last six weeks. A year later
it was still gathering stride, with the police
chief, Sir Terence Lewis, under suspension
along with two senior Cabinet ministers, and a
vast amount of corruption conceded by officers
who had accepted offers of immunity from
prosecution in exchange for sworn evidence.
Early in the proceedings the Commissioner had
persuaded the Government to broaden the terms
of reference, so that some historical perspective
might be gained. Corruption, it quickly
emerged, was no creation of the middle and late
1980s. It had been entrenched in the
Queensland police system for a long time.*

The inquiry embraced some of the most

powerful figures in Queensland, including the Premier, Sir Joh Bjelke-Petersen. It may even have been a factor in his departure from office. Certainly his successor, Mike Ahern, and the man who was deputy to both, Bill Gunn, claimed that Sir Joh's desire to terminate the inquiry prematurely was a cause of the bizarre events of November 1987, when Bjelke-Petersen tried to sack five of his own ministers and finally found himself removed from office. Sir Joh denied this vehemently, leaving only one unhappy conclusion open: that one Premier or the other was a blatant liar.

The Taxation Department was an interested observer of the Fitzgerald inquiry. Within a few months it was seeking three million dollars in unpaid taxes from two brothel owners and 800,000 dollars from a former police officer and alleged bagman, Jack Herbert, who had been arrested in London. By April 1988 more than 100 police, businessmen and criminals named at the inquiry were under investigation by a special taxation unit set up in Queensland, from which an observer attended all public sittings of the commission.

What emerged, as the Fitzgerald inquiry scrutinised the interaction between government, police, judiciary, business and organised crime, was a picture of a State where a pattern of apparently respectable roguery had developed over several decades. Practices which would have been unacceptable elsewhere were not only tolerated in Queensland, but were seen as normal and proper. For his reports on crime and corruption, Phil Dickie was awarded Australia's highest journalistic award, the Gold Walkley. Here he writes of the investigation which helped bring about the Fitzgerald inquiry (still proceeding when this book went to press):

It has been a long way down the road to Fitzgerald: all the way from a silly season news idea to an inquiry that seems destined to change Queensland.

In December, politicians go on holidays, the courts close down, the newsroom goes quiet – and chiefs of staff go through torment trying to keep journalists gainfully employed.

It was on just such a day that the former chief of staff of The Courier-Mail, Bob Gordon, who had become fascinated with a Fortitude Valley building housing a massage parlor, a tattooist, a sex shop and a dubious photographic studio, asked me to find out who owned it.

"Sin triangle," he called it. I took his assignment and thereafter muttered, "I'm working on it," whenever he asked. A month later I had a story naming who was who in two groups controlling most of the 21 Brisbane brothels I had found in that time.

It was somewhat nervously received. "If you've got any of this wrong, Dickie, it is more than your salary," said one former editorial executive.

From that story, I wrote another – and eventually a whole succession which put me, a touch nervously, into the witness box before Mr Gerald (Tony) Fitzgerald, QC.

Earlier advice for weeks from all around was that barristers ate journalists for breakfast. It isn't true.

One result of that January article was that the Police Minister, Mr Gunn, was moved to say there was "no evidence that massage parlors were used for prostitution." He wasn't widely believed, and I went on to meet some others interested in gathering evidence for him.

Notably they included Chris Masters, Debbie Whitmont and Shaun Hoyt of the ABC *Four Corners* team and one Nigel Powell, a former police officer and man of conscience who, without the backing of any large organisation like The Courier-Mail or the ABC, put his whole future on the line.

There are others too who are best not named – those who risked life and occupation to tell or to help.

Someone who had perhaps been watching too much television dubbed the other side the Black Hand Gang so we, by way of contrast, ended up as the White Hand Gang.

I am often asked why I did this at all, why I persisted with a story which at first netted nothing but official denials. My initial answer is always because it was a story – more than one – and good stories at that.

That is only a part of it. The rest is that it

was right, felt the right thing to do in the very core of me. With that feeling inside, you are somehow insulated against any array of denials, threats or chief of staff's requests to go and cover the Alderley church fete because he has no one else to do it.

That is not to say I did not sometimes feel tangibly afraid. I dare say my father well remembers the call I made from a Valley nightspot when, more than a little tired and emotional, I suddenly remembered I had two children and no will.

And my response to being caught in the roof of the carpark of an illegal casino building by Geraldo Bellino was definitely of the "Oh – ! What do I do now?" kind. I argued while an enterprising cadet photographer clicked away with his camera.

That had happened but a few days after I had gone to the District Court to watch Geraldo Bellino in a civil action, in the course of which he denied connections I had alleged back in January. I filled in a quiet spot in the evidence by sketching him in my notebook, standard issue, journalists for the use of.

It is easy, far too easy, to romanticise the shadowing, following and watching aspects of my five-month dig into the underworld and its police connections.

The truth is that a lot of even this is dead dull. All the hours when nothing happens, nothing of significance is seen and you are just tired with nothing to show for it.

Huge numbers of hours that will never make good newspaper copy are spent in front of the counters of government departments chasing bits of paper that turn out to be invaluably precious or totally useless. You get to be fairly good at reading documents upside down while some clerk, at glacial pace, decides whether you are entitled to have it in your hot little hand.

Much more interesting are the conversations you agree to have never had with people you agree to have never met. Some of them wore uniforms and risked a lot. Others work for those who have great cause to be displeased at what you write.

There can be the quick jotting down of notes outside to get some recollection of a recent conversation down, or the copying down in an unobtrusive place of the registration numbers written on your arm.

Noted Sydney journalist, Evan Whitton, hearing me detail this from the witness box, was heard to mutter: "Why didn't he use a matchbox?"

Half an armful of registration numbers is more than any matchbox will take.

The rewards now do seem worth it – first there were the magic moments when something just discovered, uncovered or heard enabled a bit more of the jigsaw puzzle to fall into place. The significance of something is just as likely to come to you in the shower or the middle of the night as when you are shuffling pieces of paper around a desk.

Then comes the satisfaction of seeing a story in print after negotiating it through the lawyers and ringing the standard questions through to get the standard denials. They become so predictable I could have written them myself.

I well remember my feelings when I realised there was to be an inquiry led by someone who didn't seem likely to take to me, the *Four Corners* team and Nigel Powell, with a bucket of whitewash.

My first reaction to the name Tony Fitzgerald was "Who?". Now it is he who has done an exemplary job of a most difficult enterprise.

I know from my knowledge of where the tangled threads lead that it will take yet more skill and courage on the part of Mr Fitzgerald and his team to pursue it to the end. I believe the man has it and I am not displeased to have had something to do with giving him his job.

My colleagues have heaped honor on me, most tangibly in the form of a Walkley Award. No matter what our critics in high places say, journalism is an honorable profession – and there is such a thing as the public interest to be defended.

1987 After nineteen years as Premier, Sir Joh makes an unwilling exit

PETER CHARLTON
Brisbane Courier-Mail, 25 November 1987

Sir Johannes Bjelke-Petersen, whom many would regard as the most successful Australian politician of his time, ruled the State of Queensland in bizarre fashion. And that is the way he left the leadership, on 1 December 1987.

Gough Whitlam, when Prime Minister, called him 'a Bible-bashing bastard . . . a paranoid, a bigot and fanatical'. Bob Hawke described him before a 1986 election as 'sick and demented', and Bill Hayden opined at the same time that he was 'dropping his marbles all over the place'. Sir Joh won that election and in fact inflicted many hurtful wounds over the years on the party led at various times by Whitlam, Hayden and Hawke.

Joh Bjelke-Petersen was a peanut farmer from Kingaroy. He was born in New Zealand, in January 1911, where his Danish-born father was a Lutheran pastor, and was two years old when the family settled in Queensland. He had little formal education, and when he entered Parliament as a Country (later National) Party member in 1947, was distinctly unimpressive. A poor mixer and a fairly stumbling speaker, with a rather wowserish, country-bumpkin image, he was later described by the Communist MP, Fred Paterson, as having looked in those early days like the only member with less chance than himself of becoming Premier. He learned quickly, though, had some good mentors and a little luck; he also possessed great reservoirs of native shrewdness, energy, determination and sheer obstinacy. On 8 August 1968 Joh became Premier of Queensland.

In January 1979, he became the State's longest-serving Premier, breaking the record of ten years, five months and five days established by Sir Francis Nicklin. During his remarkable spell in office he played a large part in forcing the Whitlam Labor government to the polls

twice (in 1974 and 1975), blocked numerous programs of that government and worked with almost passionate zeal towards its overthrow; he also established State censorship boards, retained paternalistic control over the State's Aborigines, resisted daylight saving, introduced the removal of death duties, was named (in 1974) Australian of the Year by the Australian *newspaper – for having the most 'positive impact' on Australian life – and engineered the entry of his wife Florence to the Australian Senate. He was aided by an electoral gerrymander which ensured that he could retain office even though his party received a lower total percentage of the vote than the Liberal Party and the Labor Party.*

His greatest electoral triumph came at the end of 1983, when his National Party won government in its own right (admittedly with the help of two Liberal Party ministers who decided after the election to switch sides). After twenty-six years of coalition, the National–Liberal partnership ended. The Liberals were left with only six MPs, and the Nationals were able to govern with forty-three of the eighty-two seats in Queensland's Parliament.

By December 1987 he had been a politician for forty years, and Premier for more than nineteen of them. A month away from 77, he was the oldest State or federal leader the nation had known. In his last year in office, he had been defeated and humiliated in a campaign to win the prime ministership, had backed the military coup in Fiji, had fought with his own National Party leadership, had seen his party introduce liberal policies on social issues – notably on condom vending machines and sex education – which he found abhorrent, had been embarrassed by the Fitzgerald inquiry into police corruption, had had his own popularity rating plummet by 16 points to 34 in a matter of weeks, and had been rebuffed three times in his own Cabinet where for nearly two decades he had been used to having his own way.

The end came after he attempted to sack five ministers, among them deputy leader Bill Gunn and heir-apparent Mike Ahern, for alleged disloyalty. The Governor, Sir Walter Campbell, took the unusual course of exercising discretion and declining to accept the Premier's advice; he wanted proof that Sir Joh had the support of Cabinet. Sir Joh then settled for three sackings, those of Ahern, Brian Austin and Peter McKechnie. During a week in which both Gunn and Ahern claimed that Bjelke-Petersen was motivated by a desire to close down the Fitzgerald inquiry, National parliamentarians met and elected Ahern as their leader and Gunn as deputy. Still the embattled Bjelke-Petersen refused to leave his post. When he did go, eight days after announcing the sackings that caused his downfall, he stated petulantly: 'I do not wish to lead this government any longer. Its policies are not mine.'

I offered a view of Joh, based on some close-range observation, in Time Australia of 7 December 1987:

'Joh was so durable, so convinced of his own infallibility, so deft – despite his unremitting laceration of the language – in the exploration of cobwebbed corners of constitutional law, that it is difficult to come to terms with the knowledge that he is finished; that the carnival is over. The man who demolished both a Labor federal government and a conservative coalition opposition (not to mention the graceful, century-old Belle Vue Hotel in the middle of an April night), the man who twice performed the miracle of taking a minority party into absolute power . . . he simply doesn't matter any more . . .

'Many of his philosophies belonged to yesterday, and now he has joined them. As he makes his exit, sadly without grace but with the absolute conviction that everyone around him is either a traitor or out of touch with reality – "There is no crisis, don't you worry about that", he called to reporters as his parliamentary colleagues gathered to cast him out – it is

tempting to contemplate some ramifications of the departure of this improbable 76-year-old marvel of Australian politics . . .

'Historians will have to address the contradictions of the man. He was, until his silly and final suicidal "Joh for PM" campaign, above all a winner . . . He presided over a period of great economic growth, but there are many who believe he was fortunate to do so, that his period in office coincided with (rather than caused) a demand for Queensland's natural resources, a boom in tourist development and the transformation of Brisbane from a large country town to a handsome city. He was pragmatic, but he behaved bizarrely, treating a cancer quack as a kind of savior and endorsing a car that would be fueled by water. He was a religious man who pursued the politics of hatred without much trace of compassion. He spoke for soldier settlers in cowsheds, but was beguiled by rich men with calculating eyes and white shoes. He spent forty years in parliament and still regarded the institution as a nuisance, something that stopped him from getting on with the job. He dealt in the currency of favors . . .

'For all his undoubted achievements and sheer passion for Queensland, Sir Joh was the most divisive politician of his time. He generated fear and loathing, particularly of Canberra and "the south". He stressed often to Japanese and Korean industrialists that Queensland should never be confused with Australia. To disagree with him was to be regarded as an enemy. To challenge him, as the Fraser Island environmentalist John Sinclair did, was to risk a whole future and be driven from the State. Black activists, unionists who believed they had a right to strike, homosexuals, longhairs, the Liberals – they and so many others were all the enemy. For a time he forbade his backbenchers from eating at the same table as Labor Party members in the parliamentary dining room. If the Bicentennial is to be a time of healing, of making an effort to be one nation, maybe his departure comes at an appropriate time for Australia.'

In the Courier-Mail, Peter Charlton, associate editor, leader writer and a long-time

Joh watcher, wrote of the day which changed political history:

For those people who delight in examining political entrails, yesterday was a day of portents and omens.

Firstly there was the weather: hot, thick, steamy damp, more like January or February than November.

And as Bill Gunn, Deputy Premier and Premier aspirant, announced his challenge, an almighty clap of thunder shook the city and briefly dimmed the lights.

Mr Gunn looked wryly upwards from his huge hand-printed notes – a trick he has borrowed from the Premier – and pointed. A sign of divine intervention perhaps.

The thunderstorm, like its political counterpart, had been building all day. When it came, it solved nothing, but left the city as hot, as sticky and as uncomfortable as before.

Likewise, the political heat which was expected at the 5 p.m. Cabinet meeting did not eventuate.

Last night the principal players in this political drama – the Mines and Energy Minister, Mr Austin, the Health Minister, Mr Ahern, and the Industry Minister, Mr McKechnie, were still confused and unsure whether they were, indeed, still Ministers.

Political temperatures were still on the boil and relief seemed days away.

A direct correlation between the weather and political turmoil in Queensland is worth examining further.

There was Joh Bjelke-Petersen's great 1974 electoral success, when at a December election he reduced the ALP to a derisory 11 men.

Then there was the January storm in 1985 which blacked out much of south-east Queensland and came at the height of the SEQEB strike.

Queensland summer heat and political tensions give new meaning to the word "troppo". And so it seemed yesterday. The old catchphrase "amazing scenes" hardly seemed appropriate.

Suffice it to say that Sir Joh Bjelke-Petersen, smarting over rebuffs handed to him in Cabinet on Monday, determined that he would rid himself of his burdens. But what burdens!

Who would have thought that Sir Joh would sack his loyal deputy, a man unkindly referred to as a "Joh clone" and, until recently, the man tipped by Sir Joh to take over the reins of the National Party?

For that matter, who would have thought that the Premier would administer the axe to one of the turncoat Liberals who had given him government in his own right in 1983?

And there was the third man, the politician whom the opinion polls agree would be most likely to drag the Queensland Government kicking and screaming into the 20th century.

Sir Joh's actions yesterday reflected the guidance and advice he is being given.

The Premier has lost many of his key advisers: Allen Callaghan is in jail; Ken Crooke is in another area of the public service.

Instead, he has the formidable Ms Beryl Young, a tough veteran of many battles with aviation bureaucracy; and Mr Peter MacDonald, a bulldog-solid man whose basic instinct is to go for the political jugular. Sometimes, even for his own jugular.

So there you had it. Whispers around town early yesterday morning; confirmation at 10.15 a.m. when Michael John Ahern met the Premier in a close encounter of the terse kind.

Then, a day of extraordinary meetings, counting, phone calls and hurried gestures of support culminating in a Cabinet meeting like none other held in this, the last bastion of executive-guided democracy.

Last night, the man with the constitutional keys to the solution, Sir Walter Campbell, was enjoying himself at a function run by Lorraine Martin, the training college whiz.

And amid all this, Ahern, the Downlands boy, the university graduate, and aspirant Premier, remained calm. At lunch yesterday, a hurried affair of beer and sandwiches in his office, Ahern sat back in his chair, clasped his arms behind his head and said: "I feel relaxed about it all."

"It" was his "sacking" that morning by Sir Joh Bjelke-Petersen, a sacking that did not quite take place because the Governor, Sir Walter Campbell – like Ahern, an old boy of Downlands – rejected the Premier's request that the five commissions be withdrawn.

In the office, Ahern's advisers and supporters were a curious mixture of jubilation and trepidation.

"You know what this is," said Earle Bailey, the former National member for Toowong who is one of Ahern's most enthusiastic supporters.

"This is the day that Mike lost the image of a wimp." Bailey always speaks like that.

It is a devastating image for a politician to carry, particularly in Queensland where men are men and issues black and white.

Mike Ahern was, it seemed, always too responsible, always too conciliatory, always too prepared to abide by the parliamentary conventions which were by definition and expectation ignored in the State.

The Opposition's deputy leader, Tom Burns, summed up a consensus view of Ahern when he said he had seen a miracle of modern medicine.

"Ahern's had a transplant," he said. "Someone's put some backbone into him."

The decision to stand and fight was made by Ahern, but it was urged on him by his press secretary, Finlay "Jock" McKechnie, whose lessons of political fighting were learned in the streets of Glasgow, and by Bailey, who understands what it is like to lose and to be on the outer with the Premier.

Ahern had nothing to lose yesterday morning. Had he accepted the sacking quietly, had he moved to the backbench, he would have been seen as docile and conciliatory.

In the National Party view, he would have been seen as weak – too weak, in fact, to follow a strong man whose fall from grace has been both rapid and tragic.

And particularly when he was locked in combat, not just with Sir Joh, but also with Bill Gunn, who played the day tough and close to his chest.

Ahern knows that, in the power struggle consuming Queensland politics today, he has the support of the party's king-maker, Sir Robert Sparkes. It was no coincidence that it was Ahern who went to Sparkes yesterday, not vice-versa.

After that meeting, Mr Ahern and his "sacked" ministerial colleague, Mr Brian Austin, called on the Governor.

Both said the Premier had asked for their resignations, but they had refused because they did not believe Sir Joh had the confidence of the National Party.

The Governor was appropriately discreet, given the delicacy of the situation. But it is understood that he assured the two Ministers that there would be no precipitate action and that he hoped the National Party would be able to solve what was essentially an internal party matter.

Encouraged by that advice, the two Ministers left and went then to the Executive Building for the 5 p.m. Cabinet.

The Premier kept the assembled Ministers waiting at that meeting before making an entrance.

Again he asked for the resignations, this time of the three Ministers – Ahern, Austin and McKechnie. Again they refused.

Last night David Russell QC, a member of the National Party's management committee (and coincidentally and no more, a son-in-law of the Governor) was in Mike Ahern's office.

The Health Minister – if, indeed, he is still the Health Minister – intends to play it cool over the next few days, knowing that the matter can only be resolved by a decision of the National Party parliamentary members.

1988 On our 200th birthday, some questions – and the biggest party ever

ROD FRAIL AND LINDSAY MURDOCH
Melbourne Age, 27 January 1988

It was a time for celebration mainly, but also for self-appraisal. On this day, 200 years before, Captain Arthur Phillip had christened Sydney Cove, at the heart of what he called 'the finest harbour in the world', and British civilisation, of a sort, had come to this continent.

Australia's Bicentennial, which arrived on 26 January 1988, was seen by some distinguished Australians as an event which did not warrant rejoicing. Nobel Prize novelist Patrick White expressed his disapproval by instructing that none of his works be published in 1988. The historian Manning Clark saw the 200th birthday of the coming of the British as a symbol of three great evils: violence against the original inhabitants, the Aborigines; violence against the first labour force, the convicts; and violence against the land itself.

But another, more popular, view was reflected by the columnist P. P. McGuinness in the Financial Review: *'Every country has a lot to be ashamed of and a lot to be proud of in 200 years of history. Australia has less to be ashamed of than most, and is still one of the most tolerant, democratic and egalitarian societies in the world . . . Of course there were Aborigines here when the First Fleet landed. It is probable that ever since then the Australian law has laboured under a misapprehension as to the legal doctrine under which Britain took possession of New South Wales, and then the rest of the continent. There is a history of seizure of apparently unoccupied lands and lands which were clearly not unoccupied. There is a wrong to be righted, and there is also the fact that 200 years of European settlement have clearly been devastating for the Aborigines. But no-one living bears the guilt for the treatment of the original inhabitants . . . There is a tiny number of genuine racists, and an overwhelming majority who believe that Aborigines should live in genuine equality and amity with the rest of Australians. The problem is how to overcome 200 years of demoralisation.'*

Bruce Wilson, back in Australia, from his London post, for the Bicentennial, put it more simply in the Melbourne Herald: *'Most sensible people I have spoken to in Sydney and Queensland say pretty well the same thing [about the Aborigines]. "Yes, yes, we know it's been crook for them. But just what do they want?" This is the question that no one has so far answered, at least not to my satisfaction. Of course, land rights. Of course, enshrine the rights in the constitution. But then what?'*

Other fields for contemplation and debate existed as Australia Day 1988 loomed, and some of them related to apparent contradictions in identity. This was a European civilisation, an Asian country. Urban dwellers, with largely urban values, inhabited a vast, empty, undeveloped country rich in resources and agriculture. The nation was politically independent in spirit, but it clung fondly to the British monarchy.

On the big day, though, all such questions were overshadowed by a party, the largest Australia has ever known. Its centrepoint was Sydney Harbour, so crowded with craft that D. D. McNicoll was able to claim in the Australian *that 'at 11.40 am it was possible to walk from one side to the other without getting wet'.*

Rod Frail and Lindsay Murdoch described events this way in the Melbourne Age:

The biggest crowd Australia has seen, with people drawn from almost every nation on the globe, yesterday crushed around Sydney Harbor to celebrate the arrival 200 years ago

What a party! An estimated 1.5 million people and 10,000 spectator craft crammed the shores and waters of Sydney Harbour on 26 January 1988 to commemorate the 200th anniversary of the landing of the first white settlers. Royal visitors, orchestras and choirs, replica First Fleet ships and a military fly-past entertained the revellers

of the first reluctant white settlers.

More than 1.5 million Australians travelled by foot, car, train, jet, and boat to the site where Captain Arthur Phillip and his fleet arrived unheralded on 26 January 1788.

They crammed every vantage point around the harbor foreshores, on the Harbor Bridge and at Circular Quay to watch the magnificent maritime spectacle of sunlit sailing ships and an estimated 10,000 spectator craft. Most missed seeing the official Australia Day ceremony, but they made their own birthday party, waving Australian flags and blowing trumpets.

At the ceremony on the forecourt of the

Opera House, attended by the Prince and Princess of Wales, there were lofty speeches, stirring music and fireworks as a military fly-past roared overhead.

Less than a kilometre away, more than 30,000 Aborigines mourned the same anniversary with a peaceful march and speeches in Hyde Park.

A confrontation was averted when police, confronted by a group of 3000 blacks, allowed them to pass as individuals and march to their tent embassy at Mrs Macquarie's Chair. There, they staged their own landing by Captain Phillip, but threw him back into the water.

The Royal couple, the Governor-General, Sir Ninian Stephen, and Lady Stephen, the Prime Minister and Mrs Hawke, the state Premiers and Governors, arrived for the ceremony by water at the Man O'War steps. Outside the iron fence that separated the 3000 guests, people hung from trees and from the fences.

Prince Charles told the audience that a nation of free people had emerged from a harsh penal colony.

"As history goes, 200 years is barely a heartbeat, yet look around you and see what has happened in that time – a whole new free people, a people of a whole new free country, Australia."

Referring to the Aborigines, Prince Charles said: "It must all have seemed very different and if they should say that their predicament was not yet ended it would be hard to know how to answer beyond suggesting that a country free enough to examine its own conscience is a land worth living in, a nation to be envied."

The Prince also recalled his own "transportation" to Australia 22 years ago as part of his education when he had "the Pommie bits bashed out of me". However, it was an experience he would always cherish, he said.

The Prime Minister, Mr Hawke, did not refer to the Aborigines, but said the celebration was not in the spirit of self-glorification. He said commitment was the most important word of the day.

"For our commitment to Australia is, in a very real way, the quality which best defines what it means to be an Australian in 1988," he said.

As Prince Charles finished his speech, the nine ships of the First Fleet re-enactment hove into view under full sail, anchoring in Farm Cove to cheers from the shore.

The ceremony built to a magnificent crescendo: the orchestra and choir played a medley of patriotic songs, a fly-past of about 150 military aircraft and helicopters and fireworks coincided with the release of dozens of Australian flags that parachuted into the harbor. Wearing an Akubra hat, Mrs Hawke snapped photos of the First Fleet re-enactment ships sailing up the harbor.

Bibliography

THE EARLY STRUGGLES OF THE FREE PRESS IN AUSTRALIA, by James Bonwick (Gordon and Gotch) 1890

THE AUSTRALIAN ENCYCLOPAEDIA, edited by Alec H. Chisholm (The Grolier Society of Aust. Pty Ltd) 1965

A CENTURY OF JOURNALISM — THE SYDNEY MORNING HERALD AND ITS RECORD OF AUSTRALIAN LIFE, 1831–1931 (John Fairfax and Sons Ltd) 1931

HISTORY OF AMERICAN JOURNALISM, by Melvin James Lee (Houghton Mifflin, Boston) 1917

THE CHANGING NEWSPAPER, by Allen Hutt (Gordon Fraser, London) 1973

WILD MEN OF SYDNEY, by Cyril Pearl (W. H. Allen & Co., London) 1958

MARCUS CLARKE, by Brian Elliott (Oxford University Press, London) 1958

REMEMBER SMITH'S WEEKLY ?, a biography of an uninhibited national Australian newspaper, by George Blaikie (Rigby) 1966

EARLY COLONIAL SCANDALS, THE TURBULENT TIMES OF SAMUEL MARSDEN, by Bill Wannan (Lansdowne) 1972

SELECT DOCUMENTS IN AUSTRALIAN HISTORY, 1851–1900, by C. M. H. Clark (Angus and Robertson) 1955

FOREIGN DEVIL, THIRTY YEARS OF REPORTING IN THE FAR EAST, by Richard Hughes (Andre Deutsch, London) 1972

SYDNEY REVELS OF BACCHUS, CUPID AND MOMUS, by Charles Adam Corbyn, presented by Cyril Pearl (Ure Smith) 1970

THE KINGDOM AND THE POWER, by Gay Talese (World Publishing, New York) 1969

A TREASURY OF GREAT REPORTING, edited by Louis L. Snyder and Richard B. Morris (Simon and Shuster, New York) 1949

THE EDITOR REGRETS, by Cecil Edwards (Hill of Content) 1972

HENRY LAWSON — AUTOBIOGRAPHICAL AND OTHER WRITINGS, 1887–1922, edited by Colin Roderick (Angus and Robertson) 1972

THE GREAT WHEEL, by C. Brunsdon Fletcher (Angus and Robertson) 1940

FAIR DINKUM, by Douglas Lockwood (Cassell) 1960

THE VAGABOND PAPERS, edited by Michael Cannon (Melbourne University Press) 1969

DAVID SYME — A LIFE, by C. E. Sayers (F. W. Cheshire) 1965

THE REPORTER'S TRADE, by Joseph and Stewart Alsop (Bodley Head, London) 1958

ONE FOR THE ROAD, edited by Jack Pollard, (Angus and Robertson) 1966

FEDERATED AUSTRALIA — SELECTIONS FROM LETTERS TO THE MORNING POST, by Alfred Deakin, edited by J. A. La Nauze (Melbourne University Press) 1968

BREAD AND WINE, by Kenneth Slessor (Angus and Robertson) 1970

CAPTAIN JAMES COOK, by Alan Villiers (Charles Scribner's Sons, New York) 1967

THE STORY OF A FULL LIFE, by Sir Lloyd Dumas (Sun Books) 1969

THE STORY OF JOHN FAIRFAX, by J. F. Fairfax (John Fairfax and Sons Ltd) 1941

THE BEST OF LENNIE LOWER, presented by Cyril Pearl and Wep (Lansdowne) 1963

A LATE EDUCATION, by Alan Moorehead (Hamish Hamilton, London) 1970

LOLA MONTEZ (Heritage Publications) 1973

SIR FRANK, THE FRANK PACKER STORY, by R. S. Whitington (Cassell) 1971

TRUE PATRIOTS ALL, garnered and decorated by Geoffrey C. Ingleton (Angus and Robertson) 1952

AUSTRALIA AT ARMS, edited by Norman Bartlett (Australian War Memorial) 1955

POWER WITHOUT GLORY, by Frank Hardy (T. Werner Laurie) 1962

BRUCE OF MELBOURNE, by Cecil Edwards (Heinemann) 1966

THE LAND BOOMERS, by Michael Cannon (Melbourne University Press) 1966

THE FIRST CASUALTY, by Phillip Knightley (Harcourt Brace Jovanovich, New York) 1975

TWELFTH MAN ?, by Don Whitington (Jacaranda Press) 1972

SCRIBBLERS AND STATESMEN, by George Cockerill (Bread & Cheese Club) 1944

THE BANJO OF THE BUSH, by Clement Semmler (Lansdowne) 1966

A COLONIAL CITY, edited by L. T. Hergenhan (University of Queensland Press) 1972

LOOKING BACK GAILY, by Benjamin Hoare (E. W. Cole) 1927

THE GLORIOUS YEARS, edited by Graeme Inson

and Russel Ward (Jacaranda) 1971
THE CHRONICLES OF EARLY MELBOURNE,
2 Volumes, by 'Garryowen' — Edmund Finn
(Fergusson and Mitchell) 1888
KEITH MURDOCH, JOURNALIST (The Herald
and Weekly Times Ltd) 1952
AUSTRALIANS ABROAD, edited by Charles Higham
and Michael Wilding (F. W. Cheshire) 1967
THEY CALLED ME ARTY, by Sir Arthur Fadden
(Jacaranda Press) 1969
PASSPORT, by Wilfred Burchett (Thomas Nelson)
1969
CANNIBAL CARGOES, by Hector Holthouse
(Rigby) 1969
MODERN AUSTRALIA IN DOCUMENTS, edited
by F. K. Crowley — 2 Volumes (Wren) 1973
STARLIGHT: THE MAN AND THE MYTH, by
P. H. McCarthy (Hawthorn Press) 1972
GRAB FOR POWER: ELECTION 1974, by Laurie
Oakes and David Solomon (F. W. Cheshire) 1975
THE GORTON EXPERIMENT: THE FALL OF
JOHN GREY GORTON, by Alan Reid (Shakespeare
Head Press) 1971
AUSTRALIA, NEW ZEALAND AND THE SOUTH
PACIFIC: A HANDBOOK, edited by Charles
Osborne (Anthony Blond) 1970
POLITICS IN QUEENSLAND: 1977 AND BEYOND,
edited by Margaret Bridson Cribb and P. J. Boyce
(University of Queensland Press) 1980
BOB HAWKE, A PORTRAIT, by Robert Pullan
(Methuen) 1980
125 YEARS OF AGE, edited by Geoffrey Hutton
and Les Tanner (Nelson) 1979
THE BEST OF THE AGE 1979—80, edited by
Peter Cole-Adams (Nelson) 1980
THE MAN WHO READ THE EAST WIND, A
BIOGRAPHY OF RICHARD HUGHES, by Norman
Macswan (Kangaroo Press) 1982
GAMBLE FOR POWER: HOW BOB HAWKE BEAT
MALCOLM FRASER, by Anne Summers (Thomas
Nelson) 1983
ROBERT J. HAWKE, A BIOGRAPHY, by Blanche
d'Alpuget (Schwartz, in conjunction with
Lansdowne Press) 1982, updated 1983
THE HAWKE ASCENDANCY, A DEFINITIVE
ACCOUNT OF ITS ORIGINS AND CLIMAX, by
Paul Kelly (Angus and Robertson) 1984
JOHANNES BJELKE-PETERSEN, A POLITICAL
BIOGRAPHY, by Hugh Lunn (University of
Queensland Press) 1984
GUILTY SECRETS, FREE SPEECH IN AUSTRALIA,
by Robert Pullan (Methuen) 1984
BAREFOOT REPORTER: THE BEST OF RICHARD
HUGHES COLUMNS 1971-83, edited by Mike
MacLachlan (Far East Economic Review) 1984
BIG SHOTS: WHO'S WHO IN AUSTRALIAN CRIME,
by David Wilson and Lindsay Murdoch, edited by
Bob Bottom (Sun Books) 1985
CONNECTIONS, by Bob Bottom (Sun Books) 1985

VIETNAM, A REPORTER'S WAR, by Hugh Lunn
(University of Queensland Press) 1985
WARCO: AUSTRALIAN REPORTERS AT WAR, by
Pat Burgess (Heinemann) 1986

Note: Unless otherwise stipulated, all of these books
were published in Australia.

Non-book sources included:
A series of articles of reminiscence by Montague
Grover published in various issues of the *Lone Hand*
in 1914.
An article by Alan Reid recalling personalities and
incidents in the Canberra Press Gallery published in
the *New Journalist* on 11 November 1973.
'Men Who Made the *Argus* and the *Australasian*,
1846—1923' — a typed and bound record presented
to the Victoria District of the Australian Journalists'
Association by Ross and Vincent Smith — son and
grandson of the compiler, C. P. Smith.
'Historical Records of the *Argus* and the
Australasian' — a typed and bound record presented
to the Victoria District of the Australian Journalists'
Association by Ross and Vincent Smith — son and
grandson of the compiler, C. P. Smith.

Acknowledgements

This book could not have been produced without the assistance of many individuals and institutions. Libraries contributed immeasurably: particularly the Mitchell (Sydney), the LaTrobe (Melbourne), the State Libraries of Victoria, New South Wales and Queensland, and the library of The Herald and Weekly Times Limited.

Philip V. Garrett, formerly chief research officer of the Victorian State Library, helped considerably — particularly in the tracking down of work of some of the early war correspondents.

Officials of the Australian Journalists' Association — especially Graham Walsh in Melbourne and Gordon Coleman and Syd Crosland in Sydney — were exceedingly co-operative and sympathetic.

So many people were helpful with ideas, suggestions and voluntary research that it would be almost impossible to list them all. Here are some of them: Richard Hughes, veteran Far East correspondent (who reminisced about great news stories over a meal in Hong Kong in 1970, and continued to correspond helpfully on the subject); Cyril Pearl, who would send crisp notes like, 'Have you thought of Peter (Wilfred) Burchett's world scoop in Hiroshima? . . . it was certainly one of the biggest of the war'; Laurie Power, who lent his father's unpublished book of reminiscence; the late Hugh Buggy, with whom I spent a great deal of time in research and free-ranging discussion about reporters of the 'twenties, 'thirties, 'forties and 'fifties; Frank Green, former Clerk of the House of Representatives, who took the trouble, in his eighty-third year, to write recalling Canberra Press Gallery personalities.

Also: Sir John Williams, Sir Donald Bradman, Don Whitington, R. R. Walker, King Watson, Roland Pullen, the late Clive Turnbull, the late Graham Perkin, the late John Hetherington, Ellis Glover, Leo Basser, Archer Thomas, Merton Woods, Douglas Wilkie, Ronald McKie, Colin Bingham, Hugh Bingham, Robert MacDonald, Winton H. 'Bert' Turner, the late Ronald Monson, David Aldridge, Creighton Burns, Ian Stewart, Jack Waters, Fred Morony, John Hamilton, John Holden, Alan Auldrige, Keith Dunstan, Jack Perceval, Forbes Miller, Neil Moody, Alf Brown, Noel Hawken, Rohan Rivett, Alan Reid, the late Roy Macartney, Colin Bednall, Gavin Souter, Tom Farrell, Geoffrey Hutton, Douglas Lockwood, Howard Palmer, J. Stewart Legge, Michael Courtney, Lou Leck, Tess Van Sommers, Lou D'Alpuget, Pat Burgess, Jim Hahn. Christine Cooze, Roy Terry and Colin Dawson of The Herald and Weekly Times library, and Leigh Stevens, photographic manager of the company, were particularly obliging. Special thanks are due to Brian Breingan, Chief Librarian of Queensland Newspapers.

The original publishing team deserves special thanks. Ever since this project was just an idea, Lloyd O'Neil has given total support and sympathy. At one stage, in a farmhouse at Mount Martha (Vic.), he and I covered a complete floor with wall-to-wall history, setting out each piece, each era — selecting, rejecting, looking for gaps. In production, John Currey was similarly professional and helpful, able to visualise, in a mountain of manuscript, exactly the kind of book that would emerge; editor Jenni Cunningham was always painstaking, patient, sympathetic and utterly involved.

Finally, thanks are due to these organisations for having given permission to reproduce material: The Herald and Weekly Times, John Fairfax and Sons, David Syme and Co., News Limited, West Australian Newspapers, Advertiser Newspapers, Queensland Press, Australian Consolidated Press.

Picture Acknowledgements

National Library of Australia 34, 137
La Trobe Collection, State Library of Victoria 41
State Library of South Australia 50-51, 89, 91
New South Wales Government Printer 157
James Flood Charity Trust 175
Ern McQuillan 183
Australian War Memorial 189, 197, 199, 203, 308-9, 315, 317, 325, 341, 345, 363, 367
Mr Ian Beaurepaire 219
Sydney Daily Telegraph 243
Sydney Morning Herald 251, 261
John Fairfax and Sons Ltd 273, 287, 339, 359, 417, 427
West Australian Newspapers 283
Royal Aeronautical Society (London) 301
Australian Consolidated Press 389

Publisher's Note:
All the newspaper extracts in this book are printed as they originally appeared. No alterations have been made to spelling or punctuation.

Index

Page numbers in italics refer to illustrations

Q

R

S

T